Warranties in Cross-Border Acquisitions

The International Bar Association Series

Other titles in this series:

Acquisition of Shares in a Foreign Country, (M. Gruson, S. Hutter)
ISBN: 1 85333 755 2
Arab Comparative and Commercial Law—The International Approach, Volumes 1 and 2.
Volume 1 ISBN: 0 86010 977 1.
Volume 2 ISBN: 0 86010 978 X.
Civil Appeal Procedures Worldwide, (Editor, C. Platto)
ISBN: 1 85333 725 0
Developing Global Securities Market (Editor, F.W. Neate)
ISBN: 0 86010979 8
Due Diligence, Disclosures and Warranties in the Corporate Acquisitions Practice 2nd edn. (Editors, D. Baker and R. Jillson)
ISBN: 1 85333 633 5
Energy Law 88, (Section on Energy & Natural Resources Law)
ISBN: 1 85333 097 3
Energy Law 90, (Section on Energy & Natural Resources Law)
ISBN: 1 85333 477 4
Enforcement of Foreign Judgments Worldwide, (2nd ed.) (Editors, C. Platto, W.G. Horton)
ISBN: 1 85333 757 9
Environmental Liability, (Editor, P. Thomas)
ISBN: 1 85333 561 4
Legal Opinions in International Transactions—Foreign Lawyers' Response to US Opinion Requests, (2nd ed.) (M. Gruson, S. Hutter, M. Kutschera)
ISBN: 1 85333 192 9
Life After Big Bang, (Editor, S. macLachlan)
ISBN: 0 86010 982 8
Nuclear Energy Law After Chernobyl, (Editors, P. Cameron, L. Hancher, W. Kühn)
ISBN: 1 85333 110 4
Obtaining Evidence in Another Jurisdiction in Business Disputes, (2nd ed.) (Editors, C. Platto, M. Lee)
ISBN: 1 85333 082 5
Pre-Trial and Pre-Hearing Procedures Worldwide, (Editor, C. Platto)
ISBN: 1 85333 758–7
Transnational Environmental Liability and Insurance, (Editor, R.P. Kröner)
ISBN: 1 85333 778 1
The Impact of the Freeze of Kuwaiti and Iraqi Assets—on Financial Institutions and Financial Transactions, (Editors, B. Campbell and D. Newcomb)
ISBN: 1 85333 558 4
Trial and Court Procedures Worldwide, (Editor, C. Platto)
ISBN: 1 85333 608 4
Using Set-Off as Security—A Comparative Survey for Practitioners, (Editor, F.W. Neate)
ISBN: 1 85333 363 8
Water Pollution—Law and Liability, (Editor, P. Thomas)
ISBN: 1 85333 874 5

International Bar Association Series

Warranties in Cross-Border Acquisitions

Editor

Mauro Rubino-Sammartano

Graham & Trotman
A member of the Kluwer Academic Publishers Group
LONDON/DORDRECHT/BOSTON
and
International Bar Association

Graham & Trotman Limited
Sterling House
66 Wilton Road
London SW1V 1DE
UK

Kluwer Academic Publishers Group
101 Philip Drive
Assinippi Park
Norwell, MA 02061
USA

International Bar Association
2 Harewood Place
Hanover Square
London W1R 9HB
UK

ISBN 1-85333-946-6
Series ISBN 1–85333-096–5

First published 1994

British Library Cataloguing in Publication Data is available

Library of Congress Cataloging-in-Publication Data

Warranties in cross-border acquisitions/editor, Mauro Rubino
–Sammartano.
p. cm. — (The International Bar Association series)
ISBN 1-85333-946-6
1. Warranty. 2. Export sales contracts. I. Rubino-Sammartano,
Mauro. II. Series.
K1032.C6R83 1993
346'.07—dc20
[342.67] 93-23307
CIP

Typeset in Times 10/11pt by Concept Typesetting Ltd, Salisbury, Wilts.
Printed and bound by Hartnolls Ltd, Bodmin, Cornwall.

Contents

About the IBA, The Section on Business Law and the International Sales and Related Commercial Transactions Committee

The International Bar Association (IBA) is the world's foremost international association of lawyers, with a membership of over 16,000 individual lawyers in 167 countries, as well as 146 Bar Associations and Law Societies. Its principal aims and objectives are:

— To encourage the discussion of problems relating to professional organisation and status.
— To promote an exchange of information between legal associations worldwide.
— To support the independence of the judiciary and the right of lawyers to practise their profession without interference.
— To keep abreast of developments in the law, and help in improving and making new laws.

Above all, it seeks to provide a forum in which individual lawyers can contact, and exchange ideas with other lawyers.

The IBA has three sections: the Section on Business Law, the Section on General Practice and the Section on Energy and Natural Resources Law. The largest is the Section on Business Law which has over 12,000 members. Within the Section on Business Law there are 28 Committees, each specialising in a particular area of Business Law.

Section on Business Law

The Committees of the Section on Business Law aim to study and discuss the legal and practical aspects of issues relating to their particular topic from an international viewpoint.

Members are typically partners of law firms practising in national and international business matters, or in-house or corporate lawyers of companies active in international business. Members of the judiciary and academics also join and participate in the activities of the Committees.

Committee M (International Sales and Related Commercial Transactions)

Committee M is one of the largest of the Section on Business Law Committees, with 2,000 members. Its activities focus on the main aspects of the various types of international sales and related commercial transactions, which are examined from the standpoint of different legal systems.

The Committee holds meetings each year, either at the Biennial Conference of the IBA or the Biennial Conference of the SBL, held in alternate years. It also publishes a quarterly Newsletter, the International Sales Quarterly, which contains reports of significant cases and legislation from various jurisdictions and details of Committee activities.

Further details of Committee M and the IBA and its Section on Business Law are available from:

International Bar Association
2 Harewood Place
Hanover Square
London W1R 9HB

Tel: +44 (0)71 629 1206
Fax: +44 (0)71 409 0456

List of Contributors

Jeffrey Lawton Buckland

Mr Buckland is an admitted attorney of the Supreme Court of South Africa (Witwatersrand Local Division) and formerly an articled clerk at Webber Wentzel, Johannesburg, South Africa. He graduated from the University of Stellenbosch in 1987 with a BCom.LLB in Commercial Law and was awarded an LLM in Company and Law of Taxation in 1991.

William C Conley

Mr Conley is a Partner of Blake Dawson Waldron in Sydney, Australia. He practises in the areas of corporate and commercial law. He is the Editor of the Australian section of the international publication *Mergers and Acquisitions—The Complete Guide to Principles and Practice* (in association with the *International Financing Review*); in 1986 he was seconded to Morgan Grenfell & Co Ltd in London.

Pedro de Elizalde

Dr de Elizalde is a Senior Partner of the Allende & Brea law firm in Buenos Aires, Argentina, and conducts an active practice in the fields of finance, corporate, administrative and international law. He obtained his LLB from the University of Buenos Aires in 1962.

He has served as Vice-Chairman of the Banking Law Committee of the International Bar Association since 1976 and as Co-Chairman between 1984–1988, during which period he was a member of the Council of the Section on Business Law. He is a member of the Advisory Committee of the Buenos Aires Bar Association on Financial Entities, Stock Exchanges and Securities Legislation. Dr de Elizalde is the author of several articles on these matters in specialised international publications.

Javier Faus

Mr Faus is a Senior Associate in the law firm of Bufete Cuatrecasas in Barcelona, Spain, where he is a member of the finance team. He obtained his bachelor's degree in law in 1987 from the University of Barcelona, and a master's from

Georgetown University Law School in 1988. He is a member of the Barcelona Bar Association and has also lectured at the McGeorge School of Law on Spanish law.

Rolf Giebeler

Dr Giebeler is a Partner of Pünder, Volhard, Weber & Axster in the firm's Düsseldorf and Warsaw offices, and actively practises in the areas of mergers and acquisitions as well as in general corporate practice for international clients. Since 1990 he has been advising clients on privatisation law and investment law in the former East Germany and in Poland. Dr Giebeler studied law and public administration at the Universities of Bonn, Pittsburgh, and Harvard. In 1988 he was admitted to the Bar in Frankfurt.

Glower W Jones

Mr Jones is a Partner of Smith, Currie & Hancock in Atlanta, Georgia, USA. He is a graduate of Dartmouth College and Emory Law School. He has been an active member of the American Bar Association and the International Bar Association, and is currently serving as the Chairman of the International Sales and Related Commercial Transactions Committee of the International Bar Association. He has also lectured extensively and published articles on warranties in international sales and other topics in various legal journals.

Pere Kirchner

Mr Kirchner is a Senior Associate in the law firm of Bufete Cuatrecasas, Barcelona, Spain, where he is based in the finance team. He obtained his LLB at the University of Barcelona in 1988, and an LLM at the London School of Economics. He has, during his association with Bufete Cuatrecasas, been based on placement with another law firm in London. Mr Kirchner has also lectured at the McGeorge School of Law on Spanish Law.

Delos N Lutton

Mr Lutton is a member of the Reinhart, Boerner, Van Dueren, Norris and Rieselbach s.c. law firm in Milwaukee, Wisconsin, USA. He is a graduate of DePauw University and obtained his law degree from the University of Chicago Law School. He advises clients including investment advisors, public corporations and brokers on a variety of international transactions, including foreign distribution and licence agreements, joint ventures and acquisitions, export licencing, customs, and international trade and corporate finance issues. Mr Lutton is a member of the State Bar of Wisconsin's International Section, the International Bar Association, the Union Internationale des Avocats, and the Business and International Law Sections of the American Bar Association. He has written and lectured extensively, on international law, securities and corporate law issues.

Enric Picañol

Mr Picañol is a Partner of Bufete Cuatrecasas, Barcelona, Spain. He obtained a bachelor's degree in law and an economics and business degree from the University of Barcelona in 1976 and 1977 respectively, and a master's in law in 1983 from the London School of Economics. He is a member of the Barcelona Bar Association, the International Bar Association, ASIL and the Law Society of England and Wales. Mr Picañol is also a member of the editorial boards of the *Revista Jurídica de Catalunya* and the *European Business Law Review*. He has been a lecturer at the University of Barcelona, and has also lectured extensively at the Barcelona Bar Association, McGeorge School of Law, University College, London and at other academic and commercial institutions. He is the author of the Spanish edition of *Common Market Law of Competition*.

Mauro Rubino-Sammartano

Mr Rubino-Sammartano is Head of Chambers in the law firm of Studio Rubino-Sammartano e Associati, Milan, Italy. He has chaired several international bodies and is currently Chairman of the Italian Branch of the European Court of Arbitration, Strasbourg.

He has lectured on international law at the University of Padua and has sat for some years as a Recorder of Desio. He has written extensively and is the author of *International Arbitration Law, Public Policy in Transnational Relationships* and the "Italy" section in *World Litigation Law and Practice.*

Dolf Weber

Mr Weber is the acting Senior Partner of Pünder, Volhard, Weber & Axster in Frankfurt, Germany. He was admitted to the Bar in 1963. He has an active practice in advising institutional investors and clients in multinational corporations and financial institutions, in the areas of mergers and acquisitions, corporate and real estate transactions and major restructurings, which is predominantly internationally related.

Tore Wiwen-Nilsson

Mr Wiwen-Nilsson is a Partner in Mannheimer Swartling in Malmö, Sweden. He has long advised major Swedish companies in their international transactions including industrial and construction projects, joint ventures and acquisitions. He gained his LLB in 1967 from the University of Lund. He is a member of several arbitration tribunals; the Swedish Bar Association, International Nuclear Law Association, Chairman of the Subcommittee "Turnkey Heavy Plant Contracts" in the International Bar Association, the Licensing Executive Society, Asia–Pacific Lawyers' Association and is an alternate Board Member of the Swedish Society for Construction and Consulting Law. Mr Wiwen-Nilsson lectures at the Law Faculty of the University of Lund and has published various articles.

Preface

Whilst, in view of the great interest raised by cross-border acquisitions, there is a large amount of literature on this subject, the specific issue of warranties in such transactions has been addressed much less.

Just by way of example, in several jurisdictions the very nature of the vendor's liability is argued and it is debated whether the statutory provisions on sales of goods govern also acquisitions carried out by way of transfer of shares.

As frequently happens, by studying this subject, one discovers that it is much richer than expected, and that it may have decisive relevance not only in theoretical terms.

I am consequently glad that my last task in my capacity as Chairman of the IBA's International Sales Committee—at the closing of the Cannes Conference—is to present this study.

It has been a pleasure to structure it, to select the national contributors and to liaise with them.

Mauro Rubino-Sammartano

Argentina

Pedro de Elizalde
Allende & Brea, Buenos Aires, Argentina

Purchase agreements which are drafted and executed in Argentina are traditionally short of provisions concerning seller's representations and warranties. Most acquisitions, including purchases of goods, real estate, shareholdings and on-going businesses, usually omit such clauses. In part, this is due to the fact that the purchaser is protected by statutory provisions or by compliance with specific procedures established in the law. The Statute Governing the Transfer of On-Going Businesses is a clear example along those lines.

However, contractual practice is beginning to include, especially in acquisitions of large shareholdings, long lists of representations and warranties by the seller. This change in commercial practice can be traced back to the use of Common Law-style agreements.

1. Warranty: Definition

In Argentine law, it is said that a warranty is a statement or representation made by a seller of goods, contemporaneously with and as a part of the contract of sale, though collateral to the express object of the sale, having reference to character, quality, or title of goods, and by which the seller promises or undertakes to ensure that certain facts are or shall be as he then represents them. Likewise, a warranty is briefly defined as a statement of fact reflecting the quality or character of goods sold, made by the seller to induce the sale, and relied on by the buyer, or as a promise that certain facts are truly as they are represented to be and they will remain so, subject to any specified limitations.[1]

2. Contractual and Statutory Warranties

Under Argentine contractual legislation it is important to make a distinction between contractual and statutory warranties. Even though the Civil Code and the Commercial Code contain several provisions regarding the warranties the

[1] *Black's Law Dictionary* (St. Paul Minn. West Publishing Co., 1979), 5th ed, p. 1423.

seller must make in favour of the purchaser, Article 1197 of the Civil Code establishes that the terms agreed upon in a contract between the parties are to become a rule to which the parties must submit, as if it were the law itself. This important general principle allows the parties to include in a contract whatever warranties they may consider useful, necessary or convenient for the better fulfilment of the transaction.

Even though various warranties are established by the law, it is common that parties to an agreement include many of them as well in the agreement, in order to restrict or extend the scope of the statutory warranty or waive its applicability, when the waiver does not affect public policy or morals.

3. Implied and Express Warranties

We may further say that warranties specially included by the parties in the contract are known as "express warranties", while mandatory warranties specially provided for in the Civil or Commercial Codes are not necessarily to be stated in the contract, or those that are—due to the nature of the transaction—"obviously" present, even though they are not in writing, are known as "implied warranties". In brief, we may say that whenever a warranty will be presumed, it is known as an implied warranty. Thus, Article 2164 of the Civil Code establishes that in the event that the goods being sold had, at the moment when the transaction was entered into, a hidden defect that made them unfit for use, the seller must indemnify the purchaser, regardless of whether this provision was included in the contract or not.

For the existence of an express warranty, it is not necessary that the seller use formal or special words such as "warranty", "warrant", "guarantee", etc, as long as the wording of the clause clearly sets forth the intent of the seller to provide the warranty.

4. Warranties in Negotiations (*culpa in contrahendo*)

Argentine law does not have a specific provision relating to the contractual negotiations or the pre-contractual relationship. However, Article 1071 of the Civil Code states that the law does not allow abusive exercise of rights, considering as such the exercise that contravenes the purposes of the law or exceeds the limits imposed by good faith, morals and good practice.

Our courts have always considered that the party that leaves the bargaining process in an unjustified, arbitrary and inopportune manner, behaves in a way contrary to law and therefore has to indemnify the other party for the damages caused, the expenses incurred and, in some special and defined cases, for the expected profits.

The judgment known nationwide as the leading case regarding *culpa in contrahendo*, was rendered by the National Commercial Court in re *Litvak* v *Olivetti* in which the Italian company Olivetti held negotiations with an individual looking to enter into an agency agreement. In the said decision, the Court held that the unjustified and arbitrary break of the negotiations with no prior notice, entitles the other party to the indemnification of the damages caused, which include the real cost of the preparation work performed and the wages and dismissal indemnifications paid to employees hired in order to comply with the contract.[2]

Moreover, a local court has said that for the purpose of determining the indemnification due by the party responsible for the break of the negotiations, it is important to distinguish two different terms: price and value. The first is the one agreed between the parties to the agreement while the second arises from the comparison between the first one and the generality of the agreements entered into in the market for similar objects.[3]

5. Warranties in Promises to Sell

A general principle in Argentine law says that an offer (promise) to sell may be withdrawn at any moment before it is accepted.[4] This principle allows two exceptions:

(a) when the offeror has waived the right to withdraw the offer, and
(b) when the offeror has undertaken to maintain the offer for a certain period.

The addressee of an unfulfilled contractual offer has an action against the offeror to the extent of the damages suffered arising from the unjustified withdrawal of the offer.

6. Warranties in Sale Agreements

Both the Civil Code and the Commercial Code contain several provisions regarding warranties on quality, quantity, weight, and others which may be included in sale agreements. Thus, the *ad gustum* sale consists of a sale subject to the prior test and further approval of the purchaser, who may freely terminate the contract if he or she does not like the goods so purchased.[5]

The determined quality sale is the one where the seller guarantees a certain quality of the goods to be sold, and the purchaser is required to pay the price only in the event the merchandise has the quality promised by the seller.[6]

In a case when the sale was made upon samples delivered and approved by the purchaser, he or she may not reject the merchandise if they are in accordance with the samples previously accepted.[7]

Notwithstanding the above-quoted rules, the parties are completely free to introduce in the sale agreement whatever warranties they may consider appropriate for the better fulfilment of the transaction, or to set aside by mutual agreement any of the provisions established by the Codes if no moral or public policy principles are affected.

[2] *Litvak* v *Olivetti*, National Chamber of Commerce, Court B, Federal District, 19 September, 1953, published in La Ley, Vol. 75, p. 239 and in *Jurisprudencia Argentina* Vol. 1954–II, p. 88.
[3] *Gobbi Novag SA* v *Andromar SRL*, National Chamber on Civil Matters, Court F, 11 June, 1985, published in *El Derecho*, Vol. 116, p. 643.
[4] Article 1150 Civil Code.
[5] Article 1336 Civil Code and also Article 455 Commercial Code.
[6] Article 1338 Civil Code and also Article 456 Commercial Code.
[7] Article 456 Commercial Code.

7. Warranties in Sale of On-going Business

In Argentine legislation there is a specific law which governs several matters related to the transfer of on-going businesses,[8] the main purpose of which is to protect the rights and interests of creditors of the company to be sold. For example, Article 4 of this law provides that the seller must furnish to the purchaser a document containing, among other information, all debts, names and domicile of creditors, name and domicile of the notary public who intervenes in the transaction, and amounts of debts and maturity dates.

According to the law, the parties must publish for five days in the *Official Bulletin* and in one of the local newspapers, a special report giving notice of the sale. After which, they must wait for ten days before executing the purchase agreement in order to allow any creditor to oppose the transfer, unless the amount of his credit is withheld from the purchase amount and deposited to his order in a specific bank.

Article 8 provides that no sale of an on-going business may be made for a price less than the amount of debts stated by the seller plus the amount of additional debts arising from claims filed by creditors. Creditors not listed in the seller's report and not appearing to file their claims after the notices are published in the newspapers, have no right to enforce their claims against the purchaser or the assets so transferred.

Besides the various issues relating to creditors and debts which are ruled by the above-mentioned law, the parties to an on-going business sale agreement may include all warranties necessary or convenient for executing this kind of contract.

However, it has to be taken into account that local legislation provides that the seller of an on-going business remains liable *vis-à-vis* governmental authorities for any tax, labour and/or social security claim, regardless of what may have been established in the purchase agreement.

In local practice it is common to include warranties stating that:

(a) the seller is a corporation duly organised, validly existing and in good standing under the laws of the country;
(b) the seller has full power, authority and legal right to execute and deliver the agreement;
(c) all required approvals, if any, have been obtained;
(d) the agreement constitutes a legal, valid and binding obligation of the seller, enforceable against the seller in accordance with its terms;
(e) the agreement in is proper legal form for enforcement in Argentina;
(f) so far, all taxes payable by the business have been paid and there are no tax debts nor any tax enforcement carried out by the local tax authorities against the business;
(g) except for those listed in the agreement, there are no suits and proceedings pending against the business;
(h) the seller has good and marketable title to all of the properties and assets being sold;

[8] Law No. 11.687, enacted on 9 August, 1934, as amended.

(i) prior to the closing the seller will not, without the prior consent of the purchaser:
   (i) make any material change in the conduct of its business,
   (ii) enter into or amend in any material respect any material contract or agreement except in the ordinary course of business, or
   (iii) merge or consolidate with any other company;
(j) except for those listed in the agreement, which are wholly owned by the seller, there are no other patents, trademarks, trade names and service marks, registered or not, owned by, or licensed to, the seller;
(k) the seller has not granted in favour of a third party prior to the closing, any licence for the use of any patent, trademark, trade name, etc;
(l) the moveables that are included in the sale are owned by the seller and they are free and clear of any pledge, encumbrance or lien;
(m) all insurance policies are paid up as at the date of the closing, and the coverages have the extent disclosed in the agreement;
(n) except for those listed in the agreement, the company has not entered into other contracts (agency, distribution, service, supply, etc);
(o) the list of personnel currently employed by the company truly reflects the number, position, duties, seniority status and salaries of the employees, and there are no other employees except for those mentioned in the agreement.

8. Warranties in the Transfer of Shares

In addition to the warranties listed in paragraph 7 above, which are in general also applicable to a stock purchase agreement, it is usual to include some special warranties in an agreement of this kind in which the seller declares that:

(a) the shares to be transferred are free and clear of any pledge, mortgage, encumbrance, lien, charge, or are not subject to any restriction which impedes or obstructs their free transfer to the purchaser;
(b) the total authorised capital stock of the company consists of 'X' amount of shares, stating their class, series, par value and number of votes;
(c) the seller will not increase capital without the purchaser's prior approval;
(d) advances made on account of future issuances of stock are included in the sale;
(e) the company to be sold has no rights, interests or participations in other corporations, nor is obliged to acquire any other company in the future;
(f) the closing balance sheet and the general audited balance sheet are prepared, or are to be prepared, following generally accepted accounting principles which represent truly and reasonably the economic situation of the company;
(g) there are no known liabilities which are not reflected in the closing balance sheet;
(h) the members of the Board of Directors and auditors will resign immediately prior to the closing.

9. Warranties in Stock Exchange Acquisitions

In our local stock exchange practice, all purchases of stock are carried out by means of verbal orders given by sellers or purchasers to stockbrokers who purchase and sell shares, bonds or securities on behalf of their clients, following their instructions. There are no agreements, contracts, nor any other written document reflecting these transactions, other than the transaction tickets and certificates issued by the broker. Therefore, there are no warranties other than those established by the law, the Stock Exchange's regulations, the Securities Commission's communications, and the rules established through the years by the general practice among stock agents.

These transactions are of a particular kind, since in addition to a seller and purchaser there is a third party—the broker or brokers—to whom both parties may address any claim arising from the transaction. Thus, if the shares delivered to the purchaser were forged or the securities delivered to him were previously stolen or cancelled, the broker has to indemnify his client by returning his money or by replacing the shares, securities or bonds for good ones, without prejudice to the actions the broker has against the seller and his broker. Sales in a stock market normally do not imply a liability or warranty of seller as to the condition of the company.

10. Warranties of Absence of Defects

As mentioned in paragraph 3 above, Argentine legislation expressly provides that the seller is always liable for the hidden defects that existed in the goods being sold at the time the agreement was entered into. According to Article 2164 of the Civil Code *et seq* the defects taken into consideration are those that make the goods unfit for proper use, and if the purchaser had notice of said defects before the transaction,

- he or she would not have purchased them, or
- he or she would have paid a lower price.

There is no liability if the purchaser knew the defects, or should have known them according to the circumstances.

The purchaser has to give sufficient evidence that the defects were not apparent and existed before the transaction was made. Otherwise, the courts may construe that the defects appeared subsequent to the closing.[9]

Parties are permitted to restrict, waive or extend their liability for hidden defects, unless there is wilful misconduct on the part of seller.[10] Parties may also agree that defects that normally are not considered as such, become subject to indemnification, when the seller guarantees their non-existence, or a certain quality of the goods to be purchased.[11]

The purchaser who bought goods with hidden defects, has to choose one of two possible actions:

[9] Article 2168 Civil Code.
[10] Article 2166 Civil Code.
[11] Article 2167 Civil Code.

(a) to terminate the contract returning the purchased goods and in turn receiving the price so paid, or
(b) to ask the seller for a reduction in the amount paid, according to the lesser value of the defective goods, known as *quanti minoris* action.[12]

The action described in (a) above was admitted by the Court in *Sisteco Sistemas de Computación SA* v *Sujoy, Sergio A.* In this case Sisteco filed a complaint against Mr Sujoy for the collection of the balance of the purchase price of a computer system sold to the latter. The purchaser filed a counterclaim demanding the termination of the contract due to the fact that the computer system sold and installed by the seller never worked properly. The purchaser submitted sufficient evidence to the Court to demonstrate that the computer constantly failed from the very first day and the system was so unreliable that it was completely useless to serve the purposes for which it had been bought, despite the efforts made by several technicians the seller sent to the purchaser's premises, in order to repair the system. Moreover, the expert appointed by the Court to examine the computer, concluded that the whole system, except for the printer, was unreliable due to the several errors found in the information obtained from it, evidencing serious defects in the system itself. Based on these grounds, the Court held that the purchase agreement entered into by the parties must be considered terminated and that the seller must return to the purchaser the down payment while the purchaser must deliver to the seller the defective computer system.[13]

The courts have also said that, in case of sale of merchandise with defects the purchaser must behave diligently by giving notice of such circumstance to the seller as soon as possible after the delivery of the goods. Thus, the Civil and Commercial Court of Appeals of San Martín District rejected the claim of a purchaser who did not want to pay the price of certain purchased goods five months after delivery, alleging that the merchandise was not received in good condition.[14]

If the seller knew about the existence of hidded defects but remained silent, the purchaser has, in addition to both actions referred to in the above paragraph, an action to claim for indemnification for the damages suffered, if the purchaser chooses to request the termination of the contract.[15]

11. Warranties of Clear and Marketable Title

Our legislation also contains special provisions regarding the absence of defect in title of the goods to be transmitted, which is called an "eviction warranty".

Even in the event that the sale agreement does not contain any warranty of clear title, the law considers that it is always implied (see paragraph 3 above). However, the parties may set aside, restrict or extend this principle by means of introducing in the agreement a special clause which states that the purchaser

[12] Article 2174 Civil Code.

[13] *Sisteco Sistemas de Computación SA* v *Sujoy, Sergio A*, National Court of Commerce, Court E, 26 June, 1986, published in *El Derecho*, Vol. 122, p. 437.

[14] *Belziti, Miguel C* v *Ollero, César*, Civil and Commercial Court of Appeals of San Martín District, 16 May, 1985, published in *El Derecho*, Vol. 115, p. 218.

[15] Article 2176 Civil Code.

assumes any risk arising from defective title.[16] This clause will be of no effect if the seller knew before the contract was entered into that the goods to be transmitted were of unclear title. The seller is considered in such a case to have acted with wilful misconduct.[17]

Our courts have said that the standard implied eviction warranty may be modified by the parties to an agreement by means of waiving or restricting its scope.[18] According to the language used in our law, an eviction takes place when, by virtue of a judicial decision for a cause prior or contemporaneously to the sale, the purchaser is deprived, wholly or partially, of the right to the goods he or she has acquired.[19]

In other words, the seller must indemnify the purchaser when a third party is able to demonstrate in the courts that it has better title to the sold goods. In that case the seller must:

(a) give back to the purchaser the price he had received when the sale was made,
(b) pay all the expenses incurred for entering into the contract, and
(c) reimburse the damages caused to the purchaser.[20]

Following this line of thought, our courts have stated that any clause which limits the liability arising from eviction has to be restrictively construed, as it is a waiver of a right. Moreover, the eviction warranty extends to the following items:

- the reimbursement of the monies paid, and
- the indemnification for the damages caused.

Knowledge of the danger of eviction by the purchaser may release the seller from further liability, but only in connection with the indemnification for damages; in order to release the seller from the obligation of reimbursement of the collected price, a special and express waiver provision is necessary.[21]

12. Effective Time of Warranties

As described, most of the issues regarding warranties are, under Argentine law, left to the contractual agreement of the parties. Therefore, this point, like many others may arise in connection with warranties, is generally settled—if at all—by the parties themselves. However, with regard to statutory warranties (such as those described in paragraph 11), it should be noted that, in view of the lack of specific statutory provisions, they are to be deemed effective from the time of the transaction in question.

[16] Article 2098 Civil Code.
[17] Articles 2098 and 2099 Civil Code.
[18] *Agüero 1815 SCA* v *Pittaluga, José M*, National Court on Civil Matters, Court D, 22 June, 1976, published in *El Derecho*, Vol. 71, p. 240.
[19] Article 2091 Civil Code.
[20] Article 2119 Civil Code.
[21] *Vilches, María E* v *Larrahona, Elba del V*, Civil and Commercial Court of Appeals of San Martín District, Court II, 12 June, 1984, published in *El Derecho*, Vol. 111, p. 149.

13. Duration of Warranties; Time Limitation

There are no legal requirements concerning the duration of warranties. Hence, the parties are free to stipulate any duration they consider useful, necessary or convenient for the better fulfilment of the transaction.

Regarding the time limitation for filing a judicial claim requesting the payment of a debt or the fulfilment of a certain act, our Civil Code establishes as a general principle a ten-year term. However, there are some exceptions to this general principle. For example:

(a) the statute of limitations for the action demanding the nullity of acts with vitiating factors (see paragraph 18) is two years;
(b) the statute of limitations for the action of hidden defects in the purchased goods (see paragraph 10) is three months.

14. Beneficiary of the Warranty

Although the general principle provides that warranties are established by the seller in favour of the purchaser in order to induce him to enter into the agreement, there are no restrictions in our law against appointing any beneficiary other than the purchaser. In such case, the beneficiary must be clearly identified in the contract, and a special provision should establish who will be entitled to claim a breach of the warranty—the purchaser, the beneficiary or both.

15. Warranties Limitations and Disclaimers

As mentioned above, it is possible to limit or disclaim the seller's implied warranties, as long as no public policy or moral principles are affected. The typical case in which a limitation or disclaimer will *not* be admitted is when the clause constitutes a waiver of the seller's fraud or wilful misconduct (*dolus*).

16. Formal Requirements

Article 1193 of the Civil Code provides that all agreements with an economic value in excess of a certain amount of money (which has become negligible as the consequence of inflation), must be made in writing and cannot be proved through witnesses.

Notwithstanding the above, there is no legal provision establishing that certain clauses (for example warranties and representations) must be made in writing for their validity or enforcement: once the existence of the agreement is proved (through the written document), a party may submit whatever evidence (including witnesses) for proving the existence of those clauses. Thus, the parties to an agreement may verbally agree on the sale's terms and conditions, including warranties.

17. Breach of Warranties: Conditions to Enforce Warranties

The enforcement of warranties arising under an agreement is subject to the general conditions for the enforcement of contractual provisions under the law of contract and to the conditions set forth in the respective agreement.

In turn, enforcement of statutory warranties is subject to the proof of the factual requirements set forth in the law (for example, existence of the sale, proof of the purpose of the purchase, etc).

18. Defences, Vitiating Factors and Nullity

In case of a breach of warranty, the seller may argue, in defence, the fact that the agreement the parties have entered into contains a vitiating factor which renders invalid either the agreement itself or the breached warranty or warranties.

In Argentine legislation, a vitiating factor exists whenever the parties to the agreement do not act with intention, freedom and good faith. The vitiating factors based upon the lack of intention of the party are error and *dolus*. The vitiating factor based upon the lack of freedom is violence. And the vitiating factors based upon the lack of good faith are simulation and fraud.

The party suffering vitiating factors when entering into an agreement may sue, demanding the annulment of the agreement and, if there were damages, indemnification of the damages caused by the other party.

The vitiating factors are as follows:

(a) Error: defined as the wrong knowledge an individual has of a thing. In terms of importance, the error may be:
  (i) radical (*erreur-obstacle*): one which completely negates the existence itself of the act, for the error affects its nature (*error in negotio*) or its object (*error in corpore*);
  (ii) essential: one which has to do with the person who enters into the act (*error in personam*) or with the substantial quality of the object (*error in substantia*). These errors do not negate the existence of the act but render it voidable;
  (iii) related to qualities of the object, such as its value, and does not necessarily affect the validity of the act.

  An essential error may be invoked by the party who suffered it only if it is excusable, that is, if from the circumstances of the act the party is considered not to have known and not to be reasonably required to know the error which affects the agreement.

  An error in the law is generally not invocable in our legislation, for our Civil Code establishes that the lack of knowledge of the law is not an excuse, unless the exception is expressly authorised by the law itself.[22] Our Code presumes, as a general principle, that the law is mandatory and is known by everybody.

(b) *Dolus:* according to our Code, there is *dolus* when, in order to cause the other party to enter into an agreement, a party makes false statements, hides the correct information, or uses any unfair means for such purposes.

  In order for the *dolus* to be validly invoked by a party, there are four requisites:

[22] Article 20 Civil Code.

(i) the *dolus* must have been material;
(ii) it must have been the cause of the action;
(iii) it must have caused a relevant damage;
(iv) there must have not been *dolus* from both parties.

(c) Violence: this is action caused on an individual in order to force him, against his will, to enter into an agreement. This violence may be exercised on the individual's body or against his moral beliefs or feelings, being in the latter case known as intimidation. Our Civil Code states that there is intimidation when a party, through unfair threats, inflicts on the other party the belief that he is going to suffer an action against his body, freedom, honour and assets, or those of his wife, parents or children.[23]

(d) Simulation: this takes place when the agreement has false clauses, untrue dates, false names, etc, by virtue of which the parties try to confuse third parties to their own advantage.

In this case, neither of the parties has the right to demand the nullity of the agreement alleging the existence of simulation. Such right only belongs to the third party affected by the simulated act.

(e) Fraud: this takes place when an insolvent party enters into a simulated purchase agreement in order to sell his assets so as to keep them away from the reach of his creditors.

To the extent that seller's creditors prove that an agreement of this kind is fraudulent, and the assets are still owned by the seller, the agreement will have no validity and creditors will be entitled to attack those assets for collecting their debts, regardless of the purchase agreement and of who is the supposed new owner (purchaser) of such assets.

19. Release from Liability

A release from liability in spite of a breach of warranties might have its origin in one of the following situations:

(a) By the seller's disclosures: in the event the seller gives sufficient notice to the purchaser with regard to certain circumstances, facts or qualities of the business, then there will be no grounds for the purchaser to enforce a warranty connected with the facts he was previously informed about. Thus, by means of a clear and complete disclosure made by the seller to the purchaser, the seller may waive or at least restrict his liability.

(b) By the purchaser's conduct: the purchaser's conduct may release the seller from liability in case he does not perform the obligations he has undertaken, does not apply the purchased goods to the use they were destined for, does not follow correctly the instructions for use given by the seller, etc. However, if the seller wants to release his liability under this circumstance after being sued by the purchaser, he must submit before the court sufficient evidence to convince the judge that the purchaser's conduct caused the breach of the agreement.

[23] Article 937 Civil Code.

(c) By the purchaser's awareness: the seller may be released from liability in the event he is able to evidence that the purchaser knew or should have known the fact or circumstance he is alleging, as cause for the breach.

20. Warranties Outside the Sale Agreement

Pursuant to the freedom of forms established by our Civil Code, the parties to an agreement may validly decide to list the warranties they have agreed upon in a separate document outside the main contract or even verbally (see paragraph 16 above). In the event the parties decide to proceed this way, they must take care to include sufficient references in the separate document in order to ensure without doubt that the warranties correspond to that certain agreement and that both documents must be considered and construed as if they were one and the same agreement.

Australia

William C Conley*

Blake Dawson Waldron, Sydney, Australia

Australian contract law is descended from the English common law, and in almost every respect is identical. However, just as the common law in the United States diverged from the English common law once the umbilical cords of English appellate jurisdiction and political and economic dependency were severed, so too, in Australia, the abolition of appeals to the Privy Council in stages from 1968, 1975 and 1986 may have given scope to the development of an autonomous contract law.[1] But a more material impact on the real rights of contracting parties has been made directly and indirectly by protective legislation, pre-eminently the Trade Practices Act 1974, enacted to soften the rigour of a common law shaped at a time when emphasis was given to the literal terms of contract and their form, underlined by a robust belief in the capacity of freely contracting parties to look after their own interests.

1. Common Law

At common law, pre-contractual representations are legally distinct from contractual terms. Representations given prior to the conclusion of a contract could, on the facts, be considered to be terms of the contract, but the model of formation of contract built on offer and acceptance tended to favour those contractual terms whose offer and acceptance by the parties could be most readily demonstrated. The higher ontological status of writing and, of course, its greater certainty, led to the presumption that, where there was a written contract, that written contract was the best source of the terms which had been offered and accepted by the parties. This is the "parol evidence" rule, classically formulated in the following terms:

* Partner, Blake Dawson Waldron; I acknowledge the assistance and contribution of Gilbert Elliot, solicitor (also at Blake Dawson Waldron).

[1] See comments by A. Mason (Sir Anthony Mason, Chief Justice of the High Court, writing extrajudicially), *Australian Contract Law* 1988, 1 JCL 1, 2.

> If there be a contract which has been reduced into writing, verbal evidence is not allowed to be given of what passed between the parties, either before the written instrument was made, or during the time it was in a state of preparation, so as to add to or subtract from, or in any manner to vary or qualify the written contract.[2]

While it might be possible to adduce evidence of a collateral contract which was verbal, the rule known in Australia as that in *Hoyts Pty Limited* v *Spencer*[3] has the effect of preventing the proof of a collateral contract inconsistent with the primary written contract. Though criticised by academic commentators,[4] this rule has been referred to without criticism as recently as 1986 by the High Court.[5]

Contracts are typically entered into after negotiations in which the parties make various representations as to the value of the thing they have to offer or their capacity to perform their obligations under the contract. While the obligations themselves might be spelt out with some precision in the contract, often a party would not enter into a contract, or would do so under different terms, if these various representations were not true. While at common law a representation which was knowingly or recklessly false would give the representee a right to damages for deceit, often this would be difficult to establish. Innocent misrepresentation might give a right to rescind the contract, but only in circumstances where it would be possible to put both parties back where they started. In order to be able to rely on representations, the custom developed of incorporating them into the contract as warranties. It is in this sense of a contractual promise—a term of the contract, breach of which gives rise to a right to claim damages as distinct from rescission of the contract—that reference is made to "warranty" in this chapter.

One of the most fundamental warranties in a contract for the sale of anything is that the vendor in fact has title to the thing to be sold. This is particularly important in the common law because of the doctrine of *nemo dat quod non habet*, which prevents a purchaser obtaining any more from a vendor than the vendor has to dispose of. A modern descendant of such a warranty in an offer to purchase shares is as follows:

> Subject to this Offer, and by signing the Acceptance Form and forwarding it [in accordance with clause X] you will be deemed to have represented and warranted to [the purchaser] that all the subject [XYZ] Shares will at the time of your acceptance and of the registration of the transfer to [the purchaser] be fully paid up and free from all mortgages, charges, liens and other encumbrances (whether legal or equitable) whatsoever and restrictions on transfer of any kind and that you have full power and authority to sell the subject [XYZ] Shares.

And this clause would be repeated in the first person in the acceptance form returned by the vendor to the purchaser.

> I [the Vendor] represent and warrant to [the purchaser] that . . . [etc].

[2] *Goss* v *Lord Nugent* (1833) 5 B & Ad 58; 110 ER 713 per Denman CJ at 64, 716.
[3] (1919) 27 CLR 133.
[4] J.W. Carter & D.J. Harland, *Contract Law in Australia*, Butterworths, Sydney, 1991, 179.
[5] *Gates* v *City Mutual Life Assurance Society Ltd* (1986) 160 CLR 1.

In the sale of a business, the warranties are likely to be more wide-ranging, and will normally include such warranties as:

> The facts set out in the Recitals and the Schedules to this Agreement are true, complete and accurate in all respects, and there are no material omissions therefrom.

and

> All information which has been given by or on behalf of the Vendors, the directors auditors or officers of the Company in the course of the negotiations leading to this Agreement is true and accurate in all respects.

Some idea of the breadth and complexity of the matters covered by warranties, and of the tendency to attempt to cover comprehensively matters on which a purchaser may need to rely may be obtained from the fact that the pro forma agreement from which the above warranties are taken[6] includes 51 such warranties.

One obvious purpose of incorporating warranties in writing is to establish with certainty those factors emerging from the negotiation stage which are important to the parties, and to allocate the risk for the various factual assumptions which made a contract commercially attractive. If allocation of risk is itself to be a subject for bargaining, then, as well as comprehensive and detailed warranties of matters within the parties' respective knowledge and competence, there can also be negative warranties—that the purchaser had relied on his or her own inquiries and that the vendor had made no representations. Clearly, such warranties, like any written agreement, might not always represent the true basis on which parties have entered into an agreement, yet the parol evidence rule could make it difficult for a plaintiff to establish otherwise.

In some circumstances the effect of such disclaimers or inverse warranties would be tantamount to that of an exclusion clause (that is, a clause which deprives an innocent party from recovering damages from the other for something which it would otherwise normally be liable). The common law has long been hostile to exclusion clauses, and a number of rules of construction have been developed to limit their effect. In particular, it has said that exclusion clauses will be construed strictly *contra proferentum* so as to limit the benefit they give to the party whose liability is reduced. As a rule of construction, this rule should properly only be applied where needed to resolve an ambiguity in a contractual term, but courts were once inclined readily to find an ambiguity so as to have an opportunity to apply the rule. Perhaps, however, because of the availability of statutory remedies protecting weaker bargaining parties and the assumption that parties in negotiating commercial contracts such as those for the purchase or sale of assets or a business are well informed and have access to qualified legal advice, there is a modern trend at common law, at least in relation to commercial contracts, towards treating exclusion clauses on the same basis as any other term.[7]

[6] D.R. Magarey, *Buying and Selling Businesses and Companies*, Butterworths, Sydney, 1989, 456–63.

[7] see, eg *Darlington Futures Ltd* v *Delco Australia Pty Ltd* (1986) 161 CLR 500, 510 (High Court) and J.W. Carter & D.J. Harland *Contract Law in Australia*, Butterworths, Sydney, 1991, 231–2.

2. Hard Cases: Equitable Intervention

The enforcement of warranties (or of warranties denying the existence of representations) may also be affected by equitable doctrines supplementing or vitiating the existence or exercise of legal rights. The attitude of courts may be affected by an unconscionable abuse of superior bargaining power (especially when coupled with superior knowledge), against a particularly "vulnerable" party.[8] Under the doctrines of estoppel, to the extent that the party has relied on conduct which, for instance, may had led to a belief that contractual terms would not be enforced, or that other contractual terms would be granted the "reliance interest" of that party may be protected.[9]

For instance, if, in negotiations to purchase a business on rented premises, the landlord indicated that it would consent to an assignment of the lease on its present terms, but subsequently, after the purchase of the business, refused to effect the assignment, the landlord could be compelled to make good its earlier representations by conveying the lease.

Estoppel might also effectively avoid the rule in *Hoyts* v *Spencer*.[10] For instance, if, in a sale of business, the agreement contained a wide range of representations and warranties, these might nevertheless prove unenforceable if a party could show that there had been a course of conduct between the parties which led that party to rely on a belief that the real terms of the agreement between the parties was other than expressed in the formal agreement. Where the agreement was a "boilerplate" agreement containing standard terms, it would, as a matter of evidence, be easier to establish such an estoppel than when the terms of the contract were the result of explicit negotiation between the parties.

In circumstances where parties are engaged in a joint venture or are even negotiating towards a joint venture, there may be fiduciary obligations between the parties, that is, essentially, obligations of good faith to take each other's interests into account. The High Court has made clear that the categories of fiduciary obligations are not closed, though the courts will not be quick to detect such obligations between commercial parties operating at arm's length.[11] However, they could apply where, for instance, one joint venturer was buying out another, and no contractual stipulation would be sufficient to forgive any breach of such a duty if it was not itself given without full knowledge. So that, if either the vendor or purchaser had concealed material information to the other party's detriment, that other party would be entitled to compensation for the loss suffered or the profit gained by the breach of fiduciary duty that the concealment caused. In *Gulf Pacific Pty Limited* v *Sidney Londish & Ors*[12] Londish, a land developer, was involved in a joint

[8] *Commercial Bank of Australia* v *Amadio* (1983) 151 CLR 447.

[9] *Waltons Stores (Interstate) Ltd* v *Maher* (1988) 164 CLR 387 which has taken the doctrine of "promissory estoppel" in Australia beyond its present limits in England.

[10] *supra*. fn. 3.

[11] *United Dominion* v *Brian* (1985) 157 CLR 1; *Hospital Products Ltd* v *United States Surgical Corporation* (1984) 156 CLR 91.

[12] Federal Court, unreported, 15 October 1992.

venture with Gulf in relation to an exhausted brickworks which it was proposed to develop into a golf-course and residential development. Negotiations with one prospective purchaser proved abortive, but at the time Londish bought out Gulf's interest in the venture he failed to disclose that fresh negotiations had been entered into with a second prospective purchaser, which would have made an appreciable difference to the price at which Gulf would have been prepared to sell its interest. This failure to disclose was a breach of fiduciary duty, and Londish (and other parties involved in the breach) were required to pay Gulf the difference between the price paid and the share in the profits which Gulf would have received under the terms of the original "joint venture".

2.1 Other judicial intervention

Warranties may be implied as terms of a contract by courts in order to give "business efficacy" to the contract or "by law" in recognition of the nature of the contract. In the former whether the warranty is imported depends on the express terms used and surrounding circumstances. In the latter, it is *prima facie* important if the contract is of a particular class but this presumption may be displaced by a consideration of the intentions of the parties. As Menzies J said in *Helicopter Sales Pty Limited* v *Rotorwork Pty Limited:*

> Each case must depend upon its own circumstances and upon what is found to be the intention of the parties.[13]

Such classes (which have usually applied to contracts for the sale of goods and services) are not necessarily closed and a new class of such contract will only be accepted if the term is considered necessary and reasonable to imply.[14]

In *Castlemaine Tooheys Ltd,* the New South Wales Court of Appeal referred to the nineteenth-century House of Lords decision of *Trego* v *Hunt* and the implied term (which one may categorise as a vendor's warranty) that in contracts for the sale of business a vendor will not take steps to depreciate what he has sold (goodwill) by soliciting customers of his former business. In *Castlemaine Tooheys Ltd* it was claimed that this principle is not limited to the solicitation of customers but applies generally to prohibit any action by a previous owner of a business which will depreciate the value of the goodwill sold. The Court noted that this case concerned not a contract for the sale of a business but a contract for the sale of shares in a company which carried on a business.

In Australia, as the Court also noted, there has been no decision to the effect that a *Trego* v *Hunt* term was to be implied into such a contract although the Court expressed sympathy for some term of such a kind to be implied, at least into such contracts where the business is run by a company and the vendor is selling all the shares in the company and the vendor also runs the underlying business. The Court did not need to make a final decision on whether such a term was to be implied in this case as the relevant terms and surrounding circumstances of the agreement rebutted any *prima facie* presumption that any such term was to be implied. It was neither necessary nor reasonable said the Court.

[13] (1974) 122 CLR at 6.

[14] *Castlemaine Tooheys Ltd* v *Carlton & United Breweries Ltd* (1974) 10 NSWLR 468.

The Court looked at the extensive commercial experience of the parties, the express terms of the contract, the attention by the parties to many detailed matters in those terms, the involvement of legal representatives in the long and complex negotiation and drafting process and in particular the attention given by the parties to various other matters designed to protect the goodwill acquired by the purchaser.

2.2 Statutory Intervention

During this century, various statutes have been enacted aimed at overriding the freedom generally given by the common law to parties negotiating the terms of commercial contracts. Traditionally, these statutes related to contracts for the sale of goods. More recently their reach has been extended to cover different situations and even commercial contracts relating to such matters as the sale of businesses.

2.3 Unequal Bargaining Power: Statutory Remedies

One example of such statutory intervention relates to warranties which are unfair or oppressive and which are the outcome of an unequal bargaining position. In the State of New South Wales, these may be struck down by the Contracts Review Act 1980, though this provision is essentialy limited to consumer contracts. The Commonwealth Trade Practices Act also prohibits "unconscionable conduct" in relation to consumers, and legislation recently introduced now extends this prohibition to unconscionable conduct generally. As referred to below, this statute also has State equivalents to give most of the provisions Australia-wide coverage.

3. Trade Practices Act: section 52 and State Fair Trading Acts

The principal development in recent years in Australian law concerning the terms of the bargain between Contracting Parties including warranties has come from the Trade Practices Act 1974 (Commonwealth). As well as extending traditional common law and sale of goods warranties concerning fitness for purpose, the Act, in section 52, contains a general prohibition that:

> A corporation shall not, in trade, or commerce, engage in conduct that is misleading or deceptive or is likely to mislead or deceive.

While included in Part V of that Act (headed "Consumer Protection"), the greater part of at least the reported cases involving this section have not involved "consumers", or at least have not involved consumers as plaintiffs. Actions have often been initiated by trade competitors. Australian States have enacted complementary legislation.

Claims based on misleading and deceptive conduct frequently arise in the context of a sale of business. They are particularly attractive to purchasers because not only the vendor, but also the vendor's agents or advisers may be found to be liable. For instance, in *Email (Furniture) Ltd* v *Camfia (Industries)*

Pty Ltd,[15] the vendors' accountants, who certified that the net profit was calculated in accordance with Australian Accounting Standards despite their failure to attend a stocktake and their own earlier criticisms of the accounting methods used by the business, were liable under section 42 of the Fair Trading Act (NSW),[16] though in this case, there was also a basis for liability for negligent misstatement. Similarly, in *Sevenhill Holdings Pty Ltd* v *Musovic*,[17] a case involving a sale of a "lunch-bar" business, the vendor's agent was held liable for its part in the preparation of a seriously misleading depreciation schedule. However, only the vendor was liable for misrepresentations relating to the takings of the shop in question, in which the agent had acted merely as the "conduit" of information from the vendors to the purchasers.

The salient features of section 52 of the Trade Practices Act (the "Act") in comparison with pre-existing common law rights in relation to extra-contractual representations (whether for the tort of deceit, for innocent or for negligent misrepresentation) are:

(a) The section prohibits misleading or deceptive conduct or conduct which is likely to mislead or deceive—theoretically the liability is strict.
(b) There is no "privity" of representation or contract: any person suffering loss by the conduct may seek a remedy.
(c) There is a wide range of statutory remedies.

However, each of these features has been qualified in practice by the tendency of courts to construe statutory powers according to analogous common law and equitable remedies.[18]

3.1 "A Corporation"

The form of this prohibition is to some extent shaped by constitutional division of powers in Australia. The statute relies on the Commonwealth constitutional power to regulate corporations while section 6 of the Act extends the reference to a corporation to include persons engaged in interstate trade and commerce and persons using postal, telegraphic or telephonic services (again, relying on Commonwealth constitutional authority in those areas). State legislation now applies to persons in identical terms.[19]

[15] (1992) ASC paras. 56–165. Although the accountants claimed that the certification expressed merely an opinion, Cole J. followed earlier cases in finding that an expression of opinion will be misleading and deceptive if it is made, as in this case, without a proper basis.

[16] This is in essentially the same terms as section 52 of the Trade Practices Act. See text accompanying note 19, *infra*.

[17] Federal Court, Unreported, 24 March 1992 (French J).

[18] M. Blakeney, *Old wine in new bottles: influence of the common law on the interpretation of section 52 of the Trade Practices Act* (1984) 58 ALJ 316.

[19] eg Fair Trading Act 1987 (NSW) section 42. There are also a number of other early State or territory provisions against misrepresentation, such as the Law Reform (Misrepresentation) Act 1977 (ACT) section 4(1). In *Crawford & Ors* v *Parish* (1992) ATPR (Digest) paras. 46–087 Higgins J commented that it would be hard to imagine a breach of this section (and hence presumably similar provisions in other States) which was not also a breach of section 52 of the Trade Practices Act.

3.2 "In Trade or Commerce"

The spectre of an untrammelled obligation to eschew conduct which is misleading and deceptive and perhaps a psychological reaction against the use of the Trade Practices Act to bypass the checks and balances embodied in the qualifications attached to general law remedies, have led to some judicial attempts to limit its ambit. In *Concrete Constructions (NSW) Pty Limited* v *Nelson*[20] an injured worker sought to avoid limitations on common law right to damages imposed by State workers' compensation legislation by claiming that a foreman's conduct, in advising and instructing him how a task was to be performed was misleading and deceptive conduct (by the employing corporation) in trade and commerce. On appeal to the High Court (Australia's final appellate court) two members of the Court would have excluded the workman's claim because the scheme of the Act, including the designation of Part V as referring to "Consumer Protection", limited its application to consumers, though not necessarily only private or domestic consumers. However, earlier High Court authority[21] that the express terms of the section were not to be read down in this way by reference to the heading prevailed, and the majority preferred to say that the worker's claim was excluded by the requirement that the conduct in question be "in trade and commerce". This required conduct which itself was *in* trade and commerce, rather than merely incidental to it (as for instance, a hand signal by a delivery-truck driver).

While earlier cases may need qualification in the light of the decision in *Concrete Constructions*, it seems that the sale of a private dwelling will not constitute conduct in trade and commerce by the vendor, but will constitute such conduct by the real estate agent.[22] There is no requirement, however, that the activity form part of the corporation's usual trade and commerce, and the sale of a business enterprise itself (including an owner-operated small business) has been held to be impressed with a trading and commercial character to come within the section.

4. Misleading or Deceptive Conduct

To mislead has been defined simply as "to lead into error".[23] It does not seem that the term "deceptive" adds anything to this. The additional category of "conduct which is likely to mislead or deceive" obviates any requirement to prove that any person has in fact been deceived, though actual deception will still be relevant as a matter of causation when damages or other substantive remedies between parties are sought, as opposed to corrective advertising or injunctions against the continuation of misleading conduct. "Conduct" includes representations, and the doing, or refusing or refraining to do, of any thing.[24] Remaining silent may, in certain situations, constitute misleading conduct.

[20] (1990) 92 ALR 193.

[21] *Hornsby Building Information Centre Pty Ltd* v *Sydney Building Information Centre Ltd* (1978) 140 CLR 216

[22] The agent's conduct will not then be imputed to the principal: *Argy & Anor* v *Blunts & Ors* (1990) ATPR paras. 41–015.

[23] *Weitmann* v *Katies Limited & Ors* (1977) ATPR paras. 40–041 per Franki J.

[24] Section 4(1).

The establishment of misleading or deceptive conduct involves a fourfold procedure:[25]

(a) identification of the relevant class to whom the conduct is directed, or who are exposed to the conduct (though it is not necessary that the conduct be directed to any class of the public: the conduct may be entirely private);
(b) consideration of the conduct by reference to the full range of members of that class, including the gullible and the poorly educated, where applicable;
(c) an objective determination by the court of whether the conduct was misleading or deceptive: intention, or actual deception of particular people will bear only evidentiary weight;
(d) the evaluation of the causative link between the conduct and persons being misled—this is perhaps better viewed as a check on any tendency, where actual error on the part of consumers has been established, to assume that it has been in fact caused by the conduct in question. This is essentially a question of reliance or likely reliance. Damages, when awarded, are on a reliance basis.

4.1 Representations as to Future Matters

Section 51A(1) of the Trade Practices Act provides that:

> . . . where a corporation makes a representation with respect to any future matter (including the doing of, or the refusing to do, any act) and the corporation does not have any reasonable grounds for making the representation, the representation shall be taken to be misleading.

Subsection 51A(2) imposes an evidentiary burden on a corporation[26] in any proceedings, by deeming that, unless it adduces evidence to the contrary in such cases, the corporation shall be deemed to have had no reasonable grounds. This makes the task of applicants easier, and is consistent with the objective approach of the Act to the conduct in question. In comparison, the common law approach to representations as to future matters relied on an implied representation as to the state of mind of the representor and the axiom that "the state of a man's mind is as much a fact as the state of his digestion".[27]

4.2 Importance of Findings of Fact

The section is generally worded, and has a protective purpose, supplemental to the general law. This in turn imports an emphasis on substance over form. Because actual causative links will be vital in the determination of remedies, factual findings are of crucial importance in the application of section 52. This has been particularly obvious in a number of cases concerning foreign currency loans by banks (in circumstances where foreign currency transactions had only recently in Australia been deregulated) where the success of plaintiffs under section 52 has generally depended on the extent to which they have been found

[25] *Taco Company of Australia Inc & Anor* v *Taco Bell Pty Limited & Ors* (1982) ATPR paras. 40–303, 43, 752–3.
[26] Subject to the extended applications of the term under section 6.
[27] *Edgington* v *Fitzmaurice* (1883) 29 Ch D 459, 483 per Bowen LJ.

to rely upon the bank officers as advisers rather than merely as salespersons.[28] As a matter of fact, such reliance is less likely to be found when the relationship can be characterised as an "arm's length commercial transaction".

4.3 Remedies

Section 52 is coupled with extremely broadly cast remedies in Part VI of the Act. A person (who need not be the representee) "who suffers loss or damage by conduct of another person that was done in contravention of a provision of Part IV and V" (which includes section 52) may "recover the amount of the loss or damage by action against that other person or against any person involved in the contravention".[29] There are also powers to grant injunctions[30] and a broadly cast power to make such order as the court thinks fit.[31]

4.4 Disclaimers and Attempts to "Contract Out"

There have been a number of attempts to pre-empt the operation of section 52 by the inclusion of contractual warranties that, for instance, the purchaser has not relied on any warranties other than those enumerated in the contract. Because of the obvious scope for such clauses (rather like fine print disclaimers) to circumvent the policy of the statute,[32] judges have repeatedly insisted that such terms cannot contractually exclude the operation of the section, and whether or not there has been misleading or deceptive conduct remains a question of objective fact.[33]

> A disclaimer or exclusion clause will affect liability for misleading or deceptive conduct only if it deprives the conduct of that quality or breaks the causal connection between conduct and loss. Whether it has that effect in a given case is a question of evidence and not a question of law.[34]

5. Silence as Misleading Conduct

Findings of fact are also crucial to the string of cases concerning failure to disclose information. Reference to existing legal duties of disclosure may be considered unhelpful precisely because of the remedial intent of the Act.[35] The very question that the courts are asked to decide is: notwithstanding that a party was not necessarily under a positive legal duty (other than under the section) to

[28] For instance, *Mehta & Anor* v *Commonwealth Bank of Australia* (1990) ATPR paras. 41–026, where reliance was found, but overturned on appeal, *Commonwealth Bank of Australia* v *Mehta & Anor* (1990) ATPR paras. 41–103.

[29] Section 82.

[30] Section 80.

[31] Section 87. In disputes between trade competitors, the power to order corrective advertising (section 80A) is also important.

[32] *Keen Mar Corporation Pty Limited* v *Labrador Park Shopping Centre Pty Limited & Anor* (1989) ATPR (Digest) paras. 46–068.

[33] *Henjo Investments Pty Ltd* v *Collins Marrickville Pty Ltd* (1988) 79 ALR 83.

[34] *Kewside Pty Limited* v *Warman International Ltd* (1990) ATPR (Digest) paras. 46–059 per French J at 53,222.

[35] *Elna Australia Pty Limited* v *International Computers (Australia) Pty Ltd* 75 ALR 271, 280 per Gummow J.

make certain matters known, has its failure to make them known constituted misleading or deceptive conduct?[36] Reliance will obviously be crucial to this question, and an environment of predetermined legal duties will be of assistance in establishing circumstances of reliance, but it will not be conclusive.

Section 4(2) of the Act provides that:

> (a) a reference to engaging in conduct shall be read as a reference to doing or refusing to do any act . . .
> (c) a reference to refusing to do an act includes a reference to –
> (i) refraining (otherwise than inadvertently) from doing that act.

Early consideration of silence as misleading and deceptive conduct was closely bound to these definitions. In *Bradford House Pty Limited* v *Leroy Fashion Group Ltd,*[37] the Court conceded that a duty to disclose defects in real property might exist despite the general law principle of *caveat emptor*, but were of the opinion that a person must be aware that his or her silence was conveying an erroneous impression before it could be said that the person was "refraining" from doing an act—which they thought was the relevant sense in which a failure to disclose could be characterised as "conduct".

Because of the importance of specific factual situations mentioned above, it is difficult to stipulate the "elements" of silence which constitute misleading conduct, but a cluster of four factors has been suggested as relevant:[38]

(a) proximity between the parties;
(b) knowledge of the relevant information—since without knowledge the failure to disclose will generally be "inadvertent";[39]
(c) materiality of the undisclosed information—this will go to questions of reliance;[40]
(d) the failure to disclose results in injustice to one party—this allows for some assessment of prevailing acceptable trading practices and commercial morality.

In *Rhone-Poulenc Agrochimie SA* v *UIM Chemical Services Pty Limited,*[41] the conduct complained of was the sale of a fungicide without any indication that the product was not authorised under the relevant legislation in some States, its sale was illegal, and it could be confiscated by state authorities (though this was fairly unlikely). On appeal, the majority conceded that silence could constitute conduct, but failed in the particular circumstances to find misleading or deceptive conduct, in part because the failure was inadvertent,[42] and in part because of a reluctance

[36] *Kimberley NZI Finance Ltd* v *Torero Pty Ltd* (1989) ATPR (Digest) paras. 46–054 at 53, 195.
[37] (1983) 46 ALR 305.
[38] D. Skapinker, *The Imposition of a Positive Duty of Disclosure under Section 52 of the Trade Practices Act 1974 (Cth)*, (1991) 4 JCL 75.
[39] though possibly in some circumstances, even though a party is ignorant, its conduct may be an implied representation: *Spedley Securities Limited (In Liquidation)* v *Bank of New Zealand and ors* (1991) ATPR paras. 41–143.
[40] In *Rhone-Poulenc (infra)* the majority clearly thought the unlikelihood of seizure under the State laws meant that few purchasers would have been "induced" by the failure to disclose.
[41] (1986) 68 ALR 77.
[42] *Ibid.* 83, per Bowen CJ.

to find the necessary reliance and concomitant duty.[43] Jackson J dissented, on the grounds that buyers are entitled to assume that regulated products such as fungicides are sold legally and may legally be used.[44]

In *Henjo Investments Pty Ltd* v *Collins Marrickville Pty Ltd*,[45] vendors of a restaurant failed to disclose that the then set-up of the restaurant, with seats at the bar as well as at tables, was in excess of the maximum seating capacity permitted by licensing authorities and the local council. This vitally affected the value of the business, as the vendor would well have been aware. In these circumstances, the failure to disclose was conduct which was misleading and deceptive. The conduct did not cease to be misleading and deceptive just because the purchaser's solicitor could have ascertained the true situation by further inquiries.

Krakowski & Anor v *Eurolynx Properties Limited & Anor*[46] gives a more workaday illustration of judicial attitudes to the various factors mentioned above. The plaintiff purchased an apartment from the defendant as an investment property. In requisitions in relation to the existing lease, the defendant's solicitor omitted to disclose that, although the six-year lease provided for an annual rental of $156,000, the tenant had been granted, by a collateral agreement, a three-month rent holiday and an allowance equal to a year's rent for fitting out and stocking the premises. In a falling property market and recession, the tenant subsequently defaulted, and the plaintiff claimed that the failure to disclose the collateral inducements to the tenant had misled the plaintiff into placing a higher value on the property, since the lease rental figure was not the "real" rental figure. O'Bryan J doubted whether the plaintiff had relied on the statement except as an indication of income-stream, and observed that had it not been for the default, the collateral agreement would never have concerned the plaintiff. The conduct in question had not misled the plaintiff, and any loss was more readily attributable to the tenant's default and a fall in property values. The plaintiff was sufficiently experienced in the real estate market to have inquired about tenant incentives if he had chosen to. Here, it is clear, questions of unfairness loomed large in the judicial subtext.

In *McWilliam's Wines Pty Limited* v *LS Both Wine Transport Pty Ltd*,[47] the Court rejected a contention that performance of a contract constitutes a representation of fitness for performance and hence (the defendant's tankers were, unknown to it, contaminated) misleading conduct under section 52. In this case, the terms of the consignment note expressly limited the defendant's obligations. This is perhaps another instance of Skapinker's fourth factor. Clearly the judge was happy to leave the contractual relations of the parties undisturbed by section 52:

> By presenting the tankers it did not represent that the drivers would always drive carefully, or that a valve would not spring a leak; it did not represent that there had been no carelessness in the servicing of the tankers . . . [or] that there had not been

[43] *Ibid.* 99–100 per Lockhart J.
[44] *Ibid.* 103.
[45] (1988) 79 ALR 83.
[46] (1992) VConvR paras. 54–436.
[47] (1992) ATPR (Digest) paras. 46–089.

carelessness in the cleaning of the tankers. McWilliams could not have been led to expect any such thing. What it [the defendant] represented was that the carriage of the wine, and the legal rights and obligations of it and McWilliams, would be regulated by the terms of the contract of carriage.[48]

6. Other Statutory Provisions—the Corporations Law

The Corporations Law[49] also contains provisions that impact upon the freedom of vendors and purchasers to regulate their risks and liabilities through express contractual provisions such as warranties and representations in the sales of securities.

First, there are the prospectus requirements which, unless excluded by other provisions of the Law, will apply to offers and invitations for the purchase of securities.[50] These require that a prospectus be issued and include certain information. Penalties are imposed and civil rights granted if this information is omitted or the prospectus contains false or misleading information.[51]

Secondly, there are the insider trading provisions which apply to a person possessing information which is not generally available and which could materially affect the price or value of securities if it were so available.[52] Such a person must not purchase, sell or agree to purchase or sell securities, or procure another person to do so.[53] Obviously, there will be many situations when a shareholder wishing to sell his shares in a company has information about the company's affairs which is not generally available. The scope of these provisions is very wide, and every vendor of securities and many purchasers will need to examine the state of their knowledge of a company's affairs before entering into a sale or purchase agreement.

Thirdly, there are a number of provisions prohibiting false or misleading statements as well as reckless statements in connection with a sale or purchase of securities.[54] Again, criminal and civil penalties apply. Obviously the Corporations Law will in a number of circmstances severely limit the efforts of draftsmen to reduce or eliminate the exposure of parties to liability through contractual provisions.

7. Good Faith?

Traditionally, the common law was loath to require any duty of good faith except in certain types of contract—most notably, insurance contracts, which were considered to be *uberimae fidei*. The imposition of obligations of good faith was traditionally confined to established categories of relationships where fiduciary

[48] *Ibid.*, 53,335 per Giles J.

[49] For constitutional reasons, the Corporations Law in Australia is a co-operative scheme between the States and the Commonwealth. Each State adopts as its own law the "Corporations Law" contained in section 82 of the Corporations Act 1989 (Cth) as amended.

[50] Corporations Law, section 1018, and, generally, Part 7.12, Division 2.

[51] Corporations Law, section 996 and Part 7.11, Division 4.

[52] Corporations Law, Part 7.11, Division 2A.

[53] Corporations Law, section 1002G.

[54] Corporations Law, sections 995, 996, 998; Part 7.11, Division 4.

obligations were imposed according to equitable principles. More recently, there has been a greater willingness to recognise fiduciary obligations in a wide range of situations, though there continues to be a reluctance to recognise a fiduciary relationship between "commercial parties acting at arm's length". To the extent that these attitudes are rooted in a nineteenth-century view of the capacity of freely bargaining parties to look after their own interests section 52 itself suggests that that view is now considerably qualified.

A number of recent cases concerning section 52 and implication of contractual terms indicate that the courts are now taking a less robust view of the behaviour of parties towards each other in pre-contractual negotiations and the performance of contracts, though as yet this still falls short of any general duty of good faith. Significantly, it has become increasingly common in Australia for section 52 claims to be made in conjunction with other general law claims,[55] and it is conceivable that, just as the common law originally influenced the interpretation of section 52, the spirit of section 52 is now affecting the development of general law doctrines.

In *Poseidon Limited & Anor* v *Adelaide Petroleum NL & Ors*,[56] S, an executive of the appellant ("Poseidon") made representations to the respondent ("Adelaide") concerning Poseidon's intentions in relation to a proposed takeover of Adelaide by Poseidon. In fact, these representations were false to the knowledge of S, since the board of Poseidon had passed resolutions requiring a substantially different deal. In fact the purpose of the representations was to "buy time" so that Adelaide would be diverted from concluding negotiations with a rival corporate suitor, and then, once the opportunity of the other corporate suitor had passed, would be forced to accept the (less favourable for Adelaide) terms which had really been authorised by Poseidon's board. In a decision, upheld on appeal to the Full Federal Court,[57] it was held that this conduct constituted misleading and deceptive conduct under section 52. Burchett J referred to traditional anxieties about the imposition of duties approaching good faith in circumstances when parties' interests are inherently at odds:

> I do not think it has ever been suggested that section 52 strikes at the traditional secretiveness and obliquity of the bargaining process. Traditional bargaining may be hard, without being in the statutory sense misleading or deceptive. No one expects all the cards to be on the table. But the bargaining process is not therefore to be seen as a licence to deceive.[58]

Lee J commented that "neither party to this dispute was a novice in matters of commerce",[59] and quoted from Gleeson CJ of the NSW Supreme Court in an earlier case, where, essentially for want of the necessary reliance, in

[55] This is partly because attachment of a section 52 claim to general law claims will sometimes have procedural advantages, in particular allowing plaintiffs to commence actions in the Federal Court.

[56] (1992) ATPR paras. 41–164.

[57] The intermediary appellate level of the Commonwealth court jurisdiction.

[58] (1992) ATPR paras. 41–164, 40,227.

[59] ATPR paras. 41–164, 40,244.

circumstances where no parties were commercially naïve, Gleeson CJ commented:

> Where parties are dealing at arm's length in a commercial situation in which they have conflicting interests it will often be the case that one party will be aware of information which, if known to the other, would or might cause the other party to take a different negotiating stance. This does not in itself impose any obligation on the first party to bring the information to the attention of the other party, and failure to do so would not, without more, ordinarily be regarded as dishonesty or even sharp practice.[60]

This suggests that the limits of a duty not to engage in misleading and deceptive conduct will, in general terms, coincide with a duty of honesty, rather than good faith.[61] In some circumstances, however, it may come closer to a duty of good faith.

In *Pacific Coal Pty Ltd* v *Idemitsu Queensland Pty Ltd & Ors; Agipcoal Australia Pty Ltd* v *Idemitsu Queensland Pty Ltd & Ors*,[62] the plaintiffs and defendants were joint venturers in relation to a coal deposit for which they had obtained an authority to prospect. Opinions of the joint venturers as to the commercial viability of the deposit varied, and relations between the parties became strained. In the meantime, Idemitsu, who were keen to take over the project, had various communications with the Queensland Government (who controlled the mining rights), including showing them various letters of intent from Japanese buyers, but not showing them various side letters to the letters of intent which effectively rendered the letters of intent meaningless.

Subsequently, the Queensland Government declined to renew the joint venture's Authority to Prospect and associated mineral leases, and shortly after, issued fresh Authority to a new syndicate including Idemitsu and interests associated with it. The plaintiffs claimed that Idemitsu's use of the letters of intent was misleading and deceptive conduct, which, because it caused the Queensland Government to act as it did, therefore caused loss to the plaintiffs. This claim was upheld by Ryan J in the Queensland Supreme Court. This case also illustrates tellingly how the deceptive conduct in question need not be towards the person claiming damages under section 82. Indeed, Ryan J was at pains to point out that the merits or propriety of the Queensland Government's decision were not at issue. Concurrent claims were made, and in varying degrees upheld, in relation to fiduciary and contractual duties between the joint venturers.

In *Renard Constructions (ME) Pty Ltd* v *Minister for Public Works*,[63] the plaintiff was the head contractor for the construction of two sewerage pumping

[60] *Lam* v *Ausintel Investments Australia Pty Limited & Ors* (1990) ATPR paras. 40–990, 50,880; quoted at (1992) ATPR paras. 41–164, 40,244.

[61] In *Poseidon supra*, Burchett J was of the view that the conduct of S, imputed to Poseidon, would also have constituted the common law tort of deceit; but, perhaps because section 52 appeared easier to establish at the outset, and because of the attraction of the Trade Practices Act remedies, it was not pleaded.

[62] (1992) ATPR (Digest) paras. 46–094.

[63] (1992) 26 NSWLR 234.

stations. Construction fell behind, in part because of the failure of the defendant to supply various materials on time. The contract in question provided that, on certain defaults (including, obviously, falling behind schedule) the Minister was entitled to issue a notice to the contractor requiring that it show cause why certain powers, including a power to terminate the contract, should not be exercised, and if the Minister was not so satisfied, he or she could exercise the powers in question. A majority of the NSW Court of Appeal held that there was a requirement that the Minister act reasonably in the exercise of his powers under this term.[64] Priestley JA considered it as a question of an implied term, and took the opportunity to comment at length on the emerging trend in common law countries to place weight on something approaching the civil law notion of good faith. Statutes, such as the Trade Practices Act, and case law[65] all suggested that:

> . . . people generally, including judges and other lawyers, from all strands of the community, have grown used to the courts applying standards of fairness to contract which are wholly consistent with the existence in all contracts of a duty upon the parties of good faith and fair dealing in its performance. In my view this is in these days the expected standard, and anything less is contrary to prevailing community expectations.[66]

As another sign of the increasing plausibility at common law of obligations of good faith, the NSW Court of Appeal in *Coal Cliff Collieries Pty Ltd* v *Sijehama Pty Ltd*,[67] held that it was possible to recover damages for breach of a contractual term providing that parties would negotiate in good faith. Hitherto, the common law had rejected such terms as illusory "agreements to agree".[68]

8. Conclusion

In Australia, buyers and sellers of businesses and assets can no longer consider that only the explicit terms of their written contract are relevant in determining their respective obligations or the extent of their protection from subsequent claims. As a result of approaches by courts to certain common law principles (reflecting a willingness to look beyond just the words of the contract) and the intervention of both Commonwealth and State parliaments intent on providing greater statutory protection and remedies, both buyers and sellers, as well as their advisers, need to take considerable care in their negotiations, bearing in mind at all relevant times their previous dealings as well as the nature or possible characterisation of their relationship.

[64] Meagher JA took the traditional view, that there was no requirement of reasonableness or fairness to the contractor, but that the requirement that the Minister be "satisfied" meant that the Minister had to make a properly informed decision—which had not occurred in this case.

[65] In particular, *The Commonwealth* v *Amman Aviation Pty Limited* 104 ALR 1, 21 (High Court) and (1990) 92 ALR 601, 607, 616 (Full Federal Court).

[66] (1992) 26 NSWLR 234, 268.

[67] (1991) 24 NSWLR 1.

[68] *Ridgway* v *Wharton* (1957) 6 HLC 238, 305; *Placer Development Ltd* v *Commonwealth* (1969) 121 CLR 353, 356, 360–1.

9. Various Acquisitions

9.1 Types of Acquisition

The two chief means by which businesses are acquired are by Business Sale Agreement and by Share Sale Agreement. In the first, the vendor offers those items of property which will enable the purchaser to carry on the business and generally undertakes not to operate in competition with the purchaser within a certain defined area and for a certain area of time. The business as such is not a distinct legal entity, and therefore the crucial element in such agreements is the identification of those items of property in the hands of the vendor which are to pass to the purchaser as part of the business. Because there is change in the legal person which is conducting the business, this normally requires an assignment of the benefit of all contracts and statutory authorisations necessary to carry on the business. The vendor generally retains debts owed to it prior to the sale (although in some circumstances, particularly where there are on-going trading relationships, a purchaser may wish to have some say in the way the vendor will collect these, and in some circumstances may even undertake to collect the debts on the vendor's behalf) and remains liable for all debts incurred by it in the conduct of the business prior to the sale. This method is generally used where a business has been conducted by a natural person, but also where the business to be sold is not the whole business of a company, or where, for other reasons, the company itself is not an attractive financial proposition to a purchaser.

Warranties used in these forms of agreement mainly relate to the goodwill as seen in the name of the business (and its transfer as well as the transfer of all associated marks whether or not registered trademarks); the condition and value of the assets making up the business; the currency (and "transfer") of licences or more accurately the obtaining of new licences on the same terms for the purchaser; and other permits necessary for its continuation and the performance of the business over a recent period. If other matters are dealt with in the sale (eg personnel, debts due to the vendor, restraints on trade etc) then warranties may be more extensive to recognise these additional matters.

In the share sale, the vendor sells the corporate entity which conducts the business. Its principal attraction is that the continuity of legal relations between the company conducting the business and third parties is preserved, although frequently it is a condition of many licences and authorisations, and also of larger-scale contracts (such as financial facilities, contracts with suppliers and leases), that the continuation of the licence, authorisation or contract is conditional upon notification and approval of any substantial change in the persons standing behind the company. Where the obligations of the company are secured by guarantees given by persons associated with the company, the vendors will generally seek to be released from such guarantees. This will usually require the acceptance by third parties of the purchasers in their place.

Warranties used in these agreements extend not only to the matters referred to in the business sale agreements but also to the assets actually being sold (ie shares in the company running the underlying business), the affairs of the company whose shares are being sold, its various assets, actual and contingent liabilities, affairs, records, dealings with revenue and other authorities and, of course, authorisation to contract. Where an agreement for sale covers only part of the shareholding in the company running the underlying business then the warranties usually negotiated are fewer and, unless the vendor actually ran the underlying business, mainly relate to ownership of the shares being sold, the vendor's authority to sell (eg that no other party has a lien, pledge, mortgage, encumbrance or adverse interest—such as an option or pre-emptive right) and perhaps the vendor not having knowledge of matters likely to have a materially adverse effect on the company or the underlying business.

In all these cases the warranties, the subject of negotiation between the vendor and purchaser, will cover "standard" subjects. Neither party will be surprised by a request for warranties to cover a range of matters. Many will usually be included in the relevant contract for sale. However, their form will often be the subject of intense negotiation. The exact formulation of the warranty will determine the extent of the warranty (eg it may be a categorical statement that no notices have been received from a revenue authority claiming that unpaid monies are due) or it may be restricted by reference to the vendor's actual knowledge. Also, warranties may or may not be accompanied by provisions limiting claims by reference to direct not consequential loss, minimum sums or maximum "caps", or by provisions also indemnifying a party for all types of loss, damage, cost and expense incurred in the event of a breach of warranty.

10. Warranties in the Law of Contract

As noted in the previous section, considerable statutory intervention to the common law has taken place, particularly affecting contracts for the sale of goods and more recently sales of securities, businesses and other assets. Originally, this statutory intervention related to sales of goods when statutes such as the Sale of Goods Act 1923 (NSW) came into force in the various Australian States.

This was largely modelled on the Sale of Goods Act 1893 (UK). Amendments generally followed that pattern too until recent years when a wide range of "consumer protection" legislation was introduced—principally the Trade Practices Act. This has led to the substantial lessening in importance of determining whether a statement is:

(a) an invitation to treat;
(b) mere "puffery" or sales-talk;
(c) a statement of opinion or of law;
(d) the supply of information;
(e) a representation of fact which has substantially induced the entry into the contract;

(If the presentation of fact is false it is further classified into—
  (i) an innocent misrepresentation;
  (ii) a negligent misrepresentation;
  (iii) a fraudulent misrepresentation.)

(f) a representation of intention;
(g) an independent or collateral promise or warranty.[69]

[69] *New South Wales Law Reform Commission Working Paper on The Sale of Goods Act 1975* p.17.

10.1 Warranties v Guarantees

As a term of art, "warranty" has come to mean a contractual term for which a party is entitled to claim damages but not to terminate the contract. In this chapter, and in general Australian usage, the cognate word "guarantee" is limited to contracts of surety where A (the surety or guarantor) undertakes to pay B in the event of C (the principal debtor) defaulting in C's obligations.[70]

10.2 Financial Guarantees

Both parties to an acquisition may wish to seek some kind of guarantee as to the performance by the other of its obligations under the contract. While the vendor is usually only interested in ensuring that the purchase price will be paid, the purchaser frequently will wish to be indemnified by the vendor against any damage or loss arising from breach of warranties in relation to the business. This is most important when the acquisition is by purchase of shares in a company, since then the purchaser "assumes" (indirectly via the company) all the pre-acquisition liabilities of the company. Where the company has known liabilities of an uncertain amount, the vendor may undertake to indemnify the purchaser up to a certain limit. Alternatively, the vendor may undertake to indemnify the purchaser if the liability for breach of warranty exceeds a certain amount. This entails some risk for the vendor, who may face in this way the prospect of having to meet liabilities which may be determined by litigation or negotiations between the purchaser and third parties over which the vendor has little or no control. Hence, provisions are often included as between vendor and purchaser to give the vendor, as indemnifying party, some influence or control over the purchaser in relation to the determination of any claim establishing the breach of warranty and indemnity.

Guarantees in favour of the vendor are necessarily obtained from third parties, especially, if the purchaser is a proprietary company, from natural persons associated with it, and by bank guarantee. The vendor may take real security over the subject matter of the sale, such as by mortgage of assets of the sale, a scrip lien over the shares sold (if applicable), or other security over property offered on the purchaser's behalf. Where the sale is of assets including real property, the vendor may enjoy an equitable lien over the land for the unpaid purchase price.[71] Where shares in a company are being sold, there may be statutory restrictions applicable preventing the giving of "financial assistance" in connection with the transaction.

The purchaser may likewise obtain guarantees of the vendor's obligation from third parties, including banks, and also real security (though obviously not over the assets acquired). Where the purchase is to be paid in instalments, the

[70] In fact, most contracts of guarantee are also contracts of indemnity, where A offers to indemnify B against any loss in respect of the obligations incurred by C.

[71] Strictly the lien is an equitable charge: a right to have the property sold to pay the debt, which will be defeated by a *bona fide* purchaser of the legal interest without notice. *Hewett* v *Court* (1983) 149 CLR 639; as well as over land, such a charge may exist over any subject matter for which the contract would have been specifically enforceable. See E. I. Sykes and Sally Walker, *Law of Securities* Law Book Company (1993) 199–206.

purchaser can obtain quasi-security by a right to set off liabilities of the vendor against instalments of the purchase price.

10.3 Warranties in Sales of Goods

The Sales of Goods Acts adopted a definition of "warranty" following the 1893 UK legislation and which it distinguished from a "condition". Warranty is now defined in section 5 (New South Wales Act) to mean:

> an agreement with reference to goods which are the subject of a contract for sale, but collateral to the main purpose of such contract, the breach of which gives rise to a claim for damages, but not to a right to reject the goods and treat the contract as repudiated.

while "condition" is clearly stipulated to be an undertaking or promise, the non-fulfilment of which gives the other party the right to treat the contract as at an end and to refuse to perform his side of the bargain.

The requirement that a warranty be part of a binding contract—ie that there be an intention to contract at the time the warranty is given, has been criticised.[72] Statutory intervention in legislation referred to in the preceding section, particularly the Trade Practices Act has extended protection for various parties relying on statements past, the legislative concepts applicable in the common law and original Sale of Goods legislation. Further principles such as privity of contract have been overridden by a range of legislative enactments affording statutory protection to users as well as original purchasers of certain goods (eg motor vehicles) and purchasers of houses (although not necessarily the party which contracted with the builder of the house).

Manufacturers of goods now have liability to consumers through statutory implied warranties (eg section 74B, Trade Practices Act). To some extent courts are also breaking down the much criticised privity of contract concept so as to give certain third parties the right at common law to rely on contractual provisions.[73]

10.4 Statutory Warranties

The Sale of Goods Act legislation in the various Australian States provided the first statutory incorporation of implied conditions and warranties into contracts. These included:

(a) as to the vendor's title—free of "any charge or encumbrance in favour of any party not declared or known to the buyer before or at the time when the contract is made (section 17, New South Wales);
(b) in contracts for sale by description—that the goods shall correspond with the description (section 18);
(c) as to the fitness for purpose (section 19);
(d) as to conformity with sample in the case of a contract for sale by sample (section 20).

[72] *supra.*
[73] *Trident General Insurance Co. Ltd* v *McNiece Bros Pty Ltd* (1987) (1988) 165 CLR 107.

These implied terms could, however, be excluded by contract. The Commonwealth Trade Practices Act introduced in 1974 supplemented these in relation to goods supplied by corporations (see sections 67–72) (Part V Div 2) and provided (section 68) that any term of a contract that purports to exclude, restrict or modify such implied terms is void (subject however to section 68A which in certain circumstances allows specific terms of a contract to limit liability for breach of a warranty to repair or replacement or the cost thereof). The Act also extends to the provision of services (implying a warranty) that they will be:

> rendered with due care and skill and that any materials supplied in connection with those services will be reasonably fit for the purpose for which they are supplied . . . [s.74(1)] and they . . . will be reasonably fit for (the specified) purpose. (s.74(2).)

In Division 2A privity of contract is further eroded with liability to consumers being extended further—to manufacturers and importers—in respect of goods which:

(a) are not fit for their purpose (section 74B);
(b) do not correspond with their description (section 74C);
(c) are not of merchantable quality (section 74D); or
(d) do not correspond with their sample (section 74E)

or where after an acquisition goods require repair but facilities are not reasonably available (section 74F). Further provisions extend any express warranties to ultimate consumers (section 74G).

In 1992 Part VA was introduced into the Trade Practices Act providing a statutory regime of strict liability for certain product defects regardless of contractual provisions and nexus.

11. Warranties in Promises to Sell

11.1 Relationship between Promise to Sell and Sale Agreement

Sales of businesses in Australia generally follow the classic conveyancing paradigm of negotiation and then conclusion of the terms and entry into an agreement for sale followed by a period for further investigations and satisfaction of any pre-conditions for sale culminating in an actual transfer, or "completion". (As mentioned later, this is changing in certain types of sale where investigations of the purchaser are assigned to a specific period prior to entry into the contract.) During the intermediate phase the purchaser will ordinarily make certain inquiries to satisfy itself that the thing to be sold is as promised, and that the vendor is able to sell it.

However, much of the capacity of the purchaser to inquire and investigate will depend on the contractual terms relating to this period (eg the rights of the purchaser to have access to the records of the business). In some circumstances the purchaser may have ongoing obligations, and the vendor may likewise need to satisfy itself of the purchaser's capacity to carry these out. In some instances, most notably where an assignment of a lease or other contractual entitlement is concerned, the vendor will have to satisfy important conditions as far as the purchaser is concerned. If the vendor is unable to assign its rights under contracts so as to free itself from a secondary liability to third parties, then it may also need to make further investigations concerning the purchaser and its standing as well as negotiate alternative terms to accommodate these circumstances. In most cases the agreement will, as outlined elsewhere, contain warranties by the vendor and the purchaser (in the latter case generally limited to its authority and conduct prior to completion). The vendor's warranties will be more extensive relating as well to the business and assets the subject of sale and will be expressed both in relation to the time of "completion" as well as the period from entry into the contract until completion.

The terminological distinction between promises to sell and sale agreements does not represent one familiar to Australian lawyers. Completion of agreements is generally effected not by a further agreement but by the vendor providing the necessary executed instruments of transfer in exchange for the purchaser providing the means of payment and, where there are obligations to third parties or regulatory conditions to be satisfied, whatever documents are necessary to satisfy the vendor in this regard. Where completion of the agreement is dependent on the consents of third parties and regulatory authorities, these consents (or the documentary evidence of them) are commonly expressed to be conditions precedent to completion of the agreement, with the effect that both or either party (depending on the terms of the agreement) may decline to complete the agreement unless these are forthcoming. This is usually coupled with a term requiring each party to use its best efforts to ensure that conditions precedent are satisfied or that all necessary consents are obtained. Failure to satisfy conditions precedent to completion will not itself give rise to a right to damages, but damages will flow in that case from a failure by a party to endeavour to satisfy such conditions.

11.2 Survival of Warranties in Promise to Sell not Repeated in Sale Agreement

In traditional conveyancing of interests in land, agreements were completed by a conveyance which was itself a deed. This was considered to be the final expression of the agreement between the parties, so that the agreement "merged" in the conveyance, and warranties not repeated there did not survive. Certain collateral terms, such as a promise to give compensation for errors and mis-descriptions, are excepted from the doctrine, as is a conveyance induced by fraud. More importantly, the question of merger is a matter of intention, and is commonly dealt with in contracts by an express clause in the agreement identifying which warranties or conditions are intended to continue beyond completion and which are not.

12. Warranties in Sales of Shares or of On-going Businesses

In certain share sales the manner of sale is the subject of considerable statutory regulation. So, under the Corporations Law, shares in companies having more than 15 members may, in certain circumstances, only be acquired pursuant to takeover offers or takeover schemes. These take the form of general offers to shareholders accompanied by specified information—accepted by means of the return of a signed acceptance form in the case of takeover offers or by a shareholder's broker on the Australian Stock Exchange accepting the offer on the shareholder's behalf. Contracts formed in this manner are generally not the subject of warranties. They usually include only limited conditions—relating to the title of the vendor and his authorisation to sell (ie the shares are free of all mortgages, charges, encumbrances or third party interests).

In some circumstances privately negotiated sales of shares in such companies can occur (eg where an acquisition will not, as a result, increase the entitlement of any person to more than 20 per cent of the voting shares of the corporation, section 615). However, a purchaser of such a relatively minor percentage cannot expect to obtain extensive warranties which relate to the underlying business of the company the shares of which are being sold.

Privately negotiated contracts for the acquisition of shares in such companies (rather than by way of a general offer) are permissible in certain instances such as where prior approval of shareholders is given, and in such contracts the more substantial the stake being sold the more the purchaser can realistically request by way of warranties from the vendor relating to the underlying business of the company.

In sales of shares, the form of which are not regulated by the Corporations Law, the nature and extent of the warranties included in the contract for sale will depend on the relative bargaining strengths of the parties, the extent and nature of the underlying business, key assets and potential exposures which may have a material effect on the bargain as made by the purchaser, the extent of the vendor's identity with the business (ie was he involved in its operation) as well as the other terms of sale.

Sales of shares through the mechanism of the Australian Stock Exchange will carry with them implied terms as to title and authority to sell. It is important to realise that the stockbrokers contracting on behalf of their clients are contracting as principals *inter se*. Each broker has a separate contract of agency with his client. The contract between brokers is subject to and can only be carried out in accordance with the articles of association, business rules, regulations and customs of the Exchange and its conclusion binds not only each broker but thereby its client pursuant to the terms of the respective agency contract. As such, there is also implied into the agency contract between broker and client a term that the client will also be bound by all such articles, rules, regulations and customs which bind the broker when contracting on the client's behalf.[74] Accordingly, warranties as expressed in such provisions are relevantly implied into such contracts.

13. The Subjective Element

13.1 The Subjective Element and the Warranties

The common law, with its emphasis on the enforcement of bargained-for promises, has correspondingly focused on the objective rather than the subjective

[74] *The Bell Group Ltd* v *Herald & Weekley Times Ltd* 1985 VR 613.

intention of parties—a promise means what the promisee would reasonably have taken it to mean rather than what either party subjectively meant or understood.

Warranties are treated as promissory statements whereby risk is allocated and the warrantee is freed from further inquiry. In determining whether certain statements are in fact warranties, courts may have regard to whether a matter was in the particular knowledge of a party and outside the knowledge of another, but so far as express warranties are concerned, there appears to be nothing to prevent a party relying on a warranty which it knew to be inconsistent with the facts, provided that reliance can be established and the party's conduct did not involve misleading or deceptive or unconscionable conduct under the Trade Practices Act or otherwise.

13.2 Mistake

Mistake, at common law, has a very limited scope of operation, because of the common law's "objective" view of contract.[75] Many instances of what seem to be a mistake are in fact dealt with by the courts under other bases. For instance, where the purchaser never receives what the purchaser bargained for, it will be entitled to a return of the money paid on the basis of a "total failure of consideration".[76] Mistake renders the contract void because it is considered there simply never was an agreement between the parties. More commonly, however, mistake may be a basis at equity for refusing to permit one party to enforce a contract according to its terms. This is part of the general equitable jurisdiction against unconscionability, and will occur in circumstances where the party seeking to enforce the contract knew of or contributed to the other's mistake in such a way as it would be unconscionable for that party to be permitted to enforce it.

Of much greater importance at common law is the situation where a mistake by one party has been induced by a misrepresentation of a party. The contract will then be voidable at the instance of the other party, provided that the parties can be put back in the position they where beforehand. Equitable rights, however, are always subject to legal rights acquired in good faith for value by third parties.

13.3 Common Ground and Distinction between Breach of Warranty and Mistake

Where the mistake held by the parties is so fundamental as to destroy any basis for the agreement, or prevents any common ground between the parties, the agreement will be void for mistake. This will be very rare, since the courts are more inclined to look at the nature of the agreement to see if one party (usually, in this context, the vendor) was impliedly warranting the existence of certain

[75] *McRae* v *Commonwealth Disposals Commission* (1951) 84 CLR 377, 407—per Dixon and Fullagar JJ.

[76] But the failure of consideration must be total; where a cruise ship sinks part-way through a cruise, there is not a total failure of consideration. *Dillon*.

fundamental matters.[77] Only rarely will the agreement be taken to be subject to an implied condition precedent as to the existence of the subject matter of the contract.[78]

13.4 Fraud

Where a contract has been induced by fraud, it is voidable rather than void and the representee will also have a right to damages for the tort of deceit. However, because the contract is valid until rescinded at the option of the representee, it is effective to pass property to third parties.

In practice, the law of fraudulent misrepresentation (as of negligent and innocent misrepresentation is now less important than the statutory remedies for deceptive and misleading conduct).

14. Contractual Warranties

14.1 Generally

Warranties tend to take a predictable form in many sale of business agreements or agreements for the sale of the capital of companies holding and operating a business. Where agreements involve large sums, or businesses, complex acquisitions or particular areas of potential exposure for the purchaser, the warranties will reflect more detailed negotiation and adjustment of risks as between vendor and purchaser. Some approaches as well as provisions often adopted or negotiated are referred to below.

Warranties on specific matters are often separated into schedules to the agreement and are generally preceded by general provisions in the body of the contract applicable to all the warranties. These provisions reflect such matters as:

(a) whether the warranties or some of them are also expressed as conditions (so as to give rise to an additional right of termination for breach);
(b) the extent of the warranty (eg whether unlimited) as to the truth, accuracy and completeness of each statement or whether limited and, if so, in what respect (eg "To the best of the knowledge and belief of the vendor . . ." or "As far as the vendor is aware . . .");
(c) that giving of warranties by, say, the vendor has been an inducement to the purchaser to enter the contract.
The purpose of such a statement is to record what the purchaser will want to allege in the event of breach—that he relied on the representation. Even knowledge of the falsity of a representation may not prevent reliance on it in

[77] *Svanosio* v *McNamara* (1956) 96 CLR 186. In this case, a hotel and its land were sold. Part of the hotel was actually on land not owned by the vendors. This was not a mistake but a breach of warranty, except that special rules concerning real property, and the doctrine of merger, prevented the purchaser recovering any damages once the sale was completed.

[78] *Goldsborough Mon & Co Ltd* v *Carter* (1914) 19 CLR 429, at 439. See also *Associated Japanese Bank (International) Ltd* v *Credit du Nord 3A* [1989] 1 WLR 255. Exceptionally, this is the position under the Sale of Goods Acts where the goods without the knowledge of the seller had perished at the time the contract was made. (NSW section 11; Qld section 9, SA section 6, Tas section 11, Vic section 11, WA section 6, ACT section 11, NT section 10.)

the event of the representation turning out to be false. As Hutley J said in *Gipps* v *Gipps*:

> . . . it by no means necessarily follows that complete knowledge of the falsity of representations defeats a case based on them: it is only if the knowledge is such as to destroy the effect of the misrepresentations as inducements.[79]

As the authors of the Sale of Business commentary in *The Australian Encyclopaedia of Forms and Precedents* point out:

> Therefore, the vendor might with some justification require the inclusion in the agreement of a provision which excludes from the warranties not only the matters disclosed by the vendor but also matters of which the purchaser has knowledge.[80]

(d) the operative date or duration of the warranties (eg as at the date of entry into the written contract and as at completion);
(e) whether there has to be a minimum aggregate loss suffered by a party before a claim based on breach can be made;
(f) whether a maximum "cap" liability for breach(es) by one or both parties will be included.

Initial provisions also often include warranties to the effect that the Recitals set out in the introduction to the operative provisions of the contract are true and accurate. In agreements necessarily containing substantial recitals (effectively to explain important background) such a warranty can be significant (see the various decisions leading to the Privy Council's decision in *Brinds Ltd* v *Offshore Oil NL*).[81]

Purchasers also often attempt to have vendors give a general warranty to the effect that:

> All information which has been given by or on behalf of the Vendor to the Purchaser in the course of the negotiations leading to this Agreement is true and accurate in all respects.

This is a warranty that, given the unspecified nature of the information, may potentially expose the vendor to unknown risks. A vendor is often unlikely to know everything that has been said in negotiations or what it was even intended to convey. Hence, a legitimate response of vendors to purchasers requesting such a warranty is to ask purchasers to *specify* in the contract the information on which they wish to rely rather than assume what may be a very considerable risk by the inclusion of the above form of wording.

Another form of general warranty with even more potential exposure for a vendor is a provision to the effect that:

> All information which is known to the Vendor relating to the Business or subject matter of this Agreement which is material to a purchaser for value, has been disclosed in writing to the Purchaser.

[79] (1978) 1 NSWLR 454 at 160.
[80] Volume II, 3rd ed. D. Magarey, J. Kriewaldt and E. Broderick, Butterworths, Sydney, 1991.
[81] (1986) 4 ACLC 227.

A request for the inclusion of such a provision should be vigorously resisted by a vendor. It is so general that its reach and the vendor's potential exposure cannot be assessed.

14.2 Authority

It is in the interests of both vendor and purchaser to obtain warranties (they are often in fact expressed as conditions) as to the authority and power of the other to execute the agreement, carry out its terms and obtain assurance that there are no actions, claims or proceedings pending or threatened which may have a material effect on the subject matter of the agreement. With such mutuality of interest each party is generally willing to give and receive such warranties.

14.3 Title

The vendor's warranty as to title to the assets and business (or shares) being sold is uncontroversial. They are warranted at least as at completion as being solely and beneficially owned by the vendor who has:

> ... full right, title and interest, free from any mortgage, charge, lien, option, encumbrance or any adverse claim or interest whatever.

Obviously this emphasises the importance of an accurate and comprehensive definition of the "Business".

This is also significant for a similar warranty that the assets agreed to be sold constitute all of the assets used in or in connection with the Business and necessary for its continuing conduct.

14.4 Business

Warranties here relate to such matters as:

(a) the absence of claims, demands, litigation, disputes (or notices of such) in relation to the business or assets;
(b) financial performance of the business (or company running it) that it was not affected by unusual or non-recurring items;
(c) licences, consents, permits, authorities etc—that there are no circumstances which may result in their revocation, cancellation or non-renewal of any of them and all now held are the ones necessary to carry on the business.

14.5 Assets

Warranties relating to these tend to overlap with those relating to the business. They cover such matters as:

(a) the state of repair of assets;
(b) identification of those owned and leased, the validity of relevant leases, state of compliance by the vendor (or operating company) with lease obligations and a representation that no claim, demand or threat has been made and no event exists which may give rise to litigation or termination of a lease.

A wide range of additional matters are often covered in specific warranties where the assets include significant (to the purchaser) real estate which warranties relate to such matters as the zoning, usage and development of such property and the many matters which could affect its use by and value to the purchaser.

14.6 Accounts

Specific warranties covering financial accounts on which the purchaser has based (at least in part) its purchase are generally included especially where the share capital of a company operating a business is the subject of sale.

The warranties may relate to past audited accounts as well as more recent (and unaudited) management accounts, although if these accounts are being used to determine any part of the purchase price there will generally be operative provisions of the agreement which provide for adjustments to price, finalisation of accounts on specified bases and in accordance with enumerated procedures, as well as procedures for dispute resolution.

14.7 Taxation and Other Revenue Liability

Because of the potential significance of this subject matter many transactions reflect detailed negotiation of apportionment of this liability. General warranties here will reflect representations that all documents, such as returns necessary to be lodged with a relevant authority have been lodged, all relevant assessments have issued and been paid and that there are no outstanding disputes with or notices, claims, demands from any relevant authority concerning any amount or even correspondence relating to any such matter. Often exceptions will be made to such a provision and warranties eventually negotiated here will reflect consideration by both parties. Often indemnities are also negotiated by purchasers in repsect of any additional liability of this nature required to be paid by the company being purchased so as to ensure the purchaser can receive the full amount of any additional liability finally incurred by the company (and thus fully preserve the purchaser's bargain).

Other specific subjects of warranties often relate to:

(a) intellectual property;
(b) insurance policies and claims;
(c) personnel entitlements and superannuation funds;
(d) litigation including specific cases current at the time of the agreement; and
(e) the books and records of the business or in the case of sales of shares compliance with relevant corporate legislation relating to the keeping of records and lodgement of notices and returns.

15. Form Requirements

15.1 Written Form

There is no general requirement in Australian law that a contract be in writing, with the one significant exception that contracts dealing with interests in land (including leases, but not including indirect interests in land such as shares in a company which owns land, or a beneficial interest in a trust which itself includes land) must be in writing.[82] This is the most important survival of sections 4 and 17 of the English *Statute of Frauds*.[83] In some States, other elements of the statute survive, of which the most significant is the requirement that contracts of guarantee (but not of indemnity) be in writing. However, the equitable doctrine of part performance will enable specific performance (provided the contract is one for which specific performance is available) of a contract which the parties have partly performed, even though it is not in writing. In Australia, an estoppel arising as a result of the reliance of one of the parties in reliance on the conduct of the other will also have the effect of permitting a contract, otherwise unenforceable because not in writing, to be enforced, at least to the extent of the reliance interest created.[84]

Once a contract in writing exists, there is a presumption that it is the best source of the terms which have been offered and accepted by the parties, which in any legal proceedings is given force as the "parol evidence rule". This has been classically formulated in the following terms:

> If there be a contract which has been reduced into writing, verbal evidence is not allowed to be given of what passed between the parties, either before the written instrument was made, or during the time it was in a state of preparation, so as to add or subtract from, or in any manner to vary or qualify the written contract.[85]

While it might be possible to adduce evidence of a collateral contract which was verbal, the rule known in Australia as that in *Hoyts Pty Limited* v *Spencer*[86] has the effect of preventing the proof of a collateral contract inconsistent with the primary written contract. Though criticised by academic commentators,[87] this rule has been referred to without criticism as recently as 1986 by the High Court.[88]

15.2 Further Formalities and Effect vis-à-vis the Corporation

Contracts to which a company is party can be executed under company seal, by a power of attorney or simply by a party signing as an agent of the company. It is customary to provide some evidence of a signatory's authority to execute documents of a company, usually by provision of copies of the relevant resolutions of the board of directors of the company. In general, persons dealing with a company are entitled to assume that internal requirements have been complied with in respect of execution of documents and that a person who is held out by the company as having authority to enter into a contract is in fact so

[82] Or a memorandum of the contract, in either case signed by "the person to be charged" or its lawfully authorised agent. See, for example, Conveyancing Act 1919 (NSW) section 54A(1). In Victoria the agent must be authorised in writing: Instruments Act 1958 (Vic) section 126; Sale of Goods (Vienna Convention) Act 1987 (Vic).

[83] 19 Car II c 3 (1677).

[84] *Waltons Stores (Interstate)* v *Maher* (1988) 164 CLR 387.

[85] *Goss* v *Lord Nugent* (1983) 5 B & Ad 58; 110 ER 713 per Denman CJ at 64, 716.

[86] *supra*, note 3.

[87] J.W. Carter & D.J. Harland, *Contract Law in Australia*, Butterworths, Sydney, 1991, 179.

[88] *Gates* v *City Mutual Life Assurance Society Ltd* (1986) 160 CLR 1.

authorised unless they know or ought to know that there is an irregularity.[89] Conveyancing legislation in a number of States contain special provisions in respect of deeds.[90]

15.3 Acceptance of By-Laws

The doctrine of constructive notice under which those dealing with a company were taken to have notice of its constitutive documents lodged with the relevant regulatory authority, has been abolished in Australia.[91]

15.4 Specific Acceptance of Warranties Exclusions or Limitations

In a commercial contract, warranties and exclusions or limitations to warranties will usually have effect according to their terms without any requirement for specific acknowledgement or acceptance of them.

16. Exclusions or Limitations in Sales of On-going Businesses

The growing practice of vendors in many sales of business (particularly those involving businesses previously operated by the public sector) where the business is owned by a single vendor or of the shares in the company owning the business, is to limit their warranties by affording prospective purchasers an opportunity of inspecting the books, records, premises and assets of the business being sold. This "due diligence" process may be accompanied by the provision by the vendor of relevant employees of the business to answer questions of the prospective purchaser. Another reason for the adoption of this procedure is that in some cases the sale and purchase is part of a series of transactions whereby the underlying business is being floated through a public offer of securities in the holding company. Those involved in the promotion will wish to be able to demonstrate they took "reasonable precautions and exercised due diligence" to ensure their public statements (such as in a prospectus) are accurate and that there were no material omissions from the prospectus.

Many other exclusions of or limitations to warranties which may generally be sought by purchasers are often commonly negotiated by vendors. Some of these exclusions and limitations are referred to in section 8. In addition general limitations of liability are often sought by the inclusion of "entire agreement" clauses, although these have proven through judicial and statutory invention (eg The Trade Practices Act) to be of limited utility.

17. Breach of Warranties

17.1 Is Vendor Fault Required?

No vendor fault is required for there to be a breach of warranty. Even if the thing warranted turns out to have been impossible, the warranty is taken to be a

[89] For the statutory form of this rule, see Corporations Law section 164. At general law *Northside Developments Pty Ltd* v *Registrar-General* (1990) 93 ALR 385.

[90] See generally HAL Ford, *Principles of Corporation Law* 16th ed, 1992, pp. 111–121.

[91] Corporations Law, section 165.

promise that either the thing warranted is or will be the case, or that the warrantor will make good the loss which follows from it not being so.[92]

17.2 Other Requirements to Assert the Warranty

There is no general requirement to assert a warranty other than to plead its terms, a breach and the consequent damage in any action for damages under the warranty. Express warranties, however, are often coupled with terms requiring a claim under the warranty to be made within a given time or in a given manner.

17.3 Offsetting between Effects of Warranty and Undisclosed Assets

When a purchaser sues for breach of a warranty, there is no general requirement for it to bring into account any extent to which it has acquired more than it bargained for. If, in fact, undisclosed assets have also passed to the purchaser, the vendor may make what was once termed a quasi-contractual and is now termed a claim in restitution or unjust enrichment to offset payment for this against claims based on the warranty. This option will not be available when the sale is by sale of shares, because the property sold is the shares, and the vendor cannot subsequently complain that the shares were worth more than the vendor thought they were. It would, of course, be contractually possible to qualify warranties in this way, such as, for instance, stipulating that no claims for breaches of warranties may be made unless the value of the business as a whole were less than the purchase price, or, in the case of a company, explicitly providing a set-off in favour of the vendor if the company had other, undisclosed assets.

18. Third Party Liability

Warranties are of course expressed to be in favour of another party to the contract of sale. Increasingly, beneficiaries of warranties and their associates are attempting to fix third parties involved in the negotiation of the terms of sale with liability in tort. This is particularly so with auditors whose accounts are the subject of the agreement for sale or which form some basis for the calculation of price or the entry into the agreement. The law is largely unsettled at this time with different results achieved in some cases in Australia as compared to England. In the latest Australian case the Court had reference to the internal Audit Manual of the auditors which included an express acknowledgement that "interested parties" will "read and rely upon our reports". These were stated to include not only those who employ the auditors or to whom the report is addressed. The Court concluded that thereby the auditors assumed responsibility to a wider class of persons than the company for whom the audit was being conducted and its shareholders. This class included "anyone who may reasonably and relevantly rely upon the audited accounts for the purpose of ordering their affairs", thus extending the auditors' duty of care and potential liability.[93]

[92] Carter and Harland, *op. cit.* 386.
[93] *Columbia Coffee & Tea Pty Ltd* v *Churchill* (1992) 29 NSWLR 141.

With such developments in common law and the surrounding statutory provisions referred to in this chapter, warranties as expressed in a contract for the sale of a business while continuing to be important are no longer as determinant of potential liability as they once were for either vendor, purchaser or others involved in the sale of the business.

Germany

Dolf Weber and Rolf Giebeler
Pünder, Volhard, Weber & Axster, Düsseldorf, Germany

1. Introduction

Warranties in cross-border acquisitions under German law, as probably in all jurisdictions, are as diverse as the types of businesses bought and sold in such acquisitions. The warranties used differ depending on a range of factors, including intentions of the buyer, the aspects of the business critical to the buyer, the relative bargaining power of the parties and the seller's as well as the purchaser's knowledge concerning the business to be sold. Nevertheless, certain standards have developed which can serve, at least, as a guideline for structuring the warranties in an acquisition. Whilst these guidelines are widely accepted, it should be pointed out, that many mid- to large-size German companies were and still are sold using rather short agreements, containing only a very few warranties. Purchase agreements of Anglo-American length and detail are not yet common. Thus, in drafting warranties for the purchase of a German business, one needs to walk a fine line between warranties, sufficient and necessary for the type of acquisition and an overly detailed agreement. It has happened more than once in Germany that a seller walked away from a deal because of what he considered to be an agreement with "too many warranties", a situation that is perceived to create too many risks for the seller. Often these reactions are not due to the real legal and economic content of these warranties, but to sheer detail, length and unfamiliarity of the warranties.

It is difficult to write about warranties in cross-border acquisitions without reference to German private law, in general, and contract law, in particular. This may create special difficulties for the common law practitioner who might be unfamiliar with the Civil Code legal system used in Germany. Time and space limitations prevent even the briefest attempt at outlining German private law here.[1] It is appropriate, however, to introduce the subject of this chapter by

[1] For a practitioner-oriented summary of German contract law see Mueller, Stiefel, Brücher, *Doing Business in Germany*, Ch 10, 8th ed.

highlighting a practical difference between the German and common law approach to contract.

A fundamental tenet of Anglo-American law is freedom of contract. In relatively archaic terms, the parties to the contract are "masters of the bargain". In this sense, the contract—the written document which records the bargain—provides the framework, the gist and the minutiae of the agreement reached. While the courts and legislatures have reduced the freedom of contract in certain areas, such as labour law, and in other areas of the law a set of statutory background rules has been adopted—most notably with the Uniform Commercial Code (UCC) in the United States—the Anglo American legal system provides significant incentives and/or corresponding disincentives so that parties reach and record in the form of the contract document an agreement as complete as possible. A normal result of this aspect of the Anglo-American legal system is that contracts are lengthy, detailed documents.

Although the concept of freedom of contract is also fundamental to German contract law it is—like much of the law which exists in Civil Code countries—based on statute rather than on case law. This statutory framework contains an elaborate set of rules governing a variety of contractual situations and providing various remedies. The statutory rules are, however, not binding (subject to certain exceptions). Instead, the parties are free to substitute individual contract clauses for the statutory rules as they desire. Exercising the freedom of contract in Germany usually means that the parties determine the basic economic features of the transaction and the extent to which modifications, specifications, or clarifications of or deviations from the statutory framework are desired. The existence of such a codification is important, from the perspective of this chapter, because it provides a shorthand for the drafters and the users of legal documents. The existence of a relatively dense set of background rules for a variety of contractual situations means that considerably less needs to be written into a standard contract.

In the same fashion that the UCC provides detailed rules for certain commercial transactions, German statutory law provides points of reference for an acquisition contract. The net effect of this is that, in most cases, German contracts—often (expressly or implicitly) referring to specific sections of the applicable statutes—are much "leaner" than their Anglo-American counterparts.

Furthermore, in practice there are considerable differences in the interpretation of agreements. Rather than interpreting an acquisition agreement as such, without giving much regard to the variety of circumstances surrounding the acquisition, German lawyers (as most continental lawyers) interpret the agreement according to a well-established set of rules of interpretation and guidelines, which find their basis in the Civil Code. Section 133 of the Civil Code (Bürgerliches Gesetzbuch, BGB) provides that in interpreting any legally relevant statement, the "real will" of the person making such statement has to be extracted, and that the interpreter should not limit his interpretation to the literal meaning of the statement. This interpretation rule also applies to the interpretation of contracts.[2] Section 157 of

[2] BGHZ 20, 110; Heinrichs in Palandt, Bürgerliches Gesetzbuch, section 133, note 7, 51st ed, (1992), (hereinafter Palandt/Heinrichs).

the Civil Code complements this rule by providing that contracts and agreements have to be interpreted with *bona fides* (in good faith) with due regard to established business practice. There is a virtually endless number of court decisions interpreting and applying more or less ambiguous clauses. Their essence is probably that, unless an interpretation clearly contravenes the express will of the parties, it should produce a result which conforms to the "real economic will" of the parties. Practice shows that this leads, in most cases, to an interpretation of a disputed provision which results in an "economically reasonable" resolution of the conflicting interests of the parties, at least in the view of the judges or arbitrators.

One important aspect of this practice of interpreting agreements is the "supplementary interpretation". It is used when a situation has arisen which was not foreseen by the parties or the statutes and is, therefore, neither addressed directly or indirectly in the agreement nor the statutes. In such case, an imputed contractual provision is deduced from the general principles of the existing agreement in view of what "reasonable" parties, familiar with the unforeseen situation would have agreed to.[3] The contract is then interpreted as if it contained this imputed contractual provision. As a result of these interpretive practices, German lawyers tend to rely more on a "reasonable" interpretation of an agreement or a certain provision in the future rather than on seeking to address every contingency in an agreement and using very complex language which does not leave much room for interpretation. This tendency is also evident in connection with warranties in cross-border acquisitions, because the warranties tend to use more general language and do not specifically address every detail of a business.

Thus, one of the questions arising during actual drafting of an acquisition contract between Anglo-American and German lawyers is whether to follow the relatively brief German model, or the more detailed American one. The area of representations and warranties is not immune from this tension. It is inappropriate to over-emphasise the importance of an element of legal "style" or approach; however, the explicit recognition of the existence of a tension between German and Anglo-American legal approaches should contribute to its contructive resolution. Indeed, one of the main tasks of practitioners in cross-border transactions is determining what the potential problem areas are and when to look for focused assistance from local counsel.

It is hoped that the following sections will provide practitioners with a basic understanding of the concept of warranties in acquisition agreements governed by German law. A further goal of this chapter is to provide non-German practitioners with sufficient insight into the subject of representations and warranties so that more focused inquiries can be pursued successfully.

Two further caveats must be added. The first caveat relates to the fact that warranties in an acquisition agreement are only a part of the whole agreement. The various parts of an agreement are always interconnected so that the warranties have always to be viewed together with other elements, like the amount of the purchase price, payment conditions, etc. The second caveat relates

[3] BGHZ 9, 277; Palandt/Heinrichs, *supra* note 2, section 157, note 2.

to the standard outline used for this book. This outline had to fit to the legal situation in various jurisdictions and is not specifically adapted to the situation in Germany. Therefore, it was necessary to expand item 3, ("Warranties in the law of contract") in order to give an overview of the legal situation in Germany which is consistent with the concepts and the structure of German law. Other items of the standard outline could therefore be kept rather short.

2. Concepts: Warranties v Representations and Covenants

The terms "warranty", "representation" and "covenant" are terms from Anglo-American legal terminology which cannot be used as such in the context of German law. Their original meaning in England and the United States is determined by the legal traditions in those countries.[4]

In Germany, the acquisition or sale of a business, be it in an asset deal or in a share deal, is governed by the German Civil Code (BGB), in particular the law of purchase contracts, codified in sections 433 *et seq* of the Civil Code and certain provisions of the German Commercial Code (Handelsgesetzbuch, HGB), in particular sections 22 *et seq* Commercial Code. The categories with which German law operates in this context are not always identical with the concepts of warranties, representations and covenants as they are known in the Anglo-American legal system.

A discussion of "representations and warranties" in cross-border acquisitions needs not to be burdened with differences that, in terms of German law, are more formal than real. It is sufficient to define warranties as any set of contractual and/or statutory rules which relate to the condition or relationships of the purchased business, its constituents which may give rise to the seller's liability for specific performances, damages or other remedies *vis-à-vis* the purchaser, if reality deviates from the status defined in the agreement.

3. Warranties in the Law of Contracts

3.1 Contractual v Statutory Warranties

As in most jurisdictions, German contract law provides for statutory and contractual warranties in purchase agreements. There are no statutory provisions or concepts of law which apply specifically or exclusively to business acquisitions. There are, however, various types of statutory warranties which, in the absence of an express waiver by the parties, apply to all purchase agreements, including the acquisition of businesses. Under some circumstances certain minimum statutory warranties may not even be validly waived by the parties. This applies, for example, if the seller fraudlently misrepresents the qualities or conceals the defects of the purchased item (section 476, Civil Code).

The following statutory (or quasi-statutory) warranties apply *per se* (unless waived) instead of, or in addition to, specific warranties agreed upon between the parties:

[4] For a definition of the terms see the respective entries in *Black's Law Dictionary*, 6th ed, (1990).

- warranties of good title and the absence of defects in title;
- warranties relating to the absence of material defects;
- *culpa in contrahendo* (cic).

For these types of warranties (except cic which is a quasi-statutory concept "invented" by the courts)[5] the Civil Code prescribes the conditions under which they apply, the material content of such warranties, and the remedies in case a warranty is breached (for a description of those warranties see below p.50 *et seq.*). Statutory warranties will always apply if they are not excluded by the parties.[6]

In addition to, or instead of, relying on statutory warranties, the parties may also agree on more specific contractual warranties. They may specify certain conditions under which a warranty will apply, the material content of such warranty, and the specific legal consequences and remedies available to the purchaser if a warranty is breached. These types of contractual warranties are, in part, contemplated by the Civil Code.

The Civil Code also contains provisions relating to contractual warranties which provide that the seller is liable if the purchased item does not have the qualities which the seller warranted to the purchaser ("zugesicherte Eigenschaften"—"warranted qualities") (section 459, subsection 2, Civil Code). These provisions relate, in particular, to the rights of the purchaser if such a warranty is breached. The concept of warranted qualities can therefore be considered as a combination of a statutory and a contractual warranty: the parties determine the material content of the warranty, whereas the Civil Code prescribes the legal consequences if such a warranty is breached.

Finally, the parties are generally free to agree to pure contractual warranties whose content and legal effect are both determined by agreement only. In practice, acquisition agreements often exclude statutory warranty provisions to the greatest extent possible and rely heavily on contractual warranties.

Somewhat related to contractual warranties are purchase agreement clauses providing that certain circumstances—discovered in the future—will retroactively affect the purchase price. While there is no exact borderline between a warranty and provisions governing an adjustment of the purchase price, an adjustment is typically agreed upon in cases where both parties anticipate the future clarification of economically relevant facts relating to the business which are undetermined at the time of signing.

Typical examples are cases where the purchase price was calculated on the basis of future profits or other facts not yet determined. The uncertainty with which the parties are faced could, in theory, also be addressed by a warranty. However, a seller is typically reluctant to give a formal warranty on issues which are unknown or uncertain. The main reason is probably psychological in nature, because a breached warranty has, in contrast to a purchase price adjustment, certain negative connotations. The different types of warranties (statutory,

[5] BGH, NJW 1990, 1223; BGH, NJW-RR 1989, 307; Palandt/Heinrichs, *supra* note 2, section 276, note 80 *et seq.* Aderholt, *Culpa in Contrahendo beim Unternehmenskauf*, DStR 1991, 844 *et seq.*

[6] Putzo in Palandt, Bürgerliches Gesetzbuch, Introduction to section 459, note 21 *et seq*, 51st ed, (1992) (hereinafter Palandt/Putzo).

contractual, mixed and purchase price adjustments) can apply concurrently and one set of facts may be covered by various warranties.

In the past, there has been considerable legal controversy among scholars and the German courts, in particular the "Bundesgerichtshof" (BHG) (Federal Supreme (Civil) Court) as to whether and how the statutory warranties provided by the Civil Code should be applied to the acquisition of businesses. There has been no lack of proposals as to which legal concepts should be used to address the problems connected with warranties in acquisitions.[7] However, the rulings of the Federal Supreme (Civil) Court have not been influenced to a great extent by the commentaries, and the drafting practice has adapted itself to the approach taken by the courts.[8] This chapter will therefore not describe and discuss the various legal approaches which are often of only theoretical importance today. Rather, the following sections will focus on the approach taken by the courts and the resulting drafting practice.

3.2 Statutory Warranties in Acquisitions

Two main distinctions need to be made in discussing statutory warranties in acquisitions. One distinction is between asset deals and share deals, and the other distinction is between defects relating to good title and material defects. Depending on which type of acquisition and which type of defect is present, different legal regimes apply.

3.2.1 Warranty relating to full title and to absence of defects in title

The basic warranty in an acquisition, as in all purchase agreements, concerns the seller's title to the shares or other items sold and the absence of defects in title.

3.2.1.1 WARRANTY OF GOOD TITLE AND ABSENCE OF DEFECTS IN SHARE DEALS

If shares or partnership interests[9] are purchased, the seller warrants under section 437 of the Civil Code the existence of the shares, the existence of the company

[7] G. Müller, *Haftung und Lossagungsrecht des Verkäufers von GmbH-Anteilen bei einseitiger oder gemeinsamer Fehleinschätzung der Unternehmenslage* (Diss., Bonn 1980); Canaris, *Leistungsstörungen beim Unternehmenskauf*, (ZGR 1982), 395; Grunewald, *Unerwartete Verbindlichkeiten beim Unternehmenskauf*, (ZGR 1981), 622; Hiddemann, *Leistungsstörungen beim Unternehmenskauf*, (ZGR 1982), 435; Hommelhoff, *Die Sachmängelhaftung beim Unternehmenskauf durch Anteilserwerb*, (ZHR 140 1977), 254; Hommelhoff, *Zur Abgrenzung von Unternehmenskauf und Anteilserwerb*, (ZGR 1982), 366; Huber, *Mängelhaftung beim Kauf von Geschäftanteilen*, (ZGR 1972), 395; Loos, *Mängelhaftung für schuldrechtliche Verbindlichkeiten beim Verkauf von Aktien und GmbH Anteilen*, (MDR 1962), 172; Loos, *Die Haftung für Rechts- und Sachmängel des Unternehmens beim Kauf von Aktien und GmbH-Anteilen*, (NJW 1962), 519; Müller, *Umsätze und Erträge—Eigenschaften der Kaufsache*, (ZHR 147 1983), 501; Neumann-Duesberg, *Gewährleistung von Unternehmensmängeln beim Kauf von Gesellschaftsanteilen*, (WM 1968), 494, (WM 1969), 1002; Prölss, *Die Haftung des Verkäufers von Gesellschaftsanteilen für Unternehmensmängel*, (ZIP 1981), 337; Westermann, *Neuere Entwicklungen der Verkäuferhaftung beim Kauf von Uternehmensbeteiligungen*, (ZGR 1982), 45; Wiedemann, Haftung des Verkäufers für Mängel des Unternehmens, (*Festschrift für Nipperdey* 1965 Bd. I), 815; Willemsen, *Zum Ausschluß von Sachmängelhaftung und culpa in contrahendo beim Unternehmenskauf*, (AcP 182 1982), 515.

[8] Mössle, *Leistungsstörungen beim Unternehmenskauf—neue Tendenzen*, (BB 1983), 2146 *et seq.*

[9] Unless otherwise noted, the reference to shares shall in the following also include partnership interests.

whose shares were sold, and the existence of certain rights connected with the shares.[10]

Thus, the seller of shares is liable for the continued existence of the company whose shares were bought (ie, that the company was validly incorporated and that it has not been dissolved due to bankruptcy, liquidation, or other causes).[11]

Under section 437 of the Civil Code, the seller also warrants that he has good title to the shares he is selling and that the purchaser will actually become a shareholder of the specified company with the transfer of the shares.[12] This aspect of the warranty is of particular importance if the shares of a GmbH (Gesellschaft mit beschränkter Haftung, Limited Liability Company) or partnership interests are purchased. Under German law there are no physical share certificates required of a GmbH or of a KG (partnership) which could be physically handed over by the seller and which would document or otherwise prove that the seller actually owns those shares and that he can validly transfer them. Only shares of a stock corporation (Aktiengesellschaft, AG) may exist in the form of share certificates and the ownership of these certificates evidences the status of the owner as share (stock) holder of the AG. There is also no public register, share transfer book or similar institution which would conclusively document that a certain person owns the shares of a GmbH. Therefore, the only method a seller of shares in a GmbH has available to document his ownership of the shares is to present an uninterrupted chain of transfer agreements, in the form of notarial deeds, going back to the original issue of each share, documenting that all shares of the company were at one time validly transferred to the seller(s) from the former rightful owner, and so on backward.

Not even this chain of notarial deeds completely precludes the possibility that the current, or a previous, owner of the shares has sold them twice and transferred a share at some time to a (now unknown) person. In such case, only the first transfer will be valid. In case of the sale of a partnership interest (general partnership, OHG, or limited partnership, KG), not even a chain of notarial transfer agreements is available because partnership interests can be transferred even by oral agreement and no notarial deed is necessary. Although the partners of an OHG or KG have to be registered in the Commercial Register,[13] there is no absolute guarantee of the correctness of such registration, ie, that a person who is registered as a partner is actually a partner.

Thus, there is no complete protection available to a purchaser that he will be the real (sole) owner of the shares for which he is paying. Besides the documentation by means of the notarial transfer agreements in case of the shares of a GmbH, the warranty of full title under section 437 of the Civil Code or a corresponding contractual warranty is the best protection a purchaser can obtain

[10] Zutt in Hachenburg, GmbHG, Appendix to section 15, note 19, 7th ed, (1979) (hereinafter Hachenburg/Zutt); Palandt/Putzo, *supra* note 6, section 437, note 10.

[11] RGZ 92, 73, at 76; Westermann in *Münchener Kommentar*, section 437, note 17, 2nd ed, (1988) (hereinafter MK-Westermann); Prölss, *supra* note 7, (ZIP 1981), 337.

[12] BGH, (WM 1959), 324, at 328; Hachenburg/Zutt, *supra* note 10, Appendix to section 15, note 15.

[13] Sections 106, 107, 143, 161, 162 of the Commercial Code.

under German law. It should be noted that, whilst the rather limited protection a purchaser receives in relation to the title of the seller might appear bizarre for non-German purchasers, in practice there have been very few cases where a seller did not hold full title to the shares he was selling.

A purchaser will usually notice, during the negotiations with the sellers and during the performance of the legal and financial due diligence, if the seller is actually recognised by the business as the sole shareholder or owner. Nevertheless, any well-advised purchaser of shares will insist on detailed contractual warranties, in particular, in cases where the share ownership has become fragmented over time due to the splitting of shares, sales and increases of capital.

It should be noted that only by means of a contractual warranty (and/or title search where possible) can the purchaser obtain assurance that he will be the sole shareholder of the company. This is because the statutory warranty relates only to the title of those shares sold. Section 437 of the Civil Code does not address the issue whether the shares sold are 100 per cent of the shares issued by the acquired company.

The third aspect of the statutory warranty under section 437 of the Civil Code relates to the rights directly attached to the shares, such as the voting rights and the right to receive dividends. Furthermore, under section 434 of the Civil Code, the absence of certain rights of third persons constituting a "legal defect" in a share, such as rights derived from the pledge of shares or rights attached to the share (ie obligation to pay in the nominal capital of the share), is warranted *per se* (unless waived). The absence of other, mere obligatory rights of third persons, in relation the shares (eg option rights or rights to participate in profits), are not covered by section 434 of the Civil Code. Their absence needs to be addressed in contractual warranties.

It is important to note that sections 434 and 437 do not cover any warranties relating to the value of the shares, or defects in the assets of a company or the company's financial or economic condition, even including over-indebtedness and near bankruptcy of the company.[14] Therefore, in the absence of a specific warranty as to the quality of the business or other circumstances, the seller of shares is not liable for the "economic quality" of the shares sold or the business being transferred.[15]

The legal consequences of a breach of warranty under section 437 and section 434 of the Civil Code are determined by section 440, which refers to sections 320–327 of the Civil Code. These provisions give the purchaser various choices, and the advisable course of action depends on the specific circumstances of the case. In general, the purchaser may either:

(a) continue to demand specific performance from the seller if such performance is not impossible (section 322, Civil Code); or
(b) demand payment of damages for non-performance of the obligation of the seller, if the performance by the seller was or has become impossible (section 325 or section 326, Civil Code); or

[14] BGH, (WM 1989), 2408; disputed by Winter in Scholz, GmbH Gesetz, section 15, note 112, 7th ed, (1986).

[15] BGH, (NJW 1980), 2408, at 2409; Palandt/Putzo, *supra* note 6, section 437, note 10.

(c) withhold his own performance under the agreement (in most cases payment of the purchase price), unless such a right to withhold performance was waived;
(d) rescind the contract with the seller (section 325 or section 326, Civil Code). This option may be the preferable choice only in a very few cases because the parties are obliged, if rescission is declared, to re-exchange their performances. It is obvious that the return of a running business is only a theoretical option. Furthermore, rescission of the agreement limits the right of the purchaser to demand damages, and there are also limits regarding the compensation the purchaser can receive for investments made before the rescission was declared.

In most cases the purchaser will choose to demand payment of damages and withhold—if still possible—his own performance if specific performance by the seller, is not possible. Problems arise, though, if for example, a third party owns one or more of the shares supposedly sold and is not willing to sell it or them. Depending on the number of such share(s), the purchaser might be faced with a minority interest or other practical problems. In such case, the purchaser might want to withdraw from the agreement and/or demand damages for non-performance.

The amount of damages depends on the circumstances. Generally speaking, the purchaser can demand to be put into the same financial position as if the seller had performed all his obligations and as if the warranty had not been breached.[16] For instance, if it turns out that a share was pledged to a third person, the seller would be obliged to pay to the third person the amount necessary to have the share released from the pledge.[17] Damages equal to the loss resulting from non-performance of the whole agreement or the rescission of the whole agreement are only possible if the defect in title affects the whole agreement in a way such that it would be unreasonable for the purchaser to remain a party to the agreement. For instance, the pledge of a very small percentage of the purchased shares will typically not justify damages for non-performance of the whole agreement.

Although section 437 and section 434 of the Civil Code provide the purchaser with reasonable protection against defects in title, it is standard practice also to include parallel warranties in the purchase agreement which are more detailed.

The purchaser of all shares of a company is, under the strict wording of the Civil Code, left only with these statutory warranties relating to defects in title. The Civil Code does not provide for any statutory warranties relating to the quality of the assets or the business of the company whose shares are bought. This is obviously not an equitable situation, at least in cases in which an acquisition formally relates to all shares of a company but economically relates to a complete and running business. Therefore, the courts have treated share deals as asset deals and applied the respective provisions of the Civil Code analogously to share deals if all shares of a company are bought, or if only a minuscule part

[16] Palandt/Heinrichs, *supra* note 2, introduction to section 249, note 50 *et seq.*; *Ibid.*, section 249, note 1 *et seq.*

[17] Metzger in *RGRK, Bürgerliches Gesetzbuch*, section 434, note 9, 12th ed, (1978) (hereinafter RGRK/Metzger); Palandt/Heinrichs, *supra* note 2, section 434, note 8.

of the shares (less than one per cent) is left out.[18] The respective statutory warranties are discussed in the following section.

If a substantial part of the shares is not included in a purchase, the Federal Supreme (Civil) Court decided that no fixed border line can be established to decide whether asset deal warranties or share deal warranties should be applied.[19] Rather, if the will of the parties and objective criteria indicate that the purchase was directed economically at the business itself, the provisions governing a purchase of assets will apply. The main test applied by the courts is whether the purchaser will be able to run the business without being subject to special minority rights of any remaining shareholders or whether he will be able to change the by-laws of the company without the assent of the shareholders remaining. Thus, the Federal Supreme (Civil) Court has refused to apply asset deal rules where only 50 per cent or 60 per cent of the shares were bought.[20] In those cases the purchaser of shares has only statutory warranties relating to defects of title and, perhaps, claims under cic (discussed below under 3.2.3) if no contractual warranties were agreed upon. Based on the past decisions, it is probably safe to assume that if at least 90 per cent to 95 per cent of the shares of a company are bought, the courts will treat the acquisition as if it were an asset deal and, accordingly, will apply the statutory warranties governing defects of the acquired company's assets.

3.2.1.2 WARRANTY RELATING TO GOOD TITLE IN ASSET DEALS

The legal situation as to the seller's good title is different if assets are sold. Here it is necessary to differentiate between tangible assets and intangible assets such as, accounts receivable, other claims against third parties, intellectual property rights etc. Both types of items are usually included in the assets purchased. As far as intangible assets are concerned, they are often considered "rights" under German law in the same way shares are considered rights.[21] Therefore, the provisions of section 434 and section 437 of the Civil Code which were discussed above under 3.2.1.1 apply.

A different legal regime applies to the purchase of tangible assets such as chattel or real property, referred to by the Civil Code as "Sachen". Although there is no provision in the Civil Code which directly parallels section 437 of the Civil Code and which expressly imposes a statutory warranty regarding the existence of the tangible assets and the seller's good title at the time of delivery, it is generally held that the seller, by entering into a purchase agreement, warrants that he has good title to the tangible assets he is selling and that he will be able to transfer the title to the purchaser.[22] In business acquisitions this warranty applies to all assets, which, according to the purchase agreement, constitute the business.

[18] BGH, (WM 1975), 230; (BGHZ 65), 246 (248); Hachenburg/Zutt, *supra* note 10, Appendix to section 15, note 21; Palandt/Putzo, *supra* note 6, introduction to section 459, note 15.

[19] BGH, (NJW 1980), 2408; see also BGH, (BB 1983), 2146.

[20] BGH, (WM 1980), 284.

[21] Palandt/Putzo, *supra* note 6, section 434, note 4 *et seq.*

[22] BGH, (NJW 1983), 2874; BGHZ 11, 16 at 20; Baltes in Erman, *Bürgerliches Gesetzbuch Handkommentar*, section 306, note 21, 8th ed, (1989) (hereinafter Erman-Baltes); MK-Westermann, *supra* note 11, sections 440, 441, note 2 *et seq.*

Although there are differences in detail, depending on whether the seller already lacked good title before the signing of the purchase agreement or if he lost good title after signing the purchase agreement, he is liable to the purchaser under section 440 and sections 320–327 of the Civil Code.[23] If performance by the seller is not possible, the seller is liable for damages for non-performance. Basically, the purchaser must be put into the position he would have been in had the contract been performed properly. The details as to the determination of the damages due depend on the circumstances: for example, if only a relatively unimportant business asset is missing, the purchaser will usually receive the amount necessary to buy a replacement asset and will be compensated for the losses incurred due to the missing asset. Higher amounts of compensatory damages might result if the seller used an important trademark without owning it or being licensed to use it. In that case, the purchaser might be compensated for the costs of establishing a new trademark and lost profits. In extreme cases, the purchaser may be entitled to claim rescission of the whole agreement, although such cases—in practice—are rather rare.

In so far as mere defects of title of tangible assets are concerned, for instance third parties' rights such as security right and rights to possession, section 434 of the Civil Code applies, as it applies to defects of title of shares.[24]

Such potential rights of third parties may be numerous: they include encumbrances, pledges, and also patent rights of third persons. In cases where a piece of land is sold, the purchaser can verify the existence or the lack of such encumbrances in the Land Register, which, however, does not register every kind of third party rights which might exist, for instance, rights resulting from a leasing agreement or charges and restrictions under public law. In one case relating to an acquisition, the "Reichsgericht" (the predecessor of the Federal Supreme (Civil) Court), decided that a defect in title under section 434 of the Civil Code can be present in an asset deal if the business activity is restricted to certain geographical areas by an agreement entered into by the former owner, and which still binds the purchaser by virtue of a special succession rule in the Commercial Code (section 25, HGB).[25] Furthermore, governmental rights to attach assets may be considered to constitute a defect in title.[26]

3.2.1.3 WARRANTY AS TO THE ABSENCE OF MATERIAL DEFECTS

According to section 459, subsection 1 of the Civil Code, the seller warrants that a tangible asset sold has no defects which would impair its value or its suitability for the intended use. The details of this definition are disputed, but it can be said that a material defect is present if the actual condition of the asset and the condition agreed upon by the parties (or if the parties failed to specify the conditions, the conditions typical for equivalent products) deviate from each other, and if such deviation materially reduces the value of the item or its

[23] MK-Westermann, *supra* note 11, sections 440, 441, note 2 *et seq.*
[24] Palandt/Putzo, *supra* note 6, section 434, note 4.
[25] RGZ 88, 103.
[26] RGZ 102, 292; MK-Westermann, *supra* note 11, section 434, note 10.

suitability for the intended purpose.[27] In any event, any defect must be material.

For clarification, the parties may also agree on the specifications of certain assets or other items in relation to the business, which may later serve as an indicator whether a defect is present or not. Under certain circumstances, such specifications may already be considered a warranted quality of an item which are subject to different legal rules.

The concept of material defects can be considered to constitute an implied warranty: if a material defect is present, the seller is liable without fault for such defect, unless the seller's liability is expressly excluded.

Nevertheless, the application of section 459, subsection 1 of the Civil Code to business acquisitions gives rise to significant problems. German courts have consistently ruled that a business as such cannot have a "material defect". Section 459 applies to an individual asset, such as a machine or a building. However, a business is, at least in a legal sense, not one individual asset which has specific qualities, but instead it consists of a great number of assets, rights and relationships. A business as such cannot have material defects; only its individual elements may have such legal, factual or economic defects. Accordingly, section 459 strictly speaking, cannot be applied directly to the business as a whole but instead can be applied only to each product individually. The application of section 459 of the Civil Code to the individual assets will, however, not be of much use to a purchaser. To avoid the consequences resulting from the narrow scope of section 459, the courts have applied the concept of defects as defined in section 459 to businesses by analogy, if a defect of an individual item belonging to the business is present which affects the business as a whole.[28]

According to the courts, two elements have to be present—a tangible or an intangible asset owned or used by the business (not necessarily mentioned in the purchase agreement at all)—which must be defective, and this defect, which may be a defect in title or any other material defect as defined by section 459, must negatively and substantially influence the economic basis of the business. This may apply if essential machinery fails to operate properly, or if certain assets necessary to operate the business are missing.[29] Certain assets may be considered defective solely because they cannot be used as anticipated, for example, if the production facility does not have access to a railway line, as the parties expected it to,[30] or if due to public law restrictions, the real estate or machinery of the business cannot be used as intended.[31] Furthermore, the status of legal relationships to third parties may, in principle, constitute a defect of a business. In one case it was decided that if a business was run on leased premises, the refusal of the lessor to lease the premises to the new owner of the business may constitute a defect of the whole business.[32]

27 Palandt/Putzo, *supra* note 6, introduction to section 459, note 15; Hiddemann, *supra* note 7, (ZGR 1982), 435, at 444.

28 BGH, (NJW 1988), 1700; BGH, (NJW 1970), 556; (RGZ 63), 57.

29 BGH, (NJW 1979), 33; BGH, (WM 1974), 312.

30 RG, (HRR 1930), No 1313.

31 RGZ 138, 354, at 356.

32 BGH, (NJW 1970), 556.

Even the lack of certain business opportunities may be a defect. In one case a purchaser bought shares of a GmbH from a seller and from the circumstances it was clear that the economic goal of the acquisition was to obtain the right to build and sell a certain apparatus. As it turned out later, this apparatus did not work and could not be marketed. The Federal Supreme (Civil) Court held that the defect of the apparatus and the resulting loss of the business opportunity constituted a defect of the whole business because the opportunities connected with the apparatus were the economic core of the business.[33] In the latter case it would also be possible to argue that there was no defect, but that the seller simply had not performed his main obligation under the agreement.[34]

Not all negative deviations of the purchased item from the expectations of the purchaser, or even of both parties, constitute a defect. The most frequent type of deviation is lower than expected profits or a lower than expected asset value of a business. The Federal Supreme (Civil) Court has, with considerable criticism from scholars,[35] consistently held that such deviations do not constitute a defect, because they are only a product of other factors which together result in the value or profitability of a business.[36] Furthermore, incorrect information contained in the financial statements of a company, for example, profits and turnover, is not considered a defect because it also only indirectly relates to the "business as such".[37]

The remedies for a defect in the purchased business are determined by section 462 of the Civil Code, according to which the purchaser may choose either to reduce the purchase price appropriately or to rescind the agreement. Although the amelioration of defects is not provided for by the Civil Code in connection with purchases in the absence of an agreement by the parties, it has been proposed in the literature that improvements can be demanded by the purchaser even in the absence of a specific agreement.[38]

A claim by a purchaser is excluded under section 460 if the purchaser knew about the defect at the time he entered into the agreement. Thus, if the purchaser finds problems with the business which might constitute a defect during the financial or legal due diligence, the seller will not be liable for such defects if the agreement is concluded despite the purchaser's knowledge. Under section 166, subsection 1 of the Civil Code, the knowledge of the advisers and other persons assisting the purchaser, is generally attributed to the purchaser.[39] It is not sufficient, however, if there is merely a strong suspicion of the existence of a defect; only actual knowledge of the purchaser of all facts and their (legal) relevance will protect the seller from liability under all circumstances.[40]

[33] BGH, (WM 1978), 59, at 60.

[34] V Friesen, *Der Fehlbestand beim Unternehemskauf*, (NJW 1979), 2288 *et seq.*

[35] Putzo, (NJW 1970), 653; Immenga, *Fehler oder zugesicherte Eigenschaften*, (AcP 171), 1.

[36] BGH, (BB 1974), 231; BGH, (NJW 1970), 653; RGZ 67, 86.

[37] BGH, (WM 1970), 132; MK-Westermann, *supra* note 11, section 459, note 50; Hiddemann, *supra* note 7, (ZGR 1982), 435 at 445.

[38] Palandt/Putzo, *supra* note 6, introduction to section 459, note 15; Hiddemann, *supra* note 7, (ZGR 1982), 435 at 442.

[39] Palandt/Heinrichs, *supra* note 2, section 166, note 3.

[40] BGH, (NJW 1961), 1860, (RGZ 149), 402; Palandt/Putzo, *supra* note 6, section 460, note 6.

If, due to gross negligence on behalf of the purchaser, he has not discovered a certain defect, the seller is only liable for such defect if he fraudulently failed to disclose it (section 460, Civil Code). This does not apply, however, if the seller has specifically warranted the absence of such defect. In those cases, the seller remains liable, regardless of gross negligence on the side of the purchaser.

Overall, the scope of sections 434, 437 and 459 of the Civil Code is not well suited to achieve the protection the buyer of a business expects. Only part of the qualities which a business might have (or might not have) are covered by the statutory concept of defects, and there is also considerable uncertainty whether a specific lack of quality constitutes a defect in the meaning of the statute. In cases where less than substantially all shares of a company are bought, the purchaser might even be left without any meaningful statutory warranty relating to the business. Therefore, this limited statutory concept is in fact supplemented or even replaced by other types of warranties.

3.2.2 *Culpa in contrahendo*

Culpa in contrahendo (cic) is the Latin term for a type of liability based on pre-contractual conduct of a party, which may lead to a liability equivalent or similar to that for breach of a warranty. The German Civil Code does not specifically mention *culpa in contrahendo*, but the concept is generally recognised and considered to be a part of the legal system.[41] It is derived from a number of legal provisions which relate to the obligations of good faith conduct of parties when negotiating and entering into agreements.

In connection with business acquisitions, cic can, *inter alia*, be interpreted as the (implied) warranty of the seller that the information given to the purchaser before and during negotiations, be it implicitly, orally or in writing, is correct and complete so as to enable the purchaser reasonably to assess the business to be purchased.[42]

Since the concept of defects is limited in scope,[43] the Federal Supreme (Civil) Court has supplemented this concept with the concept of *culpa in contrahendo*. The scope of cic is also quite limited in connection with acquisitions. It has mainly been applied in two types of situations where the statutory provisions governing defects do not apply:

- in cases in which the deviation of quality is not related to specific items of the business but rather to the general state of the business, which in itself is not sufficient to constitute a material defect or a defect in title in a legal sense;[44]

41 (BGHZ 6), 330, at 333; (RGZ 78), 239, at 240; Palandt/Heinrichs, *supra* note 2, section 276, note 65 *et seq*, Wiedemann in Soergel, BGB, introduction to section 275, note 857, 12th ed, (1991) (hereinafter Soergel-Wiedemann); Aderhold, *supra* note 5, at 846.

42 BGH, (BB 1991), 496; Aderhold, *supra* note 5, at 846.

43 See *supra* p. 56.

44 Soergel-Wiedmann, *supra* note 41, introduction to section 275, note 277.

- in cases where there is a defect of a specific item owned or used by the business, but such defect does not sufficiently affect the economic basis of the whole business, that is, in situations where there is no defect of the business as a whole.[45]

In these situations, the courts have taken the position that under cic there is an obligation on the part of the seller to inform completely and correctly a potential purchaser about all relevant facts and circumstances which have, under the circumstances, a clear influence upon the decision of the purchaser to buy or not to buy the business at a certain price. In addition, of course, the seller may not give wrong or misleading information to the purchaser.

There is, however, an important difference between cic and the statutory warranties. Whereas the latter apply regardless whether the seller is at fault, cic—as the term culpa already indicates—applies only if the seller culpably violates a legal obligation to state correctly and disclose certain facts relating to the business. Such an obligation exists only if the seller (or a person acting on his behalf) knows or should have known that certain information would be important for the decision of the purchaser to acquire the business under the specific conditions agreed upon between the parties, and if the seller himself knows about those facts and circumstances. It is not sufficient for the seller to wait for the purchaser to ask for specific facts and other information in relation to the business; as soon as the seller notices that specific information is important for the purchaser in his decision-making process the seller has to disclose such information to the purchaser.[46]

Cic is thus only applicable if there is no defect of the business as a whole and if the seller had an obligation to inform the purchaser about certain facts or circumstances in relation to the business which he culpably did not fulfil.

Cic has usually been applied by the courts in cases where the financial situation of a business was not correctly, or not completely, disclosed to a purchaser in the course of the negotiations.[47] However, the applicability of cic is not limited to that type of information. Any information relating to the business which was withheld from the purchaser can potentially serve as a basis for a claim under cic. The exact scope of the seller's obligation to inform depends, of course, on a large number of circumstances, and no general rule can be given. Such facts include the experience of a seller and purchaser in conducting acquisitions, the intensity with which the purchaser indicated to the seller the points and items important for the purchaser's decision and the total amount of information given by the seller to the purchaser.[48]

In this context, the legal and financial due diligence performed by the purchaser also gains importance. If due diligence was performed and certain important information was not uncovered by the purchaser or his advisers,

[45] Hiddemann, *supra* note 7, (ZGR 1982), 435, at 44; Mössle, *supra* note 8, (BB 1983), 2146, at 2148.

[46] BGH, (NJW 1970), 653, at 655.

[47] (BGHZ 69), 53 (profits); (BGHZ 65), 246 (debt); BGH, (WM 1988), 1700 (turnover); BGH, WM 1988, 124 (costs); BGH, (NJW 1970), 653 (turnover); BGH, (NJW 1969), 184 (debt).

[48] BGH, (NJW 1977), 1536.

although such information could have been discovered, the degree of responsibility of the seller might be reduced. The purchaser is, however, not obliged to perform such a review of the business to retain warranty claims against the seller.

As the Civil Codes does not prescribe specific legal consequences for the seller's breach of his obligations under cic, the courts have granted two types of remedies. The first option available to the purchaser is to rescind the agreement.[49] The purchaser may also demand from the seller an adequate reduction of the purchase price. The amount of the reduction is determined by the difference in value of the business between its actual condition and the condition which was (implicitly) warranted by the seller.[50] The details of calculating this difference can be rather difficult and depend on the circumstances of the individual case. The purchaser's freedom to choose between two alternative remedies is only limited by *bona fide* considerations, for instance, he may not rescind the agreement if he has only suffered minor damage which the seller is willing to compensate adequately.[51]

One important respect in which the courts assist a purchaser in cic cases is the shift of the burden of proof. If the general rules governing the burden of proof were applied, a purchaser would have to prove that he would not have bought the business, or would have paid a greatly reduced price, had he known the information which the seller withheld. Since this obstacle can, in practice, rarely be overcome by a purchaser the courts decided that the burden of proof must be shifted by eliminating the purchaser's obligation to prove his alternative behaviour. The Federal Supreme (Civil) Court went even further in one case and decided that the seller is barred from proving the opposite—that the purchaser would have paid the same purchase price had he known about the real situation of the business.[52]

The seller's liability based on cic can be excluded in the purchase agreement. This is frequently done, because cic is a rather vague concept and the outcome of any dispute basing a claim under cic will rarely be certain. Therefore, the purchaser has no strong interest in relying on cic, and the seller has a strong interest in avoiding the uncertainty connected with potential claims under cic.

3.2.3 Warranted qualities

Whereas the implied statutory warranties described above (absence of defects, cic) apply even without any specific language in the purchase agreement (unless the parties have expressly provided otherwise), the Civil Code also provides for express warranties in purchase agreements. Section 459, subsection 2 of the Civil Code provides for a no-fault liability of the seller that the purchased item has the qualities which where expressly warranted to the purchaser by the seller ("zugesicherte Eigenschaften"). Quality of the purchased item in the meaning of this provision is any quality that is directly related to the purchased item,

[49] Aderhold, *supra* note 5, (DStR 1991), 846; Soergel-Wiedemann, *supra* note 41, section 275, note 277.

[50] (BGHZ 69), 53; Soergel-Wiedemann, *supra* note 41, introduction to section 275, note 277.

[51] BGH, (NJW 1977), 1536; Hiddemann, *supra* note 7, (ZGR 1982), 435, at 448.

[52] BGH, (NJW 1980), 2408; BGH, (NJW 1977), 1536.

including its economic, legal or other aspects, and which is relevant to its value, the future use of the purchased item or other important reasons of the purchaser.[53]

The absence of a quality expressly warranted in accordance with section 459, subsection 2, does not, however, automatically constitute a defect within the meaning of section 459, subsection 1. While the two liability theories will often overlap, the concept of expressly warranted qualities is much broader than the concept of absence of material defects, because the parties are basically free to agree as to what specific qualities a purchased item should have.

Particular examples of expressly warranted qualities in connection with business acquisitions are the past profitability of a business[54] or the past asset value or debt of a business. It should be noted that the past turnover is not recognised as a "quality" of a business.[55]

The main legal problems connected with expressly warranted qualities concern the question of whether certain language used in the agreement or certain information given in the purchase agreement is sufficient to constitute an expressly warranted quality. This question has both a formal and a material aspect. On the formal side, it is clear that warranted qualities have to be warranted expressly and that an implied warranty can only be assumed to be present under very limited circumstances, in particular if the purchase agreement has been recorded in a notarial deed, as is the case when shares in a GmbH are transferred.[56] On the material side, the question is whether certain language used by the parties in the agreement can actually be considered to constitute a warranted quality and what, specifically, is covered by such language.

A frequently occurring example of this is when a seller warrants "the correctness of the financial statements" of the business sold, if later the profitability of the business turns out to be less than expected or the debts turn out to be higher than expected. This type of a general language warranty poses the problem of what specifically was warranted under such a clause. As the Federal (Civil) Supreme Court has explained, there is a large amount of information which might potentially be important to the purchaser, and it is not possible to refer generally to the correctness of the financial statements and then to define specific aspects as specifically warranted qualities.[57] Thus, a contractual warranty relating to the last balance sheet of a company is only of limited value to the purchaser. Only in extreme cases, such as where the seller manipulated the situation of a business in such a way as to ensure a favourable balance sheet, can a claim under cic be considered.[58]

It has also been decided by the courts that an unqualified balance sheet warranty cannot be interpreted to warrant a certain level of profitability over

[53] BGH, (NJW 1981), 1600; Palandt/Putzo, *supra* note 6, section 459, note 20.

[54] BGH, (NJW 1977), 1536; (RGZ 63), 57.

[55] BGH, (WM 1988), 1700; BGH, (WM 1977), 999; BGH, (WM 1974), 51; BGH, (NJW 1970), 653; (RGZ 146), 120.

[56] Huber in Soergel, BGB_, section 459, note 155 *et seq*, 12 ed, (1991) (hereinafter Soergel-Huber).

[57] BGH, (JW 1977), 1536; BGH, (WM 1974), 51.

[58] BGH, (WM 1974), 51.

time.[59] On the contrary, it has been held that as long as the balance sheet, to which the warranty refers is correct, there exists no valid basis for a claim for breach of warranty if profits are much lower in later years.[60] The reason for this conclusion is that the balance sheet is drawn up only at a certain point in time and that such a snapshot of information or quality, determined at a past point in time, cannot be interpreted to warrant any qualities relating to the development of the business in the future. Therefore, if it is important to a purchaser that a business has a certain level of profitability, then at least the last three balance sheets should be made the subject of an express warranty or the profitability issue should be addressed specifically. *Mutatis mutandis*, this requirement for specificity applies also to items like turnover, debt, or asset value, which are either warranted under cic or a separate guarantee.

The often-heard argument from seller's counsel that specific warranties in relation to the various balance sheet items are unnecessary and redundant is very dangerous for the purchaser. The fact that for an accountant the business is condensed in the financial statements does not mean that all factual information and assessments which went into the preparation of the balance sheet are also a warranted quality in the legal sense.

The legal consequences of a breach of a warranty under section 459, subsection 2 of the Civil Code are governed by sections 462 and 463. According to these provisions, the purchaser has a choice of demanding a reduction of the purchase price, rescinding the agreement, or demanding damages for non-performance.

3.2.4 Warranties relating to future conditions of the business and other circumstances surrounding the business (Garantien)

The applicability of the liability theory of section 459, subsection 2 of the Civil Code is somewhat limited and not available if a warranty should cover circumstances which lie outside the business or which do not concern a "quality" of the business in the narrow legal meaning of the term. For instance, a warranty of the seller that a certain customer will continue to buy the products of the business or that the business is not producing faulty products. Moreover, in order to qualify as a "quality", the respective circumstances must be present at the time of transfer of the assets or the shares of a business. Technically, this is the exact point in time when the risk of accidental destruction of the purchased item is assumed by the purchaser. This timing does not protect a purchaser against any negative events which take place only after such transfer.

In order to provide the parties with an instrument to cover circumstances not considered to constitute qualities of the business sold, the concept of guarantees ("Garantien")—which are not to be confused with guarantees of a third party used as security instruments—is applied.[61] Such guarantees are warranties encompassing those circumstances which do not qualify as "qualities" and

[59] BGH, (NJW 1977), 1536; BGH, (WM 1974), 51; see also Hiddemann, *supra* note 6, (ZGR 1982), 435, at 446.

[60] BGH, WM 1990, 1344; BGH, NJW 1970, 653.

[61] BGH, (NJW 1981), 1600; BGH, (WM 1977), 999, at 1000; Soergel-Huber, *supra* note 56, section 459, note 281.

which, accordingly, do not fall within the purview of section 459. Under the general principle of freedom of contract the seller may warrant almost anything under a guarantee (within the general framework of law) without being limited by narrow legal concepts such as defect in title or material defect. In particular, in a guarantee the seller may assume liability for a specific outcome or for certain risks connected with the business concerning the time after the transfer of the assets or the shares.

A guarantee is considered, at least in theory, as an agreement that is distinct from the purchase agreement.[62] This does not have practical implications, and drafting practice does not strictly distinguish between warranties and guarantees. It is often difficult to decide whether a warranty is, in effect, an expressly warranted quality or a guarantee, so purchase agreements refer typically to all express warranties as "warrantied qualities and guarantees" (Zusicherungen und Garantien).

The legal consequences of a breach of a guarantee are not, however, identical to those which apply if a warranted quality is found not to be present. As a guarantee is considered technically to be a separate "guarantee agreement", the legal consequences are either determined by the applicable general provisions of the Civil Code or the provisions of the purchase agreement. Thus, a purchaser would have a claim for damages for non-performance or, depending on the circumstances, a right to withdraw from the agreement. In many cases, the parties will not rely on the general provisions of the Civil Code but rather agree on specific remedies equivalent or similar to a claim for damages for non-performance.

3.2.5 Waiver by agreement

The statutory warranties (including cic) which were described above are often expressly waived in purchase agreements and/or completely replaced by contractual waranties (ie warranted qualities and guarantees.) However, section 476 of the Civil Code, which is compulsory and cannot be waived by the parties, provides that an exclusion of the statutory warranties is void, if the seller fraudulently fails to disclose a defect. Although section 476 does not apply to circmstances covered by cic, a waiver of liability under cic may also be invalid if the seller fraudulently failed to disclose those circumstances.[63]

3.3 Contractual Warranties and Guarantees

Although there is no *caveat emptor* doctrine in Germany, as discussed above, the interests of the seller and the purchaser in acquisitions are not addressed very well by the provisions of the Civil Code as they have been interpreted by the Federal Supreme (Civil) Court.

The main reasons are the very limited scope of protection a purchaser receives under the statutory warranties and the level of uncertainty for the parties in assessing the risks which they assume in relying on statutory warranties. In addition, the acquisition of a complete entity such as a running business, requires

[62] Soergel-Huber, *supra* note 56, section 459, note 281.

[63] (BGHZ 63), 369, at 375; OLG Düsseldorf, (OLGZ 1978), 317, at 319.

more flexibility than the prefabricated liability theories that the Civil Code can provide. Moreover, the legal remedies available under statutory liability theories may not suit the intentions of the parties. The seller may not favour a (unilateral) reduction of the purchase price, in particular if the standard by which such reduction is measured is not entirely clear. Neither is the rescission of an agreement in the interest of the parties: the purchaser might have operated the business for a while and altered its nature so that the return of the business will be impractical, if not altogether impossible. In the final analysis, then, both parties often have an interest to deviate from the statutory solutions and agree on specific warranties and remedies. This is strongly advised by most writers on the subject of business acquisitions.[64]

In practice, the parties to an acquisition will replace the statutory framework for warranties with their own framework of contractual warranties and guarantees, including the legal consequences in case of a breach of warranties.

From a seller's point of view, the best result would be specifically to exclude all liability or as much as possible. From the purchaser's point of view, the agreement should cover as many risks as possible, in particular since a purchaser knows—at least in most cases—little or nothing about the business to be acquired and in any event is limited to such information as the seller has provided.

The usual approach is to describe the qualities which the business should have at the time of signing, or closing, or at a certain other point in time specified in the agreement. Although no general concept will ever apply to all cases, a good conceptual starting point for describing and setting the minimum qualities of a business is the idea that the warranties should separate the risks of the past from the risks of the future and distribute them between seller and purchaser. Typically, a purchaser will not, unless specific circumstances are present, assume the risks of the past.

As to the specific contents of such warranty catalogues, the imagination of the purchaser and his advisers is unlimited. Past practice has come up with endless, albeit in specific cases often incomplete, lists that provide examples of contractual warranties and guarantees.[65] It would be beyond the scope of this chapter to describe and discuss all issues which, in theory, could be covered by warranties. From the adviser's point of view, it is important to obtain a clear understanding as to the purchaser's expectations and plans regarding the business. The adviser should then be in a position to prepare specific warranties which suit the purchaser's individual needs and not lose focus or waste resources or goodwill on marginal points. Otherwise, there is the risk that all kind of non-crucial issues will be addressed while the purchaser's real concerns are neglected.

Individual issues are typically discovered and addressed during the legal and financial due diligence process or during negotiations, and can then be specifically dealt with on a case-by-case basis. Drafting practice in Germany tends to use warranties which cover a relatively wide scope of issues in broad language,

[64] Hommelhoff, (ZHR 140), 254, at 273; Aderhold, *supra* note 5, (DStR 1991), 884, at 847.

[65] Holzapfel/Pöllath, Recht and Praxis des Unternehmenskaufs, 5th ed, (1990), note 403 *et seq.* Günther in Münchener Vertragshandbuch, Band 2, 441 *et seq*, 2nd ed, (1987).

leaving it to future interpreters of the agreement to find the "real economic will" of the parties.[66] While both parties take an unavoidable if (limited) risk with this approach there would be an even greater danger if a large number of specific warranties were spelled out in the agreement, because unforeseen and therefore unaddressed events might not be recognised by the courts to be covered by the warranties. The argument for that result could be, roughly, as follows: because the parties addressed all kinds of specific contingencies in the agreement, their goal was to limit the warranties to those contingencies which were specifically addressed and not evenly to distribute the economic risk. In the interest of a purchaser, drafting practice therefore needs to follow an approach which mixes general language warranties with warranties that address the important specific issues.

There are, however, certain issues which are of importance in all acquisitions and which are indispensable to achieve a layer of basic protection for the purchaser. Three of those issues have been selected to be discussed here in detail.

(a) warranties relating to the shares and the legal structure of the business;
(b) warranties relating to the financial statements (balance sheet warranties);
(c) warranties addressing issues not reflected in a balance sheet.

The first type of warranty applies only in share deals and not in asset deals, and the second type applies not in all deals (for example, if an entity is bought which is organisationally and financially integrated into a bigger entity). As share deals are more frequent in cross-border acquisitions, it is appropriate to address the warranties used in share deals more extensively than asset deals.

3.4 Specific Contractual Warranties

3.4.1 Warranties relating to the shares and the company

3.4.1.1 SHARE WARRANTIES

In most acquisitions, the purchaser intends to acquire 100 per cent of the shares of a company. One group of warranties is used to ensure that the purchaser receives the legal control of an existing legal entity from the purchaser. To do this, the seller is required to warrant that the shares sold represent 100 per cent of the shares of the company to be sold. If not all shares are subject to the purchase agreement, the purchaser should be aware of any minority rights of remaining shareholders and have such minority rights fully disclosed. Minority rights can be divided into statutory minority rights and additional contractual minority rights. The latter can be found in the articles of association/by-laws of the company or in additional agreements amongst the shareholders.

In this connection, it should be noted again that in a German GmbH, and also in a KG, there are no physical shares which would prove that the seller actually owns the shares he is selling. There is also no share register. Thus, a purchaser should never rely on a warranty of the seller alone, but should at the same time complement the warranty by ascertaining that (in the case of a GmbH), there is

[66] *Supra.*

a chain of notarial deeds which goes back to the incorporation of the company or the increase of the share capital and issue of new shares, respectively. In case of partnership interests of a KG, the registration of the partners in the Commercial Register provides reasonable certainty as to the status of the sellers as partners of the KG. Nevertheless, an appropriate warranty is indispensable.

The fact that the seller owns all the shares does not necessarily mean that the seller can transfer those shares freely to a purchaser. There may be a number of rights of third parties or liens (pledges or other security interests) connected with the shares which might render any transfer of the shares ineffective or at least cause disputes with third parties. The sale of the shares might also trigger rights of third parties, for instance, option rights, which might complicate the transaction. Therefore, a seller should also always warrant that he is free to dispose of the shares, that there are no rights or option rights of third parties, and that the approval or co-operation of third parties is not necessary.

Furthermore, a seller should also warrant that there is no remaining obligation for a purchaser to pay any unpaid share capital to the company, that the shares have been fully paid up at their nominal value, and that the share capital has not been refunded to the shareholder(s). The concept of refund of share capital is interpreted by the courts to go beyond the literal meaning of "refund".[67]

3.4.1.2 WARRANTIES RELATING TO THE LEGAL STATUS OF THE COMPANY

In addition to warranties relating to the shares, a purchase agreement should also contain warranties relating to the company itself.

Under German law, the basic documents relating to a GmbH are the excerpt from the Commercial Register and the articles of association/by-laws, so the seller should warrant the correctness and completeness of those documents (which should be included as an annex to the purchase agreement). The seller should also warrant that there are no shareholders, resolutions or other events which have not yet been registered in the Commercial Register to assure that there are no pending registrations of matters which might negatively influence the position of the purchaser.

Warranties relating to the excerpt from the Commercial Register and the articles of association/by-laws are an important means to ensure that the purchaser will have legal control over the company to be bought.

The excerpt from the Commercial Register not only shows that the GmbH actually exists, but also provides information such as the correct name, the share capital and the names of the person(s) who may legally bind the company as managing director(s) ("Geschäftsführer") and holders of power of attorney ("Prokuristen"). The amount of the total share capital is important information for the purchaser because it enables him to ascertain what percentage of the shares of the company he has bought.[68] The articles of association of the company are also important to the purchaser because they contain information or restrictions on the transfer of shares or special minority rights. In addition, the fact that a profit and loss transfer agreement and/or corporate control agreement

[67] Meyer-Landrut in Meyer-Landrut, Miller, Niehus, *GmbH-Gesetz*, section 30, note 1 *et seq.*

[68] This assumes, of course, that the seller is the actual owner of the shares; see above p.65.

with another company has been concluded must be registered in the Commercial Register.[69]

If the company to be bought is a stock corporation (AG), similar concepts apply. If partnership interests are bought, the respective warranties look somewhat different because, in that case, nearly all information in the Commercial Register is only of declaratory nature (although there is some good faith protection) and because the partnership agreement need not be filed in the Commercial Register.

3.4.2 Warranties relating to the financial statements (balance sheet warranties)

3.4.2.1 GENERAL REMARKS

The core of warranties in business acquisitions is often the warranties relating to financial statements (balance sheet, profit and loss statement and, where applicable, an annex giving a general description of the business situation).[70] In asset deals, financial statements may be lacking if the business to be sold was integrated organisationally and financially into a bigger entity. (In the latter case, however, the seller may have prepared pro forma financial statements.)

The financial statements to which the warranties refer should be those for the last three or four completed business years and, if possible, specifically drawn up interim financial statements. Interim financial statements as of closing should be prepared for at least three reasons:

(a) They provide the most up-to-date information as to the economic and financial situation of the business.
(b) They save the parties from the need of negotiating extensive provisions for "bringing up" the balance sheet warranties from the last account date to the date of closing; the longer the period, the more difficult this issue might be.
(c) They provide the purchaser and his advisers with the opportunity to have a closer look into the operation of the business in the course of the preparation of the interim financial statements (eg observance of stock-taking) than might otherwise be possible.

The financial statements should provide, within limits, a condensed description of the economic and financial conditions of a company (if they are complete and correct). They should also describe its financial status in relation to net assets and profit level, which often is the basis for the decision of the purchaser to buy the company at a certain price.

The financial statements are also a valuable tool for the purchaser, because the seller is not free to decide how to prepare such financial statements. On the contrary, the seller is bound by a number of statutory provisions in sections 238 *et seq* of the Commercial Code as to the rules governing the preparation and

[69] (BGHZ 105), 224; this position has recently been disputed by OLG Düsseldorf, GmbHR 1991, 526.

[70] For a general outline see: Binz/Freudenberg, *Die Bilanzgarantie im Unternehmenskaufvertrag*, (DStR 1991), 1629 *et seq*.

content of financial statements. The provisions of sections 238 *et seq* have codified in detail the necessary content of a balance sheet and the rules and procedures applicable for valuing assets and liabilities of a business. The generally accepted accounting principles in Germany which are not codified but referred to by the Commercial Code, supplement the statutory rules to provide an extensive set of rules which govern the preparation of financial statements.

All of those rules are aimed at producing as accurate as possible a description of the economic and financial situation of a company. One should take advantage of the financial statements because they provide the parties, in particular the purchaser, with standardised key information on the condition of the business.

For drafting balance sheet warranties, a good starting point is the warranty of the seller that the financial statements (for one or more specific years) have been prepared in accordance with all applicable provisions of the Commercial Code and in accordance with the generally accepted accounting principles applicable in Germany. This general balance sheet warranty can then be supplemented by specific warranties in relation to individual items on the balance sheet and/or highlight issues of particular significance, like a warranty concerning the formal and material continuity of the balance sheet, a warranty requiring balance sheet identity, or a warranty stating that the financial statements give a "true and fair view" of the business. The latter should be included, in particular, if a KG is bought. This is because, when the object of the purchase is shares of a GmbH or AG, the "true and fair view" requirement is already codified in section 264, subsection 2 of the Commercial Code.

Specific balance sheet warranties should address the individual items of the balance sheet. The degree of specificity depends on the circumstances. In most cases, it will suffice shortly to address the main items on the asset side and the liability side. It should be remembered, however, that as was pointed out above,[71] the courts in Germany tend to treat "plain" warranties relating to financial statements (ie a bald assertion that they are "correct") rather cautiously. This caution is justified because such a plain warranty does not indicate which specific piece of information or quality of the business, as it appears in the financial statements or can be derived therefrom, was considered by the parties as a quality to be warranted. If it is important for the purchaser that a company has a general level of profitability, the balance sheet warranties should cover the financial statements for at least the last three business years, if there is no separate guarantee regarding profitability.[72]

One issue which will frequently be a subject of the discussions between seller and purchaser is the question whether the warranties relating to the financial statements should be measured against reality or merely against good accounting practice. In the first case a seller would be liable for a breach of warranty in case of any deviation between the content of the financial statements and reality, even if all accounting principles were observed. For instance, if a debtor of the business were to go bankrupt unexpectedly, the seller might be liable for any resulting losses in that case. On the other hand, if the financial statements would

[71] *Supra.*
[72] BGH, (WM 1990), 1344; BGH, (NJW 1977), 1536; BGH, (WM 1970), 132, at 133.

be measured only against good accounting practice, no liability would attach, because if the bankruptcy was unexpected, no reserve would have been needed. In practice, the parties will differentiate between the various balance sheet items and, ultimately, the outcome of the negotiations will depend on the relative bargaining power of the parties.

3.4.2.2. ASSET SIDE

Typical warranties relating to items on the asset side of the balance sheet are the following:

(i) Full title to and completeness of the fixed and current assets which are reflected in the balance sheet. Also, the non-existence of rights of third parties, in particular security interests, should be warranted. Typically, this warranty is supplemented by a reference to the observance of valuation principles for current assets, eg the valuation under the lower-of-cost or market-value principle and the principle of precaution. Other warranties relating to assets may address more specific issues like the good status of repair of the machinery.

(ii) Full collectability of all accounts receivable (except to the extent that reserves have been formed) is also one of the standard warranties concerning the asset side of the balance sheet. A matter of discussion between the parties is often the issue whether the seller should also warrant that there will be no additional bad debts in the future.

3.4.2.3 LIABILITY SIDE

On the liability side of the balance sheet, the core of all balance sheet guarantees can be found, namely the warranty that the net equity of the business is equal to a certain amount of money which should, in the case of a GmbH/AG be no less than the registered capital. The reason for the importance of the net equity warranty is that all negative effects on the business which influence the balance sheet as of the relevant date (ie closing), will result in a reduction of the net equity (if not set off by corresponding positive effects). This warranty can therefore serve as protection of last resort for the purchaser in relation to all issues not specifically addressed in the balance sheet warranty catalogue.[73]

Of somewhat similar importance are the warranties that there are no obligations of the business which are not reflected in the balance sheet and there is no need to form additional reserves or increase already existing reserves. The purchaser is thereby protected from actual or potential obligations of the business which have already reached a reasonable degree of probability of materializing in the future. Accordingly, all other warranties addressing potential obligations and liabilities need only to address contingencies which have not yet reached any degree of probability.

3.4.2.4 LIMITS OF BALANCE SHEET WARRANTIES

Despite the important function that balance sheet warranties have in protecting the purchaser from risks in connection with the acquisition of a business, they

[73] Binz/Freudenberg, *supra* note 70, (DStR 1991), 1629.

have their serious limits and they are by no means a substitute for other warranties.

One obvious shortfall is that any balance sheet warranty can only apply as of a specific date, which is, in most cases, not identical with the date of transfer of the shares or the "closing". Also, the financial statements present only a static picture and do not represent a "living business", so that issues like labour relations and business relationships are not reflected. Besides these structural deficiencies, a financial statement does not reflect means of production to which no value can be assessed, such as permits, licences or business opportunities. On the other hand, the potential liabilities of a business are only included in a balance sheet as a reserve if there is a reasonable probability that a liability will materialize. This is, at least in most cases, not a satisfactory standard for a purchaser, who would like to ascertain that no events of the past, regardless of whether there is a reasonable probability of a liability could lead to a liability for him or for the business.

3.4.3 Warranties complementing the balance sheet warranties

3.4.3.1 WARRANTIES TO BRING FINANCIAL STATEMENT WARRANTIES UP TO CLOSING

Since the purchase agreement containing the warranties agreed upon between the parties will usually refer to financial statements which were prepared at least several months ago, warranties are necessary to bridge the gap between the last accounts date and the date relevant for the warranties.

Typically, this gap is bridged by a provision that, since the last financial statements, (a) there have been no transactions outside the ordinary course of business and (b) no events have occurred which could negatively influence the economic or financial situation of the business.

Although the wording of those warranties (guarantees) is not very specific, they are indispensable for reasonably protecting the purchaser. It is possible, of course, to specify those warranties by including a catalogue of exemplary transactions or events.

Also, if the relevant date for the balance sheet warranties is after the signing of the agreement, it is advisable to include a clause according to which the seller and/or the management of the business will not enter into any extraordinary transactions or bring about any other changes of the business, not in line with the warranties of the purchase agreement.

3.4.3.2 WARRANTIES ON RESOURCES NOT REFLECTED ON THE BALANCE SHEET

A business consists not only of the tangible and intangible assets reflected in the balance sheet but also of various other resources which are not reflected there but which may be as important. Examples include know-how, governmental permits and licences. In order to make sure that the business has those types of resources available, specific warranties should also address them, where necessary.

3.4.3.3 WARRANTIES ON HIDDEN LIABILITIES

Although the bookkeeping of a company should reflect as well as possible all potential or "hidden" liabilities of a business, a certain degree of probability is necessary before an accountant will include such liabilities in a balance sheet. A purchaser, when buying a business, will often not be satisfied with the accounting standard; the purchaser needs to be certain that there are no risks connected with the business that he will be responsible for in the future. This is of particular relevance because, for example, the tax authorities and tax courts are quite reluctant to recognise the need for accruals for the removal of soil contamination; one tax court has ruled that only if action is required in the near future and if the scope of the required measures is sufficiently clear may respective accruals be recognised.[74]

Therefore, many potential "hidden" liabilities are addressed in warranty catalogues. Examples include the absence of soil and ground water contaminations, the absence of asbestos in buildings used by the business, the compliance with all governmental rules and regulations, and the absence of any conditions which might give rise to product liability claims. The topic of "hidden" liabilities is, in particular, prone to expand the catalogue of warranties considerably because, in theory, any business can be subject to any number of claims.

3.4.3.4 WARRANTIES RELATING TO THE ON-GOING BUSINESS

In asset deals particularly, but also in share deals, it is important to make sure that the change of ownership of the company or the business does not impair the continued operation of the business. Respective additional warranties have to complement the static picture given by the balance sheet warranties. One warranty which is often used provides that after the closing, the business can continue to be conducted as before. In doing this, the seller warrants that he has given the purchaser control over all assets and other (ie intangible) items or services which are necessary for the conduct of the business. At the same time, the seller warrants that the fact that the business (either in the form of its assets or the shares of the company) is being purchased will not have any effect on the legal relationship between the business and third parties. While this clause is rather broad and has not yet been tested in a court, if effective it provides a purchaser with a certain amount of protection. It can also be supplemented by specific provisions relating to matters such as the continued validity of all permits and licences, continuity of business relationships etc.

Related to this warranty are provisions for the continued validity of all agreements to which the business is a party after the purchase agreement takes effect. In share deals this warranty is of a limited importance because in Germany agreements depend only rarely on the person of the shareholder of a GmbH or the partner of a KG. Only where the shareholder has an economic function as the guarantor of a GmbH's business may this issue be of relevance. More importantly, the purchaser of a business in an asset deal should be aware that the rights and obligations of the business (except for certain liabilities) are not attached to the business itself (as is the case with a GmbH, AG or KG) but to the former

[74] FG Münster, (NVwZ 1991), 1024.

owner. Therefore, it has to be made sure that customers, suppliers, landlords and other persons will agree to the assignment of their contracts to the new owner.

There is a growing tendency in Germany to include warranties in the purchase agreement which go far beyond the original concept of a warranty to protect the purchaser from negative effects. More and more, warranties are becoming descriptive, that is, they attempt to describe the business to be purchased as completely as possible (by means of annexes) based on the results of the legal and financial due diligence, regardless of whether they concern a potential "defect" or not.

3.5 Legal Consequences

As pointed out above, statutory provisions relating to defects, warranted qualities and cic, provide for legal remedies which often do not serve the best interest of either party. The right to rescind the agreement, which is a frequent remedy provided by the Civil Code, is rather impractical, and therefore it is an undesirable remedy which both parties typically try to avoid. A unilateral reduction of the purchase price by the purchaser is often unacceptable to the seller, at least if there is no clear standard by which to determine the amount of the reduction. Therefore, a practice, in relation to remedies has developed of replacing the statutory remedies with special contractual remedies. Typically, both parties agree to a two-step type of remedy, in the event a contractual warranty is broken:

(a) Claim for specific performance by the seller plus compensation for damages incurred due to the performance not being made on time.
(b) If specific performance is not possible or desired by the purchaser, claim for cash payments as damages either to the purchaser or to the acquired business.

Acquisition agreements will therefore provide routinely for such obligations on the part of the seller. From a purchaser's point of view, it may not be sufficient to be left only with claims for damages, because this would only entitle him to compensation in cash, whereas it may be more important to him to receive a missing asset, like a trademark, or receive specific services or information from the seller or a third person. This can be dealt with providing that the seller has an obligation to put the company which was bought, or the purchaser himself, into a position as good as if the warranties were not broken. In situations where specific assets are missing (eg trademarks), the transfer of the asset plus damages (such as lost profits or replacement costs) will be the appropriate remedy.

Only if specific performance turns out to be impossible or impracticable would the purchaser have an exclusive claim for damages payable in cash. The amount of the cash damages will be that necessary to procure a situation as if all obligations of the seller had been fulfilled (ie creation, registration and introduction of a new trademark) and to compensate for lost profits.

One variance of the general concept of liability is an indemnity clause by which the seller is obliged to hold the purchaser harmless from third party claims, sometimes in exchange for the right to defend the claim against the claimant. The terms of payment for such damages depend on the agreement: if the purchaser has retained a percentage of the purchase price he may be entitled to satisfy himself from the escrow, or he may draw damages from a bank guarantee provided by the seller; or he may have to demand payment directly from the seller or a third party liable to pay damages to the purchaser.

4. Implied and Express Warranties

Within the general description of warranties above, the concepts of cic and absence of defects can be considered as implied warranties, as the obligations of the seller arise without the use of specific language in a purchase agreement. However, there is also room for implied warranties in relation to warranted qualities. Technically, not all contractual warranties need to be specifically mentioned in the purchase agreement, as long as the will of the parties can be inferred from the contents. Therefore, certain express warranties, or other indications as to the intent of the parties, may be used by the courts or arbitration panels as the framework to find warranties implied in the agreement as the "real economic will" of the parties.

An important caveat exists however, in that while implied warranties do exist in the sense that they can be interpreted in or inferred from the agreement, they may not arise orally or by "mutual understanding" if the objects of the acquisitions include land, buildings or shares of a GmbH. In those cases, the complete agreement must be notarised.[75] Any "silent" warranties are not recognised as part of the agreement (if they cannot be inferred by interpretation of the agreement as economic will of the parties), or at least, they can hardly be proven to exist because a notarial deed is legally presumed to be complete.[76]

5. Warranties in Acquisitions: General v Special Warranties

The difference in the Anglo-American legal system between general and special warranties has no parallel in Germany.

6. Warranties in Sale of Going Business; in Sale of Entire Equity; in the Transfer of Shares; and in Stock Exchange Acquisitions

The type and quality of a warranty in an acquisition varies depending on the legal object of the sale and depending on the degree of knowledge of the parties about the business to be sold. In some cases, a business can be sold with only a minor part of its assets, so that in essence the mere "goodwill" of a business is sold. In an international context, such transactions are rare because they occur almost exclusively in situations where a business is not based on assets, but rather the personal qualities of the previous owner (eg doctors' offices or small legal practices).

[75] Section 313 of the Civil Code; section 15, subsection 3 and 4 Law Governing Limited Liability Companies.

[76] Palandt/Heinrichs, *supra* note 2, section 125, note 6.

The second major form of acquisition which is more frequent, is sale of all of the assets of a business, including the goodwill. In particular, this kind of transaction takes place when larger corporations dispose of certain businesses which are not incorporated separately. In such cases, it is necessary to transfer all assets separately, at least in a technical sense. While most of the specific warranties relating to assets, liabilities and legal relationships of the business will not be substantially different from warranties in a share deal, not much may be known about the operation of the business on an on-going basis so that the warranties will have to address this issue more specifically. Similarly, in these cases there are no separate financial statements for the business, which are normally the core for all warranties.[77] Therefore, no warranties relating to financial statements can be given unless the seller has made the effort to prepare a pro forma balance sheet. As a result, warranties relating to (future) turnover or profits will also be difficult to insert into the purchase agreement in these cases.

The most common form which acquisitions take in Germany is a sale of shares involving a limited liability company (GmbH) or partnership interests of a limited partnership (Kommandit Gesellschaft, KG). Limited partnerships are rather popular among German middle-sized (family) businesses, where they often take the form of a "GmbH & Co KG". In such entity, the general partner is a GmbH and the limited partners and the shareholders of the GmbH are one or more members of the owning family. In acquiring such an entity, the purchaser has to buy the shares of the GmbH and the limited partners' interests. The third type of share acquisition involves the purchase of the stock of a stock corporation (AG). The total number of stock corporations is significantly lower than the number of the GmbHs and KGs. Depending on the structure of the stock holdings, a potential buyer will be able to acquire all stock from one or more persons or may only be able to buy certain percentages of the total stock from one or more persons or on the stock market.

In all those cases, a business is not bought directly, but indirectly by the acquisition of shares, partnership interests or stock of the entity which already owns and operates the business. In this type of agreement, statutory warranties as to the absence of defects in quality are not applicable except if almost all the shares are bought.[78] As a consequence, warranties in relation to financial statements can be made and it is much easier to ascertain that the business operates profitably on its own. Additional warranties are necessary, however, in relation to the existence and status of the company or partnership, and also the shares, partnership interests or stock. While the warranties, in relation to the business of a GmbH, KG or AG, are not substantially different from each other, the warranties in relation to the shares and the legal status of the company differ somewhat because of German corporate law.

No specific warranties exist if the stock of a stock corporation is purchased on the stock exchange. In a typical stock exchange transaction there is no detailed purchase agreement, but the provisions of the Civil Code apply. The possible

[77] *Supra.*
[78] *Supra* p.71.

warranties are therefore limited to the provisions of section 437 of the Civil Code, which only creates a warranty as to the existence of the stock sold and the seller's ability to dispose freely of it.[79] This warranty does not cover the value of the stock or any material aspects of the business. Warranties relating to the business of the AG will rarely be given because an individual (minority) stockholder has only limited means to be informed in detail about the business or to influence the behaviour of the management, both of which are a pre-condition for being able to give warranties to a purchaser. There can also be no liability as a result of cic unless extraordinary circumstances are present, because there are typically no negotiations or even pre-sale contacts between buyer and seller.

If stock is not bought on the stock exchange but directly from another individual or entity, the warranties can be agreed upon as in any other acquisition, if the seller is willing to supply them. If a majority stock interest is bought (that is more than 90 per cent), the statutory warranties relating to the absence of defects in quality may be applicable and the cic warranty may apply.

If an acquisition is the result of an issuance of new stock, special statutory provisions apply in relation to the completeness and accurateness of the prospectus advertising the new stock (Prospekthaftung).[80]

7. Warranties in Negotiations: *Culpa in Contrahendo*

The concept of cic and its role for warranties in business acquisitions was discussed above under item 3.2.3. It should be noted that cic not only has the function of a quasi-statutory warranty but that the general concept of "good faith" in negotiations also has other implications not directly relating to warranties. For example, a party who gave the impression that an agreement will be reached may be liable for damages to the other party if such party arbitrarily refuses to continue negotiations in good faith or even in some circumstances to close a deal. However, this effect of cic is limited where notarial deeds are required, eg, if the transfer of shares in a GmbH or the transfer of real property is concerned.[81]

8. Warranties in Promises to Sell

German civil law, unlike the law in most other jurisdictions, strictly differentiates between an agreement which establishes a legally binding promise (*obligatory agreement*) and the performance of such promise. If the obligatory agreement requires the parties to transfer title to certain assets, a second agreement—the so-called *transfer agreement*—is essential to pass title to the respective assets from one party to the other. The agreement to purchase in any acquisition is an obligatory agreement which by itself merely constitutes a promise to do something in the future. Often (but not always), in the document which is referred to as the "purchase agreement", the parties agree to the purchase and will at the same time also agree to transfer title to the respective assets. The agreement to purchase governs the rights and obligations of the parties and in most cases contains all the warranties.

[79] *Supra.*
[80] Soergel-Wiedemann, *supra* note 41, introduction to section 275, note 328 *et seq.*
[81] BGH, (NJW 1975), 44; OLG Stuttgart, (DB 1989), 1817.

The transfer agreement, whether or not it is contained in a separate document, is usually of a technical nature and typically does not contain additional rights, obligations or warranties. This is in particular because under German law all warranties survive the "closing".

There may also be agreements preceding a purchase agreement, which is frequently reached only after long negotiations between the parties. There may be letters of intent, pre-agreements or partial agreements. It is therefore possible to include certain warranties in these agreements. They might typically address subjects such as the management of the business in the interim phase or access to information for the due diligence review or they might be warranties that the business will conform to certain specifications at the time of signing the future purchase agreement. If the pre-agreement relates to shares of a GmbH to be sold in the future, any related promise to sell has to be given in notarial form in order to be enforceable.

9. Warranties in Sale Agreements

As pointed out above, the warranties on which the parties agree are typically spelled out in the sale agreement concluded between them. See item 3.6.

10. Warranties and the Closing

The concept of a "closing" does not have a ready equivalent in German law, and the term is used rather indiscriminately in connection with acquisitions. The term may apply to the signing of the sale and/or transfer agreement, the moment when the shares or assets are actually transferred or other events or points in time. The signing and the transfer may coincide or may be apart by days or weeks. In as far as a "closing" might be relevant for the validity of the warranties, the parties should specifically agree on the closing date. In most cases, the parties will choose the moment of the transfer of the shares or the assets, because this is typically the point in time when the purchaser is able to exert control over the company. It is important to note that under German law there is no concept whereby warranties which are to apply for a period after the closing have to be repeated at the time of closing. Although there is the notional difference between warranty and guarantee, there are usually no legal consequences attached to it in the context of business acquisitions. The question whether, when and for how long a warranty applies is determined exclusively by the agreement of the parties and its interpretation and not by formal concepts.

11. Warranty of Clear Title

As discussed above under item 3.2.1., under German contract law there is a *per se* statutory warranty that the seller has clear title to the item he is selling. In acquisitions, it is not unusual to repeat and specify this type of warranty. Its exact wording depends, on whether shares, partnership interests or assets are sold (see above p.50).

12. Warranties as to Specific Assets

(a) **Trademarks.** If the business produces and sells consumer products, an important part of its value may derive from its trademarks. A purchaser has to assure, therefore, that he will receive (either directly or through the company to be bought) all trademarks (or licences) used or owned by the business, and that there are no obstacles for him to use such trademarks in the future. In a share deal, a separate transfer of the trademarks will not be necessary, but warranties should, nevertheless, refer to the specific trademarks and, in addition, provide that these are all trademarks used by the company. This issue is particularly important if the company to be bought is part of a group of companies, as it is not unusual that trademarks are owned by one company but used by another company.

In asset deals, the trademarks have to be assigned separately, or licences to use them have to be granted. For trademarks which are owned by the business or which are transferred separately, the respective warranties should establish at the least that:

(i) the company or seller is the sole and unrestricted owner of the trademarks to be transferred;
(ii) the current or anticipated use of trademarks does not violate rights of third parties;
(iii) third parties have not taken any action against the trademarks nor is there any reason to anticipate such action;
(iv) all necessary measures to maintain the trademarks have been taken.

(b) **Real Estate.** Warranties relating to the land of a company which is to be bought usually cover the issues of ownership of the land, disclosure of liens and encumbrances on the land, and such environmental issues as possible contamination of the soil or the groundwater.[82] If the purchaser plans to use the site for construction purposes, a warranty that there are no restrictions to construction (eg zoning) should be considered.

(c) **Financial Accounts.** Warranties relating to the financial accounts are discussed above under item 3.4.2.

(d) **Profits.** It was pointed out above that there are two types of warranties relating to past or even future profits of a business. When a seller has warranted the correctness of, at least the last three balance sheets, in many cases this has been recognised by German courts as a warranty of the general profit level of the business.[83] A safer, more explicit warranty is one of specific amounts of profits that were reached in the past or a guarantee that specific amounts will be reached in the current business year or in the future.

As to the remedies for breach of a profit warranty, it is important to clarify that, the lower profits are not caused by a single event but because profits were generally lower than warranted the seller will have to compensate for reduced profits not only for one year but for a number of years. It is preferable for the parties to agree on a compensation formula in case the business fails to generate the profits which were warranted.

[82] Volhard, Weber, Usinger, *Real Property in Germany*, 4th ed, (1991), p. 8, *et seq.*
[83] *Supra.*

(e) **Plant**. Warranties relating to plant and equipment usually deal with their proper maintenance in the past and to their proper condition for the purposes of the business. Recently, there has been a trend also to include a warranty that no asbestos was used in the building either as insulating material or for construction purposes. The removal of asbestos, if mandated by public authorities, can be rather expensive. In addition, there is a risk that the business will be liable to its employees for health damage caused by asbestos.

It should also be made sure that the warranty catalogue addresses the issue of compliance of the plant and its operation with workplace safety rules and governmental or quasi-governmental rules to protect the environment, including the observance of building permit and licensing requirements.

(f) **Distributors**. The warranties should assure that the distribution network of the business exists and that there are no unusual provisions in the distribution agreements. Attention should be paid to possible claims of agents for compensation under section 89b of the Commercial Code. The latter can become a heavy burden to a business, because terminated agents may claim up to one year's remuneration (calculated on the basis of the average of the last five years).

Since it would be quite difficult to draft clear warranties which address all contingencies in regard to distribution network, the due diligence review should include an analysis of these agreements in detail. The warranty then would ensure only that the reviewed agreements are valid and there are no agreements other than those reviewed.

(g) **Commercial Network**. A warranty relating to the "commercial network" of a business deals with two aspects of the business. First, it is designed to ensure that after the sale of the business it will operate for a reasonable period of time in the same way as before the sale. This first goal is typically addressed by a warranty to the effect that no agreements can be voided or cancelled by a third party because of the transfer of the business and, in addition, that all relationships with important suppliers and customers are in order and will be continued. The second goal is to assure that the business has no outstanding obligations with unfavourable or unusual terms and conditions. The absence of such obligations should also be warranted. In this case also due diligence and the catalogue of warranties should supplement each other.

(h) **Inventory**. Regarding the inventory of a business, German acquisition agreements usually contain a warranty that the inventory (finished products, semi-finished products and raw materials) has been valued in the balance sheet according to valuation specified principles in the purchase agreement (eg lower-of-cost or market value).

In asset deals, such a reference to the balance sheet cannot be made, unless the parties have agreed to the drafting of a "special transfer balance sheet". A warranty should therefore state a minimum value and the contents of the inventory. In addition, it should be warranted that the inventory can be fully used in the business or can be sold at a price not less than the costs of such inventory item for the business.

(i) **Intellectual Property.** The remarks made above in connection with trademarks also apply to other intellectual property rights, such as patents, registered designs etc. Special attention is required if the business operates with intellectual property rights or other intangible assets which are not protected in the name of the business. In such cases, the business might infringe third parties' rights, or others might copy the company's know-how and thus reduce the value of the goodwill substantially.

(j) **Insurance.** Warranties relating to insurance typically guarantee that the business is adequately insured against all risks to the extent that the insurance is usually obtained in the respective industry. Such a warranty may not suit the interest of both parties, because a seller normally does not want to make an assessment of the adequacy of the insurance and the purchaser might not want to rely on the assessment of the seller. It is often provided, therefore, that the insurance agreements of the business being transferred to the purchaser will still be in full force after the transfer of the business. The purchaser may then decide by himself whether there is adequate insurance.

(k) **Contracts.** Another warranty which is designed to give an incentive to the seller to disclose the legal relationships of the business is a warranty to the effect that the business is only bound by those agreements of a certain kind, type or size which are disclosed in the agreement or, vice versa, that there are no contracts of a certain type. In asset deals, the purchaser does not automatically take over the contracts to which the business/seller is a party. Therefore, if the purchaser wishes to take over such contracts, the agreement should provide for a guarantee that the seller will procure the consent of the respective other party to the assumption of the contractual obligations by the buyer.

(l) **Good Standing.** The concept of "good standing" is not known in Germany and is therefore not subject to warranties.

(m) **Compliance with Laws and Regulations.** In order to assure the buyer that the business cannot be closed down by public authorities and that no substantial investment for compliance with laws and regulations will be necessary, the seller should warrant that the business has all permits and licences necessary to conduct its business and that the business is operated in accordance with the terms and conditions of such permits, licences and any other applicable law or regulation. The main material areas of compliance are environmental issues (air, water, waste disposal), fire protection, and workplace safety. Depending on the type of business, additional areas of law may apply.

(n) **Negative Warranties.** Negative warranties concern actual or potential liabilities to which a purchaser or a purchased business might continue to be exposed after the acquisition. When the shares of a GmbH are bought, its liabilities remain with the company acquired; the purchaser himself is not exposed to liabilities *vis-à-vis* third parties. If only the assets of a business are bought, the purchaser is personally liable for all liabilities of the business if he continues to run the business under its old name (section 25, subsection 1 of the Commercial Code). Similarly, special liability rules may apply, for instance section 75 of the Tax Code (Abgabenordnung, or AO) which provides for the liability of the purchaser of a complete business for all tax liabilities of that business. Due to the risks connected with the various forms of continued liability, the purchaser of a business has a substantial interest in limiting his exposure by having any potential liabilities disclosed and/or by having upper limits for business liabilities set in the purchase agreement. The typical remedy for a breach of these kinds of warranties is that the seller has to hold the purchaser/purchased business harmless from claims of third persons. One negative warranty which is of relevance both in share deals and in asset deals concerns the personal liability of a purchaser for debts of a seller, if all or substantially all assets of the seller are acquired; section 419, BGB. This statutory liability cannot be excluded by agreement, and the seller should, therefore, warrant that he is not disposing all or substantially all of his assets. It should be noted, however, that the remedies for a purchaser are rather limited for obvious reasons in case the warranty turns out to be wrong.

(o) **Undisclosed Liabilities**. Purchase agreements frequently provide for a warranty to the effect that there are no undisclosed liabilities. In a share deal, all actual or contingent liabilities should be included in the balance sheet. Accordingly, a warranty as to the completeness of this item in the balance sheet should, in theory, suffice. However, this issue should, if possible, be addressed specifically because, as it was pointed out above, it is not entirely certain that the German courts would view an unqualified balance sheet warranty as a bundle of warranties concerning the correctness of all individual items on the balance sheet.

There may also be hidden liabilities which become apparent only in the future, such as tax liabilities which can only be uncovered in future field audits or liabilities resulting from unknown soil or groundwater contamination. Because such hidden liabilities are not reflected in a balance sheet, it is advisable to address them separately by means of specific warranties.

(p) **Litigation**. The risks connected with any actual or threatened litigation should appear as reserves in the financial statements of the company, but there should also be a specific warranty relating to litigation. It mainly serves to force the seller to disclose any knowledge he has about actual or threatened litigation.

(q) **Tax Claims**. Another important warranty is the one that states that there are no outstanding claims of tax, customs, social security or similar authorities for which the purchaser or the business itself would be liable. This warranty has various aspects. First, the seller has to warrant that all tax or similar payments which became due before a certain date were actually paid by the company or the business. For such taxes which concern periods or events in the past, but which were not yet paid, sufficient accruals have to be established.

Next, the warranty has to apply to the situation in which future field audits assess taxes for periods or events that occurred before the purchaser took over the business. Typically, the seller assumes liability for such taxes, although the exact mechanism to determine the amount to be paid can be rather complicated, depending on the circumstances. It is not unusual for the seller to be granted the right to assist the purchaser in the event of such future field audits and even to appeal any tax assessments (at his own cost).

(r) **Employees' Rights**. Warranties in relation to employees' rights mainly concern the adequacy of the disclosure by the seller of all monetary or non-monetary benefits (including shop agreements) which employees receive. This is of particular importance in the case of company pension plans. As the net present value of such pension obligations is very difficult to determine, and the real costs appear only many years later after all escrow accounts or similar instruments have been emptied, a warranty that the net present value of pension obligations does not exceed a certain amount is not very helpful. In any event, the present value of future pension benefits should always be assessed by a reputed firm of pension specialists. It is important to note that German law (section 613a of the Civil Code) provides that in asset deals an employee may not be terminated, and the conditions of employment may not be changed to the disadvantage of an employee in connection with a business acquisition.

(s) **Rights of Third Parties**. Rights of third parties in connection with the business may concern rights attached to the subject of the acquisition (eg option rights in relation to the shares or the assets) or may concern contractual or other legal relationships with the business to be sold. The absence of such rights and relationships should be warranted specifically or, if they exist, should be disclosed by the seller.

13. Warranties of Merchantable Quality and Fitness for Use

Discussed above under item 3.2.2.2.

14. Warranties of Absence of Defects

Discussed above under item 3.2.2.2.

15. Effective Time of Warranties

In the absence of specific agreements between the parties, warranties become effective at the time of transfer if title rights, including shares, are sold (sections 434, 437 of the Civil Code) or at the time the purchaser takes possession of the assets if assets are sold (section 459, Civil Code; technically, at the point in time when the risk of accidental destruction of the assets passes). In practice, the parties usually agree on a certain point in time, often the time of transfer, as the effective time of the warranties. Insofar as warranties concern future events (eg amount of profits for the current business year), different effective dates apply which may be specified in the agreement or which may have to be determined by way of interpretation.

16. Duration of Warranties, Survival of Warranties, Time Limitation

As was pointed out above, under German law, warranties survive the closing *per se*. The duration of a warranty is therefore determined by its material content, and no "survival clause" is necessary. There are, however, time limitations which determine when a claim for breach of warranty will become time-barred.

Due to the variety of statutory warranty provisions, the applicable statutes of limitation are also quite diverse. Claims based on defects of title (section 437 of the Civil Code) are time-barred 30 years after a claim arose, (eg 30 years after the conclusion of the agreement; section 195 and section 198 of the Civil Code). The 30-year period generally also applies for claims on the basis of cic.[84]

In contrast, claims based on the warranties for material defects of a business or warranted qualities are time barred after only six months (section 477 of the Civil Code). The short six-month period may also apply if the defect relates to a piece of land which is purchased as part of an acquisition, although the period of limitation for defects relating to real estate is normally one year.[85] With regard to guarantees given by the purchaser, the regular limitation period of 30 years applies. The 30-years limitation also applies if the seller has fraudulently failed to disclose certain defects of the business. While it is fairly certain which limitation period applies, once the applicable legal doctrine has been determined, it is less clear which legal doctrine governs a particular defect.[86]

The uncertainty resulting from disputes as to the applicable legal doctrine as well as the fact that the statutory limitation periods appear arbitrarily and unreasonable—they are either too long in the case of 30 years, or they are too short in the case of six months—lead to a standard practice in acquisitions of replacing the statutory periods by contractual limitations. Such contractual limitations also avoid the need to apply several limitation periods to one acquisition. The limitation period stipulated is typically between 18 months and 48 months. The idea which gave rise to this practice is that the purchaser should have at least one and if possible, three full business years, plus a reasonable period to prepare financial statements for those business years, to gain a thorough insight and understanding of the business. Within this time the purchaser should be able to decide if a warranty or guarantee of the seller has been breached.

The parties frequently stipulate individual limitation periods for certain individual items. The first concerns taxes arising out of the time before the transfer of business, which often are only revealed as being due by field audits which may occur up to five or six years after the purchase. In addition, any such tax assessment might be appealed, which means that for another couple of years the amount of the tax to be paid is not final and binding. It is therefore routinely agreed that warranty claims relating to taxes are only time-barred some months after the tax assessment is no longer subject to appeal. Comparable provisions can often be found in relation to other third party claims.

[84] BHG, (DB 1990), 1911.
[85] RGZ 138, 354.
[86] *Supra*.

Another exception is often demanded by the purchaser in relation to soil and groundwater contamination. Since such contaminations constitute potential long-term risk or may only be uncovered after some years, the limitation period is often extended to five or more years. In all respects, of course, the parties are free to set specific time limitations for other warranties as may suit them.

If a warranty claim arises only shortly before the limitation of claims becomes effective, the beneficiary of the warranties must file suit to prolong the limitation period, if no prolongation arrangement can be made with the seller.

17. Beneficiary of the Warranty

The parties are free to decide who should have claims against the seller in case of a breach of warranty. In the absence of any other agreement, only the purchaser himself, as party to the contract with the seller, has such claims. The purchaser may, however, assign his claims to any third person, in particular to any related company or even the purchased business itself, even without consent of the seller. Often the purchase agreement itself already provides for such an assignment. Also, the purchased company itself may be nominated as beneficiary of warranty claims against the seller.

18. Warranty Limitations and Disclaimers

German law does not have any formal concept of a disclaimer. The parties are free to agree as to the scope and content of a warranty and may exclude certain aspects of a business from the warranties. Such exclusion will serve as a "disclaimer", unless the seller fraudulently fails to disclose a defect. The only legal requirement is that such a "disclaimer" has to be reflected in the agreement, be it expressly or implicitly.

19. Requirements as to Form

As a general rule, there are no requirements as to form for the acquisition. In theory, the assets of a business or the partnership interests in a KG (if not sold together with shares of a GmbH; see following paragraph) can be bought by oral contract. If a part of the assets purchased is a piece of land, however, the complete agreement (in the case of an asset deal) must be concluded in notarial form (section 313 of the Civil Code). Both the purchase and the transfer agreement in a business acquisition must thus be notarized, including all side agreements or related agreements or even annexes, which the parties consider to be part of one economic subject matter. If the notarial requirements as to form are not complied with, the whole agreement is null and void.

The most frequent type of a business acquisition, the purchase of shares in a GmbH, also requires notarial form. Under section 15, subsections 3 and 4 of the GmbH law, an obligation to buy and sell the shares of a GmbH, the transfer of the shares, and all related agreements have to be notarized. All related agreements and annexes must also be notarized in this case in order to be effective. The same applies if a GmbH & Co KG (limited partnership with a GmbH as general partner) is sold, for instance, when the partnership interests and the shares in the GmbH are sold together. Because the process of notarization is rather burdensome (the entire agreement and all annexes have to be read aloud by the Notary!), the parties often resort to the procedure of not notarizing the (long) purchase agreement with all its annexes etc, which is simply signed. Thereafter, they have a short transfer agreement signed in notarial form which according to the GmbH law rectifies the initially void purchase agreement containing the warranties. The by-laws of a GmbH may impose additional requirements for the transfer of shares, such as the approval of the shareholders.

The sale and transfer of stock in an AG or of partnership interests does not require notarial or other form, unless the endorsement of shares or the approval of the company is required.

20. Applicable Law

The parties are free to determine which law should govern the acquisition agreement (section 27, subsection 1 of the Introductory Law to the Civil Code, Einführungsgesetz zum BGB, EGBGB), in as far as the obligatory part of the agreement is concerned. In the absence of an express choice of governing law, section 28 of the EGBGB applies, which provides that the applicable law is that of the country to which the agreement has the closest economic connection. Thus, if the seller is a German national or a German entity selling a German business, German law will apply, regardless of the nationality of the purchaser. If both parties are foreigners, doubts may arise as to whether German law applies, and the decision will depend on an assessment of all circumstances. Nevertheless, it is advisable to choose German law if a German business is to be sold, because agreements governed by foreign law might not correctly address the issues which are relevant if a German business is concerned. The part of the agreement which deals with the transfer of assets or shares should in any event be governed by German law, because otherwise the transfer of title might not be recognized by a German court. This applies in particular to the formal requirements (notarization) if real estate or shares of a GmbH are bought.

To avoid contracts which could be regarded as void by the competent German court, it is recommended to have the notarial deeds executed in Germany according to German law. While the requirement of notarization by a German notary applies without exception for the transfer of real estate, a (limited) practice has developed of having the transfer of shares in a GmbH notarized in the Netherlands or certain cantons of Switzerland. This is because of the significantly lower costs charged by the notaries in those cantons. German courts have recognised the validity of such notarial deeds due to the substantial comparability of Dutch and some Swiss notaries.[87]

[87] (BGHZ, 80), 76; OLG Düsseldorf, (DB 1989), 569; LG Nürnberg-Fürth, (DB 1991), 2029.

21. Breach of Warranties; Balance with Supervening Increases of Value; Conditions to Enforce Warranties; Review by Purchaser

All of these topics are usually also governed primarily by the agreement between the parties. If a breach of a specific warranty has occurred, the purchaser must, in the absence of any other specifically agreed-upon procedure, give notice to the seller. To assure that no specific time limit applies for such notice, except the time limitation described in item 15, section 377 of the Commercial Code and section 464 of the Civil Code should be excluded. If a claim for breach of warranty is not brought immediately against the seller, the purchaser should be careful not to create the impression that he will not assert his claims, because this could be regarded either as an implicit waiver or a forfeiture of his claims. German courts have held that, regardless of the applicable statute of limitations, a claim may be waived or forfeited, if the person having the claim gives the other party the impression that the claim will not be brought forward.[88]

The enforcement of a warranty, by invoking an arbitration proceeding or initiating a law suit, may depend on the fulfilment of certain contractual and statutory conditions. A quite typical contractual condition is that the amount claimed for the breach of warranties has to exceed a certain amount of money, either for each individual example of breach, or in the aggregate. This contractual threshold is frequently included to avoid disputes over petty amounts. On the other hand, the seller may limit his liability to a certain amount.

Statutory conditions for the enforcement of a warranty include the requirements that the seller be given notice of which warranty in particular is breached and what the background facts of the breach are. The proceedings thereafter depend on the type of remedy available to the purchaser and the actual situation. The most common ocurrence is that the purchaser demands money as compensation from the seller; specifies the exact amount demanded; and sets a date by which payment has to be made. If this date passes without payment, the purchaser may sue the seller or initiate arbitration proceedings.

If under certain circumstances an estimation of damages may not be possible, the purchaser may demand from the seller a declaration to pay any damages once they have been established. Often the purchaser has retained some of the purchase price or has other means, such as an escrow account, to satisfy any demands made against the seller, subject to the conditions of the purchase agreement.

Any damages of a purchaser are, in principle, balanced by corresponding increases in value of the business or other benefits to the purchaser.[89] Two conditions have to be fulfilled according to the Federal Supreme (Civil) Court for such a balancing or compensation to apply: these must be a reasonable causal relationship between damage and benefit, and, in the specific case, the compensation must not inequitably release the seller from his liability. Thus, accidental increases in the value of the business or its assets after the purchase cannot serve to reduce any claims for damages. Probably the most important example for

[88] Palandt/Heinrichs, *supra* note 2, section 242, note 92 *et seq.*
[89] Palandt/Heinrichs, *supra* note 2, introduction to section 249, note 119 *et seq.*

setting off damages and benefits in connection with warranties in business acquisitions is the case that the tax inspector retroactively decreases depreciation allowances, which results in higher profits and a higher tax liability. The resulting damage claim will, however, not be the full increased tax liability. Instead, such tax liability has to be reduced by the net present value of the future tax benefits resulting from the now increased basis available for depreciation.

22. Remedies

(a) **Contractual Remedies.** As already pointed out above, the parties to a business acquisition routinely replace the statutory scheme of remedies with remedies on which they specifically agree. The parties may agree either to a general clause which applies to all possible breaches of individual warranties or on specific remedies in case a certain warranty is breached. The content of such specific remedies depends mainly on the specific circumstances, and the parties are free to agree on whatever remedy suits them best. In particular, acquisition agreements often provide for detailed remedies as to tax warranties.

General contractual remedies typically provide for a two-step process in case of breach of a warranty. The primary obligation of the seller in case of a broken warranty is to establish conditions which conform to the warranties given by the seller (specific performance). This applies mainly to missing assets which can be delivered by the seller or the performance of certain services (eg bringing over of customers) by the seller. This first remedy is thus not directed at the payment of monetary damages.

The second-step remedy comes into play only if specific performance is not possible or desirable for factual or legal reasons. The seller then is obliged to pay monetary damages to the purchaser or the purchased business. The amount of such monetary damages is measured by the amount necessary either to establish conditions which comply with the warranted conditions or to compensate the purchaser or the business for the lost profits and/or recompensable expenses incurred due to the broken warranty (eg creation of a new trademark if a trademark which was warranted to belong to the business did not exist).

A typical clause by which a purchaser will try to secure a position in which he can demand the widest variety of remedies and full compensation for all damages will provide that the seller, in case of a broken warranty, will put the purchaser or, at the purchaser's choice, the purchased business into a position as if the warranty had not been broken. However, a seller will often try to exclude liability for lost profits, or at least, limit the period of his liability for long-term effects (eg lower than expected level of profitability).

Although it would be possible under German law to agree to contractual penalties in case of broken warranty, it is rather unusual to provide for them. Only in connection with personal obligations of the seller (eg a covenant not to compete) or in cases where damage would be difficult to prove are contractual penalties often agreed to.

(b) **Tortious Remedies.** As pointed out above, if the seller has fraudulently misrepresented the business sold to the purchaser, the purchaser may have the right to void the agreement. Instead or in addition he may also claim damages for the tortious conduct of the seller (section 823, subsection 2 or section 826 of the Civil Code in connection with section 263 of the Criminal Code in case of fraud). The amount of damages claimed by the purchaser may not, however, be higher than those to be claimed under contractual damages. In particular, German law does not provide for punitive damages.

(c) **More Warrantors.** Normally, only the person or the persons actually selling a business will be liable to the purchaser in case of a broken warranty. If there is more than one seller, section 427 of the Civil Code provides that, if not stipulated otherwise, all sellers are jointly and severally liable to a purchaser. Nevertheless, it is advisable also specifically to provide that all sellers will be jointly and severally liable.

If there is no joint and several liability, be it by operation of statute or contract, it will be quite difficult for the purchaser to allocate the responsibility for a broken warranty to individual sellers. In any event, a prorated responsibility of various sellers is usually difficult to enforce. In share deals, all remedies may become of only theoretical relevance if the purchaser has acquired minor percentages of shares from a great number of sellers. Instead of agreeing to hold all sellers jointly and severally liable, it may, under particular circumstances, be acceptable to provide for the individual liabilities of only one seller, if such individual has sufficient resources to cover any warranty claim. It is, of course, also possible that persons or entities not directly related to the seller(s), act as guarantors for the seller's obligation. In addition, other options to secure the payment for a breach of warranty, such as withholding parts of the purchase price or a bank guarantee, should be considered.

23. Defences

As a result of the concept of warranties and guarantees under German law (which exist as one of the forms of no-fault liability), the defences available to a seller under contractual warranties, aside from disputing the facts underlying the claim of the purchaser, are quite limited.

In particular, the lack of knowledge of certain circumstances by the seller is, in principle, not a defence for him. The seller is liable for the warranties and guarantees given by him, regardless of his knowledge or fault, unless his liability is clearly restricted by the agreement. Such restriction may not, however, relieve the seller from liability for wilful misconduct, such as fraudulent concealment or wilful misrepresentation. Sellers, in particular those who have not operated the business themselves, often try to obtain a clause in the agreement that limits their liability to those instances where they knew about any facts or circumstances constituting a breach of warranty. If such a clause is at all acceptable to the purchaser, it should be provided in the agreement that the seller has carefully questioned all persons who should know whether there is any important information relating to the warranties. In addition, unless provided otherwise in the agreement, the fact that a third party is responsible for any breach of warranty is no defence for the seller in relation to the claim of the purchaser. It might only give the seller a claim against such a third party.

The best defence strategy available to a seller is the disclosure of all information which could later serve as a basis for an action for breach of warranty prior to finalising the agreement to a purchaser. Section 460 of the Civil Code embodies the general principle that a seller is not liable for a material defect if the purchaser did know about the defect or if he did not know about the defect due to gross negligence on his part at the time of the purchase. Section 460 of the Civil Code is also applicable, in part to warranted qualities, but only in case of knowledge and not in case of gross negligence on the part of the purchaser. Similarly, section 439 provides that the seller is not liable for defects of title under section 437 if the purchaser knew about such defects prior to concluding the agreement.

A seller can therefore protect himself by disclosing as much information as possible to the purchaser (if such disclosure is compatible with the potential seller's desire for confidentiality). This is also often in the interest of the purchaser. For reasons of documentation and future evidence, it is important, however, that all such disclosures are made part of the agreement by means of annexes. As mentioned above, such annexes have also to be part of the notarial deed if the agreement requires notarial form.

A defence of last resort for a seller is that the performance of an obligation, required of him under a guarantee, has become objectively impossible to perform for reasons for which the seller is not responsible. However, the conditions for such a defence will rarely be fulfilled.

If the claim against a seller is based on cic, the seller has more defences available, because such a claim only exists on the basis of a culpable act or omission by or on behalf of the seller. The seller can, therefore, defend himself by claiming and proving that he did not negligently or intentionally fail to disclose information to the purchaser, which he knew would be important for the purchaser.

24. Warranties Outside the Sale Agreement

Warranties need not necessarily be contained in the sale agreement. Warranties can also be given in separate agreements or letters, unless notarial form is required. If the law requires notarial form, all collateral clauses and understandings have to be contained in the notarized agreement. However, if the form requirement is merely based on section 15, subsection 3, sentence 1 GmbH Law as for shares of a GmbH, the lack of notarization will be cured if the shares are transferred in proper form, ie by a notarial deed. This applies even if the notarized transfer is contained in the same notarial deed as the (incomplete) sales agreement.

25. Vitiating Factors

Under German law, an agreement is void if the agreement or its execution is prohibited by law or violates public order (sections 134 and 138 of the Civil

Code). Also, if the formal requirements of a notarization are not observed, the agreement is void.[90] Furthermore, an agreement can be voided by one party if the agreement was concluded only because of fraud or threats from the other party (section 123) or, under certain circumstances, because of one party's error as to the contents of the contract or as to such qualities of the subject matter of the agreement which are generally considered important (section 119 of the Civil Code). Finally, both parties can always agree mutually to nullify an agreement. In the above-mentioned cases, the warranties will automatically become void if the contract itself is void, voided or nullified.

On the other hand, it may be that only the contents of a specific warranty infringe the law or German public order requirements. In this case, it depends on the interpretation of the contract whether the other parts of the contract will be affected by the nullity of the void warranty or not. As most acquisition agreements contain a severability clause, the contract will normally remain valid, with the exception of the voided clause.

One reason for which an acquisition agreement may be voided is the fraudulent misrepresentation or non-representation of facts by one of the parties to the agreement. If the seller has fraudulently misrepresented facts relating to the business, the purchaser may void the agreement, regardless if such facts were warranted or not (section 123 of the Civil Code). The right to void the agreement due to fraud or threats cannot be waived and it is available to the purchaser, in addition to other remedies, though a claim cannot be based on warranties after the contract has been voided. The time limit for the notice of voidance is one year. Avoidance cannot be declared after the contract has been knowingly confirmed by the party entitled to void the contract. As mentioned above, an agreement also can be voided due to an error on the part of the purchaser relating to an important quality of the purchased business. In such a case, however, the notice has to be given without delay and the purchaser is liable for damages to the seller. Furthermore, such avoidance according to section 119, para 2 of the Civil Code cannot be based on circumstances which are considered to be a breach of warranties. Under certain circumstances, cic may also give one of the parties the right to demand the cancellation of the agreement.

26. Warranties as Substitute for Investigation; Information Concealed by Seller

To a limited extent, warranties can serve as a substitute for disclosure (eg if there is time pressure or if the seller does not want to disclose the internal affairs of a business, because the potential purchaser is a competitor). There is a balance between warranties and disclosure. Although not all sellers realise this, in most situations they should disclose as much as possible, warrant the correctness of the disclosed information and make all warranties subject to the information disclosed to the seller.

In the case of fraudulently concealed information, the purchaser retains any claims based on the concept of defects, even if such liability was specifically

[90] See *supra* p.88.

excluded (section 460 and section 476 of the Civil Code). This applies accordingly to claims which are based on cic or in connection with warranted qualities or guarantees. Furthermore, a purchaser might have a right to void the agreement under section 123 of the Civil Code.[91]

27. Liability and Joint Liability of Third Parties for Breach of Warranties

If the seller is an entity which might not survive the entire warranty period (eg if it is a mere shell after the sale of business or if it is part of a group of companies which might be reorganised in the future, or if the seller does not have sufficient other assets to cover potential claims), the purchaser will insist that a third party (either the ultimate owner or a larger parent company) join in the seller's obligations. Basically, this can be achieved by two means: the third party may either join fully in the obligations of the seller, or the third party may issue guarantees, letters of comfort or similar instruments. It is important to note that such obligations usually are assumed with respect only to monetary claims and not in relation to claims for specific performance. For instance, a third party might have difficulties in fulfilling a claim for delivery of a missing truck if that truck is owned by another company.

28. Conclusion

Within the scope of this chapter it is not, of course, possible to give a comprehensive description of the law and practice of business acquisitions in Germany. The variety of situations which arise in practice and the variety of concepts employed to address the concerns of sellers and purchasers would doom any such attempt to failure. Also, a comprehensive description would inevitably lead to the writing of a treatise on German Civil Law.

This chapter could therefore attempt only to highlight certain aspects of the law and practice of business acquisitions in Germany, in particular those problems which appear regularly in many acquisitions and those aspects which might be surprising for a foreign investor.

Because of the complexity of business acquisitions in all jurisdictions, this chapter cannot be regarded as a guide to business acquisitions in Germany. Any acquisition will require the guidance of resourceful and experienced advisers.

[91] See *supra* p.89.

Italy

Mauro Rubino-Sammartano

Studio Rubino-Sammartano e Associati, Milan, Italy

1. Various Acquisitions, Various Warranties, Other Representations and Undertakings

Warranties in acquisitions is a broad concept that is relatively unexplored.

1.1 Various Acquisitions

This subject is wide, because warranties are related to sales of ongoing businesses (as well as subscriptions of capital increases made by contributing an ongoing business). Topics to consider are:

- mergers;
- sales of single assets;
- direct sales of shares between the contracting parties;
- public takeover bids;
- acquisitions in the stock exchange;
- sales of parts of limited liability companies;
- sales of partnership interests.

1.2 Statutory v Contractual Warranties

This subject is unexplored because of its broad nature, which is complicated by the existence of both statutory and contractual warranties.

Whether statutory warranties apply and whether they may be excluded or limited must be determined. Contractual warranties must then be ascertained and whether they are modified by statute or public policy. Eventually the available remedies for breach of statutory or contractual warranties are to be analysed.

1.3 Warranties v Undertakings and Representations

Before analysing warranties, one should distinguish them from undertakings and representations. By undertakings one refers to commitments, normally written, through which a contracting party undertakes to continue, or to refrain from, certain conduct. An illustration of this is the case of a non-competition commitment by the vendor as well as a confidentiality clause are to be treated as undertakings. This applies also to commitments issued, in respect of a given negotiation, not to negotiate, similar deals with third parties, or with other shareholders, at the same time or for a given period of time after it.

Representations cover a different ground than warranties and undertakings. Representations, depending on the way they are drafted (if written), or the expressions used orally or by conduct, may or may not be a source of liability for the party which makes them.

For example, a statement that no brokers have been involved, if inaccurate, may be a source of liability. Similarly, a statement that the vendor has seven Board members, while in effect there are eight, is normally not in itself a source of liability.

2. Warranties in the Law of Contract

2.1 Warranties v Financial Guarantees

The Italian word for warranties (*garanzie*) has two meanings: it covers warranties as well as financial guarantees. In its second sense, it covers guarantees having financial content. The purchaser will, for example, provide a guarantee for his deferred payment. The seller will provide a guarantee for payment of damages, in case he defaults in his delivery of the sold assets or under a warranty. Guarantees may be real or personal. Real guarantees are a pledge, or a mortgage, or a lien. Personal guarantees are *fideiussioni*[1] or *garanzie astratte a prima domanda.*[2]

The Italian law of contract ignores the British distinction between warranties, conditions and more recently innominate terms. The best evidence of this is provided by the warranty of absence of defects, which under Italian law entitles the non-breaching party to rescission. This dismisses any possible view that warranties relate to collateral matters and that breach of warranties does not entitle the purchaser to reject the goods.

The *sequestro convenzionale* (escrow agreement) serves the same purpose of a traditional guarantee, by placing an amount of money under the control of a neutral third party.

2.2 Various Warranties

Warranties are to be found in sale agreements,[3] in building contracts,[4] in rent agreements,[5] for damages in carriage of goods,[6] and general storage for safe-

[1] From the Roman *fidejussio*, ie a guarantee that a third party (the principal debtor) will pay.

[2] A primary (on demand) guarantee, for those who see it as different from *fidejussio*, which is a secondary obligation. Against this distinction is Rubino-Sammartano, *Accessorietà delle Fidejussioni Bancarie di Buon Adempimento* (Ancillary Nature of Performance Guarantees) (*Foro pad.*, 1982), 1, 87, *Ibid.* "Performance Bonds and Interlocutory Injunctions", *The Law Society's Gazette*, (February 1981); *Ibid. Performance Bonds*, in *International Business Transactions*, Kluwer 1987, Chapter 4–A.

[3] Section 1476 *et seq* of the Civil Code.

[4] Sections 1667 and 1669 of the Civil Code.

[5] Sections 1578 and 1585 of the Civil Code.

[6] Sections 1681 and 1693 of the Civil Code.

keeping.[7] Liability which exists, unless that party can prove the absence of its fault is to be distinguished from a typical warranty.

On the one hand, one must distinguish between statutory and contractual warranties. However, the distinction between express and implied warranties does not seem to be of much help under Italian law, where contractual warranties have to be express.

2.3 Nature of Warranties

Three main theories exist as to the nature of warranties:

(a) that the warranty is based on breach of contract;
(b) that the warranty applies even in the absence of fault;
(c) that the warranty derives from a statutory responsibility to the seller, or contractor, for the risk of non-conformity to the required or promised standards.

The last theory is examined by many writers, including Redenti,[8] Barbero[9] and Rubino.[10] The prevailing precedents[11] hold that the warranty is due even in the absence of fault. However, it should be stressed that one is not always faced with a systematic approach to warranties. In fact, when dealing with building contracts, and namely with the contractor's warranty under section 1667 of the Italian Civil Code, for non-conformity or defects of the works, several precedents[12] reject the idea that there would automatically be a warranty even without fault.

It has been suggested that one should distinguish between the seller's warranty and the contractor's warranty insomuch as, in the latter's contract, the duty is to provide a result.[13] Apart from the indisputable differences between the two contracts, the duty to transfer ownership of goods in the first contract and to perform works in the second contract each seem to imply absence of defects in the goods to be supplied or manufactured and absence of defects of construction incorporated in such goods.

Warranty seems to be an addition to the seller's and contractor's duties already arising from the law of contract. If one accepts that such warranties do not derogate but add to the law of contract, the warranty, in both contracts, must have the function of strengthening the statutory protection of the purchaser or

[7] Section 1787 of the Civil Code.

[8] Redenti, *Dei contratti di alienazione a titolo oneroso* (Sales against Consideration) (Padova, 1935), at 340.

[9] Barbero, *Sistema del diritto privato italiano*, (The system of Italian private law) (Torino, 1965), II, 251.

[10] D. Rubino, *La compravendita* (The Sale of Goods), (Milano, 1952) at 506.

[11] See *Capitti* v *Biondo*, Court of Cassation, 19 July [1983], No 4980, *Rep. Foro It.* (1983) item Vendita (Sale), 1983, 78. See also *Fiori & Germany* v *Caglioni & Muscolari*, Court of Cassation, 21 October, No 3438 [1969], *Giust. Civ. Mass.* 1969, 1737.

[12] See *Fante Trosciani* v *Bardin*, Court of Cassation, 7 February No 1016 [1983], *Giust. Civ.* (1984) I, 1273 with note by Marinelli. See also *Crovace* v *Carrubba*, Court of Cassation, 10 October No 2430 [1966], *Giust. Civ. Mass.* 1966, 1399.

[13] For research on the possibility of a unitary doctrine of warranty, see L. Cabella-Pisu, *Quaderni di giurisprudenza commerciale* (Commercial precedents), (Milan, 1983), No 45 at 92.

employer. They warrant that both will obtain what they are entitled to expect, and that such an entitlement is not dependent on demonstrating the fault of the seller or contractor. Through this approach, one might come to a general concept of warranty as distinguished from the duty to perform which already exists under the law of contract.[14]

The doctrine of allocation of risk provides for liability of the seller or contractor, even in the absence of his fault. This doctrine, rather than amounting to strict liability, independent from fault, places the risk on the seller and on the contractor—an approach more acceptable to civil law which generally does not favour the latter.

However, apart from the attractiveness of its presentation, the practical effects seem not to be that different.

3. Warranties in Sales of Goods

The Italian legal system sets out specific warranties in sales of goods, which are to be added to the general remedies provided for by the law of contract and which must be distinguished between statutory and voluntary contractual warranties.

3.1 Statutory and Contractual Warranties

Under Italian law, the statutory warranties are:

(a) the warranty of clear title;
(b) the warranty of absence of defects;
(c) the warranty of merchantable quality;
(d) the *aliud pro alio* rule,

while the contractual (or voluntary) warranties are:

(e) the warranty of proper functioning;
(f) the warranty of fitness for a specific use;
(g) a general warranty;
(h) specific warranties.

Each of these warranties shall be considered, by way of introduction and subsequently will be addressed in detail as they relate to acquisitions.

3.2 Statutory Warranties

3.2.1 Warranty of clear title

The vendor is under a duty to sell assets to which he holds full and clear title. This duty is dealt with in several statutory provisions, such as section 1483 of the Civil Code:

> If the Purchaser is totally deprived of the purchased assets in consequence of rights asserted by a third party, the Vendor is under a duty to pay damages according to Section 1479, Civil Code. . . . . .

and section 1484 of the Civil Code.

[14] M. Rubino-Sammartano, "Lack of Conformity and Various Reliefs in Sales of Moveable Goods in Italy", in *Survey of the International Sales of Goods* Lafili *et al.* eds, (Kluwer 1986), at 243.

> If the Purchaser is partially deprived of the purchased asset, the provisions of sections 1480 *et seq*, Civil Code apply as well as those of section 1483.

This involves the purchaser's right to rescind the contract and to claim damages if, depending upon the circumstances, it appears that he would have not purchased the asset without it being substantially different. Alternatively, he may claim a price reduction and damages.

Section 1486 of the Civil Code provides that:

> If the Purchaser has avoided the consequences of the third party's claim by making a payment, the Vendor may be relieved of any consequence of his warranty by reimbursing to the Purchaser the amount paid by him, together with interest as well as all the expenses which he has met.

Section 1487 of the Civil Code states:

> The parties to a sale agreement may increase or reduce the effect of the warranty and may exclude it. In the latter case, the Vendor is liable for the Purchaser's loss of the purchased asset due to the Vendor's conduct. Any agreement to the contrary is null and void.

Section 1488 of the Civil Code provides:

> If the warranty has been excluded, the provisions of sections 1479 and 1480 do not apply. If the Purchaser is deprived of the purchased asset, he may claim from the Vendor only to be reimbursed the purchase price and his expenses. The Vendor is released also from such obligation when the sale has been agreed to be at the Purchaser's risk.

and eventually section 1489 states:

> Whenever the sold item is subject to non-apparent burdens or rights, which diminish its free use and which have not been declared in the sale contract, the Purchaser, who has not been aware of them, may claim rescission of contract or a reduction of the sale price, as provided for by section 1480. The provisions of sections 1481, 1485, 1486, 1487 and 1488 are further to be complied with.

3.2.2 Warranty of absence of defects

This warranty results from the following provisions:

Section 1490 of the Civil Code:

> A Vendor is bound to warrant that the sold item is free from defects which make it unfit for the use for which it is intended or which appreciably diminish its value. An agreement excluding or limiting such warranty has no effect if the Vendor has, in bad faith, omitted to mention such defects to the Purchaser.

Section 1491 of the Civil Code:

> The warranty is not applicable if the Purchaser knew of the defects in the sold asset at the time of the contract; likewise, it is not effective if the defects were easily detectable, unless, in this case, the Vendor has declared that the sold asset had no defects.

Section 1492 of the Civil Code:

> In the situations provided for by section 1490, the Purchaser can at his discretion demand rescission of the contract (section 1453) or a price reduction, unless, for certain defects, usage bars rescission. The choice is irrevocable when made in court proceedings. If the delivered goods are destroyed as a result of the defects, the Purchaser is entitled to rescission (section 1543) of the contract; if instead they are destroyed as the result of a fortuitous event or through the fault of the Purchaser, or if the Purchaser has sold or transformed them, he may only claim a price reduction.

Section 1493 of the Civil Code:

> In case of contract rescission, the Vendor shall return the price and reimburse to the Purchaser the expenses and payments legitimately made by him in connection with the sale (section 1475). The Purchaser must return the purchased asset, unless destroyed as a result of its defects (section 1492).

Section 1494 of the Civil Code:

> In any event, the Vendor is bound to pay damages to the Purchaser unless he proves that he had no knowledge, without fault, of the defect. The Vendor shall also reimburse to the Purchaser the damages caused by defects in the sold item.

Finally, section 1495 of the Civil Code:

> The Purchaser forfeits his right to the warranty if he fails to notify the Vendor of the defects in the sold item within eight days from his discovery, unless a different time limit has been agreed by the parties or is established by a statutory provision. No notice is necessary if the Vendor has acknowledged the existence of the defect or has concealed it. In any event, the action is time barred in one year from delivery; but the Purchaser who is sued for performance of the contract can always plead warranty as a defence, provided that the defect in the sold item was notified within eight days from discovery and within one year from delivery.

3.2.3 Warranty of merchantable quality

This warranty is governed by section 1497 of the Civil Code:

> When the sold item lacks the promised qualities or those essential for the use for which it is intended, the purchaser is entitled to obtain contract rescission according to the general provisions on rescission for non-performance (section 1453), provided lack of quality exceeds the limits of tolerance established by usage. However, the right to obtain rescission is subject to forfeiture and to time limitation as set forth in section 1495.

3.2.4 *Aliud pro alio*

The purchaser enjoys a further protection, which is not exclusive to sale agreements, which applies in case of delivery of *aliud pro alio*,[15] ie in case of delivery of an asset which is different from the agreed one.

Delivery of *aliud pro alio* is to be distinguished from the sale of an asset which is defective or lacks some quality, since while in the latter the delivered goods correspond to the contractual ones (except for that defect or lack of quality) in the former the delivered item is totally different. In *Giugliano* v *Fond. Off. Mecc.*[16] the former has been described "as the most macroscopic form of breach by the seller". Since there is no statutory provision expressly dealing with it, *aliud pro alio* might also be seen as an implied warranty. However, the requirement of a breach suggests not to treat it as a warranty but as a fundamental breach of contract.

In the absence of *aliud pro alio*, the purchaser would have no remedy, since the premise of the warranties is a defect, or unfitness or lack of merchantable quality or improper functioning and the different item which is delivered may have none of these defects.

3.3 Voluntary Warranties

3.3.1 Warranty of proper functioning

The lack of proper functioning of the sold item is one of its various possible defects and, as such, it is covered by the statutory warranty. This means that under domestic law if the defect is apparent, the purchaser is protected only if he notifies the seller of it within eight days after delivery. If the defect is hidden, the purchaser is protected if he notifies the seller within eight days after discovery of the defect but in no event beyond one year after delivery.

In addition to the statutory warranty, a voluntary warranty may be given, which assures proper working for a specific time period. Section 1512 of the Civil Code provides:

> If the Vendor has warranted the proper functioning of the sold item for a specific time period, the Purchaser, unless otherwise agreed, shall notify the malfunctioning to the Vendor within thirty days after discovering it; in the absence of this, he shall forfeit (section 2964) this remedy. The right of action is time barred within six months from discovery. Depending on the circumstances, the court may grant to the Vendor a time period to substitute or to repair the sold item to assure its functioning, without prejudice to the right to damages. Usage, providing that the warranty of proper functioning applies even in the absence of an express agreement, remains.

The duration of the voluntary warranty will tend to be longer than the statutory warranty for hidden defects. In this respect one should mention that duration in general has been defined as a quality by itself.[17] Proper working has been defined in *Soc. Valdarno c. Soc. Defendenti* as a due result.[18] A further characteristic of this warranty is that its remedy is replacement or repair. The purchaser, in order to succeed, has to prove malfunctioning, while he has no duty to show the reason for it.

[15] ie, literally: delivery of something for something else.
[16] Court of Cassation, 13 February, No 452 [1973] *Racc. Dec. Cass.* item *Vendita* 9818, No 275
[17] Bianca, *Op. cit.* at 270.
[18] Court of Cassation, 8 April, No 1031 [1959], *Foro pad.* 1959, I, 658.

3.3.2 Warranty of fitness for use

The vendor may warrant that the sold asset is fit for a specific use. This warranty, which is voluntary, is then governed by the statutory warranty of merchantable quality, which covers also promised qualities. Fitness for a special use is included as a promised quality. It has been argued whether the specific use is to be added to the normal use or replaces it.[19]

There is probably not a uniform answer to the question. Whether the specific use may or may not replace the normal use depends upon the contract. What must be pointed out is that the warranting of a specific use is optional. Therefore, such a warranty is voluntary but, once the warranty has been given, it is governed by the statutory provision on merchantable quality.

3.3.3 General v specific warranties

The vendor may issue a general warranty or specific warranties related to one or more given aspects or matters[20] instead of, or in addition to, a warranty of proper functioning.

3.3.4 Distinction between *aliud pro alio* warranty of absence of defects and warranty of merchantable quality

The distinction between delivery of *aliud pro alio* and of defective goods is clear. In the case of *aliud pro alio*, different goods are provided as a substitute for those described in the contract. In the case of defective goods, the delivered goods are the contractual ones, but they are also defective.

The distinction between *aliud pro alio* and lack of quality may be difficult when, because of the lack of quality, the delivered item may be seen as different from the contractual one. In *Sucato & Dori* v *Dori*[21] the Court of Cassation held that there is a delivery of *aliud pro alio*, "when the delivered goods belong to a completely different genus".[22]

This being the test, one has to establish when there is a difference of genus. Leaving aside obvious situations, like the sale of a car instead of a truck, less clear situations do arise. For example, contrast the sale of a normal horse[23] instead of the contracted race horse. Is it a lack of quality or *aliud pro alio*? To overcome the rigidness of the distinction between genus and species,[24] the notion of sub-genus (a subcategory of a given asset) has been introduced. In *Sucato & Dai* v *Dai*[25] the Court of Cassation held that:

> The identification of the *genus* can only be made on the basis of the *economic and social destination* of the thing, such as expressly or implicitly provided for by the contracting parties, with the consequence that one is no more in the area of a mere lack of quality but in the area of *aliud pro alio*, whenever the lack of certain qualities

[19] D. Rubino, *Op. cit.* see *supra* Chapter 2, note 10.
[20] The specific warranties will be dealt with later, see *infra* at Chapter 13.
[21] Court of Cassation 21 January, No 268 [1978] *Racc. Dec. Cass.* 1972–1982 item *Vendita* (Sale) 9776 No 39.
[22] ie type.
[23] Rubino-Sammartano, *Op. cit.*, see *supra* at Chapter 2 note 14, at 247.
[24] A specific *item* which belongs to a wider family (the *genus*).
[25] See *supra* note 7.

> degrades the delivered goods into a different *genus* or *sub-genus*. This is because the lack of quality has a direct effect on the use to which the sold item is destined. Therefore *aliud pro alio* cannot be reduced to a simple structural difference, since alteration in quality may determine a degeneration of the goods, if the defect or lack of quality, compared with what has been agreed between the parties, changes the thing into something different and unsuitable for its contractual purpose.

Moving to more specific situations, in *Vivirito* v *Sia*[26] the Court of Cassation held that the delivery of a repaired article instead of the agreed new one was not *aliud pro alio*. While in *Di Giminiani* v *Onesti*[27] the delivery of a car of a make or type, different from the agreed one, was treated as *aliud pro alio*.

3.3.5 Distinction between defect and lack of quality

Even the distinction between a defect and lack of quality may be difficult in various situations such as in *Pistoni* v *Caroni*[28] where the "dampness of premises" of an enterprise was in issue.

To avoid confusion, the difference between a defect and lack of quality, should remain focused on the concept respectively of defect as a deficiency of the asset and of quality as a merit of the asset, (for example, top quality, or a superior level, or a given colour). A product may then have a quality and also a defect. It may be a stainless steel bar but be broken, or a bar which is not broken but which is not stainless.

3.3.6 Distinction between a defect and improper functioning

One has to start by acknowledging that improper functioning is, by itself not only a defect, but a very serious one. Furthermore improper functioning is a defect which relates exclusively to the functioning, while other defects concern other areas, like the weight, size and so on.

Eventually one may wonder whether, in the absence of a voluntary warranty of proper functioning, such defect falls within the area of defects covered by the statutory warranty of absence of defects. As discussed earlier, the answer to this question seems to be positive.

4. Warranties in Negotiations

Warranties might be created not only in final agreements, such as a sale agreement, but even at earlier stages, such as during negotiations, or in promises to sell. One may wonder whether, aside or instead of the previous warranties, other warranties are to be found at the negotiations stage.

4.1 Confidentiality Agreements

Frequently the parties, at the beginning of negotiations, enter into an agreement neither to disclose the information to third parties, which they will acquire during the negotiations, nor to use it for their own purposes. This seems to amount to an

[26] Court of Cassation, 4 August, No 3512 [1977] *Racc. Dec. Cass.* 1972–1982 item *Vendita* (Sale) 9775 No 37.

[27] Court of Cassation, 7 June, No 1263 [1967] *Rep. Foro. It.* item *Vendita* (Sale) 1967, 2716, 122.

[28] Court of Cassation, 31 March, No 880 [1952] *Rep. Foro It.* 1952, item *Vendita* (Sale) 2462, 169–171.

undertaking and not to a warranty. Its breach is consequently subject to the statutory provisions and time bars of undertakings, which do not coincide with those of warranties.

4.2 Anti-Insider Trading Agreements

The negotiating parties, and more specifically the vendor, may take precautions against insider trading by the purchaser's officers or employees. In reality this might also be seen as a variety of terms of confidentiality agreements.

4.3 Anti-Hostile Takeover Agreements

Through anti-hostile takeover agreements, the purchaser or—as the case may be—either party, may undertake to refrain from any attempt to take over, during the negotiations as well as for a given period of time after their possibly negative conclusion, the other company and or the target company, by using other means.

4.4 Standstill Agreements

A further agreement, which the parties may enter into, at the beginning of or during the negotiations, is a commitment not to entertain parallel negotiations with other parties. That would be the case if the vendor were to conduct parallel negotiations with various potential purchasers, since in this way the purchaser could be placed in a very weak position. In fact, the vendor might be enticed by these potential bargaining profits not to behave in good faith, but simply to use one bidder against the other, in an attempt to improve the terms of his deal. In some situations as in *Penzoil*[29] and in *Sme* v *Buitoni*[30] the vendor himself has been charged with such behaviour.

4.5 The Nature of such Agreements

One might be tempted to treat such commitments as warranties. However, through them, a party does not take a risk, but merely undertakes to answer for his own breach. They consequently seem to belong to the class of undertakings and not to warranties.

5. Warranties in Promises to Sell

5.1 Relationship between Promise to Sell and Sale Agreement

In several civil law jurisdictions, and certainly in Italy, contrary to the common law practice of entering for large or sophisticated deals into an agreement for sale which provides for a subsequent closing, the normal structure of a sale is to enter

[29] *Penzoil* v *Texaco*, and *Sme* v *Buitoni*: in Rubino-Sammartano, *In Medio Stat Virtus*? (Is the right position midway?), (*Foro pad.*, 1987); see also Draetta, *Documenti precontrattuali relativi ad acquisti di societa': confidentialitv agreements e protezione contro hostile takeovers* (Pre-contractual documents concerning corporate acquisitions: confidentiality agreements and protection against hostile takeovers), *Diritto del Commercio Internazionale* (1988), 181.

[30] Court of Cassation, 25 March, No 209 [1986] *Foro It.* 1986, 1, 204.

first into a *contratto preliminare*,[31] followed by the sale agreement itself. The time between the two agreements gives to one or to all the parties the opportunity to prepare for the second agreement, for example, by raising funds and by vacating the factory, when the sold business manufactures its products, or by completing a production phase.

Normally the promise to sell does not include the draft sale agreement. It frequently does not even detail the main terms and conditions of the future sale, although doing so could avoid or reduce subsequent disputes.

5.2 Survival of Warranties in a Promise to Sell, when not Repeated in the Sale Agreement

Warranties may be provided in the sale agreement which were not provided in the previous promise to sell. This sequence of events generally causes no significant problem when considering contract warranties later. However, warranties which were included in the promise to sell but which are excluded from the sale agreement, do not survive unless the intention of the parties may be construed otherwise.

6. Notion of Shares and Applicability of Statutory Provisions on Sales of Goods

6.1 The Share as a Negotiable Instrument or merely as a Document Certifying the Position of a Party to a Contract

The basic issue under Italian law is one of which statutory provisions are applicable to shares, and more particularly whether sales of equity are governed or not by the statutory provisions on sales of goods. Since the statutory provisions which are to be applied, depend on the classification of the transaction, the answer to the question depends on the classification of shares.

6.2 Distinction between Sale of Shares and Sale of the Assets of the Corporation

Before dealing with this subject, it seems preferable to clarify two issues:

- the distinction to be made between a sale of shares and a sale of the assets of that corporation;
- the distinction between a normal sale of some shares and the sale of all the shares of a corporation as an instrument to transfer the corporate assets.

As to the first issue, the precedents concur that a sale of shares does not amount to a sale of the corporate assets. In *Pastore* v *Galimberti*[32] the Court of Appeal held that, "the sale of shares does not involve a transfer of corporate assets".

In *Cattaneo della Volta* v *Raggio*[33] the Court of Cassation[34] has held that:

> the sale of equity amongst shareholders cannot be confused with the sale of a part of the corporation . . .

[31] ie a promise respectively to sell and to purchase within a given time limit.
[32] Court of Appeal, Milan, 21 October, 1933, in *Riv. dir. comm.*, 1935, II, 122.
[33] Court of Cassation, 29 March, 1935 *Riv. dir. comm.*, 1935, 411.
[34] The highest Court of the Republic of Italy.

As to the second issue, in *Piacentini* v *Simonini et Zecchinato*[35] it has been emphasised that:

> the sale of all the shares of a corporation does not amount to a transfer of all the assets of the corporation.

In *Benedetti* v *Bellini*[36] it has been confirmed that:

> even the transfer of the entire equity does not transfer all the corporate assets to the purchaser

In *Cerruti* v *Tedeschi*[37] the Court has stated, "the transfer of corporate shares . . . produces no effect on the corporate assets". This view, expressed also in *Bianchini* v *De Molinari*[38] and in *Berlingeri* v *Berlingeri*[39], was more recently confirmed in *Immobiliare Caccia* v *Mirolo Bankruptcy et al*:[40]

> the sale of the corporate assets cannot be achieved through the sale of corporate *quotas* (note: parts of a limited liability company, which as such have to be distinguished from shares certificates) since these two sales are different from each other and produce results which cannot be reconciled.

The sale of corporate shares is consequently clearly to be distinguished from a sale of corporate assets. However, an exception to this is whenever the sale of the shares clearly is simply a means to sell the corporate assets. This was held in *Raggio* v *Raggio*,[41] where the Court of Cassation, after defining the corporation in issue as a family corporation, the access to which was not allowed to third parties, held that: "the apparent sale of the shares in reality was a sale of the business".

However, the Court in *Cattaneo della Volta* v *Raggio*,[42] held:

> Once it has been established that a corporation is not a mere façade, that its shares are owned by various members of a family and that they may not be transferred to third parties, one cannot confuse a sale of corporate shares with a sale of part of that business.

The sale of the entire stock capital has been contemplated as a sale of the corporate assets, consisting of a large farm, by the Court of Milan in *Mauro* v *Martinotti*[43]

> since the shares, objectively and in the contemplation of the parties, represented the land owned by the corporation and the shares are a second degree property, their sale is in the substance to be compared to a direct sale of that land.

[35] Court of Cassation, 4 August, No 2736 [1941] *Foro it.*, 1942, 1, 197.
[36] Court of Cassation, 10 May, No 559 [1946] *Dir. Fall.*, 1946, 2, 88.
[37] Court of Cassation, 14 February, No 325 [1963] *Giust. Civ.*, 1963, 1, 743.
[38] Court of Cassation, 18 October, No 3259 [1975] *Giust. civ.*, 1956, I, 743.
[39] Court of Cassation, 22 September, No 2598 [1959] *Dir Fall.*, 1959, 2, 911.
[40] Court of Cassation, 21 June, No 1836 [1974] *Giust. civ.*, 1975, I, 832.
[41] Court of Cassation, 27 July, [1933] *Riv. dir. comm.* 1935, II, 121.
[42] Court of Cassation, 29 March, [1935] *Riv. Dir. comm.* 1935, 135.
[43] Court of Milan, 27 June, [1988] *Le Società* 1988, 1164.

However, this classification was disregarded by the Court of Appeal of Milan while hearing an appeal against that judgment.[44] The Court held that the transaction was a sale of shares and was not comparable to a direct sale of the land owned by such corporation. The former view was followed by the Court of Appeal, Milan in *Pastore* v *Galimberti*[45] and in *Della Giovanna* v *De Francischi*[46] but both judgments were set aside by the Court of Cassation.

The view taken by the prevailing precedents is also shared by the large majority of writers.[47] This general view is that a sale of shares is to be firmly distinguished from the sale of the corporate assets, except when the shares have been treated like a mere instrument to transfer the assets. In fact, in the latter situation the corporation is just a façade to own assets which are used by the majority shareholder while ignoring the concept that the corporation is an independent legal entity. Nevertheless Mossa[48] and Salandra[49] have held that the sale of all the shares of a corporation must be seen as the sale of the assets of that corporation, a view which, as discussed earlier, has been opposed by many writers including Fré.[50]

6.3 Legal Notion of Shares

Having discussed these two preliminary issues, one can now turn to examine the nature of corporate shares, keeping it separate from the issues of the sale of all the shares amounting to the sale of the assets of that corporation, and of a corporation which is a mere façade.

Shares have been classified in many ways: as a joint ownership right; as a negotiable instrument; as an asset belonging to the category of personal estate; as a document merely certifying that its holder (either because of the initial subscription or because of a subsequent assignment) is in the position of party to the deed of incorporation of that company, and therefore, that he holds the position of party to a contract. In the latter case, the transfer of the shares may amount to an assignment of that contract, in the former case it is a transfer of a negotiable instrument. This opens the door to a further dilemma—whether the transfer is merely governed by the statutory provisions governing transfers of negotiable instruments, or whether this is a special instrument, the sale of which is governed also by the law of sale. One may further wonder whether before the actual transfer there is an underlying contract which—if a sale—brings in the

44 Court of Appeal, Milan, 5 June, [1990] *Giur. It.* 1991, 1, II, 387.

45 see *supra* note 32.

46 Court of Appeal, Milan, 5 July, [1935] *Banca Borsa e Titoli di Credito*, 1937, 2, 86.

47 Bonelli, *Giurisprudenza e dottrina su acquisizioni di società e di pacchetti azionari di riferimento* (Precedents and writers on acquisition of shares and of relevant quantities of shares), *Acquisizioni di società e di pacchetti azionari di riferimento*, (Acquisitions of Corporations and of relevant quantities of corporate shares) (Giuffre' 1990), 3; Bianca, "Vendita, Diritto Vigente", (Sales, Present Legislation), *Nov. Dig. It.*, (Turin 1975), 612; Ascarelli, "In tema di vendita di azioni e responsabilità di amministratori", (Sales of shares and directors' liability), *Foro It.*, (1953), 1, 1639.

48 Mossa, "La vendita dell' impresa sociale", (The Sale of a Business), *Annuario dir. comp.*, VII, 3, 157.

49 Salandra, "In tema di vendita di pacchetti azionari", (Sales of Shares), *Foro it.*, (1936), 1, 207.

50 Fré, "Delle società per azioni", (Corporations), *Commentario Scialoja e Branca.*, (1982), at 238.

statutory provisions of the law of sale, some of which are cogent and other ones may be derogated from.

The various doctrines shall be examined. Although, before doing so, one must state what the three main doctrines are: the doctrine of assignment of contract, the doctrine of transfer of a negotiable instrument; and the doctrine of the law of sale, adjusted to its object being a *sui generis* instrument.

6.3.1 Shares as a joint ownership right

Manara[51] and Ferri[52] have held that a corporate share is a joint ownership right of the corporate assets. Ferri further points out that the parliamentary works which preceded the Civil Code[53] expressly state that the joint ownership of the corporate assets is basically different from the traditional joint ownership.

6.3.2 Shares as intangible property

Shares have been considered as intangible property by Bonelli[54] and Visentini.[55]

6.3.3 Shares as tangible property

A reference to the nature of tangible property of shares is made by Santini[56] although he focuses on the nature of parts of limited liability companies as representing the position of holder of a contractual relationship. As a *res* (tangible property), negotiable instruments are expressly defined by Ascarelli[57] and Messineo.[58]

In *Bastolfi* v *Alifin Italiana*[59] it has been held that:

> as it has been repeated on many occasions, there is no doubt that the *sale* (emphasis added) of shares may be treated as a sale of tangible property, ie of the share, which besides representing a part of the stock capital, represents the right of the holder to participate, in proportion to that share, to the corporate assets.

6.3.4 Shares as second degree tangible property

Ascarelli[60] expressly refers to shares as tangible property which does not represent the corporate assets, but the rights of their holder on the corporation, and only indirectly then on the corporate assets. This allows them to be described

[51] Manara, *Delle società e delle Associazioni Commerciali*, (Corporations and Trade Associations), (Turin 1902), 1, at 572.

[52] Ferri, "Delle Società" (Corporations) *Commentario Scialoja e Branca*, (1981), 9.

[53] *Lavori preparatori al Codice Civile* (Preparatory works to the Civil Code) I, No 482.

[54] Bonelli, "I concetti di comunione e di personalità nella teoria delle società commerciali", (The concept of joint ownership and of personality in the structure of commercial corporations), *Riv. dir. comm.*, (1903), I, 1304.

[55] Visentini "Azioni di società" (Corporate shares) *Enciclopedia del diritto*, (Milan 1959), 969.

[56] Santini, "Natura e vicende della quota di società a responsabilità limitata" (Nature and life of parts of limited liability companies), *Riv. dir. civ.*, (1962), 437.

[57] Ascarelli, *Saggi di diritti commerciale* (Essays of commercial law), (Milano, 1955), at 239.

[58] Messineo, *Manuale di diritto civile e commerciale* (Manual of Civil and Commercial Law) IV at 384.

[59] Court of Milan, 17 April, [1989], in *Acquisizioni di società e di pacchetti azionari di riferimenti*, *Op. cit.* (1990) at 70.

[60] See *supra* note 57, at 242.

as a second degree property, since through them one owns indirectly the corporate property.

6.3.5 Shares as Negotiable Instruments

The prevailing opinion defines shares as negotiable instruments. Among the writers, one can mention Brunetti,[61] Messineo,[62] Ferri,[63] De Gregorio,[64] Fré,[65] and Ascarelli.[66]

Fré[67] points out that the word share has many meanings. First, it is a part of the capital stock, it also represents—as pointed out by Ascarelli[68]—the status of shareholder, and thirdly it is the document, negotiable as other instruments, which embodies such relationship. Fré infers from this that a document which is transferable and which represents a bundle of rights, arising from a relationship, must be defined as a negotiable instrument.

Some of these writers, like Fré,[69] further admit that shares are special instruments. In fact shares lack two elements which have been traditionally considered essential to negotiable instruments: the *letteralità*[70] and the *astrattezza.*[71]

Shares do not refer specifically to all the rights and duties arising from them. Such rights and duties result only from the corporate by-laws, from their amendments and from other sources, such as pending notices published in the *Official Gazette*. If for example the corporate capital has been recently reduced, by reducing the nominal value of the shares, that will not result from the by-laws.

It follows from this that even when—as it frequently happens—a reference to the by-laws is made in the share certificate, there will still be further sources of such rights and duties which cannot be found on the face of the instrument. Likewise the independence of the share from the underlying relationship is only partial.

The contents of the share may, in fact, have to be completed or amended based on what results from the corporate life, which may prevail over the face of the certificate. In *Cappelletti* v *Sind. Industriale Commerciale*[72] the Court of Cassation has held that one can bind a shareholder to the entries on the Companies Registry, or other duly published changes, even if there is no reference to them in the share certificate.

[61] Brunetti, *Trattato del diritto di società*, (Treatise on company law), (Milan 1950), III, at 113.

[62] Messineo, *Op. cit.* III, at 530.

[63] Ferri, *I titoli di credito, Tratt. dir. civ. diretto da Vassalli*, (Torino, 1950), at 90.

[64] De Gregorio, "Delle Società" (Corporations) *Commentario UTET*, (Turin, 1938) at 256.

[65] Fré, *Op. cit.* see *supra* at 50.

[66] Ascarelli, "Riflessioni in tema di titoli azionari e società tra società" (Comments on shares and corporations formed by other corporations), in *Saggi di diritto commerciale*, (1955), at 219.

[67] Fré, *Op. cit.*, see *supra* at note 50.

[68] Ascarelli, *Op. cit.*, see *supra* at note 66.

[69] Fré, *Op. cit.*, at 170.

[70] ie that the instrument embodies only the rights stated on its face value since it is based on its literal contents.

[71] ie its being independent from the underlying relationship.

[72] Court of Cassation, 10 October, No 3702 [1957] *Mass. Giust. civ.*, (1957), 1389.

It follows from this that the share is an instrument which is neither literal nor abstract. But since these two requirements are no longer considered essential,[73] as discussed earlier, this does not prevent shares from being considered negotiable instruments. Messineo[74] defines a share as a *titolo di credito causale* (a non-abstract negotiable instrument); this view is shared by Cottino[75] and Panzarini.[76] Shares have been treated as a negotiable instrument also in *Isotta Fraschini* v *Banco di Roma*[77] and in *Della Giovanna* v *De Francisci*.[78]

An independent position has been taken by Carnelutti[79] that the share represents a credit of the shareholder towards the corporation, if it is examined from the point of view of the shareholder's right to receive the performance to which he is entitled, and also as a right *in rem*, if considered from the point of view that such right may be asserted against any third party.

6.3.6 Shares as *sui generis* instruments

The peculiarities of shares, *vis-à-vis* ordinary negotiable instruments, have brought some writers to treat shares as a subdivision of negotiable instruments, such as *titoli di contratto*[80] as they were defined by Santini[81] or as *sui generis rights* as they were defined by Asquini[82] or as having *poteri eterogenei*[83] as it was held by Candian.[84] Carnelutti[85] places shares between titles of property and a negotiable instrument, while Stolfi,[86] and Buonocore[87] are of the view that the title of property and the negotiable instrument co-exist in the share.

In *Citi* v *Nebioli et Stipel*,[88] it was held:

> the shares of a corporation are instruments which embody the rights related to the status of shareholder and therefore represent the shareholders' participation to the corporation

[73] Asquini, *I titoli di credito* (Negotiable instruments), (Padua, 1966) at 104; Gasperoni, *Le azioni di società* (Corporate shares) at 75; *Ibid.* "Azioni di società" (Corporate shares) *Nov. Dig. It.*, *Ferri, I titoli di credito* (Negotiable instruments) *Op. cit.*, at 97; Fiorentino II 104; "Le azioni di società come titoli di credito", (Shares as negotiable instruments), *Banca Borsa e Titoli di Credito* (1948), 1, 49.

[74] Messineo, *Op. cit.*, IV, 385.

[75] Cottino, *Diritto Commerciale*, Vol. II, (Padua, 1978) at 249.

[76] Panzarini, "La tutela dell' acquirente nella vendita di titoli azionari", (The Purchaser's protection in acquisitions of corporate shares), *Riv. dir. comm.*, (1959), I, 257.

[77] Court of Milan, 11 April, 1935, *Banca Borsa Titoli di Credito* (1936), II, 169.

[78] Court of Appeal, Milan, 5 July, 1935, *Banca Borsa e Titoli di Credito* (1937), II, 86.

[79] Carnelutti, *Teoria della circolazione*, op. cit. see *infra* at note 85.

[80] Instruments representing a contract.

[81] Santini, see *supra*, at 438.

[82] Asquini, *Titoli di credito*, (Negotiable instruments), (Padova, 1951), at 109.

[83] Heterogeneous rights, or as a bundle of different rights.

[84] Candian, "Il diritto del socio nelle c.d. società di capitali, Natura giuridica", (The shareholder's rights in corporations—Legal nature), *Dir. fall.* (1961), 1, 267.

[85] Carnelutti, *Teoria giuridica della circolazione*, (Legal Rules on Transfers), (Padova, 1933), at 39.

[86] Stolfi, *La liquidazione delle società commerciali*, (The liquidation of corporations), (Milan, 1938), at 98.

[87] Bunonocore, *Le situazioni soggettive dell'azionista* (The subjective position of shareholders), (Naples, 1960), at 221.

[88] Court of Cassation, 6 May, No 1479 [1958], *Dir. fall.* (1958), II, 223.

which combines the acknowledgment of the special contents of a share with its belonging to the wider class of negotiable instruments.

6.3.7 Shares as a mere document merely certifying the position of "party to the contract"

Other writers[89] have distinguished between the financial rights, to which the holder of a share is entitled, and the non-financial rights and duties related to such a position. They have questioned whether, rather than an instrument or a right, a share does not simply certify the position of its holder as a party to the contract, which has given birth to the corporation, as possibly subsequently amended.

De Ferra sees shares as a bundle of rights, (ie a plurality of rights and duties arising from the contract existing between the shareholders). This classification was shared in *Nivoni* v *Bonacchi*[90] even in respect of limited liability companies:

> the *quotas* (parts of limited liability companies) express the measure of the participation by each part-holder to that company and his rights and duties.

In *Cremaleasing* v *Sarceni*[91] the Court of Milan has held that the share

> . . . discharges the task of a document which entitles its holder to exercise the rights arising from the *status* of shareholder of that corporation.

6.3.8 Suggested classification

It is submitted that the classification of shares as a special subcategory of negotiable instruments is the most suitable one, since it avoids two opposite excesses. On the one hand, the excess to consider the share as an ordinary negotiable instrument, which does not take into account that it includes a bundle of rights, for instance, not only financial but also other rights, (even if as De Ferra acknowledges,[92] the non-financial rights are accessory to the financial ones) as well as duties. On the other hand the other excess, which consists of treating the share not as an instrument, but a mere certificate as to the position of party to the contract.

6.4 Transfer of Shares: a Sale or an Assignment of Contract

Up to this point, common law lawyers may have believed to have been faced with a typical civil lawyers' involved argument—which I described—by applying Ancel's definition,[93] made in another context, as a *pêché d'analyse*.[94] They might feel entitled to conclude that in practice such an analysis produces little practical result.

[89] De Ferra, *La circolazione delle partecipazioni azionarie*, (The Transfer of shareholdings), (Giuffre', 1964), at 6.

[90] Court of Cassation, 31 July, No 2452 [1952] *Foro it.*, (1953), I, 1644.

[91] Court of Milan, 6 July, [1989] in *Acquisizioni di società e di pacchetti azionari*, *op. cit.* at 74.

[92] De Ferra *supra* at 89.

[93] B. Ancel, comments on *Epoux A.* v *Préfet de Paris* Tribunal de Grande Instance de Paris, 18 November, (1980) *Rev. cr. droit. int. privé*, (1981), 63.

[94] The sin of analysis.

However, very practical and highly relevant results derive from the classification of shares. The doctrine of "party to the contract" brings its reasoning to its natural conclusions by suggesting that a transfer of shares is not a sale, but merely an assignment of contract, while the doctrine, which sees shares as ordinary negotiable instruments, draws from this the conclusion that only the provisions related to transfers of negotiable instruments apply to them.

According to both such doctrines the transfer of shares would not be subject to the statutory provisions on sales of goods (which include the vendor's statutory warranties), and that the *only statutory warranty* of the assignor would be that the assigned contract exists and is valid.

The issue of the proper classification is then of the greatest importance from a practical point of view also, since the classification of the transaction produces the result that the statutory provisions governing that transaction, supplement the contractual ones, and replace those provisions which it is not possible to derogate from in such transactions. Thus, such provisions apply even if they have not been taken into account by the parties or the parties have tried to regulate that matter in a different way[95] from the statutory requirement. One of the various consequences of this, as it will be subsequently discussed, is that if the law of sale applies, several warranties, in order to be validly asserted, require action by the purchaser within very short time limits.

6.4.1 Criticism of the doctrine of assignment of contract

The doctrine of assignment of contact produces the result that the assignee takes over the entire contractual position of the assignor, and consequently all the rights and duties arising to the vendor from the deed of incorporation as amended, and gives to the assignee effective from that time, the position of shareholder. This doctrine completes its structure by replacing the need for the consent of the assigned contractual party, with an inherent right to the free transfer of the shares.

6.4.1.1 AUTOMATIC ACCEPTANCE OF THE BY-LAWS

According to this doctrine, the assignee would consequently be bound by the corporate by-laws as an automatic effect of the assignment.

However, this consequence is not so automatic. If, for example, the by-laws include an arbitration clause, it has been debated whether the purchaser is automatically bound by it simply because of his purchase, or whether his acceptance[96] is required. In *Ente Maremma* v *Acea Roma*[97] the purchasers' specific acceptance was required. Even if in *Carnevali* v *Ass. Romana Sincronizzatori*[98] as well as in *Bisconi* v *Aldini*,[99] the Court of Cassation ruled to the contrary, the answer to this question is not as automatic as it should be if the

[95] Rubino-Sammartano, The "Italy" Section, in *World Litigation Law and Practice*, (Matthew Bender, 1986 and Transnational Juris 1989; Myrick gen. ed).

[96] A specific acceptance being required since the clause deprives of the right or access to courts and consequently falls under the category of oppressive clause.

[97] Court of Cassation, 4 April, No 2214 [1980] *Mass. Giust. Civ.* (1980), 964.

[98] Court of Cassation, 23 February, No 353 [1968] *Foro It.*, (1968), I, 3057.

[99] Court of Cassation, 18 February, No 1367 [1985] *Mass. Foro It.*, (1985), 270.

doctrine of assignment applied. The absence, or the arguability, of this effect seems then not to be in line with the doctrine of assignment of contract.

6.4.1.2 VENDOR'S SALE ONLY OF PART OF ITS SHARES

Furthermore, if a vendor, who owns 2,000,000 shares, sells only 1,000,000 of them, for example, while he keeps the balance, one can hardly say that he has assigned his position of party to the contract, since he keeps it as to the shares which he has not sold. This argument has been resisted by De Ferra[100] on the ground that each share would represent its holder's position of party to the contract, and that consequently if the vendor keeps some shares, he keeps such a position since he still holds other shares.

However, this remark by itself shows that this is not a case of an assignment of contract, but just of a transfer of an instrument which embodies certain rights and duties, and that the fact that the purchaser becomes a party to the deed of incorporation, as amended, is just a consequence of the acquistion of the vendor's rights and duties.

The sale only of a part of the shares does not affect then the right to attack a shareholder's resolution, which depends on the status of shareholder and not on the number of shares owned. The vendor keeps such right even if he keeps one share. It has been held that the purchaser of shares does not acquire the right to attack the shareholders' resolution by taking over the vendor's right but that it acquires it of its own right. See *Soc. Gruppo Lepetit* v *Soc. Ravelli e Micheli.*[101] This voice is echoed by Angelici.[102]

Another situation where the transfer of the shares does not imply an assignment of the rights of the shareholder *vis-à-vis* the corporation is when there is a sale of shares between the parties, but they do not notify the corporation of the transaction. One should mention, in this respect, that some other writers look at the shareholder's position *vis-à-vis* the corporation, embodied by the shares, as Glaübigerrechte[103] (ie creditor's rights).

6.4.1.3 DISTINCTION BETWEEN ENTERING INTO THE CORPORATE CONTRACT AND HOLDING A SHARE

It has been further held[104] that a funding member becomes a shareholder by entering into the contract and not because he becomes the holder of the shares.[105] This further confirms that there is a difference between being a party to the contract and holding a share.

6.4.1.4 SITUATIONS NOT OPPOSABLE BY THE CORPORATION TO THE PURCHASER

It is further arguable whether some relationships between the corporation and the vendor are opposable to the purchaser. An example is the case of waivers to the

[100] De Ferra, see *supra* at 89.
[101] Court of Cassation, 9 August, No 2280 (1973) *Foro it.*, (1973), I, 1975.
[102] *Trattato delle Società per Azioni* (Treatise on Corporations Limited by shares) Vol. 2 at 105.
[103] Angelici, in *Trattato delle Società per Azioni*, *Op. cit.* at 124.
[104] *Giorgetti* v *Strocchi*, Court of Cassation, 26 February, No 105 (1948), *Banca Borsa e Titoli di Credito* (1949), II, 227, *Columella* v *Paleani* Court of Cassation, 22 January, No 82 (1949) *Banca Borsa e Titoli di Credito*, (1949), II, 222.
[105] De Ferra, *Op. cit.* at 18.

dividend[106] which, according to Angelici,[107] would not be opposable to the purchaser, and of shares paid through a conferment of assets, instead of cash, if the value of the conferred assets later results to be lower.[108]

Furthermore, if a share, which has not been fully paid to the corporation, is sold, in spite of a forbiddance to do so, the sale as a rule produces effects not *vis-à-vis* the corporation, but only *inter partes*.[109] Likewise, if a dividend has been paid in breach of statutory provisions[110] and the vendor acted in bad faith, the purchaser is not bound to return it. Even these situations seem to show that the vendor's position has not been fully transferred to the purchaser.

6.4.1.5 PLEDGE USUFRUCT AND ENFORCEMENT PROCEEDINGS ON SHARES

Similarly if shares simply represent the position of party to the contract arising between shareholders from the deed of incorporation, as possibly later amended, such a position perhaps may not be the object of a pledge or of usufruct or of enforcement proceedings, while all such steps may be taken on a negotiable instrument.

De Ferra[111] asserts that the share consists of financial and non-financial rights, and that the latter rights are merely accessory to the former, which allows the share to be subject to pledge, usufruct or enforcement proceedings. However, this argument seems far from convincing because in this way nothing remains of the view that a transfer of shares is an assignment of contract.

6.4.1.6 SHARES WHICH ENTITLE THE HOLDER ONLY TO THE DIVIDEND AND TO THE PROCEEDS OF LIQUIDATION

Reference to the various rights and duties, on which this doctrine bases its distinction between shares and negotiable instruments, seems weaker when it comes to *azioni di risparmio*[112] and to *azioni di godimento*.[113] These do not grant rights to vote, but merely rights to the dividends and to the proceeds of the liquidation of the corporation.

6.4.1.7 ACQUISITION BY A CORPORATION OF ITS OWN SHARES

The doctrine of assignment of contract seems to meet a further obstacle in the right granted to a corporation to acquire its own shares.[114] In fact the assignment by one contracting party of its rights and duties to the very body which is the object of such rights does not fit well into that scheme.

6.4.1.8 CONCLUSION

In conclusion it is submitted that the equation between a share and the position of party to the contract (which has given birth to the corporation and which keeps

[106] Angelici, *Trattato delle Società per Azioni, Op. cit.* at 234.
[107] Angelici, *Trattato delle società per Azioni* at 131.
[108] Section 2343 last para. of the Civil Code.
[109] Between the parties to the sale contract.
[110] Section 2433.
[111] De Ferra, *Op. cit.* at 13.
[112] Saving shares.
[113] ie shares which entitle only to the dividend and to a share of the liquidation proceeds.
[114] Section 2357 of the Civil Code provides: "A corporation may not purchase its shares unless the acquisition is approved by the shareholders' meeting, it is effected by using money coming from duly approved net profits and the shares have been totally paid."

it alive), does not seem tenable, and that shares are *non-abstract negotiable instruments* and precisely a special subcategory of negotiable instruments, since they embody not only financial, but even non-financial rights and duties.

6.5 Transfer of Shares as a Transfer of a Negotiable Instrument

A decisive argument against the doctrine, according to which shares represent "the position of party to a contract", seems to come from the statutory provisions which govern the transfer of shares, which treat them as negotiable instruments. Section 2006 of the Civil Code, for example, expressly mentions shares among the instruments to be amortised. Likewise, shares are included among the negotiable instruments which may be the object of stock exchange carry-over transactions.

De Ferra himself,[115] recognises that:

> It is beyond doubt that Parliament has included shares amongst negotiable instruments.
> Even if included amongst negotiable instruments, shares are a special instrument. . . . .

In fact the transfer of shares is governed by sections 2021 to 2027 of the Civil Code which are headed "Negotiable instruments—Subsection Registered Instruments". Also, the special legislation which has forbidden shares to be to the bearer[116] is in line with this approach.

6.6 Transfer of Shares Referred to by the Statutory Provisions as Sale

Furthermore, in several statutory provisions the terms *sale* or *purchase* are used in respect of transfers of shares. Section 2355 provides that, "the deed of incorporation may submit the *sale* of shares to some conditions" (emphasis added).

Section 2357 states that, "A corporation may not *purchase* its own shares" (emphasis added).

Section 2359 heading recites, "*Purchase* of shares of a corporation by corporations controlled by the same" (emphasis added).

Finally section 1531 states "if the *sale* concerns shares. . . " The courts also regularly refer to a "sale of share" which is the case in *Istituto Bancario S. Paolo di Torino* v *Colombo, Ilssa Viola et al*[117] and in *Piccole Partecipazioni S.p.A. Lloyd Adriatico S.p.A.*[118]

6.6.1 Sale by the heir of the estate of a deceased

Eventually the sale, by an heir of the estate to which he is entitled by succession on death, is expressly governed by statutory provisions. Section 1542 provides:

[115] De Ferra, *Op. cit.* at 37.
[116] Royal Decree 25 October, 1942 No 1148, modified by Statute 9 February, 1943, integrated by Royal Decree 29 March, 1943 No 239.
[117] Court of Cassation, 25 March No 1464 [1989] *Giur. Comm.*, (1990), 734.
[118] Court of Justice, Trieste, 3 July, [1987] *Giur. Comm.*, (1990), 873.

> He who *sells the estate* of the deceased of which he is the heir, without specifying its contents, must only warrant his title as heir. (Emphasis added.)

Now an estate is a bundle of multiple and non-homogenous assets as well as of liabilities for the estate debts. It is submitted that even if the sale of an estate is different from the sale of a share, both of them involve the transfer of a bundle of rights and duties and, therefore, the legal system has no objection in principle to a sale of a bundle of rights and obligations.

As mentioned earlier, the consequence of classification of shares on warranties is decisive. In this respect, it is suggested that, in examining this matter, it is preferable to assume that the parties have added no other warranties to the deal, and that one consequently is merely facing the statutory warranties. If shares merely reflect the position of party to a contract, their transfer is just an assignment of contract and the assignor's statutory warranty relates—as discussed earlier—only to the existence and validity of the assigned contract (ie the deed amongst funding shareholders which has incorporated and keeps—subject to the possible subsequent amendments—the corporation alive). If consequently that corporation is validly in existence, the assignor has no further statutory duties in this respect.

Thus, while shares are a *sui generis* negotiable instrument, and their transfer is statutorily treated as a sale, then, as in all other sales, the vendor is subject to the vendor's statutory warranties.

6.7 *The Doctrine according to which Transfers of Shares are Governed Exclusively by the Provisions on Transfer of Negotiable Instruments*

Between these two opposite doctrines, a third position holds that since shares are negotiable instruments, their transfer must not be subject to the statutory provisions which apply to sale agreements. Rather, subject exclusively to the rules which govern the transfer of the negotiable instruments, like the instrument *par excellence*, the promissory note[119] under which the assignee (the endorsee) answers only for non-payment of that instrument[120] by the issuer.

This view was held by Gasperoni[121] according to whom,

> . . . it is the rules on the transfer of negotiable instruments which govern the sale of shares. It follows from this that the Vendor, besides the duty to deliver the share, must accomplish all the formalities required to transfer his rights of holder of said shares.

This is similar to an endorsement of cheques, where the endorsee is liable only in case of non-payment by the bank.

This position is echoed by Angelici[122] who—after defining the share as a negotiable instrument which reflects rights, instead of creating them itself—

[119] Royal Decree 14 December, 1933 No 1669.
[120] And for non-acceptance, in case of bills of exchange.
[121] Gasperoni, *Le azioni di società*, (Padova, 1942), at 219.
[122] Angelici, *Trattato delle Società per Azioni Op. cit.* at 230.

distinguishes between the organisational aspects and the individual life of that instrument and focuses his attention on the corporation's defences *vis-à-vis* the legitimate holder of the share. It seems preferable to follow the more traditional distinction between the effects arising from a sale of shares between the parties as compared to its effects, *vis-à-vis* the corporation. The latter take place only when the corporation has been submitted a duly endorsed share certificate, or a notarised sale agreement, and is so requested by a duly identified party, in which case an entry related to the transfer is made by the corporation on the corporate ledger book or a new share certificate is issued to the purchaser.

6.8 Conclusion

Such a research of the various defences which are available to a corporation *vis-à-vis* the purchaser of its shares, risks confining the results of the research to the effects of that sale. The same negative result would be achieved if, for example, one should confine its analysis to the endorsement of the traditional, and abstract, negotiable instrument, (which is the only source of the credit, which it embodies and which must be read exclusively for what it contains).

When one considers instruments which are not abstract and which are not confined to what is contained on their face value, (since the shareholder is entitled to exercise rights towards the corporation and is subject to the limits and duties set out in the by-laws and corporate resolutions), one may not limit the effects of their transfer to their face value.

Rather than proceeding to a further analysis of these other issues, which are certainly important but are outside the ambit of this research, it is suggested to abandon them noting that by treating a transfer of shares, just as an endorsement of a bill of exchange, one goes back to a formalistic approach, as the one discussed earlier of assignment of a contract. Such a position may not be shared because, within the enlarged family of negotiable instruments, the regime of literal and autonomous instruments (which amount to the right to a certain performance, which is based exclusively on the literal wording of the instrument and has no relationship with any underlying transaction) cannot be applied to the other instruments, which represent rights arising from a well-identified relationship referred to therein, rather than being independent from it. While as to instruments issued to the bearer[123] the effect of the endorsement consists, in assigning the rights inherent to the title, as to certificates which represent goods, delivery of the certificate entitles the bearer to receive possession of the goods,[124] the sale of the goods takes place outside of the certificate, and even if one refers to a sale on documents, this does not amount to a sale of the documents;[125] the transfer of the document amounts to delivery of the goods.[126]

[123] Section 2011 of the Civil Code.

[124] D. Rubino, *La compravendita, Op. cit.* at 423 *et seq.*; Bianca, "La Vendita e la permuta" (Sale and Barter) *Tratt. dir. civ. it.*, (Torino, 1972), at 401 *et seq.*; Greco-Cottino, *Della compravendita, Comm. Scialoja-Branca*, Article 1527, 2, at 381 *et seq.*

[125] Panzarini, "La tutela dell' acquirente nella vendita dei titoli di credito", *Riv. dir. comm.* (1959), I, 256.

[126] Bianca, "La vendita e la permuta" (Sale and Barter) *Tratt. dir. civ. it.*, (Torino, 1972) at 401.

In a sale of shares, the transfer necessarily relates not merely—as in the former class of negotiable instruments—to the instrument itself, but also to rights which exist before the issue of the instrument, and which continue to exist after such issue. Even if one leaves aside the special provisions related to the endorsement of a bill of exchange and of a cheque, it is suggested that the statutory provisions dealing with the transfer of negotiable instruments deal only with the *form* of the transfer of the instrument (between the parties and *vis-à-vis* the corporation): they do not deal at all with the transferor's duties and warranties to the transferee and the transferee's duties to the transferor.

Therefore, the view that those negotiable instruments which are shares certificates are governed, as to the effects of their transfer, exclusively by the statutory provisions which deal with their transfer, cannot be accepted. Firstly, because shares, as discussed earlier, are instruments *sui generis*. Secondly, because one may not disregard the fact that the transfer of the share certificate is the performance of a preceding transaction, which may be a sale but may also be a payment, or a donation, or a guarantee.

The relationship between the parties cannot, consequently, be limited to the transfer of the instrument, since this is merely the mechanical implementation of the previous underlying contract.[127]

This explains why full effects of the transfer of *titoli nominativi* (ie a negotiable instrument issued in favour of a specific registered beneficiary) are not dealt with in the specific statutory provisions dealing with such negotiable instruments, although some reference to them is made as to *titoli al portatore* (ie instruments transferable by mere delivery) and to *titoli all' ordine* (ie instruments transferable by mere endorsement without need to state the name of the transferee).

This explains also why the provisions concerning *titoli all' ordine*[128] which establish the effects of the transfer as far as the rights on the instruments are concerned[129] by stating, "The endorsement transfers all the rights to the instrument" and, as far as the transferor's responsibility is concerned,[130] by stating:

> Unless the contrary is set out by a statutory provision, or by a mention to the contrary in the negotiable instrument, the transferor is not liable for non-performance by the issuer of the negotiable instrument

have not been referred to in the statutory provisions which govern *titoli nominativi*,[131] such as shares.

[127] Amongst the authors Santini, *L'azione causale nel diritto cambiario*, (Claims based on the underlying relationship in the law of bills of exchange), (Padova, 1968), at 23; Pavone La Rosa, "La cambiale" (The promissory note) *Trattato Cicu-Messineo*, (Milan, 1982), at 156; Bianca, "La vendita e la permuta", (Sale and Barter), *Trattato Vassalli*, (Turin, 1972); Partesotti, *I titoli all'ordine*, (Negotiable instruments transferable by mere endorsement), (Giuffre', 1991), at 108 and 152.

[128] See *supra* at 6.2.3.

[129] Section 2011 of the Civil Code.

[130] Section 2012 of the Civil Code.

[131] Section 2012 of the Civil Code.

The purpose of the statutory provisions on transfers of registered negotiable instruments is merely to deal with the "mechanical transfer", the effects of which are:[132]

> The holder of a negotiable instrument is entitled to the performance stated in the instrument against delivery of that instrument provided he is entitled to hold it.

In fact, the transferor's duties are governed by the underlying contract and consequently may vary considerably depending on it. For example, a vendor's duties are inevitably different from those of a donor.

It is submitted that it follows from this that, whenever shares are sold, the statutory provisions on sale contracts apply and—as discussed earlier—they automatically include the warranties of clear title, of absence of defects, of merchantable quality and *aliud pro alio*.

No written contract, as earlier set forth by several precedents as in *Bellini* v *Bertazzoni*,[133] is required for the sale. The contract for sale of shares may then be even oral and the statutory requirements of written form concern its implementation, ie the actual transfer of the share certificate.

It follows from the above comments that a transfer of a share certificate, which is admittedly a *sui generis* instrument since it embodies financial and non-financial rights as well as duties, cannot be imprisoned within the cage of a bill of exchange or in general of abstract instruments, in order to refuse to the purchaser the normal protection which any purchaser is entitled to receive from its vendor. Even more so when the statutory provisions (in our case the Civil Code) expressly define that transfer on many occasions as a sale contract, which calls for the application of the statutory provisions of the law of sale. This is because of the underlying sale contract which precedes the mere transfer and of the *sui generis* nature of share certificates.

This approach seems to be shared by several authors like Bigiavi,[134] Gasperoni,[135] Stolfi,[136] Rubino,[137] Santini,[138] and Panzarini[139] according to whom the shares are transferred under the statutory provisions of the law of sale[140] rather than under the provisions which deal with the formalities to be complied with in order to implement the transfer of a negotiable instrument.

In line with this approach is *Sessa et al* v *Mantovani et al*[141] which holds:

> . . . there is no doubt that the sale of *quote* (parts) or of shares can be treated as a sale of goods, the sold item being a portion of the capital and expressing its participation to the corporate net worth.

[132] Section 1992 of the Civil Code.
[133] Court of Cassation, 6 June, No 2084 [1957], *Banca Borsa Titoli di Credito* (1957), II, 379.
[134] Bigiavi, "II trasferimento dei titoli nominativi" (The transfer of nominative instruments) in *Riv. trim. dir. proc. civ.* (1950), 1.
[135] Gasperoni, *Le azioni di società* (Corporate shares), (Padova, 1942) *Op. cit. supra*, note 128.
[136] Stolfi, "Osservazioni sul trasferimento di titoli azionari", (Comments on transfer of shares), *Banca Borsa e Titoli di Credito*, (1950), I, 169.
[137] D. Rubino, *La compravendita* (The sale contract), *Op. cit.* at 234.
[138] Santini, "Natura e vicende della quota di società a responsabilità limitata" (Notion and life of parts of a company limited by shares) in *Riv. Dir. civ.* (1962), I. 442.
[139] Panzarini, *La tutela dell' acquirente nella vendita dei titoli di credito*, *Op. cit.* at 265.
[140] Sections 2003, 2011, 2022, 2023 of the Civil Code.
[141] Court of Milan, 5 July, [1990] *Giur. It.*, (1991), I, II, 39.

Our preferred view is that a sale of shares involves the vendor's statutory warranties governed by the law of sale. However, one should bear in mind that this is neither the only, nor the prevailing opinion. It may then be advisable to take into account at least the three main views in examining which warranties—if any—are applicable to the various types of acquisitions which are under examination. For instance, sales of ongoing businesses; mergers; sales of the entire stock capital; sales of shares between the parties; public takeover bids; sales of equity in the stock exchange; sales of parts of limited liability companies; and sales of interest in partnerships. After this general survey, the specific warranties shall be examined one by one.

7. Warranties in Sales of Shares and of On-going Business

7.1 Warranties in Sales of On-going Businesses

The doctrine of assignment of contract discussed previously does not have an opportunity to apply to sales of ongoing businesses. In fact, a business, even if it is a *universitas rerum*,[142] is certainly a saleable item, and as such it is automatically subject to the statutory warranties of clear title, of absence of defects and of merchantable quality.

This does not prevent the parties from adding other "voluntary" warranties, which are also referred to as "contractual", and from limiting or excluding the statutory warranties within the permitted limits. The same obviously applies to the sale of a branch of a business.

These concepts seem to apply also to contributions of businesses, such as when a capital increase of corporation A is subscribed by corporation B, (provided A has resolved that such a subscription may be made through the contribution of a business or branch of its business, instead of by paying cash).

The conferment by a company of its business, or of a branch of it, in order to subscribe shares of another company, is generally held to amount to a sale of that business.[143] The same applies when a new corporation is formed and its capital is subscribed partly by company A and partly by company B, each of them conferring their respective businesses or a branch of them.

7.2 Warranties in Mergers

Mergers may take place either by one corporation absorbing the other one or by two corporations merging into a third one (which has frequently been incorporated just for this purpose). In either case the shareholders of the merged corporation or corporations receive, in exchange for their conferment of the shares of the merged corporation, shares of the merging or of the new corporation. The subscription of shares of a corporation through conferment of the shares of another one is also to be seen as a sale of shares.

[142] ie a conglomerate of different types of assets and liabilities taken altogether.

[143] See *Fall. to SICMA S.p.A.* v *Scattolin*, Court of Cassation, 25 October, No 3844 [1976], *Giur. Comm.* (1977), II at 9; Colombo, *Trattato di Diritto Commerciale e di Diritto Pubblico dell'Economia* by Galgano, (Cedam, 1979), at 50; Bianca, *La vendita e la Permuta, Op. cit.*, at 195.

The issue of warranties seems to arise here at two levels. Firstly, at the level of the merged corporation. If one sees a conferment—such as the one which was considered in the immediately preceding subparagraph—as a sale, then the shareholder who confers, ie sells those shares, should be subject to the vendor's statutory warranties. In the event of both corporations being merged into a third and new one, this should apply to the shareholders of each of them.

Secondly, since the transfer of shares of the merging corporation, or of the third new corporation, to the shareholders of the merged corporation or corporations, is a direct transfer of shares between the parties, it is suggested that it amounts to a sale of shares and that it is also subject to the warranties which apply to the transaction, depending on the doctrine which will be followed.

7.3 Warranties in Sales of the Entire Capital Stock

The dispute between those who treat a sale of the entire stock capital like the sale of just one share, and those who see it as the sale of the entire business has been dealt with earlier. The ground has already been cleared from two possible misunderstandings. First, a sale of shares does not amount to a direct sale of the assets of the corporation. Second, one has taken into account that whenever a corporation has been established just to facilitate—taxwise or for other reasons—the sale of a given business, and it clearly results that the sale of the shares is only a facade, while *de facto* the parties have intended to transfer its business, this may play an important role in how to construe the whole transaction, warranties included.

One considers here the normal situation, ie a sale of the entire stock capital. This will inevitably produce as a consequence, but only as an indirect one, the transfer of that business. It is not easy to generalise and it is perhaps wiser to say that each transaction will have to be considered depending on its own structure. In very general terms, and subject to the said caution, one perhaps may venture to say that the sale would basically remain a sale of shares, but also that because it concerns the entire business, the contemplation of that by the parties may play a role as to possible wider applications of warranties.

7.4 Warranties in Sales of Shares between the Parties

One is eventually facing a straightforward sale of shares, directly negotiated between the parties. For those who construe it as an assignment of contract, only the very limited warranty related to assignments, ie that the assigned contract exists and is valid, shall apply. For those who treat it as an endorsement of an abstract instrument,[144] not even performance by the issuer would be statutorily warranted. For those who see it as a sale, not only the warranty of clear title, but also the other statutory warranties of absence of defects and of merchantable quality should apply.

However, as it will be discussed, the prevailing opinion does not draw from this premise all its possible consequences and tends, on the one hand, to exclude the warranty for defects and of merchantable quality, allowing only the warranty

[144] Under section 2012 of the Civil Procedure Code.

of clear title, and on the other hand, to limit the latter to title to the share, not applying it then to the corporate assets.

This position is very clearly expressed in *Cremaleasing* v *Sarcem*:[145]

> This is the reason why the warranty for defects is not to be considered as a natural effect of sales of shares. The only statutory warranty is warranty of title pursuant to section 1483, Civil Code. Once the share has been transferred free of burdens and liens, it is entirely suitable to discharge its role . . .

The sale of *aliud pro alio* applies under both doctrines, and will be discussed later.

As discussed earlier, the parties will be free to limit and exclude the statutory warranties up to the allowed limits, and to add other contractual warranties—as will be considered in subsequent sections.

7.5 Warranties in Public Takeover Bids

Public takeover bids probably place themselves between a sale between the parties, at the end of a direct negotiation, and sales in the stock exchange, where the parties deal only through brokers and their identity is generally of little or of no relevance. In stock exchange transactions the parties are in contact exclusively through brokers while in a takeover bid they are in direct relationship between themselves. However, this direct contact is limited, since the sale takes place through a mere acceptance of the public bid.

In takeover bids the generally active role of the vendor is frequently limited to his acceptance or refusal of the bid. Here the initiative, also as to the terms of the sale, lies with the purchaser. Although in given situations a vendor of a relevant number of shares may obtain a different deal, the majority of holders of few shares will either have to accept the purchaser's bid or refuse it. It is, consequently, unlikely that the vendor has an opportunity to exclude or limit his statutory warranties unless this is dealt with in the purchaser's bid.

In spite of this link with both types of sale, sales under a takeover bid seem to belong to the area of direct sales between the parties. The statutory warranties should consequently apply to them unless waived.

7.6 Warranties in Sales of Equity in the Stock Exchange

The special features of stock exchange transactions produce the normal result of a lack of negotiations between the purchaser and the vendor, while even their respective brokers confine their exchange to offering a sale or a purchase price and to accepting it. This has been seen by Angelici as resulting in a lack of any protection of the purchaser.[146]

Rather than affecting the nature of the transaction, this may play a substantial role because the intention of the parties seems to be confined to the purchase and sale of a definite quantity of shares of a given corporation for a certain price. There is no room for contractual warranties, and the applicability of the statutory provisions has been challenged, as will be discussed.

[145] See *supra* Chapter 6, note 95.

[146] Angelici, *Trattato delle Società per Azioni* (Treatise on Corporations Limited by shares) *Op. cit.* Vol. 2, at 113.

7.7 Warranties in Sales of Parts of Limited Liability Companies

Apart from the non-issue of share certificates in limited liability companies, the *quote* (parts) represent—as do the shares—the participation of the quota-holders in the corporation. However, the absence of a share certificate excludes any possible reference to negotiable instruments.

Quotas are to be distinguished from shares also because, while each share represents a unity, based on which the shareholding is measured, in companies with limited liability it is the quota-holder and not the *quota* which matters. Each quota-holder's portion of the corporate capital is then independent of its value. Quotas consequently may have, and do have, a different value.

Apart from this, parts may be the object of all the various above considered transactions except for sales in the stock exchange.

7.8 Warranties in Sales of Interest in Partnerships

Except for companies limited by shares or with limited liabilities, which are legal entities, the Italian legal system allows other structures like *società semplici*,[147] *società in nome collettivo*[148] and *società in accomandita semplice*.[149]

These structures, widely speaking, belong to the area of partnerships, some of them having also limited partners, others having exclusively unlimited partners. In such partnerships, in the absence of negotiable instruments as well as of *quote* (parts), each partner's interest in the partnership is transferred by assigning it, ie through an assignment of all the rights and duties arising from the contract. The assignment produces the result of a change in the parties to the partnership agreement. Transfer of such interest is consequently to be treated in a quite different way from a sale of shares. This difference will be examined when dealing with the single warranties.

The consent of the other partners to the transfer is required,[150] unless the partnership agreement relieves the parties from seeking such a consent.[151] It has consequently been held in *Magazzini Giovanna* v *Credito It.*[152] that an assignment of an interest, which has not been authorised in general or specifically, produces the result to transfer all the financial rights related to it, but not also the status of partner of that partnership.

8. Statutory Warranty of Clear Title

8.1 Ambit of the Warranty

The statutory warranty of clear title aims to protect the purchaser from situations arising out of successful claims by a third party against the purchaser, made after the sale has been entered into, which deprive the purchaser totally or partly of the purchased item. This warranty shall first be discussed as to sales in general, and then as to stock acquisitions.

[147] Partnership, with only unlimited partners, which may not trade.
[148] Partnerships, with only unlimited partners, which may trade.
[149] Partnerships, in which some of the partners may have a limited liability, which may trade.
[150] Di Sabato, *Manuale delle società* at 130.
[151] Ferrara-Corsi, *Imprenditori e società*, *Op. cit.*, at 282.
[152] Court of Trieste, 2 July, [1984] *Rep. Foro It.*, (1985), Società, 245.

In some situations, claims will be addressed only against the vendor while the purchaser will not be involved. In other situations the purchaser may be involved at various levels.

Full or partial title may be claimed against the purchaser and consequently by the purchaser against the vendor under this warranty:

> A purchases some property from B. After the sale is consummated, C makes a claim for full title or for 50 per cent of owner's right, on the sold property.

The third party may interfere even before the closing:

> C sues both A and B, before the closing, claiming that A has sold to C, before selling the given item to B, and claiming delivery of that item. C may also seek an interlocutory injunction against A refraining A from delivering it to B.

The third party may also interfere after the closing:

> C sues B, submitting that the buildable land which B has purchased from A, did not belong to A but to C, and that B must return it to C, leaving to B to claim damages against A. If C's title is duly registered with the Land Registry, his claim will succeed.

In other situations, C will merely claim a preferential title:

> A sells specified equipment to B. C, having become aware of this, asserts a pledge granted to him on it before its sale. If the preferential title is duly established, B has not received clear title and is entitled to be indemnified by A under the statutory warranty.

Similarly,

> A sells some buildable land to B. C, having a mortgage on it, is entitled to assert it against the new owner. B has then not received clear title and is entitled to be indemnified by A.

Finally, the third party may claim the right to use the sold item.

> A sells a factory to B and does not disclose that C has an usufruct on it. C does not vacate the sold factory and succeeds in asserting its usufruct. A has breached his warranty of clear title and is liable to B.

8.2 The Warranty in the Various Acquisitions

8.2.1 Applicability of this warranty to acquisitions in general

The existence of a warranty of clear title as to the corporate assets has been excluded in situations involving a sale of the entire stock capital. In *Cattaneo della Volta* v *Raggio*[153] it was held on the grounds that:

> When the very existence of that corporation is not in issue, the sale of its shares may not be treated as the sale of the corporate assets. Therefore, unless the vendor has issued a contractual warranty, he does not warrant clear title to the corporate assets nor undertake liability for the corporate financial conditions.

[153] Court of Cassation, 29 March, [1935], *Foro It.*, (1935), 1, 1627.

This judgment has reversed the ruling of the Court of Appeal, Milan,[154] which had held that

> a sale of shares of a corporation between shareholders may, depending on the intention of the parties, amount to a sale of the corporate business, particularly if the value of the shares has been based on an estimate of its assets . . . if so the vendor is bound by the warranty of clear title.

The statutory warranty of clear title, related to the assets of the corporation, was excluded by the Court of Cassation also in *Galimberti* v *Pastore*:[155]

> The sale of the entire stock capital of a corporation to a sole purchaser does not give rise to a statutory warranty of clear title, unless the vendor has contractually warranted the existence of the corporate assets.

This view was shortly afterwards followed by the Court of Appeal, Bologna in *Raggio* v *Cattaneo*.[156] The same view was also expressed as to sale of some shares, instead of the entire capital stock, in *Della Giovanna* v *De Francisci*:[157]

> It follows from this that normally a sale of shares does not transfer title to the single corporate assets, which continue to belong to that corporation; it will produce the result that the vendor is bound by the warranty of clear title as to his ownership of the share treated as a *res*[158] and furthermore as to the rights to the share, considered as a negotiable instrument, pursuant to section 1542 (validity, genuineness and assignability of the instrument) but it will not give rise to a warranty of clear title also as to the single assets of that corporation . . .

Much more recently in *Cremaleasing* v *Sarcem*[159] it has been held that:

> the sole statutory warranty which applies in this situation (note: sale of shares) is the warranty of clear title set out by section 1483, Civil Code . . . Once the share has been transferred clear of burdens and liens, it is totally fit to discharge its role . . .

According to such precedents, the warranty of clear title is applied to shares sales but the warranty is limited to title to the share so that title is clear of burdens. This view is shared among writers including Ascarelli,[160] Vivante,[161] Pugliatti,[162] Greco,[163] and Panzarini.[164]

[154] Court of Appeal, Milan, 1 May, [1934] *Foro It.*, 1935, 1, 1622.
[155] Court of Cassation, 3 July, [1935] *Riv. dir. comm.*, 1936, II, 113.
[156] Court of Appeal, Bologna, 31 November, [1935] *Riv. dir. comm.* 1936, II, 213.
[157] Court of Appeal, Milan, 31 July, [1935] *Banca Borsa e Titoli di Credito*, (1937), 86.
[158] ie a thing.
[159] See *supra* Chapter 7, note 145.
[160] Ascarelli, Comments to *Cattaneo della Volta* v *Raggio, Foro it.*, (1935), 1, 1628.
[161] Vivante, *Trattato* (Treatise), IV, at 146.
[162] Publiatti, "Vendita di azioni e garanzia per evizione", (Sale of shares and warranty of clear title), *Banca Borsa e Titoli di Credito* (1937), 86.
[163] Greco, "Le societa' di comodo e la vendita delle loro azioni", (Corporations formed merely to suit their shareholder and sale of their shares) *Riv. dir. comm.*, (1935), II, 122.
[164] Panzarini, *Op. cit.* at 287.

8.2.2 In sales of ongoing businesses

In sales of ongoing businesses, the warranty of clear title shall apply to the business itself and to its assets, as in any other sale of goods.

> If A sells to B an ongoing business but later title to the factory, or to the equipment of that business, is established by a third party *vis-à-vis* the purchaser on grounds prior to the sale, the vendor is liable under the warranty.

The same applies if the ongoing business is conferred in payment of subscribed shares.

8.2.3 In direct sales of shares between the parties

The prevailing opinion applies the warranty of clear title limitedly to the share certificate itself. The warranty consequently protects the purchaser in case title to the share does not exist. For example:

> A sells to C shares of corporation B, but the share certificates have been forged.
> A sells to B shares of corporation C, but the share certificates have been amortized.
> A sells to B shares of corporation C, but the shares are not transferable or the procedures to be followed for transfer have not been complied with.
> A sells to B shares of corporation C but the shares are pledged.

According to the prevailing opinion, the warranty is not extended to the sold corporation. We shall examine subsequently whether and if so in which way the prevailing opinion may or may not be followed.

8.2.4 In sales in the stock exchange

Sales of shares in the stock exchange would seem to be subject to this warranty in the same way as direct sales between the parties.

> A sells to B in the stock exchange, through brokers, shares of corporation C. If the transferred title does not exist or is not clear, the warranty shall apply.

8.2.5 In sales of parts of limited liability corporations

The warranty shall apply here too, by adjusting the above comments to the situation arising from the absence of share certificates.

> A sells to B parts of corporation C. If the parts have been pledge or attached before the closing, A shall answer under the warranty.
> Likewise if the corporation refuses to register the transfer since the procedures set forth for transfers in its by-laws have not been complied with.

8.2.6 In transfers of interest in partnerships

In transfers of interest in a partnership, the position is different since this is not a sale but an assignment of the position of the partner as party to the partnership agreement. The vendor will consequently be liable not under the vendor's warranty of clear title but under the statutory provisions which regulate assignments of contracts.[165]

[165] Section 1410 of the Civil Code.

The Assignor is here liable if the partnership agreement does not exist, or is null and void, or if the assignor had already assigned his interest to a third party.

9. Statutory Warranty of Absence of Defects

9.1 The Ambit of the Warranty

This warranty aims to protect the purchaser against defects. Defect was defined in *Erreffe* v *Cavalli*[166] as an imperfection of the manufacturing process of the sold item, in *System* v *Pavani*,[167] as a deficiency of the general structure of the sold goods, and by Mirabelli[168] as a deficiency in structure or in composition or in the external aspect.

The defects which fall under this warranty are those which make the sold asset unfit for its normal purpose. As it was held in *Cinemeccanica* v *Mormino*[169] special purposes are not relevant in this respect, unless as it was held in *Braccini* v *Nuti*[170] they have been agreed upon specifically. There is disagreement amongst writers[171] as to whether unfitness has to be relevant. It has been held[172] that the silence of the statutory provisions as to the requirement of relevance of unfitness, compared with the express provision of relevance of the defects, which reduce the value of the sold item, might have to be construed as an absence of an intention by Parliament to impose that requirement. However, the need for relevance of the defects derives from the general principle barring actions on breaches of little importance. If that were not so, complaints by purchasers for defects of little importance would be encouraged, which must have not been the intention of Parliament.

Unfitness has then to be relevant. Even defects which diminish, in a relevant way, the value of the sold asset, trigger this warranty.

The warranty applies when the defects pre-exist the sale, the purchaser is not aware of them at the time of the sale, and they are not easily discernible. Hidden and apparent defects are to be complained of within a time limit, which is not the same for the two types of defects.

9.2 The Warranty and the Various Corporate Acquisitions

9.2.1 Applicability of this warranty to acquisitions

The applicability of the statutory warranty of absence of defects to acquisitions is excluded both by the doctrine of assignment of contract and by the doctrine of sale of a negotiable instrument. For the latter the warranty concerns only

[166] Court of Cassation, 17 January, No 206 [1978] *Mass. Foro It.*, (1978), 40.
[167] Court of Cassation, 20 January, No 177 [1976] *Mass. Foro It.*, (1976), 45.
[168] Mirabelli, "Dei singoli contratti", (Specific Contracts), *Commentario Scialoja e Branca*, Vol. II, (Turin, 1967), at 1582.
[169] Court of Cassation, 6 April, No 1013 [1971] *Rep. Foro It.*, item *Vendita* (Sale), (1971), 3219, 56.
[170] Court of Cassation, 23 March, No 827 [1959] *Rep. Foro It.*, item *Vendita* (Sale), (1959), 2622, 87–90.
[171] see D. Rubino, *La compravendita* (The Sale Agreement) (Milan, 1952), at 776, *contra* Luzzatto, *La compravendita* (The Sale), (Naples, 1959) at 15.
[172] Rubino-Sammartano, *Lack of conformity, Op. cit.*, at 256.

"physical" defects in the delivered asset, and the sale concerns the share itself and not the corporate assets.

In order to avoid the consequence of Rubino's[173] definition of defects as physical defects, that would restrict consideration exclusively to physical defects of the share certificate; Panzarini,[174] following Corrado[175] and Segré,[176] has held that there is a defect whenever the right to exercise the status of shareholder is reduced, stayed or prejudiced as if the progressive number of a stolen certificate is forged or if the affidavit, issued by a bank to inform the purchaser about the history of earlier circulation of the shares, is falsified. Similar results occurred, as reported by Weiss,[177] when Dutch share certificates which had been stolen by Germans and which the Dutch Government had ordered to be out of trade, were sold in Switzerland. All these defects are treated as affecting the right to exercise the status of shareholder.

It is suggested that if one tries to expand the defects warranty beyond these illustrations, he must start by distinguishing defects of the corporate assets from defects of the corporate *patrimonio*.[178]

As to the former, since the share represents the participation of the shareholder to the corporation, the sale of the share is normally not affected by a single corporate asset.

> A defect in some of the cars of the corporation, or in a product which is stored in the corporation's warehouse, does not entitle the Purchaser to claim under this warranty.

However, if the corporation is affected by a relevant defect, which is unknown to the purchaser, and of which he had no reason to be aware at the time the sale agreement was entered into, that defect may be relevant. This does not aim to detract from the distinction to be made between the sale of shares and the sale of corporate assets. To the contrary, it is based on the fact that the share embodies the participation to the corporation, and the purchaser of a share has in mind becoming owner of a part of that corporation considered as a *universitas rerum*.

If that *universitas* is totally different from what was to be expected, one may rely on *aliud pro alio*. The principle should not change if the difference, rather than being total, consists of a defect.

For example A purchases from B 100 per cent of the shares of corporation C, which owns a skyscraper as its only asset. A finds out shortly after the sale—to the surprise of both parties—that the skyscraper is affected by a defect in its

173 D. Rubino, *La compravendita, Op. cit.* at 607.

174 Panzarini, *La tutela dell' acquirente nella vendita di titoli, Op. cit.* 370.

175 Corrado, "I contratti di borsa" (Stock Exchange contracts), 2nd ed, in *Tratt. dir. civ.* (Vassalli, Torino, 1960), 391.

176 Segré, "Questioni riguardanti titoli al portatore emessi all'estero rubati e falsificati nei numeri progressivi", (Issue abroad of stolen and forged bearer shares) *Riv. dir. comm.* (1917), II, 328 e ss.

177 Weiss, "Il compratore in buona fede e l'evizione e la responsabilità per vizi nel' acquisto di titoli di credito", (The Good Faith Purchaser, eviction and liability for defects in sales of negotiable instruments) in *Nuova riv. dir. comm.*, (1950), I, 229–241.

178 In this sense, the corporate net worth.

foundations which produces the result that the weight which the foundations can bear must be reduced. In consequence of this only 70 per cent of the skyscraper's space can be used. It is submitted that this defect affects the corporation, and consequently the right of the holder of its shares to participate to it and that it might be treated by the purchaser as a defect, ie a lower value of the participation to that corporation which he intended to purchase and which he has indeed purchased.

As it has been held in *Bonini* v *Ronchieri*[179] the purchaser of shares acquires them merely as a means to become shareholder of that corporation and its main reason for doing so is normally the financial benefit which it expects from it.

Another situation which may trigger the warranty is:

> Corporation A has large labour disputes which appreciably diminish the efficiency of its staff, and consequently its value.

Likewise,

> The factory of Corporation A (the shares of which have been sold) which is its main item, is not in good condition and this considerably decreases its value.

Similarly,

> Corporation A has manufacturing problems which reduce considerably its value.

Likewise,

> Corporation A is a real estate corporation. It turns out that all its buildings are in very bad maintenance condition. This decreases the value of the corporation.

It has been held that this may not support a claim for annulment of the sale on the ground of mistake, since the lower value of a corporation does not fall within the category of a quality of the shares which are being sold. However the sale of shares of a different corporation from the one which was intended by the purchaser entitles the purchaser to complain for sale of *aliud pro alio*. If the shares concern a corporation, which is not different from the intended one, but defective, one may wonder why the purchaser would not be entitled to complain for that defect of that corporation.

9.2.2 In sales of on-going businesses

In a sale of an on-going business, the warranty of absence of defects applies to the business itself and to its assets.

9.2.3 In direct sales of shares between the parties

The prevailing opinion among writers limits this warranty to defects in the holder's right to exercise his position of shareholder. This view is shared by the general approach of precedents to the issue of quality of the corporate assets, even if no specific precedent relates to this warranty.

It is suggested that defects of the corporation, (be they defects which interfere with its corporate structure, or functioning, or make it difficult to run it, or defects

[179] Court of Cassation, 10 February, No 338 [1967] *Dir. fall* (1967), 475.

as to its value), may be relevant from the point of view of warranty. A lower net worth, for example by 50 per cent may not be totally irrelevant. This concern is echoed in *Mauro* v *Martinotti*:[180]

> One cannot avoid to notice that the value of a corporate asset undoubtedly contributes to form the value of the share.

Although the Court then, in view of the difficulty in establishing the value of the shares, refused to conclude that the sale of the shares involved a promise as to their quality.

Admittedly, when the way the sale price has been calculated is not known, a further difficulty will arise in establishing the financial consequences of the defects. Inevitably, the position will depend very much on the circumstances of the single transaction. Although a detailed breakdown of the computation of the purchase price would more accurately and easily take into account the consequences of the defect, a lump sum sale price which is not linked to the balance sheet or to another firm reference, and which frequently has a subjective mark up on the top of the book value, will give rise to evaluation problems.

Furthermore, defects will not be a basis for a warranty action if they have been taken into account by the purchaser or the purchaser could have detected them easily.

9.2.4 In sales of shares in the stock exchange

It is submitted that, even in stock exchange transactions, defects of the corporation may be relevant not only in case of *aliud pro alio* but also in case of a "defective" corporation.

In these transactions the price determination mechanism is entirely based on the offer and its acceptance. In spite of that, some mechanism to reduce the sale price, depending on the circumstances, might be taken into account. For example, one could establish the ratio between the book value resulting from the last audited balance sheet and the market value based on the sale price. One could then adjust the book value in consequence of the defect of the corporation and then apply the above established ratio to the revised book value.

9.2.5 In sales of parts of limited liability corporations

The warranty of absence of defects seems to apply to sales of parts of limited liability coporations as well as to sales of shares.

9.2.6 In transfers of interest in partnership

The warranty of absence of defects does not apply to assignments of interest in partnerships. In the absence of a contractual warranty, the assignee should have difficulties in basing his claim on the law of contract, since the specific statutory provisions on assignments of contract do not provide a statutory warranty remedy.

[180] Court of Appeal of Milan 5 June, [1990] *Giust civ* 1, II, 387.

10. Statutory Warranty of Merchantable Quality

10.1 The Ambit of the Warranty

The warranty of merchantable quality aims to protect the purchaser against what has been defined by writers as[181] a "lack of contractual requirements" while in *Gingliano* v *Fondiaria*[182] and in *Prenestina Costruzioni* v *Giacomazza*[183] it has been defined as goods belonging, by nature or because of component elements, to a *species* (type) different from the agreed one. This, as well as other definitions, creates risk of confusion.

It has been suggested[184] that the category of lack of quality may remain homogenous only if its notion remains centred on the concept of quality as a merit of the goods, consisting of a desired characteristic of the goods. In this way the lack of quality remains separate from defects, which are, as held in *Fico* v *Sovera*[185] a deficiency of the sold asset.

Qualities covered by the statutory warranty are those essential for normal use as well as promised qualities, ie qualities expressly provided for in the sale agreement. The statutory warranties will be dealt with first.

10.2 The Warranty and the Various Corporate Acquisitions

10.2.1 Applicability of this warranty to corporate acquisitions

The applicability of the statutory warranty of merchantable quality to the value of the corporation is excluded in corporate acquisitions, both by the doctrine of assignment of contract and by the doctrine of transfer of a negotiable instrument. Panzarini,[186] while dealing jointly with defects and lack of quality, is of the view that they can both exist limitedly to the holder's right to exercise its status of shareholder. He then treats the affidavit, (which some banks outside Italy issue to the purchaser, and which contains the history of that share), as a quality of the share even if it arises from a separate statement. Even the listing of the share in the stock exchange is seen as a quality of the share.

As to precedents, in *Bonini* v *Ronchieri*[187] the providing by the vendor of the balance sheet of the corporation, at the time of the sale of the shares, is treated as a quality of the share (a promise as to the sold shares):

> if by quality one means an element which characterises the *res*, in order that it becomes more apt to suit the concrete needs of the purchaser, based on the common financial and social needs.

[181] Mirabelli, "Dei singoli contratti", (Specific Contracts) *Commentario Scialoja e Branca*, Vol. II, (Turin, 1967), at 1605.

[182] Court of Cassation, 13 February, No 452 [1973] *Racc. Dec. Cass.* item *Vendita* (Sale) 9773, No 30.

[183] Court of Cassation, 20 April, No 1141 [1973] *Racc. Dec. Cass.* item *Vendita* (Sale) 9779, No 31.

[184] Rubino-Sammartano, *Lack of Conformity, Op. cit.*, at 225.

[185] Court of Cassation, 3 December, No 2544 [1970] *Rep. Foro It.*, (1971), item *Vendita* (Sale) 88.

[186] Panzarini, *La tutela dell' acquirente nella vendita dei titoli di credito, Op. cit.* 371.

[187] Court of Cassation, 10 February, No 338 [1967] *Dir. fall.*, (1967), 475.

The acknowledgment that this is a quality of the share, fortifies the previously expressed view, since it is a quality concerning the value of the share. If so, even the other qualities, as well as the defects relating to its value, should be taken into account.

However in *Bastogi* v *Alifin Italiana*[188] the Court held that the lower value of the shares, due to the discovery of an undisclosed liability, does not amount to a lack of quality for the purposes of the statutory warranty and that the mere mention of the net worth of a corporation does not by itself mean that the net worth is warranted to be the precise result of corporate accounts.

Furthermore, in *Cremaleasing* v *Sarcem*[189] it has been held that

> in case of a sale of shares, the lower value of the same because of liabilities ignored by the purchaser; may not be treated as a hidden defect. The warranty of lack of quality is not a natural effect of a sale of shares.

This confirms the general tendency, which it is suggested, should not be followed, to exclude the warranties of absence of defects and of lack of quality as to the value of the shares.

10.2.2 In sales of on-going businesses

In sales of on-going businesses, the warranty against lack of quality applies to the business itself and to its assets.

10.2.3 In direct sales of shares between the parties

The prevailing opinion is that this statutory warranty does not apply to the value of the shares. It is suggested that, to the contrary—as discussed earlier—qualities apply not only to the share itself, seen as an instrument (such as its listing in the stock exchange), but also to the qualities of the corporation and consequently to its *net worth*, while the warranty does not admittedly apply to the quality of one or more given assets (unless they are so important as to effect the corporate net worth).

This view is confirmed by the ruling in *Bonini* v *Ronchieri*,[190] which in a situation where a non-statutory warranty had been given, it was held that the matter was governed by the subcategory "promised qualities" of the statutory provisions on lack of quality.

When one moves from principles to their practical application, the two above-mentioned subcategories have to be examined closer. As to promised qualities, one is not facing a totally statutory warranty. While the warranties of clear title and of absence of defects are automatically governed by statutory provisions, the promised quality is voluntary, rather than an automatic consequence of the legal system. Once that promise is made, the statutory provisions automatically deal with its consequences, unless the party, by voluntarily undertaking that warranty, has gone further and has added to the statutory provisions as to the consequences of its possible breach.

[188] Court of Milan, 17 April, [1989] in *Acquisizioni di società* at 65.
[189] Court of Milan, 20 April, [1989] in *Acquisizioni di società, Op. cit.* at 64.
[190] See *supra* at note 187.

The promised quality consequently shares elements belonging to voluntary and to statutory warranties. In view of the voluntary nature of the promise, it shall be dealt with in a subsequent section as a contractual warranty.

As to the other subcategory of this warranty, represented by qualities essential for the normal use of the sold item, the distinction between it and a deficiency of the sold item requires careful examination. Such a problem exists also in sales of shares, where it may be even less easy to identify essential qualities.

10.2.4 In sales of shares in the stock exchange

In theory it is suggested that the lack of a quality of the corporation, the shares of which are sold, goes beyond mere defects of that corporation and amounts to *aliud pro alio*. In practice it may not be easy to establish the lack of an essential quality, and one should not forget that the majority opinion does not recognise a statutory warranty for lack of quality in sales of shares.

10.2.5 In sales of parts of limited liability corporations

The warranty of lack of quality seems to apply to sales of parts of limited liability corporations in the same way as to sales of shares.

10.2.6 In transfers of interest in partnership

A transfer of an interest in a partnership being treated as an assignment of contract, the transferor's statutory warranty is governed by the assignment of contract and, under section 1420 of the Civil Code, is limited to the validity of the contract, while the issue of the further warranty that the contract will be performed, is left to the free decision of the parties.

The statutory warranty, if examined in a restrictive way, would simply mean that the transferor must only warrant that the contract is not invalid. However, upon closer examination, one may be inclined to consider that this formalistic distinction does not apply so easily to a transfer of interest in a partnership. First, matters in a partnership tend to be less formal than in companies. Furthermore, one cannot confine the notion of validity of the contract to compliance with formal legal requirements.

It is suggested that validity should include the capacity of the contract to produce results, ie that the partner obtains financial results from the partnership.

If there is an *aliud pro alio* situation, the assignee of that interest seems entitled to complain. Likewise if the corporation is "defective" or lacks a quality essential to it, even this might be seen as affecting the validity of the assigned interest.

11. The Subjective Element and Warranties: Mistake; Fraud; Lack of Commonly Assumed Factual Basis

11.1 The Subjective Element and the Warranties

Up to this point, our attention has been focused on the objective element. However, the importance of the subjective element is not meant to be disregarded. The subjective element plays a different role in warranties as compared with an action for annulment of contract.

In a warranty, knowledge by the purchaser is relevant in several situations. The purchaser's knowledge that the purchased item was not owned by the vendor deprives the purchaser of the right to rescind the contract.[191] Likewise, the purchaser is entitled to rescind the contract or to claim a price reduction only if he was unaware of the existence of a pledge, lien or other burden on the purchased asset.[192]

Similarly, the warranty of absence of defects does not apply if the purchaser was aware of the defect, or if it could be easily identified, except if the seller has expressly confirmed the absence of defects.[193]

The above situations deal with the subjective position of the purchaser as an element which does not trigger the warranty or reduces its effects. The subjective element plays a minor role as to the vendor, since the warranty works even in the absence of the vendor's fault.

However, the vendor's lack of care generally plays a role as to the consequences of breach of warranty. The vendor is consequently under a duty to reimburse all the costs incurred by the purchaser, even the unnecessary ones, if the vendor was in bad faith.[194] Furthermore, even if the warranty of clear title has been excluded, the vendor is liable when title is challenged because of the vendor's act, and any contrary agreement is null and void.[195] Likewise in warranties of absence of defects, the exclusion of the warranty is not valid as to the defects which the vendor has hidden in bad faith.[196]

Without prejudice to the other remedies available to the purchaser, the vendor is liable for damages unless he proves that he did not know and, in the exercise of normal care, should not have known that the sold item was defective.[197]

The position is quite different if one moves from the area of warranties to the area of a mistake by the purchaser, which affects the purchase agreement, or of fraud by the vendor.

11.1.1 Vitiating elements

Here the general law of contract applies, providing for annulment of the contract. Mistake and fraud shall be considered next, leaving aside the rather rare situations of duress.

11.2 Mistake

The sale contract may be set aside when the consent of one of the parties was vitiated by mistake. For this purpose, mistake must be recognisable by the other contracting party and essential.[198] It is recognisable, when it can be detected by using the normal care, regard having been had to the circumstances and to the quality of the contracting parties.[199]

[191] Section 1479 of the Civil Code.
[192] Section 1489 of the Civil Code.
[193] Section 1491 of the Civil Code.
[194] Section 1479 of the Civil Code.
[195] Section 1487 of the Civil Code.
[196] Section 1490 of the Civil Code.
[197] Section 1494 of the Civil Code.
[198] Section 1428 of the Civil Code.
[199] Section 1431 of the Civil Code.

It is essential when it concerns the nature or the object of the contract, the identity of the performance to be made under it, or a quality of the same, or the identity or a quality of the other contracting party, if decisive for that party's consent or, if it is an error in law, if it has been the only, or the main reason for that party's consent.[200]

As far as sales of shares are concerned, the prevailing opinion is that a mistake on the value of the corporation does not amount to an "essential" mistake within the meaning of the above quoted statutory provisions, since it does not concern a quality of the shares, but of the corporation. This view is expressed by Ferri,[201] Greco,[202] and Romano-Pavoni[203] while it is opposed by Ascarelli[204] who is of the view that matters affecting the corporate assets cannot be automatically excluded from the area of the qualities of shares, and also by Nicolo'.[205] Among precedents, a mistake on the value of the shares was held not to be essential in *Baldovino* v *Cova e Soc. Rosier.*[206]

It is submitted that the lack of value of the shares, or their much lower value, may not be always irrelevant, as the opposite doctrine suggests.

In *Rancilio* v *Parrini*[207] it was held that a mistake on the value of the shares would not be recognisable by the vendor, since such a value is based on subjective and not on objective criteria. This view was shared by Nicolo'.[208] In some situations this view might be correct, while in others it would not; one may consequently not exclude at all times that the mistake be recognisable.

In *Comune di Trento* v *Isap*[209] the Court of Cassation has held that if there is an unbalance between the sale price of the shares and their value, the only remedy available would be the setting aside of the contract based on the unbalance if that party has entered into the contract in a state of need or danger.[210]

Since this remedy may apply only if there is a special element, consisting of a state of need or of danger, this does not necessarily deprive a contracting party of the right, granted by the law of contract, to attack a contract, if there is a mistake. In other words, the remedy of setting aside the contract due to unbalance should not been seen as excluding the different remedy of annulment of the contract due to mistake as to the value of the shares.

200 Section 1429 of the Civil Code.
201 G. Ferri, *Le società, Op. cit.*, p. 493.
202 Greco, "Le società di comodo e la vendita delle lorgo azioni", *Riv. dir. comm.*, (1935), II 133.
203 Romano-Pavoni, "In tema di azioni e quote di società: vendita di aliud pro alio", (Corporate shares and *quotas*: sale of *aliud pro alio*) in *Banca Borsa e Titoli di Credito*, (1963), 1627.
204 Ascarelli, in *Foro It.*, (1935), 1627.
205 Nicolo', "Vendita di azioni e errore sul prezzo", (Sale of shares and mistake as to their price), *Banca Borsa e Titoli di Credito*, (1936), II, 1656.
206 Court of Cassation, 16 February, No 721 [1977] *Foro It.*, 1977, 1, 2275.
207 Court of Appeal, Milan, 13 April, [1951] *Foro It.*, 1951, 1, 607.
208 Nicolo', see *supra* note 205.
209 Court of Cassation, 24 April, No 1249, [1968] *Foro It.*, 1968, 1, 1457.
210 A remedy admitted under Italian law, and by some other civil law systems.

11.3 Common Ground and Distinctions between Breach of Warranty of Merchantable Quality and Mistake

There is a breach of the warranty of merchantable quality when the sold item lacks a quality, which is essential for its use, or a promised quality. The purchaser's mistake is relevant when it concerns a quality which, based on the specific circumstances of the sale or on general assessment, was decisive for the purchaser's consent. According to the general opinion, qualities which are decisive for any purchaser, amount to a quality essential for the use of the sold item.

As to the second category of qualities, relevant for the warranty of merchantable quality, ie those promised by the vendor, if the purchaser requests that the vendor warrants a given quality, this shows that such a quality was important for him and—depending on the circumstances—may be seen as decisive for the purchaser. Therefore, in general, the qualities, the absence of which gives rise to a breach of warranty and to a mistake, are in substance the same. One might draw from this the conclusion that, if any of such qualities is absent, the purchaser has both remedies at its disposal. However, mistake and breach of warranty are not compatible and there may be either mistake or breach of warranty.

When there has been a mistake, the purchaser is entitled to receive goods which are different from the ones which he ordered. Annulment because of that mistake (which allows the purchaser to receive not the goods contracted for, but the goods, different from the ones which he ordered, which in reality he wanted) avoids this consequence by setting aside the sale agreement.

For example, contractor A purchases from supplier B iron bars to reinforce concrete. Believing the diameter of the bars to be smaller, the contractor orders bars the diameter of which is rejected for this reason by the engineer. In this situation, the contractor has received exactly what it had ordered but not the steel to reinforce concrete which he intended to buy. His intention was consequently affected by mistake on a decisive quality, and the supplier was in a position to recognise it, being in the trade. The sale contract may be set aside because of mistake.

When, on the other hand, there is a breach of warranty, the delivered goods are different from the contracted ones, (ie from those which the purchaser intended to purchase). For example, contractor A orders to supplier B iron bars having a certain diameter, after seeing them in the supplier's warehouse. The supplier warrants that those bars have the required diameter. The supplier delivers bars not having that diameter. Even if the contractor made a mistake during his inspection, that mistake is superseded by the supplier's warranty. This is consequently a case of breach of warranty.[211]

11.4 Fraud

As reported by Bonelli[212] there is a consensus amongst authors that even a contract for the sale of shares may be set aside if there has been fraud by the

[211] An analysis of the relationship between breach of warranty and mistake, as well as the above examples, are due to Amorth, *Errore e inadempimento nel contratto* (Mistake and breach of contract), (Giuffre', 1967), at 92.

[212] Bonelli, *Op. cit.* at 22.

vendor. This was affirmed in *Mecheri* v *Finanziaria Italo-Britannica*[213] where the existence of fraud by the vendor was established, since he had not disclosed the existence of administrative proceedings aiming to expropriate the only asset of the corporation which he had sold.

11.5 Contract Entered into in State of Need or Danger

A sale contract, as the other contracts, may be set aside, if—as discussed earlier—it was entered into in a state of need or danger, which caused that party to accept the unbalance between the respective performances.[214]

This is exactly what happened in *Cerruti* v *Tedeschi*[215] where the owners of the shares of a corporation, who were of Jewish religion, sold them at a much lower price since, under the anti-jewish legislation enacted at that time, they could no longer own them and were obliged to sell them, rather than having them confiscated. The Court of Cassation has ruled that such a remedy exists even in sales of shares, remitting the case to another court of appeal to establish whether the complained of unbalance existed.

11.6 Failure of the Basic Premises of the Meeting of the Minds

The doctrine of the basic premise of the contract is based on the old rule of Roman law, referred to as *rebus sic stantibus* (ie on the basis of the existing situation).[216] The change of the external basic factual situation presumed by both parties has been held to entitle the parties to terminate the contract. In order for such basic premise to be relevant, it must be:

- external to the parties;
- factual;
- inferrable from the contract, even in the absence of an express reference to them;
- it must have failed, independently of the parties.

This remedy, which for a long time was denied, was eventually allowed by the Court of Cassation. Among the precedents in favour of it are *Venini* v *Orio*[217] and *Turcotti* v *Barberis and others.*[218] Bonelli[219] refers also to an award[220] which held that in theory this remedy would be available also to sales of shares.

12. Sale of *Aliud Pro Alio*

As it was discussed earlier, there is a sale of *aliud pro alio*, whenever the vendor delivers an item which is different from the agreed one. This means that it must

213 Court of Appeal, Rome, 21 July [1933] *Riv. dir. com.*, (1933) II, 121.
214 Sections 1447 and 1448 of the Civil Code.
215 Court of Cassation, 14 February, No 325 [1963] *Giust. Civ.*, (1963), I, 743.
216 See Yelpaala–Rubino-Sammartano–Campbell, *Drafting and Enforcing Contracts in Civil and Common Law Jurisdictions*, (Kluwer, 1986), at 69.
217 Court of Cassation, 9 May, No 3074 [1981] *Mass. Foro It.*, 1, 621.
218 Court of Cassation, 3 October, No 2829 [1972] *Mass. Foro It.*, (1972), 856.
219 Bonelli, *Op. cit.* at 24.
220 Rendered on 14 March, 1986 quoted in Bonelli, *Op. cit.* at 82.

not be just a matter of a defect or of a lack of quality, but of a basic difference.

Aliud pro alio applies when the item to be sold is different from the agreed one, without any mistake having been made by the purchaser, because in this case it would become a matter of annulment of the contract by mistake. The remedies in actions for *aliud pro alio* are provided for by the general law of contract, ie specific performance or rescission and/or damages.

12.1 In Sales of On-going Businesses

Aliud pro alio applies to sales of on-going businesses as to the sale of any other item.

12.2 In Direct Sales of Shares between the Parties

Aliud pro alio applies even to direct sales of shares. In *Nironi* v *Bonacchi*[221] the vendor had warranted that the corporation, the shares of which were being sold, had certain characteristics and owned an industrial plant. After the closing, it turned out that the corporation did not have those characteristics and that the plant was not working, so that the corporation could not be used for industrial purposes. The Court of Cassation held that the sold shares were an *aliud pro alio*, and went further holding that the contract could be set aside.

Even if this was a case of a voluntary (ie contractual) warranty, this precedent shows that the *aliud pro alio* doctrine is applicable to sales of shares. Many writers have criticised the decision, on the ground that defects of the corporation would not amount to defects or lack of quality of the shares.[222] Similarly, in case of a sale of a corporation which is known for a patent, if that patent is declared null and void during the sale or immediately after it, the corporation becomes different from the one contemplated by the parties and that may amount to an *aliud pro alio*.

12.3 In Sales of Shares in the Stock Exchange

It might seem that there is no room for *aliud pro alio* in sales in the stock exchange. However, it is submitted that this is not the case. For example, A instructs its broker to purchase 500,000 shares of Hilton Ruritania Ltd which owns the Ruritania Hilton Hotel. The broker purchases the shares in the stock exchange. It turns out that Hilton Ruritania Ltd Hotel's licence had been withdrawn that very day. The sold shares were then not the shares of a corporation running a hotel.

Another example is: a Canadian Company instructs its broker to purchase at the Tokyo stock exchange shares of a Japanese Insurance Company. After the sale has taken place, it turns out that the Japanese Government had just withdrawn its licence to that corporation to run insurance business (or to deal with a given major area of that business). Here too the sold shares were different

[221] Court of Cassation, 28 August, No 2784 [1952] *Foro It.*, (1953), 1, 1639, with comments by Ascarelli.

[222] Amongst such authors see Panzarini, *Op. cit.* at 290; and Romano-Pavoni, Comments to this judgment, *Banca Borsa e Titoli di Credito*, (1953), II, 150.

from the agreed ones. Therefore, *aliud pro alio* seems then to apply in both situations.

12.4 In Sales of Parts of a Limited Liability Corporation

Aliud pro alio seems to apply to parts of limited liability corporations as well as to sales of shares.

12.5 In Transfers of Interest in Partnerships

It is submitted that *aliud pro alio* applies also in this instance. A owns an interest in a partnership, which trades as stock exchange broker and transfers it to B. It turns out that, just before the transfer, the Stock Exchange has withdrawn its authorisation to the partnership to trade as brokers. The argument that the partnership agreement existed and was valid from a legal point of view would seem to be no defence against a claim for *aliud pro alio*.

There is *aliud pro alio* also if A sells to B, through brokers, shares of a corporation which has just been declared bankrupt.

As discussed earlier, *aliud pro alio* is not a warranty but a normal breach of contract. The vendor answers in case of breach for any difference between the agreed and the transferred shares. This involves no objective liability.

13. Contractual Warranties

13.1 General and Special Warranties

The contents of a voluntary, ie a contractual, warranty are a consequence of the parties' freedom to contract. Their variety and their great number is another main characteristic. The first distinction to be made among warranties is between general and specific warranties: a general warranty is a comprehensive warranty which aims to assure the purchaser that the corporation, the shares of which are sold, has a given global situation. An example of which is there is a general warranty when the vendor warrants, for example, the net worth of the sold corporation; he is then subject to the duty to pay to the purchaser the possibly negative difference which should result between the effective net worth of the corporation and the warranted one.

By comparison, each specific warranty aims to assure the purchaser—as the term states—as to a specific situation.

13.2 Classes of Contractual Warranties

Before examining the contractual warranties in detail, it may be useful to distinguish them in several classes such as:

(a) warranties of proper functioning and of good standing;
(b) warranties as to the transfer of the shares;
(c) warranties as to the corporate financial conditions;
(d) warranties as to the corporate profitability;
(e) warranties as to the corporate operational conditions;
(f) warranties as to the conduct of the corporate business until the closing;
(g) warranties of no materially adverse financial change.

13.3 Warranties as to the Transfer of the Shares

The first class of warranties aims merely to strengthen, to widen or to repeat the statutory warranty of clear title. Such warranties consequently relate to the absence of pre-emption rights, of corporate agreements restricting the sale, of other sale agreements as well as to the absence of statutory provisions or other commitments which prevent or limit the shares' transferability.

13.4 Warranty of Proper Functioning (and Warranty of Good Standing)

The warranty of proper functioning, which is expressly regulated,[223] is traditionally a warranty related to goods. It applies, for example, to the functioning of a computer system or of an engine.

For those who limit the deal to the transfer of a valid document, (which represents the position of a party to the contract which has formed and keeps the corporation alive) it would be inconceivable to adjust it to a sale of shares. Such an adjustment is difficult even for those who do not share this doctrine. Nevertheless, nothing seems to prevent the vendor from warranting that the corporation functions properly.

The so-called legal warranties aim exactly to that. This is the warranty that the company is duly organised and existing (which is also referred to as warranty of good standing), and that it has complied with all applicable regulations and provisions.

The vendor may also warrant the operational functioning of the corporation. This will be made either through a general warranty or through specific warranties. This last aspect will be dealt with in the following paragraph.

13.5 Warranties as to the Corporate Financial Conditions

The most known warranty as to the corporate financial conditions relates to:

- the existence of the assets resulting from the financial conditions and from their breakdown;
- the inexistence of greater or undisclosed liabilities in respect of the financial conditions and of their breakdown.

While even only one of such warranties may be agreed upon, it is frequent that both be given. However, even if these warranties are quite comprehensive, they may not provide sufficient protection to the purchaser if they are not combined with a third warranty: that the assets and liabilities have been correctly assessed.

If this third warranty were left in such general terms, it might be insufficient, since it would leave a large margin to different subjective criteria to assess them. A reference will consequently be generally found to an objective criterion. This may be the generally accepted accounting principles, or consistency with the criteria followed in the previous fiscal years.

[223] Section 1512 of the Civil Code.

An even wider protection may be achieved by adding to the first criterion that any dispute between the parties will be finally settled by an auditing firm of absolute, direct and indirect, neutrality both at the time of its appointment[224] and at the time the dispute arises. This warranty is particularly significant since the purchaser requires precise information as to the existing financial situation and to be covered, in case of differences arising in respect of it.

In turn the vendor, once the purchaser accepts that the sale be based on such a financial situation, is protected against possible subsequent claims, which are inconsistent with such an agreement. However, if the warranty stops at this stage, one aspect of this matter may remain open to disputes.

In fact, in case of transfers of shares which involve directly or indirectly the control of the corporation, once the purchaser takes over its management, it may run it in a different way. This may reflect on non-collection of credits resulting from the warranted financial situation, or on the arising, or increasing, of liabilities.

As to collection of credits, for example, the purchaser may, for various reasons, be of the view that it is not worth insisting to collect certain credits, or may approach the customer in a different and negative way, or may decide to give up a part of the old credits in order to obtain new contracts. It may consequently be useful to provide that the purchaser's right under this warranty be conditional upon compliance with given guidelines or more vaguely upon a uniformity of policy being respected.

Here too, in case of doubt, the difference should be resolved through arbitration, by someone expert in business management, more than in the law, or by a panel including also a neutral business manager.

The vendor may try to obtain an even wider protection by introducing a limit, below which the possibly lower value will not entitle to make a claim. This is an alternative to, or combined with, setting off negative differences with positive differences, since such a limit[225] should provide a wider protection to the vendor.

One may come across more specific warranties as to single items of the financial conditions. Different types of assets are analysed; for instance, warehouses, immoveables, receivables, shares of other corporations. For a warehouse, its value is frequently warranted with reference to a given accounting system. This warranty may be extended to the value of worked or semi-worked materials. Likewise it may extend to the absence of non-saleable or of slow-moving items. As to receivables, their amount and the absence of complaints or claims by the debtors are frequently warranted. Particularly when the purchaser has not already checked this, the vendor may warrant also that the receivables are due and payable. The immoveables give rise to various warranties as to their full and clear title, as to their maintenance conditions, as to compliance with building permits and regulations. The ownership by the corporation of a shareholding in another corporation, as well as its providing control over it, may also give rise to warranties.

[224] Preferably to take place at the time of the sale agreement.
[225] ie those situations in which a given asset or liability is respectively higher or lower.

13.6 Warranty as to Profitability

The profitability of the acquired shares being a mere consequence of the profitability of that corporation, is in reality a warranty as to profitability of the corporation. Such a warranty is very important and consequently most delicate. In fact, it is based both on past performance and on future expectations. Since the future may depend on many supervening political and other circumstances, it is practically impossible to assure future profits.

Already past profits are reluctantly warranted as such, ie as a specific item and not as part of the balance sheet, and even so with qualifications normally as to the criteria followed. Apart from any amount of future profits, the tendency of the corporation to produce profits in the future, in the absence of any negative supervening circumstances, is frequently a basic premise of acquisitions. Also the vendor, if requested, frequently would have no hesitation in asserting that the corporation of the shares of which he is selling will produce profits.

It follows that, while a warranty of precise profits cannot be expected, a warranty of profitability, subject to the absence of materially adverse changes, may not be automatically excluded.

13.7 Warranty as to Operational Conditions

Since the future of the acquired corporation does not depend exclusively on its accounts, but also on its operational conditions, warranties may concern even this separate aspect. Depending on the industry in which the corporation is trading, this warranty shall concern, *inter alia*—as to positive warranties—patents, trademarks, know-how, licences, plants, orders received, the commercial network, joint ventures, co-operation agreements, long-duration contacts, procurement contracts—and as to negative warranties—the absence of litigation, of tax claims, of environmental problems, of special labour contracts, of labour disputes, of rights of third parties. The practice shows a variety of such warranties, frequently with a certain minimum or maximum ceiling, with qualifications and with reference to some objective criterion to assess the effects of the warranty, and occasionally to assess mechanisms to resolve disputes.

13.8 Warranty as to the Conduct of the Business until the Closing

The above warranties provided at the time the sale agreement is entered into, frequently have to be combined with a warranty as to the conduct of the business in the period between the time the agreement is entered into and the closing. There is a similar need if the deal is structured through a promise to sell and to purchase[226] and the entering into of a sale agreement. Consequently a purchaser frequently negotiates a warranty to cover that time period.

There are different ways to express the vendor's duty during such period. One goes from a duty to conduct the corporate business in a way consistent with its previous management, to a reference to the diligence of the *bonus pater*

[226] In Italian *contratto preliminare.*

familias[227] to restrictions excluding extraordinary management to a duty to consult the purchaser, to a mechanism allowing quick decisions on the main issues to be made jointly by the parties or—if they disagree—by a neutral body. In a given situation, the breach of this warranty may just reduce the increase of business and still produce profits, even if lower than what they could have been, had the corporate business been handled otherwise.

In other circumstances the theoretically negative change, which would have been caused by a certain conduct of the corporate business, will be offset by positive results due to independent events, or to the vendor's action in other areas.

The precise time at which compliance with this warranty is to be established, ie whether it is the closing or a subsequent moment, and if so which one, is also to be addressed by the parties.

13.9 Warranty of No Materially Adverse Change

The warranty of no material adverse change between the promise to sell and the sale, or between the sale agreement and the closing, covers the same area of the warranty related to the conduct of the business. However, while through the warranty of conduct the vendor undertakes to maintain a certain conduct, the warranty of no material adverse change applies if the change occurs even if the vendor's conduct is unreproachable.

Here too, the determination of the adverse change, its materiality, its exclusion in case of events beyond the vendor's reasonable control, the effects of the combination of this warranty with the warranty related to the conduct of the business, the possible offsetting between adverse and positive changes or conducts, all should be taken into account and a mechanism to determine it and to resolve disputes should be considered.

13.10 The Contractual Warranties in the Various Types of Acquisitions and in Sales of On-going Businesses

Contractual warranties are perfectly feasible in acquisitions.

13.10.1 In direct sales between the parties

Contractual warranties are quite frequently agreed upon for sales of shares which are of significance either from the point of view of the control of the corporation or, even if not, because of their intrinsic value.

13.10.2 In sales of shares in the stock exchange

To the contrary, contractual warranties are not to be found in stock exchange transactions, because of the very way in which such transactions are consummated, ie through brokers merely consenting as to price.

13.10.3 In sales of parts of limited liability corporations

There is no obstacle to contractual warranties being agreed upon even in sales of parts of limited liability corporations.

[227] ie the care of a good father in dealing with his family's matters.

13.10.4 In transfers of interest in partnerships

In transfers of interest in partnerships, contractual warranties may well be inserted.

Finally, subject to the subsequent comments as to exclusions or restrictions,[228] the parties' freedom to contract finds no obstacle in this area, except for stock exchange transactions, and here too merely because of the way they are consummated.

14. Form Requirements

14.1 Written Form and Shares Sale Agreement

The form of the warranty is very closely linked to the form of the shares sale agreement. As to the form of the latter, a distinction is to be made between the agreement to sell shares and the transfer of title to them.

The sale agreement—according to the prevailing opinion—would not be subject to any form requirement, but would produce only the duty to transfer title to the shares. See *Masaero* v *Giacchero.*[229]

This view seems to be in line with the tendency to dematerialise share certificates, which is expressed also by a recent enactment[230] related to share certificates, which gives to the banks, which have been delivered shares under a safekeeping agreement, the possibility to deposit them with an *ad hoc* corporation, *Monte Titoli.*

The transfer of title requires the delivery of the shares and the *transfert*, ie the double registration of the name of the purchaser both on the share certificate and on the corporate ledger book. An alternative to the double registration is represented by the endorsement of the shares, followed by the registration of this on the corporate ledger book. See *Columella* v *Palcani,*[231] *Levis* v *Fall. Cassinese*[232] and *Masoero* v *Giacchero.*[233] This is also held, amongst the writers, by Ferrara,[234] Visentini,[235] and Mengoni.[236]

This provision is not in line with section 1376 of the Civil Code, which requires just the meeting of the minds of the parties for the transfer of title, and of section 1378, as to unidentified fungible assets, which requires their identification or compliance with the transfer procedures set out by the parties. The general rules have then been modified, as far as the transfer of title to the shares is concerned, by the specific rules related to the transfer of shares.

228 See *supra* section 7.
229 Court of Cassation, 28 April, No 2557 [1981] *Giust. Civ. Mass.*, (1981) at 966.
230 Statute 19 June, 1986, No 289 (*Monte Titoli S.p.A.*).
231 Court of Cassation, 22 January, [1949] *Banca Borsa e Titoli di Credito*, (1949), II, 222.
232 Court of Cassation, 26 June, No 1534 [1961] *Mass. Giur. It.*, (1961), 662.
233 Court of Cassation, 28 April, No 2557 [1981] *Mass. Giur. It.*, (1981), 966.
234 Ferrara, *La girata* (The endorsement) at 428.
235 Visentini, "Azioni di società". (Corporate shares) *Enciclopedia dell Diritto*, (Milan, 1959), 996.
236 Mengoni, "La regola 'Possesso vale Titolo' nella circolazione dei titoli di credito", (The rule: Possession is Title in the circulation of negotiable instruments), *Banca Borsa e Titoli di Credito*, (1949), I, 28.

A further consequence of the distinction between the shares sale agreement and the transfer of title is that the shares may be transferred by their mere endorsement which produces effects only between the parties. Only when the shares, bearing that endorsement, are presented to the corporation and the latter registers on its shareholders' ledger book the name of the last endorsee, the transfer produces effects *vis-à-vis* the corporation.

It has also been debated whether, in case of two purchasers, one through a registration of his title on the corporate ledger book and the other one through an endorsement of the share certificates and their delivery to the purchaser, the former or the latter would prevail. It was held that the latter should prevail since the former, not having delivered the shares, would have not purchased them.

In consequence of the entering into force of Statute 29 December, 1962, No 1741, the registration of title on the corporate ledger book is not even necessary in order to be entitled to attend a shareholders' meeting. To this effect the mere filing of the shares certificates is sufficient, since the corporation must make note of the transfer and record it on the ledger book However, this change is not meant to modify the requirements for the transfer of title, which consequently remain unaltered.

One must eventually mention the *fissato bollato*, a transfer form which is to be issued in respect of the sale of shares, and which has the purpose to secure the payment of the stamp duty which is levied on transfers of shares.[237]

The form requirements as to warranties are consequently to be considered within the framework of the form requirements for sale agreements.

14.2 The Written Form of Warranties in the Various Types of Acquisitions

14.2.1 Warranties in sales of on-going businesses

Sale agreements of on-going businesses are to be filed with the Companies Registrar.[238] Warranties consequently seem to require the written form.

14.2.2 Direct sales of shares

Even if, as discussed earlier, there might be an oral sale agreement, nevertheless the transfer of title requires the written form. The oral warranty might then, in theory, be effective but would be difficult to prove, because of statutory limits to oral evidence of contracts.

It is arguable whether the issue of the *fissato bollato* (the transfer form) transforms an oral agreement into a written agreement that might affect also the form of the warranties. If one follows the view that the *fissato bollato* has exclusively the purpose of complying with tax requirements, it does not produce the result of obliging the parties, which have entered into an oral sale agreement, to repeat the various terms and conditions in written form.

When the sale agreement is in writing, even the warranty requires the written form. Any alleged simultaneous or earlier oral warranty would not be allowed in evidence[239] under the general rule which does not allow evidence through

[237] Statute 20 December, 1932, No 1607, as subsequently amended.
[238] Section 2556 of the Civil Code.
[239] Section 2722 of the Civil Code.

witnesses of oral agreements simultaneous with, or earlier than a written agreement. Subsequent oral agreements may be allowed in evidence by the court, to the discretion of which this decision is left.[240] Contractual warranties should then be in writing at all times. In some situations this is even mandatory.

14.2.3 Sales in the stock exchange

Here traditionally sales take place orally and they are later followed by the endorsement of the shares either from the vendor's broker to the purchaser's broker, or directly to the purchaser, or to the *stanza di compensazione* (the clearing system).

Transfers to the *stanza di compensazione* are effected on the day which the stock exchange regulations set out each month for the settlement of the transactions consummated by each broker during the preceding month.

The transfer takes place by each broker delivering to the head of the clearing system a schedule showing the shares respectively sold and purchased by him, the so-called *stato di liquidazione* (statement of the financial results of such transactions, ie the cash amount due or to be collected) and as to each corporation, the quantity of shares, if any, which is the difference between his purchases and his sales.

Said shares are endorsed using the following formula: "to the Head of the Clearing System, and for him to. . . ." The Head of the Clearing System fills the endorsement with the name of the purchaser and certifies this insertion with the date and the stamp of the Clearing System.

This formula achieves the result of simplifying the circulation of the shares which, otherwise would have to be transferred from one vendor to his purchaser, from that purchaser to his own purchaser and so on. In such sales, traditionally, there is no room for contractural warranties. The only applicable warranties are consequently, as a rule, the statutory ones.

14.2.4 Warranties in sales of interest in partnerships

The sale of interest in partnerships is not dealt with by a specific statutory provision as to *società semplici*[241] and *società in nome collecttivo*,[242] while it is regulated as to *società in accomandita semplice*.[243]

The sale of an interest in the first two partnerships must take place by amending the partnership agreement, while as to the last type of partnership, it requires the consent of the partners who represent the majority of the partnership's capital. In all such situations the agreement must be in writing and the same requirement applies to the warranties.

[240] Section 2723 of the Civil Code.

[241] ie partnerships the scope of which is not commercial, and which can be amended, even as far as partners are concerned, only by consent of all partners (section 2251 of the Italian Civil Code).

[242] ie partnerships which may trade consisting only of fully liable partners, and which are governed by the statutory provisions of *società semplici*, as to matters statutorily not otherwise governed (section 2291 of the Italian Civil Code).

[243] Partnerships both with unlimitedly liable and with limitedly liable partners (section 2322 of the Italian Civil Code).

14.3 Further Formalities and Effects vis-à-vis the Corporation

The sale agreement, be it oral or written, is followed by the transfer or by like formalities. As discussed earlier, under recently enacted legislation[244] the sold shares rather than being physically delivered to the purchaser, may be delivered directly to the purchaser's bank, and deposited by the latter with an *ad hoc* corporation, *Monte Titoli S.p.A.* These formalities do not seem to affect the possible earlier, oral or written, warranties.

Warranties do not directly concern the corporation, since the latter is merely in the background of the sale. This may be different only if the management of the sold corporation issues direct warranties.

14.4 Acceptance of the By-laws

It has been argued that the purchase of shares implies the automatic acceptance of the corporate by-laws. This issue has been debated. On the one hand, express acceptance of the by-laws has been requested in *Carnevali* v *Ass. Romana Sincronizzatori*[245] and in *Biserni* v *Aldini*.[246]

On the other hand, it has been held that the acceptance of the by-laws is not subject to specific acceptance since, at least normally, they have not been prepared by the vendor nor entered into by using standard forms.

14.5 Specific Acceptance of Statutory Warranties—Exclusions or Restrictions

A situation different from the issue of contractual warranties exists when the parties aim to exclude or limit the statutory warranties. Here not only the written form is required, but the further requirement of specific acceptance exists. The purpose of this requirement is to protect the weaker contracting party, by providing that oppressive clauses are of no effect unless that party has known them or should have known them by using normal care.

To ensure this, oppressive clauses are mentioned specifically at the bottom of the agreement, after the parties' subscription, and such reference is to be accepted by subscribing a second time, below it and separately from the former subscription. Limitations of responsibility (such as exclusions or restrictions of statutory warranties) are among oppressive clauses and consequently need that specific acceptance to be valid.

15. Applicable Law Rules and Conflict of Laws Rules

15.1 The Traditional Italian Conflict Rules

The conflicts of laws rules are codified in the Italian legal system. The rule on the form of acts provides:[247]

[244] See *supra* note 230.
[245] Court of Cassation, 3 February, No 353 [1968] *Foro It.*, (1968), I, 3053.
[246] Court of Cassation, 19 February, No 1367 [1985] *Mass. Foro It.*, (1985), 270.
[247] Section 26, Preliminary Provisions to the Civil Code.

> The form requirements of transactions *inter vivos* (ie amongst existing persons or corporate bodies) and *mortis causa* (ie from successions) is governed by the law of the place where the transaction is performed or which governs the contents of the transaction, or by the national law of the party, or of the contracting parties, if common to them. The form of the publicity required in order to give origin to, to transfer or to extinguish, rights on an asset are governed by the law of the place where such asset is located.

As to the physical persons' or corporate bodies' capacity to act, the statutory provision states:[248]

> The status and the capacity of the persons and their family relationships are governed by the law of the State to which they belong. Nevertheless if a foreigner performs, in the territory of the Republic, a transaction for which he lacks capacity under his national law, he is treated as having such a capacity if under Italian law the Italian citizen has such a capacity, except in case of family relationships, of successions, of grants, or of sales of immoveables located outside Italy.

As to the contents of the contract, the traditional Italian rule[249] provides:

> The duties arising from a contract are governed by the national law of the contracting parties, if common to them; if not, by the law of the place where the contract has been entered into. In any event, the choice of the parties takes priority. Liability in tort is governed by the law of the place where the act, from which it derives, has taken place.

The choice of the parties is consequently the master criterion.

Aside from an express choice, the role of the *tacit* choice of the parties, which, on the one hand, excludes the part of their national laws which is different (and then normally unknown to them), and on the other hand, accepts the part of such national laws which is common to them, has been developed in Italy where the *tronc commun* (common body) doctrine was developed.[250]

15.2 International Conventions

The conflict rules have been affected by the international conventions.

15.2.1 The Hague (1955) Convention

The Hague (1955) Convention[251] recognises the right of the contracting parties to choose the law applicable to international sales of moveable goods. In the absence of their choice, it establishes that such sales are governed by the law of the State where the vendor operates. The law of the State where the purchaser operates applies only if the vendor has received the purchaser's order in the latter's State.

[248] Section 17, Preliminary Provisions to the Civil Code.

[249] Set forth in section 25, Preliminary Provisions to the Civil Code.

[250] See Rubino-Sammartano, *International Arbitration Law*, (Kluwer, 1990), at 274; and B. Ancel, "The Tronc Commun Doctrine: Logic and Experience in International Arbitration", in *Journal of International Arbitration* (1990), at 654.

[251] Convention concerning the Law Applicable to the International Sale of Moveable Goods, The Hague, 15 June, 1955.

The Hague (1955) Convention does not apply to sales of parts of limited liability companies, of interests in partnerships, of on-going businesses or to sales of shares. The first group of sales are excluded since they are not transactions on moveable goods, while sales of shares are expressly excluded since the Convention excludes[252] "*ventes de titres*" which includes share certificates.

15.2.2 The Rome (1980) Convention

The universality of the Convention is[253] generally asserted as arising from its provision[254] which states:

> The law designated by this Convention applies also if it is the law of a non-contracting State.

This inference does not seem correct.[255] But even if universality is not stated expressly, the Convention may be construed, based on its Article 11, and on its general purposes, as asserting it. It is submitted that the Convention's universality amounts to its being applicable, by each Member State, to any contract entered into it or into another adhering State, or in a non-Member-State but governed by the law of a Member State.

The Convention concerns only those contracts which have a foreign element, and are therefore international,[256] including those in which all the elements are localised in one country but the law of a different country has been chosen.

The Rome Convention mainly deals with the form and substance of contracts. However, the Convention does not apply[257] *inter alia* to:

> obligations arising from drafts, cheques, promissory notes and other negotiable instruments, when the obligations arising from them result from their negotiable character.

The Official Report on the Convention, which is due to Giuliano and Lagarde,[258] does not make any reference to shares, either to include or to exclude them. They may be excluded from the Convention as Giuliano and Lagarde suggest, if the classification of negotiable instruments is to be made *lege fori*.[259]

They seem not to be excluded from it, if one looks for a uniform solution, as advocated by the Convention itself,[260] and one tends to base oneself on the notion

[252] Article 1.2.

[253] Convention on the Law Applicable to Contractual Obligations entered into in Rome on 19 June, 1980 between the EEC Member States and entered into force on 1 April, 1991.

[254] Article 2(1).

[255] See Rubino-Sammartano, "Nuovi spazi all' autonomia delle parti: La Convenzione di Roma", (New spaces to the freedom of the parties to choose the applicable law: The Rome Convention) *Foro pad.*, (1991), II, 41.

[256] Article 1.

[257] Article 1(c).

[258] Title I, Article 1 item 4.

[259] ie according to the *lex fori*.

[260] Article 18.

of negotiable instruments as instruments which are validly purchased even if the vendor is not their owner.[261] In this respect it has been held[262] that only *titoli al portatore*[263] and *titoli all' ordine*[264] are negotiable instruments within this meaning, while *titoli nominativi*,[265] like shares, do not allow a *bona fide* purchase and therefore would not be excluded from the Convention.

In this respect it is interesting to note that another Convention, the Vienna Convention,[266] lists negotiable instruments after stocks and shares. The express mention of shares would have not been necessary if shares were already included amongst negotiable instruments. This seems to support the view that shares are not negotiable instruments.

Be that as it may, the relevance of this issue is superseded by the remark that—even if they were to be treated as negotiable instruments—neither the contract under which said instruments are issued, nor the agreement for their sale are considered by the learned rapporteurs as excluded from the ambit of the Convention. It seems to follow from these first comments that sales both of businesses and of shares are within the sphere of application of the Rome Convention.

The law applicable as to the capacity of physical persons is excluded from the Convention. The Convention limits itself to provide that a person who has the capacity to contract under the law of the place where the parties are, at the time the contract was entered into, may prove its lack of capacity to contract under a different law only if it establishes that such a lack of capacity was, or should have been, known to the other contracting party.[267]

The form of contracts entered into between parties, which at that time are located in the same State, is governed by the law which governs the substance of the contract or by the law of that place. If at that time the parties are located in different places, it is governed by the law which governs the substance of the contract or by the law of one of such places.[268]

But the major change concerns the law applicable to the substance of the contract, which is the law of the State with which the contract has the *closest connection*.[269] The Convention presumes that the closest connection exists with the State where the party, which must provide the characteristic performance, has his residence or, if a corporate body, its seat.[270]

The Convention does not supersede other conventions. It seems to follow from this that, for example, The Hague 1955 Convention on the Law Applicable to International Sales of Goods prevails on the Rome Convention.

261 The so-called *a non domino* purchases.
262 Bonomi, "Il nuovo diritto internazionale privato dei contratti", *Banca Borsa Titoli di Credito*, (1992).
263 Instruments to the bearer, transferable by mere delivery.
264 Instruments transferable by mere endorsement, without stating the name of the transferee.
265 Registered instruments.
266 Article 2.
267 Article 11.
268 Article 9.
269 Article 4 No 1.
270 Article 4.2.

15.2.3 The Vienna (1980) Convention

The Vienna Convention[271] has not changed the conflict rules but has unified[272] the substantive law governing sales of goods:

> this Convention applies to contracts of sale of goods between parties whose places of businesses are in different States. (a) when the States are Contracting States; or (b) when the rules of private international law lead to the application of the law of a contracting state.

The Vienna Convention deals, *inter alia* with the form, the formation of the contract, the obligations of the parties, conformity and remedies. Its adoption produces the result that the Convention automatically applies, replacing the domestic conflict rules, to sales between parties belonging to Member States. In the other situations the domestic conflict rules are to be applied but they may produce the result that the Vienna Convention applies if, under them, the law of a contracting State is applicable.

However, the Convention does not apply[273] to sales

> . . . (d) of stocks, shares, investments securities, negotiable instruments or money

15.2.4 Impact of the various conventions

The situation after the Vienna Convention seems then to be the following:

(a) the national law still applies to wholly domestic sales;
(b) The Hague (1955) Convention applies to identify the law applicable to international sales of *moveable goods* (which excludes sales of shares and should exclude also sales of on-going business, of interest in partnership, and sales of quotas of companies with limited liability);
(c) the Vienna Convention applies to sales between parties whose place of business is in different States but it does not apply to sales of shares (while it may apply to sales of quotas, ie of parts of limited liability companies), and it applies to sales of an on-going business, or of a partner's interest in a partnership, between parties whose place of business is in two contracting States or when the law of a contracting state applies under the applicable conflict rules;
(d) as to sales of shares, of on-going businesses, of interest in partnership and sales of quotas of companies with limited liability under contracts entered into in a Rome Convention Member State or governed by the law of one of them, the domestic rules on conflicts of laws are replaced by the Rome Convention when such contract is subsequent to the Convention and provided that, as discussed earlier, it contains a foreign element;
(e) only as to sale contracts entered into outside the ambit of The Hague (1955) and of the Rome Conventions, the domestic conflict rules may apply to international sales. However, this situation will not be frequent in an EEC framework since both conventions are construed as replacing entirely the

[271] United Nations Convention on Contracts for International Sales of Goods entered into on 11 April, 1980, and entered into force on 11 January, 1988.
[272] Article 1.
[273] Article 2.

domestic conflicts rule. That will be the case as to contracts entered into in a State which is adhering neither to The Hague (1955) nor the Rome (1980) Convention. If so, the Italian courts will then apply their domestic rules on conflicts in such cases.

As to sales in general, where The Hague Convention prevails on the Rome Convention, the situation may occur where The Hague (1955) Convention does not apply and where the Rome (1980) Convention applies, such as an international sale entered into in a State which has not adhered to The Hague Convention (for example Great Britain) if one construes the ambit of the former as totally replacing the domestic rules on conflicts (ie not only as to relationships between Member States or governed by the law of one of them); this is the view expressed by the majority of writers.

However, this potential conflict between the two Conventions will not arise as to the types of sales here considered and, therefore, to warranties in acquisitions, since The Hague Convention does not apply to shares or corporate acquisitions.

Within this framework the *lex societatis*[274] and the *lex rei sitae*[275] would not seems to play a role[276] in identifying the law which governs warranties.

15.3. Application of the International Conventions to the Various Situations

15.3.1 Sale in Italy of an on-going business between two parties of which one is not Italian

The Hague Convention does not apply to sales of on-going businesses, partnership interests or quotas of limited liability companies.

The capacity of each party is governed by its national law subject to Article 11 of the Rome (1980) Convention, when applicable. The form of the sale agreement is governed by Article 9 of the Rome Convention (1980).

The substance of the sale agreement shall be governed by the law chosen by the parties or, in its absence, will be determined—based on the Rome Convention—under the *closest connection* criterion according to the presumption that this criterion is provided for by the characteristic performance.

The Vienna Convention (1980) comes into play, if applicable (as discussed above).

15.3.2 Sales in Italy of shares between two parties one of which is non-Italian

The Rome Convention (1980) seems to apply as to the form and as to the substance of the contract, while The Hague (1955) and the Vienna Convention (1980) seem not to apply.

[274] The law which governs the corporation, over the shares of which one is disputing.

[275] The law of the place where the asset is located, law which governs the effects of the sale on the share.

[276] Both referred to in Carbone, "Conflitti di leggi e tra giurisdizioni nella disciplina dei trasferimenti di pacchetti azionari di riferimento", (Conflicts of laws and amongst Courts over jurisdiction on the discipline of sales of shares) *Riv. dir. int. priv. proc.*, (1991), 77.

15.3.3 Sales outside Italy of an on-going business between two parties one of which is Italian

The Hague (1955) Convention for International Sales of Moveable Goods, does not apply. As to contracts governed by the law of a Member State of the Rome Convention or entered into in one of such States, the Rome (1980) Convention applies.

If, under it, the law of a State, which is a party to the Vienna Convention applies, the Vienna Convention shall apply. If the contracting parties do not belong to a State which is a party to the Vienna Convention, the Convention does not apply and the law of a State Member of the Rome Convention does not apply to them, the applicable law, in the absence of a choice by the parties, is to be determined in that State, under other applicable international conventions or based on its domestic conflict rules and Italian courts shall, if other requirements exist, recognise judgments based on such law.

15.3.4 Sales outside Italy of shares between parties one of which is Italian

If the agreement is governed by the law of a State adhering to the Rome Convention or is entered into in it, the Italian Courts should apply the conflict rules provided by the Rome (1980) Convention. Otherwise the Italian courts apply their domestic conflict rules. Neither The Hague (1955) Convention nor the Vienna Convention (1980) apply.

15.4 Italian International Public Policy

Whatever the applicable law, Italian international public policy cannot be derogated by it. Whenever this is the case, either the Italian court will not apply the conflicting foreign provision, or it will not register the foreign judgment or award, based on it.

Italian international public policy principles apply to all contracts and specifically are identifiable in the areas of the object of the contract to be ascertained or ascertainable; of waivers of fundamental rights being excluded; of all defences not being excluded; of the role of nullity to be respected; of the need for proportion between liability and damages; of the need for provisions not to be oppressive; and for time bars or estoppels not to be too short.

As to the sale contracts, one must mention that the limit to a non-resident's right to purchase has been upheld by several precedents[277] as arising from statutory provisions:[278]

> Aliens are entitled to the same civil rights as Italian citizens, conditional upon reciprocity and subject to statutory provisions. This provision also applies to foreign legal entities.

[277] *Goffraniha et al* v *Boccetti*, Court of Cassation, 30 August, [1989] *Foro pad.*, 1991, 204; *Vartanian* Constitutional Court, 29 July, No 952 [1988] *Riv. Dir. Int. Priv. Proc.* 1989, 568; *Toscogerma*, Court of Prato, 4 July, 1986, *Foro It.*, 1986, I, 2963 and *Giosan*, Court of Florence, 18 January, 1989, *Foro Pad.* 1990, I, 76.

[278] Article 16 Preliminary Provisions to the Civil Code.

16. The Time Element in Warranties

16.1 The Closing

As discussed earlier, in the technique of sale agreements of shares or on-going businesses there is a major alternative. In some legal systems the parties enter directly into the sale agreement and generally condition its effects, including delivery and transfer of title, to several conditions precedent which are to occur within a given time period. The end of such a time period is repersented by the closing. In other legal systems, as in Italy, the practice is to enter into a *contratto prelimanare* (ie preliminary agreement) based on a *promessa di vendita* (ie promise to sell), ie, into an undertaking to sell at a subsequent stage.

The main difference between the two mechanisms is that the sale agreement aims to transfer title, even if subject to conditions, while the *contratto preliminare* amounts to a mere undertaking to sell at a subsequent stage.

The closing is consequently a part only of the former mechanism. It takes place, subject to the conditions precedent having occurred and the other activities provided for in the contract having been accomplished at the time at which the parties have agreed that the effects of the sale agreement must take place. In the *contratto preliminare*, the closing will be replaced by the date at which the sale agreement itself must be entered into.

16.2 Warranties not Incorporated in the Closing Documents

The effects of non-repetition of the warranties in the "final document" may be different, depending on whether the deal is based on a *contratto preliminare* or on a sale agreement. In the former case their non-repetition in the sale agreement may amount to their having been abandoned for one reason or the other. In the latter case, the solution will inevitably depend firstly on whether there was any need to repeat the warranties in the final documents. If the answer to this question is negative, the problem shall not arise. If their repetition was provided for, the intention of the parties will have to be construed to establish whether their non-repetition amounts to a waiver to them.

Italian law construes waivers in a restrictive way and requires a clear expression and not an ambiguous intention.[279]

16.3 Survival of Warranties

One generally refers to the survival of warranties with regard to the time period subsequent to the closing. However, this view seems based on the assumption that the natural expiry of the warranties *is* the closing. The opposite should be asserted, since the natural purpose of warranties seems to be to produce effects both before and after the closing.

The exception to this rule might be represented by those warranties the limited aim of which is to help the purchaser in the control which he is to make before and in view of the closing. However, in order for them to be construed so

[279] As to ambiguous statements see *Unione Prod. Frutta S. Maria* v *Grasso*, Court of Cassation, 27 October, No 3498 [1958] *Mass. Foro It.*, (1958), 1259.

restrictively, such an intention should be expressed, or should clearly transpire from the very purpose of that warranty.

16.4 Two Time Barriers to the Purchaser's Remedies

The Italian legal system is based on two barriers to the purchaser's right to benefit of the legal remedies. They are (i) the notice of non-conformity and (ii) time limitation. The writers have discussed at length the distinction between them.

It has been held that *decadenza* (ie estoppel) is a sanction, for not complying with the duty to perform within a definite time, that the legal system has set out in order that a substantive right be asserted, while *prescrizione* (ie time limitation) extinguishes the right of action because a waiver to it is legally presumed if, within a given time limit, that right has not been enforced. See *Laminatoio di Buttino S.p.A.* v *ENEL.*[280]

Regardless of possible differences between the two, the fact remains that in order to assert and pursue rights under a warranty, the purchaser has to take into account both such barriers.

16.5 Notice of Non-Conformity

The first barrier then, is the notice of non-conformity, to be given under domestic law by the purchaser within a short time limit which, as to defects or lack of quality, is eight days. Such a term runs from "delivery" as to apparent defects and from discovery as to the latent ones. In case of non-proper functioning, the term is 30 days from discovery. As to the warranty of clear title, there is no requirement for a notice.

The rationale of the short statutory term is to allow the vendor to make controls as to the complaint. The longer the notice, the more difficult it is for the vendor to control and, therefore, to resist the claim. The difference between such terms and the longer term in case of non-proper functioning is due to the fact that the vendor has less urgency to control the alleged malfunctioning than to control a defect or a lack of quality. As to clear title, then, if the purchaser's title is challenged, such an urgency does not exist and there is consequently no need for a short notice period. The consequence of the lack of the notice is the *decadenza* (a term which somehow corresponds to a conclusive estoppel of the holder from asserting his right).

The parties are not allowed to amend by consent the statutory provisions when the estoppel concerns rights of which the parties are not entitled to dispose:[281]

> The parties may neither amend the statutory provisions on *decadenza* nor waive them, as to rights of which the parties may not dispose.

Except in this situation, the parties may amend the statutory term for *decadenza* either by increasing it or by reducing it. However,[282]

[280] Court of Cassation, 21 August, No 2690 [1972] *Giust. Civ.*, (1972) (1) 1930.
[281] Section 2968 of the Civil Code.
[282] Section 2965 of the Civil Code.

> The agreement whereby the parties set out a term, within which the notice, in order to avoid the *decadenza*, is to be given, which makes it too difficult for a party to exercise his right, is null and void.

The term to prevent the *decadenza* of the right cannot be interrupted.[283]

> The *decadenza* is avoided only by performing the act which is provided for by the statutory provision or by the contract. Nevertheless, if the term is set out by contract or by a statutory provision which does not concern rights of which their holder cannot dispose, the *decadenza* may be avoided also by an acknowledgement made by the party against which that right is to be exercised.

The notice may be given even verbally.[284] As held in *Ditta Ing. A. Linn* v *Ditta SADECA*[285] the notice does not need to go into details.

16.6 Time Limitation

The *rationale* of time limitation is different from the *rationale* of estoppel. It aims to avoid permitting disputes to remain pending as a Damocles' sword for too long a time. Contrary to estoppel, time limitation concerns the right of action and not the substantive right itself.

Time limitation, in case of defects or lack of quality, is one year from delivery. Nevertheless, the purchaser, if sued for payment, after the expiry of such term, may oppose the defect as a defence, even if he can no longer bring an action under it, provided he has given notice of that defect, or lack of quality, within eight days after discovery and not later than one year after delivery.[286]

Time limitation is six months from discovery in case of non-proper functioning.[287] Claims for breach of the warranty of clear title are subject to the ordinary ten-years limitation.[288] Time limitation cannot be asserted by courts *ex officio* (ie of their own motion). It runs[289] "from the day on which that right may be asserted". It may not be amended by the parties.[290]

> Any agreement aiming to modify the statutory provisions on time limitation is null and void

It may be interrupted:[291]

> by service of a writ or application to a Court, be it for ordinary or for enforcement proceedings, or aiming to interlocutory measures. It is also interrupted by a claim made during court proceedings. Its effects remain even if the Court seised has no jurisdiction. Limitation is also interrupted by any other act which aims to place another party in breach.

283 Section 2977 of the Civil Code.
284 Greco-Cottino, *Commentario Scialoja-Branca*, (1981), at 1495; D. Rubino, *La compravendita*, *Op. cit.* at 640.
285 Court of Cassation, 18 September, No 2591 [1959] *Giust. Civ. Mass*, (1959) at 880.
286 Sections 1495 and 1497 of the Civil Code.
287 Section 1512 of the Civil Code.
288 Section 2946 of the Civil Code.
289 Section 2935 of the Civil Code.
290 Section 2936 of the Civil Code.
291 Section 2942 of the Civil Code.

This provision is construed as normally (but not always) allowing interruption to be made even by a request made in writing, and therefore also by a letter. In *Buccilli* v *Enel*[292] it was held that a creditor may prove by any means that the notice has been given in writing and duly received.

17. Beneficiary of the Warranty

17.1 The Purchaser

The natural beneficiary of a warranty, in a sale of an on-going business or of shares or parts, or in the assignment of the interest in a partnership, is the purchaser. The purchaser will generally, but not always, be the payor. In fact, apart from the general situation, one may envisage also a sale agreement whereby the payor is different from the purchaser. This may take place either if the payor is a physical person and the purchaser, a legal entity or vice versa. In fact it may happen that a physical person pays while it agrees that title passes from the vendor to another physical person or to a legal entity.

It may also happen that a legal entity pays but at the same time agrees that title be transferred to another legal entity or to a physical person, the latter being conceivable, but rare.

This deal will be classified as a contract for the benefit of a third party and will be subject to the specific statutory provisions which regulate such contracts.[293] The contract will be valid, "if the party entering into it (note: the payor) has an interest in it".

For this purpose, interest is construed as a very wide notion, including non-financial interest, as held in *Obbialero* v *Cremona*.[294] As a consequence of such a deal, the third party may become the beneficiary of the vendor's warranties.

17.2 Resale by the Purchaser

If the purchaser resells the on-going business, or shares or quotas or interest, do the vendor's warranties automatically transfer to the third purchaser? The answer should normally be negative, since the warranty derives from the sale agreement and consequently requires privity of contract between vendor and purchaser. In the absence of a different agreement, the third purchaser has consequently no claim on warranty against the original vendor, but only against its own vendor. Generally then, in case of a resale, the original vendor has no liability under the warranty to those who purchase from his purchaser.

17.3 Third Parties as Beneficiaries

However, the purchaser may, in his subsequent resale, assign his rights to his own purchaser. It has been held by precedents[295] and writers[296] that the right of action under the warranty cannot be transferred alone but together with the substantive right itself.

[292] Court of Cassation, 12 March, No 1618 [1982] *Rep. Foro. It.*, (1982), 2230.
[293] Sections 1411 to 1414 of the Civil Code.
[294] Court of Cassation, 3 July, No 3749 [1979] *Rep. Foro It.*, (1979), 659.
[295] Court of Cassation, 4 August, No 2164 [1949] in *Giur. It.*, (1950), 1, I, 399.
[296] Bianca, *La vendita e la permuta*, at 840–845.

Even in the absence of an assignment, the purchaser, if the requirements for this exist, such as if the purchaser is an unsatisfied creditor of the vendor, may act against the original vendor in subrogation of his vendor, asserting the latter's right.[297]

> The creditor, to ensure that his rights be satisfied or protected, may exercise the rights and actions which belong to his debtor and which the latter omits to exercise, provided those rights or actions have financial contents and do not belong to the class of rights and actions which may be asserted only by their holder.

The practice of the vendor's assignment of his rights under warranties[298] has become so frequent that it has been held to be tacitly included in the resale, with the consequence that the ultimate purchaser would be entitled to assert it *jure proprio*,[299] even if no assignment has taken place. However, this view is not universally accepted.

A further situation, where a third party may assert a right under a warranty against the vendor, is a sale of an on-going business which has, before such transfer, purchased shares or another on-going business. In fact, as a rule, the purchaser assumes the rights and duties of the purchased business.[300]

The rights under a warranty are transferred also in case of a merger of the corporation, (which has made such a purchase) into the merging, or into a third *ad hoc* formed corporation.[301]

18. Warranties, Disclaimers and Restrictions

18.1 Exclusions or Restrictions in Sales of On-going Businesses

18.1.1 Warranty of clear title

The special statutory provisions which regulate the warranty of clear title provide:[302]

> The parties may increase or reduce the effects of the warranty and may further agree that the Vendor be subject to no warranty at all.

This rule suffers one exception,

> Even in the event of the warranty having been excluded, the Vendor is always liable if title is not clear due to his own act. Any contrary agreement is null and void.

18.1.2 Warranty of absence of defects

The warranty of absence of defects is not due[303] "if at the time of the sale agreement the purchaser was aware of the defect". It is also not due "if the

[297] Section 2900 of the Civil Code.
[298] A practice which goes back to the *obligatio cedendarum actionum* (ie undertaking to assign rights of actions) of Roman law.
[299] ie of his own right.
[300] Sections 2555–2562 of the Civil Code.
[301] Sections 2498–2500 of the Civil Code.
[302] Section 1487 para. 1 of the Civil Code.
[303] Section 1491 of the Civil Code.

defects were easily identifiable, unless the vendor has represented that the goods have no defects".[304]

The special statutory provisions dealing with this warranty provide for exclusion or restrictions of this warranty unless the vendor has acted in bad faith in not disclosing the defects.[305]

18.1.3 Warranty of merchantable quality

The statutory provision dealing with merchantable quality[306] does not deal with exclusions or with limitations. While it makes reference, as to estoppel and time bar, to the discipline of the warranty of absence of defects, it makes no reference to exclusion of the warranty for absence of defects.

It is submitted that this silence may be construed as not being intentional. Consequently disclaimers and restrictions seem available as to this warranty also.

18.1.4 Warranty of proper functioning

Since the warranty of proper functioning is based on consent and not on statutory provisions, the matter of its exclusion does not arise. The parties are free to agree on the warranty, and they may also agree to restrict it at their discretion, provided, that in so doing, they do not deprive the purchaser of the possibility to assert the very right which has just been granted to him, by setting out a term for the notice of complaint which, being too short, makes it too difficult to assert it.

18.2 Exclusions or Restrictions in Sales of Shares

As to those who are of the view that the warranty applies only as to title to the shares, exclusion or restrictions will be applicable only to such a warranty. For those for whom sales of shares are subject to all the above warranties, exclusion and restriction of the warranty may be subject to the above wider comments.

19. Breach of Warranties

When asserting a right under a warranty, it is not enough for the plaintiff to satisfy the court that the warranty has not been met. Several other elements or requirements exist in order that an action on warranty succeeds.

19.1 Is the Vendor's Fault Required?

Vendor's fault is not always required in order that a breach of warranty exists. As to a sale of *aliud pro alio* (ie of different goods) the claim being based on breach of contract, the vendor's fault is required. To the contrary, a breach of the warranty of *absence of defects* exists, in case of a deficiency, even if it is not due to the vendor's breach.

[304] Section 1491 of the Civil Code.
[305] Section 1490 of the Civil Code.
[306] Section 1497 of the Civil Code.

A breach of the warranty of *merchantable quality* exists, according to some writers, only in the presence of the vendor's breach. However,[307] the remedy of rescission of the contract seems applicable whenever there is a lack of quality, whether due to the vendor's fault or otherwise.

A breach of the *warranty of proper functioning* does not require the vendor's fault. The same view has been expressed by Bianca[308] for a breach of the warranty of clear title.

19.2 Other Requirements to Assert the Warranty

The plaintiff will have to establish, *inter alia* that the warranty is either statutory or by consent, that the notice of non-conformity has been given and that the action is not barred by time limitation. The last two issues in particular may not be raised by the court *ex officio* (of its own motion); they require that the defendant raises them among his defences. The issue has been debated whether, once the defence of *decadenza* (estoppel) has been raised, the burden of proof lies on the vendor or on the purchaser. While for a long time it has been held that it was up to the purchaser to establish—if this was challenged—that he had given timely notice, in the last years in *Sige S.p.A* v *Fai S.p.A*[309] and in *Ford It.* v *Soc. Svai*[310] it has been held by some precedents that the burden of proof must be subject to the general rule. Therefore *excipiendi est onus probandi*[311] applies so that evidence of not receiving any notice of non conformity within the statutory or contractual deadline, would have to be provided by the vendor.

However, the Court of Cassation has recently gone back to its original approach, holding in *Scala* v *Soc. Peru*[312] that, since the timely notice of complaint is a pre-condition of the right of action, when it is challenged, the burden of proofs lies on the purchaser.

19.3 Offsetting between Effects of Warranty and Undisclosed Assets

The tendency to concentrate entirely on one aspect of the deal, when the vendor has broken his warranty, risks leaving critical offsetting issues and rights in the dark. Even when a breach of warranty has been established, its consequences may be mitigated, or even offset, whenever the damage arising from that breach of warranty is balanced by undisclosed assets, or by disclosed assets which have a higher value than stated in the balance sheet or in financial reports or in the contract.

Although this aspect is not frequently addressed, if one complains for lower value of some items, or for undisclosed liabilities, he might also have to allow, in principle, for the value of other items higher than stated in the financial

[307] Rubino-Sammartano, "Lack of Conformity and Various Reliefs in Sales of Moveable Goods to Italy", in *Survey of the International Sales of Goods*, (Lafili *et al* gen. eds.) (Kluwer, 1985) at 259.

[308] Bianca, *La vendita e la permuta, Op. cit.* at 791.

[309] Court of Cassation, 14 March, No 1888 [1983] in *Giur. It.*, 1, 336.

[310] Court of Cassation, 26 January, No 507 [1982] *Giust. Civ.*, (1982) at 178.

[311] ie he who raises a defence, must prove it.

[312] Court of Cassation, 27 February, No 2107 [1991] *Mass. Foro It.*, (1991), 194.

conditions. In any event, the solution of this issue will depend on the specific wording of the respective contract.

20. Remedies

20.1 Actions in Contract

20.1.1 Title not clear

Breach by the vendor of the statutory warranty of clear title consists—in this context—in selling shares or a business of which he does not have full and exclusive title[313] or on which third parties have some right like a pledge or lien or usufruct.[314] The vendor is liable even if this is not due to his fault.[315] The purchaser is entitled to claim rescission or a price reduction. For a claim for damages fault will be required.

The action becomes time barred with the expiry of ten years after the time it can be exercised.

20.1.2 *Aliud pro alio*

Transfer by the vendor of shares or of a business different from the agreed one entitles the purchaser to the general action for breach of contract.[316] The available remedies are consequently specific performance, or rescission and/or damages. The vendor's fault is required.

The action is barred with the expiry of ten years after the time it can be exercised.

20.1.3 Defects

In case of breach of the warranty for absence of defects, the purchaser is entitled to the special action on warranty. The vendor may claim either rescission or price reduction[317] unless trade usages exclude rescission.

This right is subject—as discussed earlier—to a notice of defects to be given within eight days after delivery (for apparent defects) or after discovery (for latent defects) and in any event within one year after delivery. The action is further subject to a time bar of one year after delivery, subject to the purchaser's right to use this a defence—even after the expiry of such term—provided the notice of the defect was given within said eight days' term.

The statutory provision provides[318] that if the sold item no longer exists because of defects, the purchaser is entitled to rescind the contract, while if this is due to a fortuitous event or to the purchaser's fault, or if the sold item has been sold by the purchaser or converted, the available remedy is only price reduction. This situation will rarely occur in respect of the sale of a business and might even not be applicable to a sale of shares.

[313] Sections 1478–1480 of the Civil Code.
[314] Section 1482 of the Civil Code.
[315] Bianca, *La vendita e la permuta* (Sale and Barter) (Torino (UTET), 1952) at 400.
[316] Section 1453 of the Civil Code.
[317] Section 1492 of the Civil Code.
[318] Section 1492 of the Civil Code.

The purchaser is entitled as an alternative, or in addition to the above remedies, to claim damages unless the vendor proves that he had no knowledge of the defect without his fault.

The action for damages is subject to a ten-year time bar, while the notice of complaint is to be given as above.

As an alternative to the special action on warranty, the purchaser may sue the vendor under the general action for breach of contract. To claim rescission of the contract, the vendor's fault is then required.

The other remedy of specific performance, available under the general action for breach of contract, which in this case would lead to repair or replacement of the defective item, has been denied by the prevailing opinion[319] on the ground that the vendor's duty is to *dare* (ie to give, to deliver) and not to *facere* (ie to do). This view has been criticised[320] on the ground that it disregards that the vendor's performance, consisting in transferring and delivering, is preceded by several other activities which include manufacturing, or buying, transporting and so on, in other words a series of "doings". The vendor's fault seems not to be required for such an action.[321] Replacement will be possible if the sold item is fungible, while only repair will be available as to non-fungible goods. In the writers' opinion, this action will become time barred with the expiry of ten years after the time it can be exercised but the above notice of defects will be needed.

20.1.4 Non-merchantable quality

In case of breach of warranty for non-merchantable quality, the purchaser is entitled to contract rescission.[322] It is argued whether the vendor's fault is required. It is suggested that the answer should be positive. It is also argued whether the purchaser is entitled to specific performance and/or to damages.

Within this framework, the non-mention of the remedy of price reduction in the statutory provision seems voluntary. It follows from this that the purchaser, when confronted with a lack of an essential quality, has to decide whether to rescind the contract or not. Then, through the remedy of reimbursement of damages, which should remain available[323] if the seller is at fault, the purchaser may in the end obtain a result which is close to price reduction.

20.1.5 Non-proper functioning

Among contractual warranties, the warranty of proper functioning is statutorily regulated. The purchaser's rights do not depend here on the vendor's fault.[324]

The remedies available under this warranty are repair or replacement. To keep that right, a notice of defect is to be given within 30 days after delivery, as to apparent defects, or after discovery, as to hidden defects. The action is then subject to a time bar of six months after discovery.

[319] Bianca, *La vendita e la permuta, Op. cit.* at 879.

[320] Rubino-Sammartano, "Lack of Conformity and Various Reliefs in Sales of Moveable Goods in Italy", in *Survey of the International Sale of Goods* (Lafili, Gewurts, Campbell gen. eds.) (Kluwer, 1985), at 243.

[321] D. Rubino, *La compravendita* (The sale contract) (Milan, Giuffre', 1952), at 644.

[322] Section 1497 of the Civil Code.

[323] Under sections 1219 *et seq.* of the Civil Code.

[324] Court of Cassation, 14 May, No 4441 [1987] *Giust. Civ.*, (1987), I, 1628.

As a alternative to the action under the special warranty, the purchaser is deemed to be entitled to the general action for breach of contract. Proof of the vendor's fault is required. The remedies available include, rescission or specific performance, and damages, as discussed above, are an alternative remedy.

20.1.6 Breach of other contractual warranties

In case of breach of other contractual warranties, the purchaser shall be entitled to avail himself of the general action for breach of contract, which has been earlier discussed. This does not prevent the parties from agreeing on other remedies as long as they do not conflict with public policy.

20.2 Actions in Tort

The traditional view was that an action in tort is not available if an action in contract is available. This concept has been reviewed and, even if the tendency is to concentrate on the contractual basis for warranty claims, actions in tort are being heard by the courts and sometimes allowed. The Court of Cassation has affirmed this principle on several occasions, such as in *Inail* v *Ratil* and in *Ass. Generali* v *Musgolio*.[325]

Actions in tort are then no more excluded in principle in case of breach of warranty, even if an action in contract will normally be available. An action in tort will come into consideration whenever the action in contract is no longer available, for example, because the notice of complaint was not timely.

On the other hand, the action in tort is not just allowed whenever a party has lost his action in contract. Its specific requirements will have to exist, namely negligence (or malice), and unjust damage and finally an actual and direct causation link between the act and the damage.[326]

20.2.1 Availability in case of breach of warranty

An action in tort is consequently available in principle in a situation amounting to a breach of warranty,[327] provided the violated right is *erga omnes*.[328] However, actions in tort will not be frequent in warranty situations.

20.2.2 Action available for breach of competition clause, of undertakings not to hire staff, not to use confidential information, or for circulating negative information

Having identified the framework within which the various actions are available to the purchaser, one may examine specific situations. Breach of a competition clause seems to allow an action in contract or in tort when the breach may amount to unfair competition.

Likewise, a breach of a commitment not to hire staff may arise whenever a branch of a business is sold but the undertaking concerns other branches of that business which have not been sold, or whenever the commitment is entered into

[325] Court of Cassation, 14 May, No 2773 [1979] *Giust. Civ.*, (1979), I, 1899.
[326] Section 2043 of the Civil Code, see Torrente, *Manuale di diritto privato* (Private Law Manual), (Milano, Giuffre', 1985), at 694 *et seq.*
[327] Bianca, *La vendita e la permuta*, (Torino, (UTET), 1952), pp. 879 *et seq.*
[328] ie a right which can be asserted by its holder against anybody.

in view of the sale of a business, if that sale does not occur but, in spite of this, staff of that business is hired by the party which negotiated the purchase.

Aside of the breach of contract, the tort of unfair competition may exist if this is carried out by unfair means.

A commitment not to use confidential information will amount to breach of contract or of an undertaking may constitute the tort of unfair competition, and may even constitute a criminal offence.

Similarly, circulating negative information on the other contracting party, either after the sale is consummated or in case it is not, may be the basis for an action for breach of contract or of an undertaking, or in tort (for unfair competition) and may even constitute a criminal offence.

20.3 More Warrantors

The traditional scenario provides for one vendor and for one purchaser. However, more vendors and/or more purchasers may participate to one transaction, for example because they are joint owners, or purchasers, of the same business or shares, which are the object of the transaction.

One transaction may include a sale to the same purchaser of a business of one corporation and at the same time of shares of another corporation, which is owned separately. In this case, each vendor, depending on the agreement of the parties, may warrant for his part of the deal, or only one general warranty may be agreed upon.

Furthermore, although it is not frequent, the warrantor may be a person or entity different from the vendor, or may add his warranty to the vendor's one.

All these are situations where more warrantors stand in front of the purchaser. If so, their liability may be joint or several, depending on the agreement of the parties or, even in its absence, on the statutory provision[329] under which, whenever more parties are under a duty to perform under the same transaction, they are jointly liable unless a statutory provision or the contract provides otherwise.

21. Defences

Although it is not possible to cover exhaustively, within this framework, all the possible defences which can be raised by the vendor in respect of a claim from the purchaser and, in some occasions, also in respect of a claim, for breach of warranty, the general defences will be examined here. Classes of defence may include:

- the non-existence of the obligation;
- the obligation being still undue;
- performance;
- extinction of the obligation;
- State interventions;
- acquisition of the right;
- earlier termination of the contract;

[329] Section 1294 of the Civil Code.

- voidability;
- right to stay performance;
- time bar;
- procedural defences.

A short summary of some of these defences will be set forth here, but more detailed studies are available elsewhere.[330]

21.1 Acquisition Null and Void

Nullity must be distinguished from non-existence and voidability. Nullity—according to the traditional position—may concern the entire sale contract,[331] or the warranty itself, or another part of the contract,[332] which was essential for the parties in order to enter into the contract and which consequently involves the nullity of the entire agreement.

Nullity may be due, *inter alia*, to breach of mandatory rules, such as a prohibition to sell shares or businesses belonging to a certain area due to security, or to other public policy reasons, or to the absence of a basic requirement of the contract, such as the meeting of the minds.

21.2 Voidability

The voidability of the sale agreement will be based[333] on the traditional grounds such as lack of capacity of a party, or a vitiating factor as mistake, duress or fraud.

Whether the warranty is directly affected by the vitiating factor or follows the destiny of the whole agreement, the defence of voidability will be available, if its requirements exist.

21.3 Creation of an Only Apparent Contract

The situation of the parties entering only apparently into a contract, while in reality either they intended to enter into no contract at all or into a different contract, may occur also as to acquisitions. That may be, and was, the case of sales made by physical persons or legal entities which were prohibited, or feared to be going to be prohibited, by new legislation from owning business or shares.

The effect of such circumstances is the nullity of the contract. Partial nullity may result from the nullity of the apparent contract as well as the validity of the hidden contract, if its requirements as to form and substance are complied with by the apparent contract.

Evidence of this type of transaction may encounter limits in disputes between the parties.[334] Evidence by witnesses is not allowed unless it aims to establish that the hidden contract is unlawful. While total or partial appearance will be

[330] Amongst which Rubino-Sammartano, "Defences to enforcement (and State Interventions) on Civil Law", in *Drafting and enforcing contracts in civil and common law jurisdictions* (gen. eds. Yelpaala–Rubino–Sammartano–Campbell) *Op. cit.*

[331] Section 1418 of the Civil Code.

[332] Section 1419 of the Civil Code.

[333] Sections 1425 to 1446 of the Civil Code.

[334] Sections 1417 and 2722 of the Civil Code.

frequently the base for a claim, it may also be used as a defence, if the apparent contract has not yet been performed and the apparent purchaser seeks performance.

21.4 Conditions Precedent and Subsequent

Whenever a sale contract of a business or of shares is subject to a condition precedent,[335] such as the carrying out of an inspection by the purchaser, and the vendor does not allow it to take place but, in spite of this, he seeks performance of the contract, the purchaser shall be entitled to base his defence on no occurrence of that condition precedent.

Likewise, if an acquisition is subject to a condition subsequent, such as a positive independent inspection by a third party subsequent to the sale, but its result is negative, the purchaser shall be entitled either to base on it a claim for rescission of the acquisition, or to use it as a defence if, in spite of this, the vendor seeks payment of the balance.

21.5 Novation

As it is known, novation exists when the parties replace their original obligations by a new obligation, or whenever the original debtor is replaced by a new debtor.[336]

Even if this will not be frequent in acquisitions, one may conceive that the purchaser's duty to pay cash be replaced, by a subsequent agreement, by a duty to deliver shares of his own company, or of another company. Whenever the vendor should seek performance of the original obligation, the purchaser would be entitled to rely upon novation.

Similarly, if the purchaser has been replaced, with the vendor's consent, by another debtor, and the vendor should, in spite of this, seek performance by the purchaser, the latter would be entitled to use novation as a defence.

21.6 Impossibility not due to Debtor's Fault

Whenever the obligation has become impossible without the debtor's fault, and the impossibility is only of a temporary nature, the debtor is not liable for delay. If the impossibility lasts until the creditor has no more interest to receive it, or the debtor may no longer be held to be under a duty to perform, then the duty to perform is extinguished.[337]

For the obligation to be cancelled due to impossibility, the impossibility must be objective and not subjective, ie that it is such as to prevent any obligor, and not just that person or legal entity, from performing.

Impossibility to perform without debtor's fault may arise also in businesses acquisitions. The sale of a business or of shares, by a resident to a non-resident would be extinguished by impossibility, for example, if after the sale agreement legislation were introduced preventing sales in that manufacturing or commercial area to non-residents.

[335] Sections 1353 to 1361 of the Civil Code.
[336] Sections 1230 to 1235 of the Civil Code.
[337] Sections 1256 to 1259 of the Civil Code.

21.7 *Force Majeure*

Force majeure is a very close to impossibility without purchaser's fault.[338] Contrary to the latter, which is generally used as a base for a claim for a declaratory judgment extinguishing the obligation, *force majeure* is generally used as a defence in order to avoid payment of damages for non-performance or for delay. *Force majeure* may be, and is, used as a defence in acquisitions also. For example, if delivery of a factory is delayed or prevented by fire, the vendor will use *force majeure* as a defence to a claim for damages.

21.8 *Set-Off*

Set off is a legal device which aims to avoid duplicate proceedings between the same parties and the risk of determining the rights of one party without simultaneously considering the rights of the other party. For example, whenever two parties are each the debtor of the other, each party has to pay the other. One of them may pay without being able in turn to collect, or having to wait for a long time before collecting from the other. The concept of set-off is to prevent this perceived unfairness. Three types of set off exist.[339]

The *statutory* set-off, under which when two parties are each under the obligation to pay the other one, and both debts are ascertained and due, they are simultaneously extinguished or, if one of the two is higher than the other one, they are extinguished up to the lower amount. Aside of the statutory set-off, *judicial* set-off applies when the debt opposed by the debtor is not yet ascertained but can be ascertained in an expeditious way. In such situations, the Court has a discretion to apply the set-off to the part of that debt, which in its view has already been established, and to stay its order as to the balance, until the rest of the corresponding credit has been established.

The last-type of set-off is the one *by consent* which occurs when the parties voluntarily extinguish some reciprocal debts, which would not qualify for statutory set-off.

The co-existence of the two debts does not automatically extinguish them. To achieve that purpose, the intention to take advantage of it has to be expressed. There is no reason why set off could not be applied to sale of shares or of on-going businesses, quotas and interest in partnership.

21.9 *State Interventions*

An important defence is represented by State intervention, ie by the *factum principis*.[340]

Whenever new legislation, or an administrative order, prevents performance of a duty, any claim to obtain such a performance may be met by the defence of the Act of the Sovereign. That may, in special situations, be the case as to sales to non-residents or, as it has been recently experienced, as to freezing of transactions related to Iraq and to Kuwait.[341]

338 Section 1218 of the Civil Code.

339 Sections 124–1251 of the Civil Code.

340 ie the Act of the Sovereign.

341 Statute 5 October, 1990, No 278 and Statute 3 October, 1990 No 271, the latter abrogated by Statute 19 July, 1991 No 224.

21.10 Right to Stay Performance because of Breach by the Other Contracting Party

Each party to a contract is entitled to refuse its performance when the other party, which had to perform first, or which has to perform simultaneously, has not performed or does not perform.[342] This defence is frequently referred to as *inadimplenti non est adimplendum.*[343]

This right may be exercised as a defence to a claim to obtain performance. Here too, there is no reason why this defence cannot be used also in the field of sales of shares or of businesses.

It may happen that each party raises the same defence. In this situation, the Court will compare the conduct of the parties and establish which party is entitled to this defence, based on succession in time and on proportion and causation of the respective breaches.

21.11 Failure of the Joint Factual Base of the Meeting of the Minds

The doctrine of the basic premise of the meeting of the minds is based on the old rule of Roman law *rebus sic stantibus.*[344] One can reasonably assume that the persistence of a factual situation was assumed by the parties.

The failure of such basic premise has been held by some precedents as in *Venini* v *Orio*[345] and in *Sorlini* v *Mariani*[346] to produce the termination of the contract. Such a doctrine may be applied as a defence also to a claim for performance in sales of shares or businesses.

21.12 Transactions in State of Need or Danger

The Italian legal system entitles a party to terminate an agreement which was entered into either in a state of need or of danger.

The contract may be terminated if there is an unbalance between the performance of the two parties, which was due to the state of need of one of them, and the other party has taken advantage of it. The requirements for termination are: (i) there has been a state of need, (ii) the decision to enter into the contract was made because of that need, and (iii) the damage is *ultra dimidium.*[347] Termination because of a state of need was held in *Cinti, Luciani, Tabellini* v *Veggetti.*[348]

This doctrine may either be applied as a defence to a claim to perform the contract or may give rise to a cause of action to set the sale aside. Furthermore, whenever a contract is entered into on unfair terms in order to save oneself (or others) from danger, the contract may be terminated if (i) there is a causation link

[342] Section 1460 of the Civil Code.

[343] ie there is no duty to perform to a non-performing debtor.

[344] ie based on the existing situation.

[345] Court of Cassation, 9 May, No 3074 [1981] *Mass. Foro it.*, (1981), 621.

[346] Court of Cassation, 3 October, No 2828 [1972] *Mass. Foro It.*, (1972), 856.

[347] ie that it exceeds 50 per cent of the value of the sold asset; (section 1448, Civil Code).

[348] Court of Cassation, 17 March, No 687 [1970] *Giur. It.*, (1970), I, 1, 1180.

between that state of danger and that party's decision to enter into the contract and (ii) the other party has, or should have, realised that it was taking advantage of it.[349]

Even this doctrine may be applied to sales of shares or businesses and may work either as a defence to a claim for performance or as a cause of action to set aside the contract. It cannot be raised as a defence when the claim is time barred.[350]

The party, against which this defence is raised, may avoid its consequences by proposing to change the contract in such a way as to put an end to the unbalance.[351]

21.13 Events Occurring between the Sale Agreement and the Closing

Whenever the transaction is structured as an agreement providing for a later closing, the possibility exists that events occurring, between the entering into the agreement and the closing may affect it. Examples of such events include the case of State interventions between the agreement and the closing, or of a novation or set off.

21.14 Termination for Excessive Hardship

This doctrine aims to provide relief to a party who is under a duty to perform a contract when performance has become excessively harsh for him. In order for this doctrine to apply, the hardship must be due to an event which is extraordinary and unpredictable. Excessive hardship entitles the party to terminate the contract and, as such, gives rise either to a cause of action or to a defence.[352]

However, the other party to the contract is entitled to avoid this consequence, by offering to modify the contract in order that it becomes fair. Excessive hardship has been held in *Sanesi* v *Galeotti*.[353]

Excessive hardship may occur also in sales of shares or businesses, namely in the period of time between the agreement and the closing.

21.15 Late Notice

The vendor may use, as a defence, lateness of the purchaser's notice of defect, when applicable. In fact, as earlier discussed, whenever the notice concerns a defect or a lack of quality, a notice of defect is to be given within a certain time limit, and its lateness prevents the purchaser from asserting its right.[354]

It has been argued whether the burden of proof of lateness lies on the party which so alleges. For a long time it has been held that it lay on the vendor. However, in the last years the Court of Cassation has held on some occasions that it is not enough to allege lateness, but that the vendor had to prove it. The matter

[349] Section 1447 of the Civil Code.
[350] Section 1449 of the Civil Code.
[351] Section 1450 of the Civil Code.
[352] Section 1467 of the Civil Code.
[353] Court of Cassation, 6 May, No 1272 [1955] *Giust. Civ.*, (1955), 1, 1079.
[354] Section 2964 *et seq.*, Civil Code.

is, consequently–as discussed earlier–still open. Among the various precedents, one may quote *Ford* v *Svai*[355] and *Società SIGE* v *Società FAI*.[356]

21.16 Time Bar

One of the last but most effective defences, available to the vendor, when faced with a claim, and therefore also with a claim for breach of warranty, is time bar.[357] This defence is based on the short and different terms set out by the various statutory provisions.[358]

22. Investigations and Substitutes for Warranties

22.1 Warranty Excluded by Right to Conduct a Previous Inspection

A vendor, sued under his warranty, may use the defence that the purchaser has made, or had been authorised to make, an inspection before entering into the contract, or in the time period between it and the closing, if the factual situation allows it. The practice of conducting inspections, before the agreement is entered into or performed, has largely developed and is referred to as the Due Diligence Exercise.[359]

Such a defence may stand on a statutory basis, if the defect or lack of quality was known by the purchaser when he entered into the contract, or that inspection discovered or should have discovered a defect, or lack of quality, and no timely notice of complaint has been given.

Apart from this statutory basis, the vendor may base such a defence on the contract. The inspection made by the purchaser may automatically relieve the vendor from warranties. In any event the success of this defence will frequently depend on the contract's wording.

22.2 Effects of Purchaser's Other Checking or Knowledge

Apart from inspections agreed between vendor and purchaser, the purchaser occasionally conducts other checkings, on his own, or through independent auditors. Audits are not necessarily limited to accounts and may concern also the legal, commercial, labour, warehouse or other areas.

The effects of this *ex parte* checking will depend on each specific contract. A vendor's liability may be released by knowledge by the purchaser of a defect or lack of quality[360] or if such were easily detectable, unless the vendor has expressly warranted absence of defects.

[355] Court of Cassation, 26 January, No 507 [1982] *Giust. Civ. Mass.*, (1982), 178.
[356] Court of Cassation, 14 March, No 1888 [1983] *Giur. It.*, (1984), I, 336.
[357] Sections 2946 *et seq.*, Civil Code.
[358] Sections 1495, 1497, 1512 of the Civil Code.
[359] See *Due Diligence, Disclosures and Warranties*, (Graham & Trotman, 1988).
[360] Section 1491 of the Civil Code.

22.3 Vendor's Special Conduct and Liability

The vendor's liability may be affected by the vendor hiding a defect or lack of quality or by the vendor causing the defect or lack of quality. The consequence of this may be that disclaimers of, or restrictions to, statutory warranties become void and of no effect.[361] The vendor's liability may also be affected by the vendor hiding information.

23. Third Parties' Liability

23.1 Intermediaries

Several intermediaries may be liable to a party to an acquisition, if their conduct causes, or contributes to cause a damage to the purchaser or to the vendor. Examples include providing wrong information, in case of brokers or other agents or withholding of information.

23.2 Auditors

The auditors' liability has been asserted on several occasions in other jurisdictions. For example, where an audit was made on the purchaser's instructions, if the auditor's conclusions make the purchaser erroneously believe that the audited shares or business have a different value or characteristics and make him act accordingly, the auditor may be liable in contract.

The practice of acquisitions has also produced situations where auditors, instructed by the vendor or by the target company, have conducted such an audit knowing that either their results were to be submitted to the purchaser, or that the purchaser would have relied upon them. In these situations, if the purchaser relies on the audit in deciding on the acquisition, or on its price, the auditor may be liable to the purchaser in tort.

23.3 Banks

In principle banks may be liable under various headings to the purchaser or the vendor, in sales of shares or business acquisitions. Such liability may arise from providing wrong information to a party to the contract, or, in certain situations, from withholding it.

Banks may also be liable for providing wrong information on specific items, like the cash situation, or timely payments, or lines of credit. In a different scenario, banks may be liable under guarantees issued by them for one of the parties, such as for the vendor's liability for breach of warranties.

23.4 Target Company's Officers

One of the classes of third parties which is most exposed to claims related to sale acquisitions is that of the target company's directors and employees. Prospective purchasers, before entering into sale agreements, frequently have contacts with them. The directors, managers and employees of the target company may then voluntarily or involuntarily convey to the purchaser, or withhold from him,

[361] Section 1490 of the Civil Code.

relevant information which affects its basic decision, ie whether to purchase or not, and if so, on which terms.

The purchaser consequently may turn to them, when such information is inaccurate. Their liability to the purchaser would generally be in tort.

They may also be liable to the purchaser for their conduct during the time period between the contract and the closing, whenever that conduct causes, or contributes to cause, a relevant adverse change in the target company or business's situation.

The target company's officers and employees may alternatively be liable to the vendor.

23.5 Professionals

Even professionals may incur into liability in contract to their client, or, in tort, to the other contracting party in respect of a sale of shares or business acquisition. Accountants, engineers, advisers and attorneys are to be included among them.

Their liability in tort will not be frequent, and will be generally limited to situations where they have had direct contacts with the other contracting party or have made representations to it. Their liability will arise in situations where their representations have been relied upon by their client, or by the other party and eventually—even though admittedly rare—when the professional himself has given rise to defects or lack of quality, or has not avoided or limited them, when he could have done so.

South Africa

Jeffrey Lawton Buckland*

Webber Wentzel, Johannesburg, South Africa

The two most common methods of acquiring control of the assets of a company are, either to purchase the assets from the company, or to purchase the shares which confer voting control in general meeting from the members of the company. In either case the general principles of contract, and in particular the principles of contract of sale and purchase, apply. In South Africa the principles of contract emanate from and are embedded in our Roman-Dutch legal heritage, as influenced from time to time by English legal concepts and terminology.

The disparate interests and concerns of the seller and purchaser will differ from case to case. Accordingly, each acquisition has to be dealt with on its own merits which necessitates in each case a balancing of interests, concerns and needs between the parties. On the one hand, the seller will require sufficient security from the purchaser for payment of the purchase price, and on the other hand, the purchaser will require legal safeguards adequately to protect his investment.

Against this background we have been asked to comment on and discuss a wide range of legal concepts, with particular emphasis on the concept, nature and scope of warranties, generally, in South African law.

1. Various Acquisitions, Various Warranties, other Representations and Covenants

1.1 Various Acquisitions

1.1.1 The meaning of "acquisition"

The ordinary meaning of "to acquire" is either "to gain, or get as one's own" or "to receive or come into possession of " [1] and an "acquistion" means "the action of acquiring" or "a thing acquired". The acquisition of a thing can therefore mean

*This chapter has also been edited by John Jarvis, Edward Southey and Leora Blumberg, Partners at Webber Wentzel.

[1] C. T. Onions (ed), *The Shorter Oxford English Dictionary on Historical Principles*, Vol. A (3rd ed, 1980), at 18.

either to gain the right to possess or actual possession of a thing, or to gain the right to own or ownership of a thing.

1.1.2 Possession

Possession of a thing is a matter of fact and is endowed with certain important legal consequences.[2] Possession is a requisite for certain modes of passing ownership of things, such as transfer (*traditio*). Once in possession of a thing, a person may protect that possession by various legal remedies, namely, an application for the recovery of possession (the *mandament van spolie*), interdicts and possessory actions. Furthermore, possession plays an important role in the law of security because possession of a thing is required for a valid pledge or right of retention.[3]

In order to possess a thing a person must exercise physical control over it and have the intention to possess it. The law recognises quasi-possession (*possessio iuris*), which relates to the control exercised over an incorporeal thing, such as a share. Quasi-possession signifies the factual control exercised intermittently over an incorporeal thing in accordance with a legal right to the thing.[4]

A person is said to have the right to possess (*ius possidendi*) when he has a right to possess arising either from a personal right against the owner of the thing, for example as borrower or lessee, or from a real right in the thing, for example, as owner or usufructuary. A person with the right to possess a thing need not necessarily be in actual possession of that thing.

A purchaser purchasing an asset should ascertain who has possession of the asset forming the subject matter of the sale, and whether any third party has a right to possess the asset in question. In order to safeguard his concerns in this regard, the purchaser may require the seller to give certain warranties in relation to possession of the asset sold.

1.1.3 Ownership

Ownership of a thing is a composite real right consisting of a conglomeration of severable rights which include the right to use (*ius utendi*), the right to enjoy the fruits (*ius fruendi*), the right to abuse (*ius abutendi*), the right to possess (*ius possidendi*), the right to alienate (*ius dispondi*), the right to reclaim the thing from anyone who wrongfully withholds it (*ius vindicandi*) and the right to resist any unlawful invasion of the right (*ius negandi*).[5]

The acquisition of ownership of a thing is said to be derivative if the ownership is derived from and dependent on the ownership of a previous owner.[6] Therefore, if the seller is not owner of the thing and is not able to procure ownership of the thing, the purchaser may request the seller to warrant against eviction (see 2.3.4.2 and 2.3.4.3 below). The most important derivative modes of acquisition of

[2] Lee and Honore, *Family, Things and Succession*, eds. Erasmus, Van der Merwe and Van Wyk, (2nd ed, 1983) at 241.

[3] Lee and Honore *Op. cit.* at 244; see 2.2.4.3 and 2.2.4.4 below.

[4] *Op. cit.* at 241.

[5] *Op. cit.* at 260.

[6] *Op. cit.* at 267.

ownership are delivery of the thing in the case of moveable things, and registration in the Deeds Office in the case of immoveable things.[7]

For the passing of ownership by either delivery or registration, the following requirements must be complied with:[8] the thing must be susceptible of private ownership (a *res in commercio*); the transferor must be capable of transferring ownership; the transferee must be capable of acquiring ownership; the transferor must have the intention to transfer ownership (*animus transferendi dominii*) and the transferee must have the intention to acquire ownership (*animus accipiendi dominii*). In the case of a contract of sale the special rule applies that ownership does not pass, notwithstanding delivery of the thing sold, unless either the purchase price is paid or security or credit for its payment is given.

Ownership in a moveable corporeal thing is transferred by delivery, in other words, by the transfer of possession.[9] Transfer of possession will normally be effected by transferring the actual physical control of the thing from the transferor to the transferee, but certain instances of constructive delivery where actual transfer of possession does not occur, are also recognised.[10]

Ownership in an immoveable corporeal thing (land) is transferred by the registration of a deed of transfer prepared by a conveyancer and executed in the presence of the Registrar of Deeds by the landowner or by a conveyancer authorised by power of attorney to act on his behalf.[11] Registration takes place when the Registrar of Deeds affixes his signature to the deed.[12]

Therefore, when a purcaser acquires the moveable and immoveable assets of a company, while ownership of the moveable assets is transferred to the purchaser on delivery of those assets, a separate deed of transfer is required in order to transfer the immoveable property to him. Furthermore, no alienation of land is of any force or effect unless it is contained in a deed of alienation signed by the parties thereto or by their agents acting on their written authority.[13]

Ownership of moveable incorporeal property, such as a share in a company, is transferred by cession, in other words, by an agreement between cedent and cessionary to transfer the real right of ownership. Delivery of the share certificate is not required to transfer beneficial ownership. Although, as between cedent and cessionary beneficial ownership in a share may be transferred by a valid contract of cession, the company has regard only for the member of a company whose name is recorded in the company's share register. Therefore the company will pay dividends to and recognise the votes in general meeting of only registered members. If the beneficial owner of the shares wishes to enforce his rights against the company, he must first exercise his right to claim rectification of the share register (see 6.1 below).

1.1.4 The thing sold (*res vendita*)

All that is necessary in non-statutory law to conclude a contract of sale is that there be agreement between the seller and the purchaser on the thing to be sold

[7] *Op. cit.* at 280.
[8] *Op. cit.* at 281–282.
[9] *Op. cit.* at 282.
[10] *Op. cit.* at 282–285.
[11] Section 16 of the Deeds Registries Act 47 of 1937.
[12] Section 13(1) of the Deeds Registries Act.
[13] Section 2(1) of the Alientation of Land Act 68 of 1981; and see 21.1.3 below.

and the price to be paid. These two elements are the *essentialia* of a contract of sale. A "thing" is traditionally defined as meaning a corporeal object external to man which has a separate legal existence, which can be subjected to juristic control and which is useful and valuable to mankind.[14] The traditional definition has been extended over time to include incorporeal objects, such as shares.

A "company" is not a "thing" and therefore will not form the subject matter of any agreement of sale and purchase. A company is an artificial legal *persona* which can be created in South Africa only in terms of the Companies Act 61 of 1973, as amended ("the Companies Act"). In order to acquire control of a company's assets, therefore, the purchaser must purchase either the shares from the members, or the assets from the company. In the case of a purchase of shares the things sold are the shares sold, whereas in the case of the purchase of a business as a going concern, the things sold comprise, *inter alia,* all the assets required to run the business as a going concern.

It is essential to classify the shares or each of the assets of a business separately according to their nature in order to ensure that ownership in and possession of each share or asset is correctly transferred from the seller to the purchaser.

Assets may be classified into those which are not susceptible to private ownership and therefore cannot be acquired by any individual person, and those which are susceptible to private ownership and can be acquired and owned by any individual person. Traditionally the *res non commercio* are divided into things common to every person (the air, the sea and running water), public things (harbours, public rivers, public road, national parks and the seashore), and divine things (tombstones and graveyards).

Assets which are susceptible to private ownership are divided according to their nature into corporeal and incorporeal things, single and compound things, tangible and intangible things, consumable and non-consumable things, divisible and indivisible things and moveable and immoveable things. The classification of each asset falls within the ambit of the "Law of Things" and is beyond the scope of this publication.

1.1.5 Different types of South African companies

Two types of companies may be formed and incorporated under the Companies Act, namely, a company having a share capital, or a company not having a share capital and having the liability of its members limited by its memorandum of association.

A company not having a share capital and having the liability of its members limited by its memorandum is termed "a company limited by guarantee" (section 19(1) of the Companies Act). The name of a company limited by guarantee must include the word "Limited" as its last word, and the statement "(Limited by Guarantee)" must be subjoined to its name.

This publication is concerned with companies having a share capital. A company having a share capital may be either a public company or a private company having shares of par value or shares of no par value.[15]

[14] Lee and Honore, *Op. cit.* at 223.

[15] Section 19(2) of the Companies Act.

1.1.6 Public and private companies

The name of a public company having a share capital must include, as its last word, the word "Limited", and the transferability of its shares and the number of its shareholders are not limited in any way.

A public company may apply for and be listed on a registered stock exchange in South Africa. There is, at present, only one stock exchange in the Republic of South Africa, namely, The Johannesburg Stock Exchange ("the JSE"). The executive authority which manages the affairs of the JSE is the Committee.[16] The Committee has the sole and unfettered power, subject to the provisions of the Stock Exchanges Control Act, to include in the list of securities which securities may be traded on the JSE, to review the listing annually and to suspend or terminate a listing of securities.[17] A "public listed company" is therefore a public company which has its shares listed on the JSE. A sale of shares in a public listed company is subject to the regulations set out in The Securities Regulation Code on Take-Overs and Mergers (see 1.1.12.1 below).

The name of a private company having a share capital shall include, as its last two words, the words "(Proprietary) Limited".[18] The expression "private company" means a company having a share capital and which, by its articles, restricts the right to transfer its shares, limits the number of its members (exclusive of persons who are in the employment of the company and of persons who having been formally in the employment of the company were, while in such employment, and have continued after the termination of such employment to be, members of the company) to 50, and prohibits any offer to the public for the subscription of any shares or debentures of the company.[19] The shares of a private company are not listed on the JSE and a sale of such shares is not—except in certain circumstances—subject to the regulations set out in The Securities Regulation Code on Take-Overs and Mergers (see 1.1.12.1 below).

1.1.7 Associations not for gain

A "Section 21 company" is an incorporation of an association not for gain (section 21 of the Companies Act). The statement "Association incorporated under section 21" must be included and subjoined to the name of the association not for gain. Any association formed for any lawful purpose which has as its main object the promotion of religion, arts, sciences, education, charity, recreation, or any other cultural or social activity or communal or group interests, and which intends to apply its profits (if any) or other income in promoting its said main object, and which prohibits the payment of any dividend to its members, may be incorporated as a company limited by guarantee.

Furthermore, a branch established in the Republic of South Africa of a company or other association of persons incorporated outside the Republic of South Africa, or, an association of persons which is not incorporated and has its head office in a foreign country, may also be incorporated under section 21 if it

16 Section 1 of the Stock Exchanges Control Act, 1 of 1985 sv "committee".

17 Rule 1.40.2.2.5 read with rule 1.50 and 10.10.1 of the Rules and Directives of the JSE, 26 February 1984, as amended.

18 Section 49(1)(b) of the Companies Act.

19 Section 20(1) of the Companies Act.

is an association not for gain and complies with the provisions of sections 21A and 21 of the Companies Act.

1.1.8 External companies

An "external company" is merely a branch of a company or other association of persons incorporated outside the Republic of South Africa, the memorandum of which has been lodged with the Registrar of Companies prior to 1 January 1974, or which has, subsequent to 1 January 1974, established a place of business in the Republic.[20] A "place of business" means any place where the company in question transacts or holds itself out as transacting business and includes a share transfer or share registration office.[21] There must be included in the name of any external company the statement "Incorporated in _________ (stating the name of the foreign country concerned)".[22]

Every external company must, within 21 days after the establishment of a place of business in the Republic of South Africa, lodge with the Registrar of Companies a certified copy of the memorandum of association of the company, and if the said memorandum is not in one of the official languages of the Republic of South Africa (English or Afrikaans), a certified translation thereof in one of those languages, as well as the other documents referred to in section 322(1) of the Companies Act must be lodged with the Registrar of Companies. Upon the registration of the memorandum of association of an external company the external company shall be a body corporate in the Republic of South Africa subject to the applicable provisions of the Companies Act (section 323). No external company shall be capable of acquiring the ownership of immoveable property in the Republic of South Africa unless its memorandum of association has been or is deemed to be registered under section 322 of the Companies Act (section 324).

1.1.9 Close corporations

The Close Corporations Act, 69 of 1984 has, with effect from 1 January 1985, introduced in the Republic of South Africa the close corporation as an alternative corporate form for a business venture. The abbreviation "CC" or "BK", in capital letters, must be subjoined to the English or Afrikaans name, as the case may be, of a corporation.[23]

The close corporation is a juristic person distinct from its members which consequently enjoys perpetual succession and its members have limited liability in respect of the corporation's debts. It is granted the capacity and powers of a natural person in so far as these are appropriate to a legal person.[24]

Close corporations do not issue shares and therefore do not have a share capital or shareholders, but only members' interests and members. Instead of shares a member becomes entitled to a member's interest as a consideration for his contribution. A close corporation may be formed with one or more members but

[20] Section 1 of the Companies Act sv "external company".
[21] Section 1 of the Companies Act sv "place of business".
[22] Section 49(2) of the Companies Act.
[23] Section 22 of the Close Corporations Act.
[24] H.S. Cilliers, M.L. Berade, J.J. Henning (ed), E.M. de la Rey and J.J. Plessis, Close Corporations Service, 1–5.

at no time may there be more than ten members.[25] Subject to a certain number of explicitly restricted exceptions only natural persons may be members of a close corporation. No juristic person may directly or indirectly, hold a member's interest in a close corporation. Consequently a company or a close corporation may not become a member of a close corporation; if they do, they risk personal liability for corporation debts. However, a close corporation may be a shareholder in a company and may even become a holding company and enter into partnerships with other companies or close corporations.

1.1.10 Groups of companies

A company may be a member of another company and in this way a network of interrelated companies can be formed to form a "group" of companies. A "group" of companies is not and has not been elevated to the status of a separate legal persona, and each company in the group retains its separate legal identity.

A group of companies consists of a holding company and its subsidiaries. The definitions of a subsidiary company in the Companies Act permit a company to have more than one holding company. For the purposes of the Companies Act, a company is deemed to be a subsidiary of another company if that other company is a member of it and either holds a majority of the voting rights in it, or has the right to appoint or remove directors holding a majority of the voting rights at meetings of the board, or has the sole control of a majority of the voting rights in it, whether pursuant to an agreement with other members or otherwise (section 1 of the Companies Act, as amended by section 1 of the Companies Amendment Act, 1992).

In determining whether a company holds the majority of the voting rights in another company, section 1 of the Companies Amendment Act, 1992, provides that:

(i) voting rights which are exercisable only in certain circumstances shall be taken into account only:
   (aa) when those circumstances have arisen, and for so long as they continue; or
   (bb) when those circumstances are under the control of the person holding the voting rights;

(ii) voting rights held by a person in a fiduciary capacity shall be treated as not held by him but by the beneficiary of such voting rights;

(iii) voting rights held by a person as nominee for another person shall be treated as not held by him but by that other person, and voting rights shall be deemed to be held by a nominee for another person if they are exercisable only on the instructions or with the consent or concurrence of that other person.

Furthermore, a body corporate or other undertaking which would have been a subsidiary of a company had the body corporate or other undertaking been a company shall be deemed to be a subsidiary of that company.[26]

[25] Section 28 of the Close Corporations Act.

[26] Section 1, subsection 3(c) of the definition of "subsidiary" of the Companies Amendment Act, 1992.

1.1.11 Acquiring the shares of a company or the business as a going concern

When those who trade or invest through the medium of a company wish to dispose of their business they are faced with a choice of methods.[27] The company can sell its business as a going concern, or the shareholders of the company can sell their shares in the company. The sale of shares method tends to be popular, not only because it is a simpler transaction, involving a transfer of ownership only of the shares in the company, but also for tax reasons.[28]

A company is a separate legal person which has the capacity not only of owning assets but also of incurring contractual, delictual and criminal liabilities. When a purchaser elects to purchase the business as a going concern from the company, the purchaser may select which assets and which liabilities he is prepared to acquire. Such selection will form the basis of negotiations between the seller and the purchaser in respect of the proposed sale. On the other hand, when a purchaser elects to purchase the controlling shares of the company from the shareholders or from a shareholder, he will be acquiring control of a company with all its existing assets and liabilities, and disclosed or undisclosed contingent liabilities. It is necessary in both instances to concentrate upon and attempt to identify the assets and liabilities of the company itself.

Although investigation by the purchaser into the affairs of a company may go some way to establishing whether or not a company owns the assets which it is said to own, the most intensive and searching inquiries cannot conclusively establish the extent of a company's liabilities. Therefore, whether the purchaser purchases the shares in the company from the shareholders or the business as a going concern from the company, it is usual practice for the purchaser to require a comprehensive set of warranties and indemnities from the sellers in respect of the company's affairs. It is also usual for the sellers to attempt to avoid giving any warranties or, failing that, at least to limit the scope of any warranties given.

1.1.12 Acquisition of shares

1.1.12.1 ACQUISITION OF SHARES IN A PUBLIC COMPANY AND CERTAIN PRIVATE COMPANIES

The rules which affect a takeover bid for a public listed company are those rules set out in The Securities Regulation Code on Take-Overs and Mergers ("the code"). The code emanates from the Securities Regulation Panel ("the panel"), which was established in 1989 in terms of the Companies Act.[29] The panel is empowered and required to make rules to, *inter alia,* regulate all transactions and schemes which constitute "affected transactions" and all proposals which on completion or implementation would become "affected transactions", and rules relating to the duties of the offeror and the duties of the offeree company during an "affected transaction".[30]

[27] W.J.L. Knight, *The Acquisition of Private Companies* (3rd ed., 1983), at 1.
[28] *Ibid.* Also, E.B. Broomberg, *Tax Strategy,* (2nd ed., 1983), at 35.
[29] Section 440B of the Companies Act.
[30] Section 440C(1), (3) and (4) of the Companies Act.

The code which contains the rules is based to a large extent on the City Code on Take-overs and Mergers issued by the London Panel on Take-overs and Mergers. The code, as laid down and applied by the panel, is intended to operate principally to ensure fair and equal treatment of all holders of relevant securities in relation to affected transactions. The code also provides an orderly framework within which affected transactions are to be conducted.

The code enjoys the force of law. An affected transaction must comply with the code.[31] The panel may enforce the code by application to court for an order for specific performance and/or for an interdict and/or for a declaratory order and/or by notification to interested parties and/or by general publication of an announcement that the requirements of the code have not been complied with and/or that a particular offer is not or was not valid, with the consequences flowing therefrom.[32]

In the determination of whether or not the code applies, it is the nature of the company which is the offeree or potential offeree company, or in which control (as defined) may change, that is relevant. The code applies where the offeree company is a public company, whether or not listed on the JSE, and to statutory corporations, which are or are deemed to be resident in the Republic of South Africa. For the purposes of the code a company shall be deemed to be resident in the Republic of South Africa if it is incorporated or registered in the Republic of South Africa, or has its head office and/or place of central management in the Republic of South Africa.

The code also applies where the offeree company is a private company which is or which is deemed to be so resident, but only where the shareholder's interests valued at the offered price, and the shareholder's loan capital, exceed R5 million and there are more than ten beneficial shareholders, provided that the executive director of the panel may exempt any particular transaction affecting a private company if satisfied that there can be no prejudice to minority shareholders.

"An affected transaction" for the purposes of the code means any transaction including a transaction which forms part of a series of transactions or schemes whatever form it may take, which:

(a) taking into account any securities held before such transaction or scheme, has or will have the effect of:
    (i) vesting control of any company (excluding a close corporation) in any person or two or more persons acting in concert, in whom control did not vest prior to such transactional scheme; or
    (ii) any person, or two or more persons acting in concert, acquiring or becoming the sole holder or holders of, all the securities, or all the securities of a particular class, of any company (excluding a close corporation); or

(b) involves the acquisition by any person, or two or more persons acting in concert, in whom control of any company (excluding a close corporation) vests on or after 1 February 1991, of further securities of that company in excess of the limits prescribed in the rules.

[31] Section 440L of the Companies Act.
[32] Sections 440C(1)(b), 440C(4)(e) and 440M of the Companies Act.

An affected transaction will include a reverse takeover of a public listed company. A reverse takeover involves the acquisition for shares by a public listed company of an unlisted one in circumstances in which the number of shares issued as consideration by the public listed company is so great that a change in the control of a listed company results. In such cases the panel claims authority and full compliance with the code is required.

For the purpose of the definition of an "affected transaction", "control" is defined to mean the holding of shares in a company giving the holders the right to exercise the "specified percentage" or more of the voting rights in the company. The "specified percentage" has been set at 30 per cent and for the purpose of (b) of the definition of "affected transactions" the rules include as such a transaction, the acquisition in any 12 month period of additional shares carrying more than 5 per cent of the votes, by any person holding together with persons acting in concert with him, shares representing between 30 per cent and 50 per cent of the votes in the company.

"Acting in concert" is widely defined to include the activities of two or more persons pursuant to an agreement, arrangement or understanding, whether formal or informal.

The consequences of a transaction which is an "affected transaction" is that a similar offer be made to the minority shareholders, in other words, those not involved in the affected transaction.

1.1.12.2 ACQUISITION OF SHARES IN PRIVATE COMPANIES

Taxation apart, there is little legislation which has specific application to the transfer of ownership in shares of private companies. Some sections of the Companies Act place restraints upon some aspects of the transaction, but there is, for instance, no legislation which implies any term to an agreement for the sale of shares. Schemes of arrangement between the company and its members under section 311 of the Companies Act are rarely used as a method of acquiring the controlling shares in a private company.

1.1.12.3 ACQUISITION OF SHARES BY A FOREIGN INVESTOR

The acquisition of shares by a foreign investor of a South African company is dealt with more fully in section 15 below.

1.1.13 Acquisition of a business as a going concern

What the "business" of a company is, is a question of fact. The memorandum of association of a company must state the purpose for which it is to be formed and incorporated and must describe the main business which the company is to carry on.[33] If the main business actually carried on at any time by a company falls within the capacity of the company by virtue only of an object stated in its memorandum, such main business shall be deemed to be the main object of that company (section 33(2) of the Companies Act).

A "business" has been defined as "anything which occupies the time and

[33] Section 52(1) of the Companies Act.

attention and labours of a man for profit",[34] although it has also been said the profit motive is not essential.[35]

The meaning of "to carry on business" has also been interpreted for the purposes of section 42 of the South African Income Tax Act, 58 of 1962 as amended ("the Income Tax Act"). The definition of "trade" in the Income Tax Act enumerates a number of activities, including "business". It may be suggested that the legislature by using the words "carrying on business" in section 42 of the Income Tax Act did not intend them in the wide sense just mentioned but in a narrower sense, namely a business falling outside the other activities specifically included in the definition of "trade". If this view be correct, then, for example, the letting of property or the use of a patent, or the exercise of a profession, because of their specific mention in the definition of trade, do not establish the carrying on of a business. The courts do not appear, however, to have approached the question of what is "carrying on business" in this way.[36]

The more general view has been that the words should be given their ordinary significance in the commercial sense,[37] in other words, their common-sense and business meaning.[38] What appears to be envisaged is a continuity of activities and not merely isolated transactions, and much will depend upon the circumstances of each case. The case of a company may be different from that of an individual where that company is formed for a particular purpose and carries it out, because from the very nature of the association the idea of continuity is inferred.[39] Essentially, however, to establish whether a company carries on a business one needs to consider its activities in the light of the intention with which it undertakes them.[40]

It is, therefore, a factual inquiry whether or not the commercial activities of a company amount to the carrying on of a business. In order to acquire a "business", in this sense, as a going concern, would mean that all the assets required in order to carry on such business in succession from the seller would need to be acquired by the purchaser.

The importance of selling a business as a going concern or a part of an enterprise where that part is capable of separate operation, as opposed merely to selling certain business assets, is that the supply of the "goods" comprising the business as a going concern is currently charged with value added tax at the rate of zero per cent.[41]

1.2 Statutory v *Contractual Warranties*

Apart from the warranty contained in section 138 of the Companies Act, there are no warranties implied by any South African statute in the sale of either shares in or assets of a company (see 1.3.5.3 below).

[34] *Smith* v *Anderson* (1980) 15 Ch D 247,

[35] D. Meyerowitz and E. Spiro, *Income Tax* (CapeTown—Taxpayer, 1990, looseleaf) at 568(A1); *Modderfontein Deep Levels Ltd* v *Feinstein* 1920 TPD 288; *Platt* v *CIR* 1922 AD 42 at 50.

[36] Meyerowitz and Spiro, *op cit.* at 568(A1).

[37] *Joel* v *CIR* 1922 WLD 35; Meyerowitz, *ibid.*

[38] *Rhodesian Railways Limited* v *CoT* 1925 AD 438 at 462.

[39] *Stephan* v *CIR* 1919 WLD 1; *Platt* v *CIR* 1922 AD 42 at 51.

[40] *Op. cit.* at 569.

[41] Section 11(1)(e) of the Value Added Tax Act, 89 of 1991.

Where shares are transferred, then for the purpose of the registration of the transfer of the shares in the company's share register, section 138 of the Companies Act imposes a statutory warranty on the person lodging with the company any document relating to that transfer. That person, and if he is acting as an agent, then his principal, is deemed to warrant that such document is genuine and that he and his principal, jointly and severally with him, indemnify the said company against any claim made upon it and against any loss or damage suffered by it arising out of a transfer registered by the company of the shares referred to in such document. The warranty and indemnity contained in section 138 of the Companies Act are aimed at protecting the company and not the purchaser and seller of the shares sold.

Like any other term of a contract, a warranty may be included as a term of a contract either by express agreement between the parties, or by implication, and, in the latter case, either by operation of law or from the surrounding circumstances. In most cases the parties will, by express agreement, decide which warranties they wish to include in or exclude from their contract. A discussion of certain express warranties, implied warranties and tacit warranties follows.

1.3 Warranties v *Commitments and Statements*

1.3.1 Introduction

The terms of a contract are the promises agreed upon by the parties which together make up the contract.[42] The parties will negotiate the terms of the contract, and once agreement is reached on what terms should be included there is a verbal contract which is binding on the parties. Usually, however, either party may require that legal advisers or they themselves, record the terms of the proposed verbal agreement in writing, pending signature of which there will be no binding agreement between the parties. A further period of protracted negotiation may then ensue during which the terms of the proposed written contract are settled by the parties.

It is not uncommon for the parties to record the progress they have made in a partial agreement, thus clearing the points on which they are agreed out of the way and facilitating discussion on the points that remain outstanding. If for one or other reason the intended contract is never concluded, one party may attempt to hold the other to the partial agreement. The partial agreement, though, is incomplete and provisional and the parties lack the necessary intention to contract.[43] The approach adopted by the courts in these types of situations is to inquire whether the undertaking by the one party was an offer made with the intention to contract (*animo contrahendi*), which upon acceptance would give rise to an enforceable contract, or whether it was merely a proposal made while the parties were in the process of negotiating and feeling their way towards a more precise and comprehensive agreement.[44] The "contract" may also be regarded as being "void for vagueness".[45]

[42] R.H. Christie, *The Law of Contract in South Africa*, (2nd ed., 1991) at 141.

[43] *Op. cit.*, at 37.

[44] *Pitout* v *North Cape Livestock Co-op Ltd* 1977 (4) SA 842 (A) at 850 D.

[45] *Levenstein* v *Levenstein* 1955 (3) SA 615 (SR) at 619; and see 21.1.11 below.

When both parties are satisfied that the written contract correctly records the terms of their agreement, it is signed. The parties may (and usually do) agree that the signed written contract be regarded as the exclusive memorial of the agreement between the parties, to the exclusion of all statements made by either party during the preparations and negotiations of that contract. Where, however, the contract does not accurately record the common intention of the parties, either party may in certain circumstances claim rectification of the contract (see 1.3.3.2 below).

When there is no written contract, however, and there is doubt or a dispute about what statements, whether oral or written, should be included in the alleged verbal contract as terms the court may have to conduct a two-stage inquiry to decide first, what was said, written or done during the negotiations and, second, whether it must be included among the terms of the alleged verbal contract.

1.3.2 Statements made during negotiations

Statements made by parties when negotiating the terms of a contract (prior to agreement) may conceivably take the status of a puff or commendation, the expression of an opinion, a representation of fact or an undertaking. Undertakings are commonly referred to as warranties and, in this respect, a warranty denotes a promise which gives rise to a contractual obligation.[46] It is necessary to analyse each statement made during negotiations and to categorise it, as each such category affords the parties different legal remedies. Once such a statement is found to be a term of the verbal contract it may be either a condition or a warranty (see 1.3.2.5 below for a discussion on warranties; and 21.4 below for a discussion on conditions).

1.3.2.1 PUFFS AND COMMENDATIONS

A statement by the seller may be a puff or a commendation. Bearing in mind that a contract is an agreement seriously and deliberately made and that its terms are usually intended by the parties to be enforceable at law, it is unlikely that mere puffing or praise of the *res vendita* will be intended by the seller to be a promise susceptible of enforcement.[47]

Sellers are in the habit of praising their wares and such sales talk cannot be treated as a term of a contract unless cast in the form of a promise that will be taken seriously by the buyer.[48] There is a great difference, therefore, between saying something in order merely to recommend the *res vendita* (a puff or commendation) and promising to make good what has been said (a warranty). A puff or commendation is, therefore, not intended to be, and is not, a term of the contract and, if subsequently found to be incorrect, affords the buyer no remedies against the seller.[49]

[46] *Petit* v *Abramson* 1946 NPD 673 at 679.
[47] *Op. cit.* at 179.
[48] *Mazza & another* v *Jones* 1973(2) SA 740 (RAD).
[49] J.T.R. Gibson, *South African Mercantile and Company Law*, (5th ed., 1983) at 74; *Geldenhuys & Neethling* v *Beuthin* 1918 AD at 435.

1.3.2.2 OPINIONS

A statement may be merely an expression of opinion or forecast of the future. For example, the seller may advise the tentative purchaser of a farm that he need not fear drought. The reference to fear of drought being placed out of consideration is not a statement of fact, but merely a confident anticipation of future events based on opinion.[50] If the honest opinion subsequently turns out to be incorrect, it affords the purchaser no remedies against the seller, based on either misrepresentation or otherwise.

On the other hand, a statement by the seller that he holds a certain opinion is a representation by the seller about his state of mind and its correctness is a question of fact. In other words, a statement of expectation or a statement in the future tense may impliedly say something as to the existing position and so import an implied representation.[51] For example, a statement of opinion by the seller of shares in a company that owned a restaurant that if the turnover of the company's restaurant business were maintained at the same level as before, the net income produced would be sufficient to pay the instalments on the price and cover the purchaser's living expenses, involves two representations of existing facts.[52] Firstly, there is an implied representation that at its present level of turnover the restaurant is earning substantial profits, and secondly, there is an express representation by the seller of his state of mind, namely that he believed that if that level of turnover were maintained, its net income would be sufficient to cover the purchase price and the purchaser's living expenses.[53] If both representations are false the purchaser will be entitled to the normal remedies available for misrepresentation, (see 1.3.2.3 below). Where the misrepresentations are fraudulent or negligent, the purchaser will also be entitled to institute a claim for damages for fraudulent or negligent misrepresentation inducing a contract, which are claims in delict, not contract.[54]

Therefore, an erroneous opinion about an event which is to take place in the future may form the basis of an action for the rescission of the contract of sale on the ground of misrepresentation, but in such the cause of action will be the misrepresentation by the person about the state of his own mind when he gave expression to the erroneous opinion, and not the mere fact that the opinion afterwards proved to be wrong.[55]

1.3.2.3 REPRESENTATIONS

A statement may be a representation of fact, in other words, a statement made by one party to the other before or at the time of the contract of some matter or circumstance relating to it, which may induce the other party to enter into the

[50] *Adam, No* v *The Curlews Citrus Farms Ltd* 1930 TPD 68 at 82.

[51] *Feinstein* v *Niggli and another* 1981(2) SA 684(A) at 695D; Halsbury *Laws of England* 3rd ed. Vol. 26 para. 1520.

[52] *Feinstein* v *Niggli and another* 1981(2) SA 684(A) at 694 E–696 C.

[53] A.J. Kerr, *The Principles of the Law of Contract*, (3rd ed., 1980) at 187–8.

[54] *Trotman* v *Edwich* 1951 (1) SA 443 (A) at 449B.

[55] *Ruto Flour Mills (Pty) Ltd* v *Adelson* 1959(4) SA 120 (T) at 122G–123A; *Novick and another* v *Comair Holdings Ltd and Others* 1979 (2) SA 116 (W) at 149F; *Van Heerden and another* v *Smith* 1956(3) SA 273 (OPD); Gibson *Op. cit.* at 75.

contract.[56] A representation is merely an inducement to contract. It does not become a term of the contract unless the parties specifically include it as a term of the contract. Where the representation is included as a term of the contract, then the remedies for breach of contract will be available where the representation is found to be false.

If the representation is incorrect, it is a misrepresentation. South African law allows a contract induced by misrepresentation to be set aside at the election of the representee irrespective of fault on the part of the representer. The contract is therefore voidable and the party seeking to avoid the contract on the ground of the misrepresentation must be able to prove the following six elements of his case:[57] firstly, that the representation relied upon was made; secondly, that it was a representation as to a fact. A promise, prediction, opinion or estimate or exercise of discretion is not a representation as to the truth or accuracy of its content although it can often be construed as a representation that the person making it is of a particular state of mind (see 1.3.2.2 above);[58] thirdly, that the representation was false. In relation to an ordinary representation of fact, what must be shown is that the fact was not as represented. When a prediction, opinion or estimate is relied upon, what must be shown is not merely that it was, or turned out to be erroneous, but that it did not represent the *bona fide* view, at the time when it was expressed, of the person who expressed it; fourthly, that it was material, in the sense that it was such as would have influenced a reasonable man to enter into the contract in issue; fifthly, that it was intended to induce the person to whom it was made to enter into the transaction sought to be avoided; and finally, that the representation did in fact induce the contract.

Misrepresentation may also provide a ground for a delictual action for damages. In such cases the aggrieved party enjoys an election between the alternative causes of action.[59]

Where the misrepresentation is made fraudulently, the representee, induced to enter the contract on the basis of such statement, has, in addition to his contractual remedies, a claim for delictual damages, in other words, for consequential loss.[60] The remedies available to an aggrieved party in the case where he has been induced to enter into a contract on the ground of fraudulent misrepresentation differ from those where his complaint is that the other party has failed to make good a warranty incorporated as a term of the contract. In the first case the aggrieved party's action is based on delict and if he chooses not to claim rescission of the contract he may content himself with a claim for damages, the measure of which is determined by the extent of the loss suffered by the aggrieved party by reason of the falsity of the representation, in other words, he may be placed in the same position he would have been in if the misrepresentation had not

[56] Kerr, *Op. cit.* at 185; Gibson *Op. cit.* at 72.

[57] *Karoo and Eastern Board of Executors & Trust Co* v *Farr & Others* 1921 AD at 415; *Novick and Another* v *Comair Holdings Limited and Others* 1979(2) SA 116 (W) at 149D–150C; Gibson *Op. cit.* at 73:

[58] *Naude* v *Harrison* 1925 CPD 84; *Lamb* v *Walters* 1926 AD 358.

[59] *Prima Toy Holding (Pty) Ltd* v *Rosenberg* 1974(2) SA 477 (C).

[60] *Caxton Printing Works (Pty) Ltd* v *Transvaal Advertising Contractors Ltd* 1936 TPD 209; *Ranger* v *Wykerd & another* 1977(2) SA 976 (A).

been made.[61] In an action on the breach of warranty the party responsible for the misrepresentation can be compelled to make good what he has promised, in other words, he can claim to be placed in the same financial position he would have been in if there had been no breach of the warranty and there had been proper performance of the warranty.[62]

Where the misrepresentation which induced the contract is made negligently, the representee also has a delictual action for damages for consequential loss.[63] Prior to the decision in *Bayer South Africa (Pty) Ltd v Frost* in 1992, the South African courts enforced the conservative rule that in the case of a *bona fide* negligent misrepresentation which induced a contract, no right to consequential damages existed.[64]

Where the misrepresentation is made innocently, the law relating to a delictual claim for consequential damages arising from a negligent misrepresentation which induces a contract of sale prior to the *Bayer South Africa (Pty) Ltd* v *Frost* case applies, and no claim for consequential loss is available.[65] An innocent misrepresentation made by the seller, which induces a contract of sale and which falls within the ambit of the concept of a *dictum et promissum* (see 1.3.2.4 below) which is not made good, however, affords the purchaser a claim for the reduction of the purchase price under the *actio quanti minoris*, or a claim for the return of the thing sold under the *actio redhibitoria.*[66]

1.3.2.4 MATERIAL STATEMENTS (*DICTA ET PROMISSA*)

A statement may be a *dictum et promissum*, in other words, a material statement made by the seller to the purchaser during the negotiations bearing on the quality of the *res vendita* and going beyond mere praise and commendation. A *dictum et promissum,* therefore, falls somewhere between a puff or commendation and a representation bearing on the quality of the *res vendita.* All three categories of statements do not form part of the contract.

In *Naude* v *Harrison*[67] the phrase *dicta et promissa* was interpreted as referring in the *dicta* part to representations and in the *promissa* part to warranties. In the case of *Phame (Pty) Ltd v Paizes*[68] it was authoritatively decided, however, that the phrase *dictum et promissum* referred not to two different concepts but to a single concept in contracts of sale. The court defined *dictum et promissum* as being a material statement made by the seller to the purchaser during the negotiations, bearing on the quality of the *res vendita* and going beyond mere praise and commendation, and which does not form part of the contract.

[61] *Trotman and Another* v *Edwick* 1951 (1) SA 443 (A) at 449; *Scheepers* v *Handley* 1960 (3) SA 54 (A).

[62] *Whitfield* v *Phillips and another* 1957 (3) SA 318 (A) at 325.

[63] *Administrateur, Natal* v *Trust Bank van Afrika Bpk* 1979 (3) SA 824(A); *Bayer South Africa (pty)* v *Frost* 1992 (4) SA 559 (A) at 568.

[64] *Dickson & Co* v *Levy* (1894)11 SC 33; *Hamman* v *Moolman* 1968 (4) SA 340(A); *Du Plessis* v *Semmelinck* 1976 (2) SA 500 (T); Gibson *Op. cit.* at 80–82.

[65] *Breedt* v *Elsie Motors (Edms) Beperk* 1963 (3) 525 (A) at 529 A–G.

[66] *Phame (Pty) Ltd* v *Paizes* 1973 (3) SA 397 (A) at 415 B and H.

[67] *Naude* v *Harrison* 1925 CPD 84.

[68] *Phame (Pty) Ltd* v *Paizes*, 1973 (3) SA 397 (A).

It is unnecessary and confusing to try to fit the concept of a *dictum et promissum* into some modern juristic niche like warranty or term, and then to draw conclusions therefrom as to the purchaser's rights.[69] The Latin words *dictum* and *promissum* are therefore not equivalent to the English words "representation", which is a statement inducing but not incorporated as a term of the contract and "promise" or warranty, which is an undertaking incorporated as a term of a contract, respectively.[70] Whether a statement by the seller goes beyond mere praise or commendation will depend on the circumstances of each case.

Relevant considerations could include the following: whether the statement was made in answer to a question from the purchaser; its materiality to the known purpose for which the purchaser was interested in purchasing; whether the statement was one of fact or of personal opinion and whether it would be obvious even to the gullible that the seller was merely singing the praises of his wares, as sellers have ever been wont to do.[71]

The remedies available to a purchaser where the seller has made a *dictum et promissum* are the *actio quanti minoris* (action for the reduction of the price) and the *actio redhibitoria* (action for the return of the thing sold), which are aedilitian remedies which have descended to use from Roman law, via the Roman–Dutch Law. The aedilitian remedies were granted to the purchaser if the seller had made a *dictum et promissum* relative to the quality of the thing sold, and it fell short of this.[72] The description of the ambit of the aedilitian edict in *Phame (Pty) Ltd* v *Paizes* is wide enough to allow some concurrence between the aedilitian remedies available to a purchaser in respect of the qualities of the thing sold and those remedies based on breach of warranty and misrepresentation.

1.3.2.5 WARRANTIES

The word "warranty" is one of the more unfortunate importations into our law from English legal terminology, because in English law it has so many different meanings.[73] A warranty in English law may mean, generically, a term of the contract as opposed to a mere puff or a representation; or it may mean, specifically, a term not going to the root of the contract as opposed to a condition in the sense of a term going to the root of a contract; or it may, especially when described as a collateral warranty, mean a term of a contract prior to and inducing the main contract.

The proper significance of the word "warranty" in the law of England is an agreement which refers to the subject matter of the contract, but, not being an essential part of the contract either intrinsically or by agreement, is collateral to the main purpose of such contract.[74] Consequently, a breach of a "warranty" in English law does not give rise to a right of rescission, the warrantee being left with only a claim for damages.

[69] *Phame (Pty) Ltd v Paizes* 1973 (3) SA 397(A) at 416H.
[70] Christie *Op. cit.* at 143.
[71] *Phame (Pty) Ltd* v *Paizes* 1973 (3) SA 397(A) at 418A–B.
[72] *Phame (Pty) Ltd* v *Paizes* 1973 (3) SA 397 (A) at 410 D.
[73] Christie *Op. cit.* at 180; *Small* v *Smith* 1954 (3) SA 434 (SWA) at 437.
[74] W.R Anson, *Principles of the English Law of Contract,* (1959), at 114.

The English "warranty" must be distinguished from the English "condition" which may be defined as a statement of fact, or a promise, which forms a term of the contract, and which if unfulfilled, allows the party to repudiate the contract (Anson, 110). Consequently, in English law, the non-fulfilment of the condition gives rise to a right of rescission.

In South Africa a true "condition" is a qualification which renders the operation and consequences of the whole contract dependent upon an uncertain event, in other words, the parties introduce contingency as to the existence or otherwise of the contract.[75]

In South Africa the term "warranty" usually means a promise which gives rise to a contractual obligation and is a term of the contract.[76] A warranty may, therefore, like any other term of a contract, be either an express term of the contract (an *accidentalium*) or implied into the contract either by the law (a *naturalium*) or by the facts (see 1.3.4.1 below).

The word "warranties" is normally used of undertakings by the warrantor that the skill with which an obligation will be performed, or the quality or quantity of the subject matter of the contract, or the absence of defects in the subject matter, or the possible future eviction of the transferee, or other similar topics, is or shall be as it is stated or promised to be by the warrantor.[77] The test for whether a statement is a warranty generally is whether both parties intended to contract that the thing sold, or performance or other circumstance should be as represented.[78] A warranty therefore relates to the characteristics of the subject matter of the contract and it can be described as an additional term of the contract which affects the content of the obligations of the warrantor arising from the contract.

Where the warranty has not been met, in other words, where there is a "breach of a warranty", the normal principles applicable to breach of contract are relevant. The breach of a warranty, like the breach of any other term of the contract, may be classified as either a major or as a minor breach. The law concerning the remedy or remedies for major or minor breaches is complicated and is best approached by considering the three classes of warranties—namely express, implied and tacit—separately. The various remedies available for breach of warranties are discussed in sections 19 and 20 below.

1.3.3 Statements forming part of a contract of sale

Once the court has categorised the particular statement made by either of the parties, it is then necessary to determine whether that statement should be included as a term of the contract. The importance of such inclusion as a term of the contract lies in the fact that a statement made during negotiations which becomes a term of the contract is enforceable and binding on the parties, whereas a statement made during negotiations which does not become a term of the contract is not enforceable or binding on the parties. It is notoriously difficult to decide which statements are intended to be included in the contract as terms and which are not.

[75] *R v Katz* 1959 (S) SA 408 (C) at 417; and see 21.4 below.

[76] *Petit* v *Abramson* 1946 NPD 673 at 679, R. Sharrock, *Business Transactions Law*, (2nd ed., 1989), at 135.

[77] Kerr, *Op. cit.* at 351.

[78] *Naude v Harrison* 1925 CPD 84 at 90.

1.3.3.1 VERBAL CONTRACTS

A statement made seriously and deliberately during the negotiation of a verbal contract becomes a term of the contract if the parties by mutual intention either expressed or implied it to be a term of that contract.[79]

Therefore, a statement which amounts to a warranty will become a term of the verbal contract if the parties intended it to be a term of their contract, and it makes no difference whether it is stated in so many words to constitute a warranty or not, so long as it was intended to convey to the mind of the purchaser that the seller intended the affirmation to constitute a promise.[80]

Whether or not the statement was made in answer to a question from the purchaser is merely one of the factors to be considered.[81] Therefore, it is incorrect to say that it is impossible to treat a plain and unqualified answer given to an equally plain and direct question as constituting a warranty in every case.[82] In most cases a direct answer given to a direct question will constitute a warranty, but it is by no means impossible to conceive of a direct question producing a direct answer that does not find its way into the contract as a warranty but must be treated as a representation inducing the contract.[83]

1.3.3.2 WRITTEN CONTRACTS

In a written contract it is usually easier to identify the terms of a contract because statements falling into the categories of mere puffs, commendations, opinions and representations inducing the contract are not normally included in the written document. It has also become a common practice for parties to insert in their written contracts exemption (sometimes called "exception") clauses, in terms of which a party purports to modify, limit or exclude altogether some or all of his common law duties that would normally arise under the contract (see Section 18 below). The primary object of a deed of sale is to record in writing the terms of a contract between the parties, and it follows that any statement in such a document *prima facie* constitutes a term of a contract unless it appears from the contract itself or other admissible evidence that the parties did not so intend.[84]

Therefore, the statements which the parties make during the course of negotiations which they consider to be the binding terms of the contract are agreed upon and then reduced to writing, or alternatively, reduced to writing and settled by the parties before they sign the contract. When a verbal contract has been reduced to writing, the writing is, in general, subject to any claim for rectification thereof, regarded as the exclusive memorial of the transaction and in a suit between the parties no evidence to prove its terms may be given save the document or secondary evidence of its contents, nor may the contents of such document be contradicted, altered, added to or varied by parol evidence.[85]

[79] *Small* v *Smith* 1954 (3) SA 434 (SWA) at 436G; *Heilbut, Symonds & Co* v *Buckleton* 1913 AC 30 at 49.

[80] *Bell* v *Ramsay* 1929 NPD 265.

[81] *Phame (Pty) Ltd* v *Paizes* 1973 (3) SA 397 (A) at 418 A–B.

[82] *cf Corbett* v *Harris* 1914 CPD 535 at 545.

[83] Christie, *Op. cit.* at 182.

[84] *Schmidt* v *Dwyer* 1959 (3) SA 896 (C) at 899 A.

[85] *Union Government* v *Viaini Ferro-Concrete Pipes (Pty) Ltd* 1941 AD 43 at 47; *National Board (Pretoria) (Pty) Ltd and another* v *Estate Swanepoel* 1975 (3) SA16 (A) at 27 A–B.

1.3.4 Terms of the contract

1.3.4.1 ESSENTIALIA, NATURALIA *AND* ACCIDENTALIA

The terms of a contract, whether express or implied, may be classified into *essentialia, naturalia* and *accidentalia*. The *essentialia* of a contract are those things which identity a particular type of contract, such as a sale or a lease, and are of the essence of the contract. Without the *essentialia* such contract cannot subsist, and there is either no contract, or a contract of a different kind.[86] The *essentialia* of a contract of sale, for example, are, firstly, that there be a thing sold, and secondly, a price for which it is sold.

If the *essentialia* of a contract are present, then certain legal results, (the *naturalia*) will follow. The *naturalia* are those things which are of the nature of a contract and which form a part of it by operation of law, even though they may not be expressly mentioned by the parties. It is therefore of the nature of the contract that the *naturalia* are included in the contract and understood. The *naturalia* differ from the *essentialia* in that a contract may subsist without them, and they may be excluded by the express agreement of the parties.[87]

The *naturalia* of the contract of sale are, *inter alia*, the obligation of the seller to take care of the thing until it is handed over, to make the thing sold available to the purchaser, to transfer ownership if he has it or can obtain it, failing which, to warrant against eviction, to warrant against latent defects, to warrant fitness for purpose, to warrant reasonable merchantable quality and to warrant the skill of his art. The implied warranty against latent defects, for example, which may be expressly excluded by a sale containing a clause whereby the thing is sold "as is", the so-called "voetstoots" clause, makes it clear that *naturalia* are terms implied by law in every contract of a particular type, unless expressly excluded.

The *accidentalia* of a contract, not being of the nature of the contract, can be included in it only by express agreement. Examples of *accidentalia* are the allowance of a certain time for paying the money due, or the liberty of paying it by instalments, and any warranties which the parties by express agreement may include in their contract.

1.3.4.2 EXPRESS, IMPLIED AND TACIT TERMS

The classification of the terms of the contract into *essentialia, naturalia* and *accidentalia* is valuable for the purpose of guiding the analysis of different types of contract. However, it is misleading when used for the different purpose of ascertaining the terms of a particular contract, for it gives the impression that the terms must be either express (*essentialia* and *accidentalia*) or implied by law (*naturalia*). Terms can also be implied into a contract from trade usage or from the facts, namely, the express wording of a contract or the surrounding circumstances or both.[88]

The most convenient method of ascertaining the full terms of a contract is, therefore, first to identify the express terms and then, in the light of those express terms, to consider whether any additional terms are to be implied either by law

[86] Christie, *Op. cit.* at 183.
[87] *Op. cit.* at 184.
[88] *Ibid.*

or from trade usage, or from the express terms and the surrounding circumstances.

1.3.5 Terms implied by law

The expression "implied term" may mean either a term implied by the law or a term implied by the facts.[89] In *Alfred McAlpine & Son (Pty) Ltd* v *Transvaal Provincial Administration* the first meaning of an "implied term" was explained thus:

> In legal parlance the expression "implied term" is an ambiguous one in that it is often used, without discrimination, to denote two, possibly three, distinct concepts. In the first place, it is used to describe an unexpressed provision of a contract which the law imports therein, generally as a matter of course, without reference to the actual intention of the parties. The intention of the parties is not totally ignored. Such a term is not normally implied if it is in conflict with the express provisions of the contract. On the other hand, it does not originate in the contractual consensus: it is imposed by the law from without. Indeed, terms are often implied by the law in cases where it is by no means clear that the parties would have agreed to incorporate them in their contract. Ready examples of such terms implied by law are to be found in the law of sale, eg the seller's implied guarantee or warranty against defects . . . Such implied terms may derive from the common law, trade usage or custom, or from statute. In a sense "implied term" is, in this context, a misnomer in that in content it simply represents a legal duty (giving rise to a correlative right) imposed by law, unless excluded by the parties, in the case of certain classes of contracts. It is a naturalium of the contract in question.

An obligation imposed by law on a contracting party has all the characteristics and consequences of an agreed term, except agreement, and therefore it is appropriate to call it a "term". The implied term is essentially a standardised one, amounting to a rule of law which the court will apply unless validly excluded by the contract itself. These terms implied by law without reference to the actual intention of the parties do not mean that the actual or presumed intention of the parties has been ignored in the historical process by which the law was made.[90] The origin of many terms now implied by law was the idea that any, or at least any honest, party entering into a particular type of contract would want to include such a term in it. Once the law has settled on that particular term it is then fruitless to inquire into the intention of the parties except to the extent of ascertaining whether they have exercised their privilege of expressly excluding the term that would otherwise be implied, as when a sale is made "voetstoots". The terms implied into the contract by operation of the law may derive from trade usage, custom, statute or common law.

1.3.5.1 TERMS IMPLIED BY TRADE USAGE

Terms implied by trade usage really occupy an intermediate position between terms implied by law and terms implied from the facts.[91]

If the trade usage is known to both parties their knowledge will be one of the surrounding circumstances indicating that the trade usage ought to be incorporated

[89] *Alfred McAlpine & Son (Pty) Ltd* v *Transvaal Provincial Administration* 1974 (3) SA 506 (A) at 531E–H.
[90] Christie *Op. cit.* at 185.
[91] *Op. cit.* at 187; and see 1.3.6 below.

in their contract as a term implied from the facts. The implication will not be made by law but from the presumed common intention of the parties to include a term customarily included to the knowledge of both of them.

However, if one party cannot prove that the other knew of a trade usage it is not a case where the trade usage could be said to have been incorporated as an implied term in the contract. Despite that party's ignorance of the trade usage in question, that party will be bound by, and the contract in question would be subject to, the alleged trade usage, provided it is shown to be universally and uniformly observed within the particular trade concerned, long established, notorious, reasonable and certain, and does not conflict with positive law (in a sense of altering a rule of law which the parties could not alter by their agreement) or with the clear provisions of the contract.[92]

1.3.5.2 TERMS IMPLIED BY CUSTOM

The old Roman–Dutch Law did not recognise the English distinction between custom and trade usage.[93] However, the English distinction has been adopted into South African law in so many cases which have referred to and applied the English authorities that a return to the pure Roman–Dutch law would be justified only if it could be shown that South African law would be improved thereby.[94] It is now generally accepted that South African law recognises and applies the English distinction between custom and trade usage.

Many of South African cases take the English law from *Halsbury*[95] which defines a custom thus:

> a custom is a particular rule which has existed either actually or presumptively from time immemorial and obtained the force of law in a particular locality although contrary to, or not consistent with, the general common law of the realm . . . A custom cannot extend to the whole realm, nor can it embrace every member of the public, for, in either case, it would then amount to the common law of the land.

Usage is distinguished from custom (paragraph 405):

> Immemorial local customs are clearly distinguishable from particular trade or local usages, although in practice frequently confused with them. The latter have chiefly to be considered in cases where they have been, or it is intended that they should be, imported as express or implied terms into commercial or other contracts: they lack three of the distinguishing features of customs properly so called. Firstly, they need not have existed from time immemorial. Secondly, they need not necessarily be confined to a limited locality, but they may in fact be thus confined, as in the case of agricultural usages. Thirdly, usages, however extensive, if contrary to positive law will not be sanctioned by the court, while customs may be inconsistent with the general law of the realm.

1.3.5.3 TERMS IMPLIED BY STATUTE

A term may be implied into a contract by statute. In South Africa, apart from section 138 of the Companies Act, there are no statutory obligations implied into

[92] *Golden Cape Fruits (Pty) Ltd* v *Fotoplate (Pty) Ltd* 1973 (2) SA 642 (C) at 645 G; *Crook* v *Pedersen Ltd* 1927 WLD 62 at 71; *Op. cit.* at 150–156.

[93] *Coutts* v *Jacobs* 1927 EDL 120 at 128.

[94] *Op. cit.* at 189.

[95] *Halsbury*, 4th ed, Vol. 12, paras. 401–2.

a sale of shares or of businesses as going concerns. Often, though, a party to the contract may expressly warrant that that party has complied with all of its statutory obligations, and in particular its obligations arising from the Companies Act and/or the relevant Tax Acts, such as the South African Income Tax Act, 1962, and Value Added Tax Act 1991.

The legislature may prohibit, in certain circumstances any attempt by the parties expressly to exclude a term implied by statute or common law in their contract (Christie, 186). An example of a statutory entrenchment of a term implied by common law is the Credit Agreements Act 75 of 1980. Section 6(1)(d) of the Credit Agreements Act states:

> 6(1) A credit agreement or any other agreement or document shall not contain a provision to the effect that—. . . (d) the liability of the credit grantor in terms of any guarantee or warranty which would, but for such provision, be implied in a credit agreement, is excluded or restricted;

An obligation imposed by a statute on a contracting party may not affect the validity of the contract, for it is merely a general proposition that when the legislature penalises an act it impliedly prohibits it, and that the effect of the prohibition is to render the act null and void (see 21.1.1 below).

1.3.5.4 TERMS IMPLIED BY THE COMMON LAW

In the absence of any agreement on the point, the law will impose certain obligations on the parties. These obligations imposed by the common law on the parties and implied into the contract are discussed in 2.3.4 below.

1.3.6 Terms implied from the facts ("tacit terms")

In *Alfred McAlpine & Son (Pty) Ltd* v *Transvaal Provincial Administration*[96] the second meaning of an "implied term" was explained thus:

> In the second place, "implied term" is used to denote an unexpressed provision of the contract which derives from the common intention of the parties, as inferred by the court from the express terms of the contract and the surrounding circumstances. In supplying such an implied term the Court, in truth, declares the whole contract entered into by the parties.

Because such terms differ from terms implied by law by being based on the unexpressed or tacit common intention of the parties, they are sometimes described as tacit terms. An "implied term" can therefore mean either a term implied by law or a term implied from the facts.

In order to decide whether a term is to be implied from the facts one must first examine the express terms of the contract.[97] A term may not be implied into a contract from the facts if the express terms deliberately exclude the possibility of implying terms of a particular type, or the parties have applied their minds to that issue and have made express provision in the contract for it. A tacit term is

[96] 1974(3) SA 506 (A) at 531H–532A.

[97] *Pan American World Airways Inc v SA Fire and Accident Insurance Co Ltd* 1965 (3) SA 150 (A) 175 C.

therefore sought to be implied in an agreement for the very reason that the parties fail to agree expressly thereon.

Where the parties have expressly agreed upon a term and given expression to that agreement in the written contract in unambiguous terms, no reference can be had to surrounding circumstances in order to subvert the meaning to be derived from a consideration of the language of the agreement only[98] and no term covering the same question can be implied. But if it is dealt with ambiguously, then the door may be left wide open to imply a term into the contract.

The express terms may also exclude the possibility of tacit terms even when they do not expressly cover the question, but when they give rise to the inference that the parties did not wish to include the term in question.[99] Therefore, if a contract, in its existing form, is efficacious and complete it will need no addition in the form of a tacit term.[100]

If an examination of the express terms does not immediately exclude the possibility of implying a tacit term the next question is what general tests the court should apply in order to decide whether the implication of a tacit term would be appropriate. The law of England on this matter is identical with our own.[101]

The most popular test applied by the South African courts is the test of business efficacy and of the officious bystander which is set out in *Reigate* v *Union Manufacturing Co (Ramsbottom)* as follows:[102]

> a term can only be implied if it is necessary in the business sense to give efficacy to the contract; ie if it is such a term that it can confidently be said that if at the time the contract was being negotiated someone had said to the parties: "what will happen in such a case?" They would both have replied: "of course so and so will happen; we did not trouble to say that; it is too clear".

The first part of this test, necessity in the business sense to give efficacy to the contract, means that the implication must be necessary and reasonable.[103] It is not sufficient to show that the term would be reasonable or convenient to one or other or even both of the parties.[104] The term will also not be implied merely because if one of the parties had suggested it, only an unreasonable person would have disagreed. Both parties must agree to the term being included in the contract. However, the concept of necessity should not be pushed to the extreme of requiring that the whole contract would be frustrated unless the term were implied.[105]

[98] *SA Mutual Aid Society* v *Cape Town Chamber of Commerce* 1962 (1) SA 598 (A) 615 D; *Delmas Milling Co Ltd* v *Du Plessis* 1955 (3) SA 447 (A) at 454.

[99] *Union Government (Minister of Railways)* v *Faux Ltd* 1916 AD 105 at 112.

[100] *Cassim* v *Kadir* 1962 (2) SA 473 (N) at 475 B.

[101] Christie, *Op. cit.* at 196; *Techni-Pak Sales (Pty) Ltd* v *Hall* 1968 (3) SA 231 (W) at 237 D.

[102] *Reigate* v *Union Maufacturing Co (Ramsbottom)* [1918] (1) KB 592 605.

[103] *Hamlyn & Co* v *Wood & Co* [1891] 2 QB 494; *Union Government (Minister of Railways)* v *Faux Ltd* 1916 AD 105; Christie, *Op. cit.* at 197.

[104] *Rapp & Maister* v *Aronovsky* 1943 WLD 68 at 74–5.

[105] *Van Boeschoten and Lorentz* v *Minister of Mines* 1933 TPD 169.

The second part of the test, the officious bystander test, was formulated in *Shirlaw* v *Southern Foundries* (1926) as follows:[106]

> *Prima facie* that which in any contract is left to be implied and need not be expressed is something so obvious that it goes without saying; so that, if, while the parties were making their bargain, an officious bystander were to suggest some express provision for it in their agreement, they would testily suppress him with a common "Oh, of course!"

Although the officious bystander test is expressed in a subjective form, it must be applied objectively in two respects.[107] Firstly, it is not necessary to prove that the parties ever directed their minds to the question: thus, the parties need not consciously have visualised the situation in which the term would come into operation. It does not matter, therefore, if the negotiating parties failed to think of a situation in which the term would be required, provided that the common intention was such that a reference to such a possible situation would have evoked from them a prompt and unanimous assertion of a term which was to govern it.[108] Secondly, the parties to the contract must be assumed to be reasonable men.[109] The court will determine from all the circumstances what a reasonable and honest person who enters into such a transaction would had done, not what a crafty person might have done who has a tendency to trick the other party into an omission of the term. A term would probably be included in circumstances where a crafty person has conducted himself in such a way as to lead the other reasonably to believe that he was tacitly assenting to the term which any reasonable man would assume would tacitly be incorporated in the contract, and the other party enters into the contract on that belief.[110]

Another test of general application is that the term sought to be implied must be capable of clear and exact formulation. Therefore, the term to be implied must be as certain (although it was never mentioned between the parties) as if it had been carefully drawn up and embodied in a written deed.[111]

2. Warranties in the Law of Contract

2.1 Warranties v Guarantees

The expression "guarantee" is often used synonymously with the expressions "suretyship" and "warranty".[112] Warranties are terms of the contract which may be classified as either *naturalia, accidentalia* or tacit terms (see 1.3.2.5 above). A warranty gives rise to a contractual obligation.

[106] *Shirlaw* v *Southern Foundries (1926) Ltd* [1939] 2 KB 206 at 227.
[107] *Greenfield Engineering Works (Pty) Ltd* v *N K R Construction (Pty) Ltd* 1978 (4) SA 901 (N) at 909.
[108] *Techni-Pak Sale (Pty) Ltd* v *Hall* 1968 (3) SA 231 (W) at 236–7; *Van den Berg* v *Tenner* 1975 (2) SA 268 (A) at 277 D.
[109] *Administrator (Tvl)* v *Industrial & Commercial Timber Supply Co Ltd* 1932 AD 25 at 33.
[110] Christie, *Op. cit.* at 199.
[111] *OK Bazaars* v *Bloch,* 1929 WLD 37 at 44; *Op. cit.* at 200.
[112] Lee and Honore, *Op. cit.* at 169.

The term "guarantee" is used generically to refer to all forms of security used to secure the performance by a contracting party of its obligations arising from the contract. Non-performance by a contracting party of its obligations in terms of a contract simply gives the other party to the contract certain contractual remedies, such as a claim for specific performance. Such remedies may take time to implement and are often valueless to the party seeking relief, especially where the defaulting party is a "man of straw". Parties intending to contract will therefore often seek ways of securing the performance by the other party of its obligations.[113] The most common forms of security used in South Africa are a mortgage of immoveable property, a notarial bond over moveable property, a pledge of moveables, liens and suretyship (or guarantee). A "guarantee" in the narrow sense of the word means a contract of suretyship (see 2.2.4.6 below).

When assets are encumbered in any way, the person holding the security over the assets encumbered may exercise its rights to the assets at any time in accordance with the provisions of the relevant guarantee (used here in its generic sense). In order to avoid the consequences of such a conflict, the purchaser may insist that the seller warrant that the assets sold are free of all encumbrances, and if they are not, to pay the purchaser appropriate compensation.

In the sale of moveables, unless agreed to the contrary, payment and delivery should take place simultaneously. In a sale of land, due to the South African system of land registration, it is not possible to achieve the desirable straight exchange of land ownership and money because the seller's conveyancer, having lodged the documents of transfer, cannot be sure exactly when they will be approved and registered and ownership will pass. It is, therefore, necessary to resort to a device in order to achieve, as nearly as possible, the desired reciprocity of payment and transfer. The standard device is the furnishing by the purchaser, when called upon to do so by the seller's conveyancers who are ready to lodge, of a "bank guarantee" payable on completion of the transfer. The purchaser could also furnish any other guarantee, or pay the money to an agreed stakeholder (a so-called "escrow" agreement) or, if the purchaser is prepared to take the risk, it could pay the seller in advance of lodging, in order to discharge its obligation to pay. In all cases where the purchaser or the debtor is required to provide a guarantee of payment, the provisions of the guarantee does not in itself amount to payment, so if the guarantee is withdrawn the debtor remains liable to pay.[114]

Therefore, on the instructions of the purchaser, the bank (or other third party) undertakes to the seller that it is holding the purchase price, and that upon and against proof of the registration of a mortgage bond over the property sold (or other property) in favour of the bank (or other third party), it will pay the amount of the purchase price to the seller. Such undertakings are usually referred to as "guarantees".

The various forms of security (mortgage bond, notarial bond, pledge and suretyship) are ancillary in nature, in other words, the right which secures the fulfilment of the obligation is always ancillary to a principal obligation and

[113] Gibson, *Op. cit.* at 617.
[114] Christie, *Op. cit.* at 495–6.

cannot exist without such a valid principal obligation. Therefore, the validity of the principal obligation of the purchaser to pay the purchase price is fundamental to the existence of any form of security securing the performance by the purchaser of its obligation.[115]

2.2 *Financial Guarantees*

2.2.1 By the purchaser as to payment of the purchase price

In order to secure payment of the purchase price by the purchaser, the seller may require the purchaser to procure that a creditworthy third party or third parties stand surety for the payment of the purchase price by the purchaser, or that the purchaser pass a mortgage bond over any immoveable property it owns in favour of the seller, or a notarial bond over moveable property, or that the purchaser pledge to the seller certain of its moveable property to secure the said obligation.

The seller may insist that the purchaser raise a loan with a third party and make payment of the purchase price in full against delivery of the thing sold. The problem then of the creditworthiness of the purchaser and of obtaining adequate security for the purchaser's obligations shifts from the seller to the lender of the money.

2.2.2 By the vendor as to possible repayment of part of the purchase price

In circumstances where the purchaser has paid the seller, but the purchase price is subject to an adjustment at a later date, and the agreed adjustment results in a reduction of the purchase price, the seller would then be obliged to repay to the purchaser a portion of the amount received by it from the purchaser. The seller may then have to procure the necessary security at the date of conclusion of the sale for its contingent obligation to repay that portion of the purchase price which falls to be repaid as a result of any adjustment.

2.2.3 By the purchaser or vendor as to payment of damages

Where one of the parties envisages a claim for damages being brought against it by a third party in the event of a breach by the other party of its obligations and/or warranties, that party will normally require an indemnity from the other party against any such damages or loss. An "indemnity" is a contract by which the party giving the indemnity undertakes an original and independent obligation.[116] The party giving the indemnity will try to limit the extent and scope of the indemnity, by, for example, limiting the circumstances giving rise to its liability to pay damages, and the amount of damages payable by it should the circumstances contemplated in the indemnity ever arise. The party seeking the indemnity would then be at risk to the extent that the amount of any claim for damages exceeded the agreed limit.

[115] Silberberg and J. Schoeman, *The Law of Property*, (2nd ed. 1983) at 428.
[116] N. Sinclair, *Warranties and Indemnities on Share Sales*, (2nd ed., UK 1989) at 193.

2.2.4 Real and personal securities

2.2.4.1 SPECIAL MORTGAGES OF IMMOVEABLE PROPERTY

A mortgage bond in the traditional form contains an acknowledgment of debt by the mortgagor for the amount of the bond, including a recital of the principal obligation which the bond secures, and a declaration binding specific immoveable property as security for the payment of an existing principal debt and the fulfilment of all other obligations imposed on the mortgagor in terms of the bond. Thus, a mortgage bond in this form fulfils three functions: firstly, it constitutes an instrument of hypothecation; secondly, it constitutes a record of the terms and conditions of the obligation in respect of which the hypothecation is to create a security; and thirdly, it constitutes an acknowledgment of debt or other admission of liability. Its primary function is to provide a real security for an obligation. For a discussion on the essential elements of a mortgage bond as an instrument of hypothecation see *Thienhaus* v *Ziegler Ltd.*[117]

A special mortgage of immoveable property is based on an agreement in terms of which the mortgagor (the purchaser) undertakes the obligation to pass a mortgage bond over specified immoveable property in favour of the mortgagee (the seller). This agreement confers and imposes only personal rights and duties on the parties, but provided that it is a valid contract, the mortgagee will be granted a decree of specific performance if the mortgagor should attempt to resile from it.

The mortgage bond must be prepared by a conveyancer practising within the province within which the deeds registry concerned is situated (section 15 of the Deeds Registries Act 47 of 1937), and must be executed by the owner of the immoveable property or by a conveyancer authorised by a formal power of attorney granted to him by the mortgagor (section 50(1) of the Deeds Registries Act 47 of 1937). The real right in the mortgaged property which the bond confers on the mortgagee, comes into existence only when it has been registered, in other words, as soon as it has been signed by the Registrar of Deeds.[118]

It is usual to distinguish between different types of bonds according to the type of principal obligation a bond is designed to secure. The most usual type is a bond to secure the repayment of a loan of money in a fixed amount.

A "covering bond" is designed to secure a debt or debts to be incurred at a future date.[119] A covering bond is used, for example, to secure overdraft facilities or the purchase price of goods to be sold and delivered in such quantities and at such times as the mortgagor may require.[120] In these cases a covering bond secures a fluctuating debt and the bond must contain an express statement to the effect that it is intended to secure future debts in general and the maximum amount which it shall secure (section 51(1) of the Deeds Registries Act 47 of 1937). Interest may be secured under a covering bond in addition to the maximum amount provided for.[121] A covering bond may also be drafted in such

[117] *Thienhaus* v *Ziegler Ltd* 1965 (3) SA 24 (A).
[118] *Smith* v *Farrelly's Trustee* 1904 TS 949 at 955.
[119] *Rooth & Wessels* v *Benjamin's Trustee and the Natal Bank Ltd* 1905 TS 625.
[120] Silberberg and Schoeman, *Op. cit.* at 439.
[121] *Lipschitz* v *Saambou-Nasionale Bouvereeniging* 1979 (1) SA 527 (T) at 530–531; *Ibid.*

a form as to remain in force even if the debt, for example, an overdraft, is temporarily extinguished. In the event of the insolvency of the mortgagor, the preference conferred by a covering bond on the mortgagee depends on its date of registration, and not on the date upon which the debt comes into existence (section 87 of the Insolvency Act 24 of 1936).

A "surety bond" is a bond passed by a mortgagor (the surety) over immoveable property owned by the mortgagor in order to provide security for a debt incurred or to be incurred by a third party (the purchaser). In practice, the mortgagor will almost invariably be required to bind itself and its property as surety and co-principal debtor.

A "kustingbrief" is a mortgage bond passed to secure the purchase price (or any portion thereof) of land. It need not be in favour of the seller, but may be passed in favour of any person that has lent or advanced money to the mortgagor towards the purchase price of the land to be mortgaged. It is of the essence of a kustingbrief that it is passed simultaneously with the transfer of the property. A kustingbrief confers certain privileges on the mortgagee in the event of the mortgagor's insolvency.[122]

Section 88 of the Insolvency Act 24 of 1936 reads as follows:

> 88. Certain mortgages are invalid.—A mortgage bond, other than a kustingbrief, whether special or general passed for the purpose of securing the payment of a debt not previously secured, which was incurred more than 2 months prior to the lodging of the bond with the Registrar of Deeds concerned for registration or for the purpose of securing the payment of a debt incurred in novation of or substitution for any such first-mentioned debt, shall not confer any preference if the estate of the mortgaged debtor is sequestrated within a period of 6 months after such lodging: provided that a mortgage bond shall be deemed not to have been lodged as aforesaid, if it was withdrawn from registration.

A clause in a mortgage bond which purports to authorise the mortgagee to take over and retain the mortgaged property as its property if the mortgagor defaults and the bond is called up is known as a *pactum commissorium* and is altogether invalid (although it is, within certain limits, allowed in a contract of sale). But a clause in a bond entitling the mortgagee to take over the property at a fair price, in other words, fair in the light of the value of the property as at the date on which the debt becomes due, is valid.[123]

An agreement for *parate executie* in a mortgage bond—in other words, a clause which purports to empower the mortgagee to sell the property out of hand or otherwise without an order of court on such terms and for such a price as it may determine—is invalid if it relates to immoveable property.[124]

It is often difficult to discover, let alone formulate, any principle which governs the respective rights and duties of a first and second bond holder.[125] However, it appears that as long as a bond holder exercises its rights in good faith it need not consider the interests of others whose bonds rank below its own. In general, therefore, the intervention of a second bond holder cannot affect its

[122] section 88 of the Insolvency Act 24 of 1936; *Op. cit.* at 440.
[123] *Op. cit.* at 446.
[124] *Ibid.*
[125] *SA Timber and Joining Works (Pty) Ltd* v *The Sheriff* 1955 (4) SA 56 (0) at 62B.

rights or impose on it fresh or further liabilities or obligations. A first bond holder is not the custodian of the second bond holder's interests.[126]

2.2.4.2 NOTARIAL BONDS OVER MOVEABLE PROPERTY

A "notarial bond" means a bond attested by a notary public and registered in the appropriate Deeds Registry Office hypothecating moveable property generally or specially (section 102 of the Deeds Registries Act 47 of 1937). A notarial bond provides a means by which a debtor may hypothecate moveable property without delivering it to the creditor in whose favour the bond is passed. A "general notarial bond" binds all the moveable property of a debtor (including moveables which it may subsequently acquire), and a "special notarial bond" binds only specific moveables described in the bond.

In the absence of delivery of the moveables to the creditor, however, the creditor does not obtain (except in the province of Natal) a real right in the moveables which the debtor purports to hypothecate in terms of the bond, but obtains in the case of a general notarial bond, but not in the case of a special notarial bond, a preference over concurrent creditors in the event of the debtor's insolvency. A distinction is drawn in this regard between a general and a special notarial bond. In the case of a general notarial bond the preference conferred upon the holder of the bond over concurrent creditors extends to all moveables owned by the debtor when it is liquidated.[127]

In the case of a special notarial bond the holder of the special notarial bond enjoys no preference over concurrent creditors in respect of the free residue of the estate of the debtor, including the moveable assets specified in the bond, on the basis that it was not the intention of the legislature to afford preference to the holder of a special notarial bond.[128] The holder of a special notarial bond would therefore appear to be merely a concurrent creditor.

The judgment in *Cooper No en Andere* v *Die Meester en 'n ander* does not affect general notarial bonds, which will continue to give the holder a preference over concurrent creditors but below all other secured and preferent creditors. Notarial bonds registered in Natal under the Notarial Bonds (Natal) Act, 1932, are also unaffected by that judgment and continue to give the holder the rights of a pledgee over the bonded assets.

In the province of Natal, as opposed to the remainder of South Africa, moveables specially hypothecated by a notarial bond are "deemed to have been pledged to the holder of the bond as security for the debt secured by the bond in the same manner as if they had been delivered to him as a pledge" except that they shall be subject to a landlord's hypothec.[129]

The notarial bond over moveables is of limited application because the debtor remains in possession of the moveable assets and is entitled to alienate its moveable assets despite the passing of a general or special notarial bond over

[126] *Op. cit.* at 454.
[127] *Op. cit.* at 469.
[128] *Cooper NO en Andere* v *Die Meester en 'n ander* 1992 (3) SA 60 (A).
[129] Section 2 of the Notarial Bonds (Natal) Act, of 1932; *Mahomed* v *Karim* 1948 (3) SA 636 (N).

them. Therefore, a trading company may continue to trade and sell its stock in the course of its business. Furthermore, even if the debtor alienates or pledges its property in contravention of the terms of the notarial bond, the creditor is not protected against the claims of *bona fide* third parties who have acquired it for value or attached it in execution of a judgment, unless such third party acted *mala fide*. A third party must have actual knowledge of the existence of a notarial bond before he will be held to have acted *mala fide*.[130]

2.2.4.3 PLEDGE OF CORPOREAL MOVEABLES

After conclusion of a contract of sale the seller may, without the knowledge of the purchaser, pledge the moveable assets comprising the subject matter of the sale and deliver them to a third party to secure a debt owed by the seller to that third party. The purchaser will then find the moveable assets sold in the possession of a pledgee. The purchaser would then have its normal contractual remedies against the seller for breach of contract, namely, the right either to cancel the contract and claim damages, or to uphold the contract and claim specific performance.

The purchaser usually requires the seller to warrant that the moveable assets have not been pledged, and that, if they have been pledged, appropriate compensation shall be paid to the purchaser. Where in breach of the warranty the assets have been pledged, the purchaser would have a claim against the seller/warrantor for specific performance of the warranty, namely, a claim for payment of compensation in terms of the warranty.

The general principles governing mortgages apply to a pledge of moveables in every respect. Thus, there must be a valid principal obligation which the pledge is intended to secure, but the pledgor need not be the person who owes that debt (so that a pledge may be validly given by a surety) and it may be constituted to secure a future debt (for a fixed or fluctuating amount). A pledge cannot be created by agreement alone. The agreement must be accompanied by delivery of possession of the moveable assets to the pledgee.[131]

The object of a pledge is to confer on the pledgee a real right in the thing pledged which it can enforce against all other creditors of the pledgor. It is essential, therefore, that the pledgee is given possession of the subject matter of the pledge. In the context of pledge a transfer of possession by a mere change in mental attitude, the pledgor retaining physical control, will not suffice. The debtor must divest itself of the control of the subject matter of the pledge and effectively transfer it to the creditor.[132] A pledgee's possession must not only be effective, but also continuous and it will generally lose its security if it returns the thing to the pledgor or otherwise allows it to leave its possession and fails to recover it before *bona fide* third parties have acquired rights in it.[133]

The pledgee is obliged to exercise reasonable care of the thing while it is in its possession and to safeguard the pledgor's interest in it. The pledgee is not permitted to use it for its own purposes without authority from the pledgor and

[130] *Meyer* v *Botha and Hergenroder* (1982) 1 SAR 47.
[131] *Op. cit.* at 471; *Vasco Dry Cleaners* v *Twycross* 1979 (1) SA 603 (A) at 611.
[132] *Op. cit.* at 472.
[133] *Op. cit.* at 473.

neither is it entitled to take any fruits it may yield. The pledgor is obliged to pay all expenses which the pledgee may incur, for example, safe deposit fees, insurance premiums and the cost of its maintenance and necessary repairs. A pledgee may not repledge the thing pledged to it by merely ceding the debt and delivering the asset to the cessionary so as to prevent the original pledgor from demanding its return when the original pledge is extinguished.[134]

As in the case of a mortgage bond, a clause in the pledge agreement which purports to authorise the pledgee to take over and retain the pledged property if the pledgor defaults, a *pactum commissorium*, is void, and the pledgee may acquire ownership in the article pledged only in terms of a clause entitling the pledgee to take over the property pledged at a fair price, in other words, fair in the light of the value of the property as at the date on which the debt becomes due.

On the other hand, an agreement for *parate executie*—in other words, a clause which purports to empower the pledgee to sell the property pledged out of hand or otherwise without an order of court on such terms and for such price as the pledgee may determine—is permissible in relation to a pledge, provided that it is always open to a pledgor to seek the protection of the court if the pledgor can show that, in effecting a sale, the pledgee has acted in a manner which has prejudiced the pledgor in its rights.[135] In the absence of any agreement the pledgee may institute proceedings and have the property sold in execution. If the pledgor is liquidated the pledgee is a secured creditor, in other words the pledged property may either be taken over by the pledgee at a valuation agreed to by the liquidator or, if sold, the proceeds will be applied to the satisfaction of the pledgee's claim in preference to all other creditors.

2.2.4.4 LIENS

A purchaser purchasing the business of a company as a going concern, including the assets of the business, or the shares of a company, should always be aware that a third party might be in possession of and have a lien over the moveable assets of the seller. A lien is a right of retention which arises from the fact that one man has put money or monies' worth into the property of another.[136] Liens are divided into enrichment liens on the one hand and debtor-and-creditor liens on the other hand.

An "enrichment lien" is a real right in the moveable property in the possession of the lien holder and may take the form of either improvement or salvage liens, depending on whether they are related to useful or necessary expenses, respectively.[137]

A "debtor-and-creditor lien" is a personal right of retention which is conferred on a person who has done work on another's property or rendered a service in pursuance of a contract, other than in the course of a contract of employment.[138]

[134] *Deutschmann* v *Mpeta* 1917 CDP 79 at 82.

[135] *Osry* v *Hirsch, Loubser and Co Ltd* 122 CPD 531 at 547; *Aitken* v *Miller* 1951 (1) SA 153 (SR).

[136] *Op. cit.* at 479; *United Building Society* v *Smookler's Trustees and Golombick's Trustee* 1906 TS 632 at 627–628.

[137] *Brooklyn House Furnishers (Pty) Ltd* v *Knoetze and Sons* 1970 (3) SA 264 (A) at 271.

[138] *D Glazer and Sons (Pty) Ltd* v *The Master* 1979 (4) SA 780 (C).

The rights of retention conferred by a debtor-and-creditor lien are not strictly contractual rights insofar as they are conferred not by virtue of the contact, but by operation of law when money or monies' worth is put into the property of another in consequence of a prior contractual relationship, although that contract may provide for the exclusion of a debtor-and-creditor's lien. The debtor-and-creditor lien remains a personal right insofar as the lien is not available against the owner, except where the owner was a party to the contract, or against *bona fide* third parties acquiring rights to the property.[139]

A lien is essentially a weapon of defence and therefore the holder of a lien has no right to insist on the realisation of the property in its possession to satisfy its claim.[140] If the creditor has an independent right of action the creditor may sue its debtor and then have the property attached to be sold in execution. However, once the holder of the lien relinquishes possession of the property the protection afforded by the lien is lost. Attachment in execution is akin to loss of possession.[141]

In the event of the debtor's insolvency the lien holder's security is preserved if the property is delivered to the liquidator at the latter's request and the lien holder notifies the liquidator in writing of its rights. On insolvency an enrichment lien outranks even a prior mortgage bond, while the personal debtor and creditor lien ranks after a mortgage bond even if created prior to registration of the bond.[142] Although, a lien over books of account and similar documents affords no security or preference in insolvency (section 47 of the Insolvency Act 24 of 1936).

The lien holder must maintain the property in good order and will be liable if it deteriorates, or is damaged or lost as a result of the lien holder's negligence. The lien will cover the lien holder's expenses to maintain and preserve the property, but it is not entitled to any storage charges merely for keeping the property on its premises.[143]

2.2.4.5 CESSION OF RIGHTS AS SECURITY

While a right of action may properly be used to secure a debt, it can effectively be so used only by way of a cession of the right of action to the creditor coupled with an agreement, as between cedent and cessionary, that on payment of the "secured" debt, the cessionary shall be obliged to re-cede to the cedent the ceded right of action. The effect of such a cession, generally known as a cession *in securitatem debiti*, is in all respects the same as that of an ordinary cession, but coupled with the agreement mentioned.[144] Where cession is made as security for a debt, it does not signify that the cedent, in fact, retains any rights in the subject matter of the cession.[145]

139 *Op. cit.* at 480.
140 *Op. cit.* at 488.
141 *Savory* v *Baldochi* 1907 TS 523; *Orbit Motors (Pty) Ltd* v *Reeds (Cape) Ltd* 1975 (2) SA 333 (C).
142 *Op. cit.* at 489.
143 *Ibid.*; but cf *Brooklyn House Furnishers (Pty) Ltd* v *Knoetze and Sons* 1970 (3) SA 264 (A) at 270.
144 *Trust Bank of Africa Ltd* v *Standard Bank of South Africa Ltd* 1968 (3) SA 166 (A) at 189B.
145 *Lief* v *Dettmann* 1964 (2) (SA) 252 (A) at 271.

It frequently happens that a trader cedes its entire book debts (present and future) as security for a debt which it in turn owes to its creditor.[146] The validity of such cessions is governed by the general rules relating to cessions *in securitatum debiti*.[147]

2.2.4.6 SURETYSHIP

A "guarantee" (suretyship) is a collateral contract in terms of which, for example, the seller contracts with a third party (the surety) that the surety will pay the whole or part of the performance due by the purchaser to the seller on default by the purchaser.[148] The suretyship is itself a contract between the seller (the creditor) and the surety and creates only personal rights. The effect of the suretyship is that the seller has extended its right against the purchaser to a right against two or more persons (the purchaser and the surety/ies) who are jointly and severally liable with the purchaser for the performance, by the purchaser, of its obligations under the contract.[149]

In terms of section 6 of the General Law Amendment Act 50 of 1956, as amended, no contract of suretyship is valid unless the terms are embodied in a written document signed by or on behalf of the surety. An agent who signs on behalf of the surety is not required to be authorised in writing.[150]

2.2.4.7 ESCROW AGREEMENTS

The term "escrow" is an English law term signifying a deed or agreement delivered to a third party in trust, pending the fulfilment of some condition specified therein in favour of the other party to the deed or agreement. If the condition is performed it becomes a binding obligation, otherwise it fails.

The term "escrow" is also applied to a payment to a third party in trust pending the performance of some condition, such as the transfer of land.

2.3 Warranties in the Law of Contract

2.3.1 Warranties in sales of goods

Where the purchaser intends to purchase from the company the business of the company as a going concern the subject matter of the sale will comprise all the assets of the company which are required to enable it to carry on the business as a going concern. For the purpose of identifying the subject matter of the sale it is necessary to categorise each asset to be purchased. If the purchaser has little or no knowledge about the assets, it will require either comprehensive warranties in relation to the assets and business of the target company or the opportunity of conducting a thorough investigation into the affairs of the target company, in which event the need for warranties may fall away.

The warranties which may be required when purchasing and selling a business as a going concern may conveniently be categorised under various headings (see

[146] *Jenkins* v *Roberts* 1912 CPD 937; *Schreuder* v *Steenkamp* 1962 (4) SA 74(0); *Rand Bank* v *Morris* 1977 (2) SA 21 (SEC); *Muller* v *Trust Bank of Africa Ltd* 1981 (2) SA 117 (N) at 128 G.

[147] *Op. cit.* at 478.

[148] Sinclair, *Op. cit.* at 193; Gibson, *Op. cit.* at 617.

[149] Gibson, *Op. cit.* at 617.

[150] *Fourlamel (Pty) Ltd* v *Maddison* 1977 (1) SA 333 (A) at 343; Christie, *Op. cit.* at 147.

13.1 below). The purchaser may further require the seller to provide certain indemnities and to clarify the position *vis-à-vis* claims under warranties and claims under indemnities. The seller may, on the other hand, require the purchaser to provide certain warranties in respect of the continuation of the business as a going concern subsequent to the completion date of the sale.

In respect of a sale of assets under South African law, and in the absence of any express agreement to the contrary, the law imposes certain obligations on the seller and on the purchaser respectively. These common law implied warranties are dealt with in 2.3.4 below, and various express contractual warranties relating to a sale of a business as a going concern are dealt with in section 13. The parties usually negotiate and agree the terms of the contract, including what warranties are to be included, and exclude the implied warranties where such exclusion is not prohibited by statute (see 1.3.5.3 above).

2.3.2 Warranties in lease

The *essentialia* of a contract of lease are that there be a price paid (rent) and ascertainable premises let. The lessor is obliged to fulfil all obligations which it expressly or impliedly undertook to fulfil and, failing express or implied agreements on any of the following points, the lessor is obliged by law firstly to deliver the property let; secondly, to refrain from disturbing the lessee in its enjoyment of the property; thirdly, to place and maintain the property in the condition agreed upon, or failing agreement in a condition reasonably fit for the purpose for which the property is let; fourthly, to warrant against defects; fifthly, to warrant against eviction by a third person with better title; and finally, to pay the relevant rates and taxes.

The lessee is also obliged to fulfil all obligations which it expressly or impliedly undertook to fulfil, and, failing express or implied agreement on any of the following points, the lessee is obliged, firstly, to pay the rent; secondly, to take good care of the property let and not to use it for a purpose other than that for which it was let; and thirdly, on termination of the lease to restore the property in the same good order and condition as it was in when it was received (reasonable wear and tear excepted).

2.3.3 Warranties in carriage contracts v liability under carriage of goods or under safekeeping agreements

The common law contract of carriage arises when one person (the carrier) undertakes, for reward or otherwise, to convey another person or his goods from one place to another.[151] A contract of carriage for reward in money—termed a fare or freight—is a species of the contract for the letting and hiring of services.

The contract is formed, therefore, when agreement has been reached on what is to be carried, the manner of carriage, the places from which and to which carriage is to be effected and the freight, if any, payable. No formalities for the formation of a contract of carriage are prescribed at common law.

Not every contract of carriage concerning the carriage of goods to the Republic of South Africa from another country is governed by South African law. The

[151] Gibson, *Op. cit.* at 598.

initial inquiry will be to determine, in accordance with the rules for the resolution of a conflict of laws, which system of law governs the contract or that aspect of the contract in dispute (see section 15 below).

The Carriage of Goods by Sea Act 1 of 1986 ("COGSA") governs the carriage of goods by sea in ships leaving a South African port and bound for any port, whether in or outside South Africa. The Hague Rules, as amended in 1968 by the Brussels Protocol, then came to be known as the Hague–Visby Rules, were enacted into South African law by COGSA on 4 July 1986. COGSA applies the Hague–Visby Rules compulsorily to the carriage of goods by sea under a bill of lading contract, firstly, when the goods are shipped from a South African port, whether the bill of lading incorporates the Rules, or purports to exclude them, or is silent about them, and secondly, wherever the port of shipment may be, if the bill of lading expressly provides that the Hague–Visby Rules shall govern the contract.

The Hague–Visby Rules do not apply to charter party agreements (Gibson, 603), save by clear agreement; but with occasional exceptions they do apply to bills of lading issued under or pursuant to a charter party agreement.[152]

By mercantile usage a CIF (cost, insurance, freight) sale is a sale of goods by the seller to the purchaser requiring shipment subject to the following terms of performance: firstly, the seller is required to contract with a carrier for the carriage of the goods to the agreed destination, ship the goods at the port of shipment and procure a bill of lading from the carrier; secondly, the seller is required to arrange insurance cover for the goods on the terms usual in the trade; thirdly, the goods are invoiced to the buyer; and finally, delivery of the goods is effected by symbolical delivery of "the shipping documents" (namely, the bill of lading, the policy of insurance and the invoice) and the purchaser is not entitled to actual physical delivery.[153]

In the absence of some special agreement the purchaser can only demand delivery of the shipping documents and normally its obligation to pay, or assume liability to pay, the invoice price arises upon tender to it of the shipping documents by the seller. The CIF sale is an unconditional sale and risk in and to the goods will pass to the purchaser immediately the parties have reached agreement.[154] The purchaser is covered by the contract of insurance against the risk that at the time of tender of the shipping documents, or subsequently, the goods themselves have become, or became lost or destroyed. Ownership in the goods normally passes to the purchaser upon transfer of the bill of lading and concurrent payment.[155]

The term FOB (free on board) is simply a term of delivery. The seller undertakes to deliver the goods on board a ship at a named port. The carrier is, in such a case, the agent of the purchaser and delivery to the carrier is

152 Article 1(b); cf *Intercontinental Export Co (Pty) Ltd* v *M V Dien Danielsen* 1982 (3) SA 534 (N).
153 *Standard Bank of South Africa Ltd* v *Efroiken & Newman* 1924 AD at 191; Gibson *op. cit.* at 169.
154 *Thomas & Co* v *Whyte & Co* 1923 NPD 413; *Op. cit.* at 169.
155 *Lendalease Finance Ltd v Corporacion de Mercades Agricola & Others* 1976 (4) SA 464 (A) at 491–2.

accordingly delivery to the purchaser sufficient for the purpose of transferring ownership.[156]

At common law the carrier of goods by sea is subject to a strict liability for the safe carriage of the goods, but is free to contract out of the liability. However, the general effect of the Hague–Visby Rules is to substitute a fault liability on the part of a sea carrier under a bill of lading contract for its strict common law liability, but at the same time to invalidate attempts to contract out of that fault liability.

On the other hand, the common law fault liability of the carrier, with regard to injury to or the death of a passenger, has not been affected or altered by COGSA. Thus, where two ships in collision are at fault, the liability of the carriers is joint and several, but provision is made for a contribution pursuant to an apportionment of liability in accordance with the degree of fault of each ship (sections 256 and 257 of The Merchant Shipping Act 57 of 1951). However, the liability for damage to goods in this situation is joint, that is, for the proportion relevant to the degree of fault only (section 255 of The Merchant Shipping Act 57 of 1951). In cases where a carrier is liable vicariously (in other words, without its actual fault or privity), the quantum of damages for personal injury and damage to property, including cargo, is limited by reference to the ship's tonnage.[157]

The duty of the carrier is to carry the goods from the place of delivery to their destination safely and without undue delay. The carrier's general liability for safe carriage and delay is subject to the overriding qualification that in most cases it shall not be liable for damage or injury due to the negligence or default of the consignor or passenger. Its duty, and hence its liability for safe carriage, commences when the goods are delivered to it (or to its agent or servant) actually or constructively.[158] The carrier's liability terminates upon actual or constructive delivery of the goods to the consignee at the place and in the manner agreed.[159]

2.3.4 Express and implied warranties

On the formation of a contract of sale each party is bound by the obligations which it has expressly or impliedly undertaken and by those which the law imposes upon it in the absence of such express or implied agreement.[160]

Therefore, in the absence of agreement on any of the following points, the law will impose on the seller the obligations to take care of the thing sold until it is handed over, to make the thing sold available to the buyer, to transfer ownership if the seller has it or can obtain it, failing which, to warrant against eviction, and to warrant against latent defects. In appropriate circumstances certain warranties will also be implied by operation of law, namely, the warranties of fitness for

[156] *Anderson & Colman Ltd v Universal Trading Co* 1948 (1) SA 1277 (W); *Op. cit.* at 171.

[157] section 261 of The Merchant Shipping Act 57 of 1951; *Atlantic Harvesters of Namibia (Pty) Ltd* v *Unterweser Reederci GmGH of Bremen* 1986(4) SA 865 (C).

[158] Lee and Honore, *The South African Law of Obligations* (eds.) E. Newman and D. J. McQuoid-Mason (2nd ed, 1987) at *Op. cit.* at para. 522.

[159] Lee and Honore, "Obligations" *Op. cit.* at para. 523; cf *South British Ins Co Ltd* v *Unicorn Shipping Lines (Pty) Ltd* 1976 (1) SA 708 (A).

[160] A. J. Kerr *The Law of Sale and Lease* (1984) at 94.

purpose, of reasonable merchantable quality, and/or of the skill of his art. These obligations imposed by operation of law and incorporated into the contract as implied terms are the *naturalia* of a contract of sale (see 1.3.4.1 above).

2.3.4.1 THE SELLER'S IMPLIED OBLIGATION TO TAKE CARE OF A THING UNTIL IT IS HANDED OVER

In the absence of an express provision in the contract, the obligation imposed by law on the seller is to take care of the thing sold from the date of the completion of the sale until delivery is effected.[161] In some instances the thing sold will be handed over at the time of sale, in others only after an interval of time. In the latter instance, subject to any modification which there may be in particular circumstances in which the rules of default come into operation, the seller is obliged by operation of law to take care of the thing until it is handed over.[162]

The risk in and to the thing sold is ordinarily transferred from the seller to the purchaser upon conclusion of the agreement, and not upon delivery, unless the parties otherwise agree. The seller may therefore be liable if the thing sold is injured, diminished, lost, or destroyed whilst in the seller's possession prior to delivery either because the seller has not shown the standard of care required, or the injury, diminution, loss or destruction results from the acts of one for whom it is responsible, (ie, its employee). If the thing sold is injured, diminished, lost or destroyed by act of God or accidental occurrence then the rules applicable to both those concepts will apply (see 21.7 below). If a third person, for whom the seller is not responsible, injures or destroys the thing, the seller is free of liability but must cede its action for damages against the third party to the purchaser.

The seller may undertake a greater responsibility than the law casts upon it, by express agreement and in such a case will be bound by its undertaking.[163] This express agreement may cover any of the events causing loss or damage for which the seller would not otherwise be liable. The seller may even agree to accept liability for all loss, destruction or damage, however caused. If it does so, the ordinary rule whereby the risk passes to the purchaser on the conclusion of the contract is reversed and until delivery of the thing to the purchaser, the risk shall remain with the seller. If the purchaser fails to accept delivery then the seller's liability immediately diminishes and the seller is answerable only for gross negligence or fraud.[164]

Where the seller has not taken due care of the thing sold between the date of sale and delivery, and the thing delivered is materially different from the thing tendered as a result thereof, the purchaser is entitled to cancel the contract and refuse to take delivery.[165]

[161] H.G. Mackeurtan and G.R.S. Mackwill (eds.) *Mackeurtan's Sale of Goods in South Africa*, (5th ed, 1984) at 82).

[162] Kerr, *Sale and Lease, Op. cit.* at 95; *Frumer* v *Maitland* 1954 (3) SA 840 (A) at 845 C–D.

[163] Mackeurtan, *Op. cit.* at 85.

[164] *Op. cit.* at 86.

[165] *Op. cit.* at 87; Kerr, *Sale and Lease*, *Op. cit.* at 96; *Frumer* v *Maitland* 1954 (3) SA 840 (A) at 845 D.

2.3.4.2 THE SELLER'S IMPLIED OBLIGATION TO MAKE THE THING SOLD AVAILABLE

It is of the essence of a contract of sale that the seller is obliged to make the thing sold available to the purchaser.[166] If there is no custom or trade usage to the contrary, the legal obligation imposed by the law on the seller is that the seller put the thing sold at the disposal of the purchaser so that the purchaser may take it away. Therefore, if a quantity of things sold has to be weighed, counted, or measured, the seller must do this, and if the thing sold is pledged, the seller must redeem it from the pledgee.

In the absence of any agreement to the contrary, when the thing sold is placed at the purchaser's disposal, the purchaser is then obliged to remove it from where it is at the time of the sale at its own cost. However, if after the sale is concluded the seller removes the thing sold to a place further away from where it was at the time of the sale, any extra cost of transporting the thing sold from the new location shall be for the account of the seller.

If the seller is aware or is deemed to be aware of the conditions under which the thing sold are to be transported and of any precautions which should be taken to ensure its safety during removal, and that the buyer is not or is unlikely to be, aware of the need for such precautions, or of what precautions should be taken, the seller is obliged to see that the thing sold is in a state fit to be transported by that method or to point out to the purchaser what needs to be done. If the seller does not, the seller will be in breach of contract and will be liable to the purchaser for any damaged caused as a result thereof to the thing sold.[167]

In the case of immoveable property, the seller is obliged to admit the buyer to possession[168] and, if transfer of ownership is envisaged, to do what is necessary to bring about transfer in the relevant deeds office.

In *York & Co (Pvt) Ltd* v *Jones No* Murray CJ stated the law succinctly thus:[169]

> A seller of immoveable property is under at least three duties to the purchaser in regard to the delivery of the property. He is firstly bound to effect transfer in the Deeds Office into the purchaser's name. Secondly he is obliged to give physical possession of the property to the purchaser on or before the stipulated date. Thirdly he is under duty, even after transfer and giving of possession, to guarantee the purchaser against eviction, ie, subsequent dispossession, total or partial, by third parties claiming a title superior to that which the purchaser has obtained from the seller.
> . . . .When the duty to give possession is to be considered, it appears to me that it is entirely irrelevant whether the so-called trespassers are there under colour of right or not. The mere fact of their physical presence, if it results in a deprivation of the purchaser's right to secure the enjoyment in possession of his purchase (provided, of course, that the deprivation is to an extent and for a time sufficient to make it material) is enough to justify the purchaser in claiming that the seller has failed to carry out his obligation.

[166] Kerr, *Sale and Lease, Op. cit.* at 97.
[167] *Vlotman* v *Buysell* 1946 NPD 412 at 413.
[168] *Sweet* v *Ragerguhara NO & others* 1978 (1) SA 131 (D & CLD) at 134D–135A
[169] *York & Co (Pvt) Ltd* v *Jones NO.*

The obligation to give vacant occupation, which is expressly stipulated for in a contract of sale (or implied into the agreement by law) is a vital or important term of the contract and, if the seller is in breach of this obligation, the purchaser is entitled to cancel the contract.[170]

The seller is bound to make available what was sold. Therefore, if a principal thing was sold with accessories and appurtenances this is what must be made available and not another thing even though the thing tendered is similar to that sold.[171]

If a number or an amount of unascertained things are sold it is the duty of the seller to select the things answering the description and to tender delivery of those things to the purchaser. The seller must tender the exact quality and quantity in terms of the contract.[172] If things are sold be description the seller is bound to make available a sound article corresponding exactly to the description of the one sold.[173]

The rule imposed by operation of law in the absence of agreement, custom, or trade usage on the point, is that a specific thing sold is to be handed over where it is at the time of sale, or, if it still has to be manufactured, at the place of manufacture.[174] However, there will frequently be an express or implied agreement with custom or trade usage on the point.

Furthermore, the seller is obliged to make the thing sold available immediately if performance is possible at the time of sale.[175] The seller's obligation is to make available at the same time all that is sold. If there is no express or implied agreement or custom or trade usage on the point, the seller is not entitled to deliver an instalment at the time of sale and to deliver the remainder later.

As payment and handing over are reciprocal obligations in a contract of sale, a purchaser who demands the thing before the purchaser has paid or tendered, payment may be met with an exception on the ground that it is in default and therefore cannot demand performance (the *exceptio non adimpleti contractus* see 21.10 below). A seller who fails to make the thing available at the time provided for in the contract, whether that time be agreed upon expressly or impliedly, or failing such agreement, set by operation of law will be in default (*mora debitoris*). If the seller does make the goods available at the correct time and the buyer fails to remove them or, if they are brought to the purchaser, to receive them, the purchaser is in default (*mora creditoris*).[176]

Failure to make the goods sold available on due date is a major breach of the contract by the seller entitling the purchaser to cancel the contract, provided that either promptness in performance is a matter of major importance or the rules on

170 *Sweet* v *Ragerguhara NO & Others* 1978 (1) SA 131 (D CLD) at 137G.
171 *BK Tooling (Edms) Bpk v Scope Precision Engineering (Edms) Bpk* 1979 (1) SA 391 (A) at 433D–H; *Tuckers Land and Development Corporation (Pty) Limited v Aleco Investments* 1981 (1) SA 852 (T).
172 *Cedarmont Store* v *Webster & Co* 1922 TPD 106 at 113–114; *Hersman* v *Shapiro & Co* 1926 TPD 367 at 377.
173 Kerr, *Sale and Lease, Op. cit.* at 99.
174 Kerr, *Op. cit.* at 100.
175 Kerr, *Op. cit.* at 101.
176 *Ibid.*

default have been complied with.[177] The purchaser may therefore cancel the contract and claim repayment of the purchase price. If something is tendered that is not what is sold the buyer is entitled to cancel the contract even though what is tendered is similar to what was was sold.[178]

The purchaser who wishes to have the thing rather than cancellation and/or damages may claim specific performance subject to the court's discretion to refuse it.

2.3.4.3 THE SELLER'S IMPLIED OBLIGATION TO TRANSFER OWNERSHIP IF HE HAS IT OR CAN OBTAIN IT, FAILING WHICH TO WARRANT AGAINST EVICTION

It is a recognised principle of South African law that a seller need not be the owner of the thing it sells. If the seller is the owner, it is obliged to transfer ownership to the purchaser.[179] A company may, therefore, sell things even though it is neither the owner nor the possessor but expects to become owner and possessor before the date when it will be bound to transfer the things and the ownership therein. In such circumstances the seller is obliged to obtain ownership to enable it to transfer it to the purchaser.

In some circumstances, if ownership is not acquired and transferred to the purchaser, the seller is not obliged to do any more than to give the purchaser undisturbed possession, that is, possession such that the purchaser can acquire ownership by prescription if no one with better title evicts it. This rule applies where the seller knows that it is not owner or doubts whether it is owner and informs the purchaser of the fact. The seller, therefore, who warrants against eviction is one who is not owner but in good faith believes itself to be owner.[180]

In the absence of express or implied agreement on the point, notwithstanding the fact that possession is transferred to the purchaser following a sale, ownership does not pass unless and until the price is paid or credit is given.[181]

2.3.4.4 THE WARRANTY AGAINST EVICTION

Usually, in a sale of shares or of assets comprising a business, the seller expressly warrants that it is the owner of the thing sold and that no other party has better legal title to the thing sold than it, and that upon transfer of possession of the thing sold to the purchaser, the purchaser shall not be evicted by any third party who might claim to have better title. In the absence of agreement between the parties, the warranty against eviction is implied into the contract by operation of law.

The scope of the warranty against eviction is limited, and applies only where the purchaser is evicted by someone with better legal title.[182] Thus, the eviction of the purchaser, in regard to which the warranty exists, must be one in respect

[177] *Landau* v *City Auction Mart* 1940 AD 284 at 294.
[178] *Ayob & Co Clouts* 1925 WLD 199; Kerr, *Op. cit.* at 102.
[179] Kerr, *Op. cit.* at 110–111.
[180] *Op. cit.* at 112.
[181] *Lendalease Finance (Pty) Ltd* v *Corporacion de Mercadeo Agricola and others* 1976 (4) SA 464 (A) at 490 DE; *Eriksen Motors (Welkon) Ltd* v *Protea Motors, Warrenton & Another* 1973 (3) SA 685 (A); Kerr, *Op. cit.* at 114–119.
[182] *Lammers & Lammers* v *Giovannoni* 1955 (3) SA 385 (A) at 397 B–C.

of a flaw in the title of the seller which either existed at the time of the sale or, if arising subsequent thereto, is due to some act on the part of the seller.[183] If another party claims and obtains the thing sold before transfer of possession to the purchaser, the purchaser's remedy is an action for breach of contract, namely, for failure to give transfer.

The most common form of eviction takes place after transfer of possession of the thing sold to the purchaser where the purchaser is deprived of that possession by the true owner.[184] It may happen, however, that the purchaser is deprived of possession of a part only of the thing sold, or that a third party is successful in claiming the existence of a right which diminishes the purchaser's enjoyment of one or other of the incidences of ownership though the purchaser retains possession of the thing sold. Thus, a successful claim by a third party to patent rights in the thing sold is an "eviction". Furthermore, this principle would seem to apply also to successful claims by third parties to copyright.[185]

The warranty against eviction is implied by law so it does not form part of any contract from which the parties expressly or impliedly exclude it. Therefore, if there is an express clause in the contract to the effect that the purchaser purchases the thing sold "as it stands", a clause referred to as a "voetstoots" clause, the clause and its context should be scrutinised with care.[186] Where parties include a "voetstoots" clause they may intend to exclude the warranty against eviction, but this would need to be proved because the usual meaning of such a clause is that all that is excluded is liability for defects.[187] The warranty against eviction is distinct from a warranty against defects.

Where both the seller and the purchaser *bona fide* and reasonably believe that a thing which they know is not the seller's is available for sale, the purchaser, on eviction, is entitled to the return of the actual loss suffered by it as a result of the breach of contract. In other words, the purchase price paid, but is not entitled to the return of any prospective loss, such as any profit which has not been made by it as a result of the breach of contract.[188] The term *id quod interest* is the expression used for damages or the loss sustained for which compensation is recoverable and comprises not only actual loss, but also prospective loss or the profit which has not been made by reason of the breach of a contract.[189]

When one party knows that the seller is not owner and the other does not, the position differs with the circumstances. If the seller knows that it is not owner and does not disclose this to a purchaser who does not know it, the purchaser has an action for its actual and prospective loss as soon as it finds out what the true position is.[190]

183 *Van Staden* v *Pretorius* 1965 (1) SA 852 (T) at 853 H.
184 *Par Excellence Colour Printing (Pty) Ltd* v *Ronnie Cox Graphic Supplies (Pty) Ltd* 1983 (1) SA 295 (A) at 307 A; Kerr, *Op. cit.* at 122.
185 *Ibid.*
186 *Op. cit.* at 84–87.
187 *Wright* v *Pandell* 1949 (2) SA 279 (C) at 284–285.
188 *Van der Westhuizen* v *Yskor Werknemers Se Onderlinge Bystandsvereniging* 1960 (4) SA 803 (T) at 811 G and 812 B.
189 *Union Government* v *Warneke* 1911 AD 657 at 665.
190 Kerr, *Op. cit.* at 123.

If the seller *bona fide* believes itself to be the owner, the purchaser has no action unless and until the purchaser is evicted or is threatened with eviction by a third party with better legal title than the seller.[191]

If the purchaser knows that the seller is not owner, and, concealing this knowledge from the seller which is ignorant of it, sees to it that the contract contains an express warranty against eviction, the clause does not entitle the purchaser to its actual or prospective loss (*id quod interest*). It is doubtful whether the purchaser may recover even the purchase price in these circumstances.

Where the seller is in breach of its obligation to transfer ownership, the purchaser's remedy is for breach of contract, namely, failure to transfer ownership. An action for specific performance, namely to transfer ownership, is one arising from the agreement of sale and purchase (*ex empto*).[192] The action *ex empto* entitles the purchaser to claim delivery of possession of the thing with its titles and fruits and everything dependent upon it.

Where a third party claims better legal title to the thing sold, the seller is regarded as being "in breach" of its warranty that the purchaser will not be evicted. The warranty against eviction binds the seller to compensate the purchaser if certain circmstances, specified in the warranty, arise. If such circumstances arise, the purchaser's remedy is an action for performance of the warranty, not for breach of it. Performance, however, involves the payment of compensation, so one often finds references to "damages" in this context.

When a third party claims ownership of the thing sold and transfer of possession, the purchaser should inform the seller and call upon the seller to assist in the defence.[193] The basic obligation of the seller is to protect the purchaser in its possession.[194] The purchaser may bring an action for compensation against the seller if the purchaser can show that the seller has admitted the demand of the third party claiming better title and has legally bound itself to comply with it[195] and that the seller had no title that could have made resistance to the true owner possible.[196]

The purchaser therefore need show only that the third party claiming ownership has a legally unassailable claim to the thing. If the purchaser can prove this, the purchaser need not force the third party claiming ownership to take it to court. In a doubtful case, however, particularly if the purchaser cannot find the seller and so cannot notify the seller, the purchaser should conduct a proper and competent defence. If the purchaser does so and loses, this will enable it to show the seller that the third party's claim is legally unassailable. In theory this conclusion is final only if the case has been to the highest court, but because one can generally rely on a judgment, there is no general requirement that a purchaser who loses in the court of first instance should appeal. The costs of a defence can

[191] *Westeel Engineering (Pty) Ltd* v *Sydney Clow & Co Ltd* 1968 (3) SA 458 (T); *Louis Botha Motors* v *James & Slabbert Motors (Pty) Ltd* 1983 (3) SA 793 (A).

[192] Kerr, *Op. cit.* at 124.

[193] *Ibid.* 124.

[194] *Lammers & Lammers* v *Giovannoni* 1955 (3) SA 385 (A) at 309 A.

[195] *Olivier* v *Van der Bergh* 1956 (1) SA 802 (C) at 805 H

[196] *Ibid.*

be recovered from the seller whenever the *id quod interest* is the measure of compensation. However, if the purchaser defends and wins the purchaser cannot claim reimbursement from the seller because, by winning, it has shown that its title is better than the third party's and the seller does not warrant against attempts to evict by third parties with inferior title.[197]

It may happen that possession of the thing sold is transferred to the purchaser before the price is paid and that a third party then makes a claim to its ownership. In such circumstances the purchaser can demand security from the seller before paying the price if the claim can be shown to be seriously intended.[198]

The benefit which the purchaser receives from notifying the seller in all the above cases and calling upon the seller to assist the purchaser, as is recommended, is that the purchaser can claim compensation from the seller. In other words, a seller who is called upon to defend the purchaser in its possession but who then refuses to assist, cannot raise the defence against a claim by the purchaser that the purchaser could or should have resisted a third party's claim more energetically or skilfully, for it was open to the seller to have taken steps to protect the purchaser and itself.[199]

The purchaser claiming performance of a warranty against eviction is entitled, except in the case of eviction from a rapidly depreciating asset or from a diminishing one, to repayment of the price or of whatever portion it has paid (actual loss) and, if loss over and above the amount of the price can be shown (prospective loss), compensation for such loss, provided that the amount does not exceed what was contemplated or foreseeable by the parties at the time of conclusion of the agreement.[200]

2.3.4.5 WARRANTY OF FITNESS FOR SPECIFIC USE

There will often be an express, or in certain circumstances an implied, warranty that the thing sold is fit for the purpose for which it is sold.[201] The warranty of fitness for a specific use is a warranty relating to the quality of the thing sold and will be implied into a contract of sale in the absence of any express agreement if the seller knows or is deemed to know the purpose for which the thing sold is to be used. Furthermore, in some circumstances the rules on misrepresentation and non-disclosure will be applicable.

Where the seller knows or is deemed to know the purpose for which the purchaser requires the thing purchased, then there is an implied warranty that the thing sold is fit for that purpose. As soon as the purchaser discovers that the thing sold is not fit for the purpose for which it is sold, the purchaser is entitled to cancel the contract. If the purchaser has not yet paid the purchase price it may return the thing sold to the seller and refuse to pay the purchase price.[202]

[197] Kerr, *Op. cit.* at 125.
[198] *Shaw* v *Arami* 1913 WLD 105.
[199] *Lammers & Lammers* v *Giovanoni* 1955 (3) SA 385 (A) at 392 G.
[200] Kerr, *Op. cit.* at 126; *Alpha Trust (Pty) Ltd* v *Van der Watt* 1975 (3) SA 734 (A).
[201] *Minister van Landbou – Tegniese Dienste* v *Scholtz* 1971 (3) SA 188 (A).
[202] *Wheeler* v *Woodhouse* (1990) 21 NLR 162; *Hugo* v *Henwood* 1905 TS 578; *Kroomer* v *Hess & Co* 1919 AD 204.

The warranty may be implied in certain contracts, not in all. The warranty of fitness for a specific use is clearly not applicable to a sale of shares, and may only in certain circumstances be applicable in a sale of a business as a going concern. In the latter instance the purchaser, in any event, will have some knowledge of the business which it is intent on purchasing. If the business is a manufacturing business the purchaser may require a warranty to the effect that the fixed capital assets are fit for the purpose for which they are being bought, namely, for manufacturing the particular product which the purchaser hopes later to sell at a profit. It is clear that where a business is being purchased the purpose of the purchase is to continue running the business as a going concern and the seller will be aware of the purpose. In such circumstances, the warranty may be implied into the contract of sale.

When the purpose of a contract is referred to, what is meant is a purpose of which both parties are, or are deemed to be, aware, not a purpose which only the purchaser has in mind and which the purchaser keeps secret.[203] The purpose of the contract may be communicated by the purchaser to the seller beforehand, or it may be deducible from the circumstances. Thus, if a business is sold as a going concern the parties cannot be heard to argue that it was not understood that the purchaser or somebody else with its consent, would continue to run that business as a going concern and use the assets purchased for that purpose.

It is convenient to consider questions of fitness under three headings. Firstly, things may be unfit for the purpose for which they are sold though they are, in themselves, sound. Secondly, things may be unfit for the purpose for which they are sold because they are suffering from a patent defect. Thirdly, things may be unfit for the purpose for which they are sold because they are suffering from a latent defect.[204]

Firstly, a thing may be sound, but unfit for the purpose for which it is required. If a fixed asset is being used in a successful business, and the business is sold as a going concern, it is unlikely that the fixed asset will be unfit for the purpose for which it was bought. But each case will have to be dealt with on its own merits, and a purchaser should be careful if the seller attempts to exclude the warranty.

The question whether a particular asset sold is "sound" or "defective" may cause difficulty. In practice, absolute perfection is normally unattainable and what may seem to be a "defect" in an asset of a low standard may not be recognised as a defect in law, entitiling the purchaser to cancel the contract and claim damages.[205] In a supply contract for the supply of assets, a "sound" asset means an asset supplied by the seller which is as fit as any answering the description in the order.[206] Therefore, although an asset may be sound and have nothing wrong with it, it may still be unfit for the purpose for which it was purchased. Thus, in considering fitness and soundness the intended or specified method of use is important.

[203] Kerr, *Op. cit.* at 131.
[204] *Op. cit.*, at 131–137.
[205] *Curtain Crafts (Pty) Ltd* v *Wilson* 1969 (4) SA 221 (E).
[206] *Hall & Co* v *Kearns* (1983) 10 SC 152 at 155.

Secondly, an asset may be unfit for the purpose for which it is sold because it is patently defective, in other words, upon an examination of the asset sold by the purchaser, the purchaser could have observed the defect. Whether or not a thing is patently defective is a question of fact. The aedilitian remedies (the action for reduction of the purchase price and the action for the return of the purchase price if the thing sold is found to have a latent defect—discussed in 2.3.4.8 below) are not available if the thing sold is patently defective. The purchaser, however, has the ordinary remedies for breach of contract unless there is a "voetstoots" clause and the purchaser accepts the thing sold as it is. If at the time of the sale the assets are unascertained and are described with precision, delivery of patently defective things will allow the purchaser to reject them on either of two grounds: firstly, that what is tendered is not what was sold because it does not comply with the description, or secondly, unfitness for purpose.[207]

Thirdly, apart from special cases such as those manufacturers, merchant sellers, or others who come within the rule *spondet peritiam artis* (discussed in 2.3.4.7 below), the seller of latently defective goods is not liable on the implied warranty of fitness for purpose.[208] Thus where the defects are latent, the purchaser must rely on the aedilitian remedies against the seller. In the alternative, the purchaser may, after cession of action from the seller, bring action against the manufacturer of the thing sold on the warranty given by the manufacturer relating to the skill of his art.[209]

There does not seem to be a South African case concerning the period during which the thing sold is warranted to be fit for the purpose for which it is sold nor on the effect of the warranty on the observed change in the thing.

2.3.4.6 WARRANTY OF REASONABLE MERCHANTABLE QUALITY

Where the purpose for which a thing sold is not known to the seller it is a question of fact whether the thing sold is "unmerchantable" or not of a reasonable quality, and entirely useless to any person. If the thing sold is entirely useless, so that it is of no value to the purchaser, the purchaser may demand that the thing sold shall be declared to have been "unmerchantable" or not of a reasonable quality, and the seller consequently condemned to take it back and to restore and return the money received by it, with damages (including consequential loss) and interest.[210]

The purchaser does not lose its right to cancel and claim restitution and damages if it does not inspect the goods immediately on delivery, but the longer the purchaser delays, the more difficult it will be to prove that the goods were not reasonably merchantable when delivered. South African law in this regard is in accord with the principles of English law on the point.[211]

In the absence of definition in South African law on the meaning of the words "reasonable merchantable quality", one South African writer, Christie, suggests

[207] Kerr, *Ibid.*, 133.
[208] *Kroonstad Westelike Boere-Ko-Operatiewe Vereeniging Bpk* v *Botha and another* 1964 (3) SA 561 (A).
[209] Kerr, *Ibid.*
[210] Kerr, *Ibid.*
[211] See for example *Fergusson* v *Wood Bros* (1885) 4 SC 111.

that the terms of subsection 2 of paragraph 2–314 of the American Uniform Commercial Code may well be considered in their interpretation:

(2) Goods to be merchantable must be at least such as
- (a) pass without objection in the trade under the contract description;
- (b) in the case of fungible goods, are of average quality within the description; and
- (c) are fit for the ordinary purposes for which such goods are used; and
- (d) run, within the variations permitted by the agreement, of even kind, quality and quantity within each unit and among all units involved; and
- (e) are adequately contained, packaged, and labelled as the agreement may require; and
- (f) conform to the promises or affirmations of fact made on the container or label if any.

2.3.4.7 WARRANTY OF THE SKILL OF HIS ART

In the absence of agreement to the contrary, manufacturers and merchant sellers warrant the skill of their respective arts, which means of their respective professions, pursuits, or callings. The term comes from the Latin phrase *spondet peritiam artis*, which means "he promises the skill of his art".[212] The warranty of the skill of his art is not applicable to a sale of shares or of businesses as going concerns, but is applicable where a merchant seller or trader sells his wares to the public.

Where the merchant trader purchases things suffering from latent defects from the manufacturer, the manufacturer's liability may be either contractual (based on breach of the warranty against latent defects) or delictual (based on the negligence or intention of the manufacturer).[213] Where the merchant trader on-sells the things to a purchaser, this ontract may contain the implied warranty *spondet peritiam artis* and the purchaser will be entitled to rely on breach of the implied warranty to cancel the contract and claim restitution.[214] Where there is *dolus* (intention) or *culpa* (negligence) on the part of the merchant seller it seems that actions can be taken in either contract or delict. Where there is no *dolus* or *culpa* on the merchant seller's part, there is no liability in delict.[215]

It is relatively easy to see that a carpenter selling wood to be used for a known purpose is liable for consequential loss if the wood is used for that purpose and is defective, and also that a seller who did not know of the defect and is not acting in the course of his business is not so liable. It is much more difficult to decide what the position is with regard to a merchant or dealer who, in practising his trade, sells an article which both he and the customer know has come from a manufacturer packaged in such a way that it is obviously intended to be opened only by the purchaser and not by the merchant. In *Hackett* v *G & G Radio &*

[212] Kerr, *Contract, Op. cit.* at 287.

[213] *Holmdene Brickworks (Pty) Ltd* v *Roberts Construction Co Ltd* 1977 (3) SA 670 (A) at 686 F–687 B.

[214] Kerr, *Ibid.*

[215] *Ibid.*

Refrigerate Corporation[216] Schreiner J A made some observations on the question. He said (at 692, 693):

> The decisions in the Provincial Divisions broadly speaking recognise the justice of the generalisation that a seller who manufactures or deals in a kind of goods should be treated as having given the purchaser of such goods from him his expert assurance that the goods are free of latent defects. It seems to me that this recognition accords with the present day needs of the community . . . Motor-cars, for instance, are often assembled in South Africa out of parts manufactured overseas—possibly in several different countries and certainly by several different persons—and are then sold by dealers whom alone the purchasers know and on whose standing as experts they rely . . . It seems reasonable in general to give the purchaser a right of full compensation against his seller where the latter is a dealer in goods of that kind and does not show that his being such a dealer did not influence the mind of a purchaser in entering into the sale.

The question arose for decision in *Kroonstad Westelike-Boere-Ko Operatiewe Vereniging Bpk* v *Botha and another.*[217] The Appellate Division stated, and it must now be recognised to be law, that:

> Liability for consequential damage caused by latent defect attaches to a merchant seller, who was unaware of the defect, where he publicly professes to have attributes of skill and expert knowledge in relation to the kind of goods sold. (It is not intended here to draw any distinction between the words "*merchant*" and "*dealer*".) Whether a seller falls within the category mentioned will be a question of fact and degree to be decided from all the circumstances of the case. Once it is established that he does fall within that category, the law irrebuttably attaches to him the liability in question save only where he has expressly or by implication contracted out of it.

2.3.4.8 WARRANTY AGAINST LATENT DEFECTS

The warranty against latent defects is not applicable to a sale of shares, but may be applicable to the sale of businesses as going concerns where assets are sold.

The aedilitian remedies, namely an action for cancellation of the contract and restitution (*the actio redhibitoria*), and the action for the return of portion of the purchase price (*the actio quanti minoris*) are available in South African law where an asset sold is found to be latently defective, but not where the asset sold is patently defective.[218] When the assets sold are delivered to the purchaser, the purchaser is entitled to reject any patently defective assets, cancel the contract and claim damages for the breach. If the purchaser does not reject and return the patently defective assets to the seller, but uses them in its business, it will not be entitled to cancel the contract. Instead, the purchaser will be left with a claim against the seller for damages arising from the seller's breach of contract, namely its failure to deliver assets according to the terms of the contract.

[216] 1949 (3) SA 664 (A).

[217] 1964 (3) SA 561 (A).

[218] *SA Oil and Fat Industries Ltd* v *Park Rynie Whaling Co Ltd* 1916 AD 400 at 413; *SA Wood Turning Mills Ltd* v *Price Bros Ltd* 1962 (4) SA 263 (T) at 266.

A purchaser relying on a latent defect may avail itself of an aedilitian remedy or of the relevant general contractual remedy.[219] The phrase "the right of action for rescission of a contract on account of a latent defect" should not be used without qualification, because cancellation and restitution, either alone or in combination with another remedy, may be sought by more than one action, such as an action on fraudulent, negligent or innocent misrepresentation, an action on the contract where an express or implied warranty is involved, or the *actio redhibitoria*.[220]

The *actio redhibitoria* lies if at the time of the sale the thing sold suffered from any "disease or defect" not declared by the seller, even if it was one of which the seller had no knowledge, or if a thing is sold "in contravention of what was stated and promised" (see 1.3.2.4 above in respect of *dicta et promissa*). Whether or not the thing sold suffered from a disease or defect at the time of sale is a question of fact.[221] The aedilitian remedies, therefore, do not lie if the thing sold was sound at the time of the sale although it had previously suffered from a disease or defect, or if it became diseased or defective thereafter.[222]

This does not mean to say that in all circumstances where a defective part of, say, an engine, is replaced or repaired so that at the time of sale the engine is functioning properly no action will lie. If the engine were finally to collapse and the replaced or repaired part is found to function properly they may still be a causal connection between the defect and the damage which supervened after delivery. The deterioration of the engine is a progressive process so that although the defective part was repaired or replaced when it ceased to function properly, other parts of the engine will have been affected. The deterioration of the engine increased each time the moving part was so abused until the engine develops what one might call a "propensity to seizure".[223] Thus, although the thing sold may function properly at the time of sale, if a part of it has been replaced or repaired and, on the evidence, it is shown that the thing sold ceases to function as a result of a "propensity to seizure", then the aedilitian remedies will lie.

The mere fact that a disease or defect manifests itself or is discovered shortly after the sale may not lead to an inference that the disease or defect existed at the time of the sale. The burden of proof rests on the purchaser to show on the balance of probabilities that the disease or defect did so exist.[224] The purchaser does not have to prove that the disease or defect was apparent at the time of the sale. It is sufficient to prove that at the time the thing sold had within it the beginnings of what is later seen to be a disease or defect.[225]

A disease has been defined as "some condition of the body which renders it less able to perform the functions for which nature has bestowed upon as

219 Kerr, *Sale and Lease Op. cit.* at 55, *Landau* v *City Auction Mart* 1940 AD 284.

220 Kerr, *Ibid.; Hackett* v *G&G Radio & Refrigerator Corporation* 1949 (3) SA 664 (A) at 685; *Minister van Landbou-tgniese Dienste* v *Scholtz* 1971 (3) SA 188 at 198 C–E.

221 *Sebeko* v *Soll* 1949 (3) SA 337 (T) at 350.

222 Kerr, *Op. cit.* at 56.

223 *Schwarzer* v *John Roderick's Motors (Pty) Ltd* 1940 OPD 170 at 180; Kerr, *Ibid.*

224 Kerr, *Op. cit.* at 57.

225 *Pelunsky & Mervis* v *Friedman & Joffe* 1907 TH 73.

corporeal health".[226] However, the maxim that the law does not take account of trifling matters (*de minimus non curat lex*) applies, so the only diseases such as those which interfere with the use and services of the thing sold are taken into account. Where the disease is of such a nature that it is not trifling but does not entitle the purchaser to rely on the *actio redhibitoria* because it is not material, the purchaser will be able to resort to the *actio quanti minoris* as its remedy.

Not all imperfections in the thing sold amount to a defect which will give rise to the aedilitian remedies. Those which do may be termed "aedilitian defects" and those which give rise to an *actio redhibitoria* as "redhibitory defects".[227]

Two important factors to be considered in determining whether or not an imperfection is an aedilitian defect are the class of goods into which the thing sold falls and the purpose for which the thing is, or is deemed to be, sold. An imperfection in the thing sold can only be described as a defect giving rise to a legal action by the purchaser if it is shown that such imperfection is of a type or nature which a reasonable man would not expect to exist in other articles of substantial identity with the thing sold.[228]

2.3.5 Contractual v statutory warranties

Except for the statutory warranty referred to in section 138 of the Companies Act, which in any event protects the company and not the seller or the purchaser of the shares (see 1.2 above), there are no statutory warranties implied into contracts for the sale of shares or of businesses as going concerns.

The parties to a contract of sale may therefore rely on either the implied warranties discussed in 2.3.4 above in the absence of agreement, or, the contract warranties they expressly wish to include as terms of the contract. The various express warranties are discussed in subsequent sections.

3. Warranties in Sales of Goods

3.1 Statutory Warranties

In South African law the parties to a contract of sale enjoy the freedom of agreeing which warranties, if any, they wish to include in or exclude from their contract. There are no South African statutes which imply warranties into such contracts (see 1.3.5.3 above) and, in the absence of agreement, the *naturalia* discussed above will, where relevant, be implied into the contract by operation of law (see 2.3 above).

3.1.1 Statutory warranty of good standing

There is no statutory, or in the absence of agreement between the parties any implied, warranty of good standing applicable in the Republic of South Africa.

[226] Kerr, *Ibid.*
[227] *Op. cit.* at 58; *Dibley* v *Furter* 1951 (4) SA 73 (C).
[228] *Curtaincrafts (Pty) Ltd* v *Wilson* 1969 (4) SA 221 (E).

3.1.2 Statutory warranty of clear title

There is no statutory, or in the absence of agreement between the parties any implied, warranty of clear title applicable in the Republic of South Africa. There is an implied obligation on the part of the seller to transfer ownership and, if he cannot, to warrant against eviction (see 2.3.4.3 above).

3.1.3 Statutory warranty of absence of defects

There is no statutory warranty of absence of defects applicable in the Republic of South Africa, but the common law aedilitian remedies are available to the purchaser if the thing sold is found to be latently defective at the time of the sale (see 2.3.4.8 above).

3.1.4 Statutory warranty of merchantable quality

There is no statutory warranty of merchantable quality applicable in the Republic of South Africa, but there may be an express, or in certain circumstances an implied, warranty of merchantable quality (see 2.3.4.6 above).

3.2 Contractual Warranties

3.2.1 Warranty of proper functioning

A thing will not function properly if it is defective or is unfit for the purpose for which it is bought or is unmerchantable. These concepts have been discussed above (see 2.3.4.5, 2.3.4.6 and 2.3.4.8). If the seller expressly warrants that the thing sold "will function properly" as at the date of sale, and it does not, then the purchaser will be entitled to either the general contractual remedies based on breach of the aforesaid express warranty, or any of the remedies applicable if the purchaser can prove that the thing sold was defective and unfit for the purpose for which it was sold or unmerchantable. The purchaser may then elect which remedy it wishes to rely on.

The question whether or not the thing sold does or does not function properly in accordance with the terms of the warranty given will be a question of fact, to be decided on the facts of each particular case.

3.2.2 Warranty of fitness for specific use

The common law position, with regard to the implied warranty of fitness for a specific use, has been discussed above (see 2.3.4.5 above). In the absence of any agreement, therefore, the warranty of fitness for a specific use will be implied into the contract only in certain contracts, not in all. Thus, a cautious purchaser which wishes to ensure protection under the implied warranty may verbally advise the seller of the purpose for which the thing sold is to be used.

The parties may agree either expressly to include the warranty, or exclude the warranty. The seller will usually wish expressly to exclude this warranty, particularly in circumstances where the thing sold notoriously does not perform as the purchaser wishes it to perform.

An example would be the sale of software, where at most the seller may be prepared to warrant that the software package will operate in accordance only with its instructions and specifications.

3.2.3 General warranty

General contractual warranties relating to the sale of the assets comprising a business as a going concern are discussed in section 13.

3.2.4 Specific warranties

Specific contractual warranties relating to the sale of assets comprising a business as a going concern are discussed in section 13.

4. Warranties in Negotiations

4.1 Confidentiality Agreements

The parties to an agreement may acknowledge to each other and record in their agreement that each of them intends to retain strict confidentiality regarding their negotiations, the subject matter and contents of their agreement, and any other information regarding their activities which may be classified as confidential. Each party, therefore, may undertake to the other party to treat all negotiations, the content and subject matter of the agreement and any other matters relating to the agreement, and any confidential information, in strict confidence and not either to disclose any of the aforementioned to any third party without the prior written consent of all the other parties, except where it is necessary to do so in order to ensure the fulfilment of any suspensive condition (see 21.4 for a discussion on conditions), or use any confidential information to the detriment of the other party.

Should any of the parties be in breach of the provisions of their undertaking, as recorded in the agreement, then the other party would be entitled to its normal contractual remedies for breach of contract and, in appropriate circumstances prior to the disclosure or use of any confidential information, to apply to court on an urgent basis for a temporary or final interdict restraining the other party from disclosing the information to any person, or using the confidential information.

4.2 Non-Insider Trading Agreements

In the light of the provisions of section 440F(1) of the Companies Act, the concept of "non-insider trading agreements" is virtually unknown in the Republic of South Africa. Section 440F(1) of the Companies Act (which came into force on 1 February 1991) states that:

> Any person who, whether directly or indirectly, knowingly deals in a security on the basis of unpublished price-sensitive information in respect of that security, shall be guilty of an offence if such person knows that such information has been obtained—
> (a) by virtue of a relationship of trust or any other contractual relationship, whether or not the person concerned is a party to that relationship; or
> (b) through espionage, theft, bribery, fraud, misrepresentation or any other wrongful method, irrespective of the nature thereof.

"Unpublished price-sensitive information" in respect of a security, means information which relates to matters in respect of the internal affairs of a company or its operations, assets, earning power or involvement as offeror or offeree company in an affected transaction or proposed affected transaction (see 1.1.11.1 above for the meaning of an "affected transaction"), which information is not generally available to the reasonable investor in the relevant markets for that security, and which information would reasonably be expected to affect materially the price of such security if it were generally available (section 440F(2)(a) and (b) of the Companies Act).

A "security" means any shares in the capital of a company and includes stock and debentures convertible into shares and any rights or interest in a company or in respect of any such shares, stock or debentures, and any "financial instrument" as defined in the Financial Markets Control Act, 1989 (section 440A(1) of the Companies Act).

Section 440F(1) of the Companies Act has the effect of extending criminal liability for insider trading to three categories of persons. Firstly, there are those persons who have access to inside information by virtue of a relationship of trust or any other contractual relationship. Such persons have been termed the "primary" insiders and would probably include within the ambit of fiduciary relationships, the relationship between a company and its directors, attorneys, advocates, accountants, bankers, brokers, certain civil servants and even, perhaps, financial journalists. Secondly, there are those persons who may be referred to as "tippees", who obtain inside information from a "primary" insider or another "tippee". Thirdly, there are those persons who have access to inside information through espionage, theft, bribery, fraud, misrepresentation or any other wrongful method.

Where a person has been found guilty of the crime of insider trading such person shall be liable to any other person for any loss or damage suffered by that person as a result of such contravention. The plaintiff in a civil suit for recovery of such loss or damage in the case of insider trading in securities on the JSE or a financial market as defined in section 1 of the Financial Markets Control Act, 1989, shall not need to prove intention or negligence towards him or it (section 440F(4)(a) and (b) of the Companies Act).

The provisions of section 440F of the Companies Act apply to dealings in securities in public listed companies and in private companies, but not to dealing in members' interest in a close corporation (section 440F(5) of the Companies Act).

The criminal aspects of, and recovery of loss or damage in a civil suit arising from, insider trading are therefore dealt with by statute (section 440F of the Companies Act). It may, therefore, be superfluous to include a clause in a contract of sale of shares or of a business as a going concern recording a contractual undertaking not to participate in criminal activity. Any aggrieved person who believes that insider trading in securities has impacted on a proposed deal to his detriment may report the alleged insider trading to the Securities Regulation Panel for investigation. Such an investigation is at the expense of the State and may or may not lead to a criminal prosecution. Where a criminal prosecution results in the conviction of a person of the crime of insider trading, then that person may be sued for recovery of any loss or damage caused to the aggrieved party as a result of the contravention.

4.3 Non-Hostile Takeover Agreements

Where the shares in a company change hands with the approval of the board of directors of that company the danger of obstructive action on the part of the directors is less likely to occur. In the case of a closely held private company the shareholders are often also the directors of the company. It is then normal to provide in the agreement of sale that payment of the purchase price will be made against delivery to the purchaser by the seller of the relevant share certificates and share transfer forms, together with the written resignation of those directors appointed to the board of directors by the selling shareholder. The new controlling shareholder is then free to appoint directors of his choice.

In the case of a takeover of control of any company other than a private company with less than ten members or a value of less than R10,000,000, special provisions in the Companies Act apply which are designed to protect minority shareholders (see 1.1.12.1 above).

4.4 Standstill Agreements

A debtor is always free to negotiate a moratorium in respect of payments or a compromise with its creditors. The legal consequences of a compromise are discussed in 21.5.3 below. The fact that a debtor enters into a compromise or an arrangement or a moratorium with its debtors generally may constitute a ground of default in terms of other contracts entered into by the debtor, entitling the other parties to those contracts to terminate the contract in question. Furthermore, if the debtor acknowledges that it cannot pay its debts this acknowledgment may constitute an act of insolvency in terms of section 345(1)(c) read with section 344(b) of the Companies Act, in which event any of its creditors may attempt to wind it up. Therefore, an attempt by a company to enter into a compromise or other arrangement with its creditors may sound the death knell for that company.

The only statutory reference to "standstill agreements" can be found in the Currency and Exchanges Act, 1933. In 1985 the South African Government declared a moratorium in respect of the payments to foreign creditors on debts arising before 28 August 1985. Debts arising after 28 August 1985 are not subject to the moratorium. Although the effect of the moratorium has been extended only to 31 December 1993, the period of the standstill arrangement may again be extended.

The moratorium extends to all instruments of debt, including overdrafts Euro facilities, discounting of bills, banker's acceptances, outstanding commitments under lines of credit and all trade debt excluding supplier credit in respect of services or goods received in the Republic of South Africa on or after 1 January 1985.

The standstill regulations prohibit any person from making payment to or in favour of any foreign creditor in respect of the above debts except payment into a special restricted account. A "special restricted account" means an account opened with the Public Investment Commissioner for the purpose of the payment into such account of any amount which may not be paid to or in favour of a foreign creditor.[229]

[229] Regulation 2 Government Notice R 603 GG 10166, 27 March 1986, as amended.

Any payment of commercial rand made by a debtor into a special restricted account in terms of these regulations shall, to the extent of the sum so paid and upon the issuance by the Public Investment Commissioner of a confirmation of deposit, operate as a valid discharge to the person so making payment. The sum standing to the credit of a special restricted account bears interest which is calculated and payable in a manner and at a rate which is determined from time to time by the Minister of Finance. Such a credit is regarded as a debt due by and repayable by the Public Investment Commissioner in such manner and in such instalments of commercial rand and on such conditions as may be determined from time to time by the Minister of Finance, to the foreign creditor in whose favour such sum has been paid into the special restricted account. All the obligations and liabilities of the Public Investment Commissioner with regard to amounts paid into special restricted accounts in any resulting deposits are the obligations and liabilities of the South African State.

The Minister of Finance is empowered in terms of the above mentioned regulations in his discretion to exempt any person from any of or all the provisions of the regulations and may at any time amend or withdraw such exemption or condition.

Any person who contravenes or fails to comply with the regulations shall be guilty of an offence and liable on conviction to a fine not exceeding R250, 000 or to imprisonment for a period not exceeding five years, or to both such fine or such imprisonment.

5. Warranties in Promises to Sell

5.1 Relationship between a Promise to Sell and an Agreement of Sale

5.1.1 The concept of an offer

A contract is formed when parties who have the requisite intention and who comply with the requirements of the law agree. The intention which is requisite is one to enter into a legal relationship, the same legal relationship, with each other, in other words, the parties must enter into the transaction "seriously and deliberately and with the intention that a lawful obligation should be established".[230]

The general principles of offer and acceptance in the law of contract apply when determining whether a contract has been formed. A person is said to make an offer when he puts forward a proposal with the intention that by its mere acceptance, without more, a contract should be formed.[231] A distinction is therefore made in our law between an offer requiring a straight affirmative answer in order to create a contract, and a promise which was not intended to be accepted by anyone.[232] What distinguishes a true offer from any other proposal

[230] Kerr, *Contract, Op. cit.* at 33; *Conradie* v *Rossouw* 1919 AD 279 at 324; *Tobacco Manufacturers Committee* v *Jacob Gree and Sons* 1953 (3) SA 480 (A) at 493–2; *Froman* v *Robertson* 1971 (1) SA 115 (A) at 121 D.

[231] Christie, *Op. cit.* at 29.

[232] *Saambou-Nasionale Bouvereniging* v *Friedman* 1979 (3) SA 978 (A) at 991 G.

or statement is the express or implied intention to be bound by the offeree's acceptance.[233]

Where the intention to enter into a legal relationship is lacking, even though the parties are serious, there is no contract: such as when promises are made with fairness and a real design of accomplishing them, but without any intention of giving the person to whom they are made a right of demanding their performance, or where a person makes a promise, intimating at the same time that he does not mean to engage himself, or when such a reservation can be implied from the circumstances of the case, or from the relative characters of the person making the promise and the person to whom it is made. Each case will depend on the facts, so the nature of the offer, including the words in which it is expressed, the relationship between the parties and the circumstances surrounding the making of the offer must all be examined before it can be decided whether an offer was made with or without the intention to contract.[234]

Therefore, where a valid offer to sell is made and this offer is accepted, then a contract of sale comes into existence provided that the terms of the offer, whether express or implied, cover both the minimum requirements of the proposed contract (the *essentialia*) and any matters which the parties intend to negotiate themselves (the *accidentalia*); in other words, matters which they do not wish to be regulated by the common law (the *naturalia*).[235]

5.1.2 Rights of pre-emption and option contracts

Although an offer normally invites the offeree to enter into one of the commoner contracts, for example, to buy, to hire, to accept a mandate or to serve, an offer may also be an invitation to enter into a contract of which the subject matter is the offer in a different contract. For example, there may be a contract to give preference if an offer to purchase is made in future, or to keep open an offer to purchase which has been, or is being, or will be, made.[236] These are two of the forms an agreement to conclude a contract, a *pactum de contrahendo,* may take.[237]

One of the forms of an agreement to conclude a contract is a contract whereby one party gives to the other a preference if an offer is made, thus granting a right of pre-emption which is a preferent conditional right to purchase.[238] The grantor of a right of pre-emption undertakes to and is obliged to make an offer to purchase to the grantee before making an offer to someone else.[239] The conditional right to purchase conferred upon the grantee does not normally impose any corresponding enforceable positive obligation upon the grantor to sell, save under the conditions prescribed in the agreement creating the right.[240] Normally, in a right of pre-emption, the condition is that if the grantor of the right of pre-emption decides or desires or proposes to sell, he shall first offer the

233 *Op. cit.* at 20.
234 *Op. cit.* at 32.
235 Kerr, *Contract, Op. cit.* at 59.
236 Kerr, *Op. cit.* at 65.
237 *Hirschowitz* v *Moolman and others* 1985 (3) SA 739 (A).
238 *Aronson* v *Sternberg Brothers (Pty) Ltd* 1985 (1) SA 613 (A) at 621L–622C.
239 *Soteriou* v *Retco Poyntons (Pty) Ltd* 1985 (2) SA 922 (A) at 932H, 935B–D.
240 *Owsianick* v *African Consolidated Theatres (Pty) Ltd* 1967 (3) SA 310(A) at 321F.

property to the grantee of the right of pre-emption. The grant of a right of pre-emption, therefore, does not compel the grantor to sell, it only compels him to give the grantee the preference in case he sells at all. Consequently, it prevents him from selling to third persons during the existence of the right.

Where the grantor of the right of pre-emption makes an offer to sell to a third person in breach of the aforesaid right, the grantee of the right of pre-emption may either interdict acceptance by the offeree (the third person), or interdict the grantor of the right from making offers to anyone else, or claim specific performance of his right to receive the first offer; that is, claim that the offer be made to him, or by a unilateral declaration of intent take the place of the offeree and accept the offer.[241] This follows from the fact that the grantor of a right of pre-emption is in breach of his obligation as soon as he offers the thing to a third person. If the grantor of a right of pre-emption sells to another and transfers the thing to that other before the holder of the right discovers what has happened, and if the other was unaware of the holder's rights, transfer to the holder of the right is not normally ordered, the holder being left with a claim for damages.[242]

Another common form of an agreement to conclude a contract is the option contract. Such a contract is an agreement between two parties whereby one party undertakes, sometimes for a consideration, to keep open an offer which he has made or is making or will make.[243] There are therefore two offers to be considered in option cases: firstly, the offer in the contract of sale, and secondly, an offer to keep the offer in the contract of sale open. Normally these two offers are made to the same person and are often combined in one proposition. The offer to keep open the offer to sell may be irrevocable or limited by time. If an option holder sues for damages for breach of the option the onus is on him to prove that he has suffered damage, which involves proving that he would have exercised the option.[244]

5.1.3 The distinction between an offer to sell and an agreement of sale

An agreement of sale will come into existence only once the offeree accepts the offer made by the offeror. Prior to acceptance by the offeree, and provided there is no option contract in terms of which the offeror has undertaken to keep the offer open for a specified period, the offeror may, at any time, withdraw the offer. Should the offer, which may include certain warranties, be accepted, such warranties will be included in the contract of sale.

5.2 *Survival of Warranties in Promise to Sell not Repeated in Sale Agreement*

As mentioned in 5.1 above, the terms of an offer to sell, including any warranties contained therein, become binding between the parties only once the offer has

[241] *Associated South African Bakeries (Pty) Ltd* v *Oryx and Vereinigt Bäckerein (Pty) Ltd* 1982 (3) SA 893(A).

[242] *Owsianick* v *African Consolidated Theatres (Pty) Ltd* 1967 (3) SA 310 (A) at 319E-F; *Associated South African Bakeries (Pty) Ltd* v *Oryx and Vereinigt Bäckerein (Pty) Ltd* 322A-B 1982 (3) SA 893 (A) at 909D–9 1OH.

[243] *Hersch* v *Nel* 1948 (3) SA 686 (A) at 693, 695; Kerr, *Contract Op. cit.* at 67.

[244] *Sommer* v *Wilding* 1984 (3) SA 647(A).

been accepted by the offeree. If the offeree does not accept the terms of the offer, there is no contract of sale, in which event any warranties which may have been included in the offer will not survive the promise to sell.

6. Warranties in Sale of Shares

6.1 Shares as Negotiable Instruments or as Contractual Position? Consequent Sale of Instrument or Assignment of Contract

Nominative shares are not negotiable instruments,[245] the reason being that a share certificate lacks an essential attribute of negotiability, namely that mere delivery of a share certificate, or delivery coupled with endorsement, cannot suffice (no matter with what intention delivery is made) to transfer ownership of the shares.[246]

A "share" means a share in the share capital of a company.[247] The term "share" does not refer to a right of ownership in the net assets of the company, such ownership being vested in the company as a separate legal person. A share in a company consists of a bundle, or conglomerate, of personal rights entitling the holder thereof to a certain interest in the company, its assets and dividends.[248] By contrast, a share certificate is *prima facie* evidence of the shareholder's title to the shares.

The memorandum of association and the articles of association, when registered, bind the company and its registered members to the same extent as if they had been signed by each member,[249] and constitute a contract between the company and its members, *qua* members, as well as between the members *inter se*. A non-member acquires no rights under the articles.[250]

An important distinction must therefore be made in relation to shares in a company between the beneficial owner of those shares and the person registered as a member of the company in respect of those shares. In company law a company need have regard only for its registered members, and not for any person not registered as a member. For each right which attaches to the shares issued by a company there exists a corresponding obligation on the company. Although the rights may be ceded to a third party, who may not be a registered member of the company in respect of those shares, the obligations of the company, including the obligation to pay dividends when declared, are owed

245 Hahlo & Kahn, *Hahlo's South African Company Law through the Cases* J.T. Pretorius (gen. ed.), P.A. Delport, M. Havenga, M. Vermaas (5th ed. 1991), at 272; *United South African Association Ltd* v *Cohn* 1904 TS 733 at 738–9.

246 B.V.Cowen and L. Gering, *The Law of Negotiable Instruments* (5th ed, Juta 1985) *v.1*: *General Principles*. 285; *Oakland Nominees* v *Gelria* 1976 (1) SA 441 (A) at 452 H; *Randfontein Estates Gold Mining Co Ltd* v *Custodian of Enemy Property* 1923 AD 576 at 582.

247 *Borland's Trustee* v *Steel Brothers & Co Ltd* [1901] 1 Ch 279 at 288; *Liquidators, Union Share Agency* v *Hatton* 1927 AD 240 at 250–l.

248 *Standard Bank of SA Ltd* v *Ocean Commodities Inc* 1983 (1) SA 276 (A) at 288.

249 Section 65(2) read with section 103(2) of the Companies Act; Hahlo & Kahn, *op. cit.* at 113,

250 Hahlo & Kahn, *Ibid.*; *Hickman* v *Kent or Romney Marsh Sheep-Breeder's Association* [1915] 1 Ch 881 at 900.

only to its registered members. Therefore, when the company pays dividends to its registered members its obligation to pay dividends is discharged in full, notwithstanding the cession by the registered member of its rights to receive dividends to a third party. A registered member may have antecedently divested himself of beneficial ownership in the shares so that the rights attaching to the shares, as between cedent and cessionary, no longer vest in the cedent but are vested in the cessionary. If the statutory formalities for the transfer of the shares, such as the registration of the transfer in the register of members of the company have not been executed, the company need not take cognisance of the cession of the beneficial ownership of the rights attaching to the shares. A cessionary wishing to enforce his rights against the company and step into the public domain must first apply for the registration of the transfer of the shares by the company and rectification of its register of members.

A person may acquire beneficial ownership of shares from another by purchase. Transmissions of beneficial ownership of shares may also arise by operation of law on the death, bankruptcy or liquidation of a member (section 103(3) of the Companies Act). A beneficial shareholder has a *prima facie* right to claim registration of the transfer of his shares into his own name and to be registered as a member of the company.[251] To transfer title to shares registration of the name of the transferee as the new owner must be made in the books of the company pursuant to the signing of a share transfer form.[252] In regard to shares, the word "transfer", in its full and technical sense, is not a single act but consists of a series of steps, namely an agreement to transfer, the execution of a deed of transfer and, finally, the registration of the transfer.[253]

Most transfers take place in pursuance of a contract of purchase and sale. No formalities are required. By virtue of this contract the seller may be obliged to deliver the shares to the purchaser.[254] The formalities of the transfer (as distinguished from the agreement to transfer, which requires no formalities) are regulated by sections 133 ff of the Companies Act and the company's articles of association.[255]

Unless otherwise provided in its constitution, shares in a public company are freely transferable (section 91 of the Companies Act). The shares and debentures of a public company may be traded on a stock exchange, such as the JSE, only if the company has the status of a listed company within the meaning of section 16 of the Stock Exchange Control Act 1 of 1985.

A private company must restrict the right to transfer its shares in its articles (section 20(1)(a) of the Companies Act). This requirement would be met if the articles provide for pre-emption rights, namely, that any shareholder wishing to withdraw from the company is obliged to offer his shares to the remaining shareholders before he is allowed to sell them to an outsider (articles 21–24 of Schedule 1—Table B of the Companies Act).

[251] *Op. cit.* at 257.
[252] Cowen, *op. cit.* at 285; Hahlo & Kahn, *Ibid*; section 103 of the Companies Act.
[253] *Inland Property Development Corporation (Pty) Ltd* v *Cillier* 1973 (3) SA 245 (A) at 251.
[254] *Moosa* v *Lalloo* 1956 (2) SA 237 (D) at 238.
[255] Hahlo & Kahn, *Op. cit.* at 258.

It is clear, therefore, that property in shares passes under the ordinary principles of a cession, but that registration of the transfer of the shares undoubtedly has important effects on the rights of the owner of those shares in his relation with the company and in relation to all other persons other than the transferor.[256]

6.2 Warranties in Sales of Businesses as Going Concerns

The different categories of warranties relating to sales of businesses as going concerns is dealt with fully in section 13.

6.3 Warranties in Mergers

There are generally two methods of achieving a "merger" of companies: there can be a merger by absorption, or a merger through the formation of a new company. In either case the shareholders of the target company cause assets to be transferred to the acquiring company usually in exchange for shares in that company. The target company may or may not continue in existence.

Mergers and acquisitions may be effected by outright bid or by a scheme of arrangement approved by the courts and usually take the form of:

(a) a privately negotiated agreement with the controlling shareholders of the target company; or
(b) procuring the controlling shareholders of the target company to procure that the target company issue new shares to the offeror; or
(c) a general offer to the shareholders of the target company for all or a specified number of shares in the target company for a stated consideration; or
(d) arrangements whereby:
    (i) all the shares held by the shareholders of the target company are cancelled;
    (ii) shares in the offeror company are issued to those shareholders of the target company in compensation for the shares cancelled; and
    (iii) shares in the target company are issued to the acquiring company in lieu of those cancelled; or
(e) the acquisition of control by the purchase of shares through the stock exchange.

In principle the interests and concerns of the acquiring company with regard to the nature and scope of the warranties which may be sought in relation to the target company are similar to those sought in a purchase of the entire issued share capital of the target company. Usually, however, the acquiring company will either have conducted a thorough investigation into the affairs of the target company prior to any approval of the shareholders of the target company, or the business of the target company is known to the acquiring company, so that few warranties, if any, are required.

[256] *Farrar's Estate* v *Commissioner for Inland Revenue* 1926 TPD 501 at 508; *Jeffrey* v *Pollak and Freemantle* 1938 AD 1 at 22; *Standard Bank of SA Ltd* v *Ocean Commodities Inc* 1980 (2) SA 175 (T) at 180.

6.4 Warranties in Sale of the Entire Issued Share Capital

Ownership of the entire issued share capital of a company confers on the sole shareholder absolute control of the company, together with all the attendant risks in and to and control of the assets owned by the company, as well as the liabilities (contractual, delictual or criminal) and whether contingent or not, which may have been incurred by the company.

The form that warranties may take where the entire issued share capital of a company is purchased, is infinitely variable and no standard set of warranties can be entirely suitable for any specific case.[257] In selecting which warranties are appropriate for a particular transaction, it is helpful to have a comprehensive standard form available which can be suitably edited to deal with that transaction. It is not the purpose of this publication to provide such a set of warranties, the purpose is merely to discuss in general terms the nature and scope of warranties which are commonly in use.

For a systematic approach, it is essential, as well as good practice, for the warranties to be grouped into sections dealing with related subject matters. It should be noted that the warranties, or the comments in relation to them, may not be appropriate in all cases for sales of shares.

6.4.1 Capacity and authority of sellers and warrantors

A company has neither a soul to be damned nor a body to be kicked. It is a legal fiction and can be represented only by human agents. A lack of contractual capacity to act or to represent a company may arise in the case of minors, unrehabilitated insolvents, persons of unsound mind and companies which do not have appropriate provisions in their memoranda of association. Accordingly, it is necessary when a natural person represents a company, that that person has authority to represent the company in question. Where the seller or the purchaser of the shares is a company it should warrant that it has full power and authority to enter into and perform the agreement, and that the agreement, when executed, will constitute binding obligations on the seller and the purchaser, in accordance with the terms of the agreement.

As a precaution against the possibility of the seller or the purchaser—if they are companies—later denying that the director or person who signed on their behalf had the necessary authorisation to do so, the other party may insist upon annexing to the agreement a certified copy of an extract from the relevant board meeting minuting the resolution of the board of directors to the effect that the individual who signs on behalf of the company has authority to sign on behalf of the company.

6.4.2 Good standing of the company

The company which issued the shares forming the subject matter of the sale must in fact exist, and must be registered in accordance with the South African company laws. The purchaser of the shares may conduct a search at the Registrar of Companies' office to ascertain that the company which issued the shares is, in fact, registered.

[257] Sinclair, *Op. cit.* at 133.

The seller should, therefore, warrant that prior to and as at the date of delivery of the shares, the target company is a company duly registered in the Republic of South Africa in accordance with the provisions of the Companies Act, and that no steps will have been taken or contemplated in respect of the target company in terms of section 73 of the Companies Act. Section 73 of the Companies Act deals with the procedure whereby the Registrar of Companies may deregister a company if the Registrar has reasonable cause to believe that a company is not carrying on business or is not in operation.

6.4.3 Capital structure and the shares

Another potential danger which awaits the unwary purchaser is that after conclusion of the sale but prior to delivery of the shares sold, the company may issue shares to a third party. In the result, the purchaser may acquire less than the expected voting control in the company. The seller should warrant to the purchaser:

(a) the quantity of the authorised and issued share capital of the target company prior to and as at the date of delivery of the shares sold; and
(b) that during such period the issued share capital of the target company will be the total or part of the authorised share capital of the target company; and
(c) that the shares so issued are fully paid and rank *pari passu* in every respect; and
(d) that neither the target company nor its directors have issued or agreed to issue any further shares (including bonus or capitalisation shares) in the capital of the target company, nor have they passed or agreed to pass any resolution for the increase or reduction of its capital, or for the creation or issue of any debentures or securities, or for the alteration of its memorandum or articles of association, during the relevant period.

The shares of the company may be issued at a premium and the amount of such premium must be transferred to an account called the share premium account (section 76(1) of the Companies Act). The share premium account may be applied by the company in three ways: firstly, in paying up unissued shares of the company to be issued to members of the company as fully paid capitalisation shares; secondly, in writing off the preliminary expenses of the company and the expenses of, or the commission paid or discount allowed on, the creation or issue of any shares; or thirdly, subject to three provisos, in providing for the premium payable on redemption of any redeemable preference shares of the company. The first proviso is that, such premium shall not be so provided unless it is payable according to the terms of issue of the shares concerned and such terms have been embodied in the articles of the company as from a date prior to the date on which such shares were allotted and issued or on such later date as may be allowed by the court on application to it. The second proviso is that, in the case of ordinary shares which are converted into redeemable preference shares redeemable at a premium, only that portion of the amount standing to the credit of the share premium account which arose on the original issue of such shares may be applied in providing for the premium payable on redemption. The third proviso is that, the first and second provisos referred to above do not apply in respect of redeemable preference shares issued before 1 July 1992 (section 76 of the Companies Act, as amended by section 3 of the Companies Amendment Act, 1992).

The purchaser will, therefore, wish to ensure that the share premium account, if any, is protected and may require the seller to warrant that prior to delivery of the shares sold, the target company's share premium account, if any, will not have been reduced in any manner and the company will not have transferred any amount from its reserves (including its share premium account) or undistributed profits to its share capital or its share premium account.

6.4.4 Ownership of the shares and other encumbrances

The seller may be either the registered member of the company and the beneficial shareholder in respect of the shares sold, or it may be the beneficial shareholder but the shares are registered in the name of a nominee, or it may be the registered member and apparently be the beneficial shareholder but, in fact, may have antecedently divested itself of its rights (including its voting rights) attaching to the shares (see 6.1 above).

The purchaser of the shares would be unwise merely to accept the *prima facie* evidence of the share certificate as to legal title to the shares in question. It is advisable, therefore, that the purchaser ensure as best it can that the seller is able to transfer beneficial ownership in the shares free of any encumbrances. Details of registered shareholders are obtainable from the company's share register which any member of the public is entitled, by section 113 of the Companies Act, to inspect.

Accordingly, the seller should warrant to the purchaser that prior to and as at the date of delivery of the shares sold:

(a) the seller is and will be the sole registered member and beneficial owner of the shares sold;
(b) the seller is and will be reflected in the register of members of the target company as the sole owner of the shares sold;
(c) no person has or will have any right to obtain an order for the rectification of the register of members of the target company;
(d) no person has any right or option or right of first refusal (see 5.1.2 above) to acquire any shares in the target company, or to subscribe for or take up any of the unissued shares in the target company, nor are any of the shares sold subject to any lien or other preferential right;
(e) the seller is entitled to dispose of the shares sold and is or will be entitled and able to give unencumbered title to the shares and that on delivery the purchaser will be the beneficial owner of the shares sold to the exclusion of all others;
(f) none of the shares sold is the subject of a disposition without value, or a voidable or undue preference or a collusive dealing (within the respective meanings of those expressions in section 26, 29, 30 or 31 of the Insolvency Act 24 of 1936) within the period of two years prior to the effective date of the sale of shares sold; and
(g) the seller is not a party to any shareholder's or other voting agreement, and the seller is entitled to attend and vote in general meeting and exercise its vote freely and in its sole discretion.

6.4.5 The financial statements

It is not unusual for the purchaser to request audited financial statements of the target company as at the effective date of sale and to base its decision to purchase the shares on the information contained in the audited financial statements as at a certain date. These financial statements are hereinafter referred to as the "effective financial statements".

Clearly the accuracy of the information recorded in the effective financial statements is of utmost importance to the purchaser, and apart from the remedies available to a purchaser which bases its decision on the effective financial statements against the auditors who prepared the same (see 23.2 below), the purchaser may further protect itself if the seller will warrant that the effective financial statements (which may be attached to the agreement as an annexure):

(a) were prepared in conformity with generally accepted accounting principles and on a basis of accounting similar to that employed for all previous accounting periods for which financial statements are available;
(b) fairly present the assets, liabilities and profit of the target company;
(c) comply with all technical and legal requirements required by any law;
(d) fully disclose all the assets of the company;
(e) correctly reflect the book value of assets so that no amount included in the effective financial statements in respect of any asset, whether fixed or current, exceeds its purchase price or production cost, or in the case of current assets, its estimated net realisable value at the date of the effective financial statements;
(f) make appropriate provision for all redundant, obsolete and slow-moving stock in trade and that such stock in trade has been written off or written down where appropriate;
(g) correctly and properly make provision for the depreciation of the fixed assets of the target company in accordance with generally accepted accounting principles;
(h) fully disclose all the liabilities of the company, and make full provision or reserve for all liabilities and capital commitments of the target company, whether ascertained or contingent, including all taxation of whatsoever nature, and for all bad and doubtful debts, possible overvaluation of inventories and stocks and for leave pay;
(i) make provision or reserve, in accordance with the principles set out in the notes in the last audited accounts, for all taxation likely to be assessed on the target company, or for which it may be accountable, in respect of the period ended on the date of the effective financial statements;
(j) adequately and properly provide for any deferred taxation, and that where provision for deferred taxation is not made in the effective financial statements, full details of the amount of deferred taxation shall have been fully disclosed in a disclosure letter;
(k) adequately and properly provide for bad or doubtful debts, and that no part of the amounts included in the effective financial statements as owing by any debtors is overdue by more than, say, 12 weeks, or has been released on terms that any debtor pays less than the full book value of his debt, or has

been written off, or has proved to any extent to be irrecoverable, or is now regarded by the company as irrecoverable in whole or in part, and that none of the debts is subject to any counter-claim or set-off.

6.4.6 Books, records and registers

The articles of association of the company and certain provisions of the Companies Act require the company to keep proper accounting records and certain registers (of members, directors, share transfers, and assets). Upon completion of the sale, possession of these accounting records and registers will and must remain with the company, and it is essential to the purchaser, which may require the disposing shareholder to warrant, that all such accounts, books, ledgers, financial and other records and registers, of whatsoever kind and in whatever form, of the company:

(a) are in the possession of the company;
(b) have been fully, properly and accurately kept and completed;
(c) do not contain any material inaccuracies or discrepancies of any kind;
(d) give and reflect a true and fair view of the company's trading transactions, and its financial, contractual and trading position, and of its current and past members, directors and assets.

6.4.7 Auditing and tax returns

It is important when purchasing shares and assuming control of the target company that all its obligations relating to previous years of assessment for tax purposes arising prior to the effective date of the sale should have been discharged by the target company and accounted for by the seller. Accordingly, the seller should warrant that as at the date of delivery of the shares sold:

(a) no work remained to be performed, and no expense not reflected in the effective financial statements remained to be incurred in connection with the completion and auditing of the target company's financial statements in respect of any of its financial years ended prior to the effective date of sale; and
(b) all income tax returns in respect of any of its financial years ended prior to the effective date of sale have been properly submitted to the relevant authority and that any other return required by law to have been submitted by the target company to any competent authority prior to such date, has been so submitted.

6.4.8 Capital commitments

Apart from the capital commitments recorded in the effective financial statements, the target company may have covertly committed itself further and the purchaser would be wise to ascertain, if possible, whether or not the company has overreached itself by committing itself too heavily in future capital purchases.

The purchaser should, therefore, request the seller to warrant that:

(a) there are no commitments on capital account outstanding as at the date of the effective financial statements; and
(b) since the date of the effective financial statements and prior to delivery of the shares sold, the company has not made or agreed to make any material

capital expenditure, or incurred or agreed to incur any material capital commitments, nor has it disposed of, or realised, any material capital assets or any interest in such assets.

6.4.9 Dividends and distribution

Prior to delivery of the shares sold to the purchaser and registration of the transfer by the company, the seller could, without the knowledge or consent of the purchaser, procure the declaration and payment of a substantial dividend to the then registered members of the company. Clearly, such a distribution would be prejudicial to the purchaser, who should require the seller to warrant that since the date of the effective financial statements, no dividend or other distribution has been or is treated as having been declared, paid or made by the company. It is advisable that the purchaser extend the meaning of dividends to include any distribution which would have the effect of a deliberate reduction of shareholders' funds between the end of the last accounting period and the delivery and registration of transfer of the shares sold.[258]

Where there are different classes of shares the purchaser may also wish the seller to warrant that all dividends and distributions declared, paid or made by the company have been declared, paid or made in accordance with the articles of association of the company and the applicable provisions of the Companies Act. This warranty is intended to protect the purchaser of the shares sold in circumstances where a prior payment of a dividend or distribution to a particular class of shareholders has not been declared, paid or made in accordance with the relevant provisions of its articles of association and the Companies Act, and an aggrieved shareholder then proceeds to assert his claim against the company.

6.4.10 Bank and other borrowings

Knowledge of the company's financing arrangements and limits is important for the purchaser. One method of highlighting the importance of this information is to require the seller to warrant that full details of all limits on the company's bank overdraft facilities and of all other financing arrangements are accurately set out in a disclosure letter.[259]

The disposing shareholder should also be requested to warrant that the total amount borrowed by the company from each of its bankers does not exceed its respective current overdraft facilities, or any limitation on its borrowing powers contained in its articles of association, or in any debenture or other deed or document binding upon it.[260]

The purchaser should be wary of debt factoring by the company. Debt factoring is a method of financing which is off balance sheet and involves the sale of debts. Where factoring has taken place, it would be appropriate to ensure that the target company has not given any warranty to the purchaser of the debts sold, that the debts will be recoverable in full or to any specified extent. Accordingly, the seller should warrant that the company has no outstanding debts, and has not agreed to create or issue any loan capital; and that it has neither factored any of

[258] Sinclair, *Op. cit.* at 156.
[259] *Op. cit.* at 157.
[260] *Ibid.*

its debts, nor engaged in any financing of a type which would not require to be shown or reflected in the effective financial statements, nor has it borrowed any money which it has not repaid, save for borrowings not exceeding the amounts shown in the effective financial statements.[261]

It is also possible that the company may be in default in respect of a loan, thus creating an early or accelerated repayment obligation in respect of that loan. Accordingly, the seller should warrant that the company has not, since the date of the effective financial statements, repaid, or became liable to repay, any loan or indebtedness in advance of its stated maturity by reason of its default (or for any reason whatsoever), and that no notification has been received by the company since the date of the effective financial statements of such liability.[262]

The purchaser is entitled to ensure that the financial facilities apparently available to the company have not been withdrawn.

Accordingly, the disposing shareholder should warrant that the company has not received notice (whether formal or informal) from any lenders of money to the company, requiring repayment or intimating the enforcement by the lender of any security which it may hold over any assets of the company, and also that, so far as the seller is aware, there are no circumstances likely to give rise to such a notice.

6.4.11 Loans by and debts due to the company

The purchaser is entitled to ensure that the company has made no prohibited loans. Section 226 of the Companies Act deals with certain prohibited loans by the company to *inter alia* its directors and managers. Accordingly, the seller should be made to warrant that the company has not lent any money which has not been repaid to it other than debts which have arisen in the ordinary course of its business, and that the company has not made any loan contrary to the Companies Act.

6.4.12 Liabilities

A liability is outstanding so long as it remains in existence. The purchaser should require the seller to warrant that there are no liabilities (including contingent liabilities) which are outstanding on the part of the company, other than those liabilities disclosed in the effective financial statements or incurred in the ordinary and proper course of trading since the date of the effective financial statements.[263]

Furthermore, the purchaser should ensure that there has been no exercise, purported exercise or claim for any charge, lien or other encumbrance over any of the fixed or moveable assets of the company which remains outstanding and that there is no dispute directly or indirectly relating to any such assets.[264]

Where the company was the original lessee of premises but ceded its rights and assigned its obligations under the lease to a third party, without first seeking the

[261] *Op. cit.* at 158.
[262] *Ibid.*
[263] *Op. cit.* at 160.
[264] *Ibid.*

consent of the lessor, it will remain liable to the lessor by virtue of the privity of contract between them (see 21.5.5 and 21.5.6 below). Thus, the company will remain contingently liable to the lessor for the payments arising out of the lease, the contingency being the new tenant defaulting under the lease. Accordingly, the purchaser should request the seller to warrant that the company has not been the tenant of, or a guarantor in respect of any leased property other than the premises which it now occupies (Sinclair, 161).

Another possible undisclosed contingent liability, which only the seller may have knowledge of, may be that the company has signed a suretyship (see 2.1 above). Accordingly, the seller should warrant that the company is not bound by any suretyship for the obligations of any person, or by any other guarantee or indemnity.

6.4.13 Bank accounts

The examination of the company's bank statements and comparison with the information recorded in the effective financial statements are valuable for reconciliation purposes and for calculating any adjustment in the cash position of the company which could impact on the amount of the purchase price. Accordingly, the seller should warrant that since the date of each bank statement there have been no payments out of the account to which the statement relates, except for payments in the ordinary and proper course of business; and that the balances on current accounts are not substantially different from the balances shown on such bank statements.

6.4.14 Working capital

The purchaser may require the seller to warrant that, having regard to existing bank and other facilities, the company has sufficient working capital for the purposes of continuing to carry on its business, in its present form and at its present level of turnover, for the period of 12 months after the closing date and for the purposes of executing, carrying out and fulfilling, in accordance with their terms, all orders, projects and contractual obligations which are binding upon it and remain outstanding.

6.4.15 Litigation

The seller should warrant to the purchaser that the company is not party to any legal proceedings (whether civil or criminal) or arbitration proceedings, or labour disputes or statutory inquiries or investigations, other than normal debt collections, and the seller is not aware of any legal proceedings threatened or instituted against the company or of any facts which are likely to give rise to those proceedings.

Should any such proceedings, at any time, be threatened or instituted against the company arising out of circumstances preceding the closing date, then the purchaser should be entitled to give written notice to the seller of the fact that proceedings have been threatened or instituted. The seller should then be entitled to elect by written notice to the purchaser within such period as may be reasonable, not exceeding ten days, that the proceedings are to be opposed, subject to the following:

(a) if such notice is not given by the seller, the seller shall be deemed to have elected not to oppose the proceedings. If the seller elects to oppose the proceedings, it shall indemnify the purchaser against any judgment, order or award that may be granted against the company and any fine that may be imposed on the company and any costs that may be incurred by or awarded against the company. The seller shall, at the time of giving the notice of the election, furnish the purchaser with a guarantee in respect of the indemnity which is acceptable to the purchaser in its entire discretion. The purchaser shall procure that the company opposes the proceedings under the direction of the seller and the seller shall provide all necessary clerical, accounting or legal assistance for the conduct of the proceedings;

(b) if the seller does not elect to oppose the proceedings, or, if it does so elect, fails to furnish the guarantee referred to above, the seller shall forthwith, if the claim is capable of being discharged by the seller, place the purchaser in a position to do so, or if the claim is not capable of being discharged by the seller, indemnify the purchaser against any loss the purchaser may suffer.

6.4.16 Statutory requirements

Although there are no statutory warranties included as terms in a contract for the sale of shares there are a number of statutes which impose various obligations on a company. Therefore, the seller should warrant that:

(a) the company will have complied with all the provisions of the Companies Act, the laws relating to taxation and all other laws and by-laws which affect it and its property;

(b) all statutory requirements of the Receiver of Revenue, the Registrar of Companies and all other authorities, governmental whether central, provincial, municipal or otherwise, have been complied with and there will be no matters outstanding in connection with the rendering of returns and the payment of dues and levies;

(c) if after the date of delivery of the shares the company receives any income tax assessments relating to the period prior to the signature date, the purchaser shall forthwith furnish a copy to the seller, and the seller shall be entitled to elect that the assessments be objected to, in which event the provisions in 6.4.15 above dealing with the seller's right to elect to oppose litigation and arbitration proceedings shall apply, in particular all necessary clerical, accounting or legal assistance for the conduct of the proceedings shall be provided by the seller.

6.4.17 Taxation

For the purpose of the warranties set out in this clause, the word "tax" shall, unless the context indicates the contrary, mean any tax including, but not limited to, income tax, general sales tax, value added tax, non-resident shareholders tax, and any duty or levy (including any penalty or interest) imposed by any law administered by the Commissioner for Inland Revenue or his lawful representative or any other authority entitled to administer taxes in the Republic of South Africa.

The seller should warrant that as at the closing date:

(a) the company has paid all tax where the due date for payment of the tax arose on or before the closing date; in respect of any tax which is due for payment after the closing date, adequate provision or reserves for the payment of that tax will have been made in the effective financial statements. Consequently any new assessments raised by any relevant authority within the warranty period will be recoverable from the seller;
(b) the company is not a party to any tax objection or appeal nor are any such proceedings threatened against or likely to be instituted by or against the company nor is the seller aware of any circumstances which may give rise to the institution of any such proceedings;
(c) no queries have been addressed to the company or any of its representatives by any official administering any tax, nor have any objections with regard to any tax been lodged by the company which have not been fully disposed of;
(d) the company will not be liable to pay any penalty or interest in connection with any claim for tax;
(e) the company will not be subject to any liability as a result of the reopening of any tax assessment or assessments to be raised thereafter;
(f) all necessary information, notices and returns (all of which are true and accurate and none of which is disputed by the Commissioner for Inland Revenue, his lawful representative or any other appropriate authority) will have been properly and timeously submitted by the company and there is no reason to suppose that any such information or return will not in due course be accepted as true and accurate by the Commissioner for Inland Revenue, his lawful representative or any other appropriate authorities;
(g) the company has properly operated the PAYE system and the SITE system, has deducted tax as required from all payments made to or treated as made to employees or former employees of the company or any other payment from which tax is required to be deducted in terms of the fourth schedule of the Income Tax Act and has accounted to the Commissioner for Inland Revenue, his lawful representative or any other appropriate authority for all tax so deducted;
(h) the company has withheld all taxes which it is liable to withhold and has paid such taxes to the Commissioner for Inland Revenue, his lawful representative or any other appropriate authorities;
(i) no notice has been served on the company in terms of which the company has been appointed as a representative taxpayer;
(j) the company has timeously lodged a claim for any refund of tax to which the company may be entitled;
(k) neither the seller nor the company is a party to any agreement with the Commissioner of Inland Revenue bearing upon or relating to the manner or circumstances in which tax will or might be levied on the company nor has the Commissioner granted the company any allowance in terms ot section 24 or section 24(c) of the Income Tax Act;
(l) the company is registered as a value added tax vendor in terms of the Value Added Tax Act, 1991, and at the delivery of the shares, it will have fully and

completely complied with all of its obligations in terms of the Value Added Tax Act, and will have paid all value added tax that it is obliged to pay;

(m) the company has lawfully and fully withheld and paid to the Commissioner for Inland Revenue all non-resident shareholders tax that it is obliged by law to do;

(n) the effective financial statements make provision, in accordance with the principles set out in the notes to the effective financial statements, for all tax (including deferred tax) for which the company has become or will become liable to pay;

(o) the company has not acquired from any other companies under any scheme of arrangement or reconstruction of any companies or its affairs (including any scheme for the amalgamation of two or more companies and any other scheme) which is sanctioned by any order of court on or after 1 April 1981, any asset which is, in terms of section 22A of the Income Tax Act, deemed to be trading stock of the companies;

(p) the company is not a party to any agreement with the Commissioner for Inland Revenue of the nature referred to in section 24A of the Income Tax Act;

(q) no rents, interest, annual payments or other simiiar expenditure incurred or to be incurred by the company will be disallowed as a deduction wholly or in part from the income of the company;

(r) the company is not a party to any transaction, operation or scheme of the nature referred to in section 103(1) of the Income Tax Act or section 73 of the Value Added Tax Act;

(s) there are no circumstances affecting the company under which the provisions of section 7(7) of the Income Tax Act can operate;

(t) the company has not made or received any donation on which donations tax can be levied and nor has the company made any donation at the instance of a third party;

(u) the company has paid all stamp duty for which the company is or may be liable and there is no liability for any penalty in respect of such duty nor are there any circumstances or transactions to which the company is or has been a party which may result in the company becoming liable for any such duty or penalty.

6.4.18 List of disclosures

The list of disclosures which may be annexed to the agreement of sale reflects all material off balance sheet liabilities of the company including commitments and obligations under leases of moveables and foreign exchange liabilities and losses as at the date of signature of the agreement of sale.

6.4.19 Premises, laws, regulations, consents, licences and permits

Another unwanted potential interference with the conduct of the business by the company after delivery of the shares sold may arise if, prior to delivery of the shares, the company were to lose its licences or its right to occupy its business premises, or failed to comply with any relevant by-laws. Accordingly, the seller should warrant that:

(a) the premises in which the company carries on business comply with all government, provincial and local authority requirements, with the conditions of title of land on which such premises are situated and with the conditions of any lease applicable to those premises, and that it knows of no facts or circumstances, the effect of which may in future give rise to any government, provincial or local authority objecting to the manner in which the company carries on its business;
(b) the company will have complied with all laws and regulations affecting its affairs and business, except only to the extent that any infringement of those laws and regulations can readily be rectified;
(c) the company is in possession of all consents, permits and licences necessary for the conduct of its business and its affairs, and the seller is not aware of any facts which may give rise to the cancellation of, or failure to renew, any such licences, permits or consents or only being renewed subject to the imposition of onerous conditions not presently applicable thereto.

6.4.20 Labour laws, regulations, determinations, agreements and disputes

Labour relations between employers and employees in South Africa are governed by a number of statutes, including the Labour Relations Act, 1956, as amended. Certain statutory remedies are available to an employer and an employee if either commits an unfair labour practice. An "unfair labour practice" means any act or omission, other than a strike or lock-out, which has or may have the effect that, firstly, any employee of class or employees is or may be unfairly affected or that his or their employment opportunities or work security is or may be prejudiced or jeopardised thereby; or secondly, the business of any employer or class of employers is or may be unfairly affected or disrupted thereby; or thirdly, labour unrest is or may be created or promoted thereby, or finally, the labour relationship between employer and employee is or may be detrimentally affected thereby (section 1 definition of "unfair labour practice", Labour Relations Act, 1956).

In order to avoid a labour dispute or committing an unfair labour practice the purchaser of the entire issued share capital of a company needs to ensure that the company has not fallen and does not fall within the ambit of the unfair labour practice legislation.

The purchaser should, therefore, request the seller to warrant that the company:

(a) has complied with all determinations and industrial conciliation agreements made in terms of the Labour Relations Act, 1956, which apply to it, its business and its employees;
(b) has complied with any grievance procedures agreed to by it and its employees with regard to grievances of and relations with its employees;
(c) has complied with the trade union recognition agreement (if any) to which it is a party;
(d) is not party to any labour disputes and is not obliged by law, agreement, judgment or order of court, to reinstate employees that have been dismissed or will be dismissed;

(e) is not a party to any unfair labour practice suit, nor has it committed any unfair labour practice.

6.4.21 Employment, leave, remuneration and pension

Clearly, the employees of the company and their employment terms and conditions should not be altered by the seller prior to delivery of the shares sold. Therefore, it is essential that the seller should warrant that:

(a) the company will not be party to any contract with any of its directors or employees requiring more than one month's notice of termination, or entitling any of them to compensation on termination of employment, or to participation in or entitlement to a commission on profit;
(b) no employee or official of the company will be entitled to any exceptional leave privileges, accumulated leave, pension or the like;
(c) the company will not in any material respect have improved the terms of employment of or remuneration payable to any of its employees;
(d) there was no unfunded deficit in respect of any future liability of any pension fund of which any of the company's employees were members; provided that if there is any such deficit in respect of services of any such employees for periods up to the signature date, as certified by any actuary for the time being of the pension fund, whether the company has any liability in respect thereof or not, then without prejudice to the purchaser's right as a result of the breach of this warranty the purchaser will be entitled to claim payment from the seller of an amount equal to the amount of such unfunded deficit;
(e) the company's pension fund will be fully funded and a certificate to this effect by the pension fund's actuary will have been delivered to the purchaser by the signature date.

6.4.22 Restraint of trade

The purchaser will not want to assume control of the company and its business only to find that the company is a party to a restraint of trade agreement. Accordingly the seller should warrant that the company is not and will not be bound by any restraint of trade agreement.

6.4.23 Insurance

It is important that the assets of the company are adequately insured by the company prior to the delivery of the shares, and for at least enough time thereafter to enable the purchaser to obtain insurance cover. Accordingly the seller should warrant that:

(a) the company carries insurance cover against loss arising from *inter alia* accident, fire, earthquake, flood, burglary, theft, employer's liability, workmen's compensation, public liability, storm damage, civil commotion, riot or political risk and loss of profits, and such insurance will continue to be effective for a period of 14 days after date of delivery;
(b) all premiums due in respect of such insurance will have been paid and the company will have complied with all of the conditions to which the liability of the insurers under the policies of insurance will be subject;

(c) it is not aware of any facts, matters or circumstances which may give rise to the cancellation of the policies of insurance or the repudiation of any claims thereunder or to such policies not being renewed in the future or only being renewed subject to the imposition of onerous conditions not presently applicable.

6.4.24 Resolutions

In order to ensure that the seller does not disrupt the ordinary business activities of the company, the purchaser should require the seller to warrant that no resolutions will have been passed by the members or directors of the company between the date of signing of the agreement (or the date of the effective financial statements) and the date of delivery of the shares, save for such resolutions as may be necessary to give effect to the agreement and such resolutions as shall have been passed in the ordinary course of business or as shall be approved by the purchaser in writing which approval may not be unreasonably withheld.

6.5 Warranties in Sale of Shares between the Parties

A shareholder of a company who purchases additional shares in that company from a co-shareholder would clearly require fewer (if any) warranties from the seller. Such a shareholder would probably have sufficient knowledge of the affairs of the company not to require warranties from the seller. The main concerns of the purchaser in these circumstances would be that no more shares in the company are issued (see 6.4.3 above), that the shares sold are free of any liens, pledge or other encumbrance and that the seller is able to transfer beneficial ownership in such shares to the purchaser (see 6.4.4 above).

6.6 Warranties in Public Takeover Bids

Stock exchanges provide organised markets for trading in securities of companies. The requirements of the JSE for listed companies are designed to achieve two objectives, namely, public disclosure of the fullest possible information about a company's activities, and fair and equal treatment for all shareholders (see 1.1.12.1 above).

The rules which affect a takeover bid for a public listed company are contained in The Securities Regulation Code on Take-Overs and Mergers (see 1.1.12.1 above). It is unlikely that the seller/s will furnish any warranties where a purchaser makes a takeover bid for control of a public listed company, arguably because sufficient information about the affairs of the company is already disclosed to the public in its financial reports and statements, and because usually the purchaser will have conducted a thorough analysis of the target company's affairs prior to making the takeover bid. If any warranties are given, and subject to negotiation between the parties, such warranties may not differ substantially from the warranties given by the seller and discussed in 6.4.

6.7 Warranties in Sales of Equity in the Stock Exchange

The transferor of listed securities, and the transferee, never meet and may be unaware of each other's identity. In these circumstances it is unlikely that the transferor or the transferee will furnish any warranties in relation to the purchase and sale of the listed securities.

Purchases and sales of listed securities by stockbrokers are governed by sections 22–27 of the Stock Exchanges Control Act, and the stock exchange rules relating to "transactions". In terms of section 135(1) of the Companies Act listed securities may be transferred either by "a securities transfer form", or a "securities transfer form" in conjunction with a "broker's transfer form". The securities transfer form is signed by the transferor alone; the name of the transferee is left blank and it is indicated that the securities will be transferred to the transferee whose name is entered in part B of the form. The securities transfer form together with the broker's transfer form is used when transfer is made to several transferees whilst only one securities transfer form and a single certificate is available. It is signed by the selling broker who certifies the signature of the transferor on the "securities transfer form" whereafter both forms are stamped by the broker for lodgement and registration. In doing so the broker warrants that the signature and other documents of the transferor are genuine.[265]

When the transferee lodges the "scrip" and the transfer form with the company, the company substitutes his name for that of the transferor in the share register and sends him a share certificate, made out in his name (section 140 of the Companies Act). By registration, the transferee becomes a member of the company.[266]

Section 136 of the Companies Act deals with certification by a company that a security has been lodged with it. It is taken as a representation by the company to any person acting on the faith of the certification that the necessary documents relating to the securities mentioned in the instrument of transfer have been lodged with it and that it appears from these documents that the title to the securities is held by the transferor named in the instrument, but not as a representation that he has in fact good title.[267] Persons lodging instruments of transfer in respect of a security are deemed to warrant that the instruments are genuine and have to indemnify the company if they are not (section 138 of the Companies Act).

6.8 Warranties in Sales of Parts of Limited Liability Companies

A company may conduct a number of businesses as separate going concerns under one corporate umbrella. When a company sells a going concern the assets comprising the "business" to be sold must be clearly identified and separated from the other activities or "businesses" of the company. Often a company will have separated each activity for convenience and administrative purposes into separate profit centres, divisions or "parts" and may even have conducted each separate activity in different subsidiary companies. Whatever the factual situation may be in each case the warranties furnished by the seller in relation to the "division" or "part" of its activities comprising the separate business as a going

[265] Hahlo and Kahn, *Op. cit.* at 258.

[266] *Op. cit.* at 259.

[267] Section 136(2) of the Companies Act; *Oakland Nominees (Pty) Ltd* v *Gelria Mining & Investment Co (Pty) Ltd* 1876 (1) SA 441 (A); Hahlo and Kahn, *Ibid.*

concern, will not differ substantially from the type of warranties discussed in Section 13 below.

6.9 Warranties in Transfers of Interest in Partnerships

As a general principle any change of membership of the partners comprising a partnership for whatever reason destroys the identity of the partnership. But the outgoing partner/s may transfer all the rights and liabilities of the partnership concern to the incoming partner/s, and such transfer will be binding as between themselves. The principles governing delegation of liabilities (see 21.5.4 below) and cession of rights (see 21.5.5 and 21.5.6 below) will apply.

7. Statutory Warranty of Clear Title

7.1 Ambit of the Warranty

There is no statutory warranty of clear title applicable in the Republic of South Africa but there is in the absence of any agreement between the parties an obligation implied by the common law and imposed on the seller to transfer ownership if he has it or can obtain it, and, if he cannot, to warrant against eviction (see 2.3.4.3 above).

8. Statutory Warranty of Absence of Defects

8.1 The Ambit of the Warranty

There is no statutory warranty of absence of defects applicable in the Republic of South Africa, but the common law aedilitian remedies, namely the action for the reduction of the purchase price (the *actio quanti minoris*) and the action for cancellation of the contract and restitution (the *actio redhibitoria*) are available to the purchaser by operation of law if the thing sold is found to be defective at the time of the sale (see 2.3.4.7 above).

9. Statutory Warranty of Merchantable Quality

9.1 The Ambit of the Warranty

There is no statutory warranty of merchantable quality applicable in the Republic of South Africa, but there is in certain instances in the absence of agreement between the parties an implied warranty of merchantable quality (see 2.3.4.5 above).

10. The Subjective Element

10.1 The Subjective Element and the Warranties

In South African law, if two or more persons of sound mind and capable of contracting, enter into a lawful agreement, a valid and enforceable contract arises between them. The promise made by the one party must have been made with the intention that it should be accepted by the other. Thus, the only element that our law requires for a valid contract to come into existence is consensus.[268]

The agreement between the parties must be a true agreement in the sense of a "meeting of the minds" or "coincidence of the wills" of the contracting parties, or *consensus ad idem*.[269] If, through a mistake or misunderstanding in the mind of one or both parties, there is no true subjective agreement between the parties, there will be no contract. However, the English law doctrine of quasi-mutual assent has been imported and accepted into our law of contract.[270] Thus, where one party relies on a mistake to escape a contract but whatever his real intention may have been, he so conducts himself that a reasonable man would believe that he was assenting to the terms proposed by the other party, and that other party upon that belief enters into the contract with him, the first party thus conducting himself would be equally bound as if he had intended to agree to the other party's terms.[271] In these circumstances, any unexpressed reservations hidden in the mind of the first party are irrelevant and he cannot be heard to say that he meant his promise to be subject to a condition which he omitted to mention, and of which the other party was unaware.[272]

10.2 Mistake

The word "mistake" is used in connection with contracts to describe a number of different factual situations. It is important to bear in mind that where the parties find themselves in "disagreement" what is meant is that there is no contract because although the parties may think that they have reached a successful conclusion to their negotiations, there is neither actual nor apparent agreement.[273] Where one party is mistaken, and the mistake is a reasonable mistake (*iustus error*) or an operative mistake, then certain legal consequences will flow from such mistake. The law does not make a distinction between mistake and ignorance in this regard, so a person who is ignorant of a particular fact may be said to be mistaken about it.

A mistake may relate to the subject matter of the contract (*error in corpore*), or to the identity of the other contracting party (*error in persona*), or to the motive of the other contracting party, or to the materials or substance of which the asset sold is made (*error in substantia*). There are, generally, three classes of mistake which have legal consequences: namely unilateral, mutual and common mistakes.

10.2.1 Unilateral mistake

There is a unilateral mistake when one party to the contract is mistaken but the other is not. If the mistake relates to something other than the other party's state of mind the existence of the mistake may or may not be known to the other party,

268 *Conradie* v *Rossouw* 1919 AD 279 at 288, 320 and 324; Christie, *Op. cit.* at 10.
269 *Op. cit.* at 11.
270 *Pieters & Co* v *Salomon* 1911 AD 121 at 130.
271 *Smith* v *Hughes* (1871) LR 6 QB 597 at 607.
272 *Pieters & Co* v *Salomon* 1911 AD 121 at 137; *Benjamin* v *Gurewitz* 1973 (1) SA 418 (A) at 425.
273 Kerr, *Contract, Op. cit.* at 167.

but if it relates to his state of mind it cannot be described as unilateral unless it is known or at least ought to be known to him.[274]

The relationship between unilateral mistake and the doctrine of quasi-mutual assent is the following: where the party who is trying to resile from the contract has been to blame in the sense that by his conduct he has led the other party, as a reasonable man, to believe that he was binding himself to a contractual term, he will be bound by the agreement.[275] However, if his mistake is due to a misrepresentation, innocent or fraudulent, by the other party, then it is the other party who is to blame and the first party is not bound.[276] But where the other party has not made any misrepresentation and has not appreciated at the time of acceptance that his offer was being accepted under a misapprehension the scope of a defence of unilateral mistake is very narrow, if it exists at all. At least the mistake would have to be reasonable (*iustus*) and it would have to be pleaded.[277]

This summary of the law is borne out by the cases which show the possibility of *iustus error* to be very limited, unless the other party knew or ought to have known of or caused the mistake. In other words, as explained by Coetzee J in *Horty Investments (Pty) Ltd* v *Interior Acoustics (Pty) Ltd*,[278] the fault principle applies to both parties.[279]

If a purchaser institutes action for the delivery of the thing he purported to purchase, the ordinary rules on the onus of proof require him to prove a contract entitling him to make such a claim for specific performance. All that the seller need do at the outset is to deny that there is such a contract if that is his case. If the purchaser cannot prove either actual or apparent agreement to buy and sell he must lose his action. If, on the other hand, the purchaser puts in evidence a written document purporting to be a signed contract of sale then the burden of adducing evidence in rebuttal is on the seller.[280] What the seller needs to show in rebuttal is his reasonable unilateral mistake, for example, that his view of the circumstances that he was selling something else and not what the purchaser is claiming was reasonable.[281]

The most common way in which this can be achieved occurs when he can show that he has been misled by the other party (Kerr, "Contract", 170), but this is not the only way to discharge the onus of adducing evidence in rebuttal.

10.2.1.1 WHERE NO KNOWLEDGE OR FAULT IS IMPUTABLE TO THE OTHER PARTY

Where the seller (the mistaken party) cannot prove that the purchaser knew of his unilateral mistake, or that as a reasonable man he ought to have known of

[274] Christie, *Op. cit.* at 382.

[275] *Pieters & Co* v *Salomon* 1911 AD 121 at 130 and 137.

[276] *George* v *Fairmead (Pty) Ltd* 1958 (2) SA 465 (A) at 471.

[277] *National and Overseas Distributors Corp (Pty) Ltd* v *Potato Board* 1958(2) SA 473(A) at 479.

[278] 1984 (3) SA 537(W) at 540 C–D,

[279] *Op. cit.* at 383.

[280] *George* v *Fairmead (Pty) Ltd* 1958 (2) SA 465 (A) at 470(A); *Allen* v *Sixteen Stirling Investments (Pty) Ltd* 1974 (4) SA (D); *Soobramoney and another* v *R Acutt & Sons (Pty) Ltd* 1965 (2) SA 899 (D) at 905–906.

[281] *Papadopoulous* v *Trans-State Properties and Investments Ltd* 1979 (1) SA 682 (W) at 689 D–E.

it, or that he caused it, the onus of showing that the unilateral mistake was a reasonable one justifying release from the contractual bond will not be easy to discharge.[282]

The seller will first have to show that his mistake relates to a material matter.[283] The law identifies different categories of mistake, such as a mistake as to the motive or identity of the other party, or as to the subject matter of the contract, or as to the meaning of the terms of a written contract. Thus, an error in motive or about the identity of the other party to the contract may be immaterial.[284]

However material the mistake, the mistaken party will nevertheless not be able to escape from the contract if his mistake was due to his own fault. Thus, the mistaken party will be bound by the terms of the contract if, due to his own fault, he failed to carry out reasonably necessary investigations before committing himself to the contract,[285] or he did not bother to read the contract before signing,[286] or he carelessly misread one of its terms,[287] or he did not bother to have the contract explained to him in a language understood by him,[288] or where he misinterprets a clear and unambiguous term.[289] In all of these circumstances the mistake was due to the mistaken party's own fault, namely his carelessness or inattention, and he could not prove that his mistake was reasonable.[290]

10.2.1.2 WHEN KNOWLEDGE OR FAULT IS IMPUTABLE TO THE OTHER PARTY

If the mistaken party has so conducted himself as to give the other party reasonably to believe that he was contracting with him on certain terms, he is bound, unless there is some special reason for classifying his mistake, as an *iustus error*. One such reason exists when the other party either knew of the mistake or, if he did not, he ought reasonably to have known it. Only a person in the position of a reasonable man can rely on the doctrine of quasi-mutual assent, and a person who has not acquired the knowledge of a reasonable man would have acquired is not in that position.[291]

Actual knowledge disables the party having knowledge of the mistake from relying on the doctrine of quasi-mutual assent, so the mistaken party will be able to rescind the contract if his mistake was material,[292] and provided the mistaken party can show that he would not have entered into the contract if he had known the truth.[293]

282 Christie, *Op. cit.* at 383.
283 *National and Grindlays Bank Ltd* v *Yelverton* 1972 CA SA 114 CR) at 117 D; *Op. cit.* at 384.
284 *Op. cit.* at 384–385.
285 *Acacia Mines Ltd* v *Boshoff* 1957 (1) SA 93 (T) at 101–2; *Diedericks* v *Minister of Lands* 1964 (1) SA 49 (N) at 57; *Springvale Ltd* v *Edwards* 1969 (1) SA 464 (RA) at 468 and 470(H),
286 *Ex-Parte Rosenstein* 1952 (2) SA 324 (T).
287 *Patel* v *Le Clus (Pty) Ltd* 1946 TPD 30.
288 *Mathole* v *Mothle* 1951 (1) SA 256 (T).
289 *Van Pletzen* v *Henning* 1913 AD 82 at 89.
290 Christie, *Op. cit.* at 385.
291 *Op. cit.* at 387.
292 *George* v *Fairmead (Pty) Ltd* 1958 (2) SA 465 (A); *National & Overseas Distributors Corporation (Pty) Ltd* 1958 (2) SA 473 (A); *Op. cit.* at 388.
293 *Khan* v *Naidoo* 1989 (3) SA 724 (N).

Once a unilateral mistake has been established and the question of the fault of either party has been determined, the next question is whether the unilateral mistake is of such a nature as to render the contract voidable at the instance of the mistaken party, or whether there was no contract at all, in other words, the "contract" was void *ab initio*. There is in this regard an important distinction to be made between a "material" and "fundamental" mistake. A mistake may sometimes be fundamental in the sense that because of its existence agreement is so completely lacking that it is impossible to say there is any contract at all and therefore the "contract" is void *ab initio*, or the mistake may be material in the sense that agreement is not so completely lacking, but is sufficiently lacking to make the agreement voidable at the instance of either party.[294]

10.2.2 Mutual mistake

There is a mutual mistake when each party is mistaken about the other's state of mind, for they are at cross purposes. If a purported acceptance does not correspond with the offer there is no contract because the parties are not *ad idem* ("of one mind"). When this non-correspondence of offer and acceptance is not apparent at the time the contract is purported to be entered into, but only becomes apparent later, we are in the field of mutual mistake.[295]

Thus, if the seller and the purchaser are at cross purposes and the seller's understanding of what has been agreed is reasonable but the purchaser's understanding is unreasonable, then the seller can rely on the doctrine of quasi-mutual assent but the purchaser cannot, and an enforceable contract will exist in accordance with the seller's understanding of the terms of the contract.

Where, however, each party's understanding of what was purportedly agreed is reasonable, then both parties could rely on the doctrine of quasi-mutual assent. Obviously both reasonable versions of the contract cannot be enforced so that the only alternative is to enforce neither, by declaring the contract void from its commencement, in other words, there was no contract because the parties were not *ad idem* (Christie, 394).

Where the terms of a contract are clear and unambiguous a party who misinterprets that term cannot rely on his unilateral mistake in order to absolve himself of liability under the contract. However, if the term is incurably ambiguous then the misinterpretation and the mistake becomes relevant, not as a mistake about the true meaning of the term, for there is none, but as a mistake about the agreed meaning of the term or a mistake about the other party's state of mind in relation to the meaning of the term. The parties in fact, are at cross purposes so that the contract cannot be enforced against either. It is a case of mutual mistake (Christie, 386). The same result can be reached by saying that the contract or the particular term if it is non-essential, is void for vagueness, each party being equally justified in his interpretation.

Where a mutual mistake comes to light there is no contract because if the offer and acceptance do not correspond there is no agreement. Furthermore, the distinction between material and fundamental mistake, so important in unilateral

[294] *Op. cit.* at 391.
[295] *Op. cit.* at 393.

mistake in order to decide whether the contract is voidable at the option of the mistaken party or void *ab initio*, does not apply. Instead the distinction must be between true non-correspondence of offer and acceptance which may be ignored on the maxim *de minimus non curat lex.*[296]

10.2.3 Common mistake

There is a common mistake when both parties are of one mind and share the same mistake about anything other than the state of each other's mind.[297]

Common mistake differs from mutual mistake in a very fundamental way. Parties who are mutually mistaken are by definition not *ad idem* so that provided the mistake of each is reasonable (*iustus*) the "contract" is void *ab initio*, and if the mistake of one is reasonable but the other not then the doctrine of quasi-mutual assent applies.[298] Parties who are commonly mistaken are by definition *ad idem*, so no question of quasi-mutual assent can arise and the effect of the mistake on the contract must necessarily be decided on different principles.

The reasonableness of the common mistake is irrelevant.[299] This principle would be appropriate and applicable in circumstances where both parties were unreasonable in making the same mistake, or where one party has reasonably made a mistake and the other party has unreasonably made the same mistake. The matter is different if the common mistake is caused by one of the parties only.

The party who was not responsible for the common mistake ought to be able to seek relief from the obligations of the contract if the common mistake works against him, but the party who was responsible for the mistake ought not to be able to obtain relief from his obligations under the contract if the common mistake works against him, as he was the author of his own loss.[300]

Common mistake will render the contract void *ab initio* only if it leads the parties to make a "contract" which is impossible of performance, such as a sale of a thing which is extinct.

The effect of a joint mistake not giving rise to initial impossibility on the agreement founded upon such mistake, is that the agreement can be set aside, formally if necessary, or treated as set aside and so invalid without any process or proceedings to do so.[301]

10.3 Common Ground and Distinction between Breach of Warranty and Mistake

In South African law, unlike English law, a breach of warranty, as in the case of other breaches, may or may not be a major breach and if it is a major breach the aggrieved party may cancel the contract.[302] Thus, a breach of warranty does not

[296] *Op. cit.* at 397.
[297] *Op. cit.* at 313.
[298] *Op. cit.* at 397.
[299] *Tshoba Colliery (Natal) Ltd* v *Tshoba Coal Syndicate Ltd* 1926 NPD 526; *Op. cit.* at 398.
[300] *Fienberg* v *Jardine* 1915 NPD 439 at 445; Christie, *Ibid.*
[301] *Huddersfield Banking Co Ltd* v *Henry Lister & Son Ltd* [1895] 2 Ch 273; *Dickinson Motors (Pty) Ltd* v *Oberholzer* 1952 (1) SA 443 (A) at 450; Christie, *Ibid.*; see 21.6 below.
[302] Kerr, *Contract, Op. cit.* at 351; *Small* v *Smith* 1954 (3) SA 434 (SWA).

in itself bring the contract to an end.[303] It gives the aggrieved party a choice of remedies, the options varying with the nature of the breach. In the case of a major breach the aggrieved party may terminate the contract by cancelling it. In the case of a minor breach he may not cancel, his choice, normally, being between a claim for specific performance and damages. The onus of proving that a breach is a major one is on the party asserting it.

On the other hand, where a party proves mistake, he is relying on the fact that there was no agreement and therefore no contract between the parties. For example, if there was a mutual mistake in the sense that one of the terms of the contract is incurably ambiguous, then there was no agreement *ab initio* as there was a mistake about the agreed meaning of the term in question.

10.4 Fraud

Fraud is a delict which may relate to the making of a contract or to a misrepresentation inducing a contract. A claim for damages for fraudulent misrepresentation is therefore a claim in delict, not contract (see 1.3.2.3 above). The claim will lie against a third party who fraudulently induced the contract but was not a party to it. The innocent party may bring a delictual claim for damages for fraud and either claim for rescission of the contract or for specific performance of the contract.[304] Therefore, a claim for damages for fraud and a claim for damages for breach of contract may be combined in the same action.[305]

The innocent party's reason for not claiming rescission may be that the fraudulent misrepresentation did not induce him to enter into the contract so he is not entitled to rescind,[306] or that he is unable to give restitution, or that he has committed himself to other contracts on the strength of the contract,[307] or simply that he does not wish to rescind it.[308]

Fraud is proved when it is shown that a false representation has been made knowingly or without belief in its truth or recklessly, careless whether it be true or false.[309]

If a fraudulent misrepresentation induces disagreement or a mistake there is no contract.[310] An innocent party may still claim damages for fraud, irrespective of whether there was a contract or not, if he can prove the elements of the delict.

10.5 Contract Entered into a State of Need or Danger

In South African law a contract entered into in a state of duress or undue influence is either voidable or void *ab initio*, depending on the facts of the case.

303 *Stewart Wrightson (Pty) Ltd* v *Thorpe* 1977 (2) SA 943 (A) at 952A; Kerr, *Op. cit.* at 445.
304 *Claassens* v *Pretorius* 1950 (1) SA 37 (O) at 42.
305 *Pockets Holdings (Pvt) Ltd* v *Lobel's Holdings (Pvt) Ltd* 1966 (4) SA 238 (R).
306 *Ranger* v *Wykerd* 1977 (2) SA 976 (A) at 990 H.
307 *Trotman* v *Edwick* 1951 (1) SA 443 (A) at 448 H.
308 Christie, *Op. cit.* at 357.
309 *Derry* v *Peek* (14 AC 337) at 374, approved in *R* v *Myers* 1948 (1) SA 375 (A) at 382–5, and *Vereeniging Consolidated Mills Ltd* v *Newman* 1958 (2) SA 20 (C) at 23–4.
310 *Preller and others* v *Jordaan* 1956 (1) SA 483 (A) at 496 F; *Cornelissen NO* v *Universal Caravan Sales (Pty) Ltd* 1971 (3) SA 158 (A) at 170 F; *Janowski* v *Fourie* 1978 (3) SA 16 (o); *Saambou-Nasionale Bouvereniging* v *Friedman* 1979 (3) SA 978 (A) at 1000B.

10.5.1 Duress

A person may act under "duress" if his actions are caused by force, threats or fear. The effect of absolute force (*vis absoluta*) on a "contract" is that the "contract" is void *ab initio*, and what may appear to be a contract is not a contract at all. Such cases are rare but one example would be where a stronger person physically overcomes a weaker, puts a pen in his hand and physically forces his hand to write his "signature" on a written contract.[311]

The other way in which force may affect the making of a contract is by fear of its repetition or continuance or by a threat inducing fear of its initiation. What really operates on the mind of the victim is fear, and the legal significance of this fear as affecting his consent may be the same whether he has been beaten, is being beaten or is about to be beaten. A fear of equal legal significance may be aroused in the mind by causes quite unconnected with physical force. Because a person who is induced by legally significant fear can probably be said to have consented, his contract is voidable at his option, not void *ab initio* like the contract of the person whose hand is physically forced (Christie, 367).

The requirements for setting a contract aside and claiming restitution on the ground of duress are, generally, that there must be actual violence or reasonable fear, which fear must be caused by the threat of some considerable evil to the party or his family (or to his property or people other than his family). The threat must be of an imminent or inevitable evil, and must be contrary to public policy (*contra bonos mores*) and the moral pressure used must have caused damage.[312]

10.5.2 Undue influence

The term "undue influence" found its way into our law from English law.[313] However, the use of the English term does not mean that we have taken over the English rules, though they have often proved helpful in explaining the concepts. The grounds of restitution in the Roman–Dutch law are wide enough to cover the case where one person obtains an influence over another which weakens the latter's resistance and makes his will pliable, and where such a person then brings his influence to bear in an unprincipled manner in order to prevail upon the other to agree to a prejudicial transaction which he would not normally have entered into of his own free will.[314]

In determining whether a transaction, induced by fraud or undue influence, is void or merely voidable, the test is whether the person seeking to have it set aside entered into the transaction wilfully and knowingly, with the intention to bring about the legal consequences which are entailed, or not. If so, then it is a valid transaction until it is declared invalid, although it may be voidable at his instance on the ground that he was induced to enter into it in an unlawful manner. If, however, it was not his intention to enter into the transaction, then the

[311] Christie, *Op. cit.* at 367.

[312] J.W. Wessels, The Law of Contract in *South Africa* (2nd ed., v. 1, Durban, Butterworths 1951), para. 1167; Christie, *Op. cit.* at 368–369.

[313] *Mauerberger* v *Mauerberger* 1948 (4) SA 902(C); *Op. cit.* at 377.

[314] *Preller and Others* v *Jordaan* 1956(1) SA 483(A).

transaction (apart from whatever effect estoppel might have) has no legal consequences.[315]

The South African case law shows that undue influence may exist in a variety of circumstances: between doctor and patient thought to be dying;[316] husband and wife;[317] attorney and client.[318] It is not necessary that there be a special relationship between the parties.[319] If the contract was due to the folly, imprudence or lack of foresight of the party seeking relief, his claim to set it aside will fail for lack of causation, in other words, the influence did not induce the contract (Christie, 379).

The question whether one party has exercised an undue influence over another is a question of fact. In South African law, unlike English law, the existence of a confidential relationship between persons, though relevant, does not create any presumption of undue influence. English law places the onus on the party seeking to set aside the contract to show the existence of an undue influence unless one of a number of special relationships exists between the parties, in which case the onus is on the other party to prove that he did not abuse the confidential relationship or his position of trust.[320]

Although the English rule, namely that the existence of a special relationship reverses the normal onus, does not appear to be part of South African law, the attorney/client relationship may present a special case.[321] The rule that an attorney cannot enforce a contract between himself and his client unless it is manifestly fair to the client or the client took independent legal advice before entering into the contract, in effect requires the attorney to prove that he brought no undue influence to bare on the client.[322]

10.6 Failure of the Basic Premises of the Meeting of the Minds

Where there is no "meeting of the minds" or "coincidence of the wills" of the contracting parties, or no *consensus ad idem*, then there may be no contract between them (see 10.1 above).

11. Sale of *Aliud Pro Alio*

11.1 Applicability to Sold Shares

The Latin phrase *"aliud pro alio invito creditori soleri non potest"* means "payment cannot be made to a creditor by giving him one thing in exchange for another without his consent".[322a]

In order for a valid contract of sale to come into existence the parties must agree upon a purchase price. This is an *essentialia* of a contract of sale (see 1.3.4.1 above). The parties must either fix the amount of that price in their

[315] *Preller and Others* v *Jordaan* 1956 (1) SA 483 (A).
[316] *Preller* v *Jordaan* 1956 (1) SA 483 (A).
[317] *Ratane* v *Maharaj* 1950 (2) SA 438 (0).
[318] *Miller* v *Muller* 1965 (4) SA 458 (C).
[319] *Patel* v *Grobbelaar* 1974 (l) SA 532 (A).
[320] *Op. cit.* at 378.
[321] *Op. cit.* at 379.
[322] *Armitage Trustees* v *Alison* 1911 NPD 88 at 107; Christie, *Ibid, Op. cit.*
[322a] Paulus *Digest*, included in Hus-chke Jurisprudentiae Ante-justinianae.

contract or agree upon some method whereby it will be possible to determine the price without further reference to them. In other words, the purchase price must be certain or at least ascertainable. The purchase price must also sound in money, or partly in money and partly in goods.[323]

As a general rule the purchaser must pay to the seller the purchase price agreed upon, whether that price sounds in money, or partly in money and partly in goods, and the seller cannot be compelled to receive any other thing in the place of that which is due, even if what is tendered as payment is more valuable than the agreed purchase price.[324] This follows from the principle that the terms of contracts are determined in accordance with the agreement arrived at.

Furthermore, although the object of the obligation of the purchaser to pay the purchase price is physically capable of division, from a legal point of view the debt is one and indivisible, and therefore the purchaser cannot, without the consent of the seller, tender payment of the debt in instalments. The purchaser must pay the debt in its entirety and at the moment when he undertakes to perform his obligation.[325] If the purchaser could pay by instalments he would be entitled to alter the debt of a single amount into a number of smaller debts, each corresponding to the instalment paid.

Accordingly, when shares in a company are sold, the purchaser must pay to the disposing shareholder the purchase price agreed upon in the contract when he undertook to perform.

11.2 Applicability to On-going Businesses

The principles enunciated above would apply equally to a sale of a business as a going concern. The purchaser's obligation must be performed and the purchase price paid in accordance with the terms of the contract. Payment of the purchase price cannot be discharged in any other manner except with the consent of the seller.

11.3 Applicability to the Company, When the Shares are Sold

The company is not a party to an agreement for the sale of shares, its only function being to register the transfer of the shares in its share register when called upon to do so and upon lodgement of the requisite documents. Therefore, the obligation of the purchaser to pay the purchase price for the shares sold is of no concern to the company.

11.4 Extent of Applicability

If the purchaser does not pay the purchase price, the seller may, against tender by the seller to perform its obligations under the sale, claim the purchase price from

[323] *Burroughs Machines* v *Chenille Corporation of SA (Pty) Ltd* 1964 (1) SA 669 (W) at 670 C–D; *Hattingh* v *Van Rensburg* 1964 (1) SA 578 (T) at 582 C; Kerr, *Sale and Lease*, *Op. cit.* at 23.

[324] Wessels, *Op. cit.* at para. 2208.

[325] Wessels, *Op. cit.* at para. 2237; *Bernitz* v *Euvrard* 1943 AD 595 at 602–3.

the purchaser (its actual loss) as well as any prospective loss which the seller can prove, in other words its *id quod interest*.[326]

The seller may also cancel the contract and claim damages, but then the rule on mitigation of loss comes into operation, as it does when the seller seeks specific performance but this is refused by the court in the exercise of its discretion.[327] Thus, a seller aggrieved by the non-payment of the purchase price who has an opportunity to sell the shares to another and so mitigate his loss and does not take the opportunity will find that he is responsible for whatever portion of the loss is attributed to his failure to mitigate. The normal method of mitigation open to the seller is to sell the shares to someone else.[328]

12. Warranty of Proper Functioning

In a sale of a business as a going concern the purchaser may require the seller to warrant that the tangible assets sold are and will be in good working order and repair, fair wear and tear excepted, and that they have been and will be properly maintained until the date of delivery. The purpose of this warranty is to ensure that the assets sold are functioning properly and will be able to perform for the purpose for which they have been bought.

Where the tangible assets sold are defective, or were defective and repaired prior to delivery, the purchaser will have available at common law, the remedies discussed in 2.3.4.5 (implied warranty of fitness for specific use) and in 2.3.4.8 (warranty against latent defects), if applicable.

13. Warranties in Sales of Businesses as Going Concerns

13.1 Introduction

The nature of the business being sold, and the assets and liabilities comprising that business, will determine the warranties which may be required by the purchaser or the seller of that business. Each case must be dealt with on its own merits and the comments above (see 6.4) in connection with the infinite variety of warranties which may be included is equally applicable in sales of businesses as going concerns.

The meaning of a "business" has been discussed above (see 1.1.13). The Insolvency Act does not define the word "business", but does define the word "trader" as:

> any person who carries on any trade, business, industry or undertaking in which property is sold, or is bought, exchanged or manufactured for purpose of sale or exchange, or in which building operations of whatever nature are performed, or an object whereof is public entertainment, or who carries on the business of an hotel keeper or boarding-house keeper, or who acts as a broker or agent of any person in the sale or purchase of any property or in the letting or hiring of immoveable property; and any person shall be deemed to be a trader for the purpose of this Act (except for the purposes of sub-section (10) of section 21) unless it is proved that he is not a trader as hereinbefore defined: Provided that if any person carries on the

[326] Kerr, *Sale and Lease, Op. cit.* at 144.
[327] Kerr, *Op. cit.* at 146–7.
[328] *Ibid.*

> trade, business, industry or undertaking of selling property which he produced (either personally or through any servant) by means of farming operations, the provisions of this Act relating to traders only shall not apply to him in connection with his said trade, business, industry or undertaking.

It must be borne in mind that a business as such is not a legal persona, it is in fact a collection of assets and liabilities used by a trader in a specific way with a profit motive. These assets and liabilities are normally the following:

(a) goodwill;
(b) the rights and obligations in terms of an agreement of lease, in respect of the premises housing the business operation;
(c) stock in trade;
(d) the debtors of such business operation;
(e) the rights and obligations in terms of any other agreements relating to that business operation.

The right to conduct such business is dependent upon the obtaining of a trading licence in terms of the Licensing Ordinances application to the various provinces of the Republic of South Africa.

The warranties which may be relevant and applicable in sales of businesses as going concerns will now be discussed in general.

13.2 Warranties as to Financial Conditions

The financial statements of the company selling the business as a going concern (the seller) will set out the known assets and liabilities of the seller as at a particular date, as well as other important information relating to the business of the seller.

Not all of the information contained in the financial statements is relevant to the purchase of specific assets. The main advantage of purchasing a business is that the purchaser may select which assets and which liabilities, if any, it will purchase. Often a purchaser will base its decision to purchase certain assets comprising a business on the information recorded in the audited financial statements of the seller as at a particular date. It may be that in practice certain assets or liabilities are not disclosed in the financial statements. The purchaser should be aware of the possibility of the existence of these so-called off balance sheet assets and liabilities, which the seller may disclose to the purchaser in a disclosure letter. Otherwise the existence of such undisclosed assets is irrelevant to the purchaser because such assets or liabilities will not form part of the subject matter of the sale.

It is essential (if the purchaser relies on the financial statements to select the assets it wishes to purchase) that the information recorded in the financial statements fairly represent the assets and liabilities of the company as at a certain date. Accordingly, the seller should warrant that the effective financial statements:

(a) were prepared in conformity with generally accepted accounting principles and on a basis of accounting similar to that employed for all previous accounting periods for which financial statements are available;

(b) fairly present the assets, liabilities and profit of the seller;
(c) fully disclose all the assets of the seller;
(d) correctly reflect the book value of assets so that no amount included in the effective financial statements in respect of any asset, whether fixed or current, exceeds its purchase price or production cost, or in the case of current assets, its estimated net realisable value at the date of the effective financial statements;
(e) fully disclose all the liabilities of the seller, and make full provision or reserve for all liabilities of the seller, whether ascertained or contingent, including provision for all bad and doubtful debts and possible over-valuation of inventories and stocks;
(f) adequately and properly provide for bad or doubtful debts, and that no part of the amounts included in the effective financial statements as owing by any debtors is overdue by more than, say, 12 weeks, or has been released on terms that any debtor pays less than the full book value of his debt, or has been written off, or has proved to any extent to be irrecoverable, or is now regarded by the company as irrecoverable in whole or in part, and that none of the debts is subject to any counter-claim or set-off.

13.3 Warranty as to Profitability

It is unlikely that a seller will warrant the future turnover of the business sold. Such a warranty will be too risky for the seller because there are so many variables present. The seller may furnish a warranty in regard to past turnover if the warranty can be substantiated by a certificate from the seller's auditors certifying the turnover for the relevant period.

13.4 Warranty as to Operational Conditions

13.4.1 Contracts

The nature of the business carried on by the seller will determine what contracts, if any, it has entered into with third parties in order to carry on its business. The purchaser may wish to "take over" some or all of these contracts by way of a cession of the rights and delegation of the obligations in terms thereof by the seller to the purchaser. The purchaser will usually analyse each of the contracts in question in order to ascertain whether there are any obstacles to such cession and delegation and what effect the sale of the business may have on each contract. Such an investigation is termed a "due diligence" investigation.

The purchaser will usually request copies of all the relevant contracts in existence as at the closing date. The seller should warrant that copies of all the contracts in existence as at the closing date and specified in the agreement of sale have been submitted to the purchaser (a list of such contracts should be attached as an annexure to the agreement of sale), and that such copies of the contracts fully and correctly reflect all the terms and conditions thereof, will not be subject to any claim for rectification, and will not have been amended in any respect.

With regard to its various contracts with various creditors, in respect of *inter alia,* the supply of stock in trade or other materials, the seller should warrant that all such contracts have been entered into by the seller under normal credit terms and will be subject to payment in accordance with those terms.

It is essential for the continuity of the business as a going concern after the closing date that the validity of any of the contracts taken over by the purchaser should not be attacked on the basis that they are not arm's length transactions, or that the contracts benefit the other parties to them to the detriment of the seller, or that they are too onerous on the seller, or that the seller is in default of any of their provisions. Therefore, the seller should warrant, in respect of the agreements to be taken over by the purchaser, that it is not a party to any agreement which has not been entered into on an arm's length basis and on terms which are normal having regard to the nature of its business, and that the seller is not in breach of any such agreements and that it has complied in all material respects with its obligations under such agreements, and that it is not aware of any facts, matters or circumstances which may give rise to the cancellation of any of the contracts to which the seller is bound as a result of any breach of it by the seller.

To the extent that any contract imposes obligations on the seller, the seller should warrant that the other party to the contract being taken over by the purchaser, has consented to the delegation of such obligations (see 21.5.4 below). The purchaser could go further and make delivery of the relevant written consents to it prior to the closing date a suspensive condition of the agreement of sale (see 21.4.1 below).

13.4.2 Intellectual property rights

The goodwill of the seller and the popularity of the products it manufactures and/or sells or of the services it renders will depend, to a large extent, on the reputation of its trademarks, name or logo in the market-place. It would clearly be detrimental, even fatal, to the business if a third party were to succeed in an application to enforce better legal title to such intellectual property rights. Accordingly if these rights are to be ceded to the purchaser as part of the rights comprising the business as a going concern, the seller should warrant that:

(a) the business conducted by the seller will and does not infringe any patent, copyright, trademark or other intellectual property rights and no person is entitled to an order requiring the seller to change its name, its trading style, or any of the marks and designs applied by it to its products;
(b) no person is entitled to an order requiring the seller to change its name, its trading style or any of the marks and designs applied by it to its products.

13.5 Warranty as to the Conduct of Business until the Closing

The purchaser is particularly vulnerable to events occurring between the date of the signing of the contract and the date of delivery of the assets comprising the business which could detrimentally affect the financial position of the business.

Accordingly, the following list of warranties could assist the purchaser in reducing the aforesaid vulnerability. Thus, the seller should warrant to the purchaser, that as between the signing date and the closing date and as at the closing date:

(a) the seller will have continued to operate in the normal and regular course of its business, and such business will have been carried on in a proper and regular manner;
(b) the seller will not have changed its normal manner and method of carrying on business;
(c) no assets will have been acquired or sold otherwise than in the ordinary, normal and regular course of the seller's business;
(d) no liabilities will have been incurred without adequate value having been received;
(e) the seller will not have done or omitted to do anything which will materially prejudice its continued goodwill; reduce the scope of its business; or result in any of its business associates or customers ceasing to transact business with it or to vary the terms upon which it transacts business with the seller;
(f) the books and records of the seller will be up to date and will have been properly kept according to law and will be capable of being written up within a reasonable time so as to record all of the transactions of the seller.

13.6 Property

The following warranties regarding property should be obtained from the seller:

13.6.1 Assets

(a) The seller owns the assets which are reflected in the effective financial statements and has good and marketable title thereto, and that except for agreements entered into in the ordinary course of business between the date of the statements and the closing date, no other persons have any rights to or in respect of such assets, and this position will prevail on the closing date in respect of assets acquired since the date of the effective financial statements.
(b) The assets sold are in good order and condition and fully operational apart from breakdowns (in the ordinary course) and any loss or damage to or destruction of such assets beyond the control of the seller; provided that any such loss, damage or destruction will have been fully insured for the benefit of the seller.
(c) None of the assets sold is subject to any mortgage, debenture, notarial bond, cession or pledge or any other encumbrance, or was purchased under any hire-purchase or suspensive sale agreement or is subject to any lease.
(d) None of the assets sold is subject to any option or right of first refusal in favour of any person.

13.6.2 Debtors

All amounts owing to the seller by its debtors will be recovered by the seller from those debtors in full by not later than six months after the closing date and in the event of any amounts owing by those debtors in excess of the bad debt provision in the effective financial statements not being recovered by such date, those amounts shall be recoverable from the seller by the purchaser, provided that the purchaser shall cede to the seller or its nominee their claims against the debtors in question.

13.6.3 Immoveable property

With regard to any immoveable properties sold to the purchaser, the seller should warrant that:

(a) the seller will be the sole registered owner thereof;
(b) save as reflected in the effective financial statements, none of those properties is subject to any mortgage, hypothec or other charge nor does any party have any right of occupation of the properties;
(c) the properties are not subject to any restrictive conditions or servitudes which are not reflected in the title deeds under which they are held and any applicable town planning or similar scheme.

13.7 Other Statutory Requirements

13.7.1 Section 228 of the Companies Act

Section 228 of the Companies Act provides that:

> 228. Disposal of undertaking or greater part of assets of company
> (1) Notwithstanding anything contained in its memorandum or articles, the directors of a company shall not have the power, save with the approval of a general meeting of the company, to dispose of—
> (a) the whole or substantially the whole of the undertaking of the company; or
> (b) the whole or the greater part of the assets of the company.
> (2) No resolution of the company approving any such disposal shall have effect unless it authorises or ratifies in terms of the specific transaction.

Accordingly, the seller should warrant that it has complied with the provisions of section 228 of the Companies Act.

13.7.2 Section 34 of the Insolvency Act

Section 34 of the Insolvency Act provides that:

> 34. Voidable sale of business
> (1) If a trader transfers in terms of a contract any business belonging to him, or the goodwill of such business, or any goods or property forming part thereof (except in the ordinary course of that business or for securing the payment of a debt), and such trader has not published a notice of such intended transfer in the Gazette, and in two issues of an Afrikaans and two issues of an English newspaper circulating in the district in which that business is carried on, within a period not less than thirty days and not more than sixty days before the date of such transfer, the said transfer shall be void as against his creditors for a period of six months after such transfer, and shall be void against the trustee of his estate, if his estate is sequestrated at any time within the said period.
> (2) As soon as any such notice is published, every liquidated liability of the said trader in connection with the said business, which would become due at some future date, shall fall due forthwith, if the creditor concerned demands payment of such liability: Provided that if such liability bears no interest, the amount of such liability which would have been payable at

such future date if such demand had not been made, shall be reduced at the rate of eight per cent per annum of that amount, over the period between the date when payment is made and that future date.

(3) If any person who has any claim against the said trader in connection with the said business, has before such transfer, for the purpose of enforcing his claim, instituted proceedings against the said trader—
   (a) in any court of law, and the person to whom the said business was transferred knew at the time of the transfer that those proceedings had been instituted; or
   (b) in a Division of the Supreme Court having jurisdiction in the district in which the said business is carried on or in the magistrates' court of that district, the transfer shall be void as against him for the purpose of such enforcement.

(4) For the purposes of this section "transfer" when used as a noun, includes actual or constructive transfer of possession, and, when used as a verb, has a corresponding meaning.

Often the seller does not wish to publish details of the sale of the assets in the business in terms of section 34(1) of the Insolvency Act and the purchaser may consent to such non-publication on the condition that the seller (or another third party) furnish an appropriate indemnity to the purchaser. Accordingly, the seller (or the relevant third party) should indemnify the purchaser against any loss or damage (including consequential losses) which the purchaser may suffer by reason of the failure by the seller to publish details of the sale.

14. Form Requirements

14.1 Written Form

South African law has accepted the simple Roman–Dutch concept of a contract as a serious and deliberate agreement.[329] As a general rule, no special formalities are required for the making of an enforceable contract, and, subject to certain exceptions, mostly statutory, any contract may be verbally entered into.[330] Therefore, an offer or an acceptance need not be in writing, nor are words essential, for an acceptance may be inferred from conduct.[331]

14.1.1 Formalities decided on by the parties

If during negotiations, mention is made of a written document, it is in each case a question of construction whether the object of the parties was merely to afford facility of proof of the verbal agreement or whether the parties intended that the writing should embody the contract. It is always open to the parties to agree that their contract shall be a written one; and in that case there will be no binding obligation until the terms have been reduced to writing and signed.[332] It follows that where the parties are shown to have been *ad idem* as to the material terms of the contract, the onus of proving an agreement that legal validity should be

[329] *Conradie* v *Rossouw* 1919 AD 279.
[330] *Goldblatt* v *Fremantle* 1920 AD 123 at 128.
[331] *Timoney and King* v *King* 1920 AD 133 at 141.
[332] *Goldblatt* v *Fremantle* 1920 AD 123 at 128–9; Christie, *Op. cit.* at 122.

postponed until the due execution of a written document lies upon the party who alleges it.[333]

This summary of South African law may be explained as follows: an agreement to confirm in writing the written terms of a contract implies that what was arranged prior thereto was merely introductory and provisional and of no binding force, and furnishes very strong evidence of intention that the writings containing the terms and the confirmation should alone form the contract. On the other hand, no such implication would arise merely from an agreement to embody in a written document terms which had been previously verbally arranged. Such an undertaking would rather be consistent with an intention to be bound by the verbal agreement, which a condition requiring confirmation in writing of written terms would not.[334]

The cases do not fit neatly into the two categories of those in which there is no contract until the execution of the written document and those in which the oral contract is binding. For example, the informal contract may refer to the execution of a formal contract in such terms that the execution of the formal contract becomes a contractual obligation under the informal contract and not a condition precedent to its validity.[335] In such a case the court may order specific performance of the obligation to sign, or damages for failure to do so.[336] On the other hand, although the informal contract refers to the execution of a formal contract it may not indicate an intention not to be bound until the execution of the formal contract, and if the parties have not yet reached even an informal agreement they will not be bound to each other.[337]

14.1.2 Signing the contract

Once the parties have decided that they will reduce their contract to writing and that they will be bound by their written contract but not by any earlier informal contract, then the contract comes into existence when, and only when, the written document containing it has been signed by all of the parties.[338] Unless the parties contemplate some particular form of signature, any sign or mark made with the intention of signifying assent to the document will suffice.[339] Initials have been held sufficient.[340]

The proper analysis of the process of signing a written bipartite contract is that the first party to sign makes an offer and the other by his signature accepts. In a multipartite contract the first signatory offers, each intermediate signatory accepts the offer of prior signatories and makes an offer to subsequent signatories, and the last signatory accepts. Usually all signatories except the last must be interpreted as subject to the condition precedent that all other proposed parties sign. A multipartite contract, in the absence of clear indications to the contrary,

[333] *Woods* v *Walters* 1921 AD 303 at 305; Christie, *Ibid.*

[334] *De Bruin* v *Brink* 1925 OPD 68 at 73; Christie, *Op. cit.* at 123.

[335] *Amoils* v *Amoils* 1924 WLD 88.

[336] *Woods* v *Walters* 1921 AD 303 at 309–11.

[337] *Op. cit.* at 124.

[338] *Goldblatt* v *Fremantle* 1920 AD 123 at 129; Christie, *Ibid.*

[339] *Ibid.*

[340] *Ariefdien* v *Socker* 1982 (2) SA 570 (C) at 578 A–E.

would presumably not bind any of the parties unless signed by all of them. For example, a surety will usually be correct in arguing that it was not intended that he should be bound unless all his proposed co-sureties signed too.[341]

14.1.3 Formalities required by law

It is a travesty of justice that a crafty party to an agreement should be allowed to admit making the contract in an informal manner, but escape its consequences by pleading that the contract was not made with the formality required by the statute.[342] That is, however, the inevitable result of any statute prescribing particular formalities for particular classes of contracts. The formality of writing has been prescribed for a number of classes of contracts, such as a sale of land, contracts of suretyship, credit agreements, negotiable instruments and insurance policies.

14.1.3.1 SALE OF SHARES

The prescribed statutory formalities for a transfer of shares are set out in sections 133 to 140 of the Companies Act. There are no formalities in respect of the sale by cession of the rights attaching to the shares (see 6.1 above). However, the new beneficial shareholder will not be entitled to enforce his rights against the company until he registers the transfer of the shares in accordance with the aforementioned provisions of the Companies Act.

14.1.3.2 SALE OF LAND

No alienation of land shall be of any force or effect unless it is contained in a deed of alienation signed by the parties thereto or by their agents acting on their written authority.[343]

14.1.3.3 CONTRACT OF SURETYSHIP

No contract of suretyship shall be valid, unless the terms thereof are embodied in a written document signed by or on behalf of the surety.[344]

14.2 Further Formalities and Effect vis-à-vis the Corporation

As stated above (see 6.1 and 14.1.3.1), the Companies Act prescribes certain formalities for the transfer of shares in a company. If these formalities are not complied with, and the transfer of shares to the transferee is not registered, the company may disregard the transferee, who until registration of the transfer, will have no rights against the company save for a claim for rectification of the share register and registration of the transfer.

14.3 Acceptance of By-laws

The memorandum of association and the articles of association, when registered, bind the company and its registered members to the same extent as if they had been signed by each member,[345] and constitute a contract between the company

[341] *Op. cit.* at 125.
[342] *Op. cit.* at 127.
[343] Section 2(1) of the Alienation of Land Act, 68 of 1981; see 21.1.3 below; see 1.1.8 above and section 324 of the Companies Act.
[344] Section 6 of the General Law Amendment Act, 50 of 1956; see 2.2.4.6 above.
[345] Section 65(2) read with section 103(2) of the Companies Act; see 6.1 above.

and its members, *qua* members, as well as between the members *inter se*. A non-member acquires no rights under the articles of association.

14.4 Specific Acceptance of Warranties, Exclusions or Limitations

Exclusion and limitation clauses in relation to warranties are dealt with in section 18 below.

14.5 Acceptance of Contractual Warranties

By signing the written contract the parties accept the terms (including the warranties) contained therein.

15. Applicable Law—Conflict of Law Rules

15.1 Sale in South Africa of South African (i) Business or (ii) Shares between a South African and a non-South African Citizen.

The conflict of laws, or private international law, is that branch of municipal law which comes into operation when a legal relationship of a private law nature has some connection with a foreign legal system and which then determines the appropriate law to govern that relationship. Because the legal system to be applied in a given case is determined by the class or character of the issue involved, classification or characterisation naturally precedes the application of a conflict rule.

15.1.1 Sale of a business in South Africa

The assets of any business may be classified into moveable and immoveable property (see 1.1.4 above). The classification into moveable and immoveable property has an important bearing upon the applicable law relating to that property. Whether property is moveable or immoveable is determined according to South African law by the law of the place where the property is situated (the *lex rei sitae*). Therefore, the applicable law relating to whether the assets of a business which are situated in South Africa are moveable or immoveable assets, and to the acquisition of ownership and transfer thereof, would be South African law.

The question of the applicable law which would determine certain aspects of a contract of sale of either the assets of a South African business, or the shares of a South African company, are dealt with in 15.1.2 below.

15.1.1.1 IMMOVEABLE PROPERTY

Where property situated in South Africa has been categorised as immoveable property then South African law will dominate all questions of rights to such immoveable property. Thus, the capacity to transfer or acquire ownership of such property or any other right therein is determined by the *lex rei sitae*. The forms and conditions prescribed by the *lex rei sitae* for the acquisition and transfer of such rights will have to be observed, for example, those prescribed by the provisions of the South African Deeds Registries Act 47 of 1937 (see 1.1.3 and

14.1.3.1 above, and 21.2.3 below). In addition the validity of any legal act creating or extinguishing property rights in respect of immoveable property situated in South Africa, as well as questions of prescription and the recognition and enforceability of hypothecs, will be determined by South African law.

15.1.1.2 MOVEABLE PROPERTY

Where property is categorised as moveable in terms of South African law, then the legal fiction in South African law that moveables follow their owner applies, so that a conflict of laws regarding moveable property will, in principle, be resolved by applying the law of the owner's domicile. Therefore, if the owner is domiciled in South Africa the applicable law relating to that person's moveable assets, wherever they may be situated in the world, would be South African law.

A company is usually regarded as being "domiciled", in this sense, in the country of its incorporation or registration. Provision has been made in the Companies Act for a change of "domicile" in the sense that an external company may apply for registration as a South African company (section 322 of the Companies Act; see 1.1.8 above).

In some instances the domicile of the owner of moveable property may be disregarded and the *lex rei sitae* may apply. For example, there is authority to the effect that the recognition and enforcement of a tacit hypothec over moveables will be governed by the *lex rei sitae*,[346] and the *lex rei sitae* will probably also govern questions of capacity and the form of alienation and acquisition of rights in moveable property.[347]

When an incorporeal moveable, such as a right of action, is ceded, the place where the cession is made will as a general rule govern its validity, while the effect of the cession will depend upon the law of the debtor's domicile.[348]

A share in a company is categorised as moveable incorporeal property. A company is required to keep a share register at its registered office (section 105 of the Companies Act).

15.1.1.3 IMMATERIAL PROPERTY

There are various statutory provisions dealing with the protection of immaterial property rights, such as copyright, patents, designs and trademarks, acquired in South Africa or elsewhere.

Works which are eligible for copyright in terms of the South African Copyright Act 98 of 1978, are original literary works, musical works, artistic works, cinematograph films, sound recordings, broadcasts, programme-carrying signals and published editions (section 2(1) of the Copyright Act). Copyright is conferred on every work, eligible for copyright, of which the author or, in the case of a work of joint authorship, any one of the authors is at the time the work or a substantial part thereof is made, a "qualified person" (section 3(1) of the

[346] *Cape Government* v *Liquidators of the Balmoral Diamond Co Ltd* 1980 TS 681 at 685.

[347] Professor Kahn in Hahlo and Kahn, *Union of SA: Development of its Laws and Constitutions* 751.

[348] *Rothschild* v *Lowndes* 1908 TS 493 at 498.

Copyright Act). In the case of an individual, a "qualified person" is a person who is a South African citizen or is domiciled or resident in South Africa, and in the case of a juristic person, is a body incorporated under the laws of South Africa. The term of copyright is 50 years commencing at various dates according to the nature of the work involved (section 3(2) of the Copyright Act).

Registration of copyright is not usually necessary to protect such copyright (but see the Registration of Copyright in Cinematograph Films Act 62 of 1977). The owner of copyright is protected by operation of statutory law (see sections 23–28 of the Copyright Act).

Section 37 of the Copyright Act provides that the South African Minister of Economic Affairs and Technology may by notice in the Government Gazette provide that any provision of the Copyright Act specified in the notice shall, in the case of any country which is party to a convention relating to copyright to which South Africa is also a party, and which country is specified in the notice, apply:

(a) in relation to literary, musical or artistic works, cinematograph films, sound recordings and published editions first published in that country as it applies in relation to literary, musical or artistic works, cinematograph films, sound recordings and published editions first published in the Republic;
(b) in relation to persons who at a material time are citizens or subjects of that country as it applies in relation to persons who at such a time are South African citizens;
(c) in relation to persons who at a material time are domiciled or resident in that country as it applies in relation to persons who at such a time are domiciled or resident in the Republic;
(d) in relation to bodies incorporated under the laws of that country as it applies in relation to bodies incorporated under the laws of the Republic;
(e) in relation to broadcasts and programme-carrying signals made or emitted to a satellite from places in that country or by one or more organisations constituted by or under the laws of that country as it applies in relation to broadcasts and programme-carrying signals made or emitted to a satellite by the Corporation.

When a foreign State fails to give adequate protection to the works of South African citizens the Minister of Economic Affairs and Technology may deny copyright to the citizens of such countries (section 37(3) of the Copyright Act).

In terms of the Patents Act 57 of 1978, Designs Act 57 of 1967 and Trade Marks Act 62 of 1963 provision has been made for the registration of patents, designs and trademarks by South African residents and non-residents.

Provision has also been made for the recognition of an application for registration of a trademark, patent and design in a convention country to the extent that the applicant or his legal representative or assignee shall, inpriority to other applicants, be entitled to registration of the trademark, patentor design, provided that the application is made within a specified period of the date on which the application was made in the convention country.[349] Such registration

[349] Section 73(1) of the Trade Marks Act; section 95 of the Patents Act 37 of 1952; section 18 of the Designs Act 57 of 1967.

shall then have the same date as the date of the final application in the convention country, but the applicant shall not be entitled by virtue of this provision to recover damages for an infringement happening prior to the actual date on which the application is first advertised.

15.1.2 Contract

Where the owner of property agrees to sell property, whether moveable or immoveable, the seller and the purchaser will enter into an agreement of sale in respect of that property. The "proper law of the contract", in other words, the law governing most of its aspects, is the law of the country which the parties have agreed or intended or are presumed to have intended shall govern it.[350] A clause in a contract stipulating that a specified system of law shall govern the contract is valid and enforceable in South African law.[351] In the absence of such an express stipulation the applicable law is that which the parties tacitly accepted as governing their contract.

The parties may, therefore, expressly or tacitly select the law governing the intrinsic validity, effect and interpretation of the contract, but their selection does not affect the objectively applicable law relating to contractual capacity, formal validity and legality, because the application thereof determines whether the agreement expressing the selection is legally effective. Therefore, matters relating to the form and validity of the contract may fall to be decided by one system of law and matters relating to its performance by another. Whether the parties may select a legal system with which their contract has no connection whatsoever is an open question, and such a selection would presumably not be effective if it were made deliberately to avoid some provision of the law which would normally appertain to the contract.

In the absence of an express choice of law by the parties the proper law is determined objectively with reference to all the connecting factors of the case. Such factors give rise to presumptions as to what the parties would have intended had they applied their minds to a choice of law. Thus, the proper law of the contract has been determined with reference to the place where the contract was entered into, where it was performed, the place where property is situated, the domicile or nationality of the parties, the form, terminology and language of a contract and the place where the offer was made.

15.2 Sale Outside South Africa of South African (i) Business or (ii) Shares between a South African and a non-South African Citizen

The general principles relating to the proper law of the contract have already been discussed (see 15.1.2 above).

[350] *Guggenheim* v *Rosenbaum* 1961 (4) SA 21 (W) at 31.
[351] *Standard Bank of SA Ltd* v *Efroiken and Newman* 1924 AD 171 at 185–186.

(a) Where a business as a going concern continues to function in South Africa after the sale of the business, and the moveable assets remain in South Africa, and the purchaser is domiciled in South Africa, then the applicable law relating to the business and its assets will be South African law.
(b) Although shares are moveable incorporeal property, the applicable law governing those shares will be determined by the place where the share register is kept, which is normally the registered offices of the company.

15.3 Sale in South Africa of a Foreign (i) Business or (ii) Shares between a South African and a non-South African Citizen

The general principles relating to the proper law of the contract have already been discussed (see 15.1.2 above).

Where the immoveable assets of a foreign business are situated in a foreign country the applicable law governing the immoveable property will be the *lex rei sitae*. However, because of the legal fiction applicable in South African law that moveables follow their owner, the domicile of the purchaser will be one of the factors to be considered when determining the question which is the applicable law governing the rights in and to such moveable assets (see 15.1.1.2 above).

15.4 Sale Outside of South Africa of a Foreign (i) Business or (ii) Shares between a South African and a non-South African Citizen

The principles set out in 15.3.1 apply. It is unlikely that South African choice of law rules or substantive law would be applied.

15.5 Applicable Multilateral and Bilateral International Conventions

South Africa is not party to any international conventions or bilateral treaties on jurisdiction or the reciprocal enforcement of foreign judgments, other than with the "independent territories" of Transkei, Bophuthatswana, Venda and Ciskei. None of these "states" is recognised by the international community.

South Africa is, however, party to the 1958 United Nations Convention on the Recognition and Enforcement of Foreign Arbitral Awards.

15.6 South African International Public Policy

In South Africa, the courts will not enforce a foreign judgment automatically; it must be made a judgment of the South African court by the institution of action, and provided that:

(i) such judgment is final and conclusive;
(ii) such judgment was not obtained by fraud;
(iii) such judgment is not contrary to public policy in the Republic;
(iv) such judgment is not contrary to natural justice;
(v) the consent of the relevant Minister has been obtained in terms of section 1 of the Protection of Businesses Act, 99 of 1978.

In this regard the Act provides that no foreign judgment in respect of, *inter alia*, the importation, exportation, use or ownership of any matter or material in the Republic shall be enforced in the Republic without the permission of the Minister.

Section 1A of the above-mentioned Act stipulates further than no foreign judgment for the payment of multiple or punitive damages shall be recognised or enforced in the Republic, irrespective of whether the Minister has granted his consent.

16. The Time Element in Warranties

16.1 Closing

Often the parties to an agreement will agree a date some time after the signing of the agreement to "close" the deal. At or before the closing, the parties will exchange documents, obtain consents from creditors in respect of the delegation of obligations and generally finalise any outstanding matters. Delivery of the assets sold, payment of the purchase price (or the first instalment thereof), and the passing of risk and ownership to and in the assets sold, usually occurs at the closing. But the parties may agree otherwise. In any event, there is a transition period during which control of the company's assets and business (whether it is a sale of shares or of the business of the company) is transferred from the seller to the purchaser.

The terms of each agreement will determine the purchaser's period of vulnerability, namely the period during which the assets remain in the control of the seller prior to the closing. The purchaser will want the seller's warranties to apply at least for the period between the date of signing the agreement and the closing date, and in certain instances to apply to the periods before the date of signing and/or after the closing date. The period of application of each warranty will be a matter of negotiation between the respective parties, the purchaser hoping to extend the period as much as possible, and the seller trying to limit the relevant period of application.

16.2 Warranties not Incorporated in Closing Documents

In a sale of shares the closing documents to be delivered by the seller to the purchaser are usually the original share certificates in respect of the shares sold; share transfer forms completed by the seller and left blank as to the transferee; the memorandum of association and articles of association of the relevant company; its certificate of incorporation and its certificate to commence business; all contracts; documents; tax records; and any other relevant records of the company; the written resignation of the board of directors of the company and the secretary and auditors of the company. The warranties relating to the various aspects of the sale of shares are incorporated in the written agreement of sale, and not in any of the "closing documents". The same applies to a sale of a business as a going concern.

16.3 Survival of Warranties

Warranties incorporated in an agreement of sale will "survive" for the period of their application stipulated in the relevant agreement. At the expiry of such period the warranties will no longer have any force or effect.

16.4 Notice of Non-conformity—Term

The parties may agree that in the event of a breach of a warranty, the aggrieved party shall give notice of non-conformity and require rectification of the breach within a specified period before he is entitled to pursue his rights following the non-rectified breach.

16.5 Time Limitation

As mentioned above (see 16.1 and 16.3), the period during which any warranty is of force and effect and binding upon the parties is the period agreed upon by the parties.

17. Beneficiary of the Warranty

17.1 The Purchaser

The warranties furnished by the seller are usually in favour of and for the benefit of the purchaser. The obligations created by the warranties will therefore be due by the seller to the purchaser.

17.2 Resale by Purchaser

Should the purchaser resell to a third party the assets forming the subject matter of an agreement of sale between the original seller and the purchaser, there will be no privity of contract between the original seller and such third party. Usually the purchaser will furnish the third party with back-to-back warranties in relation to the assets sold. Then, if there is a breach of warranty, and the third party institutes an action against the purchaser, the purchaser may in turn institute an action against the original seller, or in appropriate circumstances join the original seller as a co-defendant to the proceedings. Unless the agreement specifically prohibits a cession, the purchaser may cede to a third party (including a new purchaser) his rights in terms of the warranties given by the seller. In such event the third party will be entitled to proceed against the seller in the event of any breach of any warranty originally given by him.

17.3 Third Parties as Beneficiaries

A warrantor may give a warranty for the benefit of either the other party to the contract or for the benefit of a third party. A contract between two parties for the benefit of a third party is termed a *stipulateri alteri*.[351a] The contract between the warrantor (the seller) and the warrantee (the purchaser) creates an offer to the third party which may be communicated to the third party in any manner. When the third party accepts the offer he becomes a party to the

[351a] J.L. De Wet and A.H. Van Wyk (eds.), Die Suid-Afrikaanse Kontraktereg en Hendelsreg (4th ed. 1978), at 92–99.

contract, a *vinculum iuris* is created between him and the warrantor and the third party may therefore sue the warrantor on the contract.[352]

18. Warranties, Limitations and Disclaimers

18.1 Limitations or Disclaimers in Sales of Businesses as Going Concerns

There is an important distinction to be drawn between true exemption clauses and limitation clauses. In terms of an exemption clause a party purports to exclude altogether some or all of that party's common law duties that would normally arise under the contract, whereas a limitation clause is aimed at modifying or limiting such common law duties.[351b] The clauses purporting to exclude or limit the common law duties of the relevant parties may therefore attempt to exclude or limit liability arising from, *inter alia*, negligent acts, representations or mistake.

Where, for example, a business consists of the assembly of machinery parts, then the assembler of such parts may attempt to limit its liability and contract out of its absolute liability for defects in the manufacture of parts which it has not itself manufactured. In the ordinary course of business the assembler may offer some *quid pro quo* in the form of an undertaking to replace or repair defective parts. It will seldom, if ever, be the fault of the assembler if a part turns out to be defective through bad material or workmanship. But where the assembler of the parts may be treated as a "merchant seller" then it may, in a proper case, be held strictly liable for latent defects of which it was not aware and for which it was not to blame see 2.3.4.7 above.[353]

The assembler of the parts may, therefore, contract out of liability for consequential damage caused by latent defects in the parts for which it might otherwise be liable in terms of the strict liability principle applicable to merchant sellers. This type of clause may be described as a limitation clause rather than an exclusion or exemption clause. Bearing in mind that the assembler may have agreed to repair or replace defective parts and is not really in a position to know whether or not they are defective since the assembler is not the manufacturer, this limitation on the assembler's liability is arguably reasonable.[354]

A true exemption clause or a disclaimer or an exclusion clause is one where the assembler would attempt to contract out of any responsibility for its own work. A true exemption clause is regarded by the courts with circumspection for the contention is that, in this example, the assembler is not to be held liable for its own negligence in assembling parts which were not defective in any way.

The courts will interpret a true exemption clause very restrictively and apply a three-phase test to ascertain whether the contracting party—the assembler in this example—is liable or not: firstly, if the clause contains language which

[351b] Sharrock, *Op. cit.* at 136–137.

[352] Christie, *Op. cit.* at 136–137.

[354] see 2.3.4.7 above; *Kroonstad Westelike Boere-Ko-operatiewe Vereniging Bpk* v *Botha and Another* 1964 (3) SA 561 (A) at 571H; *Holmdene Brickworks (Pty) Ltd* v *Roberts Construction Co Ltd* 1977 (3) SA 670 (A); *Gannet Manufacturing Co (Pty) Ltd* v *Postatflex (Pty) Ltd* 1981 (3) SA 216 (C).

[354] *Transport and Crane Hire Ltd* v *Hubert Davies & Co Ltd* 1991 (4) SA 150 (ZSC) at 165 H.

expressly exempts the person in whose favour it is made ("the *proferens*") from the consequence of negligence of its own servants, effect must be given to that provision. Secondly, however, if there is no express reference to negligence, the court will consider whether the words used are wide enough, in their ordinary meaning, to cover negligence on the parts of the servants of the *proferens*. If a doubt arises at this point it must be resolved against the *proferens*. Thirdly, if, on the other hand, the words used are wide enough for the purpose of covering negligence on the part of the servants of the *proferens*, the court will then consider whether the claim for damages may be based on some other ground, other than that of negligence. This other ground must not be so remote that the *proferens* cannot be supposed to have desired protection against it and its existence is fatal to the *proferens* even if the words used are, *prima facie*, wide enough to cover negligence on the part of its servants.[355]

Therefore, generally speaking, where in law the liability for the damages which the clause purports to eliminate can rest upon negligence only the exemption must be read to exclude liability for negligence. Otherwise it would be deprived of all effect, but where in law such liability could be based on some ground other than negligence, it is excluded only to the extent to which it may be so based, and not where it is founded on negligence.[356] In order for an exemption clause to exclude liability arising from negligence there must be an express reference to negligence,[357] unless the context indicates that the exemption clause relates only to negligence.[358] Ideally, the *proferens* should add words to the effect that the other party should take out insurance to cover any possible risk of loss from negligence of the *proferens*.[359] The taking out of insurance by the other party is a major factor for excluding liability of the *proferens* for its own negligence: the agreement to insure may be a satisfactory *quid pro quo* for the exemption.

Furthermore, and despite the emphatic language of an exemption clause, the courts will assume that the parties could hardly have intended that the *proferens* would be exonerated from liability if it failed to perform its obligations at all, or if its performance proved useless, or if it committed a breach going to the root of the contract. The underlying ground for this reasoning is that the parties must have in mind that both of them would carry out the terms of the contract.[360] It is essential then to ascertain whether such a clause, having regard to the intentions of the parties to be gathered from the contract as a whole can be interpreted to cover fundamental breach. There is a rule of construction that normally an

355 *Alderslade* v *Hendon Laundry Ltd* [1945] KB 189 ([1945] 1 All ER 244 (CA); *Transport and Crane Hire Ltd* v *Hubert Davies & Co Ltd* 1991 (4) SA 150 (ZSC) at 163 J–164 C; *Canada Steamship Lines Ltd* v *Regem* [1952] AC 192 at 208 [1952] 1 All ER 305 (PC) at 310 A–D.

356 *Essa* v *Divaris* 1947 (1) SA 735 (A) at 756; *South African Railways and Harbours* v *Lyle Shipping Co Ltd* 1958 (3) SA 416 (A) at 419 C–E.

357 *Cotton Marketing Board of Zimbabwe* v *Zimbabwe National Railways* 1990 (1) SA 582 (ZS) at 597 I.

358 *Transport and Crane Hire Ltd* v *Hubert Davies & Co Ltd* 1991 (4) SA 150 (ZSC) at 165 C.

359 *Government of the Republic of South Africa* v *Fibre Spinners & Weavers (Pty) Ltd* 1978 (2) SA 794 (A).

360 *Hall-Thermotank Natal (Pty) Ltd* v *Hardman* 1968 (4) SA 818 (D) at 835 F–G.

exemption clause should be construed as not applying to a situation created by a fundamental breach of the contract. This rule is based on the presumed intention of the parties and involves the implication of a term to give the contract that business efficacy which the parties as reasonable men must have intended it to have.[361] Where there has been a fundamental breach of contract then each party is entitled to treat such fundamental breach as a repudiation to bring the contract (including the exemption clause) to an end and sue for damages.

In practice, therefore, the parties are free to agree what limits shall apply in respect of the defaulting party's liability arising in the event of a default. The limitations of liability may apply in respect of the period during which the breach must occur, the maximum quantum of damages recoverable or the exclusion of petty claims altogether unless the aggregate of such claims during a specific period exceeds a certain amount.

18.2 Limitations or Disclaimers in Sales of Shares

The comments made in 18.1 above apply *mutatis mutandis* to a sale of shares.

19. Breach of Warranties

19.1 Is Vendor's Fault Required?

The short answer to this question is: no—fault on the part of the warrantor is not required. Where, for example, the seller warrants the quantity or quality of the assets sold, and the quantity or quality of the assets sold are not what the seller promised they would be, then the seller may be in breach of the warranty, and the remedies available in law or those agreed upon by the parties if such breach did occur, are available to the purchaser.

Not every act by one party to a contract which causes loss to the other will give rise to an action on the contract. It is necessary for the plaintiff to allege and prove a breach of the contract, and that it was committed by the defendant.[362] Proof that a breach has occurred is basically a two-stage process involving, first, the factual inquiry into what was done or omitted, and second, the interpretation of the contract in order to decide whether what was done or omitted was contrary to the terms of the contract. It is, therefore, not necessary to prove fault, in other words, that what was done or omitted was done or omitted, intentionally or negligently (see 20.2.1 below), in order to establish a breach of contract entitling the innocent party to rely on its contractual remedies.

Fault is, however, a requirement for a claim for damages based on a delict (see 20.2 below).

19.2 Other Requirements to Assert the Warranty

The question whether or not there has been a breach of a warranty is first and foremost a factual one, and secondly a matter of interpretation of the meaning and scope of the warranty (see 19.1 above).

[361] *UGS Finance Ltd* v *National Mortgage Bank of Greece and National Bank of Greece* SA [1964] 1 Ll LR 446 (CA) at 453.

[362] *Goldfields Supermarket* v *Calendar and Novelties (SA) (Pty) Ltd* 1964 (4) SA 11 2(T).

19.3 Offsetting between Effects of Warranty and Undisclosed Assets

The parties may agree the consequences of a breach of any of the warranties. Thus, the parties may agree that a warranty is material and that a breach of that warranty will entitle the warrantee either to cancel the agreement or uphold the agreement and sue for damages. Alternatively, the parties may agree the amount payable to the warrantee in the event of a breach of that warranty, or that that amount shall be set off (see 21.8 below) against the value of certain assets delivered to the purchaser in terms of the agreement of sale, which value had not before the occurrence of the breach been included in the purchase price. These assets may have been "undisclosed" as at the date of their delivery to the purchaser in circumstances where for example, the seller sells and the purchaser purchases all of the assets located at the premises of the seller as at a certain date.

20. Remedies

20.1 Actions in Contract

The obligations imposed by the terms of a contract are meant to be performed, and if they are not performed at all, or performed late or performed in the wrong manner, the party on whom the duty of performance lay is said to have committed a breach of the contract or, in the first two cases, to be *in mora*, and, in the last case, to be guilty of positive malperformance.[363] South African law is opposed to the idea that breach discharges a contract, so that forfeiture clauses which state in plain words that a specified breach shall "*ipso facto* cancel and annul" the contract or that the contract "shall lapse" on such breach are interpreted as giving the innocent party the right to cancel or enforce the contract at his option,[364] since to give the wording its plain meaning would enable the wrongdoer to profit from his own wrong by committing the specified breach in order to destroy the contract against the wishes of the innocent party.[365]

In English law, a warranty is a collateral term of the contract and as such its breach gives rise only to a claim for damages and not for rescission (see 1.3.2.5 above). In South African law, a breach of a warranty, as in the case of breaches of other terms of the contract, may or may not be a major one. If it is a major breach the aggrieved party may cancel the contract.

Because of the difficulty involved in determining whether a term of the contract (including a warranty) is such that a breach of that term would amount to a major, as opposed to a minor breach, the parties may expressly agree whether or not a breach of that term will entitle the other party to rescind the contract. Usually the parties include in the contract of sale a breach clause to the effect that if either party breaches any provision of the agreement, including/excluding any or some of the warranties, and that party remains in breach for, say, 14 days after

[363] Christie, *Op. cit.* at 587.
[364] *Associated Manganese Mines of SA Ltd* v *Claassens* 1954 (3) SA 768 (A) at 774.
[365] *Op. cit.* at 588.

receipt of written notice requiring it to rectify the breach, the other party shall be entitled at its option (and without prejudice to any other rights that it may have at law) either to sue for specific performance of the defaulting party's obligations under the agreement, or to cancel the sale by notice in writing to the defaulting party and to sue for such damages as that party may have suffered as a result of the cancellation.

There is nothing in law to prevent the parties from agreeing that the breach of some obligations but not others will entitle the innocent party to cancel the contract. It seldom happens that the party in whose favour a warranty exists asks that the subject matter of the contract be put into the warranted condition. A seller may, for example, warrant the quantity of the subject matter of the contract. Where there is a shortfall, the purchaser may ask for, and be granted, an order that the quantity be made up. Such an order cannot be granted, however, if it is impossible to make up the quantity.

Where a warranty is given by a third party, and not by the seller, to the purchaser, who is influenced thereby and enters into a contract with the seller, then if the circumstances are such that there is a breach of warranty, the purchaser has a delictual action for damages based on misrepresentation against the third party.[366]

20.1.1 Title not clear

The common law position with regard to the seller's implied obligation to transfer ownership if he has it or can obtain it, failing which to warrant against eviction, is discussed in 2.3.4.3 above.

20.1.2 For defects

The common law position with regard to the seller's "warranty" against latent defects is discussed in 2.3.4.8 above. Under the common law the aedilitian remedies are available to the purchaser by operation of the law if the thing sold is found to have a latent defect. A warranty against defects is not to be understood to mean that the seller undertakes to prevent the thing sold from having those defects, for this would be an impossible undertaking if in reality it has them. If the thing sold has these defects, the seller binds itself according to the terms of the warranty either to pay such damages as the purchaser may suffer thereby, or at least to release the purchaser from the contract. On this understanding payment of the requisite sum of money, or release from the contract, is performance of the warranty, and not damages for breach of it.

20.1.3 For non-merchantable quality

The common law position with regard to the seller's warranty of reasonable merchantable quality is discussed in 2.3.4.6 above. The purchaser will be entitled to claim damages for breach of an express warranty relating to the quality of the thing sold.[367] In *Evans & Plows* v *Willis & Co*[368] the purchasers were plumbers and sanitary engineers who purchased cement from Willis and Co, who knew it was to be used by the purchasers in their trade. The purchasers had asked for a

366 Kerr, *Contract, Op. cit.* at 352.
367 *Ibid.*
368 *Evans & Plows* v *Willis & Co* 1923 CPD 496.

particular brand of cement. Not having that brand in stock, one which they had previously supplied, the sellers sold to the purchasers another brand and expressly warranted it to be as good as the brand asked for. In fact it was not and the works on which it was used cracked and broke and had to be taken up and renewed. The damages awarded included the cost of the materials and of taking up and renewing the work. Watermeyer J, Benjamin J concurring, said, at 502:

> In our law if an express warranty as to the quality of the article sold has been given by the seller and this turns out to be untrue an action for damages for breach of contract lies ...

What then is the measure of damages for breach of express warranty of quality? Watermeyer J answered the question by referring to *Victoria Falls & Transvaal Power Co Ltd* v *Consolidated Langlaagte Mines Ltd*,[369] to Pothier, and to *Hadley* v *Baxendale*[370] which are the leading authorities on the ordinary measure of damages, including consequential loss, where, on the ordinary principles, such loss is recoverable. Therefore, the general principles governing the assessment of damages for breach of contract are applicable.[371]

The decision in *Evans & Plows* v *Willis & Co* was not reached on the special rules relating to artificers or merchants:

> Molinaeus, De Eo Quod Interest, in sections 4, 5, 49 and 51, makes it clear that in the case of an express warranty the seller is liable for damages on breach of that warranty, even if he acted *bona fide*, and that this case of an express warranty by an ordinary person is additional to the admitted case of artificer and merchant who are liable on an express or implied warranty, and the case of the fraudulent seller who is liable without any warranty.

20.1.4 For improper working

With regard to warranties relating to the "proper working or functioning" of the thing sold, see 3.1.1 and 3.2.1 above. As stated above, in certain circumstances breach of an express warranty by the seller will entitle the purchaser to cancel the contract. A good example of the circumstances in which cancellation of the contract is competent is the case of *Small* v *Smith*.[372] A second-hand car was expressly warranted to be mechanically 100 per cent sound and to use no oil. In fact it used a considerable amount of oil. The court held that the aggrieved party was entitled to cancel the contract.

20.2 Actions in Delict (Tort)

In an action in delict the right enforced is a remedial or sanctioning right arising out of the breach of a duty owed by the defendant to the plaintiff, and usually consists in a claim to receive pecuniary compensation for harm suffered in consequence of the breach.[373] The elements of a delict are that there must be

[369] 1915 AD 1.
[370] (1854) 9 Ex 341: 156 ER 145.
[371] Kerr *Contract, Op. cit.* 353.
[372] *Small* v *Smith* 1954 (3) SA 434 (SWA).
[373] R.G. McKerron, *The Law of Delict: a treatise on the principles of liability for civil wrongs in the Law of South Africa.* (7th ed. Cape Town Juta, 1971) at 1.

intentional or negligent conduct (an act or omission) which is wrongful and causes harm to another, in other words, there must be fault, conduct, wrongfulness causation and harm. Fraudulent misrepresentation, negligent misstatements, unfair competition are but a few examples of delicts.

20.2.1 Availability for breach of warranty

The incorporation of a fraudulent misrepresentation (which is a delict) in a contract as a term does not confine the innocent party to a remedy for breach of contract. The innocent party may choose whether to sue on the delict or on the contract whether or not the measure of relief differs.[374]

However, breach of a contractual duty not to be negligent must be treated only as a breach of contract and will not support an action in delict, because the Aquilian action would not fit comfortably in the contractual setting).[375] Contract and delict must also be kept apart to the extent that a party which, while performing its contractual duty, injures a third party cannot rely on any contractual restriction of its liability.[376]

In certain circumstances an action in delict lies against a third party for inducing a party to a contract to commit a breach of it,[377] and for intentionally and wrongfully interfering with contractual rights.[378]

20.2.2 Action for breach of competition clause, for hiring of staff, for price dumping, for circulating negative information

Though the loss resulting from competition in trading is usually economic rather than physical, the danger of indeterminate liability is neutralised by the presence of intention as an element of all the established forms of unlawful competition.[379] The freedom to trade competitively upon which our economy is based, implies that it cannot be *prima facie* wrongful to harm another simply by competing with him. Something more is required. To be actionable the harm must result from the defendant's transgression of accepted norms of behaviour in trading. It is this element that transforms his competition with the plaintiff from the lawful into the unlawful, bringing the law's wrath upon him. So the central question in this field is: what forms of competition are wrongful?

The influence of Anglo-American law has led our courts to categorise certain common varieties of unlawful competition, such as passing-off and injurious falsehood, as causes of action having particular elements. This does not mean that they constitute "specific torts", or that liability is confined to these instances. A trader who complains of his rival's activities founds upon the Aquilian action. Therefore, in a case for which there is no precedent he is entitled to invoke the "broad and ample basis of the *lex Aquilia*" in support of his claim. A court required to draw the line between lawful and unlawful competition in a novel

[374] *Prima Toy Holdings (Pty) Ltd* v *Rosenberg* 1974 (2) SA 477 (C) at 484 H; see 1.3.2.3 above.

[375] *Lillicrap, Wassenaar and Partners* v *Pilkington Brothers (SA) (Pty) Ltd* 1985 (1) SA 475 (A).

[376] *Compass Motors Industries (Pty) Ltd* v *Callguard (Pty) Ltd* 1990 (2) SA 520 (W); Christie, *Op. cit.* at 589.

[377] *Atlas Organic Fertilizers (Pty) Ltd* v *Pikkewyn Ghwano (Pty) Ltd* 1981 (2) SA 173 (T).

[378] *Dantex Investment Holdings (Pty) Ltd* v *Brenner* 1989 (1) SA 390 (A).

[379] Boberg, *The Law of Delict,* (1984) at 149.

situation will invoke the general criterion of wrongfulness, seeking to give expression to the community's sense of fairness and honesty. And it is neither fair nor honest to filch the fruits of another's industry or expertise.[380]

Declining to define the limits of lawful competition, our courts have retained the flexibility to deal with whatever new schemes for the downfall of others the untiring imagination of the dishonest may devise. Thus, in appropriate circumstances, there may be delictual actions by one party against another based on unlawful competition,[381] misuse of confidential information,[382] stealing trade secrets,[383] injurious falsehood, in other words, circulating negative information or information disparaging of a trader's goods, service or business.[384] A company, it seems, can now sue for defamation for injury to its business reputation and it is not necessary for it to prove special damages.[385]

Insomuch as either *dolus* or *culpa* suffices for Aquilian liability, in principle there is no reason why an action for unlawful competition should not be founded upon negligence. Though there is no authority on the point, for most unlawful competition seems to be intentional, the recognition in principle of liability for negligent misstatements causing pure economic loss in *Administrateur, Natal* v *Trust Bank van Afrika Bpk*[386] has certainly smoothed the path of a plaintiff who complains of negligent injurious falsehood. At the same time, the gravity of the defendant's fault (ie whether he acted intentionally or only negligently) must remain a relevant policy factor in determining whether his competition is unreasonable and hence unlawful.[387]

The availability of an interdict, a very important remedy in this field, is not dependent upon fault. On the other hand, it does require wrongfulness, and the interference of which the plaintiff complains may not be wrongful unless it was culpable. Fault is, of course, a requirement of a claim for damages.

The delictual aspect of unlawful competition is but a segment of a much wider field. The statutory regulation of trading by instruments controlling monopolies and advertising, by the legislation governing patents, designs, trademarks and copyright, and by contractual arrangements, falls outside the scope of this book. Here we are concerned only with the common law delict of unlawful competition.[388]

20.3 More Warrantors

Where there is more than one person giving the warranty, the warrantor's liability in the event of a breach of warranty may be joint or joint and several, depending on the terms of the agreement (see 20.4 and 20.5 below).

[380] Boberg, *Op. cit.* at 149.
[381] *Stellenbosch Wine Trust Ltd* v *Oude Meester Group Ltd* 1972 (3) SA 152 (C), 1974 (1) SA 729 (A); *Rectifier & Communication Systems (Pty) Ltd* v *Harrison* 1981 (2) SA 283 (C); *Lorimar Productions Inc* v *Sterling Clothing Manufacturers (Pty) Ltd* 1981 (3) SA 1129 (T).
[382] *Knox D'Arcy Ltd and others* v *Jamieson and others* 1992 (3) SA 520 (WLD).
[383] *SA Historical Mint (Pty) Ltd* v *Sutcliffe* 1983 (2) SA 84 (C).
[384] *Atlas Organic Fertilizers (Pty) Ltd* v *Pikkewyn Ghwano (Pty) Ltd* 1981 (2) SA 173 (t) at 179.
[385] *Dhlomo* v *Natal Newspapers (Pty) Ltd* 1989 (1) SA 945 (A).
[386] 179 (3) SA 824 (A).
[387] Boberg, *Op. cit.* at 152.
[388] *Ibid.*

20.4 Joint Liability

The general principle of South African law relating to the liability of co-obligors and the rights of co-obligees is that, unless otherwise agreed upon, the liability is joint, and the rights are held in common. If, therefore, two or more persons incur a joint obligation, the general rule is that each is liable only for its share and not *in solidum*.[389]

The presumption that liability is joint and not joint and several is a strong one. Even where the obligation undertaken by the co-debtors is an indivisible one the presumption applies so that, despite the obligation not being capable of division and each co-debtor being liable for the full performance, in the event of damages being awarded for non-performance of the indivisible obligation, such damages will be awarded against each co-debtor only in proportion to its share.[390]

A joint debtor which has paid its share is discharged from liability, whatever the fate of the other joint debtors, and may protect itself from liability for non-performance by tendering payment of its share (Christie, 302). If one of the joint debtors has a good defence against the creditor's claim, or if the contract, as between it and the creditor, is voidable or void *ab initio* the liability of the other joint debtors will remain unaffected.[391]

Therefore, a defence such as misrepresentation or lack of contractual capacity may affect one joint debtor only, whereas a defence such as illegality will usually affect all joint debtors equally, unless the illegality is personal and applies to one of the contracting parties.[392]

Whether a joint debtor which has paid more than its share automatically has a right of recovery against its co-debtors which have benefited thereby is an open question.[393] If there are circumstances from which a tacit agreement can be inferred creating a right of contribution then the tacit agreement would form the basis of such a right. Otherwise the joint debtor which overpaid may rely on unjust enrichment to claim a contribution from the other joint debtors, which would necessitate an inquiry into the circumstances in which it came to overpay.[394]

20.5 Several Liability

Partners, co-parties to negotiable instruments and those on whom the contract clearly by express words or necessary implication, imposes liability *in solidum* are jointly and severally liable. Each is liable to the creditor for the full amount of the debt and the creditor can at its option claim the full debt or any lesser amount from any of them, provided the creditor does not recover in total more

389 *De Pass* v *The Colonial Government* (1886) (4) SC 383 at 390; *Tuckers* v *Carruthers* 1941 AD 251.

390 *Pocket's Holdings (Pvt) Ltd* v *Lobel's Holdings (Pvt) Ltd* 1966 (4) SA 238 (R) at 254 F; *Kistan* v *Komarasamy* 1941 NPD 56 at 62.

391 *Suburban Real Estate Ltd* v *Whall and Bocking* 1951 (3) SA 409 (C) at 413–4.

392 Christie, *Op. cit.* at 302.

393 *Koornklip Beleggings (Edms) Bpk* v *Allied Minerals Ltd* 1970 (1) SA 674 (C) at 677.

394 *Ibid.*

than the full amount of the debt, since by definition there is only one debt due (Christie, 303).

By electing to sue one debtor for the full amount, or more than one for equal or varying amounts, the creditor does not thereby commit itself to recovering from that debtor or those debtors alone and abandoning its rights to claim against the others.[395] Similarly, if the creditor receives less than the full amount of the debt from any one co-debtor it is not thereby debarred from claiming the balance from that debtor or the others.

If the creditor gives personal discharge to one of two co-debtors it discharges that co-debtor altogether and it discharges the other co-debtor to the extent to which such co-debtor would have had a claim for contribution against the debtor originally discharged. Thus, the *nexus* between the released debtor and the creditor disappears and the joint liability of the other co-debtors is reduced as a result of the compromise, by at least the whole amount of the released debtor's proportionate share, or if the amount paid by the latter is greater than that share, then by that amount. The reason for this reduction is that the common creditor has received such sum on account of the total debt and is not entitled to claim from the other co-debtors more than the balance.[396]

The creditor and one co-debtor may also enter into an agreement which has the effect of discharging the other co-debtors. Thus, a novation agreed between the creditor and one co-debtor may discharge the whole contract and therefore release all the other debtors.[397] It is also arguable that the co-debtors can take advantage of a reduction of the total debt arising from a right of set-off or *compensatio* that one of their number has against the creditor, even if the creditor elects not to sue that co-debtor.[398] Therefore, joint and several debtors may be able to raise a defence which destroys the creditor's claim wholly or in part against all of them, or one of them may be able to raise a defence which affects its liability only, in which case the liability of the other co-debtors remains.[399]

Where one of the co-debtors pays more than its share of the total debt it has an automatic right of contribution against the other co-debtors, and no cession of action is necessary.[400]

21. Defences

21.1 Acquisition Null and Void

A "contract" may be void *ab initio* on a number of grounds recognised by the law, and, where it is so void, the "transaction" will have no legal consequences. If either party has performed it will be entitled to claim restitution of its performance. A brief discussion of a few of these grounds follows.

[395] *Shillings CC* v *Cronje* 1988 (2) SA 402 (A) at 422 B; *Ibid.*
[396] *Dwyer* v *Goldseller* 1906 TS 126 at 129; *Boyce* v *Bloem* 1960 (3) SA 855 (T) at 857; *Op. cit.* at 304.
[397] *Mgweba* v *Hlepa* (1894) EDC 11.
[398] *Ibid.* Wessels. *Op. cit.* at paras. 1533–6; *African Guarantee and Indemnity Co Ltd* v *Thorpe* 1933 AD 330 at 338.
[399] *Shillings CC* v *Cronje* 1988 (2) SA 402 (A) at 422; Christie, *Op. cit.* at 305.
[400] *Dwyer* v *Goldseller* 1906 TS 126; 305.

21.1.1 Statutory illegality

No useful purpose would be served by endeavouring to list the very many statutes and statutory regulations and by-laws that may render a contract illegal.[401] The legislature may make its intentions plain by enacting that any contract which contravenes the relevant statutory requirement shall be null and void or of no force and effect. The wording of each statutory enactment will have to be interpreted and if such language is used it will normally be given its straightforward meaning and the contract will be treated as non-existent, with the corollary that it cannot be subsequently ratified nor its voidness renounced or waived.[402]

Even apparently unambiguous words such as the contract shall be "null and void" or "of no force and effect" give rise to some difficulty, for it may mean that the contract is voidable at the option of the party belonging to the class for whose benefit the statute was intended;[403] or that such a party may waive his statutory benefit unless public interests are concerned;[404] or that, although unenforceable, it might be given in evidence wherever material;[405] or that it is voidable at the option of either party provided it is not taking advantage of its own wrong;[406] or that it is not void against the parties to it, but only to their successors, for whose benefit the statute was intended.[407]

Where a contract contravenes some provision of a statute which does not expressly say the contract shall be void, the question is whether such an intention is to be imputed to the legislature. The question often presents itself in the form of whether the statutory provision is peremptory, in which case a contract which contravenes it may be void, or merely directory, in which case the validity of the contract which contravenes it is unaffected.[408]

Depending on the circumstances of the case and any relevant statutes which might have a bearing on the transaction in question, the parties may negotiate the terms of a warranty dealing with compliance with certain statutory provisions, such as those contained in the Companies Act or in the various statutes dealing with taxation, by either party. Although contravention of the statutory provision may or may not render the contract void (or voidable), such contravention may result in certain expenses, penalties or fines being incurred by either of the parties. In such a case the parties may agree that the warrantor who fails to comply with the relevant statutory requirements and is in breach of his warranty in respect thereof, will indemnify the other party in respect of any claims arising from such breach.

[401] *Op. cit.* at 409.

[402] *Neugarten* v *Standard Bank of South Africa Ltd* 1989 (1) SA 797 (A) at 813 H–I; *Op. cit.* at 409.

[403] *Brown* v *Vlok* 1925 AD 26 at 60.

[404] *Bezuidenhout* v *AA Mutual Insurance Association Ltd* 1978 (1) SA 703 (A) at 710.

[405] *Moser* v *Milton* 1945 AD 517 at 526.

[406] *Neugarten* v *Standard Bank of South Africa Ltd* 1989 (1) SA 797 (A).

[407] *Messenger of the Magistrates' Court Durban* v *Pillay* 1952 (3) SA 678 (A) at 682 H; *Op. cit.* at 410.

[408] *Ibid. Sutton* v *Scheepers* 1932 AD 165; *Standard Bank Ltd* v *Van Rhyn* 1925 AD 266; *Schierhout* v *Minister of Justice* 1926 AD 99.

In these circumstances it is necessary for the court to determine the intention of the legislature, and where the legislature is content with a penalty laid down against those who contravene the act, then the act itself may not be null and void.[409] For example, the seller of a second-hand motor vehicle is required to obtain a certificate of fitness (section 13 *bis* of Ordinance 17 of 1931(T)). Non-compliance with this requirement does not affect the validity of the contract.[410] Furthermore, this requirement is not an implied term of the contract.[411] The contract, therefore, is left unaffected whether or not there is compliance with this type of obligation.[412]

21.1.2 Common law illegality

The South African courts have the power to treat as void and to refuse in any way to recognise contracts and transactions which are against public policy or contrary to good morals. It is a power not to be hastily or rashly exercised, but once it is clear that any arrangement is against public policy, the courts will not be hesitant to declare such an arrangement void.[413] Although there are recognised categories of contracts which are contrary to public policy, such as contracts which are injurious to the State, contracts which are injurious to the administration of justice, contracts encouraging crime, delict and other unlawful acts, contracts injurious to the institution of marriage, contracts curtailing the freedom of testation (*pacta successoria*), certain restraints of trade and gambling, the list is not exhaustive.[414]

The main result of common law illegality is the unenforceability of the contract.[415] The principle of the unenforceability of illegal contracts is contained in the maxim "from a base consideration no action arises" (*ex turpi causa non oritur actio*). Unenforceability means that a claim for specific performance of the contract will not be granted,[416] nor a claim for payment, nor damages for breach,[417] nor aedilition relief, nor any other claim to enforce rights conferred by the contract, but in a proper case a declaration that the contract is null and void may be claimed.[418]

21.1.3 Contract cannot be validated

Section 2(1) of the Alienation of Land Act, 68 of 1981, provides that no alienation of land shall be of any force or effect unless it is contained in a deed of alienation signed by the parties thereto or by their agents acting on their written authority. The effect of non-compliance with the requirements of section 2(1) is that the contract shall not "be of any force or effect". It is trite law that

409 *Standard Bank* v *Estate van Rhyn* 1925 AD 266 at 274.
410 *Pottie* v *Kotze* 1954 (3) SA 719 (A).
411 *Pottie* v *Kotze* 1954 (3) SA 719 (A) at 727 A; *Pema* v *Rasmussen* 1959 (1) SA 196 (T).
412 *Cf Eastern Transvaal Garage* v *Harland* 1950(2) SA 778 (T); *General Merchandise Corp (Pty) Ltd* v *Osman* 1951 (4) SA 524 (T) 528.
413 *Eastwood* v *Stepstone* 1902 TS 294 at 302; *Kuhn* v *Karp* 1948 (4) SA 825 (T) at 838–40; *Sasfin (Pty) Ltd* v *Beukes* 1989 (1) SA 1 (A) at 9B.
414 *Op. cit.* at 419–455.
415 *Op. cit.* at 466.
416 *Essop* v *Abdullah* 1988 (1) SA 424 (A).
417 *Bobrow* v *Meyerowitz* 1947 (2) SA 885 (T).
418 *Raynath* v *Jokoy Orie* 1949 (1) SA 570 (D).

non-compliance with the provisions of section 2(1) render the transaction of no force or effect or void *ab initio*, and can under no circumstances confer any right of action.[419] So neither party can enforce the informal contract against the other, even if it has fully performed its part of the contract, as by effecting transfer of the land.[420]

However, section 28 of the Alienation of Land Act provides that if the informal contract has been fully carried out and the land has been transferred to the purchaser, the alienation shall in all respects be valid *ab initio*. On the other hand, if the informal contract has been partly carried out (which may include performance in full by one party but not the other), then each party is entitled to recover that which it has performed, and in addition the purchaser may recover interest on any payment it made and reasonable compensation for necessary expenditure on preservation of the property and for improvements. The seller may recover reasonable compensation for the purchaser's occupation, use or enjoyment and compensation for damage.[421]

21.1.4 Absolute force

The effect of absolute force (*vis absoluta*) on a contract, is that the "contract" is void *ab initio* (Christie, 367; see 10.5.1 above).

21.1.5 Fundamental unilateral mistake

A unilateral mistake which is fundamental in the sense that because of its existence agreement is so completely lacking that it is impossible to say there is any contract at all, will render the contract void *ab initio*.[422]

21.1.6 Mutual mistake

The result of a mutual mistake, namely the true non-correspondence of offer and acceptance, is that there is no contract at all, and the "contract" is void *ab initio*.[423]

21.1.7 Common mistake and impossibility

Common mistake will render the contract void *ab initio* only if it leads the parties to make a "contract" which is impossible of performance, such as a sale of a thing which is extinct.[424]

21.1.8 Misrepresentation inducing fundamental mistake

The effect of a misrepresentation, whether innocent, negligent or fraudulent, may be to induce in the mind of the innocent party a mistake of so fundamental a nature that his apparent assent to the contract is, in truth, not assent at all. In such a case, for lack of assent there is no agreement and therefore no contract, in other words, the "contract" is void *ab initio*.[425]

419 *Wilken* v *Kohler* 1913 AD 135 at 143; *Op. cit.* at 142; and see 2.2.4.6 above.
420 *Botha* v *Kelder* 1948 (3) SA 248 (T).
421 *C D Development Co. (East Rand) (Pty) Ltd* v *Novick* 1979 (2) SA 546 (C); *Op. cit.* at 143.
422 *Op cit.* at 391; see 10.2.1 above.
423 *Op. cit.* at 397; see 10.2.2 above.
424 *Op. cit.* at 398; see 10.2.3 above.
425 *Allen* v *Sixteen Stirling Investments (Pty) Ltd* 1974 (4) SA 164 (D) at 169–171; *Op. cit.* at 344–345; and see 10.2.1.2 above.

21.1.9 Undue influence inducing fundamental mistake

The effect of undue influence, as with fraud, is to make the contract void *ab initio* only if the influence induced in the mind of the party seeking relief such a fundamental mistake that his apparent assent to the contract is in truth not assent at all. In all other cases the contract is voidable at the option of the party influenced.[426]

21.1.10 Impossible condition

A condition which is impossible of performance renders the whole contract a nullity because the event can never happen.[427] Physical impossibility will not destroy the contract unless it is absolute. Thus, a condition which is impossible for the promissee or prommissor to fulfil, but which could be fulfilled by someone else, is effective.

21.1.11 Vagueness

The "void for vagueness" cases may be classified into four classes. Firstly, those cases which exemplify the maxim "a promise is unenforceable which is dependent on a condition which in fact reserves an unlimited option to the promissor". Secondly, where the vague and uncertain language justifies the implication that the parties were never *ad idem*. Thirdly, where there is no concluded contract as in the case of continuing negotiations broken off in the middle. In these three classes the element of uncertainty is fatal to the existence of the so-called contract; in the first class because there is uncertainty as to whether the promissor will ever acknowledge the existence of an obligation; in the second there is uncertainty as to what he has acknowledged as being his obligation, and in the third class there is uncertainty as to the subject matter which has still to be agreed. The fourth class concerns those cases where the unspecified details of the contract are questions of fact capable of determination by evidence.[428]

21.2 Acquisition Voidable for Vitiating Elements

It may happen that certain elements of a contract are lacking so that, although the contract is not void *ab initio*, it is voidable at the instance of either or one of the parties. The following is a discussion of some of these vitiating elements.

21.2.1 Unilateral mistake

Where one party to the contract is mistaken the distinction between a "material" and a "fundamental" mistake is important in dealing with the question whether the contract is voidable or void *ab initio*. A mistake may be material in the way that agreement is not so completely lacking, but is sufficiently lacking to make the agreement voidable at the instance of either party (see 10.2.1.2 above).

21.2.2 Common mistake

Parties who are commonly mistaken are by definition *ad idem*, so that a common mistake will only render the contract void *ab initio* if it leads the parties to make

[426] *Preller* v *Jordaan* 1956 (1) SA 483 (A); *Op. cit.* at 380; see 10.5.2 above.
[427] *Op. cit.* at 159.
[428] *Levenstein* v *Levenstein* 1955 (3) SA 615 (SR) at 619; *Op. cit.* at 111.

a contract which is impossible of performance.[429] If the contract is not impossible of performance, then an agreement founded upon a common mistake, which mistake is impliedly treated as a condition which must exist in order to bring the agreement into operation, can be set aside, formally if necessary, or treated as set aside and as invalid without any process or proceedings to do so.[430]

A common mistake of law has no effect on the validity of a contract,[431] though either party may apply for rectification of the contract.[432]

21.2.3 Misrepresentation

A party which has been induced to enter into a contract by the misrepresentation of an existing fact is entitled to rescind the contract provided the misrepresentation was material, was intended to induce that party to enter into the contract and did so induce that party.[433] It is not necessary to prove that the misrepresentation was fraudulent in order to invalidate the contract, and the innocent party is equally entitled to rescind whether the misrepresentation was fraudulent or innocent.[434]

If the effect of a misrepresentation, whether fraudulent or innocent, is to induce in the mind of the innocent party a mistake of so fundamental a nature that his apparent consent to the contract is in truth not assent at all, then the contract would be void *ab initio*. But if the mistake induced as aforesaid is only material, the contract would be voidable.[435]

21.2.4 Duress

Force, or the threat of force, may induce fear in the mind of the victim. Because a person who is induced by legally significant fear can properly be said to have consented, the contract is voidable at his option, not void *ab initio* like the contract of the person whose hand is physically forced.[436]

21.2.5 Undue influence

The effect of undue influence induced in the mind of the party seeking relief is such a fundamental mistake that his apparent assent to the contract is, in truth, not assent at all. In all other cases the contract is voidable at the option of the party influenced.[437] If the contract is voidable the position of the party influenced is the same as that of a party induced to contract by a misrepresentation, in other words, he must elect within a reasonable time whether to rescind the contract or to stand by it. He cannot both approbate and reprobate.[438]

429 *Op. cit.* at 398; see 10.2.3 above.
430 *Dickinson Motors (Pty Ltd* v *Oberholzer* 1952 (1) SA 443 (A) at 450; *Op. cit.* at 399.
431 *Sampson* v *Union and Rhodesia Wholesale Ltd* 1929 AD 468 at 481.
432 *Mouton* v *Hanekom* 1959 (3) SA 35 (A); *Op. cit.* at 401.
433 *Novick* v *Comair Holdings Ltd* 1979 (2) SA 116 (W) at 149–150; *Op. cit.* at 325; see 1.3.2.3 above.
434 *Lamb* v *Walters* 1926 AD 358 at 364; *Ibid.*
435 *Trollip* v *Jordaan* 1961 (1) SA 238 (A) at 252 H; *Allen* v *Sixteen Stirling Investments (Pty) Ltd* 1974 (4) SA 164 (D) at 169–71; *Op. cit.* at 344–5; see 10.2.1.2 above.
436 *Op. cit.* at 367; see 10.5.1 above.
437 *Preller* v *Jordaan* 1956 (1) SA 483 (A) at 496; *Op. cit.* at 380; see 10.5.2 above.
438 *Armstrong* v *Magid* 1937 AD 260 at 273–4; *Ibid.*

Undue influence brought to bear by a third party gives the party influenced no right to rescind unless the other party to the contract was aware at the time the contract was made that undue influence had been exercised.[439]

21.3 Creation of an Only Apparent Contract

In order to decide whether a contract exists one looks first for the agreement by consent of two or more parties. Such agreement may be regarded as the foundation of contract.[440] If there is no true subjective agreement between the parties there will be no contract unless the English law doctrine of quasi-mutual assent applies. The doctrine of quasi-mutual assent or an only apparent contract is dealt with in Section 10 above.

21.4 Conditions Precedent and Subsequent

A condition precedent, also referred to as a suspensive condition, suspends the operation of all or some of the obligations flowing from the contract until the occurrence of a future uncertain event, whereas a condition subsequent, also referred to as a resolutive condition, terminates all or some of the obligations flowing from the contract upon the occurrence of a future uncertain event.[441]

The correct classification may be important in order to decide the rights and duties of the parties.

21.4.1 Conditions precedent

There is authority for the proposition that a contract of sale subject to a condition precedent that has not yet been fulfilled is not a sale.[442] The better view though is that the contract is binding immediately upon its conclusion and that what may be suspended by a condition is the resultant obligation or its eligible content.[443]

In a sale subject to a suspensive condition, delivery of the *res vendita* before the fulfilment of the condition does not pass ownership to the purchaser, so the seller can vindicate from a third party, the purchaser cannot pledge the *res vendita*, nor does it pass to the liquidator of the purchaser in insolvency and the risk remains with the seller.[444] The purchaser may, although it does not yet have ownership, let the *res vendita* out on hire, provided the purchaser does not thereby prejudice the seller in regard to the enforcement of the seller's rights.[445] The seller who has not delivered may not dispose of the *res vendita* to a third party.

If the effect of a sale subject to a suspensive condition is that the contract of sale cannot be regarded as a sale until the fulfilment of the condition then statutes making a contract of sale (or other disposition) of land unenforceable unless it

[439] *Ibid.*

[440] *Op. cit.* at 10.

[441] *Design and Planning Service* v *Kruger* 1974(1) SA 689 (T) at 695C; *Op. cit.* at 161.

[442] *Op. cit.* at 163.

[443] *Odendaalsrust Municipality* v *New Nigel Estate Gold Mining Co Ltd* 1948 (2) SA 656 (O) at 667.

[444] *Martin and McElney* v *Savory* 1904 TS 180; *Roos* v *Ross & Co* 1917 CPD 303; *Op. cit.* at 164.

[445] *Leo* v *Loots* 1909 TS 366 at 372.

complies with the prescribed formalities do not apply to a sale or disposition subject to a suspensive condition.[446] The authorities for the aforementioned principle constitute a departure from the common law, which regarded a sale subject to a suspensive condition as a sale *ab initio*, and has been firmly disapproved of by the Appellate Division.[447]

21.4.2 Conditions subsequent

Pending the fulfilment of a resolutive condition the contract is fully operative, and the parties must perform their obligations.[448] Therefore, in a contract of sale subject to a resolutive condition delivery of the *res vendita* passes ownership to the purchaser, so a sale by the purchaser to a third party will pass ownership to the third party and the original seller will have no right of vindication.[449] The *res vendita* may also be attached in execution by the purchaser's creditors, but not by the seller's creditors, and will pass to the purchaser's liquidator in insolvency, and the risk and profit pass to the purchaser.[450]

The parties to a contract of sale subject to a resolutive condition are bound by the contract not to do anything inconsistent with the resolutive condition. For example, the seller could apply for an interdict restraining the purchaser from selling the *res vendita* to a third party, because if carried through it would deprive the original seller of the *spes* of recovering the *res vendita* if the resolutive condition were fulfilled. If the seller were too late to stop such a sale the seller would be entitled to such damages as it could prove, for breach of a necessarily implied term that the purchaser would not do anything inconsistent with the resolutive condition.[451]

21.5 Novation

Novation means replacing an existing obligation by a new one, the existing obligation being thereby discharged.[452] Although the effect of novation is to extinguish a debt "as if by payment" it does not constitute payment, but discharges the debtor from the original obligation to pay.[453] The dispute which usually arises between the parties is whether the first agreement can still be enforced.

As a generic term for replacing an existing obligation by a new one, novation includes voluntary novation, compulsory novation, compromise and delegation.[454]

21.5.1 Voluntary novation

An existing obligation may be replaced by a new contract between the same parties by agreement. Voluntary novation, therefore, has its origin in contract and

[446] *Op. cit.* at 158.
[447] *Tuckers Land and Development Corporation (Pty) Ltd* v *Strydom* 1984 (1) SA 1 (A).
[448] *Badenhorst* v *Van Rensburg* 1986 (3) SA 769 (A).
[449] *McHardy* v *Olifant* 1905 ORC 42.
[450] *Op. cit.* at 164.
[451] *Op. cit.* at 165.
[452] *Op. cit.* at 536.
[453] *Market Furnishers* v *Reddy* 1966 (3) SA 550 (NPD) at 553D.
[454] *Ibid.*

is essentially a matter of intention and consensus. When parties novate they intend to replace a valid contract by another valid contract.[455] The intention and consensus that must be sought is a common intention to cancel the old contract so that it can no longer be enforced and no longer exists, and replace it with a new one.[456]

There is a presumption against novation because it involves a waiver of existing rights. Thus, a creditor who has rights under an existing contract and then enters into another connected contract will be presumed to intend rather to strengthen and confirm his existing rights than to waive them and accept his rights under the new contract in substitution.[457]

The onus of proving novation therefore lies on the party who asserts that it has taken place,[458] and he must specifically plead it.[459] Where he cannot prove an express intention to novate he must prove a tacit intention, and the intention must be clearly proved and must itself be a clear and unequivocal intention to novate.[460]

21.5.2 Compulsory novation

A compulsory novation happens when an existing obligation is replaced by a judgment. It takes place by operation of law and arises out of judicial proceedings between parties whose rights and obligations are in issue between them.[461] A judgment differs from a voluntary novation to the extent to which it novates the contract. The consequences of a judgment can thus differ from case to case. For example, a judgment for cancellation of a contract and for damages will novate the entire contract, but where judgment for specific performance is granted to one party the judgment may be regarded not as novating the contract, but as strengthening or reinforcing the rights arising out of the contract. Thus, a plaintiff who has a judgment for specific performance in his favour is not precluded from suing in another action for cancellation and damages, in lieu of the decree of specific performance.[462]

A compulsory novation, when it does take place, does not release sureties so that when a judgment is obtained against a principal debtor and one surety the creditor may still proceed against the other co-sureties, whose obligations are not compulsorily novated by the judgment.[463]

455 *Swadif (Pty) Ltd* v *Dyke* 1978 (1) SA 928 (A) at 940; *Op. cit.* at 537.

456 *French* v *Sterling Finance Corpn (Pty) Ltd* 1961 (4) SA 732 (A) at 736 F; *Ibid.*

457 *Van Coppenhagen* v *Van Coppenhagen* 1947 (1) SA 576 (T) at 579; *Marendaz* v *Marendaz* 1953 (4) SA 218 (C) at 227; *Barclays National Bank Ltd* v *Smith* 1975 (4) SA 675 (D) at 683 C; *Woolfsons Credit (Pty) Ltd* v *Holdt* 1977 (3) SA 720 (N) at 724 F; *Op. cit.* at 444.

458 *Marendaz* v *Marendaz* 1953 (4) SA 218 (C) at 226–7; *Op. cit.* at 445,

459 *Stassen* v *Nel* 1912 CPD 284.

460 *Woolfsons Credit (Pty) Ltd* v *Holdt* 1977 (3) SA 720 (N) at 724 F.

461 *Swadif (Pty) Ltd* v *Dyke* 1978 (1) SA 928 (A) at 940–1; *Op. cit.* at 542.

462 *Trust Bank of Africa Ltd* v *Dhooma* 1970 (3) SA 304 (N) at 310; *Swadif (Pty) Ltd* v *Dyke* 1978 (1) SA 928 (A) at 944; *Jordan and Co Ltd* v *Bulsara* 1992 (4) SA 457 ECD at 461 D; *Op. cit.* at 543.

463 *Skelton* v *Shelvoke and Smith* (1904) 21 SC 664; *Rand Bank Ltd* v *De Jager* 1982 (3) SA 418 (C); *Op. cit.* at 544.

21.5.3 Compromise

A compromise occurs when disputed obligations are settled and replaced by a contract. It is a form of novation differing from ordinary novation in that the obligations novated by the compromise must previously have been disputed or uncertain, the essence of compromise being the final settlement by agreement of the dispute or uncertainty.[464] A compromise is thus an ordinary agreement whereby the parties settle a dispute which exists between them and is therefore governed by the common law principles which are generally applicable to contracts.

There is no authoritative statement that fraud and *iustus error* are the only grounds upon which an agreement of compromise can be challenged. Therefore, the principle that a contractual obligation can be extinguished by impossibility of performance applies to agreements of compromise.[465]

The effect of a compromise is the same as *res iudicata* on a judgment given by consent, namely, it is an absolute bar to action on the cause of action compromised. What claims were and were not included is ascertainable from the pleadings if the compromise settled an action, and from the terms of the compromise interpreted in accordance with the general rules of interpretation in any other case.[466]

The effect of repudiation or breach of the compromise agreement will depend on the nature of the agreement. In the case of a compromise not subject to a suspensive or resolutive condition the action must be brought on the compromise and there can be no question of returning to the original contract. If the compromise of an action is not fully complied with, the remedy is not to continue with the previous action but to institute a new action on the compromise, unless the defendant raises no objection to the former course. But a party who challenges the validity of the compromise is not obliged first to bring an action to set it aside before suing on the original cause of action. A plaintiff may sue on the original cause of action and leave it for the defendant to plead the compromise as a defence, unless in the circumstances the claim is frivolous or vexatious.[467]

21.5.4 Delegation

Delegation is a form of novation by which, by agreement between all concerned, a third party is introduced as debtor in substitution for the original debtor, who is discharged.[468] Therefore, the debtor is replaced by a third party but the creditor remains the same.

The creditor, the original debtor and the debtor proposed in his place must all be parties to the new contract.[469] The creditor therefore has to agree to accept the new debtor in place of the old. After a valid delegation the creditor can sue the

[464] *Ibid.*
[465] *Blou Bul Boorkontrakteurs* v *McLachlan* 1991 (4) SA 283 (T).
[466] *Op. cit.* at 550.
[467] *Ibid.*
[468] *Op. cit.* at 551.
[469] *Van Achterberg* v *Walters* 1950 (3) SA 734 (T) at 745.

new but not the original debtor.[470] The onus is on the party alleging delegation to prove it. Thus, if the creditor sues the third party he must prove that the third party has been introduced as substitute debtor by delegation, but if the creditor sues the original debtor it is for the original debtor to prove that he has been released by delegation.[471]

21.5.5 Cession

A cession is not properly regarded as a novation. It involves the substitution of a new creditor (the cessionary) for the original creditor (the cedent), the debtor remaining the same. The consent of the debtor is not always required to effect a valid cession and the cession does not replace the original agreement. The cessionary sues the debtor on the original contract.[472]

Notice to the debtor is not necessary but it is advisable for the cessionary to give it or ensure that it is given because only then does it become the debtor's duty to pay the cessionary, not the cedent (Christie, 556). A debtor who pays the cedent after notice of the cession remains liable to the cessionary, but a debtor who pays the cedent in good faith without notice of the cession is discharged, and so is a debtor in whose favour a set-off against the cedent operates before he has had notice of the cession.[473] Notice of the cession means knowledge, from whatever source obtained, but partial knowledge is insufficient provided the payment to the cedent was made in good faith.[474] Registration of the cession in the Deeds Office is deemed to be notice.[475] A debtor who has paid the cedent bears the onus of proving that at the time of payment he had no notice of the cession. It is unnecessary for the cessionary to allege or prove the giving of notice.[476]

21.5.6 Combined cession and delegation

South African law has no single term of art to describe the process by which a third party, by agreement of all concerned, steps into the shoes of one of the parties to a contract and replaces that party entirely both as creditor and debtor.[477] Stepping into another's shoes involves acquiring that party's rights, which can be done by cession without the debtor's consent (in most cases), and undertaking that party's obligations, which can be done by delegation with (or without) the creditor's consent (see 21.5.4 and 21.5.5 above). Even in the absence of the necessary consent, the contract between a party to the original contract and the party stepping in may be enforceable.[478]

A partial substitution may take place without the other party's consent when there is no evidence that the rights acquired by the party wishing to cede those

[470] *Op. cit.* at 552.
[471] *Desai* v *Inman & Co* 1971 (1) SA 43 (N) at 51.
[472] *Op. cit.* at 553.
[473] *Pillay* v *Harichand* 1976 (2) SA 681 (D); *Agricultural and Industrial Mechanisation (Vereeniging) (Pty) Ltd* v *Lombard* 1974 (3) SA 485 (O); *Op. cit.* at 557.
[474] *Brook* v *Jones* 1964 (1) SA 765 (N) at 767.
[475] *Barclays Bank (DC & O)* v *Riverside Dried Fruit Co (Pty) Ltd* 1949 (1) SA 937 (C) at 945.
[476] *Trust Bank van Afrika Bpk* v *Oosthuizen* 1962 (2) SA 307 (T).
[477] *Op. cit.* at 561.
[478] *MTK Saagmeule (Pty) Ltd* v *Killyman Estates (Pty) Ltd* 1980 (3) SA 1 (A).

rights that they have to the contract were intended to be exercised by him personally (in other words, it involves *delectus personae*), and a third party takes cession of that party's rights and undertakes that party's obligations but the cedent remains responsible for the proper performance of those obligations.[479]

21.6 Impossibility not due to Debtor's Fault

A contract is void *ab initio* if at the time of its inception its performance is impossible or if at any time thereafter its performance becomes impossible.[480] The English doctrine of frustration and the English rule that supervening impossibility does not excuse the non-performance of a contractual obligation, subject to a number of exceptions, does not apply in South African law.[481]

In applying the principle that supervening impossibility discharges the contract, "impossibility" is given the same meaning as it is given when initial impossibility is under consideration. First, the impossibility must be absolute as opposed to probable. The mere likelihood that performance will prove impossible is not sufficient to destroy the contract.[482] Second, the impossibility must be absolute as opposed to relative. Thus, if A promises something which, in general, can be done, but which A cannot do, then A is liable on the contract. Third, the impossibility must not be the fault of either party. A party who has caused the impossibility cannot take advantage of it and so will be liable on the contract.[483] Fourth, the principle must give way to the contrary common intention of the parties.

This intention may be expressed, as when a seller warrants the quantity or quality of the *res vendita*. If the quality or quantity is not as it was promised to be, the seller will be liable for breach of its promise or for its false misrepresentation if fraudulent or negligent.[484] The common intention of the parties may be implied, as in the case of a sale of property belonging to a third party. The seller impliedly undertakes to deliver the property or to pay damages if it is unable to do so.[485] Thus, the implication that the party which has promised to perform has accepted the risk that performance might prove impossible and that it will be liable for non-performance if it does will be drawn when the impossibility was contemplated by the parties at the time of contracting and no provision for it was made in the contract.[486]

21.7 Force Majeure

As stated above (see 21.6) when a contract is or becomes impossible of performance it is void, for the authorities are clear that if a person is prevented

[479] *Op. cit.* at 562.
[480] *Peters, Flamman and Co* v *Kokstad Municipality* 1919 AD 427 at 434–5; *Op. cit.* at 563.
[481] *Bayley* v *Harwood* 1953 (3) SA 239 (T) at 244 D.
[482] *Heyneke* v *Abercrombie* 1974 (3) SA 338 (T) at 345 F; *Op. cit.* at 107.
[483] *Theron Ltd* v *Gross* 1929 CPD 345.
[484] *Op. cit.* at 108.
[485] *Frye's (Pty) Ltd* v *Ries* 1957 (3) SA 575 (A) at 581.
[486] *Wilson* v *Smith* 1956 (C) SA 393 (W) at 396 D; *Ibid.*

from performing his contract by *vis maior* or *casus fortuitous*, he is discharged from liability.[487] For the purposes of this branch of the law there is no necessity to distinguish between *vis maior* and *casus fortuitous*, which between them include any happening, whether due to natural causes or human agency, that is unforeseeable with reasonable foresight and unavoidable with reasonable care.[488]

There is nothing to prevent the parties making special provision in their contract for happenings that would otherwise discharge the contract and excuse non-performance. By mentioning the possibility they may have taken the unforeseeability out of it and by making provision for it they may have taken the unavoidability out of it, so it no longer falls within the rule.

Interruption by *vis maior* or *casus fortuitous* of a contract requiring continuity of performance entitles the other party either to cancel the contract or accept the reduced performance in exchange for a reduced counter-performance. This option only arises if the interruption continues or is likely to continue for an unreasonably long time. What is an unreasonably long time may be ascertained from the nature of the contract and the surrounding circumstances.[489] It should be noted that if, in such a case, the contract does not continue it has been terminated by (justified) cancellation by the party entitled to the option, and has not been terminated by operation of law.[490]

21.8 Set-Off

Set-off or compensation or *compensatio* is a method by which contractual and other debts may be extinguished. Set-off comes into effect when two parties are reciprocally indebted to each other: if the debts are equal, both are discharged; if they are unequal, the smaller is discharged and the larger is reduced by the amount of the smaller. Set-off may be regarded as a form of payment, and even as the equivalent of payment in cash.[491]

There are two views of when the set-off takes effect. The few cases which express the view that set-off does not occur unless the defendant claims it, are unanimous in holding that, once claimed, it operates retrospectively with effect from the time the compensating debts came into existence. The overwhelming weight of authority, however, expresses the view that set-off is automatic when the debts are mutually in existence and has to be pleaded and proved only to inform the court that it has occurred.[492]

A defendant is not obliged to raise every available defence to a claim, and if he does not plead set-off and judgment is given against him he may rely on the set-off against the judgment debt and if necessary apply to stay execution on

487 *Peters, Flamman and Co* v *Kokstad Municipality* 1919 AD 427 at 435.

488 *Spolander* v *Ward* 1940 CPD 24 at 30–2; *Op. cit.* at 565.

489 *Niemand* v *Okapi Investments (Edms) Bpk* 1983 (4) SA 762 (T).

490 *Beretta* v *Rhodesia Railways Ltd* 1947 (2) SA 1075 (SR) at 1081.

491 *Joint Municipal Pension Fund (Tvl)* v *Pretoria Municipal Pension Fund* 1969 (2) SA 78 (T); *SWA Amalgameerde Afslaers (Edms) Bpk* v *Louw* 1956 (l) SA 346 (A) at 354; *Op. cit.* at 566.

492 *Great North Farms (Edms) Bpk* v *Ras* 1972 (4) SA 7 (T); *Schierhout* v *Union Government* 1926 AD 286 at 289–90; *Ibid.*

it.[493] If the judgment debtor lets this opportunity pass he can pursue his claim by separate action.[494]

The parties may also contract out of the operation of set-off, such as where the parties agree to exchange cheques for the full amounts of their respective indebtedness to each other. The effect of this method of doing business is to exclude the operation of set-off.[495]

The law requires that a debt which it is desired to oppose by way of set-off must be of a liquidated nature. It need not be liquid in the sense in which that word is now used in South African practice. The debt, if not admitted by the other side, must be capable of easy and speedy proof. A debt is liquidated when it is evident that it is due, and to what amount. Thus a disputed debt cannot be opposed in compensation unless the person who opposes it has proof at hand, and is in a position to justify his claim promptly and summarily.[496] The concept that the debt must be capable of "easy and speedy proof " is rather elastic and leaves the court some discretion in deciding whether a particular debt can be set off.[497]

A defendant whose claim against the plaintiff cannot be set off because it is not liquidated should bring a claim in reconvention and take advantage of rule 22(4) of the Uniform Rules of Court, which permits him in his plea to ask that judgment in convention be postponed until judgment in reconvention.[498] This procedure may be adopted by a surety provided his claim in reconvention is concerned with the nature, validity or existence of the principal debt.[499]

The debts must be not only liquidated but due, because set-off is equivalent to payment and a debtor cannot be required to pay until the debt is due. It makes no difference whether the debt is not due because the time for payment has not arrived, or because it is contingent or subject to a suspensive condition that has not been fulfilled. Set-off cannot come into effect until, or relate back to a time before, both debts are due.[500]

A debt which has become prescribed since the set off occurred has already been set off by operation of law, so the running out of time for prescription is immaterial. A debt that is already prescribed before the necessary mutuality of debts arises could not, under the common law, be set off, and section 10(3) of the Prescription Act 68 of 1969 does not alter this rule.[501] Section 10(3) of the Prescription Act provides that payment of a prescribed debt shall be regarded as payment of a debt.

493 *The Government* v *Regna-Adwel Business Machines Africa (Pty) Ltd* 1970 (2) SA 428 (T) at 433 F.
494 *Op. cit.* at 567.
495 *Herrigel* v *Bon Roads Construction (Pty) Ltd* 1980 (4) SA 669 (SWA); *Ibid.*
496 *Treasurer-General* v *Van Vuren* 1905 TS 582 at 589.
497 *Trinity Engineering (Pvt) Ltd* v *Anglo-African Shipping Co (Pvt) Ltd* 1986 (1) SA 700 (ZS) at 702–703.
498 *Op. cit.* at 569.
499 *Standard Bank of SA Ltd* v *SA Fire Equipment (Pty) Ltd* 1984 (2) SA 693 (C).
500 Christie *Ibid.*
501 *Op. cit.* at 570.

21.9 State Interventions

An "act of State" may qualify as one of the circumstances contemplated by the concepts *vis maior* and *casus fortuitous* (see 21.6 and 21.7 above). Thus, legislation subsequent to the making of the contract, making performance illegal either absolutely or without a specified consent which has been refused will qualify, as will refusal of a statutory consent,[502] but not obedience to a ministerial directive given without statutory authority.[503]

21.10 Right to Stay Performance because of the Other Contracting Party's Breach

The principal of reciprocity recognises the fact that in many contracts the common intention of the parties, expressed or unexpressed, is that there should be an exchange of performances, and the *exceptio non adimpleti contractus* gives effect to the recognition of this fact by serving as a defence for the defendant who is sued on the contract by a plaintiff who has not yet performed or tendered to perform.[504]

The defence of the *exceptio non adimpleti contractus* may only be used if the contract between the parties is a bilateral or synallagmatic contract; in other words, one in which each party undertakes obligations towards the other. In such a case there is a presumption that the common intention of the parties is that neither should be entitled to enforce the contract unless he has performed or is ready to perform his own obligations.[505] The defendant can only succeed on the *exceptio* if the plaintiff's performance fell due prior to or simultaneously with the performance claimed from the defendant.[506]

Thus, in a bilateral contract certain obligations may be reciprocal in the sense that the performance of one may be conditional upon the performance, or tender of performance, of the other. This reciprocity may itself be bilateral in the sense that the performance, or tender of performance, of them represent concurrent conditions, that is, each is conditional upon the other. A ready example of this would be delivery of the *res vendita* and payment of the purchase price under a cash sale.[507]

The defendant who relies on the principle of reciprocity and raises the *exceptio non adimpleti contractus* is not seeking to rescind the contract so he does not need to prove that the plaintiff is seriously in breach, or even that he is in breach at all.[508] The right to rescind the contract is a right of action based on a breach going to the root of the contract whereas the *exceptio* is a defence in the nature of a dilatory plea based on no more than the plaintiff's failure to perform or

[502] *Bekker* v *Duvenage* 1977 (3) SA 884 (E); *Ornelas* v *Andrew's Cafe* 1980 (l) SA 378 (W); *Op. cit.* at 565.

[503] *William Maine & Son (Pvt) Ltd* v *Rhodesia Railways* 1976 (4) SA 914 (R); *Ibid.*

[504] *BK Tooling (Edms) Bpk* v *Scope Precision Engineering (Edms) Bpk* 1979 (1) SA 391 (A); *Op. cit.* at 503.

[505] *Nesci* v *Meyer* 1982 (3) SA 498 (A) at 513 F.

[506] *Op. cit.* at 504.

[507] *ESE Financial Services (Pty) Ltd* v *Cramer* 1973 (2) 805 (C) at 808; *Crispette and Candy Co Ltd* v *Oscar Michaelis NO and another* 1947 (4) SA 521 (A) at 537.

[508] *Op. cit.* at 505.

tender performance. It follows that the plaintiff may always perform or tender performance should the *exceptio* be successfully raised against him and thereby rectify the position.

The plaintiff's duty is to perform fully and exactly in accordance with the contract, and his failure to do so, no matter how slight that failure may be, entitles the defendant to raise the *exceptio*, subject only to the principle *de minimus non curat lex.*[509] This is all that is meant when it is said that the plaintiff's breach or failure to perform must be material.[510]

21.11 Failure of the Joint Factual Basis for the Meeting of their Minds

The agreement between the parties must be a true agreement in the sense of a "meeting of the minds" or "coincidence of the wills" of the contractor, parties, or *consensus ad idem*. If there is on the facts no true subjective agreement between the parties, there will be no contract, unless the English law doctrine of quasi-mutual assent applies in the particular circumstances of the case. Thus, the purely subjective intention of the parties is married and subject to the objective doctrine of quasi-mutual assent, so that in certain circumstances even though there is no true subjective agreement between the parties there is an apparent agreement and the parties will be bound to the apparent agreement (see 10 above).

21.12 Sale or Acquisition in State of Need or because of Danger

The law relating to a sale or acquisition in a state of need or danger or threat of danger is dealt is in 10.5 above.

21.13 Events Occurred between the Agreement and the Closing

Usually the parties will base their decision to enter into an agreement on information at their disposal at a certain point in time. Clearly, events may occur subsequent to the agreement but prior to the date when the parties will meet to sign the contract, exchange documents and do all that is necessary to close the deal. Once agreement is reached, whether that agreement is verbal or written, the parties to it are bound by its terms and subsequent events will not affect this state of affairs unless the subsequent event renders the performance of any of the obligations of the parties impossible (see 21.6 above).

It is common, therefore, for the parties expressly to deal with events which are contemplated by the parties at the time of agreement which might impact on their agreement and on the business or shares sold, as the case may be, for the period commencing on the date of the agreement and until the delivery of the *res vendita* or the closing. The various warranties relating to sales of business as going concerns and of shares in a company during the vulnerable period are dealt with in Sections 13 and 6.4 above, respectively.

[509] *BK Tooling (Edms) Bpk* v *Scope Precision Engineering (Edms) Bpk* 1979 (1) SA 391 (A) at 419–21.

[510] *National Screenprint (Pty) Ltd* v *The Campbell-Scott Co (Pty) Ltd* 1979 (4) SA 393 (C) at 397D; *Op. cit.* at 506.

21.14 Termination for Excessive Hardship

A party to a contract may complain in vain that the contract into which he has entered contains terms that are unfair to him. The courts will not come to the assistance of an aggrieved party on the simple ground that the terms of the contract are unfair, unreasonable or oppressive to him.[511] The reason for this hands-off attitude is clear. The parties have agreed, and the whole basis of the law of contract is that the courts will enforce their agreement. Intervention by the courts would be a form of paternalism inconsistent with freedom of contract.[512] Other countries have found legislation to curb unfair contract terms successful and it seems likely that South Africa will introduce similar legislation.[513]

There is no evidence in South African common law of the existence of a general substantive defence based on equity, nor does our legal system administer a system of equity as distinct from a system of law. Roman–Dutch law is itself inherently an equitable legal system and in administering the law the Dutch courts paid due regard to considerations of equity but only where equity was not inconsistent with the principles of law. Equity could not override a clear rule of law. This is also the position of present South African courts as regards their equitable jurisdiction.

Moreover, there is no support in Roman–Dutch law for the proposition that in the South African law of contract an equitable exception or defence, similar in effect to the Roman law *exceptio doli generalis*, was used under the aegis of *bona fides*. Therefore, the Roman law *exceptio dolus generalis* is a superfluous, defunct anachronism and does not form part of current South African law.[514]

The Appeal Court in *Bank of Lisbon and South Africa Ltd* v *De Ornelas and Another* did not purport to tackle the question of how the *exceptio doli generalis* is to be replaced, or whether South African law is to manage without a general remedy against the oppressive enforcement of contractual rights.[515] The problem is still under consideration.

The courts do have and exercise a power of declaring void a contract contrary to public policy. The power to declare contracts contrary to public policy should, however, be exercised sparingly and only in the clearest of cases, lest uncertainty as to the validity of contracts result from an arbitrary and indiscriminate use of the power. One must be careful not to conclude that a contract is contrary to public policy merely because its terms (or some of them) offend one's individual sense of proprietary and fairness.[516]

A possible defence to the *caveat subscriptor* rule—namely the principle of law that a man, when he signs a contract, is taken to be bound by the ordinary meaning and effect of the words which appear above his signature—is that the

[511] *Burger* v *Central South African Railways* 1903 TS 571 at 576.
[512] *Op. cit.* at 16.
[513] *Op. cit.* at 17.
[514] *Bank of Lisbon and South Africa Ltd* v *De Ornelas and Another* 1988 (3) SA 580 (A) at 606–607.
[515] *Op. cit.* at 18.
[516] *Sasfin (Pty) Ltd* v *Beukes* 1989 (1) SA 1 (A) at 9B; *Op. cit.* at 418; see 21.1.2 above.

document which was signed without being read, contained a term or terms which the reasonable man would not expect to find therein. This defence cannot be put on the broad basis that the signatory will not be bound to any unreasonable term for the reasons stated above. Because it is a known fact of life that people habitually sign contracts without reading them only because they assume they do not contain unexpected terms, it can be argued that the unwitting signatory of a contract which does contain unexpected terms has not conducted himself in such a manner that a reasonable man would believe he was assenting to those unexpected terms. Therefore, there may be no true *consensus ad idem* and the doctrine of quasi-mutual assent would not assist the other party to the contract.[517]

Where the court has established the proper meaning of the words contained in a contract by applying the canons of construction, this meaning will not be departed from on equitable grounds. Therefore, if the parties have made an onerous or one-sided, unreasonable or even grossly inequitable contract it is not for the court to amend it out of sympathy with either or both of the parties.[518] On the other hand, the words may be modified sufficiently to avoid an absurdity *Boerne* v *Harris*,[519] or a result repugnant to or inconsistent with the contract as a whole,[520] if it is clear that the common intention of the parties was not to achieve such a result.[521]

21.15 Late Notice

There is nothing in law to prevent the parties from agreeing that any claim contract against the other party arising from them must be instituted within a specified period reckoned from the date of signature of the agreement, or from the date of discovery of the breach or event giving rise to the claim. If the claim is instituted after the period specified, the claim may be effectively barred.

21.16 Time Bar

The Prescription Act 68 of 1969 came into operation on 1 December 1970, repealing Act 18 of 1943 which, however, still applies to any debt which arose before 1 December 1970 (section 22 read with section 16(2) of the Prescription Act, 1969). The Prescription Act 1969 is not a complete codification of the law of extinctive prescription, so common law rules which are not inconsistent with the provisions of the Prescription Act 1969 remain in force.[522]

We are here concerned only with the extinctive prescription of contractual debts. The word "debt" was chosen, not with the intention of restricting the scope

517 *Op. cit.* at 205–6.

518 *Van Rensburg* v *Straughan* 1914 AD 317 at 328; *Howiland Estates (Pty) Ltd* v *McMaster* 1969 (2) SA 312 (A) at 336; *Op. cit.* at 251.

519 *Boerne* v *Harris* 1947 (l) SA 793 (A).

520 *Cameron* v *Getz* 1945 WLD 92.

521 *Ibid.*

522 *Marais* v *Commercial Union Assurance Co of SA Ltd* 1977 (2) SA 269(T) at 271–3; *Op. cit.* at 574.

of prescription, but in order to change from a "weak" prescription system of barring the remedy to a "strong" prescription system of extinguishing the right.[523] The word "debt" in the Prescription Act 1969 must be given a wide and general meaning denoting not only a debt sounding in money which is due, but also, for example, a debt for the vindication of property.[524] A debt is to be construed as the correlative of a right of action, the debt and the right of action being opposite poles of an obligation, which generally embraces a proprietary element and a duty.[525]

Although the question has not been settled authoritively by the Appeal Court, it is arguable that the contractual remedy of rescission has been affected by the Prescription Act 1969.[526] There is undoubtedly a right of action to rescind, based on breach of an obligation not to induce a contract by misrepresentation, and the correlative of that right of action is therefore a debt. To hold otherwise would be to reintroduce the common law periods of prescription for rescission which could not have been the legislature's intention.

Section 10 of the Prescription Act 1969 makes it clear that the effect of the expiration of the period specified in section 11 or any other law as applicable to a particular debt is to extinguish that debt entirely, leaving no natural obligation, except that section 10(3), apparently anomalously, provides that payment of a prescribed debt shall be regarded as payment of a debt.[527] Therefore, prescription is a matter of substantive and not procedural law and the old distinction between the complete extinction of a right by prescription and the barring of a remedy by prescription, leaving a form of natural obligation, no longer applies.

In the same way that a prescribed debt will not support a claim, so it will not support a defence. This follows logically from the change in the Prescription Act 1969 from prescription of actions to prescription of debts.[528] The effectiveness of the defence of the *exceptio non adimpleti contractus* (see 21.10 above) has been maintained because provision has been made for the simultaneous prescription of reciprocal contractual debts (section 13(2) of the Prescription Act 1969).

If the obligation not to induce a contract by misrepresentation is not a debt, the defence of rescission would be governed by the common law and seemingly would be available as long as an action on the contract remained unprescribed. In the case of a long-term contract such as a lease under which new debts become due at intervals, this could lead to a defence of rescission being raised many years after the making of the contract, unless the plaintiff could show that the defendant had waived this defence or was estopped from raising it.[529]

[523] Memorandum of Professor J.C. de Wet, the draftsman of the Prescription Act 1969, paras 71–75.

[524] *Evins* v *Shield Insurance Co Ltd* 1979 (3) SA 1136 (W) at 1141 F and confirmed on appeal—1980 (2) SA 814 (A).

[525] *Evins* v *Shield Insurance Co Ltd* 1980 (2) SA 814 (A) AT 842; *Oertel* v *Direkteur van Plaaslike Bestuur* 1983 (1) SA 354 (A) at 370; *Op. cit.* at 575.

[526] *Op. cit.* at 576.

[527] *Lipschitz* v *Dechamps Textiles GmbH* 1978 (4) SA 427 (C); *Ibid.*

[528] *Op. cit.* at 577.

[529] *Ibid.*

Section 11 of the Prescription Act 1969 sets out the periods of prescription of debts, and provides as follows:

> 11. Periods of prescription of debts.—The periods of prescription of debts shall be the following:
> (a) thirty years in respect of—
>   (i) any debt secured by mortgage bond;
>   (ii) any judgment debt;
>   (iii) any debt in respect of any taxation imposed or levied by or under any law;
>   (iv) any debt owed to the State in respect of any share of the profits, royalties or any similar consideration payable in respect of the right to mine minerals or other substances;
> (b) fifteen years in respect of any debt owed to the State and arising out of an advance or loan of money or a sale or lease of land by the State to the debtor, unless a longer period applies in respect of the debt in question in terms of paragraph (a);
> (c) six years in respect of a debt arising from a bill of exchange or other negotiable instrument or from a notarial contract, unless a longer period applies in respect of the debt in question in terms of paragraph (a) or (b);
> (d) save where an Act of Parliament provides otherwise, three years in respect of any other debt.

No distinction is drawn between written and oral or implied contracts, and contractual debts generally are subject to the three-year period. Therefore, a contractual debt, which prescribes in three years, becomes on the taking of judgment, a debt which prescribes in 30 years because there is an independent new cause of indebtedness in terms of the judgment whether or not the original debt continues in existence.[530]

Prescription commences to run as soon as the debt is due. A debt becomes due when it is recoverable, owing and already payable; immediately claimable; when the creditor acquires a complete cause of action for its recovery; or when the cause or right of action accrues, which are synonymous expressions.[531] In applying this test of recoverability a creditor is not able by his own conduct to postpone the commencement of prescription.[532]

Debts to perform contractual obligations, by their very nature, become due in accordance with the contract. Interpretation of the contract will therefore, in the absence of other relevant indicators, show when prescription starts to run.

The cases on damages for breach of contract reflect a divergence of judicial opinion.[533] On the one hand, a single breach of contract may give rise to different debts, the debt correlative to a right of action for a declaration of rights or nominal damages becoming due immediately on the breach, but the debt correlative to a right of action for damages not becoming due until the loss occurs.[534] The better view, however, is that a single breach of contract gives rise

530 *Jordan and Co Ltd* v *Bulsara* 1992 (4) SA 457 (ECD) at 461 H.

531 *Deloitte Haskins & Sells* v *Bowthorpe Hellerman Deutsch* 1991 (1) SA 525 (A) at 532; Christie, 578–9.

532 *Ibid.*

533 *Ibid.*

534 *Syfin Holdings Ltd* v *Pickering* 1982 (2) SA 225 (ZS).

to a single cause of action, and prescription begins to run from the breach whether or not the damage has become apparent.[535]

The provisions of section 12(2) and (3) of the Prescription Act 1969 make the creditor's knowledge of the facts from which the debt arises material. Section 12(2) and (3) provide as follows:

> (2) If the debtor wilfully prevents the creditor from coming to know of the existence of the debt, prescription shall not commence to run until the creditor becomes aware of the existence of the debt.
>
> (3) A debt shall not be deemed to be due until the creditor has knowledge of the identity of the debtor and of the facts from which the debt arises: Provided that a creditor shall be deemed to have such knowledge if he could have acquired it by exercising reasonable care.

Therefore, prescription does not commence to run until the creditor has knowledge or is deemed to have knowledge of the facts amounting to a breach of contract. The creditor then has three years to bring his action and if, within those three years, no damage has resulted he may bring an action for a declaration of rights. The occurrence of a loss resulting from the breach does not create a new debt with a new prescriptive period. The action for a declaration of rights is sufficient to interrupt prescription of his claim for damages.[536]

The running of prescription is interrupted by an express or tacit acknowledgment of liability by the debtor, it being necessary for this purpose to prove that the debtor intended to admit that the debt was in existence and that he was liable therefor.[537] It must be an acknowledgment of legal liability for the debt and must be made to the creditor or his agent.[538] It must be an admission of present liability, not merely an acknowledgment that an obligation was incurred.[539]

The running of prescription is also interrupted by the service on the debtor of any process (this includes a defence of set-off in a plea) whereby the creditor claims payment of the debt (section 15(1) of the Prescription Act 1969). An application for a winding-up order and an attachment order pending an action do not qualify, as a creditor does not thereby claim payment of the debt.[540]

The proper way to raise the defence of prescription is by special plea, not in the course of interlocutory proceedings, but this is not a rigid rule, as section 17 of the Prescription Act 1969 permits prescription to be invoked by any party to litigation, and section 17(2) empowers the court to allow prescription to be raised at any stage of the proceedings. The court may not take notice of prescription of its own motion, but this does not detract from the effect of section 10, which is to extinguish the debt.[541] The parties are also always free to agree to waive

[535] *Hawken* v *Olympic Pools (Pty) Ltd* 1979 (3) SA 224 (T); *Ibid.*

[536] *Cape Town Municipality* v *Allianz Insurance Co Ltd* 1990 (1) SA 3 11 (C); *Op. cit.* at 580.

[537] *Hawken* v *Olympic Pools (Pty) Ltd* 1979 (3) SA 224 (T) at 228–9; *Op. cit.* at 582.

[538] *Pentz* v *Government of the Republic of South Africa* 1983 (3) SA 584 (A).

[539] *Benson* v *Walters* 1984 (1) SA 73 (A) at 86–87; *Ibid.*

[540] *Ibid.*

[541] Section 17(1) of the Prescription Act 1969; *Standard General Insurance Co Ltd* v *Verdun Estates (Pty) Ltd* 1990 (2) SA 693 at 699; *Op. cit.* at 583.

prescription. Such a clause would not be regarded as contrary to public policy.[542]

22. Investigation as Substitute for Warranties

22.1 Warranty Excluded by Right to Conduct a Previous Control

Clearly, if the purchaser does not have any knowledge of the affairs of the company which controls the assets the purchaser wishes to acquire control of a large part of the negotiations of the terms of an agreement of sale will focus on the warranties. If the purchaser has first-hand knowledge of such affairs and enjoyed hands-on control of the assets in question, it is unlikely the seller will give any warranties and the business as a going concern, or the shares, as the case may be, will most probably be sold "voetstoots" (see 1.3.4.1 above).

22.2 Effects of Vendor's Other Controls or Knowledge

The comments made in 22.1 are equally applicable here.

22.3 Vendor's Special Conduct and Liability

If the warranties, including the common law warranties, are excluded, the seller's liability is accordingly limited. The purchaser will have no claims against the seller based on the excluded common law warranties or the express implied or tacit warranties, because they have been excluded.

23. Third Parties' Liability

23.1 Intermediaries

The purchaser or the seller, or both, may appoint an agent to represent them during the negotiations and signing of the agreement of sale. The liability of an agent appointed in terms of South African law is governed by the law of agency. Agency is either simply a contract by which the principal and the agent create rights and obligations *inter se* (as such it belongs to the category of contracts known as mandate or *mandatum* in Roman–Dutch law), or it is a representation in terms of which the agent concludes a juristic act on behalf of or in the name of the principal.

"Authorisation" is a juristic act not dependent on the existence of a contract of agency between the representative and the principal. Thus, even if a contract of agency exists between two persons and even if the task to be performed by the one in terms of the contract is the conclusion of a juristic act on behalf of the other, the agent's authority is not simply one of the rights or obligations arising from the contract, but a capacity derived from an act of authorisation, which is a unilateral juristic act distinct from the contract of agency.

Where authority is derived from an act of authorisation the scope and extent of the representative's authority are determined by the source of the authority and the authorisation.

[542] *Nedfin Bank CP* v *Meisenheimer* 1989 (4) SA 701 (T).

23.1.1 Estoppel

A person who has not authorised another to conclude a juristic act on his behalf may, nevertheless, under appropriate circumstances be estopped from denying that he had authorised the other to act on his behalf. The effect of a successful reliance on estoppel is that the person who has been estopped is liable as though he had authorised the other to act.[543]

The "third person" who relies on estoppel will have to show that he was misled by the person whom he seeks to hold liable as principal to believe that the person who acted on the latter's behalf had authority to conclude the act and that he (ie the "third person") acted on that belief to his prejudice. The burden of proof rests on the person who relies on estoppel. He has to show, firstly, that he was misled, secondly, that he was misled by the person whom he seeks to hold liable as principal or by someone for whose conduct such person is responsible, thirdly, that he acted on the faith of what he was led to believe and, fourthly, that he acted to his prejudice. Of course the third person cannot rely on estoppel where he himself is to blame for the conclusions he has drawn.[544]

23.1.2 Personal liability of the representative

Where one person concludes a juristic act on behalf of another with or against a third person the legal relationships which are created, altered or extinguished by the juristic act are legal relationships between the third person and the person represented and not legal relationships between the representative and the third person. The reason is that the representative and the third person intended the effects of the juristic act to accrue to the principal and not to the representative.

For the intended results to materialise the representative has to have authority to conclude the juristic act on behalf of the other person. If he has no authority the principal acquires no rights and incurs no obligations and his legal relationships are not affected unless he subsequently ratifies the act done on his behalf. As between the purported principal and the third person the unauthorised and unratified act has no legal effect.

The question now is whether the pretending representative is liable to the third person and, if he is liable, what the basis and extent of such liability are. On these points complete clarity does not yet exist. The proposition that a person who contracts as agent for a non-exist principal is himself bound as principal, is untenable. For the same reason the person who contracts as representative cannot acquire rights as though he were the principal.[545]

A person who fraudulently represents to a third person that he has authority to conclude juristic acts on behalf of another can be liable in delict if the third person acts on the faith of the representation. Although there are no reported cases in which liability was actually based on fraudulent representation of authority there can be no doubt that a person who commits fraud in this context will be liable. Thus, a person who knows that he has no authority to act on behalf of another or that the principal on whose behalf he professes to act does not exist,

543 W.A. Joubert, (ed) *The Law of South Africa* (Vol 1, Butterworths, 1976), at 106.
544 *Ibid.*
545 *Gardner* v *Richardt* 1974 (3) SA 768 (C); Joubert, *Op. cit.* at 108.

will be liable to the third person if he induces the third person to act to his detriment in the belief that the person who professes to be an authorised agent has authority. The damages recoverable by the third person will be assessed in terms of the principles which govern the assessment of damages for fraudulent misrepresentation in general.

A person who concludes a juristic act on behalf of another may bind himself by an ancillary contract with the third person guaranteeing that he has authority to represent the person on whose behalf he acts. If he does not have the authority he warrants to have, he is liable to the third person for breach of the ancillary contract. The extent of his liability will depend on the terms of the ancillary contract. If the extent of his liability is not fixed he will be bound to put the third person in the position in which the latter would have been if he (ie the representative) had had authority to conclude the specific act.

A person who warrants that he has authority, warrants that he has authority at the time he concludes the juristic act in the name of another with a third person, and is guilty of a breach of warranty of authority the moment he concludes the unauthorised act. Strictly speaking the third person can proceed against him without awaiting the possibility of ratification by the purported principal. Instead of warranting the existence of authority the would-be representative may contract with the third person that he will secure the ratification of an act which is admittedly an unauthorised act. Damages for failure to secure the ratification will be calculated on the same basis as that which applies to breach of warranty of authority.

Thus, the unauthorised representative does not automatically step into the shoes of the purported principal as principal. The person who acted as representative "must be held to have impliedly promised that his principal should be bound by it, and that if not he would make good to the other party the damages resulting from that fact".[546]

It is submitted that it is misleading to speak of an "implied warranty" when the "warranty" is not based on tacit consensus but on a misrepresentation and that in the absence of consensus the real basis of liability can only be misrepresentation. That this, if the position is borne out by the view that the would-be agent is not liable if the third person knows that the would-be agent has no authority or is in as good a position as the would-be agent to determine whether the latter has authority. If misrepresentation is fairly and squarely accepted as the basis of liability, in the absence of an explicit or tacit warranty of authority, the principles for assessing damages will have to be those which apply to the calculation of damages for misrepresentation in general. Where the pretending representative's liability is based on a tacit warranty of authority the representative's contractual capacity is relevant. If liability is based on misrepresentation the rules relating to capacity to commit delicts will be applicable.

23.1.3 The undisclosed principal

Direct *vincula iuris* between one person and a third person could arise out of a contract only if the intermediary contracted as representative of the former, ie

[546] *Blower* v *Van Noorden* 1909 TS 890 at 901; *op. cit.* at 111.

concluded the contract not in his own name but on behalf of that other person. Where a person concluded a contract in his own name even in terms of a contract of mandate between himself and another no *vincula iuris* were created between the mandator and the third person, but the mandatory was bound by reason of the contract of mandate to cede to the mandator the rights he had acquired against the third person.[547]

In English law on the other hand direct *vincula iuris* can arise between an undisclosed principal, as he is called, and a third person from a contract concluded with the third person by another who contracts in his own name and not as representative. Although the third person and the person with whom he contracts contemplate the creation of *vincula iuris* between themselves the undisclosed principal can emerge from obscurity and assert that he is the "real" party to the contract and therefore entitled to the rights which arise out of it. Similarly, the third person, on discovering that there is an undisclosed principal lurking in the dark, can hold him liable.

The doctrine of the undisclosed principal has been described as odd, anomalous, unsound and inconsistent with principle not only in South Africa[548] but also in England.[549] Various attempts have been made to reconcile this doctrine with basic principles but not one has been found to be sound and acceptable. The absence of a sound basis in principle renders the doctrine vague and uncertain in its application.

An undisclosed principal relationship can only arise where a person concludes a contract in his own name with another. Where he openly contracts in the name of or on behalf of another the situation is one of representation and not an undisclosed principal situation. This is the position even if the identity of the principal is not disclosed. The contract is an undisclosed principal contract even if the third person knows that there is another person in whose interest the intermediary concludes the contract in his own name, and that is the position even where the identity of the undisclosed principal is known to the third person.

Just what relationship there has to exist between one person and another so that one can be said to be the undisclosed principal of the other is not very clear. It would appear though that the required relationship only exists where the undisclosed principal has instructed the intermediary to conclude a contract either in the name of the principal or in his own name or in either as he chooses. If no such relationship exists the situation is not an undisclosed principal relationship and the alleged undisclosed principal can acquire no rights and incur no obligations from the contract.[550]

An undisclosed principal can acquire rights and incur obligations from a contract concluded by a person not authorised to contract in his name. What is required is the existence of some relationship between the intermediary and the

[547] Joubert, *op. cit.* at 112.
[548] *Cullinan* v *Noordkaaplandse Aartappelkernmoerkwekers Ko-Op Bpk* 1972 (1) SA 761 (A) at 770.
[549] *Op. cit.* at 113.
[550] *Op. cit.* at 114.

undisclosed principal as described in the preceding paragraph. Obviously a person with unfettered contractual capacity does not require another's authority to conclude a contract in his own name by which he acquires rights and incurs obligations. Whether another person, as undisclosed principal, also acquires rights and incurs obligations from that contract does not depend on whether he has authorised the intermediary to conclude the contract but on whether he has instructed him to conclude the contract.

In an undisclosed principal situation the intermediary and the third person create *vincula iuris* between themselves by the contract concluded in their own names, but also, so it is said, alternative *vincula iuris* between the undisclosed principal and the third person. The position seems to be that either the undisclosed principal or the third person can elect to transform the *vincula iuris* between the intermediary and the third person into *vincula iuris* between the undisclosed principal and the third person (Joubert, 115–116).

In *Cullinan* v *Noordkaaplandse Aartappelkernmoerkwekers Ko-op Bpk*[551] the appellate division laid down that the *vincula iuris* arising out of a contract concluded by a third person with an intermediary could not be split up between a number of undisclosed principals or even between the intermediary and a single undisclosed principal. The third person in contracting with the intermediary stipulated for a right against a single person and bound himself to a single person and that it would be inequitable to permit this right and this obligation to be split up so as to create a multiplicity of debtors or creditors for the third person.

23.1.3.1 THE LIABILITY OF THE THIRD PERSON TO THE UNDISCLOSED PRINCIPAL

The essence of the doctrine of the undisclosed principal is that the undisclosed principal can claim that he and not the intermediary, with whom the third person contracted, is the real creditor of the third person. This assertion is of course basically untrue. The third person did not contract with the undisclosed principal but with the intermediary who is the real creditor. This is borne out by the recognition of the third person's right to set-off against the undisclosed principal's claim any debt owed to him by the intermediary. For the same reason the undisclosed principal will have no claim against the third person if the latter pays the debt or performs his obligations to the intermediary before the undisclosed principal intervenes, and there is no reason in principle why the third person should not be discharged by agreement with the intermediary such as release and novation.

Primarily the third person is liable to the intermediary and not to the undisclosed principal. As a creditor the undisclosed principal only steps into the shoes of the intermediary when he elects to do so and until that time the third person is not bound to him. Mere knowledge on the part of the third person that there is an undisclosed principal in the background does not affect his position *vis-à-vis* the intermediary. The intermediary is only displaced by the undisclosed principal when the latter shows his hand.[552]

[551] 1972 1 SA 761 (A).
[552] *Op. cit.* at 116.

23.1.3.2 THE LIABILITY OF THE THIRD PERSON TO THE INTERMEDIARY

The contract is concluded between the third person and the intermediary acting in his own name. The third person is, in terms of the contract, liable to the intermediary. He cannot avoid liability to the intermediary on the ground that he is liable to the undisposed principal, unless and until the undisclosed principal elects to hold him liable.

In *Zieve* v *Verster & Co*,[553] the court as an alternative ground for deciding against the plaintiff held that the defendant could rely on a defence which he would have had against the plaintiff's undisclosed principal, had the latter been the plaintiff. This conclusion is not justified. Until the undisclosed principal elects to hold the third person liable he is a stranger to the *vincula iuris* which arise from the contract.[554]

23.1.3.3 THE LIABILITY OF THE UNDISCLOSED PRINCIPAL TO THE THIRD PERSON

The person primarily liable to the third person is of course the intermediary who contracted in his own name. On discovering that there was an undisclosed principal in the background the third person may, however, elect to hold the undisclosed principal liable instead of the intermediary. Obviously the third person cannot elect until he knows that there is an undisclosed principal, but once he has made his election he is bound by it.[555] The mere fact that the third person sued the intermediary will not prevent him from holding the undisclosed principal liable if at the time he took action against the intermediary he was unaware that there was an undisclosed principal.[556]

23.1.3.4 THE LIABILITY OF THE INTERMEDIARY TO THE THIRD PERSON

In terms of his contract with the third person the intermediary who has contracted in his own name is liable to the third person. He cannot avoid his liability by referring the third person to the undisclosed principal. He is, however, discharged from liability by the third person's election to hold the undisclosed principal liable.

23.2 Auditors

23.2.1 Duties of auditors

Section 20 of the Public Accountants' and Auditors' Act 80 of 1991 and sections 281, 282, 300 and 301 of the Companies Act impose certain statutory duties upon an auditor and provide him with certain comparative powers.

Section 20(1), (2), (3) and (4) of the Public Accountants' and Auditors' Act states the following:

[553] 1918 CPD 296 302.
[554] *Op. cit.* at 117.
[555] *Natal Trading and Milling Co Ltd* v *Inglis* 1927 TPD 724 at 727.
[556] *Op. cit.* at 118.

20. Powers and duties of auditors

(1) No person acting in the capacity of auditor to any undertaking shall, without such qualification as may be appropriate in the circumstances, pursuant to any audit carried out by him in that capacity, certify or report or express an opinion to the effect that any financial statement, including any annexure thereto, which relates to such undertaking, presents fairly, or gives a true and fair view of, or reflects correctly, the affairs of such undertaking and the results of its operations, or the matters dealt with in such financial statement or annexure, as the circumstances may require, unless:

   (a) he has carried out such audit free of any restrictions whatsoever;
   (b) proper accounting records in one of the official languages of the Republic have been kept in connection with the undertaking in question, so as to reflect and explain all its transactions and record all its assets and liabilities correctly and adequately;
   (c) he has obtained all information, vouchers and other documents which in his opinion were necessary for the proper performance of his duties;
   (d) he has, in the case of an undertaking regulated by any law, complied with all the requirements of that law relating to the audit of that undertaking;
   (e) he has by means of such methods as are reasonably appropriate having regard to the nature of the undertaking in question, satisfied himself of the existence of all assets and liabilities shown on such financial statement or annexure;
   (f) he is satisfied, as far as is reasonably practicable having regard to the nature of the undertaking in question and of the audit carried out by him, as to the fairness or the truth or the correctness, as the case may be, of such financial statement or annexure;
   (g) any matter referred to in subsection (5) had, at the date on which he so certified or reported, or expressed such opinion, been adjusted to his satisfaction.

(2) No accountant or auditor shall, when acting otherwise than pursuant to an audit, certify or report, or express an opinion, without such qualification as may be appropriate in the circumstances, to the effect that any account, financial statement (including any annexure thereto) or other document relating to the business or financial affairs of any undertaking, presents fairly, or gives a true and fair view of, or reflects correctly, the matters dealt with therein, unless he has *mutatis mutandis* complied with the provisions of sub-section (1)(a), (c) and (f).

(3) If any accountant or auditor or his partner or any person employed by him or his partner or any person working under his supervision and control or under the supervision and control of his partner, was responsible for keeping the books, records or accounts of an undertaking, except to the extent of making closing entries or assisting with any adjusting entries or framing any balance sheet, account, statement or other document from existing records, such accountant or auditor shall in certifying or reporting on anything in connection with the business or financial affairs of such undertaking, indicate that, as the case may be, he or his partner or a person employed by him or his partner or a person working under his supervision and control or under the supervision and control of his partner was responsible for keeping such books, records or accounts.

(4) Any certificate required to be given or report to be made or opinion to be expressed by an accountant or auditor in his capacity as accountant or auditor pursuant to any assignment carried out by him, shall be given or made or

> expressed within a period of four months after the date on which the assignment was completed, and if such accountant and auditor is unable to give an unqualified certificate or make an unqualified report or express an unqualified opinion, he shall within the said period give that certificate or make that report or express that opinion subject to such qualifications as he may deem necessary and may, if he considers it advisable, endorse on that certificate, report or opinion the reasons for any such qualification.

The auditors' duties under the Companies Act relate mainly to the validation of the financial statements of a company. An auditor is under no statutory obligation to give advice to the directors or management, or to the shareholders, on the company's policy and objectives or to judge the efficiency of management.

An auditor also has a statutory duty to report certain irregularities. Section 20(5), (6) and (7) of the Public Accountants' and Auditors' Act states the following:

> (5) (a) If any person acting in the capacity of auditor to any undertaking is satisfied or has reason to believe that in the conduct of the affairs of such undertaking a material irregularity has taken place or is taking place which has caused or is likely to cause financial loss to the undertaking or to any of its members or creditors, he shall forthwith despatch a report in writing to the person in charge of that undertaking giving particulars of the irregularity, at the same time drawing the attention of such person in charge to the provisions of paragraphs (b) and (c) and requesting him to acknowledge receipt of such report in writing.
>
> (b) Unless within 30 days after an auditor has despatched such a report, he has been satisfied that no such irregularity has taken place or is taking place or that adequate steps have been taken for the recovery of any such loss so caused or for the prevention of any such loss likely to be so caused, he shall forthwith furnish the board with copies of the report and of any acknowledgement of receipt thereof and reply thereto and such other particulars as he may deem fit.
>
> (c) The board may disclose any information supplied to it in terms of paragraph (b) to any attorney-general or the Registrar of Deposit-taking Institutions or any officer in the public service or any member or creditor of the undertaking concerned or any juristic person of whom the undertaking is a member or who has control over the undertaking or who has the power to take disciplinary steps against the undertaking, or to the committee of any stock exchange on which shares of the undertaking are listed.
>
> (d) For the purpose of determining whether any irregularity contemplated in this subsection has taken place or is taking place, an auditor may carry out such investigation as he may deem fit.
>
> (e) Nothing in this subsection contained shall be construed as conferring upon any person any right of action against an auditor which, but for the provisions of this subsection, he would not have had.
>
> (6) (a) If any person who was acting in the capacity of auditor to any undertaking immediately prior to its sequestration or liquidation (whether provisional or final), is satisfied or has reason to believe that at or before the date of the sequestration or liquidation a material irregularity in the conduct of the affairs of such undertaking was taking place or had taken place which had caused or was likely to cause financial loss to the undertaking or to any of

its members or creditors, and such person did not comply with the provisions of subsection (5)(a) in respect of such irregularity before the said date, he shall forthwith despatch a report in writing, giving particulars of such irregularity, to the person appointed as trustee or provisional trustee, or as liquidator or provisional liquidator, as the case may be, of such undertaking, and at the same time supply copies of such report to the person in charge of such undertaking and to the board.

(b) If any person who was acting in the capacity of auditor to any undertaking immediately prior to its sequestration or liquidation (whether provisional or final) and who has not taken action in terms of subsection (5)(a) or despatched a report in writing in terms of paragraph (a) of this subsection, is at any time requested in writing to do so by the person appointed as trustee or provisional trustee or as liquidator or provisional liquidator, as the case may be, of such undertaking, he shall forthwith inform the person so requesting whether or not a report in writing is required by paragraph (a) of this subsection, and in the event of his informing the person so requesting that such report is so required, he shall forthwith despatch the report to him, and at the same time supply copies of such report to the person in charge of such undertaking and to the board.

(c) The provisions of subsection (5)(c) shall *mutatis mutandis* apply with reference to any information supplied to the board in terms of paragraph (a) of this subsection, and the provisions of subsection (5)(e) shall *mutatis mutandis* apply with reference to any provisions of this subsection.

(7) An auditor shall, in performing any duty referred to in subsections (5) and (6), have regard to all the information which comes to his knowledge in his capacity of auditor to any undertaking and all the information which comes to his knowledge from any other source.

23.2.2 Inquiry and disciplinary hearing by the Public Accountants' and Auditors' Board

Section 20(8) of the Public Accountants' and Auditors' Act states the following:

(8) If a person who has been registered as an accountant and auditor in terms of this Act:

(a) fails to perform any duties devolving upon him in the capacity of an auditor to any undertaking with such degree of care and skill as in the opinion of the board may reasonably be expected; or

(b) is negligent in the performance of such duties, the board may, whether or not such auditor is liable to be or has been criminally charged or has been convicted in respect of such failure or negligence, inquire into the circumstances, and if such failure or negligence is proved to its satisfaction, impose upon that person any of the punishments prescribed under section 13(1)(h) which it may deem fit: provided that no such person shall incur liability to punishment by the board by reason of any opinion expressed by him in good faith as to the value or amount of any asset or liability appearance on the balance sheet in respect of the undertaking in connection with which the audit was carried out, or by reason of his having declined to express any opinion thereon, if the board is satisfied that, having regard to the nature of such asset or liability or any other circumstances, he could not reasonably have been expected to express an authoritative opinion.

23.2.3 Liability of auditors

The liability of the auditor can be divided into three sections, namely: liability towards his client, liability towards third parties, and criminal liability.

Claims that may be instituted against the auditor can be divided into two sections, namely: claims in terms of common law (breach of contract or delict), and claims in terms of statutory law. Liability under statutory law can further be subdivided into civil liability (a claim for damages as a result of wrongful conduct, breach of their fiduciary relationship or neglect of duty), or criminal liability (if the auditor infringed certain provisions of the Companies Act), and disciplinary liability (if the auditor infringed certain provisions of the Public Accountants' and Auditors' Act—see 23.2.2 above).

23.2.3.1 LIABILITY TOWARDS HIS CLIENT

When a client company appoints an auditor, a contractual relationship exists between the company and the auditor. The contract, in setting out the specific auditing services required, also places a responsibility on the auditor to exercise his duties with due professional care.

The contractual relationship exists between the auditor and his client, the company, and not with the shareholders, or creditors of the company or any other third party. The task that the auditor has to fulfil in terms of his contract may, apart from statutory duties imposed on him, differ from case to case.

The responsibility of the auditor to exercise his duties with due professional care is also acknowledged by the South African Institute of Chartered Accountants which requires, as a third general auditing standard, that due professional care must be exercised by the auditor during the examination and in the preparation of his report (statement AU 010). In deciding whether an auditor exercised the required professional care the test would be whether he complied with the generally accepted auditing standards and techniques in force at the time. In terms of the common law, the auditor's liability towards his client originates either from breach of contract or delict.

Where the auditor is held liable in terms of breach of contract, his liability will, to a great extent, depend on his contract with the client. However, the auditor of a sole proprietor or of a partnership exercises his duties according to the terms of his appointment.

If he is given an unqualified assignment to audit, there will be no limitation on his liability, on the other hand, his liability will be limited accordingly if his audit instructions are qualified in any respect. When he is instructed not to review the bank statements, he will not be held liable for losses due to fraud which could only have been discovered by an examination of the bank statements. On the other hand, the auditor of a company has a specific duty to audit the books and financial statements of the company and cannot limit his liability by means of a contract.

However, in terms of common law, an auditor who was negligent and incurred a liability towards his client, will only be liable for damages caused by his negligence. If the service provided by the auditor is not of an acceptable standard, and as a result, his client suffers a financial loss, the client can sue the auditor for damages suffered. He can sue on the grounds of the wrongful conduct (delict) and has a recourse against the auditor for loss suffered. Where a case has to be decided as to whether or not an auditor is guilty of negligence, lack of proficiency will not be taken into account. He will be judged according to the standards of his profession. Lack of proficiency is no excuse, as an auditor is not supposed to assume any mandate for which he is not fully qualified.

In an action for damages against the auditor for breach of contract, the client (company) will have to prove the contractual relationship, the breach of contract, complained of and the loss it suffered as a result of that breach. In a claim for negligence resulting from wrongful conduct (delict), the client (company) will have to prove that the auditor was at fault in that he breached his duty to the company to take care, and that it suffered loss as a result of that breach.

When a company appoints an auditor, the auditor's duties towards the company originates from the statutory provisions regulating his office and task, and the terms of his contract with the company. The statutory provisions regulating the scope of the auditor's main duties as auditor of a company are included in the Companies Act while his duties in his capacity as auditor are included in the Public Accountants' and Auditors' Act (see 23.2.1 above).

Further duties could also be specifically imposed on the auditor by contractual stipulations (for example: an instruction to manage the company's tax returns) or by implication (for example: where the company's articles include provisions in respect of the audit). Where the auditor's duties are statutorily determined, he cannot limit his rights, duties or liability by means of a contract or instructions, but he can extend them.

Section 20(9), (10), and (11) of the Public Accountants' and Auditors' Act (see also in section 8 of the Companies Act) which deal with an auditor's liability both to his client and third parties, provide that:

(9) Any person registered as an accountant and auditor in terms of this Act shall, in respect of any opinion expressed or certificate given or report or statement made or statement account or document certified by him in the ordinary course of his duties:

(a) incur no liability to his client or any third party, unless it is proved that such opinion was expressed or such certificate was given or such report or statement was made or such statement, account or document was certified maliciously or pursuant to a negligent performance of his duties; and

(b) where it is proved that such opinion was expressed or such certificate was given or such report or statement was made or such statement, account or document was certified pursuant to a negligent performance of his duties, be liable to any third party who has relied on such opinion, certificate, report, statement, account or document, for financial loss suffered as a result of having relied thereon, only if it is proved that the auditor or person so registered:

(i) knew or could in the particular circumstances reasonably have been expected to know, at the time when the negligence occurred in the performance of the duties pursuant to which such opinion was expressed or such certificate was given or such report or statement was made or such statement, account or document was certified—

(aa) that such opinion, certificate, report, statement, account or document would be used by his client to induce the third party to act or refrain from acting in some way or to enter into the specific transaction into which the third party entered, or any other transaction of a similar nature, with the client or any other person; or

(bb) that the third party would rely on such opinion, certificate, report, statement, account or document for the purpose of acting or refraining from acting in some way or of entering into the specific transaction into which the third party entered, or any other transaction of a similar nature, with the client or any other person; or

(ii) in any way represented, at any time after such opinion was expressed or such certificate was given or such report or statement was made or such statement, account or document was certified, to the third party that such opinion, certificate, report, statement, account or document was correct, while at such time he knew or could in the particular circumstances reasonably have been expected to know that the third party would rely on such representation for the purpose of acting or refraining from acting in some way or of entering into the specific transaction into which the third party entered, or any other transaction of a similar nature, with the client or any other person.

(10) For the purposes of paragraph (b) of subsection (9) the fact that an auditor or a person referred to in that paragraph performed the functions of an accountant or auditor shall not in itself be proof that he could reasonably have been expected to know that—

(a) his client would act as contemplated in subparagraph (i)(aa) of the said paragraph (b); or

(b) the third party would act as contemplated in subparagraph (i)(bb) or (ii) of the said paragraph (b).

(11) The provisions of paragraph (b) of subsection (9) shall not affect—

(a) any liability of an auditor or a person referred to in that subsection which arises from—

(i) a contract between a third party and such auditor or person; or

(ii) any statutory provision; or

(b) any disclaimer of liability by an auditor or a person referred to in that subsection.

The above-mentioned sections exclude the no-fault liability of auditors, either on account of breaching a statutory duty or on account of wrongful conduct or breach of contract.

Under statutory law the auditor can also be held civilly liable as a result of wrongful conduct where he is guilty of breaching a statutory duty. The burden of proof lies with the company which will have to prove certain things.

23.2.3.2 LIABILITY TOWARDS THIRD PARTIES

The auditor does not stand in a contractual or fiduciary relationship with third parties. Consequently, if a third party should seek to hold the auditor liable for the latter's wrongful conduct, that liability would have to be established on the basis of the general principles of common law delictual liability, as discussed under the auditor's liability towards his client. Where there is no contract with the third party, which is typically the case, the third party suffering loss as a result of relying on a negligent misstatement by accountants or auditors, can only base his claim for damages on wrongful conduct (delict).

Section 20(9)(a) of the Public Accountants' and Auditors' Act provides that an auditor shall incur no liability towards third parties, unless it is proved that he acted maliciously or pursuant to a negligent performance of his duties. In regard to an auditor's liability towards third parties, section 20(12) defines a third party as "any person other than the client concerned, and includes any member of a client which is a company or external company . . . or which is any other juristic person". Therefore, although an auditor reports to the members of the client company they are, *vis-à-vis* the auditor, in the same position as other third parties. The auditor, therefore, has no direct responsibility to a member, only because he has to report to the members of the company in terms of section 301 of the Companies Act.

The conduct giving rise to potential delictual liability to third parties will usually relate to an intentional or negligent misrepresentation by the auditor in respect of the financial position of the company concerned or aspects thereof, for example, the prospects of the company or the value of its shares. Claims for misstatement may be based on the company's annual financial statement or report or valuation by the auditor, even though it may have been a mere expression of opinion on his part.

Section 20 of the Public Accountants' and Auditors' Act provides that where the auditor is sued for negligence or misrepresentation on the grounds that he could reasonably have been expected to know that the third party would have relied on, for example, the financial statements, it would depend on the particular circumstances present and could not just be deduced from his professional position. The mere fact that a person performed the duties of an accountant or auditor is not in itself proof that he reasonably could be expected to know that his client would use his report to induce a third party to act in some or other manner. The same applies regarding the third party relying on his opinion or report. The mere fact that, for example, a client-company's shares are quoted on the stock exchange and that its financial statements are sent to the Registrar of Companies and its members, is clearly not sufficient grounds for the existence of a liability towards a third party who bought shares on account of the so-called misleading financial statements. Under these circumstances more information is needed before it could be expected from the auditor to know about the inducement of the client or the relying by the third party. Where the auditor is requested to prepare financial statements for a specific purpose (for example: a loan or the acquisition of the client-company's shares), his risk would be substantially greater.

The burden of proving that the auditor is guilty of misrepresentation lies with the third party which will have to prove the elements of the misrepresentation (see 1.3.2.3 above).

Where the auditor is guilty of intentional or negligent misrepresentation and is aware that third parties would act thereon, the auditor may be delictually liable to the third parties.

23.2.3.3 CRIMINAL LIABILITY

An auditor can incur criminal liability in terms of the Companies Act while, in terms of the Public Accountants' and Auditors' Act, he would be subject to the disciplinary jurisdiction of the Public Accountants' and Auditors' Board (see 23.2.2 above).

Therefore, where an auditor is appointed to perform a non-statutory audit, he cannot incur criminal liability in respect of the performance of his audit assignment. He can only be held liable for improper conduct as a result of negligence or breach of contract in terms of the disciplinary jurisdiction of the Public Accountants' and Auditors' Board.

An auditor can incur criminal liability under many of the provisions of the Companies Act. Although it is not feasible to attempt to state all those offences here, the following instances in which an auditor is criminally liable in terms of the Companies Act deserve to be mentioned, namely; if he knowingly makes a materially false statement, return, report, certificate, financial statement or other document required by the Act (section 249 of the Companies Act); if he conceals, destroys or falsifies any book, register, document, financial record or financial statements of a company, or with the intention to defraud makes any erasure therein (section 250 of the Companies Act); if he makes or circulates any certificate, written statement, report or financial statement in relation to any property or affairs of the company which is false in any material particular; he may, however, raise the defence that he acted with reasonable care to ensure that the report or document is true (section 251 of the Companies Act); if he acts as an auditor of a company while disqualified to do so in terms of section 275 of the Companies Act; if he fails to give notice on the prescribed form to the company (section 276(2)(5) of the Companies Act); if he fails to give notice within 14 days to the company on the prescribed form of any change in the particulars which are entered in respect of him in the register of directors and officers (section 276(3)(5) of the Companies Act).

In terms of section 441 of the Companies Act, an infringement by an auditor of any of the provisions of sections 249, 250, 251 and 275 of the Companies Act shall make him liable to be sentenced to a fine or imprisonment or both, whilst infringement of section 276(2), (3) and (5) of the Companies Act would render him liable to a fine only.

23.3 Banks

Any liability of a bank (acting as bankers to the company in respect of which the shares are sold, acting as bankers to the seller selling a business as a going concern or acting in any other capacity) will be based either on a contractual or a delictual relationship between the bank and the purchaser and the principles relating to a contractual or delictual liability, as set out in this work, will apply.

23.4 Target Company's Officers

As with bankers, officers of a target company may become liable to a purchaser because of specific contractual or delictual arrangements between any such officer and the purchaser. Again the liability principles set out in this work will apply. In addition those officers of the target company who are directors have a fiduciary duty to a company to act in its best interests and any breach of such duty will give rise to action by the company against such directors for any damages suffered. In addition the Companies Act (Section 424) makes the directors personally liable for the debts of the company in the event of the directors carrying on the business of the company recklessly or with intent to defraud creditors or for fraudulent purposes.

23.5 Professionals

The professional advisers of a company will be in the same position as banks.

Spain

Enric Picañol, Javier Faus, Pere Kirchner[1]

Bufete Cuatrecasas, Barcelona, Spain

1. Introduction

1.1 Concept of Acquisition. Various Acquisitions

Basically a company can be sold either through the sale of its assets or through the sale of its shares. The legal treatment given in every case will vary, as will vary the remedies available to the buyer. Also, in case of shares, a difference will also exist in case the parties are merely trading shares in an exchange or as a portfolio investment or actually selling and buying a business through the change in ownership of its shares.

1.2 Form of Acquisitions Agreements; Statutory and Contractual Warranties

Spanish general contract rules, and especially Article 1.278 of the Civil Code, establish the freedom of formalities when entering into a contract. However, for contracts over 1,500 pesetas to become effective in front of third parties, they have to be in writing. In practice, all deals outside the stock market are formalised in writing. Furthermore, the system establishes specific formal requirements in the case of share deals which we will examine in paragraph 6 of this chapter.

The fact that most acquisitions adopt the form of a written agreement means in practice that written contractual warranties are usually used in Spain, leaving little room for statutory provisions. Said practice can be better understood if we consider that the Spanish legal system lacks any statutory or consuetudinary rules that regulate the sale of a company as a whole, and judicial precedents are scarce.

There are indeed several statutory regulations, basically found in the Civil and Commercial Codes, the Corporation Act of 1989 and the Urban Lease Law of

[1] Mr Picañol is a Partner and Messrs. Faus and Kirchner are Senior Associates in Bufete Cuatrecasas with offices in Barcelona, Madrid, Bilbao, Girona and Brussels.

1951, which deal with specific aspects of the sale of a company. However, said regulations are not co-ordinated amongst each other, and do not foresee all the issues relevant to this work. Courts and scholars neither have, to this date, filled up the loopholes of the system. Therefore, and due to the lack of regulations, some of the conclusions of this paper have been drawn based primarily on general principles of law and analogy.

1.3 Concept of Warranty; Difference between Representation and Warranties

We believe that under the common law system a representation or condition is a term for which non-compliance by the debtor allows the creditor to terminate the contractual obligations, while the non-compliance of a warranty only allows the creditor to request damages from the debtor.

Such terminology has been transferred to Spanish acquisition agreements, usually translating representation for *manifestaciones* and warranties for *garantías*. However, the legal meaning in Spanish is not the same as the one implied by the original common law term. Any non-compliance of an obligation, regardless of its terminology, will only entitle the creditor to terminate the contract in case it is an objectively important, substantial and serious non-compliance. As Clemente Meuro states, "the criteria basically followed to value the importance of the non-compliance has an objective feature, that is, we shall focus on the objective economic importance of the non-compliance, and not on the importance to the creditor".[2] The failure to comply with any *manifestaciones* and *garantías* will give the buyer, in any case, the right to request damages.

1.4 Introduction to Statutory Warranties

The basic legal text used for our purposes is the Civil Code. It contemplates the general obligations of any seller and the remedies of any buyer. In this respect, and as a first approach, the said code provides that a seller is liable *vis-à-vis* the buyer for the following:

(a) the legal and quiet possession of the object transferred, that is, the buyer is entitled to full and good title over the object purchased. This warranty affects both shares and assets deals;
(b) the latent defects of the object transferred. This warranty also affects both share and asset deals.

Other provisions do, however, complement in some cases the general rule. For instance, when the buyer sells not a single object or asset, but a company[3] as a whole, the seller does not warrant under the Code each and every one of the

[2] Even though the parties may, as per Article 1.255 of the Civil Code already mentioned, consider that a secondary obligation is in fact important and substantial, the courts, following the good faith principle, can mitigate such clauses.

[3] Defined by De La Camara as a "group of men who work according to a plan and under a single management, using a series of impersonal elements (material and immaterial) in order to produce goods or services". (Manuel De La Camara Alvarez: "La venta de la empresa mercantil; Principales problemas que plantea" Anates de la Academia Matritense del Notariado; Tomo XXIV, 1981; pp 281–382).

assets sold but the globality of the business.[4] The statutory warranties mentioned, which will be further developed in this work; could they be superseded or limited by contractual warranties? The answer is yes, based on the general principle of contractual freedom the parties have under Article 1.255 of the Civil Code. However, as we have already seen, the courts can mitigate these contractual provisions if they consider that they act against the public order and/or good faith of the parties.

In the case where the parties are silent, the statutory warranties will indeed apply in the manner examined in the present paper.

2. Warranties in Negotiations

Before an acquisition deal is closed the parties may negotiate in depth, promise the sale or the purchase of the target company and even execute a precontract. We will first focus on the negotiations and the liabilities incurred by the parties that is, what is commonly known as *culpa in contrahendo.*

The negotiations in an acquisition agreement refer to those preliminary contacts between the parties with the aim of closing a deal in the future (eg a preliminary meeting or a telephone conversation). During the negotiations the parties may invest time and money in projecting the business, give certain information to the other party or make some investments to adapt its business to the projected agreement based on the confidence they have deposited in the other party.

The warranties in negotiations are not specifically regulated and, therefore, scholars and courts have been trying to cover the loopholes of the system applying Civil Code general rules by analogy.

The key issue is if a party who has entered into negotiations is liable *vis-à-vis* the counterpart in case it decides not to proceed with the deal. The first approach is to examine which potential liability, if any, we are referring to.

Some Spanish scholars[5] have considered, following German influences, that we are neither in the presence of contractual nor of extra-contractual relations, since (i) no contract, either oral or written, exists yet and (ii) there have already been certain contacts that would make it difficult to consider the relation merely as an extra-contractual one.

It is submitted that there is a third type of liability, one which requires, in order to be effective, a clear *animus nocendi*. That is, liability will exist only as far as one of the parties enters into the negotiations with the clear aim of ending the same without closing a deal and infringing the regulations or causing damage.

The right to be compensated for damages is contemplated under Spanish law in Article 1.101 of the Civil Code, according to which those who, when performing their obligations act with bad faith or negligence or are in breach, are subject to compensate for the damages caused. Obviously, the *animus nocendi* has to be proven by the party that claims to have been damaged.

[4] Article 1.532 of the Civil Code. See its full text in paragraph 5.1.1. below.
[5] See Puig Brutau, *Fundamentos de Derecho Civil*, II, Vol. I, Bosch, ed, pp. 227–231.

The plaintiff, when claiming under Article 1.101 of the Civil Code, will have to bring evidence on the following elements:

- The existence of negotiations that gave rise to obligations between the parties (notwithstanding any agreement had not yet been reached).
- The existence of the *animus nocendi.*
- The existence of damages caused by the said *animus nocendi.*

This is in practice a very heavy burden for a plaintiff.

3. Promise to Sell or to Buy

The promise to sell or to buy is the next step in an acquisition negotiation and is regulated in Article 1.451 of the Civil Code as follows:

> The promise to sell or to buy, existing already an agreement on the object and price, will give the parties the right to reciprocally claim the compliance of the contract. In case of impossibility of executing the promise to buy or sell, the regulation provided for the obligations and contracts in this code will be applicable.

Two approaches have been adopted by scholars as to the legal nature of the promise to sell or to buy:

(a) The first approach is influenced by Article 1.589 of the French Civil Code[6] and considers that the promise to sell equals to a sale when there is already an agreement on the object and price between the parties. Article 1.450 of the Spanish Civil Code contains a similar provision, stating that a sale is valid regardless of the fact that object has or has not been transferred, and price paid, if the parties have already defined both of them.

Following this approach, De Castro, Calvillo and Gonzalez Enríquez[7] consider that the injured party can indeed require the Court to oblige the counterpart to fulfil its obligation and proceed with the sale or the purchase.[8]

(b) The second approach states that the legislator distinguished between the "sale" and the "promise to sell" as in fact two different contracts. Clearly, they argue, a promise to sell does not imply transfer of title on the asset or share being sold.

In this respect, Puig Brutau[9] states that in the promise to sell or to buy, the parties undertake the obligation "to do something" and that it is a personal obligation *intuitu personae*. Consequently, the injured party cannot request the specific performance of the promise and would be entitled only to claim for damages.[10]

[6] "La promesse de vente vaut vente, quand il y a consentement des deux parts sur la chose et sur le prix".

[7] The three of them quoted in *Comentarios del Código Civil* v *Compilationes Forales, Revista del Derecho Privado* Tomo XIX, p. 892.

[8] See in favour of this approach Supreme Court Judgment of 1 July, 1950 (R1187).

[9] *Op. cit.* 4 p. 14.

[10] See in favour of this approach Supreme Court Judgment of 11 November, 1943.

Most precedents adopt this second approach in case there is a unilateral promise to sell or to buy, and therefore the only remedy available will be to request for damages, not being able to ask for the fulfilment of the promise. However, in case of bilateral obligations, ie one party promises to sell and the other to buy, the courts have interpreted both theories and have not given us yet a unified criteria.[11] The solution depends very much on the wording and the circumstances of each particular case.

4. Warranties in the Precontract

Finally we have the precontract. Here the parties have not only negotiated and promised to sell or to buy but they have also agreed on the main terms of the transactions and executed the said agreement in the form of a precontract. Usually they fix the most relevant issues of the transaction, being the latter held due only to legal or economic causes such as the lack of permits, documentation, etc. They can also be conditioned upon the completion of a full revision and audit of the company being purchased.

Regarding its legal effects, Spanish scholars have adopted two main approaches:

(a) The so-called classical theory considers that the precontract is a contract by means of which the parties undertake the obligation to execute a new and different contract, which will require a new acceptance by the parties.

The precontract consequently merely creates an obligation to contract in the future, that is, an obligation to do something in the future, to *facere* or *contrahere*. Under this approach the acceptance of the second contract cannot be provided by any third parties, including the court, since it is a non-coercive action based on *intuitu personae* nature.

In case of breach of the precontract, that is, of the undertaken obligation to celebrate the new contract, the counterpart can request damages but not the fulfilment of the obligation.[12]

(b) A new, more modern theory, lead by scholar De Castro, considers, however, that the precontract is a promise of contract which constitutes the first stage of a succession of acts that end up with the final contract. All of these acts form a unity, being the parties already bound by this first promissory stage.[13]

Therefore, in the event that one of the parties does not fulfil its obligation to perform the precontract, the Judge could order the execution of the specific performance, since it is understood that the party in default had

[11] La Cruz Berdejo, "Elementos de Derecho Civil II", *Derecho de Obligaciones*, Vol. Segundo, Teoría General del Contrato, p. 279.

[12] This theory has been applied during the first part of the present century by the majority of the Spanish scholars and precedents. In this respect, see Supreme Court Judgments of 16 October, 1965; 9 July, 1940; 31 October, 1955 and 19 December, 1963.

[13] This theory is widely followed by present Spanish scholars, including Diez Picazo, Puig Brutau, Albadalejo, Laguna, Román García, all of them quoted by Cruz Berdejo, *Op. cit.* 10, p. 273. See also the following Supreme Court decisions quoted by Cruzberdejo, *Op. cit.* p. 273: 1 July, 1950, 21 December, 1951, 2 May, 1959; 21 February, 1969 and 11 November, 1969.

already given his consent to the contract and therefore no new *intuitu personae* consent is necessary.[14]

This is the theory presently being mostly accepted by Spanish scholars and courts. Therefore, if a party does not comply with its obligations under a precontract, the counterpart may (i) request damages or (ii) request the fulfilment of the contract.

5. Warranty of Full Title in an Asset Deal

5.1 Applicable Rules

There are several acts and regulations to consider when examining the sale of an on-going business through the sale of its assets.

5.1.1 Civil Code

The contract by which the ownership of an on-going business is transferred is ruled in accordance to the Civil Code.[15]

Within the Civil Code we must focus our attention on Article 1.532, since it applies to the acquisition of an on-going business. This article reads as follows:

> Whomever sells, for a fixed or global price, the whole of certain rights, incomes or products, will be liable for the legitimacy of the whole as a unit; but will not however be obliged to compensate for each and everyone of the various parts or components of such unit, except in the case the buyer were deprived of all or the main part.

Precedent and scholars agree that Article 1.532 of the Civil Code applies to the sale of an on-going business,[16] despite considering that a business is much more than just *certain rights, incomes or products*.[17]

5.1.2 Corporations Act

Without prejudice to the application of the Civil Code, the Spanish Corporation Act,[18] and specially its Article 39.3, may also apply analogically[19] to the sale of an on-going business through the sale of its assets. This article reads as follows:

[14] See the following precedents ordering the specific performance of the contract itself: Supreme Court Judgment of 21 December, 1955; 28 July, 1976 and 30 December, 1980.

[15] As Garrigues says "companies are sold, inherited, pledged, leased and given in usufruct. For all those acts the civil code rules are applicable": Garrigues *Curso de Derecho Mercantil*, T.I., 7ª ed, p. 194. See also Vicent Chulia: *Delimitación del concepto de compraventa mercantil*, RDCI, p. 84.

[16] Garrigues: *Curso de Derecho Mercantil*, T.I., 7ª ed, p. 195; Garrigues Y Uria, *Comentarios a la Ley de Sociedades Anónimas*, T.I., 1, 3ª ed, p. 350; Sanchez Calero, *Instituciones de Derecho Mercantil*, 8ª ed, I. 109.

[17] De La Camara, *Op. cit.*, p. 360.

[18] "Ley de Sociedades Anónimas", *Real Decreto Legislativo 1564/89* of 22 December, 1989, published in the *Official Gazette* (BOE) No 310 of 27 December, 1989.

[19] According to Article 4.1 of the Civil Code, when an Act does not regulate a specific case, but a similar one and it is considered that there is an identical *raison d'être* for both cases, that Act will be applied analogically.

> Article 39. Non-monetary contributions. Responsibility.
> 3. If a business or establishment is contributed, the contributor will be liable for the legitimacy of the whole if the defect or the deprivation affects the totality or some part of the elements which are essential for the ordinary management of the business.
> It will also be liable for the individual legitimacy of those elements of the business contributed which are considered important as per its economic value.

We should first consider why Article 39.3 applies, since it refers not to the acquisition of a business, but to its contribution to a company in return for shares of the same. The answer is twofold:

- Article 8 of the Limited Liability Company Act[20] and Article 31 of the former Corporations Act[21] refer to Article 1.532 of the Civil Code when discussing the contribution of a business to a corporation.
- Even if the contribution is not a sale, it is indeed an act of transferability, which due to its similarity, has been equated to it. This would explain why Article 31.2 of the former Corporations Act imposed the obligation on the contributor to deliver and warrant full title of the contributed asset in the terms established in the Civil Code for the sale.[22]

5.2 *Interpretation of the Civil Code and the Corporations Act*

Now that we have seen that both the Civil Code and the Corporations Act may apply, and after having introduced Article 1.532 of the Civil Code, we are in a position to examine the different alternatives open to a buyer in case of deprivation of the assets bought. Different approaches to the problem do exist depending on the volume and substantiality of the assets purchased, that is, for instance, it has a different treatment to buy just a trademark than all the assets of a company, and even if only some assets are acquired, it will be treated differently to the purchase of essential and non-essential assets. All these considerations play a major role when considering the remedies available to a buyer. Let us examine four different situations.

5.2.1 Compensation for deprivation of the whole

Here the buyer has been deprived by a final judgment of all the assets purchased by virtue of a third party's right prior to the sale (Article 1.475 of the Civil Code).

In this case, known by precedent and scholars as *evicción total* or total deprivation, Article 1.532 of the Civil Code shall apply and the seller will have to compensate the buyer for the whole.

In a situation of total deprivation the third party who had a prior right will claim against the buyer, who will in return ask the Judge to notify the seller of the proceedings (otherwise, according to Article 1.482 of the Civil Code, the

[20] "Ley de Régimen Jurídico de las Sociedades Anónimas", of 17 July, 1953, published in the *Official Gazette* (BOE) No 199 of July 18, 1953.

[21] "Ley sobre Régimen Jurídico de las Sociedades de Responsabilidad limitada", of 17 July, 1953, published in the *Official Gazette* (BOE) No 199 of July 18, 1953.

[22] Supreme Court Judgment of 11 November,1970 and 3 December, 1981 both quoted in the Judgment of 2 April, 1990 (R. 11.206).

seller will not be liable since he has no option of defending his position against the title reclamation of the third party). Once notified, the seller may appear or not at the proceedings. If he does so, his position is that of a co-defendant and the judgment will determine his future liability against the buyer for damages.[23] In case he does not appear, the proceedings will continue against the buyer, who will have a later action against the seller.

These damages are regulated in Article 1.478 of the Civil Code which states that when the seller has warranted full title to the assets or when nothing has been agreed, the buyer will have the right to claim from the seller the following:

(a) the price of the given asset at the time of the deprivation, regardless of its sale price;
(b) the yields of the asset (if so stated in the judgment);
(c) court fees and contract expenses;
(d) in case of bad faith of the seller the buyer will also be subject to damages and lost profits.[24]

It may be agreed by the parties, however, that no compensation for deprivation of title should be paid. In that case, the seller will have to pay to the buyer only the price of the assets at the time the deprivation occurred and not the other expenses and fees established in Article 1.478 of the Civil Code seen above. In no case can the seller apply the buyer's waiver if he has acted with bad faith (Article 1.476 of the Civil Code).

If the buyer waived any rights for damages knowing the risks of the object bought, he will not even be entitled to the price of the object whose title has been deprived (Article 1.477 of the Civil Code).

5.2.2 Compensation for deprivation of the "main part" or of any of the elements which are "essential" for the management of the business

The latter are the expressions used respectively in Article 1.532 of the Civil Code and section 39.3 of the Corporations Act. They have been interpreted as synonymous, but, what do they exactly mean?

Spanish precedent and scholars have different opinions as to what has to be considered as the "main part" of the assets of a business. The leading scholars consider that it has to be understood as those assets without which the business could not achieve the goal for which it was founded. If that occurs, for instance, with just one trademark, or one patent, then such assets are by themselves a major part of the business being sold.[25]

23 Supreme Court Judgment of 12 November, 1970, (R.5104).

24 The existence of bad faith needs to be proven by the buyer. There is bad faith if the seller knew that the whole assets belonged to the third party when selling them. There is not bad faith if the seller doubted whether he was the real owner of the assets sold and explained so to the buyer, or if he was mistaken about his own rights. See *Comments to the Civil Code*, XIX, Gabriel García Albadalejo, revised by Manuel Albadelejo, p. 306.

25 Garrigues Y Uria, *Op. cit*, 16 p. 335, are of the same opinion when considering that "in each economic organisation certain elements—but not forcely the largest ones—are essential: a patent can often be the most important element, more important in fact than other larger elements which could compose a business organisation". Broseta in *La Compraventa de la Empresa*, p. 58, quotes the same example of the patent, including also trademarks and other intellectual property rights.

Other interpretations, such as considering the main part of the assets as being the numeric simple majority of the same (half plus one) is not being applied any longer by scholars or courts.[26] This interpretation, where quality prevails over quantity, also arises from Article 39.3 of the Corporations Act.

According to De La Camara, to establish the substantiality of the loss for the buyer we must take into account not only subjective but objective factors.[27] According to the circumstances of the buyer (subjective factor) it can be determined objectively what elements compose the main part.

After having considered whether the deprived asset(s) are or are not a main or an essential part, we should determine the liabilities of the seller and the remedies of the buyer. If the asset being deprived is indeed a main part of the business, the buyer will have the same rights as considered above for the case of total deprivation, that is, the seller will have to compensate the buyer according to Article 1.478 of the Civil Code, but only proportionally for the assets being deprived.

De La Camara also considers that in these cases the buyer will also have the option of applying Article 1.479 of the Civil Code, which reads as follows:

> If the buyer loses, due to deprivation, a part of the sold assets of such importance in regard to the whole that without such part he would have not bought them, he will be able to require the resolution of the contract; but with the obligation of returning the asset without greater charges that the ones it had when acquired.
> The same rule will apply when two or more assets were sold together for a fixed price, if it was clear that the buyer had not bought one without the other.

Therefore, in these cases the buyer could either (i) keep the new deprived assets and obtain compensation according to Article 1.478 of the Civil Code for the deprived assets or (ii) terminate the contract, return the non-deprived assets and obtain also the compensation established in the same article for the deprived assets.

Finally, the possibility that the buyer waives his rights as examined in section 5.2.1 above also applies in this case, as well as in all subsequent sections to be discussed below.

5.2.3 Compensation for deprivation of those business elements that, even not being essential, are important when as per its asset value

This is a possibility not regulated in the Civil Code but referred in Article 39.3 of the Corporations Act. Terminology is not at its best here, since it is clear that interpreting the term "importance" will be difficult for courts and scholars. Such legal declarations, made in an abstract way, may lead to undesired litigation on whether an asset can be qualified as important and essential or not.[28]

[26] De La Camara, *Op. cit.* 2, p. 361.

[27] *Op. cit.* 2, p. 363.

[28] Article 133 of the Companies Register Royal Decree ("Real Decreto Legislativo 1597/1987" of 29 December, 1989, published in the *Official Gazette* (BOE) No 313 of 30 December, 1989) requires, in case of the contribution of a business, to describe in a public deed those elements that can be registered at any Public Register (the most important of which are real estate and intellectual or industrial property); as for the other elements, it considers enough a mere list enclosed to the deed.

It may be agreed that the "importance" should be measured as a percentage of the total assets, and not according to its absolute value. A building can have no relative importance whatsoever in an acquisition, regardless of its high value when considered as an independent unit. The fixing of which percentage is "important" can only be decided on a case-by-case basis.

In this situation, the seller is obliged to compensate the buyer, but not over the whole of the business, as we have seen in subsection 5.2.1, but only for the specific asset that has been deprived. Since we have already stated that Article 39.3 of the Corporations Act applies also to the sale of a business, we should conclude that said compensation follows Article 1.478 and 1.479 of the Civil Code, again at the choice of buyer as referred in subsection 5.2.2 above.

5.2.4 Compensation for deprivation of elements that are neither essential nor of importance as independent units

From the literality of Article 1.532 of the Civil Code, we can infer that, except if it is otherwise provided, the contributor or seller of a company will not be liable for the deprivation of title that affects business elements that are neither essential nor important while considering its asset value.

Garrigues and Uria[29] also consider that if the business is transferred as a combined organised unit of industrial activities and assets with economic value, the effects of the deprivation of title of one of those elements cannot be extended to the whole business itself.

It seems clear from the examined Article 39.3 of the Corporations Act that, outside the two cases referred in sections 5.2.2 and 5.2.3 above, the seller does not have to compensate the buyer for deprivation of title on some of the assets of the acquired company. In these contributions the attention is not paid to the individual object which forms the business, except if in the agreement to contribute it the company or the contributor shareholder, or the existing shareholders, ask for the detailed list and data of the assets forming the whole.

However, the Civil Code allows for (i) freedom of agreements among parties as per Article 1.255 and (ii) increase the buyer's securities established in the Civil Code. In this latest respect, Article 1.475 establishes that the contracting parties may "increase, decrease or eliminate the obligation of the seller". This obligation refers to the compensation in case of deprivation of title. Therefore, we consider that the buyer of a business through the purchase of assets may increase his security by stating in the contract that the seller warrants full title to each and every one of the assets sold, attaching, therefore, a list of the same in the contract. In those cases, the general rule will not apply and the seller will be liable for every single deprivation of the assets sold.

An interesting and related issue is raised in case the buyer acquires a business with the purpose of selling its assets independently and no mention is made to the individual assets nor any list is attached. In this case, the buyer is clearly interested in having full title to all assets, and not only to the main part or the essential assets. His interest is not the business as a global unit, but each of the pieces independently. In case the buyer is deprived from the full title of a non-

[29] Garrigues Y Uria, *Op. cit.* 16, p. 354.

essential asset, does it have any further rights or only the remedies just examined? De La Camara answers in the negative, since we cannot apply one or another rule depending on the subjective will of the buyer at any given moment; but he considers that the buyer's intention must be taken into account to interpret the contract since subjective and objective factors are important when determining what are essential and important assets.[30] We agree with De La Camara, and insist on the fact that the buyer can increase his security. Therefore, it is most advisable that the buyer clearly states in the contract its interest on the good title of each and every one of the assets purchased.

6. Warranty of Full Title in a Share Deal

The sale of an on-going business through the sale of its shares—commonly known as an "indirect sale" of business—is the most common way to sell a business in Spain. Two factors contribute to selling a business. First, most businesses in Spain, either large, medium or small, are organised under a corporation form, either as a *Sociedad Anónima* or a *Sociedad de Responsabilidad Limitada*, and therefore a share deal is feasible in almost every case. Secondly, a share deal is thought generally as easier, cheaper and more flexible to execute than an asset deal.

In Spain the most common limited liability company, the *Sociedad Anónima*, shares can either be issued to the bearer, nominative or determined by book entries (*Anotaciones en Cuenta*).[31]

The sale of shares under Spanish law has to fulfil certain formal requirements to be enforceable:

- Written form: as we have seen before, and as a general rule, all contracts of sale over 1.500 pesetas have to be in written form.
- Official intermediary: it will not be required if the shares are *anotaciones en cuenta* (whether bearer or nominatives) or nominative on paper. If the buyer wants to protect himself from the possibility that he is buying *non domino* (defect in title of the seller), the shares have to be bought in the Stockmarket or legalised by a Notary or *Corredor de Comercio.*

  If the shares are bearer paper shares, according to the Third Additional Provision of the Stockmarkets Act, the sale will require the legalisation by a Notary or *Corredor de Comercio* unless the sale has been done through a *Sociedad de Valores* or an *Agencia de Valores.*

In considering the warranty of good title in a share deal we will distinguish between the liability of the seller in case the actual transfer of the title is vitiated (deprivation of the title to the shares) and the case in which the transfer is perfectly valid (no deprivation occurs, nor are there latent defects on the title) but the acquired company has been deprived from part or all of its assets.

[30] De La Camara, *Op. cit.* p. 312.

[31] All Spanish listed companies must have its shares in the form of *Anotaciones en Cuenta* according to the First Additional Provision of the Stockmarket Act ("Ley de Mercado de Valores", Law 24/88 of 24 July, 1988).

6.1 Deprivation of the Title of the Shares

As examined in the case of asset deals, a deprivation of all or part of the acquired shares could occur if ownership to the shares is taken away from the buyer by virtue of a non-appealable judgment stating that a third party had a right—with the limitations we will refer to hereinafter—to the shares prior to the sale.

When considering the deprivation of the title of the shares in an acquisition, two relationships have to be distinguished:

- the right of replevin of a third party against the new owner;
- in the event the replevin by a third party, which is the liability of the seller *vis-à-vis* the buyer.

6.1.1 Right of replevin of a third party

The Civil Code establishes that the possession of a moveable—as in the case of a share—acquired with good faith, amounts to ownership. However, those who have lost a moveable possession or have been illegally deprived from it, can revindicate it from whoever possesses it.[32]

The degree of protection that this regulation gives the good faith buyer of a share, is considered not enough, especially as to securities issued to the bearer and those structured in book entries (*anotaciones en cuenta*), whether bearer or nominative. To solve this problem, the law has established certain limitations, depending on the form the shares have, to the right of replevin by a dispossessed third party. These limitations go beyond the general regulations established for deprivation of assets examined in the first part of this chapter.

6.1.1.1 BEARER SHARES

The transfer of ownership of bearer shares occurs with delivery of the document. The buyer will not be subject to a replevin unless it has obtained possession with bad faith or grave negligence. Notwithstanding this, the real owner will keep his rights and actions against those responsible for the acts which have caused him to lose the ownership.[33]

6.1.1.2 SHARES IN BOOK ENTRIES

The sale will take place by an accounting transfer and recording, in favour of the purchaser, which will have the same effects as the delivery as referred for bearer shares.[34] If the purchaser acquires from the person appearing at the register as the owner, he will not be subject to title claims except in case of bad faith or grave negligence.[35]

6.1.1.3 NOMINAL SHARES

These can be transferred by delivery as well as by endorsement.[36] The holder of the shares will be considered legitimate when he justifies his right to the title by a non-interrupted chain of endorsements.

[32] Article 464 of the Civil Code.
[33] Article 545 of the Commercial Code, *Op. cit.*
[34] Article 9 of the Stockmarkets Act, *Op. cit.*, 30.
[35] Article 11 of the Stockmarkets Act, *Op. cit.*, 30.
[36] Article 56 of the Corporations Act, *Op. cit.*, 18.

Furthermore, it cannot be alleged, for the purposes of challenging the validity of the transfer, any defence concerning the individual situation of the seller.[37] It is worth mentioning that Spanish law allows restrictions on the transferability of nominal shares if such a possibility is contemplated in the by-laws of the company.[38]

6.1.2 Compensation for deprivation of the shares

The situation where the good faith buyer is deprived of the acquired shares is regulated in Article 1.478 of the Civil Code.[39] In case the deprivation of the shares acquired, affects a relevant amount without which the buyer would not have bought the stock package, Article 1479 of the Civil Code shall also apply[40] as an option for the buyer.

6.2 Deprivation of the Title of the Assets in a Share Deal

In case of acquiring a business through the indirect way of acquiring its shares, has the buyer any remedy against the seller in case of being deprived from all or part of the assets of the acquired company?[41] The answer should differ if the sale comprises a majority of the shares or only a minority interest (either merely for portfolio investment purposes or not).

6.2.1 Sale of a majority of the shares of a company

In this case, the aim of both the seller and the buyer is to sell an on-going business through the indirect way of selling its shares. Scholars consider that the seller should be held liable for the deprivation of the assets of the company.[42] Consequently, the applicable rules will therefore be the same as the ones in the case of deprivation of assets, which have already been previously examined in this chapter. The importance and volume of the assets deprived will also determine the type of remedy available to the buyer. Note, however, the scarcity of precedents in this area of the law.

6.2.2 Sale of a minority non-controlling stake of a company

In this case of a sale of a minority non-controlling stake of a company, it seems that the seller cannot be held responsible for any deprivation of assets *vis-à-vis* the buyer. Such burden cannot be imposed on operations where the goal is not, or cannot be presumed to be, the sale of an on-going business, but a portfolio investment.[43] The same will apply to the following two situations:

- Takeover bids where the buyer acquires a majority shareholding through the acquisition of different non-controlling minority interests in the company.
- Any portfolio disinvestment in the stockmarket.

[37] Article 56 of the Corporations Act, *Op. cit.*, 18.

[38] Article 63 of the Company Act, *Op. cit.*

[39] See Section 5.2.1. of this chapter.

[40] See Section 5.2.2. of this chapter.

[41] We will not consider here the right that the sold company itself has against the seller of the deprived asset.

[42] See De La Camara, *Op. cit.* p. 385. This scholar considers that the sale of a minority but controlling interest should also fall into the category of selling a majority interest. In this respect, to have a minority but controlling interest is a very common practice in big corporations.

[43] De La Camara, *Op. cit.*, 2, p. 312.

7. Warranty of Absence of Latent Defects

The main difference between deprivation of title, referred to in sections 5 and 6 and the warranty of absence of hidden defects is that, in the former the seller guarantee the peaceful possession of the asset being sold against any legal disturbance, whereas in the latter the guarantee is the proper economic usefulness of the sold asset.[44]

The Civil Code states in its Article 1.484 what has to be considered as hidden defects. The following are necessary features of hidden defects, which are either directly inferred from the article or taken from courts, and scholars' interpretations.

(a) The defect has to exist before the sale, although it might develop after the same.

(b) The seller has to compensate the buyer for the hidden defect even if the seller himself was unaware of the defect. The buyer may waive its right to be compensated in this case but never in the case where the seller knew of the defect—that is, in case of bad faith.

(c) The defect must be hidden, that is, must neither be known to the buyer nor be easily identifiable. Even in the case where it is not identifiable, the seller will not be obliged to compensate when the buyer is an expert who should have known the defect because of his profession.

The concept of the expert is of great importance for the issues studied in this section. An expert *perito* under the Spanish legal system is a person with special formation and knowledge in a determined area of learning, science, art or even of a practical aspect of any technical or human behaviour.[45] A *perito*, or expert, by contrast with a non-expert, has to know necessarily if a business, due to the defects in most of its elements, is worth a given price.

In the same sense, Puig Brutau[46] explains that a hidden defect is one that cannot be discovered by reasonable vigilance or merely visable, and consequently he excludes those that ought to be easily discovered either because of (i) its undoubtful features, or (ii) the fact that the buyer is an expert who, due to its profession or training, should have known it.

(d) The defect must be substantial, that is, either (i) it is of such a nature that makes the object bought unsuitable for the use it was conceived, or (ii) it diminishes its usefulness to such an extent that if it had been known to the buyer, he would have either not bought it or offered a lower price.

Therefore, it is enough that the object becomes useless for the purpose it was acquired, not being necessarily a complete objective uselessness. If nothing was agreed upon its use, we must understand that it was acquired in order to use it in accordance with its nature and the activity the buyer was, at that time, carrying out.[47]

[44] Supreme Court Judgment of 5 December, 1985, (R. 6204).

[45] Comments to the Civil Code, Ministry of Justice, Vol. II, p. 395.

[46] Puig Brutau, *Fundamentos de Derecho Civil;* T.II.V. 2nd. (2nd ed.) p. 195. Also confirmed by Supreme Court Judgment of 3 January 1970, (R. 370).

[47] Supreme Court Judgment of 1 January, 1970, (R. 370).

(e) The defect has to be of certain importance. As Manresa says,[48] any imperfection or minor defect does not imply the application of the Civil Code and the right to compensate the buyer.

The difficulty arises when establishing the degree of the defect, since mathematical solutions are clearly not applicable. As Badenes Gasset[49] states, when appreciating the importance or degree of any defect, we have to rely on the appreciation made by the courts as if it were a mere question of fact. In any case, it is not required that the defect to be a perpetual one.[50]

8. Warranty of Absence of Hidden Defects in an Asset Deal

The issue to consider is the same as studied when dealing with the warranty of full title in an asset deal, that is, what is the scope of the seller's warranty?; does it warrant that all assets included in the deal are free from latent defects?

8.1 Applicable Rules

The Civil Code, in its Articles 1.488 to 1.499, inclusive, deals with latent defects of a sold object and the subsequent compensation the seller is obliged to give the buyer.

Scholars have considered that Article 1.532 of the Civil Code, referred to in sub-section 5.1.1 of this work, in connection with the sale of an on-going business is also applicable to hidden defects and latent liabilities, regardless of the fact that it does not mention so literally.[51]

8.2 Application of the Civil Code and the Corporations Act

The potential cases arising out of the application of the Civil Code and the Corporations Act follow the same pattern as those examined when considering the deprivation of assets (ie, we should consider hidden defects as a whole, of essential and important elements, and of elements without individual importance). However, as we have seen when defining latent defects in section 7 of this chapter, the degree of expertise the buyer had when acquiring the business is a new element in the study of the hidden defects which will play an important role in determining the seller's obligations and the buyer's remedies.

If the expert (*perito*) decides to buy, regardless of the defects, it is because he has already discounted them from the global price. Therefore, if the buyer knew the defect at the moment of the execution of the contract, or he was expected to know it due to its knowledge and expertise, the seller's guarantee will not apply: in such a case, the buyer cannot consider himself deceived in his expectations,

48 Quoted by Badenes Gasset, *Op. cit.*, p. 693.

49 Badenes Gasset, *Op. cit.*, p. 693.

50 As examples recognised by Spanish jurisprudence of latent defects, we have the following: machine non-usable for the purpose it was originally manufactured, dwelling which needs important reparation work, defective construction of a building, lack of health and sanitary conditions, impossibility of using the heating system, land leaking.

51 Garrigues Y Uria, *Op. cit.*, p. 354.

as he gave his implicit approval to the state the elements were in, and he would have normally taken it into account when determining the price.[52]

The consequences of the buyer being or not being an expert are important when considering the obligation of the seller and the remedies available to the buyer. We will therefore differentiate the following two cases:

8.2.1 Sale to a non-expert buyer

It is essential in this case whether the seller knew or not the latent defects when selling the asset. Only in case the seller did not know of the existence of the latent defects does the Civil Code (Article 1.485) allow for a waiver by the buyer of the seller's liability.

According to Article 1.486 of the Civil Code, if the seller did not know the defects, the buyer may choose between either (i) to terminate the contract or (ii) to ask for a reduction in the price; if the seller knew of the hidden defects but did not notify them to the seller, he will be, in addition to (i) or (ii) above, subject to compensate the buyer for the damages caused.

A different case is raised when the asset sold is lost. In this respect, the loss could have been caused by the hidden defects or by the buyer. If the seller was not aware of the hidden defects, and the object is lost because of this, he will have to return the price and the contract expenses to the buyer; if he knew them he will be also responsible for damages (Article 1.487 of the Civil Code).

If the asset had hidden defects but was lost due to the buyer's negligence or due to *force majeure*, the seller will restitute the assets value at the time the loss took place, and only pay damages if he knew of the hidden defects (Article 1.488 of the Civil Code).

8.2.2 Sale to an expert buyer

Article 1.484 of the Civil Code is very clear when it states that when the buyer is an expert, the seller does not have the obligation to compensate him for hidden defects in the object.

8.3 Statute of Limitations when Claiming Damages for Latent Defects in Acquired Assets

Article 1.490 of the Civil Code establishes that "the remedies established in the five precedent articles (referred to hidden defects) will be extinguished in six months, starting from the delivery of the sold object" (this term cannot be interrupted).[53]

Regardless of the literality of Article 1.490 of the Civil Code, courts have considered that the parties can agree on a period during which the seller is liable for hidden defects. However,[54] the time between when the defect is found and the

52 Badenes Gasset: *Op. cit.*, p. 691.

53 Castan, *Op. cit.*, p. 129, footnote 2. The following jurisprudence determined that the six-month term cannot be interrupted: Supreme Court Judgments of 10 January, 1946; 27 May and 5 July, 1957; 22 May, 1965; 6 April, 1967; 14 October, 1968; 8 March, 1969; 18 April, 1969; 22 December, 1971; 30 November, 1972; 10 February, 1973; and 3 April, 1974.

54 By virtue of Article 1255 of the Civil Code.

seller is notified of its existence, must be a reasonable term, fixed case by case, taking into account as a reference the six-months period established by the code.

The seller does have the right to check, within a reasonable time after he has been notified, if the hidden defects really existed or not at the time of the sale. This examination will determine if the defects did occur due to the fault of the buyer or alternatively, they were already there when the object was sold.

The parties can, therefore, agree that the guarantee lasts for years. But, once the defect is discovered, the reasonable term starts to count. Otherwise, if the buyer could wait until the last day of the expiration term to notify the seller, the seller could not defend its position by checking, for example, if the defect in fact exists, its importance and if it was already there when the object was sold.[55]

8.4 Burden of Proof when Claiming Latent Defects in an Acquired Asset

In order to compel the seller to indemnify the buyer for hidden defects, the defects had to exist at the time the sale took place. Who has the burden of proving so?

Scholars are divided on this issue.[56] We consider, with Manresa,[57] that the plaintiff must prove all facts stated in the claim, that is, not only the existence of the defect when the claim is filed but also that it existed at the time of the sale. In case there is no evidence that could prove its claim, the buyer should try to apply a presumption. Under Spanish law (Article 1.253 of the Civil Code), in order to claim presumption in court it is mandatory to have a direct and precise link, analysed under ordinary human criteria, between the proved fact and the fact that is trying to be inferred. That is, the buyer would need to establish a link between the hidden defect (proved fact) and the fact that such defect occurred before the sale took place.

Returning to the evidence, courts have stated that the mere proof of the existence of the damage is not enough to prove the hidden defect.[58] They have also determined that the buyer, aside from proving the latent defects, has to give the seller the opportunity to challenge and defend its position.[59]

[55] The courts have determined that if from the time an object has been delivered until the time the buyer denies payment, no claim has been brought for defective function, it cannot be proved then the existence of hidden defects on the base of an expert report performed almost two years after the sale of the object. Court judgment of the *Audiencia Provincial de Santa Cruz de Tenerife* dated 18 April, 1982 and commented in *La Ley*, T.1983–1, p. 921, 3355–R.

[56] Badenes Gasset, *Op. cit.*, p. 695.

[57] Quoted by Badenes Gasset, *Op. cit.*, p. 695.

[58] Supreme Court Judgment of 3 December, 1957.

[59] There is a case where the buyer, even though he indeed notified the seller of the defects that, in his opinion, had he sold merchandise, he did not do so in accordance with the required procedures provided in Article 2.127 of the *Ley de Enjuiciamiento Civil*, which is the applicable one, as determined by case law (Supreme Court Judgments of 6 July, 1915 and 15 June, 1926). The buyer just verified the defective state by nominating an expert, and refused to deliver the merchandise to the seller's warehouse so the latter could also determine, by his expertise, the existence of the defects and if they existed before the sale or not. (*Audiencia Territorial de Albacete*, 1 February, 1982.)

We can, therefore, conclude that even if a longer guarantee period is agreed upon, the buyer has to notify the hidden defects to the seller within a reasonable term, so the latter will have the option to certify (i) whether these defects really exist and (ii) whether they already existed at the time of the sale (which as we have previously examined we considered have to be proven by the buyer.)

9. Warranty of Absence of Hidden Defects in a Share Deal

We have so far examined the hidden defects on assets, which obviously can be as diverse. However, when dealing with shares, the hidden defects are more limited. When we buy shares in Spain, which defects could the shares contain that could damage our position as buyers? We will examine only two situations. In both of them the key issue is if the defect is hidden, that is, if it was easily identifiable to the buyer. If it was identifiable, the buyer will not be able to claim any compensation from the seller, as we have previously examined when discussing the hidden defects on assets.

9.1 Shares with non-Voting Rights

In this case the buyer buys the shares believing that he is acquiring all the statutory rights and later finds out that he has bought non-voting rights shares. It seems difficult for the buyer to argue that he had no way of knowing this feature of the shares. Non-voting shares, under Spanish law, have to be contemplated in the by-laws of the company, which are registered at a public Mercantile Register.[60]

Secondly, Article 53.2 of the Corporations Act establishes that in the title of the non-voting shares this will be clearly identified. A buyer should obviously examine the title when acquiring shares. Also, in case titles are not issued and in its place the company issues provisional certificates (*resguardos provisionales*), the feature of non-voting shall also be clearly identifiable in the certificate.

If shares are nominative, they have to be registered at a shares book, which is kept by the company. This book should also contemplate the fact the sold shares did not enjoy the political rights. Consequently, we consider that the defect is easy to identify and therefore it cannot be considered as a hidden one subject to compensation.

9.2 Pledged Shares Sold as Free of Encumbrances

Two situations should be distinguished depending on whether the shares have been issued as titles or as *anotaciones en cuenta.*

- Titles: for the pledge to be created it is required that possession of the titles is given either to the creditor or a third party with the consent of both the creditor and the debtor. Therefore, only by fraud can pledged shares be sold as free of encumbrances. It will clearly be a case of bad faith on the part of the seller, subject to the compensations we have examined before when discussing the asset deals.

[60] By-laws of a company have to be registered at the Companies Register, which is public and open to anyone interested in them.

- Shares in book entries (*anotaciones en cuenta*): encumbrances on shares with this form can be alleged *vis-à-vis* third parties only after the encumbrance has been recorded at the Register of the affected shares. Therefore, the pledge is clearly identifiable, giving the buyer the obligation of checking at the proper registries.

10. *Aliud Pro Alio*

10.1 Definition

The expression *aliud pro alio* can be described as the delivery of an object different from the one agreed upon by the parties, without such delivery being caused by error. The delivered object, therefore, does not fit the interests, needs or expectations of the buyer and, in principle, the obligation of the seller of delivering the object for which he has been paid has not been fulfilled.

10.2 Legal Remedies Available to the Buyer in Case of Aliud Pro Alio

As a general rule, Article 1.124 of the Civil Code states that in the event that one of the parties does not fulfil its obligations, the counterpart may either (i) compel the other to comply with the obligation or (ii) terminate the relationship, having, in both cases, the right to ask for damages.[61]

As we have seen before, Spanish law establishes two terms during which the seller in a civil action has to claim against the buyer for non-compliance of its contractual obligations. If nothing is stated otherwise, the general term of the buyer to claim against the seller for hidden defects is six months. However, in case of *aluid pro alio*, we consider that we are in front of a general contractual non-compliance, and therefore, the general term of 15 years established in Article 1.964 of the Civil Code applies.

It is clear, therefore, that to consider that we as buyers have received a different object or a defective object is essential in order to consider the timetable available, that is, either six months (if not provided otherwise) or 15 years.

The Supreme Court stated in its judgment of 10 June, 1983 that there is a situation of *aliud pro alio* when there is full unfulfilment due to the inadequacy of the object, causing consequently a dissatisfaction for the buyer. In these cases the buyer should be granted the protection contemplated in Articles 1.101 and 1.124 of the Civil Code, already examined in this chapter, avoiding subsequently the application of Article 1.490 of the Civil Code.[62]

[61] Also in this area, see Article 1.101 of the Civil Code, which states that those who incur in *dolus*, negligence and delay when performing their obligations are obliged to compensate the counterpart for the damages caused. See Supreme Court Judgment of 6 March, 1985, which states that due to the unsuitability of the supplied object, which is of impossible use to the buyer, the seller has delivered a different object, or *aliud pro alio*, being therefore a real non-compliance of the contract and not a single case for defects.

[62] Other Supreme Court Judgments concerning the *aliud pro alio* doctrine are those of 30 November, 1972 (R. 4.689); 20 December, 1977 (R. 4.837); 23 March, 1982 (R. 1.500); 20 February, 1984; 20 October, 1984; 22 November, 1984; 3 December, 1984 and 19 December, 1984.

Certain scholars consider that limits have to be set to avoid the abuse of the *aliud pro alio* doctrine. In this sense, Bercovitz states[63] that it should not be applicable when the buyer claims for damages that, if acted with diligence, should have discovered within the periods established in the Civil Code.

11. Third Party Liability

The various third parties acting during an acquisition are subject to a certain level of due diligence in the performance of their activity. It should be distinguished between the general regime of liability and specific provisions for certain professional advisers.

11.1 General Regime of Liability

Spanish law provides for contractual and non-contractual liability (torts).

(a) Contractual liability is regulated in Article 1.101 (already examined above in this chapter). For the liability to be effective, Article 1.104 requires an omission in the diligence that corresponds to the nature of the obligation and the circumstances of the people involved, the time and the place. The damages that can be claimed include the loss of profits.
(b) Non-contractual liability is regulated in Article 1.902 of the Civil Code. It arises when somebody causes damages by action or omission to another, with deceit or negligence.

In both cases three requirements must be fulfilled:

(i) existence of an action or omission producing an imprudent or negligent action attributable to the defendant;
(ii) existence of damages;
(iii) relation between the damage and the action.

11.2 Special Provisions

Apart from disciplinary sanctions, to which we will not refer, the following special provisions should be noted:

(a) Stockmarket intermediaries: among the different rules of conduct it should be pointed out that they must always give priority to clients' interest and that in case of conflict of interest between clients none of them should be given priority.
(b) Auditors: civil and criminal liability must be claimed according to the general regime.[64]

    As to civil liability the auditors (or auditing company) that sign the audit are directly liable, jointly and with no limit for the damages provoked to the audited company and/or third parties. The other partners of the auditor, in case of auditing companies, will be liable subsidiarily, jointly and with no limit as to these damages.[65]

[63] Bercovitz, *Op. cit.*, No 75, pp. 2475–2476.
[64] Article 45 of the "Reglamento de Auditoría de Cuentas" ("RAC") of 20 December, 1990, published in the *Official Gazette* (BOE) No 308 of 25 December, 1990.
[65] Article 45 of the RAC.

(c) Directors of a Company: they are liable before the company, the shareholders and company creditors for damage caused by acts against the law, by-laws or performed without the diligence of a methodical businessman and a loyal representative.[66]

(d) Lawyers: they are subject to civil liability when by deceit or negligence cause damage to the interests of the client (Article 102 Estatuto General de la Abogacía Española). They will have to compensate the damages caused.[67]

(e) Public Notaries: they are subject to civil liability of the damages provoked because of their acts when they are due to deceit, negligence or unreasonable lack of knowledge. If the damages can be repaired, totally or partially, granting another deed the Notary will pay the cost arising from it, and will be liable only for the other damages.[68]

[66] Article 133 of the Corporations Act.

[67] Article 105 of the "Estatuto General de la Abogacía Española" (General By-Laws of the Spanish Bar Association), approved by Royal Decree 2090/1982 of 24 July.

[68] Article 146 of the "Reglamento Notarial", approved by Decree of 2 June, 1944.

Sweden

Tore Wiwen-Nilsson

Mannheimer Swartling Advokatbyrå, Malmö, Sweden

1. Introduction

1.1 Sweden—a Civil Law Country

Swedish law belongs to the Nordic law family, and it has, to a great extent, been influenced by the unification work commenced among the Nordic countries[1] during the 1870s and which still goes on. As a result, the laws of the Nordic countries are similar in many respects. The laws of the Nordic countries, including the laws of Sweden, are heavily influenced by European continental law with respect to terminology, notions and important principles of law.

The most important sources of Swedish law are statutes, court precedents, preparatory works, customs, trade practices, and the legal doctrine as expressed by authoritative legal writers. The legal literature in the Nordic countries can be said to have a strong position.

In Sweden, the decisions of higher courts are not formally binding on the lower courts. Thus, the so-called *stare decisis* doctrine is not applicable in Sweden. On the other hand, principles laid down by the Swedish Supreme Court (*Högsta Domstolen*) are to a large extent adhered to by the lower courts. Further, judgments by lower courts are in some instances used as guidance in other cases.

1.2 The Legal Framework

The most important Swedish statutes within the field of contract law of relevance to the topic of this report, are the Contracts Act of 1915 and the "New" Sale of Goods Act which entered into force on 1 January, 1991 (substituting the Sale of Goods Act of 1905), which both are the result of Nordic unification efforts.

The Contracts Act is the cornerstone of the general law of contracts in Sweden, while the New Sale of Goods Act occupies a similar position within the law of special contracts.

[1] The Nordic countries are Denmark, Finland, Iceland, Norway and Sweden.

The Contracts Act, which has general application within the field of commercial law, contains provisions on the formation of legally binding agreements and related matters. The basic principles contained in the Contracts Act apply to all contracts unless particular legislation exists. These basic principles are: freedom of contract, few formal requirements, "privity of contract" and "*pacta sunt servanda*".

The New Sale of Goods Act regulates the legal effects of a legally binding sales agreement. In cases where the New Sale of Goods Act is not directly applicable, and where to other legislation applies, the Act will probably (as did its predecessor, the Sale of Goods Act of 1905) often be applied indirectly within other fields of special contracts by analogy.

Through the Swedish Act on International Sales of 1987, Sweden adopted Articles 1–13 and 25–88 of the United Nations Convention on Contracts for the International Sale of Goods of 1980 ("the Vienna Convention").[2] The Swedish Act on International Sales applies (with some exceptions relating to the type of goods concerned and excluding consumer sales) exclusively if:

(a) the sale is international, ie the seller and the buyer have their respective places of business located in different States; and
(b) such States are parties to the Vienna Convention, or Swedish substantive law is applicable to the contract as a result of the application of Swedish private international law; and
(c) either of the seller and the buyer has its place of business outside the Nordic countries.[3]

The Vienna Convention and the Swedish Act on International Sales apply only to contracts relating to the sale of goods. Sales of shares are expressly excluded under both the Vienna Convention and the Swedish Act on International Sales.[4] Further, for the purposes of the Swedish Act on International Sales, the term "sale of goods" has been construed by the Swedish legal writers to exclude acquisitions of an on-going business.[5]

As a consequence, cross-border acquisitions of shares of companies are not governed by the Swedish Act on International Sales. Furthermore, it is unlikely, based upon the said opinion of Swedish legal writers, that an acquisition of an on-going business would be governed by the Swedish Act on International Sales. However, this does not preclude the possibility that the acquisition of well-defined moveable assets would be governed by the Swedish Act on International Sales, even if the assets were intended to be used in an on-going business, if the other requirements for the application of the Act are fulfilled. In acquisitions of shares or an on-going business, and in those cases where the requirements of (a)–(c) above are not met, the New Sale of Goods Act will, in principle, be applicable, if Swedish law is to govern.

[2] See Jan Hellner and Jan Ramberg, "Speciell Avtalsrätt I", *Köprätt*, (Stockholm, 1989), *Köprätt*, pp. 285–286.

[3] See Jan Hellner and Jan Ramberg, *Köprätt*, pp. 287–288.

[4] See Article 2(d) of the Vienna Convention.

[5] See for example J. Hellner and J. Ramberg, *Köprätt*, p. 287.

However, where the shares sold do not "represent the business of the company", the New Sale of Goods Act would not be applicable; instead, the principles of section 9 para. 2 of the Swedish Promissory Notes Act would govern.[6] This would be the case where the shares sold represent only a minority portion of such company's shares without any controlling possibilities. The exact borderline has not yet been defined by the Swedish courts. According to said section 9 of the Swedish Promissory Notes Act, the responsibility of the seller is limited to the authenticity of the shares and to the legality of the title of the seller to the shares.[7]

There are no specific rules with regard to warranties in the case of sales of shares listed on the Swedish or a foreign stock exchange; the principles of section 9 para. 2 of the Promissory Notes Act will apply.

With a few exceptions of no relevance to the topic of this chapter, the Contracts Act, the New Sale of Goods Act, the Swedish Act on International Sales and the Swedish Promissory Notes Act are non-mandatory, meaning that the parties are free to agree on terms deviating from these Acts.

There is also a possibility for trade practices to supplement, and sometimes even overrule, the regulations of non-mandatory statues.[8] However, this requires that the trade practices are established and commonly used. Under certain circumstances, standard contract provisions which are very often used, may become trade practices. However, the Swedish courts tend to require a well-established practice and a common use of such provisions for considering them as trade practices. In the case of acquisitions of shares or a business, no such standard contract provisions exist in Sweden.

Moreover, a contract term may be set aside or modified in accordance with section 36 of the Contracts Act. This section states that a contract term may be set aside or modified if it is found to be unreasonable, taking into account the contents of the contract, the circumstances existing at the time of conclusion of the contract, later events and other circumstances. If the term is so fundamental for the agreement, that it cannot reasonably be required that the other provisions of the contract shall remain unchanged, other terms of the contract may also be modified, or the contract may be set aside in its entirety. Although the main purpose of section 36 is to protect consumers, it is recognised that it applies also to contracts between commercial parties, especially in the case of unfair terms in standard form contracts. However, there are, to date, only a few court cases in which section 36 has been applied to contracts between commercial parties. None of the court cases is applicable to the questions discussed in this chapter, and it is reasonable to assume that section 36 will

[6] See Gunnar Karnell, *Om värdefel vid överlåtelse av rörelsdrivande aktiebolag, Festskrift till Knut Rodhe* (*Värdefel*), (1976), pp. 284–286. However, some legal writers have argued that the New Sale of Goods Act is applicable to all sale of shares. See Stefan Lindskog, *Festskrift till Grönfors*, s 306 ff and Christina Hultmark, *Kontraktsbrott vid köp av aktie*, s 85 ff.

[7] See Gunnar Karnell, *Värdefel*, pp. 284–285, Anders Knabe, *Företagsöverlåtelser, en probleminventesring*, (Stockholm, 1989) (*Företagsöverlåtelser*), pp. 73–74 and Anders Johansson, *Undersökningsplikt vid aktiebolagsförvärv*, (SvJt 1991) (*Undersökningsplikt*), pp. 81, 90–93.

[8] See Axel Adlercreutz, *Avtalsrätt II*, (Lund, 1978), pp. 49–50.

be used restrictively in cross-border acquisitions between commercial parties.[9]

The New Sale of Goods Act entered into force quite recently and most of the Swedish legal literature on acquisitions is based on its predecessor, the Sale of Goods Act of 1905. Therefore, the consequences of applying the New Sale of Goods Act in the situations dealt with herein have not yet been thoroughly discussed in the legal literature.[9a]

In accordance with Swedish practice, Swedish businessmen try to avoid involving the courts in their legal differences. Therefore, there are relatively few court cases in Sweden relating to warranties in acquisitions. The most important cited cases are, instead, a few arbitration awards that have been released for publication.

Naturally, Swedish law will be applied only if agreed upon by the parties to an international transaction, or if Swedish law would be designated as the governing law in accordance with applicable international private law (choice of law rules).

1.3 Scope of this Chapter

This chapter focuses on cross-border acquisitions where one purchaser or a group of purchasers acquires at least the main part of the shares or an on-going business of a company, from one seller or a group of sellers. Purchase agreements relating to such acquisitions normally contain a list of agreed warranties. As a matter of principle, there is no legal difference regarding the seller's liability under Swedish law between domestic and cross-border acquisitions, except that there would be some implications, for example, in the case of an acquisition of an on-going business (as distinguished from an acquisition of shares) which involved real estate located outside Sweden.

No attempt is made in this chapter to analyse the special circumstances or legal aspects relating to takeover bids or acquisitions of companies, the shares of which are registered or traded on the Swedish or a foreign stock exchange, traded so-called over-the-counter, or otherwise where the shares are widely held. Generally, warranties are not frequently used in those types of acquisitions.

This chapter will not, in principle, deal with acquisitions of individual assets belonging to an on-going business.

2. Notions in Swedish Law

Anglo-Saxon legal terms such as "warranties", "representations" and "covenants" do not have the same meaning as corresponding terms of Swedish law. Under Swedish law, other notions have been developed. The most important notions are:[10]

[9] See Jan Ramberg, *Allmän avtalsrätt, (1989)*, p. 251 and Axel Adlercreutz, *Avtalsrätt I*, 8th ed, (Lund, 1984) (*Avtalsrätt*) p. 229.

[9a] This report was finalised in December, 1991. Since then, some legal writers have dealt with the application of the New Sale of Goods Act as regards share purchases. A comprehensive study has been made by Christina Hultmark, in *Kontraktsbrott vid köp av aktie*, April, 1992.

[10] See J. Hellner and J. Ramberg, *Köprätt*, pp. 168–171, Anders Knabe, *Förstagsöverlåtelser*, p. 87 and Folke Grauers, *Fastighetsköpet*, (1984), pp. 121–125.

(a) *Garanti*: by an *garanti* a party (eg a seller) expressely assures a certain quality or a certain condition, in the sense of a state of being and in a broad sense.

(b) *Enuntiation*: there is an *enuntiation* when a seller, without giving an express *garanti*, has provided a purchaser with detailed information about the object to be acquired under such circumstances that the purchaser has a justified reason to assume the correctness of such information and rely upon the same.

Garanti and *enuntiation* will hereafter jointly be referred to as warranties, since their legal consequences in general are the same.

(c) *Konkret fel*: there is a *konkret fel* when the object to be acquired differs from what is agreed between the parties, eg when a warranty is not met. Consequently, deviations from warranties (ie *garantier* and *enuntiationer*) are considered as *konkreta fel*.

(d) *Abstrakt fel*: there is an *abstrakt fel* when the object to be acquired differs from a general standard. An *abstrakt fel* is independent of a warranty and is determined from a hypothetical general standard of objects of the same kind as the object to be acquired.

(e) *Faktiskt fel*: there is a *faktiskt fel* when there is a non-conformity with respect to a physical condition or quality.

(f) *Rådighetsfel*: there is a *rådighetsfel* when there are non-conforming restrictions or limitations as to the purchaser's use of the object acquired resulting from decisions or regulations of governmental and other authorities.

(g) *Rättsligt fel*: there is a *rättsligt fel* when there are non-conforming restrictions or limitations as to the purchaser's use of the object acquired resulting from a legal right of a third party.

3. Freedom of Contract—Implied and Express Warranties

The parties to a contract regarding the acquisition of shares or an on-going business are in principle free to stipulate the terms and conditions of their agreement. Both oral and written warranties (see the definition in section 2 above) will be binding upon the parties.

A warranty does not need to be explicit; it can be deducted from the general wording of the contract or otherwise be implicit or construed from, for example, the conduct of the seller.

It is sometimes uncertain whether or not information presented by one party to the other can be considered as specific enough to constitute an *enuntiation*. As a general rule, the information presented has to refer to the quality or conditions of the object acquired and the information has to be understood by the recipient thereof as seriously meant to be correct, in order to be considered as an *enuntiation*.

In acquisitions of shares, it has been questioned whether or not the seller could be held liable for information originating from the company sold. Based on section 18 para. 2 on the New Sale of Goods Act, (surprisingly) it has been suggested that a seller could be held liable if he has handed over documents containing such information to the purchaser or if the seller himself, orally or in writing, has invoked such information during the negotiations. Another paragraph of the same section of the New Sale of Goods Act has been invoked to support the opinion that a seller could be held liable also if the information has been furnished to the purchaser, not by the seller himself but by the management of the company sold; provided always that the purchaser had reason to believe that the information was furnished on behalf of the seller and the information had affected the purchaser's decision to purchase the company.[11]

Contracts rarely contain terms to meet all situations. Swedish law allows a written contract to be supplemented by statutes and many statutes have the function of filling gaps. Consequently, if an agreement is silent, the statutes (here the New Sale of Goods Act) will be applied.

Until recently, Swedish legal writers have been of the opinion that it is very difficult to determine a "general" standard or a "general" value of a company.[12] Consequently, *abstrakta fel* have rarely been considered as a possibility in the case of a purchase of a company. However, lately the opinion has been brought forward in the legal debate that a purchaser of a company should have an opportunity to invoke *abstrakta fel*.[13]

One example mentioned in this debate is the situation where the major asset of the purchased company deviates from what can be considered as the general standard of such asset and the deviation is substantial when considering the company as a whole.[14] Section 17 para. 2(1) and (2) of the New Sale of Goods Act has been invoked as the basis for this opinion. Further, some legal writers are of the opinion that a seller is always responsible for the compliance of the books of the company with law and generally accepted accounting principles.[15]

4. General v Special Warranties

Normally, warranties in contracts for the acquisition of shares or an on-going business with a Swedish party are directed to a named beneficiary, namely the purchaser or purchasers. Of course, a contract could contain "general" warranties in the sense that the beneficiary is an unknown group of purchasers. Such warranties would probably be construed, taking into account its generality and in principle, as binding upon the "warrantor". However, this report will focus on warranties directed to a named beneficiary and will not deal further with "general" warranties.

[11] See Ola Åhman, *Betydelseprövningen vid förestagsöverlåtelse*, (SvJt 1990), (*Betydelseprövningen*), p. 479, pp. 483–484.

[12] See Gunnar Karnell, *Värdefel*, pp. 277–278, Anders Knabe, *Företagsöverlåtelser*, p. 69.

[13] See Anders Johansson, *Undersökringsplikt*, pp. 94–96 and Ola Åhman, *Betydelseprövningen*, pp. 484–485.

[14] See Ola Åhman, *Betydelseprövningen*, p. 485.

[15] Anders Johansson, *Undersökningsplikt*, p. 94 and Stefan Lindskog, *Något om köprättsligt fel i rörelsedrivande aktiebolag, Festkrift till Gotthard Calissendorff*, (Stockholm, 1990), (*Festskrift*), p. 142.

5. Warranties in Negotiations—*Culpa in Contrahendo*

The concept of *culpa in contrahendo*[16] is recognised by Swedish law as to create legal remedies both in the situation where no contract is concluded and where there is a contract.

The basic principle according to Swedish law is that the parties negotiate at their own risk. Normally, they cannot expect to be compensated for their costs for the negotiations or for anticipated benefits of the contract, should no contract ultimately be concluded. Swedish law starts from the position that either party is free to re-evaluate its position during the negotiations and to withdraw unilaterally from such negotiations without giving any reasons and without incurring any liability towards the other party.[17] Legal consequences follow, in principle, only from an offer and its acceptance.

It has, however, been suggested that parties who engage in negotiations should have certain duties towards each other and that certain liability could result from a failure to fulfil such duties. This opinion is influenced by the originally German notion of *culpa in contrahendo*. Vaguely, the opinion has been voiced that the parties to negotiations should act loyally towards each other and diligently.[18]

Certain typical situations where a party could be held liable have been identified:

(a) a party has acted so as to lead the other party to believe that he should be compensated for his costs for the negotiations, if the negotiations do not result in a contract;
(b) a party has entered into the negotiations without ever intending to conclude the contract;
(c) the party's intention with the negotiations is only to extract commercial or technical information from the other party; etc.

The opinion has also been expressed that the deeper the parties have engaged in the negotiations and the longer the negotiations have continued, the more likely it is that a party would need to have a reasonable excuse if he should wish to withdraw.[19]

The principle that a party can be held liable to pay damages on the grounds of blameworthy behaviour during contract negotiations is considered to have been established by two decisions of the Swedish Supreme Court: *NJA* 1963 p. 105

[16] The doctrine of *culpa in contrahendo* goes back to an article by von Jhering, entitled *Culpa in contrahendo oder Schadenersats bei nictigen oder nich zur Perjektion gelangten Verträgen* (Jahrbücher für die Dogmatik des heutigen Römischen und Deutschen Privatrechts I (1861)). See also Akel Adlercreutz, *Avtalsrätt*, p. 83, Jan Hellner, *Speciell avtalsrätt II, Kontraktsrätt*, (Stockholm, 1984), (*Speciell avtalsrätt*) p. 325 and Bernhard Gomard, *Nordiska Juristmötet*, (1984), p. 307.

[17] See Axel Adlercreutz, *Avtalsrätt*, p. 83, Berhnard Gomard, *Nordiska Juristmötet*, (1984), pp. 286–288.

[18] See Axel Adlercreutz, *Avtalsrätt*, pp. 83–84, Jan Hellner, *Speciell avtalsrätt*, pp. 325–326, Lars Gorton, *Shipping and Contracting*, p. 47 and Bernhard Gomard, *Nordiska Juristmötet*, (1984), pp. 276–277, 301–302, 307.

[19] See Bernhard Gomard, *Nordiska Juristmötet*, (1984), pp. 277–278, 292, 307, 309, 446.

and *NJA* 1978 p. 147. Although the claims were rejected in the latter case, the court indicated that fault of a party during negotiations could result in liability for damages.[20]

No guidance is, however, given by Swedish court cases regarding which duties the parties owe each other or the degree of carelessness required to found a claim. Nor are there any cases defining which reasons are acceptable for a unilateral withdrawal from negotiations without incurring liability.[21] An individualistic approach where all the facts of the specific case will be considered, will most likely be adopted by the Swedish courts.

In determining the extent of compensation payable by a party liable for damages, Swedish law makes the distinction between so-called "negative interest" and so-called "positive interest". Where the injured party is compensated for his "negative interest" he is restored to the position he would have been in had he not, in our case, entered into the negotiations. In the case where the "positive interest" is compensated, he would also recover the value of the benefit anticipated from the contract, including expected profits.[22]

The position of Swedish law in respect of precontractual liability (however, not undisputed)[23] is said to allow only compensation for the negative interest of the injured party.[24]

The fact that the behaviour leading to liability "takes place" in the grey area between the rules for non-contractual and contractual liability entails certain difficulties in determining the extent of the liability and who shall bear the burden of proof, the injured party or the liable party. The position of Swedish law is most likely that the injured party has to prove the blameworthy behaviour and cause.[25]

Independent of the seriousness of the behaviour of a party, the only remedy under Swedish law is damages. Thus, the court will not "force" a contract upon the parties. Another matter is that uncertainty may exist whether or not a contract has been concluded. In such a case, the court may determine that a contract shall be considered to exist. The basis for such determination would not, however, be the wrongdoing of either of the parties, but whether the elements required for the constitution of a contract are at hand, in specific situations, a court may be ready to determine that a binding contract shall be considered to exist also when one of the parties claims lack of agreement.[26]

Further, statements and actions of one of the parties during the negotiations could, if a contract is concluded, be considered as *enuntiationer* and will as such be binding upon the warrantor.

[20] See Axel Adlercreutz, *Avtalsrätt*, p. 84.

[21] Gomard is of the opinion that serious objections about the other party and reasons beyond the party's control are acceptable reasons for a unilateral withdrawal from negotiations. An offer from a third party or reasons within the party's control is in Gomard's opinion not acceptable reasons for such withdrawal. See Bernhard Gomard, *Nordiska Juristmötet*, (1984), p. 309.

[22] See Kjetil Krokeide, *Tidskrift for rettsvidenskap*, (1979), pp. 132–227.

[23] See *NJA* 1989, section 614, p. 620. Bert Lehrberg, *Juridisk Tidskrift*, (1990–91) Nr 3, p. 406.

[24] See Bernard Gomard, *Nordiska Juristmötet*, (1984), pp. 302, 307, 310 and Jan Hellner, *Speciell avtalsrätt*, p. 326.

[25] See Göran Portin, *Nordiska Juristmötet*, (1984), p. 451.

[26] See eg *NJA* 1977 p. 92.

6. Warranties in Promises to Sell

According to the Contracts Act, an offer once communicated is binding and cannot be revoked within its time of validity. Consequently, warranties given in an offer are also binding.

Also an acceptance is binding and cannot be revoked, but a legally binding agreement does not come into existence, unless, with a great simplification, "there is a meeting of minds". An offer lapses if not accepted within the period of time during which the offer is valid. According to the Contracts Act, the time during which an offer is binding is determined either in the offer itself or, where the offer is silent on this point, by the court. The court will determine what is a reasonable period of time considering the time required to communicate the offer to the offeree, the time required by the offeree to consider the offer and the time required to communicate the answer to the offeror.[27]

Swedish law could, somewhat simplified, be said to adhere to a compromise between the reliance theory and the will theory aiming at protecting both parties. The system laid down by the Contracts Act is schematic. It only distinguishes between two situations: there is no contract or there is a contract.[28]

7. Warranties in Sale Agreements

Warranties in sale agreements are binding upon the seller. However, notwithstanding the existence of a warranty the seller may be relieved (as described below).

A general rule under the New Sale of Goods Act is that the purchaser may never invoke such defects as he was aware of before the entering into the agreement. Further, a purchaser has a duty to examine the object of acquisition before the signing, if the seller so requests. The purchaser may invoke defects which he should have found, had such examination been performed, only if the seller was acting in bad faith.[29]

If the seller has given a warranty in the sales agreement, which covers certain qualities of the object to be acquired, the purchaser is, in principle, relieved of the above-mentioned duty to examine the object with respect to such qualities.[30] However, voices have been raised in the legal literature, contending that if the seller requests the purchaser to examine a specified quality and the warranty in respect of such quality is vague, then the purchaser still has a duty to examine the object with respect to such quality.[31]

Even if the purchaser was aware of a defect before entering into the contract, he may invoke a warranty on the condition that also the seller was aware of the

[27] See Kurt Grönfors, *Avtalslagen*, (Lund, 1984), (*Avtalslagen*), pp. 23–65 and Axel Adlercreutz, *Avtalsrätt*, pp. 36–61.

[28] See Axel Adlercreutz, *Avtalsrätt*, pp. 28–29, 202–207 and Kurt Grönfors, *Avtalslagen*, pp. 138, 152–155.

[29] See section 20 of the New Sale of Goods Act and Jan Hellner and Jan Ramberg, *Köprätt*, pp. 64–65.

[30] See Jan Hellner and Jan Ramberg, *Köprätt*, p. 65 and Proposition 1988/89: 76, *NY köplag*, p. 94.

[31] See Anders Johansson, *Undersökningsplikt*, pp. 97–98.

defect and it was either agreed or implied that the seller should be liable for the defect. However, if the seller was not aware of the defect and this is known by the purchaser, the general opinion expressed by legal writers is that the purchaser has to inform the seller thereof prior to entering into the agreement, in order to be able to invoke a warranty for such a defect.[32]

8. Warranties and the Closing

Under Swedish law, the parties are free to agree on the duration of a warranty and on the period during which remedies may be available.

Section 21 of the New Sale of Goods Act lays down the basic principle that questions concerning conformity of the goods acquired are determined as of the time when the risk of loss passes to the purchaser. Normally, the purchaser has to prove that there was a non-conformity when the risk of loss passed. However, if the seller has given a warranty covering a certain quality of the object, a lack of conformity with such warranty is presumed to have existed at the time when the risk of loss passed to the purchaser, even if it occurs thereafter; ie a legal consequence of a warranty is that the burden of proof in this respect lies with the seller.[33]

It is also possible for the seller to give warranties concerning the quality of the object acquired after the time when the risk of loss has passed; for example, a warranty that the object will for a period of time remain fit for a particular purpose or will retain a specified quality. Of course, such warranties are binding upon the seller.[34]

9. Warranty of Clear Title

A warranty of "clear title" (*rättsligt fel*) is binding upon the warrantor. Even if no warranty is given, the seller is liable for deviations relating to the possibility of the purchaser to use the object as intended, due to a third party's real right or resulting from decisions or regulations of governmental and other authorities.[35]

According to section 41 of the New Sale of Goods Act, the object to be acquired must be free from any rights or claims of a third party, unless the purchaser has agreed to acquire the object subject to such rights or claims.

10. Warranties as to Specific Assets—Positive and Negative Warranties

Normally, contracts on cross-border acquisitions governed by Swedish law contain a list of warranties. Such warranties can be both positive and negative in the sense that the warranty may relate to the existence or non-existence of

[32] See Folke Grauers, *Fel i sålt skepp*, p. 219 and Anders Johansson, *Undersökningsolikt*, p. 98.
[33] See Jan Hellner and Jan Ramberg, *Köprätt*, pp. 66–67.
[34] See Jan Hellner and Jan Ramberg, *Köprätt*, p. 67.
[35] See Jan Hellner and Jan Ramberg, *Köprätt*, pp. 206–207.

something. Generally, warranties relating to the following items will be found in a contract for the acquisition of a business.

- financial information;
- share capital;
- historical profits;
- liabilities;
- immoveables;
- intellectual property;
- insurances;
- contracts;
- good standing;
- litigation;
- tax claims;
- employee's rights;
- rights of third parties;
- compliance with laws and regulations.

The contents and legal implications of a warranty depend on the wording of such warranty and other circumstances relevant to contractual interpretations. If no express warranties on the above-mentioned subjects have been included in the contract, it cannot be precluded that the New Sale of Goods Act will be applied to the effect that specific items that would have been covered by such express warranties could be deduced from the general provisions of the New Sale of Goods Act (ie section 17 para. 2) or be construed as being implicitly applicable as a liability for *abstrakta fel.*

11. Warranties of Merchantable Quality and of Fitness for Use

The legal terms "merchantable quality" and "fitness for use" are not as such legal terms under Swedish law. However, the concepts that have been developed for defining the seller's responsibility for quality in section 17 para. 2(1) and (2) of the New Sale of Goods Act, are similar to the concepts on which the Anglo-Saxon warranties of "merchantable quality" and "fitness for use" are based.

According to the above-mentioned section, the object of acquisition does not conform with the contract unless:

(a) it is fit for the purposes for which objects of the same description normally would be used; and
(b) it is fit for the particular purpose for which it was intended, if the seller at the conclusion of the contract must have been aware of such purpose, and it was reasonable for the buyer to rely on the seller's "skill" and "judgment".

As mentioned in section 3 above, due to the fact that it may not be possible to determine a general standard for a business, it is uncertain whether section 17 para. 2(1) and (2) of the New Sale of Goods Act is applicable as regards acquisitions of businesses.

12. Absence of Defects

The starting point when deciding whether or not the object to be acquired is defective is the agreement between the parties. As mentioned above, there is a *konkret fel* when the object to be acquired differs from what is agreed between the parties. Consequently, a breach of a warranty constitutes a *konkret fel.* Section 17 para. 1 of the New Sale of Goods Act emphasises that the parties must comply with their agreement.

Even if the agreement is silent and no warranty is given by the seller, a non-conformity with a general standard of objects of the same kind as the object to be acquired could be considered as an *abstrakt fel.* Further, the object to be acquired must be transferred free of any right or claim of a third party, unless otherwise agreed. These provisions are embodied in section 17 para. 2(1) and 41 of the New Sale of Goods Act. However, as mentioned above, it is uncertain to what extent *abstrakta fel* can be invoked in acquisitions of businesses.

13. Effective Time and Duration of Warranties

Normally, conformity with a warranty is determined as of the time the risk of loss of the goods passes to the purchaser, even if the lack of conformity becomes apparent after that time. This is provided for in section 21 para. 1 of the New Sale of Goods Act.

The warrantor will bear the burden of proof since a lack of conformity with a warranty is presumed to have existed at the time risk of loss passed to the purchaser, even if it occurs thereafter.[36]

Such warranty is binding upon the seller. Section 21 para. 2 of the New Sale of Goods Act states that the seller is liable for any lack of conformity with such a warranty, as well as for any lack of conformity which occurs after the risk has passed, if it is due to a breach of contract by the seller.

The parties are free to agree on the duration of a warranty. Unreasonable short time limits for the purchaser to give notice of lack of conformity with a warranty might, however, be set aside by a Swedish court if it decides to apply section 36 of the Contracts Act (see section 1.2 above).

If the contract is silent on this point, the time limit within which a notice must be given by the purchaser will be the one which is set forth in section 32 para. 2 of the New Sale of Goods Act. This section provides that the purchaser loses his rights following from lack of conformity of the object, if he does not give the seller notice of such non-conformity at the latest within a period of two years from the date on which the object was transferred to the purchaser, unless otherwise follows from an agreed warranty.

However, as dealt with in more detail in section 18 below, based on a Supreme Court judgment,[37] a legal writer contends that a purchaser has a duty to examine the acquired company and give notice of such lack of conformity which he should have discovered at such examination at the latest within one year after the

[36] See Jan Hellner and Jan Ramberg, *Köprätt*, pp. 66–67.

[37] See *NJA* 1976 section 341 (p. 352).

closing.[38] Opinions have also been presented in favour of an examination period ending within a reasonable period after the first annual closing of the accounts of the acquired company after the closing.[39]

14. Beneficiary of the Warranty

Warranties in acquisition contracts with a Swedish party is normally directed to a named beneficiary, namely to the purchaser. However, the possibility that a third party may invoke a warranty cannot be precluded. This could, for example, be possible if the purchaser assigns his rights under the contract to a third party.

Section 4.22 of the Swedish Land Law provides that a purchaser may claim damages from his seller's seller if the purchaser has to renounce the real estate acquired because of the prevailing right of a third party, and the seller cannot pay the damages. Opinions have been raised in the legal literature that this provision should be applied by analogy also to acquisitions of documents of title, such as shares.[40]

15. Limitations and Disclaimers

Limitations and disclaimers of liability as regards warranties are frequently used in contracts for the acquisition of shares and an on-going business with a Swedish party.

As a general rule, limitations and disclaimers are interpreted in Sweden in a restrictive manner, which emphasises the need of clarity. One could say that there is a presumption against the party relying on limitations and disclaimers. Furthermore, there is a (small) possibility that unreasonable limitations and disclaimers may be set aside by a Swedish court according to section 36 of the Contracts Act (see section 1.2 above).

The inclusion of express warranties in the agreement does not by itself limit the right of the purchaser to raise a claim against the seller for matters not covered by such express warranties. If the seller wants to limit his liability to such express warranties, such limitation would have to be an express term of the agreement. Thus, the mere fact that certain express warranties are included in the contract does not preclude that the seller may be held liable for matters not covered by the warranties.

16. Form Requirements

There are legally no form requirements as regards the acquisition of an on-going business or shares, except in the case of real estate included in an assets transfer, ie where the real estate itself is acquired and not the legal person owning the real estate.

[38] See Gunar Karnell, TSA 1977, "Något om reklamation och preskription vid garantianspråk beträffande aktiebolagsöverlåtelser", pp. 160–161 and 163.

[39] See Anders Johansson, *Undersökningsplikt*, p. 110.

[40] See Henrik Hessler, *Obehöriga förfaranden med värdepapper*, (1981), p. 127; and Gösta Walin, *Lagen om skuldebrew m m*, (1977), p. 80, No 2.

In summary, the following applies to the acquisitions of real estate. Contracts of sale of real estate must be in writing and signed by both the seller and the purchaser (it may be drawn up privately). The price and the registered name of the real estate has to be stated in the contract. The contract is void if the price mentioned in the contract differs from the price agreed between the parties and such difference is invoked by one of the parties.[41]

17. Applicable Law

The parties to a contract relating to a cross-border acquisition have, according to Swedish law, in principle the freedom to agree on which law shall govern. Such agreement is normally binding upon the parties and will be applied by the courts, unless, on the basis of *ordre public* or other similar reasons, the court disregards the choice made by the parties.[42]

Swedish law does not have a specific answer to the question of applicable law in cross-border acquisitions of shares or of an on-going business if the parties have not reached an agreement in this regard. Rules of general application have been developed by the courts and by the legal doctrine. The principal rule is that the law with the strongest connection to the contractual relationship of the parties will be governing. Based on this principal rule, *prima facie* rules have been developed. These rules will generally be applied, unless they are found to be inadequate in a certain case. According to one such *prima facie* rule, the law of the seller will govern the sale of goods—which has for this purpose been interpreted to include acquisitions of shares and of an on-going business.[43]

18. Breach of Warranties—Conditions to Enforce Warranties

Where a purchaser is in breach of a warranty in a cross-border acquisition, the extent to which the purchaser is able to seek remedies will largely depend on the wording of the contract. Normally, the contract will contain provisions on applicable remedies and provisions on when such remedies may be sought. Such provisions are of course normally binding upon the parties.

However, if the contract is silent in this respect some legal writers are of the opinion that both *konkreta fel* and *abstrakta fel* must be material when considering the company acquired as a whole, in order to entail the right for the purchaser to seek remedies.[44]

Consequently, these legal writers claim that even deviations from a warranty must be material when considering the acquired company as a whole in order to entail a remedy, unless otherwise follows from the wording of the contract or from the purpose of such warranty.[45] Other writers are of the opinion that the

[41] See Folke Grauers, *Fastighetsköp*, (Lund, 1984), pp. 48–49 and JB 4 kap 1.
[42] See Michael Bogdan, *Svensk Internationell Privatoch Processrätt*, (*IP*), (Lund, 1985), pp. 206–207.
[43] See Michael Bogdan, *IP*, pp. 211–212.
[44] See Gunnar Karnell, *Värdefel*, pp. 279–280, Ola Åhman, *Betydelseprövningen*, pp. 487–491 and Anders Knabe, *Företagsöverlåtelser*, p. 72.
[45] See Gunnar Karnell, *Värdefel*, p. 280 and Ola Åhman, *Betydelseprövningen*, p. 489.

seller, in all circumstances where a warranty is given, is liable for any deviation.[46] Perhaps, one should not exaggerate the importance of these differing opinions, as in practical situations the end result often may be the same.

According to section 18 of the New Sale of Goods Act, incorrect information handed over by a seller to a purchaser may entail remedies only if the incorrect information is assumed by the court to have affected the acquisition. According to the preparatory works, the purchaser has to make probable that the incorrect information provided by the seller has affected the acquisition.[47] One legal writer is of the opinion that it is sufficient that the purchaser shows that the information was not unimportant for his valuation of the acquired company.[48]

Some legal writers are of the opinion that the court should decide whether or not deviations or incorrect information are of importance or have affected the acquisition based on the situation of the individual purchaser.[49]

A question frequently raised is whether or not a seller may be relieved from liability if a negative deviation from a warranty can be "balanced" by a positive deviation. A seller could argue that this should be the case if, for example, he has given the purchaser incorrect information on the acquired company's stock but the net worth of the company is the same anyhow because some of the claims of the company which had been written off as "bad-debts" later were paid to the company. One legal writer is of the opinion that such an argument should not be accepted as a general rule in all situations. For example, the purchaser might have evaluated the company taking into account the possibility of receiving some of the depreciated claims.[50] However, the concept that a deviation from a warranty should be material when considering the acquired company as a whole in order to entail a remedy, supports the argument that there could be a right of set-off. Thus, no straight answer can be given; the final conclusion much depends on the basis on which the purchase price has been calculated, the contents of the applicable warranties and other relevant circumstances.

Even if a deviation from a warranty is material when considering the acquired company as a whole, there are possibilities for the seller to be relieved of his liability, if the purchaser fails to fulfil the duty to examine the acquired company (see section 7 above), or if he fails to give notice of a non-conformity.

Unless otherwise agreed, according to section 32 para. 1 of the New Sale of Goods Act, the purchaser has to notify the seller of a defect within a reasonable period of time after he has, or ought to have, become aware of it. This provision could be interpreted as a far-reaching duty of the purchaser to examine the acquired company after the closing. However, a judgment by the Swedish Supreme Court (*NJA* 1976, p. 341) limits this duty. The judgment can be construed such that the time period within which the purchaser shall notify the seller of a deviation from a warranty is one year after the closing.

[46] See Stefan Lindskog, *Förhandlingsspelet–om affärsförhandling och kontraktskrivining*, (1989), p. 187.

[47] See Proposition 1988/89: 76 *Ny köplag*, p. 88.

[48] See Stefan Lindskog, *Festskrift*, p. 136.

[49] See Ola Åhman, *Betydelseprövningen*, pp. 487–486, (Stockholms handelskammares skiljedomsinstituts årsskrift, 1986), p. 56 and Stefan Lindskog, *Festskrift*, pp. 134–136.

[50] See Stefan Lindskog, *Festskrift*, p. 141.

The above Supreme Court judgment was based on the former Sale of Goods Act of 1905 and its one-year limitation period for claims related to defects. According to section 32 para. 2 of the New Sale of Goods Act, the limitation period is now two years. However, one legal writer still claims that a purchaser has a duty to examine the acquired company and notify the seller within one year after the closing of defects which the purchaser has, or ought to have, noticed within such one-year period.[51] Voices have also been raised in favour of an examination period ending at the first annual closing of the accounts of the acquired company after the closing.[52]

If a deviation from a warranty has not or should not have been noticed within the one-year period, the seller is still liable for the deviation, provided that the purchaser notifies the seller within two years from the closing ("receipt of the goods"). The seller remains liable also after such limitation period, if the seller has been guilty of gross negligence or has acted in bad faith (see section 33 of the New Sale of Goods Act).

According to the Statute of Limitations, a claim is barred after ten years of its coming into existence, if the time period is not interrupted by a recognition of the claim, a written reminder of the claim or the institution of a lawsuit or arbitration proceedings.

19. Remedies

As mentioned, contracts on cross-border acquisitions with a Swedish party normally contain provisions on remedies applicable in case of a non-conformity with warranties. Such provisions are, in general, binding upon the parties. If the contract is silent in this respect, the remedies which are available to the purchaser according to the New Sale of Goods Act are:

(a) retification;
(b) reduction of the purchase price;
(c) damages;
(d) cancellation of the contract.

The parties are free to agree on terms limiting or excluding the purchaser's right to any of the remedies mentioned in (a)–(d) above.

(a) **Rectification.** If the seller fails to comply with a warranty, the purchaser has the right to require the seller to rectify, at this own cost, the defect if the seller can do so without suffering unreasonable costs or inconvenience (see section 34 of the New Sale of Goods Act).

According to section 36 of the New Sale of Goods Act, the seller also has the right to rectify, at his own cost, any defect if he can do so without causing the purchaser unreasonable inconvenience and without the risk that the purchaser will not be reimbursed by the seller for his own costs. However, according to the preparatory works of the New Sale of Goods Act, the

[51] See Gunnar Karnell, TSA 1977, "Något om reklamation och preskription vid garantianspråk beträffande aktiebolagsöverlåtelser", pp. 160–161 and 163.

[52] See Anders Johansson, *Undersökningsplikt*, p. 110.

purchaser retains his right to claim damages, notwithstanding the fact that the seller rectifies a defect.

(b) **Reduction of the Purchase Price**. According to sections 37 and 38 of the New Sale of Goods Act, the purchaser, with some exceptions of no relevance to the topic of this report, may claim a reduction of the price, if the object acquired is defective. The price may be reduced in the same proportion as the value that the object actually had at the time of delivery bears to the value that a non-defective object would have had at that time.

If there is no warranty, some legal writers are of the opinion that the right of the purchaser to reduce the purchase price is limited.[53] This opinion is based on the argument that it is difficult to determine a general standard and a general value of a company, and consequently that it is even more difficult to determine the consequences of a deviation to the company as a whole.

However, lately other legal writers have expressed the opinion that the purchaser will be entitled to have the price reduced under certain circumstances even if there is no warranty.[54] This opinion is mainly based on an arbitration award that has been published.[55] In this arbitration award, the seller had provided the purchaser with reports on the profit of the company containing incorrect information. The arbitration tribunal was of the opinion that, if the acquired company's historical profit deviates from what the purchaser had reason to assume, the purchaser is entitled to a price reduction proportionate to the decrease of the company's net worth due to such deviation. However, according to said award the seller has no liability towards the purchaser for the correctness of forecasts of the company's profit, if there is no express warranty in respect of such forecasts. The interpretation of this award has been that the arbitration tribunal did not rely on *enuntiationer* (see section 2 above).

It is important to emphasise the distinction between price reduction and damages. The aim of a price reduction is only to determine the difference in value between a non-defective object and a defective object, and then to reduce the purchase price accordingly. Consequently, a price reduction is not intended to compensate the purchaser for the entire loss he may suffer.

(c) **Damages**. Claims for damages have been raised in several court cases from the time before the New Sale of Goods Act, but where no express term for payment of damages was agreed, such claims have rarely been accepted by the courts. The general opinion from the time before the New Sale of Goods Act is that the purchaser is only entitled to damages if there is a breach of warranty or if the seller has acted fraudulently.[56]

However, the New Sale of Goods Act (section 40) provides for damages in the event of a breach of warranty, if the non-conformity is not the result of events outside the control of the seller, which he reasonably could not have expected to occur at the time of entering into the agreement and the

[53] See Anders Knabe, *Företagsöverlåtelser*, p. 76 and Gurar Karnell, *Vädefel*, p. 296.

[54] See Stefan Lindskog, *Festskrift*, pp. 139–141.

[55] "Årsskrift från Stockholms handelskammares Skiljedomsinstitut", 1986, pp. 47–58.

[56] See Anders Knabe, *Företagsöverlätelser*, pp. 77 and Gunnar Karnell, *Värdefel*, pp. 296–297.

consequences of which he reasonably could not have avoided or overcome. It is uncertain if and to what extent the New Sale of Goods Act has had the effect of changing the previous situation, making it possible for the seller to claim damages as a remedy for *abstrakta fel*.

The purpose of damages is to put the purchaser in the same economic position as if the acquired object had conformed with the contract. Where a warranty has been given, this includes compensation for lost profits.

It should be noted, however, that section 70 of the New Sale of Goods Act requires that the party suffering the damage should take all reasonable actions in order to limit his damage.

(d) **Cancellation of the Contract**. According to section 39 of the New Sale of Goods Act, a purchaser may cancel the contract due to a deviation from a warranty, if such breach of contract is of substantial importance to the purchaser and the seller was, or ought to have been, aware of this.

The fact that a breach must be of substantial importance together with the fact that a deviation from a warranty must be material when considering the acquired company as a whole, implies that cancellation of a contract on the acquisition of shares or an on-going business can be invoked by the purchaser only in rare situations.

Further, it is a common opinion in the Swedish legal literature, that the right of the purchaser to cancel the contract only exists during a very limited period of time after the closing.[57] It would, in most cases, be unreasonable if the purchaser would be permitted to cancel the contract a long time after he has taken over the control of the company. This entails that a purchaser has to make a prompt review of the acquired company in order to be able to cancel the contract, should serious deviations be found to exist. Often, the purchaser makes his investigation after the signing but before the closing.

20. Nullity and Other Defences

The Contracts Act contains provisions which deal with invalidity of legal acts. Section 36 has been mentioned above (see section 1.2). Sections 28–32 of the same Act relates to circumstances which occur at the time the contract is entered into.

Somewhat simplified, Swedish law in this respect can be described as follows. According to the above-mentioned sections of the Contracts Act, a contract can be rendered void due to duress, fraud, undue influence or mistake.

A contract can be declared void even if neither of the parties, but a third party has been guilty of duress, fraud or undue influence. However, if a party does not know and cannot reasonably be expected to know that a third party has, by such means induced the other party to enter into the contract, only duress of a more serious kind renders the contract void.

A party would not be bound by a miswriting or another mistake, if the other party realised or ought to have realised the miswriting or other mistake. This

[57] See Gunnar Karnell, *Värdefel*, pp. 295–396 and Anders Knabe, *Företagsöverlåtehlser*, p. 76.

means, *e contrario*, that the party making the mistake is bound, if the other party neither realised nor ought to have realised the mistake.

Section 33 of the Contracts Act supplements the special provisions mentioned above. According to this section, a legal act is invalid if the circumstances, at the time of its undertaking, were such that it would be contrary to good faith and fair dealing to invoke the Act with knowledge of such circumstances. In addition, the person towards whom such legal act was taken must have had such knowledge. See also section 1.2 above regarding section 36 of the Contracts Act.

Other defences that the seller may invoke in order to be released from liability have been mentioned above. These defences are:

(a) the purchaser's awareness of a defect, (see section 7 above);
(b) the purchaser's conduct, (see sections 13 and 18 above); and
(c) the seller's disclosures (see section 7 above).

21. Conclusion

As in other judisdictions, a contract for the acquisition of shares or an on-going business governed by Swedish law should be explicit on the warranties of the seller and on the remedies applicable to a non-fulfilment of the warranties. The formats frequently used in international acquisitions are in general usable also in Sweden, but may require some adjustments, especially in respect of consequences following from inspections made by the purchaser or the possible awareness of the purchaser of defects, and in respect of the time period within which claims under the warranties should be made. If a purchaser desires to have the right to claim damages instead of a price reduction, he should make such right an express term of the agreement. If the seller wants to limit his liability to only those warranties expressly given, he should make this an express term of the agreement.

United States of America

Glower W Jones and Delos Lutton
Smith, Currie & Hancock, Atlanta, Georgia, USA

1. Introduction

The globalisation of markets for products and services will surely be recorded as one of the most important economic phenomena of the late twentieth century. As businessmen and women survey the markets in other countries as potential sources of growth, and as their businesses grow beyond one country's borders, lawyers naturally become more interested in the details of foreign legal systems as applied to particular transactions of major business importance.

Perhaps no transaction of more regular importance to business people exists than the sale of an entire business as a going concern. At least, few transactions which occur with such frequency in the business world engender such large amounts of anxiety, confusion, doubt, uncertainty and risk. Accordingly, few transactions need lawyers more.

One of the ways we lawyers have created to reduce uncertainty and risk when something is sold is to suggest that the seller warrant that the thing being sold has certain qualities. This chapter focuses on the warranties that are commonly given when the assets or the stock of an on-going business are sold. We analyse, from the common law perspective, what roles warranties play in this process, what objectives the opposite sides have in negotiating warranties, and what happens when something goes wrong—when a warranty is breached.

We also touch on what remedies may be provided if the business persons (or their lawyers) do not specifically agree on a warranty or a remedy in the acquisition agreement (as of course they should, time and money permitting). Finally, we raise for special consideration, without attempting to analyse thoroughly here, some unique features of cross-border sales of businesses that may significantly affect the desired content of the warranties and the availability of practical remedies for their breach.

We hope to have provided here a fair picture of the importance of warranties in the sale of a business and the normally available remedies for their breach, all from the perspective of participants in a common law legal system. We end our introduction with the probably obvious conclusion, but one which we felt with singular force in researching and writing this chapter, that no single participant in the process of selling a business of any size is more helpful than a skilled local lawyer, familiar with both the laws and the customs of his or her jurisdiction, crafting clear and unambiguous warranties on which both parties will, in the end, rely.

2. Typical Structure of an Agreement for the Sale of Shares or Assets of a Business in the United States

In order to understand what happens when something goes wrong in the sale of a business, it is important to understand how a typical purchase agreement is structured. Apart from establishing the price, the primary purposes of the typical purchase agreement in the US today are firstly to specify clearly exactly the shares or the assets which are being purchased and what liabilities (if any) are being assumed, and secondly, specify the condition of the assets (either the assets being purchased or the assets owned by the corporation whose stock is being purchased) and the consequences which will ensue if it turns out that the assets were not, after all, in that condition.

As will be discussed more thoroughly below, the common law legal system would, even in the absence of much verbiage in the purchase agreement, probably provide some kind of a remedy for a badly mistreated buyer (see discussion of the common law system below). In order to provide greater certainty and reduce the risk of uninformed judges making a bad decision, the buyer uses the purchase agreement to specify exactly what will be treated as a compensable injury and to specify the allowable remedies in advance.

Accordingly, when something goes awry, the buyer looks first to the purchase agreement to determine its rights and remedies and only rarely relies on more general remedies, supplied by common law, for redress. Often, the recourse available to an injured party for breach of certain representations and warranties is set forth in the section of the purchase agreement dealing with indemnification.

Although there may be others, the most important types of provisions which will be found in a purchase agreement in the US are operative terms, representations and warranties, covenants, conditions, and indemnification. These sections are discussed below in detail.

2.1 Operative Terms

2.1.1 Stock purchase

In the case of a purchase of shares, the operative terms include provisions identifying the class and number of shares of stock, provisions for transferring the stock, and for dealing with the mechanics of closing the transaction and paying the purchase price. The purchaser of shares receives (in corporate form) the assets of the corporation purchased, subject to all of the liabilities associated with the assets and of the business which used the assets.

The section dealing with closing the transaction and paying the purchase price for the shares will set forth the amount the purchaser will pay the seller for the shares, the time the closing will occur and the manner by which the purchaser will pay the seller the purchase price (eg, cash, promissory notes or other compensation).

2.1.2 Asset purchase

In the case of an asset purchase, the operative terms include provisions for transferring assets, assuming liabilities, and dealing with the mechanics of closing the transaction and paying the purchase price. In the asset transfer section, the seller agrees to sell and the purchaser agrees to purchase the "purchased assets". The purchased assets will include the seller's personal property (this generally includes machinery, equipment, fixtures—ie, something which was once moveable, but has become physically attached to land and/or buildings such that its removal would damage the property—vehicles and other personal property used in the seller's business), as well as the seller's land and buildings. Schedules to the asset purchase agreement will specifically set forth those items of personal property and real property which are included as purchased assets, as well as those items which the purchaser is not buying.

The purchased assets will also generally include the seller's rights under specified leases. This includes leases of land, buildings, equipment and other tangible personal property used in connection with the operation of the business. The schedules to the agreement will set forth the leases specifically assumed, as well as those leases excluded from the asset purchase agreement.

The purchased assets also include any contracts which the purchaser assumes (ie, agrees to perform the seller's obligations in return for receiving the seller's benefits under the contract). A schedule to the asset purchase agreement will specify those contracts assumed by the purchaser, as well as those contracts the purchaser is not assuming. The purchased assets may also include the seller's intangible assets such as goodwill (that is, the result of such features of an on-going business enterprise as the existence of a good reputation, a good relationship with customers and suppliers, and the standing of the business in its community), patents, licences, trade names, trademarks, copyrights, trade secrets, confidential information, formulas, processes, techniques, know-how, and causes of action.

The purchased assets will also include the seller's rights in all government licences, approvals, permits and authorisations necessary for the operation of the seller's business. In addition, the purchased assets may include certain records and documents belonging to the seller (eg, computer software, customer lists), seller's accounts and notes receivable, cash and cash equivalents and prepaid assets (that is, an asset for which an expenditure has been made before the benefit will be enjoyed, such as rent, utility charges, or insurance premiums).

If the business manufactures goods (as we will assume for purposes of this chapter), inventory (including raw materials, work in process and finished goods) will be included in the definition of purchased assets. If the business provides only services, and not goods, the purchased assets obviously will not include inventory. The other types of assets we have mentioned above will, however, be equally important in the sale of a service business or a manufacturing business.

The operative terms will also address liabilities. Typically, the purchaser will assume certain specified liabilities relating to the seller's business. The asset purchase agreement will list those liabilities which the purchaser is assuming, as well as those it is not assuming. The agreement will typically provide that, in any event, the aggregate amount of assumed liabilities will not exceed a certain dollar value. The asset purchase agreement will also state that the seller must retain certain liabilities (eg, taxes, environmental claims, warranty claims relating to products shipped before the closing date of the purchase, and other liabilities and claims relating to events occurring prior to the closing date of the purchase, and liabilities relating to any excluded assets, excluded contracts or excluded leases).

Finally, operative terms include provisions dealing with closing the transaction and paying the purchase price. This section of the asset purchase agreement sets forth the amount the purchaser will pay the seller for the purchased assets and the time and the manner by which the purchaser will pay that amount (eg, cash, promissory notes and assumption of liabilities). The purchase price may be subject to adjustment after a post-closing audit of certain items such as inventory or accounts receivable.

2.2 Representations and Warranties

A seller's representations and warranties provide a snapshot of its business as of the date the parties sign the purchase agreement. The purchaser and the seller will each make certain representations and warranties regarding proper organisation of their businesses and authority to execute the purchase agreement and related documents. In addition, the seller will generally make a substantial number of representations and warranties to the purchaser regarding all aspects of the seller's business. These representations and warranties are the heart of the purchase agreement and therefore, the focus of this chapter.

Generally, the seller will make more representations and warranties than the purchaser. This is due, at least in part, to the fact that the purchaser generally pays for the shares or the purchased assets with cash or other liquid assets, and the parties' relationship terminates soon thereafter. In addition, the purchaser will probably be required to make extensive representations and warranties about the seller's business as a condition to receipt of its financing for the transaction. If the purchase agreement does not contain comparable representations and warranties from the seller, including remedies for breach, the purchaser risks losses due to the seller's breach, as well as default on its financing obligations.[1]

In some circumstances, however, the seller might legitimately request the purchaser to make additional representations and warranties (eg, where the consideration consists of securities of the purchaser which are not readily marketable, or where the seller is providing financing to the purchaser).[2]

[1] S. Reed and Lane & Edson, pc, *The Art of M&A: A Merger/Acquisition/Buyout Guide*, (1989), at 545.

[2] S. Lorne, *Acquisitions and Mergers: Negotiated and Contested Transactions* (1990), at F3–78.

In this chapter, we will focus primarily on the seller's representations and warranties to the purchaser. Typically, the seller will make representations and warranties to the purchaser regarding, among others, the following issues:

- financial statements.
- absence of undisclosed liabilities.
- accounts receivable.
- inventory.
- business changes.
- real property.
- planned public improvements and special assessments.
- title to shares and/or title to and condition of purchased assets.
- contracts and leases.
- litigation and proceedings.
- compliance with environmental laws.
- government licences and regulation.
- restrictions on personnel.
- taxes.
- employee benefit plans.
- labour matters.
- employment contracts.
- intangible assets.
- unlawful payments.
- compliance with law.
- insurance.
- disabled employees.
- subsidiaries.
- transactions with certain related persons.
- disclosures.

In some cases, a party will specifically exclude a warranty. For example, in a situation where the title to certain assets is in dispute, the seller may specifically state that the seller disclaims any warranty as to title to those particular assets.

In many instances, the representations and warranties of the seller's shareholders will be important. For example, consider the situation in which the seller sells substantially all of its assets to the purchaser, and the proceeds are distributed to the seller's shareholders. In this case, the seller's representations and warranties may be of limited value beyond any amount retained in escrow to cover the purchaser's claims.[3] The purchaser will want the seller's shareholders to join the seller in making representations and warranties so that the seller and the seller's shareholders would be jointly and severally responsible for any breaches of warranty.

In some cases, the beneficiary of certain of the seller's warranties may be, in addition to or instead of the purchaser, the company which is being purchased. For example, in the purchase of shares, the seller may represent and warrant to the purchaser and to the company that the seller, as an officer of the company,

[3] *Ibid.* at F3–79—F3–80.

paid all taxes to which the company was subject. The purchase agreement may provide that the seller agrees to indemnify the company against any damages if this warranty turns out to have been untrue.

You will find appended to this chapter (as Exhibit 1) a sample of a few of the representations and warranties which the seller might make in a purchase agreement. Depending upon the circumstances in a particular instance and the amount of money involved, these representations and warranties may be much longer or somewhat shorter.

2.3 Covenants

The purchase agreement will contain covenants by the purchaser and the seller. A covenant is a promise or agreement to do something or refrain from doing something over a period of time (generally, the period between the date the agreement is signed and the date of closing). While representations and warranties typically relate to the past or present, covenants relate to the future. As with representations and warranties, the seller provides the most covenants. For example, in an asset purchase, the seller will covenant to obtain shareholder approval of the sale of the business before closing. The seller will also be required to make certain negative covenants. For example, the seller might covenant not to incur any debt in connection with the business being purchased without the purchaser's prior consent.

2.4 Conditions

The purchase agreement will contain several conditions precedent. These are facts, acts or events which must exist or occur before a duty of immediate performance of a promise arises.[4] A typical condition precedent to the purchaser's obligation to close the transaction is receipt of a "comfort letter" from the seller's independent certified public accountants (ie, a letter regarding recent unaudited results of the seller's operations)[5] or the absence of any governmental objection to the purchase on antitrust law grounds. A typical condition precedent to the seller's obligation to close the transaction is the signing of any ancillary documents forming part of the bargain such as leases or employment contracts. The purchase agreement will also contain the following general types of conditions with respect to each party's obligation to close:

(a) the condition that all of the other party's representations and warranties will be true at closing as if they had been made on that date;
(b) the condition that the other party will have performed all of its covenants by closing;
(c) the condition that the other party will furnish officer's certificates verifying the foregoing conditions to be true; and
(d) the condition that the other party's lawyers will provide legal opinions on certain matters (eg, the enforceability of the purchase agreement and any related agreements) prior to closing.[6]

[4] *Restatement of Contracts*, section 250(a), (1932).
[5] J. Freund, *Anatomy of a Merger*, section 5.3.1, (1975).
[6] *Ibid.*

The purchase agreement will generally provide that if one party fails to satisfy a condition precedent to the other party's obligation to close, that other party can cancel the transaction without liability.

2.5 Indemnification

This section sets forth each party's agreement to indemnify and hold the other harmless from and against certain specified damages and liabilities. For example, the seller will agree to indemnify the purchaser against damages the purchaser subsequently realises in connection with the seller's pre-closing non-compliance with environmental regulations. While the covenants in the purchase agreement relate to obligations of the parties *prior* to closing and the conditions set forth in the agreement must be satisfied *at* closing, the indemnification provision protects the parties *after* closing. The indemnification provision serves a number of purposes including:

(a) to eliminate any question as to whether representations and warranties are intended to survive closing;
(b) to clarify that all misrepresentations (even if unintentional or minor) are indemnifiable if that is the bargain;
(c) to provide that the indemnifying party must pay certain of the indemnified party's expenses in connection with a misrepresentation (eg, attorneys' fees);
(d) to identify remedies available to the parties and method(s) of calculating damages;
(e) to establish the terms and procedures for indemnification;
(f) to include breaches of covenants and other agreements as indemnifiable claims; and
(g) to obtain indemnification for certain items which are not misrepresentations, but as to which a party insists upon being indemnified (eg, seller might agree to remain liable for damages relating to a particular pending law suit).[7]

3. Warranties in the Law of Contract

3.1 Warranties versus Guarantees

In addition to obtaining the appropriate warranties, as discussed above, the purchaser or the seller may also desire, in some instances, to obtain certain guarantees in connection with the transaction. For example, if the seller is not satisfied with the purchaser's ability to pay the purchase price, the seller may require a third party (eg, the purchaser's shareholders) to guarantee some or all of the purchase price. In addition, either the seller or the purchaser may require a personal guarantee or third party guarantee of the other party's performance in connection with a covenant or an indemnification obligation. A similar result may be obtained by requiring a third party to join in making representations and warranties and in indemnifying the other party.

[7] *Ibid.*

3.2 Warranties in Sale of Shares or Assets of a Business—Commentary Regarding Representations and Warranties

3.2.1 Representations v warranties: survival

As a practical matter, the terms "representation" and "warranty" are used interchangeably in the context of the sale of a business in the US. The consequences of breach will be the same, whether a statement is called a representation or a warranty.

Some legal commentators distinguish representations from warranties by saying that representations are limited to statements as to existing circumstances, whereas warranties may cover future circumstances. For example, a party may represent and warrant that as of a prior date total assets were worth $50,000. The party can also warrant that as of a future date, the assets will be that amount.[8]

The general rule, however, as to the time to which a warranty relates, is that "unless otherwise expressed, a warranty relates only to the time of sale and does not cover future defects not then in existence or inherent in the article".[9] Wisconsin courts have followed this general rule, stating that an ordinary warranty relates to the time of sale and, if broken at all, is broken when the sale is made.[10] Thus, we will use the terms representation and warranty interchangeably to mean statements made as to circumstances which exist at the closing date of the transaction.

The purchase agreement will often provide that representations and warranties "survive closing". Stating that the representations and warranties survive closing allows the parties to invoke whatever remedies are provided by the purchase agreement (eg, indemnification) or by other law, for breaches which are discovered after the closing, while the absence of such a statement allows the breaching party to assert that the parties did not intend that warranties have any effect after the closing. Depending upon the parties' relative bargaining power, the purchaser may agree that he has no right to seek recourse against the seller in connection with certain representations or warranties that turn out to be untrue after a shorter period of time (eg, two years) than the applicable statute of limitations would otherwise allow him. In such a case, the provision might state that certain representations and warranties (eg, relating to environmental or tax matters) survive closing for a certain period of time (eg, two years) and all other representations and warranties survive closing for their statutory period.

3.2.2 Why do we care about representations and warranties?

3.2.2.1 GENERALLY

Both the purchaser and the seller carefully negotiate the representations and warranties section of the purchase agreement. This process can take a large amount of time and effort and often results in many long pages of complex warranty language.

[8] 1 Herz & Baller, *Business Acquisitions*, section 5.401, (1981).
[9] 77 CJS *Sales*, section 321, (1952).
[10] *Dittman* v *Nagel*, 43 Wis 2d 155, 168 NW 2d 190 (1969).

When reviewing a purchase agreement drafted by an attorney in the US, anyone not familiar with the common law system will almost certainly wonder why the representations and warranties section is so long. Comprehensive representations and warranties are necessary for several reasons, most of them based on the fact that statutory remedies for breach of warranty in the sale of a business are almost non-existent (see discussion of statutory causes of action and remedies, below) and common law remedies are, in a business context, full of unacceptable uncertainties (see discussion of the US common law system, below).

First, the representations and warranties section of the purchase agreement gives the parties the opportunity to determine the point at which a breach is important enough to trigger the other party's right to back out of the deal and/or seek damages. Because judges generally are not trained business people, the purchaser and the seller do not want the judges applying their own concept of materiality to the transaction. That is, if the seller's accounts receivable are not $500,000, as represented, but rather $499,750, has the seller breached its representation to the purchaser? Even if the seller has *technically* breached its representation, is this breach material enough that the purchaser should have the right to back out of the deal or seek damages for breach of contract? Comprehensive representations and warranties allow the parties to agree in advance on applicable materiality standards.

Second, comprehensive representations and warranties, coupled with a well-drafted indemnification provision, mitigate the uncertainty of a successful claim of misrepresentation. Fraudulent misrepresentation may be difficult to prove (see discussion of fraudulent misrepresentation, below). In addition, initiating a lawsuit would be costly and time-consuming. The parties can protect themselves from these uncertainties by including comprehensive representations and warranties and an indemnification provision in the purchase agreement.

Third, the process of negotiating comprehensive representations and warranties provokes investigation and disclosure, allowing the purchaser to understand better the business of the company whose shares or assets the purchaser is purchasing. The seller's representations may raise a question in the purchaser's mind as to a particular issue, and the purchaser will be able to look into the issue further before closing the transaction. The additional disclosure will also allow the parties to adjust the purchase price appropriately either before and after signing the agreement. For example, the seller might during negotiations make a representation regarding the existence of certain pending litigation which would alert the purchaser to additional liabilities with which it or the company may be faced in the future. The purchaser would investigate the matter further, provoking additional disclosure by the seller. If the purchaser discovered that a particular pending lawsuit was likely to subject it or the company to substantial liability, the purchaser would negotiate with the seller to adjust the purchase price appropriately.

The purchaser will want to add a provision to the purchase agreement to the effect that the purchaser's pre-closing investigation—usually called a "due diligence" investigation—does not constitute a waiver of its right to indemnification or to sue the seller for breach of contract. In the absence of such a provision, in some jurisdictions, if the purchaser conducts a due diligence inquiry and completes the transaction, the purchaser may later be precluded from prevailing on a breach of warranty claim.[11] Of course, it is in the seller's best interest to prevent inclusion of such a provision. At a minimum, if the provision is included in the agreement, the seller will have additional incentive to ensure that its representations and warranties are true at the date of closing to avoid any future dispute.

Of course, extensive representations and warranties as to certain items are not always necessary. If the company whose shares or assets the purchaser is purchasing has been filing annual and quarterly reports with the Securities and Exchange Commission for some years,[12] the purchaser may be able to rely somewhat on the company's own disclosures and reports of its auditors over the years. For purposes of this chapter, however, we will assume that the company is a middle market manufacturing company whose stock is not publicly traded. Consequently, the purchaser will insist on comprehensive representations and warranties from the seller of the shares or assets.

3.2.2.2 THE PURCHASER'S PERSPECTIVE

From the purchaser's perspective, the seller's comprehensive representations and warranties are necessary to protect the purchaser from liability resulting from the seller's action (or inaction) while the seller operated the business. In an asset purchase, the purchaser also wants the warranties in order to be reassured that the purchased assets are in the condition the purchaser believes them to be. Statutory remedies which might apply to sales of goods between merchants (eg, the warranties implied by the Uniform Commercial Code or the quasi-warranties of the Convention on Contracts for the International Sale of Goods) will not necessarily apply to the sale of a business (see discussion of statutory liabilities, below). Accordingly, the purchaser of assets will want the seller to provide a "laundry list" of representations and warranties as to the nature of the purchased assets and their physical qualities. For example, the purchaser will want the seller to represent that the inventory is of a quality and quantity usable and saleable in the "ordinary course of business" (see discussion of ordinary course of business, below) consistent with the seller's past practice. Similarly, the seller will be required to represent that no repairs or maintenance outside the ordinary course of business is needed with respect to the purchased assets. The purchaser of shares will want similar representations and warranties regarding the assets of the company to ensure that the purchase price, for which the parties bargained fairly, represents the true value of the company represented by those shares.

The purchaser will also want the seller to provide representations and warranties regarding balance sheet liabilities. For example, the seller will represent that there are no liabilities or obligations of any kind relating to the assets of the company except as fully reflected on the balance sheet of the business or incurred in the ordinary course of business after the balance sheet

[11] See eg, *Faw* v *Greenwood*, 101 Idaho 387, 613 P 2d 1338 (1980).

[12] See sections 13 and 15(d) of The Securities Exchange Act of 1934, 17 USC section 78a *et. seq.*

date prior to closing. Similarly, the seller will represent that it does not owe vacation compensation or severance pay to its employees for services rendered prior to the closing date, except as disclosed in the balance sheet or on a schedule to the purchase agreement.

Finally, the purchaser will insist that the seller provide comprehensive representations and warranties regarding certain types of remote or contingent liabilities not necessarily reflected on the subject company's balance sheet. This is an important category because certain US laws can impose significant liability on the purchaser for remote or contingent liabilities arising from the subject company's action or inaction.

For example, the Employee Retirement Income Security Act of 1974 (ERISA)[13] is a complex, technical law designed to alleviate a number of problems that were affecting employee retirement plans, especially the lack of employee information and adequate safeguards concerning operation of the plans. Through various statutes and regulations, ERISA creates minimum standards to assure the equitable nature and financial soundness of employee benefit plans. These complex statutes and regulations have created a discrete legal specialty for many lawyers in the US. ERISA can subject employers to horrifyingly high liability for failure to meet the minimum standards imposed by the law (eg, an employer can be liable to a plan beneficiary for up to $100 a day from the time the employer failed to meet certain ERISA notice requirements; the plan administrator can be liable for up to $1,000 a day from the date of failure to file required annual reports). Consequently, the purchaser will want the seller to make full disclosure in the representations and warranties section concerning any employee benefit plans it has.

Another source of potentially substantial liability which might not appear on the seller's balance sheet arises under US environmental laws, particularly the Comprehensive Environmental Response, Compensation and Liability Act (CERCLA).[14] Congress enacted CERCLA in 1980 to provide for the clean up of hazardous waste sites and spills. Pursuant to CERCLA, the government is authorised to set up an environmental fund (called a "Superfund") which provides money for environmental clean up. The government can use this Superfund money to take direct action without waiting for the responsible parties to come forward with payment. The government may then hold any responsible party liable for the costs the government has incurred in cleaning the site. Alternatively, the government may insist that the party or parties responsible for the site either pay for the initial action or clean up the site themselves. Finally, a private party may clean the site and sue other parties for reimbursement.

Potentially responsible parties under CERCLA include the current owner or operator of a facility, all former owners or operators at the time of any disposal of hazardous material, all persons who transported waste to the site and all persons who generated waste that was transported to the site. Any of these parties may be held solely responsible for the *entire cost* incurred in cleaning the site,

[13] Employee Retirement Income Security Act, 29 USC section 1001 *et. seq.*

[14] Comprehensive Environmental Response, Compensation and Liability Act, 42 USC section 9601 *et. seq.*

even if the party was not negligent and had no knowledge of any wrongdoing.

The products liability laws of the US provide yet another source of potentially enormous liability for the subject company, necessitating complete disclosure by the seller. The products liability doctrine, itself a product of the common law, holds a manufacturer, or other party involved in selling a product, strictly liable (that is, liable without fault) when an article, placed into the market with knowledge that it is to be used without inspection for defects, proves to have a defect that causes a personal injury. Thus, one who sells any product in a defective condition unreasonably dangerous to the user may be liable for physical harm caused thereby, even though there is no contractual or other relationship between the seller and the user, and even though the seller has not been negligent.[15]

In the case of a purchase of shares, the purchaser itself may be protected by corporation law from direct liability for the liabilities incurred by the company whose shares were purchased. Corporation laws in the US generally insulate shareholders from liability for the debts and obligations of the company. However, if the company has violated product liability laws and, at a later date, loses one or more product liability lawsuits, the purchaser's shares will decline in value. Thus, the purchaser of shares will also want the seller to represent and warrant that no such violations have occurred.

US antitrust laws present another source of potentially serious liability. The Sherman Antitrust Act,[16] passed in 1890, prohibits unreasonable restraints upon and monopolisation of trade in interstate or foreign commerce. The statute forbids two or more persons from engaging in monopolisation (ie, where all or nearly all of an article of trade within a community is brought within the single control of one person or company, thereby excluding competition) and price fixing (ie, a combination or conspiracy formed for the purpose and with the effect of raising, depressing, fixing, pegging or stabilising the price of a commodity in interstate commerce). Other US antitrust laws prohibit tying, exclusive dealing and total requirements agreements, corporate mergers that tend substantially to lessen competition and interlocking directorates. Conviction of violating US antitrust laws can lead to severe criminal penalties (eg, up to a $10,000,000 fine for a corporation, $350,000 fine for an individual and/or three years' imprisonment) and divestiture (a court order to the offending party to rid itself of property or assets). Offenders may also be subject to substantial civil damages.

There are numerous other sources of potential liability to the purchaser not reflected on the seller's balance sheet, necessitating the seller's comprehensive disclosures in the representations and warranties section of the purchase agreement. These other areas of US law include, among others, tax laws, labour laws, securities laws and laws relating to international trade (eg, the US Foreign Corrupt Practices Act).

[15] Restatement (Second) of Torts section 402A (1977). See also, *Gray* v *Manitowoc Co, Inc*, 771 F 2d 866 (5th Cir 1985); *Goode* v *Herman Miller Inc*, 811 F 2d 866 (5th Cir 1987); *Kemp* v *Miller*, 154 Wis 2d 538, 453 NW 2d 872, (1990).

[16] Sherman Antitrust Act, 15 USC sections 1–17 (1890).

3.2.2.3 THE SELLER'S PERSPECTIVE

From the seller's perspective, it is important to minimise on-going responsibility and potential liability with respect to the shares or assets the seller is selling. The seller will want to limit the type of liability it will face (see discussion of materiality, knowledge and ordinary course of business below), as well as the amount of liability (see discussion of "basket" below).

3.2.3 Negotiating representations and warranties

3.2.3.1 THE PURCHASER'S OBJECTIVES

The purchaser generally has three main objectives when negotiating representations and warranties. These objectives are to obtain maximum disclosure regarding the seller's business, to create a means of withdrawing from the transaction if it discovers adverse information before closing, and to establish circumstances under which the seller must indemnify the purchaser for misrepresentation.[17]

First, the purchaser wants to obtain the maximum degree of disclosure regarding the business before entering into a binding commitment. The purchaser hopes to be able to obtain enough information to identify additional areas which might require further review before proceeding with the transaction. The information may also provide the purchaser with ammunition for negotiating a lower purchase price or other favourable terms in the purchase agreement.

The date that the parties sign the purchase agreement and the closing date often are not the same. The parties may delay the closing date in order to conduct due diligence (that is, to examine and verify the facts upon which the other party's representations and warranties are based) and/or pending receipt of legal approval (eg, antitrust approval from the federal government). From the purchaser's perspective, this period is one of the most important periods of the entire transaction, second only to the period during which the contract is actually drafted. This period gives the purchaser the last clear chance to avoid the difficulties inherent in a breach of warranty situation.

Thus, during the due diligence period between the signing and closing, the parties negotiate representations and warranties back and forth, establishing benchmarks against which items are tested. For example, the seller might represent that only 2 per cent of its accounts receivable are uncollectable in any given month. The purchaser will examine the seller's documentation, which should support this representation. If the purchaser discovers that the seller typically experiences 6 per cent uncollectable accounts in any given month, the purchaser will renegotiate the price or have the opportunity to walk away from the deal (see discussion of exit vehicle below). If the purchaser has accepted the seller's representation with regard to uncollectable accounts receivable, and, subsequent to the closing date, it turns out that the seller misrepresented this fact, the purchaser can seek damages.

Obviously, it is in the purchaser's best interest to conduct appropriate due diligence prior to the closing date to verify the seller's representations. Discovering the seller's misrepresentation during due diligence and negotiating an

[17] J. Freund, *Anatomy of a Merger*, section 7.1 (1975).

appropriate reduction in the purchase price is preferable to discovering the misrepresentation subsequent to closing and seeking damages. Depending upon the lapse of time since the closing date, the seller (or the seller's shareholder(s)) might be difficult to locate, insolvent or unwilling to make the purchaser whole.

Second, the purchaser wants to create a situation allowing it to walk away from the deal if it discovers information which would make it unwise to consummate the transaction. That is, the purchaser will be able to use the representations and warranties as a benchmark against which to test the underlying facts. If the facts at closing are not as the seller represented them, the purchaser can walk away from the transaction without liability because the truth of the representations and warranties at closing will be a condition precedent to the purchaser's obligation to close.

Third, and most important with respect to breach of warranty considerations, the purchaser wants to establish the circumstances under which the seller must indemnify the purchaser after the closing date for losses, should it turn out that the seller's representations were untrue (see discussion of indemnification, below). Note, however, that if the selling company is publicly held, the representations of the seller generally do not survive closing (except in cases of fraud). This is because public shareholders generally will not be willing to delay receipt of part of their consideration in order to guarantee an indemnification provision. In addition, as a practical matter, the purchaser is unlikely to be able to track down all of the public shareholders to enforce its claim.

3.2.3.2 THE SELLER'S OBJECTIVES

In drafting representations and warranties and remedies (such as indemnification), the question arises whether *every* deviation from the representations and warranties, no matter how small, will constitute a breach, entitling the other party to walk away from the deal or obtain indemnification. As a practical matter, the parties will limit the dramatic effect of technical or negligible breaches of warranty. In the US, we do this in one of several ways.

First, breaches can be limited to those violations which are "material". To avoid arguments over what "material" means, the parties may establish dollar or other quantity definitions of materiality in the purchase agreement. Second, the parties may establish a "basket" in the indemnification section of the purchase agreement. Third, the parties may limit responsibility for breach of warranty to situations in which a party had knowledge of facts or circumstances contrary to the representation or warranty. Finally, the parties may limit the effect of technical breaches in the agreement by allowance for transactions in the "ordinary course of business". These techniques for limiting the effect of technical breaches of warranties are addressed below in more detail.

If the seller had its way, it would be liable only for *material* breaches of *material* representations and warranties. In contract law, a material breach is a breach that excuses further performance by the aggrieved party and gives rise to an action for breach of contract.[18] Generally, a representation or warranty is

[18] *Barron's Law Dictionary*, 298, 2d ed., (1987).

material if it would be important to a normal, prudent investor in determining whether to make the investment.[19] This definition has been applied frequently in the context of securities transactions.[20]

For example, in *TSC Industries, Inc* v *Northway, Inc*,[21] a minority stockholder in an acquired corporation brought suit against the acquiring corporation and sellers of a controlling interest in the acquired corporation, charging violation of certain securities regulations. The US Supreme Court held that an omitted fact is "material" if there is a substantial likelihood that a reasonable shareholder would consider it important in deciding how to vote (as to whether or not to sell the corporation).

> The question of materiality, it is universally agreed, is an objective one, involving the significance of an omitted or misrepresented fact to a reasonable investor. Variations in the formulation of a general test of materiality occur in the articulation of just how significant a fact must be, or put another way, how certain it must be that the fact would affect a reasonable investor's judgment.[22]

A representation or warranty may also be deemed "material" if it was "part of the basis of the bargain" between the parties. For example, in *Ainger* v *Michigan General Corp*,[23] the sellers of a book publishing company sued the purchaser to recover certain funds they were to have received under the purchase agreement, and the purchaser counter-claimed for breach of warranty and fraud. In finding the sellers liable for breach of contract, the court noted that the sellers' warranty that it had not been notified of any claims which could give rise to litigation was material in the contract sense, as it was part of the basis of the bargain between the parties.[24] Thus, the concept of "materiality" can limit a party's liability for the type of breach (ie, a substantial violation operating to excuse further performance by the other party) and/or limit the types of representations and warranties the party would be liable for breaching (ie, those representations and warranties which are important to a normal, prudent investor in determining whether to make the investment, or which are part of the basis of the bargain between the parties).

As a result of these varying applications and broad definitions of "materiality", the parties may establish a dollar threshold (or other quantifiable benchmark) to define the materiality of a breach in particular circumstances. That is, the parties might agree that the seller will list only each claim over, for example, $10,000. If the parties adopt this approach, the purchaser may also require the seller to represent that the aggregate of lesser claims does not exceed a certain limit, for example, $50,000.[25]

[19] S. Reed and Lane & Edson, *The Art of M&A: A Merger/Acquisition/Buyout Guide*, (1989) at 548.
[20] See eg, *TSC Industries Inc* v *Northway Inc*, 426 US 438 (1976); *Virginia Bankshares Inc* v *Sandberg*, 111 S Ct 2749 (1991).
[21] *TSC Industries Inc* v *Northway Inc*, 426 US at 438.
[22] *Ibid.* at 445.
[23] 476 F Supp 1209, 1227 (SDNY 1979), aff'd, 632 F 2d 1025 2d Cir, (1980).
[24] *Ibid.*
[25] J. Freund, *Anatomy of a Merger*, section 7.3.1 (1975).

As another means of limiting liability for technical or negligible breaches of warranty, the parties may use a "basket" in the indemnification section of the agreement. This means that the purchaser would only be entitled to indemnification if the aggregate loss caused by all of the seller's misrepresentations exceeds a certain dollar figure (the "basket"), and then usually only to the extent of that excess. Sometimes, the parties will agree to split liability for the amount constituting the basket. The size of the basket will vary, depending upon the circumstances, but a basket of one per cent to two per cent of the purchase price is common.

If the parties use a basket, the purchaser may require the seller to forgo materiality (and often knowledge) limitations so that the seller does not double up on its liability limitations (ie, if non-material, not a breach; if material, falls in basket). The seller will also want to limit its responsibilities with respect to certain matters with a knowledge standard. That is, the seller will want to state that certain representations and warranties are true only "to the best of seller's knowledge".

In effect, the "best of knowledge" limitation allocates to the purchaser all risks regarding unknown defects. Although the limitation is customarily agreed to, regarding the existence of threatened litigation and third party copyright and patent infringements,[26] the purchaser may be able to negotiate the balance of the representations and warranties without it.

Generally, the seller is in the best position to know its business and will stand by its representations and warranties regarding it. In a few limited situations, the purchaser may have more knowledge about the seller's business. For example, in a management leveraged buyout, where management will own much of the seller's business and has operated the business for some time, management may be willing to accept the risk of error in the representations and warranties. Under these circumstances, management is in the best position to evaluate the risk and make an appropriate business decision.

In the end, whether a knowledge limitation is used in a particular case, depends in large part upon the relative bargaining strengths of the parties. If the purchaser wishes to impose a duty on the seller to investigate the matters represented by the seller to the best of its knowledge, the purchaser will include the words "after due inquiry" in the "best of knowledge" limitation. In the absence of the "after due inquiry" phrase, the seller's inquiry is generally assumed to be limited to the information already in its possession.[27]

Arguably, the purchaser can add to its protection by requiring the seller to make its representations and warranties "to the best of the seller's information and belief". This is because "knowledge" refers to one's perception of the truth of affirmative or negative propositions, while "belief" admits of all degrees, from the slightest suspicion to the fullest assurance.[28] Thus, for example, if the

[26] S. Reed and Lane & Edson, *The Art of M&A: A Merger/Acquisition/Buyout Guide*, (1989), at 552.

[27] *Ibid.* at 553.

[28] *Franken* v *State*, 190 Wis 424, 434, 209 NW 766 (1926) (citing *State* v *Harris*, 97 Iowa 407, 66 NW 728 (1896)).

seller represents that it has no knowledge of any pending litigation, the seller may arguably have a suspicion as to the existence of pending litigation, but yet be able to make the representation legitimately. If, on the other hand, the seller represents that, to the best of its information and belief, there is no pending litigation, the seller would have to disclose any suspicion of the existence of pending litigation in order to avoid breaching the warranty.

Finally, the seller may want to use the phrase "ordinary course of business" to exclude certain items from the representations and warranties. "Ordinary course of business" generally means according to the common practices and customs of commercial transactions. The term refers to a usual and necessary activity that is normal and incidental to the business.[29] The specific definition of "ordinary course of business" will vary, depending upon the seller's industry and the size. For example, the purchase of $50,000 of steel might be a purchase in the ordinary course of business for a large machine manufacturer, but not for a small machine repair shop. Accordingly, a warranty that no liabilities have been incurred out of the ordinary course of business since the balance sheet date allows the seller to incur the normal and usual liabilities that are typically associated with running its business without breaching the warranty.

3.3 Warranties in Other Contracts

In order to contrast the warranties used in a typical purchase agreement for the purchase of a business in the US with those used in other common types of contracts, we briefly mention here some typical contracts and some warranties associated with such contracts.

3.3.1 Sales of goods

In transactions involving the sale of goods between merchants, the provisions of the Uniform Commercial Code (the UCC) apply. Standard warranties include a warranty of merchantability and a warranty of fitness for a particular purpose. These warranties are discussed in detail in section 8 of this chapter.

3.3.2 Landlord–tenant contracts

When a landlord enters into a rental agreement, several warranties are implied by law. These warranties may be avoided by an express contractual provision to the contrary. The primary warranty which the landlord is presumed to make is that of habitability/tenantable condition.[30] Additionally, a landlord is presumed to have made a warranty of continuous use and possession.[31]

In some States, the tenant is presumed to have made an implied warranty that he or she will immediately notify the landlord of any damage or defects in the property leased.[32]

29 *Barron's Law Dictionary*, 329 2d ed., (1987).
30 *American Mut Liability Co* v *Fisher*, 206 NW 2d 152, (1973).
31 See *Evans* v *Grand Union Co*, 759 F Supp 818 (MD GA 1990) and *EMRO Marketing Co* v *Plemmons*, 855 F 2d 528 (8th Cir 1988).
32 See, eg, *First Wisconsin Trust Co* v *Wiemann Co*, 286 NW 2d 360 (Wis 1980).

3.3.3 Construction contracts

Construction contracts are generally interpreted the same as any other contract. However, in the absence of contractual provisions to the contrary, the builder and designer of a building may be held responsible for several industry-specific warranties. An architect is charged with knowledge of building codes.[33] Further, the designer of a building warrants that the design is free from defects which would cause the contractor to incur additional unanticipated costs.[34]

In the absence of express contractual provisions otherwise, a builder warrants that construction will be performed in a workmanlike manner.[35] A builder must perform its duties in a safe, timely manner in accordance with industry practice.[36] Without knowing the intended use of a building, a builder does not make an implied warranty of fitness for a particular purpose.[37] Finally, many States now impose an implied warranty of habitability upon builders/vendors of residential real estate.[38]

3.3.4 Carrier of goods

A carrier of goods is responsible for such goods from the time it takes possession of the property until it has sufficiently delivered the property pursuant to the consignor's instructions. A common carrier transports goods for any consignor. A private carrier only works for a particular shipper or group of shippers.

A common carrier must transport goods (1) properly; (2) with reasonable diligence; and (3) with reasonable care.[39] A common carrier is presumed to know the proper method of handling and storing goods which it accepts for shipment.[40]

Unless otherwise agreed, a common carrier is an insurer of the goods transported. A common carrier is generally held liable for goods lost or destroyed while in the carrier's possession.[41] The common carrier may avoid liability through any of several recognised exceptions. However, a common carrier is still liable, despite an exception, if the damage actually results from the carrier's negligence.[42] A common carrier is not responsible for damage caused by:

[33] *Gagnon* v *Ainsworth*, 186 NE 498 (Mass, 1933).

[34] *Chicago College of Osteopathic Medicine* v *George A. Fuller Co*, 719 F 2d 1335 (Ill App, 1983).

[35] *Hennes Erecting Co* v *National Union Fire Ins Co of Pittsburgh PA*, 813 F 2d 1074 (10th Cir, 1987).

[36] See, eg, *Hudson Waterways Corp* v *Coastal Marine Service Inc*, 436 F Supp 597 (DC Tex, 1977).

[37] *San Francisco Real Estate Investors* v *J.A. Jones Const, Co*, 524 F Supp 768 (DC Ohio, 1981).

[38] See, eg, *Scott* v *First Inv Corp*, 556 F Supp 782 (DC PA, 1983) (applying PA law); and *Reichelf* v *Urban Inv and Development Co*, 577 F Supp 971 (DC Ill, 1984) (applying Illinois Law).

[39] *Kuney* v *Chicago & NW Ry Co*, 197 NW 708 (Wis, 1924).

[40] *Ibid.*

[41] Some States only apply a strict liability standard when goods are lost, employing traditional negligence rules when property is damaged.

[42] *General Foods* v *Baker*, 451 F Supp 873 (DC Md, 1978).

(a) a public authority;[43]
(b) the negligence of the consignor (e.g, mispacking, mislabelling or misdirection);[44]
(c) a public enemy;
(d) an Act of God; or
(e) the inherent nature of the property.

3.3.5 Safekeeping contracts

Pursuant to most "safekeeping contracts," in the US, an owner of goods (the "bailor") pays another person or business (the "bailee" or "warehouseman") to store those goods. Because the bailee/warehouseman has been paid to store the bailor's goods, the bailee/warehouseman is generally presumed to be liable for any damage to the goods.[45]

A bailee/warehouseman may only avoid liability for the loss or damage of goods in its possession if it can demonstrate that it was not negligent and that the loss or damage was caused by (a) an Act of God, (b) a public enemy, or (c) the negligence of the bailor.[46]

3.3.6 Implied warranties

Implied warranties impose liability on a party to a transaction even though the party never expressly stated or agreed to assume such liability. Implied warranties generally attempt to impose standards commonly followed in an industry and to protect the probable "intent" of the parties. Most implied warranties can be waived by an express contractual provision to the contrary.

4. Warranties in Sales of Goods

4.1 Statutory Warranties

In transactions involving the sale of goods, the provisions of the Uniform Commercial Code (UCC) apply. The UCC has been adopted throughout the US (except in Louisiana), and sets forth the terms and conditions of sale which apply to the transaction between the parties unless otherwise agreed. Standard warranties under the UCC which apply to sales between merchants include a warranty of merchantability and a warranty of fitness for a particular purpose. These warranties are discussed in detail in section 8 of this chapter.

4.2 Contractual Warranties

As in the sale of a business, the parties may make certain representations and warranties in their agreement for the purchase and sale of goods. Such warranties generally relate to the condition of the purchased goods. The discussion in section 1 above regarding negotiating representations and warranties applies with equal force in the sale of goods or the sale of a business.

[43] *Missouri Pac RG* v *Elmore and Stahl*, 377 US 134 reh. den'd 377 US 984 (1964).
[44] *Stroh Brewery Co* v *Grand Trunk Western R Co*, 513 F Supp 827 (DC Mich, 1981).
[45] See generally, 93 *Corpus Juris Secundum*, Warehousemen section 30 (1992).
[46] *Ibid.*

5. Warranties in Negotiations

5.1 Confidentiality Agreements

During negotiations, the parties may desire to have a confidentiality agreement, whereby the prospective purchaser will agree to hold in confidence any information it acquires about the target company during negotiations. This allows the seller to provide to the prospective purchaser such information as is necessary for the prospective purchaser to make a decision as to whether or not to purchase the shares or assets of the target company. At the same time, the seller is assured that, if negotiations fall through, the prospective purchaser will not reveal information about the target company to third parties, thereby potentially damaging the target company and/or the seller's ability to negotiate a favourable deal with another prospective purchaser. In addition, the confidentiality agreement may contain provisions whereby the prospective purchaser agrees not to use the information it acquires to compete with the target company should negotiations fall through.

5.2 Non-Hostile Takeover Agreements

Even during relatively friendly merger negotiations, the management of the target corporation will attempt to minimise its vulnerability to an ultimately hostile takeover. As a condition precedent to providing the potential purchaser with information regarding the target company and entering into negotiations, the target company often insists that the potential purchaser represent and warrant that it has not commenced, and does not intend to commence, a hostile tender offer. To protect itself from a hostile takeover in the event the friendly negotiations collapse, the target may also require a standstill agreement from the potential purchaser.

5.3 Standstill Agreements

A standstill agreement is a contract between a potential purchaser and a potential target designed to prevent the potential purchaser from accumulating shares of the target's stock. The agreement states that the potential purchaser will not acquire, directly or through an affiliate, any shares of target's stock, for a specified period after the date of the agreement, without the prior written consent of the target's board of directors.

6. Warranties in Promises to Sell

Prior to entering into a purchase agreement, the parties will often execute a letter of intent. The letter of intent will set forth, in general terms, the substantive provisions which will eventually be found in the purchase agreement. In other words, the letter of intent contains the parties' basic agreement, leaving the details to be worked out later in the purchase agreement.

The letter of intent may be binding, non-binding or, as is most often the case, a hybrid version. If the letter of intent is binding, it requires the parties to proceed with the purchase of the shares or assets on the basis stated therein. If the letter of intent is non-binding, either party may back out of the deal at any time and for any reason without liability. Often, the letter of intent will provide that it is non-binding except as specifically indicated otherwise. The binding provisions may address, for example, such issues as confidentiality and exclusive dealing—ie the letter of intent may provide that the purchaser will hold in confidence all information about the target company which it acquires during negotiations. In addition, the letter of intent may provide that neither party will negotiate with any third party regarding the purchase or sale of the business for a specified time period, during which time the parties will attempt to reach final agreement.

7. Warranties in Sales of Businesses

7.1 Sales of Minority Interests v Sales of Entire Company

The breadth and type of warranties generally required of sellers will depend in large part on the per cent of ownership being sold. If only a few owners are selling a minority interest in a company, the number and type of warranties made will be much different than if the entire company is being sold. The reason for this is twofold. First, minority shareholders are often not involved in the business and cannot control its affairs and, therefore, are generally not in a position to make representations concerning the company itself. Second, a purchaser of a minority interest in a company is investing less money and is generally not as concerned about the intricacies of the company's operations. The minority purchaser is more of a passive investor who must rely on the current owners and managers to make the investment profitable. Because the minority owner generally has no control over the company, it would prefer to receive certain contractual protections from the company or its majority owners such as repurchase agreements and antidilution protection. Generally, however, neither the selling minority shareholder nor the purchaser has the bargaining power to extract these promises from the company or its other shareholders.

Although a purchaser of a minority interest generally will not require warranties as to the business itself, it should always require warranties as to the stock it is purchasing. For example, the seller almost always must warrant that it has good title to the shares being sold, free and clear of all liens and encumbrances. In addition, the seller should be required to warrant that it may sell the shares without the consent of any third party and without breaching any agreements to which the seller is bound.

7.2 Warranties in Sales of Assets Contrasted to Warranties in Sales of Shares

An asset acquisition is theoretically different from a stock acquisition in several respects. For example, in the US, the sale of substantially all of the assets of a corporation generally requires shareholder approval, while the sale of stock does not involve corporate action. Rather, the sale of stock is viewed as a transaction directly between the purchaser and the shareholders of the seller. Because each of the seller's shareholders is free to make her or his own decision, stock acquisitions are not subject to appraisal rights. The purchase of assets, however, often gives rise to appraisal rights for dissenting shareholders.[47]

The decision to acquire assets, rather than stock, may affect the timing of the transaction. In many US States, there is a minimum of 20 days' notice to the shareholders prior to the meeting at which they will approve or disapprove the sale of the company's assets. On the other hand, if the seller is a company whose shares are publicly traded (rather than a privately held concern), the necessary filings with the Securities and Exchange Commission (SEC) and mandatory tender offer period for purchases of stock can take even longer.

In addition, an asset purchase technically avoids application of rule 10b–5, promulgated under the Securities Exchange Act of 1934.[48] However, some of the substantive language of rule 10b–5 is often incorporated into the asset purchase agreement by the parties. For example, the asset purchase agreement might contain a provision stating that

> to the best of the seller's and the seller's shareholders' knowledge, there exists no fact, condition or threatened development of any nature not otherwise disclosed in this asset purchase agreement or on the schedules to this asset purchase agreement that would be materially adverse to the operation of the business. No warranty or representation by the seller or the seller's shareholders contained in this asset purchase agreement or in any writing to be furnished pursuant hereto or previously furnished to the purchaser contains or will contain any untrue statement of fact or omits or will omit to state any fact required to make the statements therein contained not misleading.

This language is very similar to the language in rule 10b–5(b).[49] Thus, although the asset purchase agreement would not be directly governed by rule 10b–5, the seller and the seller's shareholders will be held under the contract to disclosure requirements as though they were selling stock, rather than assets, to the purchaser.

The decision whether to purchase assets or stock in the US has far more to do with questions of tax consequences and liabilities than with questions of warranties or remedies. As to tax matters, the purchase of assets from a corporation will typically result in a corporate tax on any gains at the corporate level, followed by a tax on shareholders' gains when the selling corporation is dissolved and the sales proceeds are distributed; while the purchaser receives a tax basis in the assets equal to each asset's *pro rata* portion of the purchase price. A sale of shares, on the other hand, usually results only in the tax on gains at the shareholder level while the purchaser receives (in corporate form) assets whose basis remains as it was in the hands of the seller.

As to liability matters, a purchaser of assets generally receives, although the rule differs in certain circumstances in certain jurisdictions of the US, unless

[47] C. Nathan and H. Pitt, *Outline of Corporate and Securities Law Considerations and Related Legal Framework for Acquisitions in the United States by Foreign Companies*, at 6 (Practicing Law Institute, 1987).

[48] See, *Landreth Timber Co* v *Landreth*, 471 US 681 (1985).

[49] 15 USC sections 78a–78jj, (1934).

otherwise agreed, only the assets purchased and not any of the liabilities associated with the assets or the business which used the assets. A purchaser of stock, on the other hand, receives (in corporate form) the assets of the corporation purchased, subject to all of the liabilities associated with the assets and of the business which used the assets.

Accordingly, the parties will decide which form of transaction (sale of assets or sale of stock) is most advantageous under the circumstances and will normally use contract language to even out any differences in warranty protection which would otherwise result from the form of the transaction.

7.3 Warranties in Mergers

The warranties made by the selling shareholders and target company in a merger are much the same as those made in a stock purchase transaction. If the sellers will receive stock or other securities of the surviving corporation, the sellers will generally require certain warranties from the buyer concerning these securities. For example, the sellers may require in addition to a full panoply of financial warranties regarding the buyer, a warranty that the securities have been duly authorised and will, upon issuance, be fully paid and non-assessable. In addition, since a merger involves one or more corporations, each corporation will usually be asked to warrant that they are corporations duly organised, validly existing and in good standing under the laws of their respective jurisdictions of incorporation. In addition, each corporation is usually asked to warrant that the merger has been duly authorised by all necessary corporate action and that the merger agreement is binding on the corporation.

7.4 Warranties in Public Takeover Bids

When a purchaser makes a public offer to all shareholders of a publicly owned company, known as a "tender offer," the purchaser must comply with various federal and State securities laws. These securities laws require the bidder to make certain filings with the ("SEC") and disclose certain specified information to the potential sellers. For example, the bidder is required to disclose its intentions regarding the target company. In a broad sense, these statements constitute warranties of the bidder to the shareholders of the target company and to the SEC. In certain situations, the SEC or other parties may have recourse against the purchaser for breach of these warranties.

Generally, the selling shareholders of a public company will not be required to make any warranties to the purchaser other than a warranty of ownership of shares tendered. They will simply tender their shares to the purchaser in return for payment. In some tender offers, the purchaser negotiates with the seller's management to receive their recommendation of the transaction. In this situation, the seller's management may require the purchaser to make certain warranties concerning the future of the purchased company and its management. For example, the seller's management may require the purchaser to warrant that present management will be continued and that the assets of the company will not be sold for a period of time.

7.5 Warranties in Sales of Limited Liability Companies

The Limited Liability Company (LLC) is a relatively new type of entity in the US. It was first adopted by a few States some years ago, but recent indications are that the LLC will find widespread popularity over the next few years. The entity combines the most favourable taxation and limited liability aspects of partnerships and corporations and may well become the most frequently used form of entity throughout the US in the future. The American Bar Association, at the time this chapter is being written, is drafting standard guidelines for LLCs. Over time, standard representations and warranties in the sale of limited liability companies will develop as more such entities are formed and sold.

7.6 Warranties in Sales of Partnership Interests

When purchasing partnership interests from a partnership, the purchaser will generally require warranties concerning the partnership itself. These types of warranties are similar to the warranties required of a selling corporation. For example, warranties concerning the proper formation of the partnership as well as warranties concerning its operations would be appropriate. In addition, the purchaser will obviously want to receive the partnership agreement and will generally require a warranty that the agreement received is complete and correct.

8. Specific Types of Warranties in Sales of Businesses

8.1 Warranty of Clear Title

The seller of personal property impliedly warrants his title to the property.[50] Because stock constitutes a form of personal property, the seller of stock warrants title thereto. Additionally, when acquiring real property, the buyer usually demands a warranty of good title. This request is replaced, in many jurisdictions of the US, by a request for the issuance of a title insurance policy.

If the title is flawed, the buyer can recover against the seller for breach of the warranty. Although implied, most asset purchase agreements contain an express warranty of good title, such as:

> Seller is the record and beneficial owner of the Tangible Assets and his title to each such asset is good, valid, indefeasible and free and clear from all security interests, liens, encumbrances, options, calls, pledges, assessments, covenants, restrictions, reservations, commitments, obligations, liabilities and other burdens. Seller has full power and authority to sell the Tangible Assets and this Agreement is a valid and binding obligation of Seller in accordance with its terms.

However, because the buyer in a stock purchase transaction is not directly acquiring the property of the corporation, there is no implied warranty of good title to the assets of the corporation.[51] Accordingly, any such warranty must be expressly set forth in the sale agreement, as above. Additionally, stock purchase agreements usually contain an express warranty of good title to the stock.

[50] *Williston on Sales*, sections 15–16 4th ed (1974).

[51] *12A Fletcher Cyclopedia Corporations*, section 5616 (1984).

8.2 *Warranty of Merchantable Quality*

The Uniform Commercial Code ("UCC") provides general background on the merchantability of goods. The UCC implies that this warranty exists between merchant sellers and merchant purchasers. Sellers can, however, disclaim the warranty.

Briefly, to satisfy such a warranty, the seller must demonstrate that the goods sold:

(a) pass without objection in the trade under the contract description;
(b) in the case of fungible goods, are of fair, average quality within the description;
(c) are fit for the ordinary purposes for which such goods are used;
(d) run, within the variations permitted by the agreement between the seller and the purchaser, of even kind, quality and quantity within each unit and among all units involved;
(e) are adequately contained, packaged and labelled as the agreement may require; and
(f) conform to the promises or affirmations of fact made on the container, package or label, if any.

In short, the seller must prove that the goods are of a quality comparable to that quality generally acceptable in the line of trade applicable to such goods.

8.3 *Warranty of Absence of Defects*

A seller generally does not make a specific warranty with respect to the absence of defects in connection with the sale of a business. If the seller makes such a warranty, it is usually in connection with the sale of inventory items. In most cases, the seller will warrant that the goods are free from defects in materials and workmanship and are saleable in the ordinary course of business. Essentially, the seller warrants that there is no inherent problem with the goods. This concept is very similar to the concept of merchantability.

8.4 *Warranty of Fitness for a Particular Purpose*

Again, as with the warranties of merchantability and absence of defects, this warranty more often applies in the case of the sale of particular goods rather than the sale of a business. For this warranty to arise under the UCC, the purchaser must prove the following elements:

(a) the seller knew of the "particular" purpose for which the goods were required;
(b) the purchaser relied on the seller's skill or judgment to select or furnish suitable goods; and
(c) the seller did not disclaim the warranty.

Because the purchaser must actually rely on the seller, the purchaser may negate this warranty if the purchaser performs due diligence in the context of a sale of a business. In addition, the particular warranties given by the seller in connection with the assets transferred may offer more rights than this warranty.

9. Form Requirements

9.1 Common Law of Contracts

Most contracts can be oral. State legislatures have the power to require that certain contracts be in writing (see the discussion of the UCC requirements below). As a practical matter, the parties will find it difficult to prove the terms of an oral contract in the event of a dispute.

9.2 The UCC

The UCC, which is sometimes but not always held inapplicable to the sale of all assets of a business, utilises a general requirement that a contract be in writing and imposes more specific requirements in particular areas. Under the general "statute of frauds", the parties cannot enforce contracts for the sale of personal property in an amount greater than $5,000 unless there is a writing. In all cases under the UCC, only the party against whom enforcement is sought need sign the writing.

A contract for the sale of goods for the price of $500 or more is not enforceable unless there is some writing sufficient to indicate that a contract for sale has been made between the purchaser and the seller. The writing is not insufficient because it omits or incorrectly states a term agreed upon, but the contract is not enforceable beyond the quantity of goods shown in such writing. As indicated, the parties must include a quantity provision in the contract, but numerous exceptions undercut the impact of the general rule. For example, an oral contract is valid with respect to goods for which payment has been made or accepted. As another example, the parties can confirm their contract by conduct.

The UCC also provides for conflicts between purchase and sale documents (sometimes known as the "Battle of the Forms"). The purchaser and the seller will enter into a contract for the purchase and sale of goods. Under the UCC, the terms of this contract often are determined by a purchase order on the purchaser's side and a quotation, an invoice or an acknowledgment on the seller's side (the "Terms and Conditions"). If only one party uses such a form, that party can argue persuasively that its form controls. If the purchaser and the seller use forms with identical terms, they will enter into a contract consisting of such terms.

If their forms contain conflicting, additional or different language, the contract between the seller and the purchaser is deemed to consist only of those terms upon which the purchase order and the terms and conditions do not conflict. Conflicting terms automatically "fall out" and the parties are left to the so-called "gap-filler" provisions of the UCC. The gap-filler provisions supply certain terms, including damage and warranty terms, to take the place of those terms which fall out.

Although conflicting terms automatically fall out, additional terms (terms which are not addressed in the other party's form) or different terms (terms which take an alternative approach to the corresponding terms in the other party's form) may or may not become part of the contract (although a minority of courts hold that different terms also *automatically* fall out). Whether additional or different terms become part of the contract depends upon the language of the forms and the actions of the parties. If either the purchase order or the terms and conditions contain language limiting acceptance to its terms, additional or different terms should not become part of the contract. If, however, the forms do not contain language limiting acceptance, additional or different terms become part of the contract unless (i) the terms materially alter the contract or (ii) the party making the offer objects to the additional or different terms within a reasonable time after notice of such terms.

10. Cross-Border Sale of Shares or Assets of a Business

When the purchaser is acquiring the shares or assets of a foreign concern, the purchaser obviously must investigate the legal requirements of the country in which the seller is located. For example, a French purchaser of a US business must analyse the application of US federal and State securities filing requirements, federal and State antitrust or takeover restrictions and filing requirements, foreign investment laws, tax laws and other laws.

Often, parties to a transnational purchase agreement will retain local counsel in the other party's country to assist in the due diligence investigation and other aspects of the transaction. A party also may seek the legal opinion of local counsel in the foreign country as to certain issues. For example, the seller might provide the purchaser with the opinion of the seller's local counsel in the country in which one of its subsidiaries is located as to the proper organisation of the subsidiary under its local laws.[52]

The transnational sale of the shares or assets of a business may also necessitate the use of different or additional representations and warranties in the purchase agreement. For example, it may be important for a US company to obtain the foreign company's representation that it has not acted in such a way as to result in the extraterritorial application of US antitrust laws. A non-US company might request a US seller to represent that it has sufficient quality procedures in place to meet the certification standards of ISO 9000.

In addition to representations and warranties, of course, other provisions in the purchase agreement require special attention (eg, the *force majeure* provision). A detailed examination of the scope of the differences between a purchase agreement where the parties are all located in the US and a purchase agreement between parties in more than one country is, however, beyond the scope of this chapter.

Nevertheless, the issue of applicable law is of particular importance in the transnational sale of a business. In an effort to avoid conflict of law problems, the parties should specify the law they want to govern the purchase agreement, and state that it is the exclusive law to be applied. The parties should also specify the forum in which they wish any disputes to be resolved. Of course, there are no guarantees that these choices will be enforced. In order to increase the likelihood of enforcement, the law and forum chosen should have some relevance to the

[52] As to legal opinions of foreign counsel generally, see the excellent articles by Michael Gruson, "Legal Opinions of New York Counsel in International Transactions", 3 *Colum Bus L Rev.* 365 (1989), and M. Gruson and M. Kutschera, "Opinion of Counsel on Agreements Governed by Foreign Law", 19 *Vand J of Transnat'l L*, 515 (1986).

parties and the transaction. However, in some countries (eg, many Latin American countries) choice of law clauses are invalid as a matter of law.

Occasionally, the parties may choose a "least favoured choice of law/forum" clause. Under this type of clause, if the purchaser sues the seller for breach of warranty, the purchaser must bring the action in the seller's home country. Of course, the reverse is also true. These clauses are designed to encourage negotiation and settlement.

If the parties do not specify applicable law, the court exercising jurisdiction would apply its country's rule to determine applicable law. These rules vary from country to country. In the US, the law of the country having the most significant relationship to the transaction and the parties would be applied (see discussion of courts, below). In other countries, the applicable law might be the law where the contract was made, the law where the contract is performed or the law determined by another rule.

Because several texts of the purchase agreement may be drafted using several languages, the parties should specify the overriding language which will govern the agreement. As a practical matter, the governing language should be that of the chosen forum. Note that some countries (eg, People's Republic of China) have laws requiring that certain types of agreements be drafted in their language.

For resolution of disputes between the parties to a transnational purchase agreement, it is more likely that the parties will provide in the agreement for resolution of disputes through mediation, conciliation or arbitration. In the cultures of many countries outside the US, resorting to litigation is considered an acknowledgment of failure. Moreover, the court systems in some countries including the US sometimes work very slowly and resolution of a dispute could take years and become very costly. It is also possible that neither party is willing to submit to litigation in the other party's court system.

For these and other reasons, alternative dispute resolution processes are popular in agreements between parties located in different countries. The parties may resolve their dispute by negotiating in the presence of a third party, a process known as mediation or conciliation. Alternatively, arbitration offers a more formal means of dispute resolution. There are several organisations throughout the world with structured rules and/or forums for arbitration (eg, the American Arbitration Association, the International Chamber of Commerce, the Arbitration Rules of the United Nations Commission for International Trade Law).

11. Breach of Warranties and Remedies for Breach

11.1 What Constitutes a Breach of Warranty

11.1.1 The common law system

In order to understand what constitutes a breach of warranty in the US, one must be familiar with the US common law system. This is the system of jurisprudence, originating in England, which is based on judicial precedent, rather than legislative enactments. The common law is:

generally derived from principles rather than rules; it does not consist of absolute, fixed and inflexible rules, but rather of broad and comprehensive principles based on justice, reason and common sense. It is of judicial origins and promulgation. Its principles have been determined by the social needs of the community and have changed with changes in such needs. These principles are susceptible of adaptation to new conditions, interests, relations, and usages as the progress of society may require.[53]

11.1.2 Establishing a breach

Thus, what constitutes a breach of warranty is determined in the US by case law (unless the parties have agreed to a specific rule). The breach of a provision in a contract, including the breach of a representation or warranty in a purchase agreement, will be governed by general principles of contract law, as determined by case law in the US. Commentators have summarised this case law to state that a breach of contract is, in general terms, non-performance of a legal duty when due under a contract.[54] Failing to render performance promised will not be a breach of contract until the time fixed for such performance has expired and all conditions precedent have occurred.[55] For example, the purchaser will not be in breach of contract for failure to pay the purchase price until the due date and until the seller satisfies any conditions precedent to the purchaser's payment (eg, delivering a legal opinion of seller's counsel to the purchaser). When determining whether there has been a breach, a court may look for a "material" failure to fulfil the contract terms and/or failure to fulfil "material" contract terms (see discussion of materiality, above).[56] The generality of the definition of a breach of contract is due to the fact that "contract rules must operate in a wide diversity of factual situations."[57]

In order to show that the defendant breached a contract, the plaintiff must prove several elements:

(a) formation of a contract between the plaintiff and defendant;
(b) performance by the plaintiff of any depending conditions or conditions precedent;
(c) defendant's failure to perform its obligations;
(d) resulting in damage to the plaintiff.[58]

In addition, in the context of a purchase agreement, the purchaser must have relied on the warranty allegedly breached as an inducement to make the purchase in order to assert a breach of warranty claim.[59] If the purchaser has actual knowledge of the seller's breach of warranty prior to the closing date, the

[53] *Miller* v *Monsen*, 228 Minn 400, 37 NW 2d 543, 547 (1949).
[54] *Restatement (Second) of Contracts* section 260 (Tent Draft No 8, 1973).
[55] 4 *Corbin on Contracts* section 943, (1992).
[56] See eg, *Ainger* v *Michiaan General Corp*, 476 F Supp 1209, 1227 (SDNY 1979) aff'd, 632 F 2d 1025 (2d Cir, 1980).
[57] S. Burton, "Breach of Contract and the Common Law Duty to Perform in Good Faith", 94 *Harv L Rev* 369 (1980).
[58] *Republic Corp* v *Procedyne Corp*, 401 F Supp 1061 (SDNY 1975). See also 17A CJS *Contracts* section 566 (1963).
[59] *CBS Inc* v *Ziff-Davis Pub Co*, 75 NY 2d 496, 554 NYS 2d 449, 553 NE 2d 997 (1990).

purchaser cannot rely on the seller's warranty as an inducement to purchase.[60] On the other hand, the purchaser generally has no duty to attempt to determine whether the seller's representations are true. This stems from Judge Learned Hand's definition of a warranty in *Metropolitan Coal Co* v *Howard*.[61] Judge Hand defined a warranty as

> [A]n assurance by one party to a contract of the existence of a fact upon which the other party may rely. It is intended precisely to relieve the promisee of any duty to ascertain the fact for himself; it amounts to a promise to indemnify the promisee for any loss if the fact warranted proves untrue . . .[62]

Thus, as long as the purchaser has something less than actual knowledge of the seller's breach of a warranty prior to the closing date, the purchaser will be able to assert a breach of warranty claim.

11.2 Contract Remedies

In most instances, US courts will enforce the remedies the parties provide in their contract. In a few cases, however, courts will not enforce the parties' chosen remedy (eg, where the parties provide for a remedy which is obviously a penalty). Remedies the parties may use include, among others, indemnification rights, set-off rights, liquidated damages and specific performance. These remedies are addressed below.

11.2.1 Indemnification

The common law system applied in the US has many favourable attributes, but it sometimes has a tendency to produce unpredictable results. Therefore, the parties use remedies in a purchase agreement to reduce this unpredictability. Indemnification is the most important of these remedies. The indemnification section is the parties' attempt, using their right to contract freely, to create predictable outcomes for common circumstances in the absence of common law predictability. When well drafted, an indemnification section creates a self-contained remedy with its own statute of limitations. The section establishes the circumstances under which the parties can claim damages or take other action in the event of the other party's breach of a representation or warranty. Indemnification is an important addition to the parties' other rights of recourse for breach of representations or warranties. This is because the indemnification section will typically provide remedies not available under general case law (eg, recovery of reasonable attorney fees incurred in connection with breach of a representation).

The indemnification section will also provide for recovery of certain losses which result from disclosed risks. Because these risks were disclosed, the losses do not give rise to a claim for breach of a representation or warranty. As noted above in the discussion of the definition of a warranty, the purchase agreement allocates certain risks in connection with disclosed items, allowing recovery even in the absence of a breach.

[60] *DuBois Const Corp* v *United States*, 98 F Supp 590, 594 (Ct Cl, 1951).
[61] 155 F 2d 780 (2d Cir, 1946).
[62] *Ibid.*

There are several issues to address with respect to the indemnification section. For example, the seller may demand an exclusivity clause, stating that the indemnification section is the exclusive source of remedies for the parties. An exclusivity provision will not, however, apply to liability under securities laws (eg, rule 10b–5 of the Securities Exchange Act of 1934) and fraud laws.[63] If the purchaser agrees to an exclusivity provision, it may prefer that such a provision cover only monetary damages, leaving the purchaser free to pursue non-monetary remedies (eg, injunctive relief).[64]

The duration of the indemnification remedy is often subject to a great deal of negotiation. The purchaser will want the representations and warranties to "survive" the closing for a certain period of time. The term "survive closing" is incorporated into a purchase agreement to furnish a secure basis for indemnification to a party subsequent to closing for breach of a representation or warranty.[65]

Whether the seller's obligation changes when it incorporates a "survive closing" provision in the purchase agreement has not been specifically addressed in case law. However, at least one commentator has noted that the term "survive closing" may be interpreted as a basis for allowing the purchaser to seek indemnification after closing for a breach of the representations and warranties given the day of closing.[66] The purchaser is assured of a procedural right to challenge a breach of representation or warranty for some period of time after closing of the transaction. Although the seller's representations and warranties relate to circumstances existing at the date of closing, the purchaser is given an adequate period of time to discover any basis for indemnification.[67]

In order to preserve its claims, the purchaser may prefer that the purchase agreement contain language to the effect that the obligations of the seller and the seller's shareholders to indemnify and hold the purchaser harmless shall survive closing for the appropriate statute of limitations period following closing. Often, however, the seller may argue that the statutory period is too long. Thus, the parties may agree on an interim period for survival of the representations and warranties (eg, two years). However, the purchaser may insist that the seller remain subject to the appropriate statutory time limitations with respect to intentional breaches of representations or warranties.

The purchase agreement may provide that the parties will indemnify each other from breaches discovered throughout the period of indemnification, and not just for losses actually sustained during that period. For example, a lawsuit between the seller and a former customer might not be resolved until after the end of the indemnification period. If the claim arose during the indemnification period, the purchaser would be entitled to indemnification from the seller.

[63] L. Walton, *Selected Issues In Drafting Acquisition Agreements: Financial Representations and Indemnity Provisions* at 6 (1991).
[64] *Ibid.*
[65] J. McGaffey, *Buying, Selling and Merging Businesses,* section 1.04(b) (1989).
[66] J. Freund, *Anatomy of a Merger*, section 10.2.2 (1975).
[67] *Ibid.*

11.2.2 Escrows: set-off rights

The indemnification provision is useless to the purchaser unless the seller has the financial ability to back up the indemnification. Where the protection provided by the indemnification section may be inadequate, the parties may agree to place a portion of the purchase price in escrow as security for the seller's indemnification obligations. The purchaser will be able to withdraw from the escrow account upon determination of the seller's liability under the indemnification section of the purchase agreement.

Alternatively, the purchaser may retain the right to set off any losses due to breach of the purchase agreement against payments it owes to the seller. In the absence of a set-off provision in the purchase agreement, in most jurisdictions, the purchaser probably does not have the legal right to withhold payments from the seller until there is a final determination of liability under the indemnification section.[68]

11.2.3 Purchase price adjustment

Instead of providing for recovery on the basis of breach of representation or warranty, the parties may agree to a purchase price adjustment provision in the purchase agreement. The economic effect of the purchase price adjustment is similar to that of an indemnification provision, but does not imply wrongful action.[69]

11.2.4 Enforceability of liquidated damages

While some purchase agreements in the US do not specifically address damages as a remedy, other contracts contain a formula for computing damages agreed to by both parties, referred to as "liquidated damages". Most courts will enforce the liquidated damages clause, so long as the amount of damages is not excessive or an apparent penalty, and so long as the damages bear a reasonable relation to the injuries actually suffered.[70]

11.2.5 Specific performance

Where the subject matter of a contract is so unique that monetary damages are insufficient compensation, specific performance may be the appropriate remedy. The court would order the breaching party to perform the contract, exactly as written. Courts may be reluctant to require specific performance, finding other remedies to be adequate. However, courts have been increasingly willing to order performance in a wide variety of cases, including cases dealing with the sale of a business.[71]

[68] S. Reed and Lane & Edson, *The Art of M&A: A Merger/Acquisition/Buyout Guide*, (1989), at 571.

[69] International Bar Association, *Due Diligence, Disclosures and Warranties in the Corporation Acquisitions Practice* (1987), at 126.

[70] E.A. Farnsworth, *Contracts* sections 895–904 (1982).

[71] *Restatement (Second) of Contracts*, introductory note to section 357 *et. seq.*

11.3 Other Causes of Action and Remedies

11.3.1 Statutory causes of action and remedies

The UCC applies by its terms only to certain defined commercial transactions, not specifically including the sale of the assets of a business as a whole. However, there is a strong tendency for courts to apply the UCC to other commercial transactions, including the sales of businesses, because the UCC "embodies the foremost legal thought concerning commercial transactions".[72] Because the UCC has been adopted throughout the US (except in Louisiana), it is regarded as a modern restatement of the law of contracts with a seal of legislative approval.[73] Thus, courts may apply the UCC to commercial transactions not technically covered by the UCC either directly or by way of analogy.[74]

For example, in *Rose* v *Helm*,[75] the purchaser of a business sued for breach of an express warranty regarding the fitness of a building's canopy. The Court of Appeals affirmed an award of damages to the plaintiff with a statement regarding the UCC which was either intended to apply the UCC or make reference to it by way of analogy. The court stated that

> under the Uniform Commercial Code, the usual measure of damages for breach of warranty is the difference, at the time and place of acceptance, between the value of the goods accepted and the value they would have had had they been as warranted. However, this method is not exclusive where, as here, the special circumstances show proximate damages of a different amount . . . The remedies provided in the Uniform Commercial Code are to be liberally administered so as to put the aggrieved party in as good a position as if the other party had fully performed.[76]

Some courts may consider the sale of a business to be a "hybrid" transaction—that is, a combination of the sale of goods and the sale of goodwill, real estate, and other non-goods. If they find the sale of goods to be the "predominant purpose" of the transaction, many courts will apply the UCC to all aspects of the sale.[77] A few courts will apply the UCC only to the sale of goods portion of the transaction regardless of whether the sale of goods is the "predominant purpose".[78]

Thus, when interpreting an asset purchase agreement, the courts may apply or refer to the principles embodied by the UCC. In addition, the parties may specify in the asset purchase agreement that the UCC will apply, and that agreement will be given effect.[79] In the event that the UCC is applied, it will impose certain

[72] *Vitex Mfg Corp* v *Caribtex Corp*, 377 F 2d 795 (3d Cir, 1967).

[73] 1 R. Anderson, *Anderson on the Uniform Commercial Code* sections 1–101: 17 3d ed, (1981).

[74] *Basch* v *George Washington University*, 370 A 2d 1364 (DC App 1977); *Rose* v *Helm*, 501 P 2d 753 (Col App, 1972).

[75] 501 P 2d 753 (Colo Ct App 1972).

[76] *Ibid.* See also *Frank Le Roux, Inc* v *Burns*, 4 Wash App 165, 480 P 2d 213 (1971); *Jinright* v *Russell*, 123 Ga App 706, 182 SE 2d 328 (1971).

[77] J. White and R. Summers, *Uniform Commercial Code* (1991), at 26.

[78] *Ibid.*

[79] *Bartlett Bank & Trust Co* v *McJunkins*, 147 Ill. App 3d 52, 100 Ill. Dec 420, 497 NE 2d 398, (1986).

implied warranties on the parties (eg, warranties of merchantability[80] and fitness for a particular purpose[81]) even if the parties have not included these warranties in their agreement. The warranty of merchantability and the implied warranty of fitness for a particular purpose are discussed in detail in section 8 above.

The UCC also allows the parties to include other warranties in their agreement, such as those set forth above in the discussion of types of representations and warranties.[82] In addition, the UCC sets forth rules for calculating damages in the event of a breach of warranty.[83] Under UCC section 2–714(2), the purchaser can claim damages for breach of warranty in the amount of the difference between the value of the product accepted by the purchaser and the value the product would have had if it had been as warranted.

Essentially, the UCC is a comprehensive embodiment of common law cases dealing with trade and commerce. Article 2 of the UCC, dealing with sales of goods, has been adopted in all US States except Louisiana. Article 2 governs or affects many, if not most, commercial transactions in the US. For a good discussion of the UCC, see J. White and R. Summers, *Uniform Commercial Code*, (1991) or R. Anderson, *Anderson on the Uniform Commercial Code*, 3d ed., (1981).

The Convention on Contracts for the International Sale of Goods (the CISG), like the UCC, does not specifically state whether it applies to sales of entire businesses. Article 1 of the CISG states essentially that the CISG applies to contracts for the sale of goods between parties whose places of business are in different countries. The CISG does not define "goods", but specifically excludes certain items (eg, sales of stock or shares) from CISG coverage. Sales of the assets of a business are not listed among these exclusions. Thus, by implication, sales of the assets of a business could be covered by the CISG. Of course, application of the CISG depends upon whether it has been adopted by the relevant countries and whether the contract between the parties specifically excludes its application. Arguably, even if the CISG would not otherwise apply, the parties could specifically opt into it.

11.3.2 Common law causes of action and remedies

When the purchase agreement fails to provide the purchaser with a right of recourse (eg, indemnification) for the seller's breach of warranty, or when for some reason the purchaser is not satisfied with the remedies provided in the contract, the purchaser may seek recourse by pursuing a common law cause of action.

11.3.2.1 ACTION ON THE CONTRACT FOR BREACH

When one party can establish that the other party has breached their purchase agreement (see discussion of establishing a breach, above), the non-breaching party may bring an action on the contract for breach. Once the non-breaching party has established the other party's breach, they may be entitled to, among other remedies, injunctive relief, damages or rescission of the contract.

[80] UCC section 2–314.
[81] UCC section 2–315.
[82] UCC section 2–313.
[83] UCC section 2–714.

Injunctive or other equitable relief will be granted if damages are inadequate to protect the interest of the injured party. Damages are considered to be inadequate if:

(a) damages are difficult to prove with reasonable certainty, as when no monetary value can be attached to the interest of a party;
(b) the injured party cannot procure a substitute for performance through the use of money, as when goods are unique; and
(c) it is impossible or very difficult to collect damages from a party.[84]

Injunctive relief is unlikely to be granted when the assets sold include commodities or other fungible goods. However, specific performance may be available as a remedy for breach of warranty or contract when the business assets sold include land and buildings.[85]

The non-breaching party may be entitled to expectation damages or reliance damages, and possibly punitive damages. Expectation damages are intended to give the injured party the "benefit of the bargain" by placing it in as good a position as it would be in had the contract been performed.[86] Expectation damages are calculated by combining the loss of the value caused by the breach with any other incidental or consequential loss, reduced by the cost or other loss avoided by not having to perform.

The first element that must be estimated in calculating expectation damages is the loss of value caused by the breaching party's deficient performance or non-performance.[87] For example, lost value includes the expected net profit from resale of an asset that an injured party is prevented from reselling because of the breach.[88]

If a party cannot show lost value with reasonable certainty, it may be entitled to an alternative means of calculating loss of value. For example, a party may recover damages based on the rental value or interest accrued on property if a breach delays the use of the property. In other cases, the injured party might be entitled to an amount equal to the cost of remedying or repairing defects.[89]

The injured party is also entitled to damages for all losses actually suffered. These include incidental and consequential losses.[90] Incidental damages include costs incurred while attempting to avoid a loss, such as the cost of finding a suitable substitute performance.[91] Consequential damages include injuries to person or property resulting from a defective performance or breach.[92] For

[84] *Restatement (Second) of Contracts* section 360 comments b, c and d (1979).
[85] *Rand-Whitney Packaging Corp* v *Robertson Group, Inc*, 651 F Supp 520, 538 (D Mass, 1986).
[86] *Restatement (Second) of Contracts* section 344 comment b (1979). See also *Alteri* v *Heenen*, 466 NYS 2d 835, 837 (1983) (applying damages rule to breach of warranty in sale of assets); *Plasti-Line Mfg* v *Combined Communications Corp*, 741 F Supp 141, 144 (ED Tenn, 1989), aff'd, 917 F 2d 1304 (6th Cir, 1990).
[87] *Restatement (Second) of Contracts* section 347 comment b (1979).
[88] *Ibid.*
[89] *Restatement (Second) of Contracts* section 348, (1979).
[90] *Restatement (Second) of Contracts* section 347 comment c (1979).
[91] *Ibid.*
[92] *Ibid.*

example, consequential damages might include lost profits from collateral contracts that the injured party can no longer perform due to the breach.

Finally, expectation damages are reduced by the amount of costs or losses that the injured party avoided because of the breach.[93] For example, the operating costs of a business are subtracted from the injured party's damages if a breach prevented the injured party from incurring those costs.[94]

As an alternative to expectation damages, reliance damages restore the injured party to as good a position as it would have been in if the contract was never made.[95] Reliance damages are most frequently awarded when the injured party cannot prove lost profits with reasonable certainty.[96] A court will reimburse the injured party for expenditures made in performance or anticipating performance. It will subtract from this total any loss avoided by the injured party proved by the breaching party.

The non-breaching party may not, however, obtain damages for a loss that it could have avoided. That is, the injured party must make an effort to mitigate, or minimise, its own damages.[97]

Also, an injured party can only recover expectation damages if they are foreseeable. A loss is foreseeable if it follows from the breach in the ordinary course of events or is a result of special circumstances known by the breaching party.[98] If damages are not foreseeable, a court may limit the remedy of an injured party to reliance damages.[99] In *Mead* v *Johnson Group, Inc*, the seller of a business sued a buyer for failing to pay business debts and for injury to the seller's "credit reputation". The Texas Supreme Court applied the traditional rule of *Hadley* v *Baxendale*, that actual damages are awarded when the injury is a "natural, probable and foreseeable consequence of the breach".[100] The court then awarded damages to the seller for the loss of its credit reputation, holding that such damage was foreseeable and was not too speculative to be excluded from an award of consequential damages.

An additional limitation on recovery of damages exists in that a party cannot recover damages beyond an amount that can be established with reasonable certainty.[101] Punitive damages are generally not recoverable for breach of contract unless the breach also constitutes a tort for which punitive damages are available.[102] The purpose of contract damages is to compensate the injured party

93 *Restatement (Second) of Contracts* section 347 comment d, (1979).
94 *Ibid.*
95 *Restatement (Second) of Contracts* section 344 comment c, (1979).
96 *Restatement (Second) of Contracts* section 349 comment a, (1979).
97 *Restatement (Second) of Contracts* section 350 comments a and b (1979). See also, *Fateh* v *Rich*, 481 A 2d 464, 471 (DC Ct App, 1984).
98 *Restatement (Second) of Contracts* section 351 (1979).
99 *Ibid.* See also, *Mead* v *Johnson Group Inc*, 615 SW 2d 685, 687 (Tex, 1981) (citing *Hadley* v *Baxendale*, 9 Exch 341, 354 (1854)).
100 *Mead* v *Johnson Group Inc*, 615 SW 2d at 687.
101 *Restatement (Second) of Contracts* section 352 comments a and b (1979). See also, *Mead* v *Johnson Group, Inc*, 615 SW 2d at 687; *Continental Sand & Gravel* v *K&K Sand & Gravel*, 755 F 2d 87 (7th Cir, 1985).
102 *Restatement (Second) of Contracts* section 355 comment a, (1979). See also *Meinrath* v *Singer Co*, 482 F Supp 457, 461 (SDNY, 1979), aff'd 697 F 2d 293 (2d Cir, 1982).

for a loss, not to punish the breaching party. However, a court may award punitive damages when the breach is particularly wilful or egregious.[103]

In addition to injunctive relief and damages, another potential remedy available to the non-breaching party is rescission. A rescission is a unilateral disaffirmance or discontinuance of a contract.[104] A contract can be rescinded for misrepresentation for fraud, mutual mistake as to a material fact, substantial failure or want of consideration and non-performance or breach of contract.[105]

The right to rescind may be waived by a party if it continues its own performance under the contract instead of exercising its right to rescind. For example, in *Hanks* v *GAB Business Records*,[106] a party waived its right to rescind a contract for the sale of assets by retaining and continuing to operate the assets of a purchased corporation.

An injured party may be prevented from maintaining an action on the contract for breach and receiving damages if the breaching party asserts a valid defence. For example, a breaching party can assert the defence of purchaser knowledge of misrepresentation if the injured party knew that the representations and warranties of the seller were untrue before the time of purchase.[107] A party cannot rely on a warranty which it knows to be false.

Legal impossibility may also be asserted as a defence.[108] This defence is available when the performance of a contract would involve a violation of the law. For example, a seller of assets might claim that its performance of the contract would result in a monopoly, restraint of trade or combination in violation of federal antitrust laws.

Other possible defences include mistake,[109] fraud,[110] frustration,[111] failure to give timely notice of the breach, the statute of limitations, lack of injury or loss by the plaintiff and the plaintiff's failure to avoid or minimise its damages.[112]

11.3.2.2 THE TORT OF FRAUDULENT MISREPRESENTATION

> One who fraudulently makes a misrepresentation of fact, opinion, intention or law for the purpose of inducing another to act or refrain from action in reliance upon it, is subject to liability to the other in deceit for pecuniary loss caused to him by his justifiable reliance upon the misrepresentation.[113]

[103] *Restatement (Second) of Contracts* section 355 comment a, (1979). See also, *Flaks* v *Koegel*, 504 F 2d 702 (2d Cir, 1974).
[104] 17A CJS *Contracts* section 412, (1963).
[105] 17A CJS *Contracts* sections 418, 420 and 421 (1963). See also *In re Matter of Topco, Inc.* 984 F 2d 727 (5th Cir, 1990), reh'g den., 902 F 2d 955 (5th Cir, 1990).
[106] 644 SW 2d 707 (Tex, 1982).
[107] *DuBois* v *United States*, 98 F Supp 590, 594 (Ct Cl, 1951); *Royal Business Machines* v *Lorraine Corp*, 633 F 2d 34, 44 (7th Cir, 1980); *Overstreet* v *Norden Laboratories, Inc*, 669 F 2d 1286, 1291 (6th Cir, 1982).
[108] 17A CJS *Contracts* section 467 (1963).
[109] 17 CJS *Contracts* section, 135 (1963). See also *Fruth* v *Divito*, 26 Ariz App 154 (1976).
[110] *Fruth* v *Divito*, 26 Ariz App 154, (1976).
[111] *Corbin on Contracts* sections 1353–1361, (1962).
[112] 67A Am Jur 2d *Sales* section 790, (1985).
[113] *Restatement (Second) of Torts* section 525, (1977).

A misrepresentation may be defined as words spoken or written or other conduct that amounts to an assertion not in accordance with the truth.[114] The elements of a claim of fraudulent misrepresentation are discussed below.

(a) **Fraudulent Nature of the Misrepresentation**. A misrepresentation is fraudulent if the maker (i) knows or believes that the matter is not as he represented it to be, (ii) does not have the confidence in the accuracy of his representation that he states or implies, or (iii) knows that he does not have the basis for his representation that he states or implies.[115]

In an action for fraudulent misrepresentation, the basis for responsibility is the intent to deceive, proved by the fact the speaker believes his statement to be false or the representation is made without any belief in its truth. For example, in *Whipp* v *Iverson*,[116] the plaintiff purchased an automobile business from the defendant, believing it included an Oldsmobile agency and franchise. General Motors subsequently refused to transfer the franchise to the plaintiff, who then returned the business to the defendant and demanded rescission of the contract. In upholding the validity of the plaintiff's complaints, the court stated that the defendant knew or should have known that the franchise was not saleable as part of the business.

The seller also may be liable for fraudulent misrepresentation if he makes a statement capable of two interpretations, one of which he knows to be false and the other true, if he makes a statement with the intention that it be understood in the false sense, or without any belief or expectation as to how it will be understood, or with reckless indifference as to how it will be understood.[117]

On the other hand, if the seller makes a representation which he believes to be true, but the statement turns out to be, in fact, false, the seller will be liable only for negligent misrepresentation, and not fraudulent misrepresentation. For example, in *Luciani* v *Bestor*,[118] the buyers of a motel and restaurant business brought suit against the sellers, seeking damages for fraudulent misrepresentation. The buyers argued that the sellers included income and expenses in their financial statements from all of their vending machines, and not just the vending machines that were sold to the buyers. The court found no intentional fraud on the part of the sellers, but found the sellers guilty of negligence. The court stated that the focal point in distinguishing between intentional fraud and negligent misrepresentation is intent. A representation which the maker believes to be true that is, in fact, false is a negligent rather than a fraudulent misrepresentation.

If the seller makes any disclosure at all regarding an issue which is material to the transaction, he is subject to a duty to make full and fair disclosure.[119] That is, the seller cannot make a statement that refers only to

[114] *Ibid.*
[115] *Ibid.* at 526.
[116] 43 Wis 2d 166, 168 NW 2d 201, 203, (1969).
[117] *Restatement (Second) of Torts* section 527, (1977).
[118] 106 Ill App 3d 878, 62 Ill Dec 501, 436 NE 2d 251, 259, (1982).
[119] *Ragsdale* v *Kennedy*, 286 NC 130, 209 SE 2d 494, (1974).

favourable matters and omits all reference to unfavourable matters. Whether or not such a partial disclosure of facts is fraudulent misrepresentation, however, depends on whether the seller knows or believes that the undisclosed facts might affect the purchaser's conduct.[120]

Similarly, if the seller makes a true statement which, before the closing of a transaction, is rendered false by a change of circumstances of which the seller is aware, he has a duty to notify the purchaser of the change in circumstances. For example, in *Milliken* v *Green*,[121] the purchasers of a newly built residence sought damages from the vendors based on fraud and other causes of action. Two months after the parties signed an earnest money agreement, the city in which the house was built advised the sellers that the roof of the residence would have to be removed and replaced to comply with the city's building code. Subsequently, the parties closed the sale without the seller notifying the purchaser that the roof would have to be replaced.

The sellers argued that they did not know at the time the earnest money agreement was signed that the roof had to be removed, and that, consequently, they committed no fraud. The court responded that because they completed the transaction after they had such knowledge, fraud could be inferred.

Note that if the seller makes a misrepresentation with reckless indifference to error, the misrepresentation may be deemed fraudulent.[122]

The seller also may be liable for fraudulent misrepresentation if he fails to disclose or conceals a material matter of past or present fact. The purchaser must show that the relevant information was not, in fact, communicated to him.[123] In addition, the purchaser must show that the seller had a duty to disclose the undisclosed fact. For example, in *Matthews* v *Kincaid*,[124] Matthews listed his apartment building for sale with a brokerage. The property had no off-street parking, and Matthews left a blank space next to "parking units" in the listing agreement. He submitted an "as built" survey of the lot, showing no available parking, and submitted a subdivision plan which distinguished his lot from adjacent lots with off-street parking.

Kincaid purchased the property, apparently believing that the tenants would be able to park in the lot next door. Subsequently, when she learned that the tenants were not allowed to park in the lot next door, she sued Matthews and the broker for damages for fraudulent or negligent misrepresentation.

The court stated that Kincaid had to prove that Matthews had a duty to disclose information which he failed to disclose. "A duty to disclose is, however, rarely imposed where the parties deal at arm's length and where the information is the type which the buyer would be expected to discover by

120 *Restatement (Second) of Torts* section 529, (1977).
121 283 Or 283, 583 P 2d 548, (1978).
122 *Ainger* v *Michigan General Corp*, 476 F Supp 1209 (SDNY, 1979), aff'd, 632 F 2d 1025 (2d Cir, 1980).
123 *Colonial Lincoln Mercury, Inc* v *Musarave*, 749 F 2d 1092 (4th Cir, 1984); *Shenandoah Valley Poultry Co, Inc* v *Armour & Co*, 859 F 2d 1013 (7th Cir, 1988).
124 746 P 2d 470 (Alaska, 1987).

ordinary inspection and inquiry."[125] In this case, the court noted that the lack of off-street parking is an obvious fact which the ordinary purchaser would be expected to discover by ordinary inspection and inquiry before purchasing the property. In addition, the parties did not enjoy a relationship of trust and confidence which might require Matthews to discuss obvious facts. Consequently, the court stated, Kincaid acted unreasonably if she purchased the property with the belief that she was also purchasing the parking lot next door. The court saw no facts which might impose upon Matthews an affirmative duty to disclose the lack of off-street parking to Kincaid.

(b) **Expectation of Influencing Conduct**. The purchaser must show that the seller intended to influence the purchaser's conduct with its misrepresentation. For example, in *Colonial Lincoln Mercury, Inc* v *Musgrave*,[126] the sellers sold to the purchasers the assets of an automobile dealership and the stock of a related automobile leasing enterprise. The purchasers suffered operating losses following the purchase and sued the sellers alleging that the sellers concealed the existence of a programme whereby the automobiles were leased to persons who could not immediately finance purchases, but for whom financing allowing purchase later might be arranged, in order to induce reliance by the purchasers upon a false picture of profitability for the company.

The court observed that there was no evidence of deliberate concealment of the existence and discontinuance of any such plan. The sellers made available to the purchasers every item of information requested, and, consequently, the purchasers had failed to prove that the sellers intended to induce reliance upon a misrepresentation.

(c) **Justifiable Reliance**. In order to recover on a claim of fraudulent misrepresentation, the purchaser must show that it actually relied on the seller's misrepresentation.[127] In addition, the purchaser must show that its reliance on the seller's misrepresentation was justifiable.[128] The purchaser may satisfy this requirement by showing that its reliance was reasonable under the circumstances. If the purchaser shows that the misrepresentation was material (see discussion of materiality above), reliance will generally be considered to have been reasonable.[129]

Arguably, when a purchaser of a business is given the opportunity to conduct an independent investigation of the records of the business and does so, the purchaser is not entitled to rely on an alleged misrepresentation of the sellers. In *Faw* v *Greenwood*,[130] for example, the Greenwoods started a

[125] *Ibid.* at 472.

[126] 749 F 2d 1092 (4th Cir, 1984). See also, *Clouse* v *Myers*, 753 SW 2d 316 (Mo Ct App, 1988); *Mursau Cor* v *Florida Penn Oil & Gas, Inc*, 638 F Supp 259 (WD 1986), aff'd 813 F 2d 398 (3d Cir, 1987).

[127] *Peery* v *Hansen*, 120 Ariz 266, 585 P 2d 574 (Ct App 1978); *Faw* v *Greenwood*, 101 Idaho 387, 613 P 2d 1338 (1980); *Tan* v *Boyke*, 156 Ill App 3d 49, 108 Ill Dec 229, 508 NE 2d 390, appeal denied, 116 Ill 2d 577, 113 Ill Dec 318, 515 NE 2d 127, (1987).

[128] *Condios, Inc* v *Driver*, 145 Ga App 537, 244 SE 2d 85 (1978); *Arnott* v *Kruse*, 730 SW 2d 597 (Mo Ct App, 1987).

[129] *Moschelle* v *Hulse*, 190 Mont 532, 622 P 2d 155, (1980).

[130] 101 Idaho 387, 613 P 2d 1338, (1980).

business consisting of retail sales, service and installation of various electrical supplies and appliances. Six months after they started the business, the Greenwoods decided to sell the business and listed it with a sales agent.

Subsequently, the Faws approached the sales agent and received financial information about the Greenwoods' business. The sales agent did not explain how a $26,000 net profit figure was estimated, but did advise the Faws to examine the books on their own. Later that month, the Faws put $1,000 down and signed an earnest money agreement. Soon thereafter, the Faws briefly examined the Greenwoods' financial statements. The parties closed the transaction and the Faws operated the business for three months before closing it and suing the Greenwoods for fraud and misrepresentation as to the $26,000 net profit figure.

The court noted that the Faws were aware that the income projection of $26,000 was based on only six months' sales. Further, the Faws had "ample opportunity to completely examine the Greenwoods' books", and did so. Consequently, the court adhered to the rule that when a purchaser is given the opportunity to conduct an independent investigation of the records, and does so, it is not entitled to rely on the seller's alleged misrepresentation.

Other cases have stated that where both parties recognise the uncertainty of a particular fact, neither party is entitled to rely on the fact to support a claim of fraud. For instance, in *Arnott* v *Kruse*,[131] the Arnotts purchased an auction and flea market business from the Kruses. Subsequent to the purchase, the Arnotts claimed that the Kruses made fraudulent misrepresentations regarding sales and expenses.

The evidence in the case showed that at the time of entering into the agreement, the Arnotts were aware that the expenses listed by the sellers were not a complete itemisation of expenses. Both parties were aware that certain actual expenses of the auction business were uncertain. Consequently, the court held that the plaintiffs were not entitled to rely on the seller's statement of expenses as a complete itemisation.

(d) **Materiality**. Reliance upon a fraudulent misrepresentation is not justifiable unless the matter misrepresented is material. The matter is material if a reasonable person would attach importance to its existence or non-existence in determining a choice of action in the transaction *or* if the maker of the representation knows (or should know) that its recipient regards (or is likely to regard) the matter important in choosing a course of action, even if a reasonable person would not so regard it.[132]

In *Tan* v *Boyke*,[133] for example, the purchaser of apartment buildings brought a fraudulent misrepresentation action against the seller. During negotiations, the seller represented to the purchaser that the two apartment buildings contained a total of 66 units, when, in fact, at least five of the units

[131] 730 SW 2d 597 (Mo Ct App, 1987).

[132] *Restatement (Second) of Torts* section 538, (1977). See also *Peery* v *Hansen*, 120 Ariz 266, 585 P 2d 574 (Ct App 1978); *Tan* v *Boyke*, 156 Ill App 3d 49, 108 Ill Dec 229, 508 NE 2d 390, appeal denied, 116 Ill 2d 577, 113 Ill Dec 318, 515 NE 2d 127, (1987).

[133] 156 Ill App 3d 49, 108 Ill Dec 229, 508 NE 2d 390, appeal denied, 116 Ill 2d 577, 113 Ill Dec 318, 515 NE 2d 127, (1987).

were unlawful. Apparently, the seller had only received written permits to construct some of the units. The seller did not tell the purchaser about zoning and building code violations, although he knew that the purchaser believed all 66 units to have been lawfully constructed.

The court found that this constituted a misrepresentation. Because the seller knew that the purchaser intended to use all of the units, the seller had a duty to reveal the discrepancy between the number of units reported on the building permit applications and the actual number of units constructed.

(e) **Causation**. One who makes a fraudulent misrepresentation is subject to liability for pecuniary loss suffered by one who justifiably relies upon the truth of the matter misrepresented, *if* his reliance is a substantial factor in determining the course of conduct that results in his loss.[134]

(f) **Remedies**. Generally, the plaintiff's remedies are to disaffirm the agreement and rescind the transaction, or to affirm the agreement and seek damages.[135] If the plaintiff disaffirms the agreement he should receive a refund of the purchase price paid to the defendant, plus incidental damages.[136]

If the plaintiff affirms the agreement, he may recover damages. Generally, the plaintiff will be entitled to recover the difference between the value of what the plaintiff received in the transaction and its purchase price or other value given for it (ie, general damages), plus any loss suffered otherwise as a consequence of the recipient's reliance upon the misrepresentation (ie, consequential damages). In addition, the plaintiff is entitled to recover additional damages sufficient to give him the benefit of his contract, if these damages are proved with reasonable certainty.[137] This allows courts to award damages under the "benefit-of-the-bargain" rule or the "out-of-pocket" rule.

American courts generally hold that the plaintiff is entitled to the benefit of his bargain with the defendant.[138] Under the "benefit-of-the-bargain" rule, the plaintiff will be compensated for the loss suffered as measured by the difference between the actual value of the business at the time of sale and the value as represented by the defendant, plus consequential damages. In *Kalb* v *International Resorts, Inc*,[139] for example, International Resorts, Inc purchased a motel from Kalb for $750,000. This purchase price was arrived at by multiplying the gross income in a particular year (as represented by Kalb) by five (generally considered to be an appropriate multiplier in that location). Subsequently, it was determined that gross income in the year was not $150,000, as Kalb represented, but $97,565. Consequently, International Resorts sued Kalb for fraudulent misrepresentation and prevailed. The court held that International Resorts was entitled to receive the difference between the value of the property as represented and the actual value of the property

[134] *Restatement (Second) of Torts* section 546 (1977). See also, *Patel* v *Hanna*, 525 So 2d 1359 (Ala, 1988); *Canterbury Court Inc* v *Rosenberg*, 224 Kan 493, 582 P 2d 261, (1978).
[135] *Patel* v *Patel*, 706 SW 2d 3 (Ky Ct App, 1986); *LaFazia* v *Howe*, 575 A 2d 182 (RI, 1990).
[136] *Carrigg* v *Blue*, 283 SC 494, 323 SE 2d 787 (Ct App, 1984).
[137] *Restatement (Second) of Torts* section 549, (1977).
[138] *Restatement (Second) of Torts* section 546 comment g on subsection 2.
[139] 396 So 2d 199 (Dist Ct App, 1981), review denied, 407 So 2d 1104 (Fla, 1981).

at the time of sale, and remanded the case for further proceedings to determine the actual value of the property at the time of sale.

Occasionally, the "benefit-of-the-bargain" rule will not provide satisfactory compensation to the plaintiff. This would be the case if the value the plaintiff would have received if the bargain had been performed, cannot be proved with any satisfactory degree of certainty. In a case of this nature, damages may be measured by the "out-of-pocket" rule.

Under the "out-of-pocket" rule, the plaintiff will be compensated for the loss suffered as measured by the difference between the actual value of the business and the price the plaintiff paid, plus consequential damages.[140]

In addition, in some jurisdictions, the plaintiff may be entitled to punitive damages if the defendant acted in a wanton, wilful or malicious manner. For example, in *Faller Group, Inc* v *Jaffe*,[141] Faller Group purchased an insurance business from Jaffe and subsequently sued Jaffe for fraudulent misrepresentation. Faller Group proved in court that Jaffe took steps fraudulently to conceal an investigation which was being conducted by the New York State Department of Insurance into excessive fees charged by Jaffe's companies. The investigation later resulted in reduction of the fees and serious financial detriment to the insurance companies.

After finding for Faller Group on its claim of fraudulent misrepresentation, the court awarded as compensatory damages the difference on the date of sale between the price paid for the insurance companies and their fair market value. The court noted that it was not necessary to determine whether the damages should be measured by the benefit-of-the-bargain rule or the out-of-pocket rule because both formulas produced the same result. "Where fair market value (assuming the truth of the representations) is the same as the purchase price, there is no practical difference between the out-of-pocket and the benefit-of-the-bargain measures."[142]

In addition, the court awarded Faller Group $200,000 in punitive damages, noting that punitive damages are available for fraud, under New York law, upon a showing of wilful and wanton conduct.

> To impose liability only in the compensatory amount of Faller's out-of-pocket loss would do no more than deprive Jaffe of his fraudulently obtained gain. It would virtually encourage such fraud in that it would leave the defrauder no worse off then he would have been had he dealt honestly. Meanwhile Faller has suffered heavy costs in the nature of legal expenses in his efforts to recover what he was wilfully and wantonly cheated out of.[143]

(g) **Defences**. Of course, the defendant will be able to refute the plaintiff's claim of fraudulent misrepresentation by arguing that the plaintiff has not met its burden by establishing all of the foregoing elements of the cause of action. For example, the defendant might claim that the misrepresentation was a

140 *Ainger* v *Michigan General Corp*, 476 F Supp 1209 (SDNY, 1979), aff'd, 632 F 2d 1025 (2d Cir, 1980).

141 564 F Supp 1177 (SDNY, 1983).

142 *Ibid.* at 1184.

143 *Ibid.* at 1186.

non-actionable opinion, promise or statement regarding the future,[144] or that the misrepresentation or non-disclosure was immaterial to the transaction between the parties.[145]

11.3.2.3 TORT OF NEGLIGENT MISREPRESENTATION

The principal elements of the tort of negligent misrepresentation are:

(a) the defendant, owing a duty of care to the plaintiff, negligently asserts a false statement;
(b) the defendant intends that his statement will be acted upon by the plaintiff;
(c) the defendant has knowledge that the plaintiff will probably rely on the statement which, if erroneous, will cause loss or injury;
(d) the plaintiff, justifiably, takes action in reliance on the statement; and
(e) the plaintiff suffers damage proximately caused by the defendant's negligence.[146]

In *Martens Chevrolet, Inc* v *Seney*,[147] for example, the buyers of an automobile dealership sued the sellers on several grounds, including negligent misrepresentation. The sellers argued that the tort of negligent misrepresentation does not apply to statements made in connection with consummation of an arm's length transaction. The court rejected this argument.[148] The trial judge in the case had directed a verdict in favour of the sellers on the negligent misrepresentation count, apparently on the grounds that the tort did not exist in the State of Maryland or because the judge believed there was insufficient evidence to support the claim. The Court of Appeals disagreed with this ruling and remanded the case for a new trial on the question of negligent misrepresentation by the sellers.

In *Batten* v *Watts Cycle & Marine, Inc*,[149] the purchaser of a motor-cycle dealership sued the seller, alleging negligent misrepresentation in connection with the seller's advertisement for the dealership. The court held that the buyer failed to show that any of the seller's representations was false and noted that even if some of the representations were false, none of them was significant. Many of the statements were merely subjective opinions subject to the common law doctrine of *caveat emptor* (ie, let the buyer beware).

Thus, the purchaser in a transaction for the purchase of shares or assets of a business may be able to sue the seller for negligent misrepresentation. Courts in some jurisdictions, however, may be unwilling to allow the claim in an arm's length transaction.[150]

144 *Zar* v *Omni Industries, Inc*, 813 F 2d 689 (5th Cir, 1987).
145 *Ainger* v *Michigan General Corp*, 476 F Supp 1209 (SDNY, 1979), aff'd, 632 F 2d 1025 (2d Cir, 1980).
146 *Restatement (Second) of Torts* section 552 *et seq.*, (1977).
147 292 Md 328, 439 A 2d 534, (1982)
148 *Ibid.* at 540.
149 *Batten* v *Watts Cycle & Marine, Inc*, 240 Mont 113, 783 P 2d 378 cert denied, 494 US 1087, (1990).
150 *Matthews* v *Kincaid*, 746 P 2d 470 (Alaska, 1987) ("a duty to disclose is rarely imposed where the parties deal at arm's length and where the information is the type which the buyer would be expected to discover by ordinary inspection and inquiry.").

12. Third Party Liability

Accountants, attorneys and other third parties may incur liability in connection with the purchase transaction. For example, many courts will hold an accountant responsible to third parties to whom the accountant intends to supply information or to persons that the accountant knows will receive the information from the client.[151] This view is based on the Restatement (Second) of Torts, section 552, which limits liability to justifiably relying third parties for negligent misrepresentation incurred (a) by one for whose benefit the accountant, attorney or other third party intends to supply the information or knows that the recipient intends to supply it; and (b) through reliance upon the information in a transaction that the accountant, attorney or other professional intends the information to influence or knows that the recipient intends the information to influence.

Some courts have taken another approach and required that only reasonably foreseeable third parties may bring suit against the accountant, attorney or other professional.[152] For example, in *H. Rosenblum, Inc* v *Adler*, the plaintiff investors purchased stock in a corporation which subsequently went bankrupt. The plaintiff investors sued the auditors, alleging that their negligence proximately caused the plaintiffs' loss. The court stated that the plaintiff investors were entitled to recover because they were reasonably foreseeable third parties, and an accountant is in the best position to avoid costs altogether by performing a careful and complete audit. In addition, the accountants can distribute the costs more fairly by insuring against risk and passing their costs on to clients, who in turn pass their costs on to the public.[153]

Of course, once the plaintiff proves the existence of a duty by the accountant, attorney or other professional to him or her, the plaintiff must prove that the professional's conduct fell below the appropriate standard in carrying out that duty. This will be a question of fact for the plaintiff to prove. In the end, the purchaser of shares or assets of a business may be able to look to an accountant, attorney or other third party professional to make the purchaser whole if the third party professional failed to satisfy a duty owed to the purchaser in connection with the transaction.

[151] See eg, *Selden* v *Burnett*, 754 P 2d 256 (Alaska, 1988).
[152] *H Rosenblum, Inc* v *Adler*, 461 A 2d 138 (NJ, 1983).
[153] 461 A 2d at 153.

Appendix 1

EXHIBIT 1

Financial Statements

Seller has delivered to Purchaser copies of the following financial statements prepared by ________, including in each case all notes thereto, all of which are complete and correct, have been prepared from the books and records of Seller in accordance with generally accepted United States accounting principles consistently applied and maintained throughout the periods indicated (GAAP) and fairly present the financial condition of Seller as of their respective dates and the results of its operations for the periods covered thereby:

Audited balance sheets of Seller as of ____, 19 __, ____________; 19 __ and ______, 19 __ ([most recent audit date] being referred to herein as the "Balance Sheet Date") and audited statements of income, changes in shareholders' equity and cash flows of Seller for each of the years then ended; and

An unaudited balance sheet of Seller as of ______, 19 __ (the "Interim Balance Sheet") and the related unaudited statement of income, changes in shareholders' equity and cash flows for the ____, month period ending ______, 19 __ (the "Interim Balance Sheet Date").

Such statements of income do not contain any items of special or nonrecurring income or any other income not earned in the ordinary course of business except as expressly specified therein, and such interim financial statements include all adjustments, which consist only of normal recurring accruals (the effect of which will not, individually or in the aggregate, be materially adverse), necessary for such fair representation. Seller's books of account, as well as its minute books and stock records, are complete and correct and have been maintained in accordance with sound business practices, including the maintenance of an adequate system of internal controls.

Absence of Undisclosed Liabilities

There are no liabilities or obligations, direct or indirect, absolute or contingent, known or unknown, or any outstanding evidence of indebtedness arising out of or relating to the Company, the Business [in an asset purchase: or the purchased assets], including liabilities or obligations arising out of any act, omission, transaction, circumstance, sale of goods or services, state of facts or other condition which occurred or existed on or before the date hereof (or the closing date) whether or not due or payable, except (a) as fully reflected or as specifically reserved against on the Interim Balance Sheet; and (b) liabilities incurred in the ordinary course of business after the Interim Balance Sheet Date, consistent with Seller's prior practice, which, in the aggregate, do not result in any adverse change in the financial condition of the Business [in an asset purchase: or the purchased assets] from that set forth in the Interim Balance Sheet. Seller has no knowledge of any circumstances which form the basis for the assertion of any liability or obligation other than as specified in ______ of this Agreement. None of Seller's employees is now, or will in the passage of time hereafter become, entitled to receive any vacation time, vacation pay or severance pay from Purchaser attributable to services rendered prior to the closing date, except as set forth on the schedule to this section.

Accounts Receivable

Attached hereto and incorporated herein as ______ is a complete and accurate list of all Receivables of Seller as of the Interim Balance Sheet Date. All of the Receivables reflected on the Interim Balance Sheet arose in the ordinary course of business and represent amounts payable by a purchaser for goods actually sold or services actually performed and are current and collectable at the aggregate recorded amounts thereof, less the reserve for bad debts reflected on the Interim Balance Sheet and, are not subject to any counterclaims or set-offs. Receivables arising after the date of the Interim Balance Sheet have arisen in the ordinary course of business and represent amounts payable by a purchaser for goods actually sold or services actually performed, and are current and collectable at the aggregate recorded amounts thereof, less a reserve for bad debts consistent with the reserve stated on the Interim Balance Sheet.

Inventory

The Inventory is of a quality and quantity usable and saleable in the ordinary course of business consistent with past practice without discount for obsolescence. The value at which Seller carries the Inventory on the Interim Balance Sheet reflects its customary inventory valuation policy of stating inventory on the FIFO method at the lesser of cost or market all in accordance with generally accepted accounting principles. No Inventory has been consigned to others. The quantity of Inventory is sufficient and adequate for, but is not in excess of the level appropriate to, the customary conduct of the Business as it previously has been conducted. Seller has not made any purchase commitments in excess of normal, ordinary and usual requirements.

Litigation and Proceedings

There is no suit, action or legal, administrative, arbitrative or other proceeding pending or, to Seller's or the Seller Shareholders' knowledge, threatened against Seller with respect to the Business [in an asset purchase: or affecting the Purchased Assets] and Seller is not under investigation with respect to any charge concerning violation of any law or administrative regulation, foreign, federal, local or State, in respect to the operation of the Business, and no set of facts or circumstances exist or have existed which would constitute a basis for any such action, proceeding, investigation, suit or arbitration. Set forth on the schedule to this section is a summary of all claims that were made against Seller in the four-year period ended ______, 199 __, including, without limitation, those which alleged with respect to Seller's products defective workmanship or manufacture, breach of express or implied warranties, product liability, or any combination thereof. Such summary includes a brief description of each such claim, the amount or value or such claim, and a brief description of its current status or final disposition. To Seller's knowledge, there is no reason to believe that the experience of the Business following Closing will not continue to be consistent with such experience.

Disclosure

To Seller's and the Seller Shareholders' knowledge, there exists no fact, condition or threatened development of any nature not otherwise disclosed in this Agreement or on the schedules to this Agreement that would be materially adverse to the operation of the Business. No warranty or representation by Seller or the Seller Shareholders contained in this Agreement or in any writing to be furnished pursuant hereto or previously furnished to Purchaser contains or will contain any untrue statement of fact or omits or will omit to state any fact required to make the statements therein contained not misleading.